BASIC CRIMINAL LAW

The Constitution, Procedure, and Crimes

Second Edition

Anniken U. Davenport
Harrisburg Area Community College

PEARSON
Prentice
Hall

Upper Saddle River, New Jersey
Columbus, Ohio

Library of Congress
Cataloging in Publication Division CIP 20540-4320
101 Independence Avenue, S.E. 9140 East Hampton Drive
Washington, DC 20540-4320 Capitol Heights, MD 20743

Library of Congress Cataloging-in-Publication Data

Davenport, Anniken.
  Basic criminal law: the constitution, procedure, and crimes/Anniken Davenport.— 2nd ed.
    p. cm.
  Includes bibliographical references and index.
  ISBN 978-0-13-513051-3
1. Criminal law—United States. I. Title.
  KF9219.85.D38 2009
  345.73—dc22

                                                                        2008008558

Editor in Chief: Vernon Anthony
Acquisitions Editor: Gary Bauer
Development Editor: Craig Beytien, Content Connections
Editorial Assistant: Katie Rowland
Production Coordination: DeAnn Montoya, S4 Carlisle Publishing Services
Project Manager: Jessica Sykes
Senior Operations Supervisor: Pat Tonneman
Art Director: Diane Ernsberger
Cover Designer: Bryan Huber
Cover photo: Getty One
Director of Marketing: David Gesell
Marketing Manager: Leigh Ann Sims
Marketing Assistant: Alicia Dysert

This book was set in Bembo by S4Carlisle Publishing Services and was printed and bound by Edwards
Brothers. The cover was printed by Phoenix Color Corp.

Pearson Education Ltd., London   Pearson Education Australia Pty. Limited
Pearson Education Singapore Pte. Ltd.   Pearson Education North Asia Ltd., Hong Kong
Pearson Education Canada, Inc.   Pearson Educación de Mexico, S.A. de C.V.
Pearson Education—Japan   Pearson Education Malaysia Pte. Ltd.

                                                        10 9 8 7
                                              ISBN-13: 978-0-13-513051-3
                                              ISBN-10:   0-13-513051-4

CONTENTS

CHAPTER 9: *Common Law Defenses*   348

CHAPTER 10: *Constitutional Rights before Arrest*   368

CHAPTER 11: *Constitutional Rights after Arrest*   402

PREFACE

Ideally, a nation's criminal justice system protects its citizens, provides a stable set of rules on which individuals and businesses may rely, and supports the nation's economic, social, and artistic growth. More commonly, criminal justice is street-level government, where everyday citizens interact with elected officials and law enforcement professionals as victims, witnesses, jurors, defendants, or convicts. Because it is so deeply entwined in its citizens' lives, any nation's criminal justice system can serve as a barometer of the nation's standing in the world, security of its citizens, and limits of its government's powers.

In this second edition of *Basic Criminal Law*, students will take an up-to-date look at the U.S. criminal justice system, both the law and legal procedures. Like its predecessor, this second edition is designed for undergraduates and legal studies programs.

SECOND EDITION TOOLS

The second edition takes a law approach first and then a procedure approach that familiarizes students with laws, their histories, and underlying theories before proceeding to specific legal procedures. This departure from the first edition was adopted to provide students with a sound theoretical base before applying legal procedures. Generally, students who understand legal history and theory can more easily place new court decisions within a sound framework.

One of the first edition's most popular features was the use of cases to illustrate various legal concepts. The second edition continues this approach with many updated cases. Using recent court decisions serves several purposes. First, students understand that the law is a living, dynamic presence in our lives. Those choosing the law as a career will spend many hours staying up-to-date on legal issues. Thus, this edition is designed to help develop the important legal research skills employers seek.

KEY FEATURES

The second edition's many new learner-centered features are designed to spark dispute and debate among instructors and students to keep classrooms lively and the lessons memorable. They include:

- *An Integrative Case:* Throughout this book, one particular case is mentioned because it shows both the best and the worst of the U.S. criminal justice system. That case is the Duke Rape Case, which not only shows what can go wrong when public servants put political success above the pursuit of justice, but also shows that ultimately the truth came out and those falsely accused were freed. The case addresses issues of politics, race, prejudice, media hype, prosecutorial misconduct, and the "rush to judgment" mentality. Discussion questions taken from the case should provoke spirited classroom debate about all of these issues.
- *Real Court Documents:* Students will find copies of documents used in many of the cases discussed. This feature allows students to delve more deeply into the legal

concepts being studied and see how legal procedures look in the courtroom. Studying court documents such as indictments, jury selection forms, and court decisions familiarizes students with the documents they will use in the real world.

- *Historical Highlight:* New Historical Highlight boxes throughout the chapters show the historical basis for Anglo-American legal concepts and their application in the current-day criminal justice system.
- *You Make the Call:* Throughout the second edition there are new, boxed You Make the Call scenarios that put the student in a real-life circumstance, asking them to use their critical thinking ability to resolve the legal challenge.
- *Key Terms:* Key terms appear in the margin where the term is first used and are compiled in a Glossary at the end of the text for easy reference.

The second edition also provides examples of where the system failed to live up to its ideals and the lessons learned from these mistakes. Ultimately, this book seeks to show a criminal justice system run by human beings with all the idealism and folly that entails. More than 230 years after the Declaration of Independence, the U.S. criminal justice system is still a work in progress. For those who seek to work in it, a challenging, rewarding, but ultimately very human experience awaits them. This second edition will provide students with the basic skills to move into that world.

STUDENT RESOURCES

Companion Website

Go to www.prenhall.com/davenport to locate links to additional resources and test-prep quizzes.

Instructor Resources

All instructors' resources are downloadable from the Instructor Resource Center at www.prenhall.com.

Instructor's Manual

The instructor's manual contains sample syllabi, and chapter notes including a chapter outline, brief overview of topics, instructional ideas, additional readings and occasional viewing recommendations, and suggested answers to discussion questions.

Test Generator

The Test Generator allows you to generate quizzes and tests composed on questions from the Test Item File, modify them, and add your own.

PowerPoint Lecture Presentation

The PowerPoint Lecture Presentation includes key concept screens and exhibits from the textbook.

CourseConnect Online Criminal Law Course

Looking for robust online course content to reinforce and enhance your student learning? We have the solution: CourseConnect! CourseConnect courses contain customizable modules of content mapped to major learning outcomes. Each learning object contains interactive tutorials, rich media, discussion questions, MP3 downloadable lectures, assessments, and interactive activities that address different learning styles. CourseConnect Courses follow a consistent 21-step instructional design process, yet each course is developed individually by instructional designers and instructors who have taught the course online. Test questions, created by assessment professionals, were developed at all levels of Blooms Taxonomy. When you adopt a CourseConnect course, you purchase a complete package that provides you with detailed documentation you can use for your accreditation reviews. CourseConnect courses can be delivered in any commercial platform such as **WebCT, BlackBoard, Angel,** or **eCollege** platforms. For more information contact your representative or call 800-635-1579.

To access supplementary materials online, instructors need to request an instructor access code. Go to **www.pearsonhighered.com/irc,** where you can register for an instructor access code. Within 48 hours after registering, you will receive a confirming e-mail, including an instructor access code. Once you have received your code, go to the site and log on for full instructions on downloading the materials you wish to use.

ACKNOWLEDGMENTS

No work of this length and complexity is done alone. I would like to thank those who helped make this second edition possible. My researchers, Elizabeth Gonzalez, Albert Davenport, Morgan Horton, and Eric Horton, all pitched in to do much of the legwork necessary to update and enliven this second edition. Morgan Horton also contributed numerous photographs showing the *Sturm und Drang* of a working democracy.

Quite obviously, no second edition exists without a first edition. Stephanie Lingle contributed numerous hours of research to the first edition, and much of her work survives in this edition.

My "partners in crime" at Prentice Hall also deserve many thanks. Gary Bauer came on board after the first edition and has been instrumental in shepherding this project to its conclusion. Also Craig Beytien should be thanked for his infinite patience while he waited for this work to come to him reworked chapter by chapter. I can only hope it was worth the wait.

There were a number of criminal law teachers from paralegal and criminal justice programs across the country that provided very helpful feedback in the preparation of the second edition. I want to give them special recognition and my personal thanks for the constructive commentary that informed and inspired my revision of this work. I valued greatly this collaboration in making the second edition a more effective teaching and learning resource for their students.

Sally Bisson	*College of Saint Mary*
Teresa Blier	*Northern Virginia Community College*
John Burkoff	*University of Pittsburgh*
Sylvia Caballero	*Miami Dade College*
Teresa Carlo	*Pierce College—FS*
Carol Chase	*Pepperdine University*
Lora Clark	*Pitt Community College*
Nigel Cohen	*Richard Stockton College of New Jersey*
Ernest Davila	*San Jacinto College North*
Kathleen DuBois	*St. Louis Community College at Meramec*
Lisa Duncan	*Central Carolina Community College*
Garry Elliott	*Reedley*
Duane Everhart	*Wayne Community College*
Harold Ferguson	*Montclair State University*
Phyllis Gerstenfeld	*California State University—Stanislav*
Pam Gibson	*Rockford Business College*
Christopher Godialis	*Iona College*
Tim Hart	*College of the Sequoias*
Darren Henderson	*Remington College*
Warren Hodges	*Forsyth Technical Community College*

David Jaroszewski	*Lee College*
Edan Jorgensen	*University of Nebraska—Lincoln*
Alan Katz	*Cape Fear Community College*
Prahlad Kedia	*Grambling State University*
David Kemp	*Amarillo College*
Mark Lloyd	*Ivy Tech State College*
Patricia Marcus	*Consolidated School of Business*
William Marino	*Hesser College*
Susan McCabe	*Kellogg Community College*
Maya Mei-Tal	*West Virginia Wesleyan College*
James P. Murphy	*Union Institute & University*
Kathryn Myers	*Saint Mary of the Woods College*
Michael Napolitano	*City University of New York*
Judith Olean	*Central New Mexico Community College*
Jeffrey Penley	*Catawba Valley Community College*
Alex Poyuzina	*Maric College*
Peter Puleo	*Harper College*
H. L. Raburn	*Florida Metropolitan University*
Doris Rachles	*South University*
Anana Rice	*Metropolitan College*
Cliff Roberson	*Washburn University*
Thomas Sarver	*Ivy Tech Community College*
Brian Schorr	*Briarcliffe College—Interboro Institute*
Michael Seigel	*University of Florida*
Scott Silvis	*Griffin Tech*
Howard Sokol	*Athens Technical College*
Andrew J. Sosnowski	*Elgin Community College*
Claire Summerhill	*Utah Career College*
Susan Sutton	*Durham Technical Community College*
Leo Villalobos	*El Paso Community College*
Michael J. Watanabe	*Arapahoe Community College*
Lorrie C. Watson	*Orangeburg-Calhoun Tech*
Charlotte A. Weybright	*Brown Mackie College—Fort Wayne*
Mary Wilson	*Northern Essex Community College*
John Woodruff	*Bay Path College*
David Woods	*Limestone College*
Alvin Zumbrun	*University of Maryland*

What Is Criminal Law?

CHAPTER CONTENTS

We hold these truths to be self-evident, that all men are created equal, that they are endowed by their Creator with certain unalienable rights, that among these are life, liberty and the pursuit of happiness.

Declaration of Independence, 1776

CHAPTER OBJECTIVES

After studying this chapter, you should be able to:

- Explain the concept of English common law.
- Explain *stare decisis*.
- Explain *mala in se* and *mala prohibita*.
- Explain the term jurisprudence.
- List and explain the major theories of law and schools of jurisprudence.
- List and explain the difference between criminal and civil law.
- List the three categories of crimes.
- Explain the federal system and federalism.
- Explain how a criminal case is processed through the criminal justice system.
- Explain checks and balances.
- Explain the Supremacy Clause.
- Explain the Commerce Clause.
- Explain police power.
- List and explain the sources of American law.

3

Law

The body of rules of conduct created by government and enforced by the authority of government.

Jurisprudence

The study of law.

Common Law

The system of jurisprudence, originated in England and later applied in the United States, that is based on judicial precedent rather than legislative enactments.

Stare Decisis

To stand by that which was decided; rule by which courts decide new cases based on how they previously decided similar cases.

Precedent

Prior decision that a court must follow when deciding a new, similar case.

Consensus Theory

A theory developed by Emile Durkheim that postulates that laws develop out of a society's consensus of what is right and wrong.

INTRODUCTION AND HISTORICAL BACKGROUND

Every society, from the most remote tribe to the most technologically advanced culture, has rules by which it operates. Most societies have written rules governing behavior and a set of punishments for those who break the rules. These can be called the society's laws. The **law** is defined as the body of rules of conduct created by government and enforced by governmental authority. Without any rules of behavior, life in a group would be difficult, if not impossible. **Jurisprudence** is the study of law. Criminal law is a specialized part of the study of jurisprudence.

In order to master criminal law, you must understand the context in which criminal law exists. In this chapter, we will take a look at the U.S. legal system as a whole. Once you have a good grasp of that system's structure and form, you will find it easier to visualize the criminal law system as a subpart of the whole.

The United States has a system of law derived from the English system of **Common Law.** As the original English settlers arrived in the New World, they brought with them a well-developed system of justice. This English system of law was common to all persons and all areas in the English Empire, so it came to be referred to as the Common Law. Common Law is founded on the idea that if one set of facts yields a decision in one case, the same set of facts should yield the same decision in the next case. So, if a judge in Essex ruled that stealing a cow was a crime, a judge in Londonderry should rule the same way. Under Common Law, judges look to similar cases decided before and decide new cases the same way. This helps make the legal system predictable and stable. Using previous decisions in similar cases to decide a current case is called following the rule of *stare decisis.* *Stare decisis* means "to stand by the decision." The earlier case on which the court relies is called a **precedent.**

You should get familiar with these terms and the others to which you will be introduced in this textbook because they form part of the language of the law.

THEORIES OF LAW AND SCHOOLS OF JURISPRUDENCE

Law's role in society varies from era to era, culture to culture, country to country, region to region, and sometimes even town to town. Different cultures have different ideas of what is right and wrong and what should be legal or illegal. Recall that jurisprudence is the study of law. Over the years, philosophers, lawyers, and social scientists have developed theories about how laws develop and are accepted by cultures. These theories of law are referred to as "schools of jurisprudence." In the following text, you will learn some of the major theories and schools of jurisprudence. As you study these, ask yourself how each theory is reflected in the laws that affect you daily. For example, which theory do you think best reflects the almost universal prohibition against sexual relationships between blood relatives? Which theory explains laws against jaywalking or spitting on public streets?

DURKHEIM'S CONSENSUS THEORY

Emile Durkheim (1858–1917) was a Frenchman who is often referred to as the father of sociology. Durkheim developed what he called the **consensus theory.** He thought that laws develop out of a society's consensus of what is right and wrong.

According to Durkheim, crimes are crimes because the society decides they are, not because certain actions are inherently right or wrong. In his classic work, *The Division of Labor in Society*, Durkheim wrote:

> Even when a criminal act is certainly harmful to society, it is not true that the amount of harm that it does is regularly related to the intensity of the repression which it calls forth. In the penal law of most civilized people, murder is universally regarded as the greatest of crimes. However, an economic crisis, a stock-market crash . . . can disorganize the social body more severely than an isolated homicide. (T)he only common characteristic of all crimes is that they consist . . . in acts universally disapproved of by members of each society. . . . [1]

In Durkheim's view, society's collective membership decides what is a crime and what isn't. Likewise, society can change its mind. Society can outlaw specific behavior. For instance, prior to the mid-twentieth century, smoking marijuana was not a crime simply because most people had never heard of marijuana. When smoking it became popular, many states passed laws barring its use. Later, when societal attitudes changed, the behavior was decriminalized in some states. For example, some states permit individuals to grow marijuana for personal consumption. In some cases, these laws were passed by referendum (a change in the law that occurs when the majority of voters vote to make the change) showing that society has made a collective judgment that growing marijuana isn't worthy of being considered a crime. Similar changes have occurred in attitudes toward gambling, prostitution, slavery, and racial segregation.

MARX'S RULING CLASS THEORY

While Durkheim saw criminal laws as agreed upon societal norms, the sociologist Karl Marx (1818–1883) saw things very differently. He taught that laws are a reflection of the interests or ideology of the ruling class. Under Marxist theory, laws are a manifestation of ongoing class conflict. They exist merely to protect property interests of the **bourgeoisie,** or the group that controls industrial production. Private property rights are viewed as a tool of oppression of the **proletariat,** or the working classes.[2] This theory is referred to as the **elite or ruling class theory.** Related to this theory is the **Command School** theory.[3] The Command School believes that law is a set of rules developed by the ruling class or elite and imposed on the society. Under this theory, laws will change when those in power change.

BLACKSTONE'S THEORY

The great English legal analyst Sir William Blackstone (1723–1780) theorized that there are two different types of crime. Some acts are crimes because the behavior is inherently bad or evil. A crime that is bad in and of itself is defined by the Latin term *mala in se.* Other acts are crimes because society has chosen to criminalize specific behaviors. Such crimes are called *mala prohibita.*[4] For example, murder is *mala in se*, or inherently evil. Driving a car with an expired inspection sticker, however, is not inherently evil. Most traffic and auto code violations are *mala prohibita*. Think of *mala prohibita* crimes as violations of those rules your mother enforced over your objections with "because I said so, that's why."

The basis of a democratic state is liberty.
Aristotle, *The Politics* (343 B.C.)

Bourgeoisie
In Marxist theory, the class in society that controls the means of production.

Proletariat
In Marxist theory, the working class who must sell their labor in order to survive.

Elite Theory
Also known as the ruling class theory, it is the theory put forth by Karl Marx that postulates laws exist only as a means of class oppression.

Command School
The school of jurisprudence thought that posits that laws are dictated to society by the ruling class of that society.

Mala In Se
According to Blackstone, a category of crimes that are bad in and of themselves.

Mala Prohibita
According to Blackstone, a category of crimes that are crimes because society has decided they are crimes.

Natural Law School

The school of jurisprudence thought that teaches that laws are based on morality and ethics and that people have natural rights.

Moral Theory of Law

A theory subscribed to by Natural Law adherents stating that laws are based on the moral code of the society.

Let us consider the reason of the case. For nothing is law that is not reason. John Powell, English judge (1645–1713)

Historical School

The school of jurisprudence thought that believes that law is an accumulation of societal traditions.

Analytical School

The school of jurisprudence thought that believes laws are based on logic.

THE NATURAL LAW SCHOOL OF JURISPRUDENCE

The **Natural Law School** believes that people have natural rights and that laws are based on what is right. They adhere to the **moral theory of law,** the belief that law is based on morality. Much of English law reflects this school.[5] The English political philosopher John Locke (1632–1704) spoke of the natural rights of man and profoundly influenced Thomas Jefferson (1743–1826) in the writing of the Declaration of Independence. Both the Declaration of Independence and the U.S. Constitution reflect the Natural Law School of jurisprudence. For example, the introductory quote in this chapter is from the Declaration of Independence. Note the references to self-evident truths and unalienable rights. These are hallmarks of the Natural Law School of jurisprudence.

THE HISTORICAL SCHOOL

The **Historical School** of jurisprudence states that law is merely the accumulation of a society's social traditions. Historical School legal theorists believe that laws evolve to accommodate changes in society.[6] Historical legal scholars will look to previous decisions and then determine if the norms reflected by those decisions are still the norms of the society. In other words, precedent is only relied on if the society's current social norms support the rationale underlying the decision in the case.

The Historical School would likely support overturning precedent if times have changed. For example, assume that the courts have regularly ruled that children born out of wedlock can't inherit from their fathers. The Historical School would look to society's current views on illegitimate births. If such births have become commonplace and accepted by a large segment of society, the Historical School would support overturning precedent. Like Durkheim's consensus theory, the Historical School recognizes that society influences what is or should be legal and illegal.

THE ANALYTICAL SCHOOL

The **Analytical School** of jurisprudence holds that logic determines what is law. Analytical philosophers will apply theories of logic to the facts of a case to make a decision.[7] Emotional appeals hold little sway. Analytical adherents will tend to focus on the logic of a legal decision rather than on popular opinion or changing values.

THE SOCIOLOGICAL SCHOOL

The **Sociological School** of jurisprudence holds that law is a way of achieving sociological goals within a society. Also known as **realists,** sociological theorists believe that the purpose of law is to shape societal behavior.[8] Because of their activist approach, they are unlikely to place much emphasis on prior decisions. Realists propose new laws designed to shape behaviors they consider desirable for society. For example, realists seeking to encourage religious tolerance might urge the passage of laws banning religious hate crimes such as burning churches or desecrating houses of worship. In effect, realists decide on a public policy and then mold laws to achieve that policy.

THE CRIT AND THE FEM-CRIT SCHOOL OF JURISPRUDENCE

Another theory of jurisprudence that emerged in the twentieth century is the Critical Legal Studies School, or the **Crits.** Crits believe that the legal system is arbitrary and artificial, that legal neutrality and objectivity are myths to maintain the current status quo, and that the legal system perpetuates social inequality and oppression of those not in power. The **Fem-Crits** are an offshoot of the Crits. Fem-Crits apply the crit theory of oppression and control to women, arguing that the legal system perpetuates the oppression of women in society.[9]

WHICH THEORY FITS THE AMERICAN SYSTEM?

No one theory of jurisprudence explains or describes the U.S. legal system perfectly. There are elements of each theory in our legal system. For example, the introduction of a new bill to encourage more fathers to pay child support can be seen as the work of realists who want to encourage more fathers to support their children by penalizing those who don't. The law could also be the work of Analytical School proponents who see increased child support as logically reducing dependence on government aid. The Historical School would support the law because it sees increased child support collection as a necessary measure in a society that accepts a high divorce and illegitimacy rate. The Natural Law School would see a child's right to support as the natural and moral obligation of his or her father. Finally, the Realists and Fem-Crits would see the law as a way of addressing a societal problem of children living in poverty and a correction of the unequal earning power of single mothers.

CRIMINAL LAW VERSUS CIVIL LAW

Legal proceedings are classified as either criminal or civil. Criminal and civil law each have a unique set of functions, procedures, and consequences. Generally speaking, criminal law is designed to protect and vindicate public rights, while civil law is used to resolve private disputes. Criminal law seeks to protect society as a whole from the aberrant (as defined by the law) behavior of some members of that society. A **crime** is a wrong against society.

CRIMINAL LAW PROTECTS PUBLIC RIGHTS

When a murder, assault, rape, or other crime directed at a person is committed, a victim is harmed, and the public order is disturbed. People assume that a civilized society has an interest in protecting the physical safety of its citizens. Thus, actions that threaten physical safety are crimes.

    This same public interest is often also attached to property rights. In societies that believe that property can be owned (and that's not a universally held belief), it's assumed that stable property rights produce a stable society. That stability is threatened when members of the society appropriate property for their own use without permission or payment. Theft of property is therefore also a wrong against society.

Sociological School
Adherents of the Sociological School of jurisprudence believe that the purpose of law is to shape societal behavior; believers are called realists.

Realists
Belonging to the Sociological School of jurisprudence; realists believe that the purpose of law is to shape societal behavior.

Crits
A short term for the School of Critical Legal Studies who see the legal system as arbitrary and artificial.

Fem-Crits
A school of jurisprudence that holds the legal system perpetuates the oppression of women in society.

Crime
A wrong against society or the public interest.

Because criminal laws protect public interests, criminal prosecutions are brought on behalf of all of us through a state actor. The prosecutor is always a public figure, not a representative of the victim of the crime. Thus, a Pennsylvania rape case is prosecuted by a district attorney, and the case is captioned *Commonwealth of Pennsylvania v. John Doe*. A federal case is brought by a U.S. attorney and is captioned as *United States v. Jane Doe*. Both the district attorney and the U.S. attorney represent society as a whole.

CIVIL LAW PROTECTS PRIVATE RIGHTS

While criminal law deals with crimes, civil law deals with **torts,** contracts, estates, and family matters. A tort is a private or civil wrong, or injury resulting from a breach of a legal duty. It can be an intentional tort, such as an assault, or an unintentional one, such as an automobile accident. A person who commits a tort is called a **tort feasor.** Individuals seeking redress of private grievances file civil lawsuits over personal injuries, breach of contract, divorce and custody actions, or the administration of estates.

Sometimes one act can be both a crime and a tort. For example, a physical assault is both a crime and a tort. The criminal law seeks to punish the assailant on behalf of all of us, and the civil law seeks to reimburse the assault victim for any loss he or she had because of the assault. Because different rights are at stake, the assailant can be sued in both criminal court and in civil court for the same assault.

Perhaps no event in U.S. history better explains the rights vindicated by the criminal and civil system than the terrorist bombings of the Pentagon and World Trade Center on September 11, 2001. The aftermath left the entire nation in grief and feeling at least a little less secure. Clearly, the terrorists' acts harmed us all. Those same acts also killed almost 3,000 innocent men and women, whose survivors each have a potential civil tort action against the terrorists, those that financed their operations, and perhaps other parties responsible for security.

CRIMINAL LAW PENALTIES AND THE BURDEN OF PROOF

The punishment for a crime is imprisonment or death. Sometimes a fine is added to the punishment. Criminal punishments are meant to vindicate the public interest by either removing the convicted criminal from society for a period of time or permanently in the case of death or a life sentence. In the U.S. criminal law system, it is always the government that has the **burden of proof,** or has to prove that the allegations against the **defendant** are true. The criminal defendant is presumed innocent until proven guilty.

Because the consequences of conviction are so great, the prosecution has a heavy burden of proof. In criminal cases, prosecutors must prove **beyond a reasonable doubt** that the defendant did commit the criminal act with which he or she was charged. (See Chapter 12 for a full discussion of the meaning of "beyond a reasonable doubt.")

TORT PENALTIES AND THE BURDEN OF PROOF

The remedy in tort actions is a payment of money to the victim, an order to stop doing something (such as polluting a stream), or an order to do something (such as clean

---

Tort

A private or civil wrong or injury independent of contract, resulting from a breach of a legal duty.

Tort Feasor

A person who commits a tort.

Burden of Proof

The duty to go forward to prove an allegation with facts.

Defendant

In a civil case, the person against whom a suit is filed. In a criminal trial, the person accused of a crime.

Beyond a Reasonable Doubt

The burden of proof the prosecution must meet in a criminal case in order to convict the accused; the prosecutor is required to prove beyond a reasonable doubt that the defendant committed the crime with which he or she was charged. A reasonable doubt is a fair doubt based upon common sense.

up an industrial waste site). A tort feasor stands to lose money if he or she must pay a damage award or stop production. The loser in a civil trial is in no danger of imprisonment. Because only money is at stake, a different burden of proof is used in civil trials. A **plaintiff** (the person bringing the suit) in a civil case need only prove his or her case by a **preponderance of the evidence.** This concept can best be explained by picturing a blindfolded statue of justice holding her scales. If the scales tip under the weight of evidence ever so slightly to one side or the other, the side to which it tips wins the case.

Unlike criminal cases, which are prosecuted by a representative of the state or federal government, civil cases are brought by private attorneys retained to represent the plaintiff. As in criminal cases, the person bringing the suit has the burden of proving the case.

TYPES OF CRIMES

Crimes are often classified as **summary offenses, misdemeanors,** and **felonies.** The exact terminology varies from state to state. Summary offenses are generally minor violations such as speeding tickets, parking violations, and littering. They carry only the possibility of a short prison term, generally less than 90 days, and are usually punishable by the payment of a fine. Summary offenses are often tried at the lowest level of the judicial system, usually before a district magistrate or justice of the peace, and often use a streamlined procedure. A person charged with a summary offense may not receive all the procedural safeguards a defendant charged with a more serious crime would receive. For example, he or she will not have the case tried before a jury.

Plaintiff
The party who files a lawsuit.

Preponderance of the Evidence
Evidence that is more convincing than the opposing evidence; enough evidence to tip the scales of justice.

Summary Offenses
Minor offenses such as parking tickets or minor traffic violations.

Misdemeanors
Crimes punishable by relatively short prison sentences or fines; misdemeanors are less serious than felonies.

Felonies
The most serious classification of crimes punishable by long prison sentences or death.

HISTORICAL HIGHLIGHT
Different Burdens of Proof Equal Different Verdicts

On June 12, 1994, Nicole Brown Simpson and Ron Goldman were brutally murdered outside of Nicole Simpson's condominium in the Brentwood section of Los Angeles. Nicole was the former wife of football star and sportscaster O. J. Simpson. Bloody footsteps led from the scene. When police arrived at O. J.'s house, they found his white Ford Bronco parked on the street with blood stains trailing from it toward the house. Scaling the fence, Detective Mark Fuhrman claimed he found a bloody glove matching one recovered at the scene of the crime. Simpson was not home, having left earlier in the evening for a business trip to Chicago.

Upon his return from Chicago, Simpson was questioned. Suspicion quickly fell on him because the police were familiar with the violence of the Simpsons' marriage. The police made arrangements for Simpson to turn himself in, but he didn't show up. That evening a low-speed chase took place on the freeways of Los Angeles. The chase was televised live across the United States. Simpson's friend A. C. Cowlings drove the white Ford Bronco as a despondent Simpson threatened suicide in the back seat. The nation watched as the chase ended peacefully at Simpson's house when he surrendered.[10]

Simpson retained a legal "dream team" of high-profile attorneys to defend him against the charges. The prosecution expressed confidence in its ability to convict Simpson. The evidence presented by the prosecution was at first compelling. Bloody footprints at the crime scene matched exclusive, high-fashion shoes belonging to Simpson. Bloodstains in the haphazardly parked Bronco and a bloodstained sock found in Simpson's bedroom all pointed to Simpson's guilt.

The "dream team," however, found holes in the prosecution's case. The Bronco was left unsecured in police custody. In a dramatic in-court demonstration, the prosecution had Simpson try on the bloody glove, and it was too small. That led Simpson attorney Johnny Cochran to say in his summation, "If the glove doesn't fit, you must acquit." A DNA expert testified that DNA belonging neither to Simpson nor the victims was found in the blood removed from under Nicole's fingernails. When Detective Fuhrman was called to testify about the circumstances under which he found the glove, he refused to answer on the ground that the answer might incriminate *him*. In a stunningly short deliberation, the jury returned a "not guilty" verdict. The district attorney had been unable to prove beyond a reasonable doubt that O. J. Simpson had murdered his ex-wife.

Months later, Simpson was sued civilly by Nicole's parents and the family of Ron Goldman. Much the same evidence was presented. But this time Simpson lost. A judgment for $33.5 million was entered against Simpson. Why the different verdicts? The answer lies in the different burdens of proof required for criminal and civil proceedings.

Misdemeanors are more serious crimes, but crimes that are not as serious as felonies. A defendant convicted of a misdemeanor offense may serve a prison term, generally less than one year. The length of possible imprisonment varies from crime to crime and state to state. Most theft offenses are misdemeanor offenses unless they involve several thousand dollars. In some cases, repeat offenders are charged with felonies rather than misdemeanors.

Felonies are the most serious crimes. Murder, rape, and robbery are considered felonies in most states. Felonies are punishable by long prison sentences or death. Felony trials occur in state or federal courts. Procedural safeguards are more closely monitored in felony trials because of the serious nature of the potential punishment. A convicted felon faces lifelong consequences. Felons generally cannot serve in public office or on a jury and often cannot hold professional licenses. They also can't vote while imprisoned and sometimes for long periods after release. They may also lose other important benefits such as access to student grants and loans for college.

The U.S. Capitol.

Federal System

A system of governing where government is divided into different levels.

Men being . . . by Nature, all free, equal and independent, no one can be put out of this Estate, and subjected to the Political Power of another, without his own consent. John Locke, *The Second Treatise on Government* (1690)

Legislative

One of the three branches of government; the one charged with making the law.

Executive

One of the three branches of government; the branch charged with enforcing the law.

Judicial

One of the three branches of government; the branch charged with interpreting the law.

U.S. Supreme Court

The highest court in the United States.

THE U.S. JUDICIAL SYSTEM

THE FEDERAL SYSTEM

The U.S. government is a **federal system** where the task of governing is divided between different levels of government. The United States has a national government, 50 state governments plus the District of Columbia, and numerous local governments. In addition, Puerto Rico, Guam, the Northern Mariana Islands, and the U.S. Virgin Islands are governed by U.S. law.

The Constitution of the United States lays out the federal government's structure, including its court system. In addition, the Constitution guarantees that U.S. citizens and legal aliens shall enjoy liberties such as freedom of speech and religion and equal protection under the law. In many instances, these rights are even extended to those in the United States illegally. The Constitution provides important procedural safeguards for individuals charged with crimes, including the right to counsel, right to a jury trial, and freedom from cruel and unusual punishment. You will learn more about these guarantees in later chapters.

The Constitution establishes three branches of government, the **legislative,** the **executive,** and the **judicial.** The legislative branch makes laws, the executive branch enforces the laws, and the judicial branch interprets the laws. The **U.S. Supreme Court** heads the judicial branch. The Supreme Court has the last say on the constitutionality of laws, and its decisions establish the law of the land.

The U.S. Supreme Court hears appeals from the federal court system and appeals from state court systems if the issue concerns the interpretation of federal law or the U.S. Constitution or a conflict between states or citizens of different states. Generally, the Supreme Court only hears cases it considers important to the national interest. As a result, very few of the many cases presented to the court are actually heard. A litigant who wants to take his or her case to the U.S. Supreme Court must file a **petition for** *certiorari,* requesting that the court hear the case. If the court decides it wants to hear the case, it issues a ***writ of certiorari.***

The ability of the court to declare laws unconstitutional is part of the **checks and balances** system between the branches of government. The legislative branch consists of the Senate and the House of Representatives. Together, these two bodies are referred to as Congress. Congress makes law. The Senate must also approve all judges appointed to the federal bench, including to the Supreme Court, in a process called **confirmation.**

Supreme Court justices and all other federal judges are appointed for life. A federal judge or a justice of the Supreme Court can only be removed from office through **impeachment.** The Constitution specifies that a judge or justice can be impeached if he or she is convicted of "high crimes or misdemeanors." Charges are brought in the House of Representatives. If enough evidence of wrongdoing is found, the House can pass a bill of impeachment. A trial is then held in the Senate. If the judge is convicted by a two-thirds vote of the Senate, he or she is removed from office.

The executive branch of the government enforces the laws Congress enacts and constitutional protections. The president of the United States heads the executive branch, which contains numerous agencies, each responsible for enforcing laws under its **jurisdiction.** For example, the Department of Justice enforces federal criminal laws, the Department of Labor enforces wage and hour laws, and the Food and Drug Administration laws enforces governing foods and pharmaceuticals.

Petition for Certiorari
Request by a litigant that the U.S. Supreme Court hear his or her appeal.

Writ of Certiorari
Notice from the U.S. Supreme Court that the court will hear a case.

Checks and Balances
The system of restraints built into the U.S. Constitution that prevents one branch of government from dominating the others.

Confirmation
The process of approval of presidential nominees by the Senate.

Impeachment
The process by which Congress may charge a sitting judge, president, or vice president with "high crimes and misdemeanors" and convict that person in a trial before the Senate; a conviction results in removal from office.

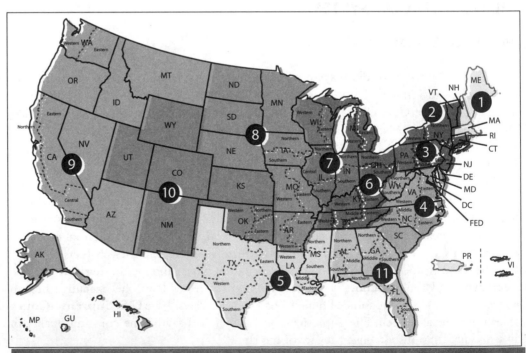

Geographic Boundaries of United States Courts of Appeals and United States District Courts.

THE FEDERAL JUDICIARY

In addition to the Supreme Court, there are **U.S. District Courts** and **U.S. Courts of Appeals.** Federal crimes are tried in the U.S. District Courts and appealed to the U.S. Courts of Appeals and ultimately to the U.S. Supreme Court if that court agrees to hear the case. Federal courts try cases when federal laws have been broken and in other areas where the federal government has been given **exclusive jurisdiction.** For example, the federal court system has exclusive jurisdiction over patent cases, federal crimes, most admiralty cases, and federal bankruptcy cases. Federal courts also have **concurrent jurisdiction** with state courts over some matters. For example, a federal court can decide a civil lawsuit filed by a citizen of one state against a citizen of another state.

The federal system is organized into **Federal Circuits.** There are 13 circuits in all. Within each circuit, there are U.S. District Courts and a U.S. Court of Appeals. The number of U.S. District Courts in a circuit depends on the size of the geographic area covered by the circuit. Each circuit has only one U.S. Court of Appeals. Within each circuit, the District Court must follow the law as interpreted by the Court of Appeals for that circuit and the rulings of the U.S. Supreme Court. That is, it must abide by *stare decisis* and rely on precedents if any are available.

The Circuit Court of Appeals must follow the rulings of the U.S. Supreme Court but don't have to follow the decisions of the other 12 Courts of Appeals. That means there can be up to 13 different interpretations of a law. These differences are referred to as "splits in the circuits." The U.S. Supreme Court often accepts cases for review to resolve these splits.

There are also special federal courts that handle specific subject matter. The U.S. Tax Court handles federal tax questions, the U.S. Bankruptcy Court handles bankruptcy cases, and the Armed Forces have their own court as well.

After the terror attacks of September 11, 2001, first the White House, and then Congress (after input from the U.S. Supreme Court) created a separate judicial process largely outside the federal court system to deal with alleged terror suspects caught in the armed conflicts in Afghanistan, Iraq, and other so-called battlefields in the **War on Terror.** The Military Commissions Act of 2006 was passed by Congress and signed into law by President George W. Bush on October 17, 2006 and provides detainees and unlawful enemy combatants with an alternative judicial process. (See Chapter 6 for more information on military tribunals and enemy combatants.)

The Constitution gives specific powers to the federal government. All other powers are reserved to the states and their citizens. It is a common misconception that powers flow from the federal government to states. In fact, all power originates at the state level. The powers given by the states to the federal government are called **enumerated powers.** These powers are primarily in areas of national and international interest. Some of the enumerated powers are described in the following sections.

THE SUPREMACY CLAUSE

The Constitution's **Supremacy Clause** establishes it as the supreme law of the land. The concept that federal law must take precedence over state and local law is called the **preemption doctrine.** When the U.S. Constitution or a federal law addresses an area within the federal government's exclusive jurisdiction, federal law is said to preempt the state or local law.

Jurisdiction
The power to hear and decide a case; jurisdiction can be divided as to subject matter, parties, or territory.

U.S. District Courts
The federal court system's trial courts.

U.S. Courts of Appeals
The federal court system's intermediate appellate courts.

Exclusive Jurisdiction
A court with exclusive jurisdiction is the only court that can hear the case.

Concurrent Jurisdiction
Jurisdiction shared by two or more courts.

Federal Circuit
One of 13 federal judicial districts, each with a U.S. District Court and a U.S. Court of Appeals.

War on Terror
The term commonly used to refer to the aftermath of the September 11, 2001 attacks and efforts to bring the masterminds of the attacks to justice.

Enumerated Powers
The powers explicitly given to the federal government in the U.S. Constitution.

"We the People" tell the government what to do, it doesn't tell us. "We the people" are the driver, the government is the car. And we decide where it should go, and by what route, and how fast.
Ronald Reagan, farewell address (January 11, 1989)

We may define a republic . . . as a government which derives all its powers directly or indirectly from the great body of the people, and is administered by persons holding their offices during pleasure, for a limited period, or during good behavior.
James Madison, *The Federalist* (January 16, 1788)

All states have their own constitutions, but state constitutions can't give the state's citizens fewer rights than given under the U.S. Constitution. In other words, states can give their citizens greater rights than the U.S. Constitution gives, but never fewer rights. The U.S. Constitution serves as the minimum standard below which the states may not go.

THE COMMERCE CLAUSE

Initially, the jurisdiction of the federal courts was very limited. However, as transportation and communications linked the states more closely, some standardization of laws was necessary. The Constitution gives the federal government jurisdiction over matters of **interstate commerce.** In the early days of the republic, the **Commerce Clause** of the Constitution was interpreted narrowly. However, as commerce grew more complex, the federal government assumed jurisdiction over anything affecting interstate commerce. For example, Congress passed the Civil Rights Act of 1964, which guarantees equal civil rights to all regardless of race, sex, religion, or national origin, under the authority of the Commerce Clause.

As the federal government's role expanded, so did the number of federal laws. Crimes that involved interstate flight posed problems for state and local law enforcement. The advent of the automobile made flight easier and created a whole new category of crime—

HISTORICAL HIGHLIGHT
Acquitted in State Court but Convicted in Federal Court

Early in the morning of March 2, 1991, Rodney King and two friends were drinking and apparently decided to go for a ride. Driving erratically and at high speed, King soon drew the attention of the California Highway Patrol and some Los Angeles Police Department officers. After a high-speed chase down the freeway, King headed down city streets. While driving at a moderate rate of speed, he ran several red lights in an attempt to elude the police. Eventually, he pulled over.

The police ordered the men out of the car. King's two friends quickly complied, but King did not. Slowly, he got out of the car while yelling at police and refusing to comply with their orders to lie down on the ground. Sergeant Stacey Koon tried to get King to lie down by administering an electrical charge from a Taser. The shock had no effect.

Ultimately, King lay down. At that point, a resident of the area, Mr. George Holliday, began to videotape the scene. King got up and attempted to run away. As he ran, Officer Laurence Powell struck him on the side of the head, and he fell. King was still trying to escape as other officers struck him with their batons.

King eventually rolled over, and Officer Koon reached for his handcuffs. Then Officer Theodore Briseno stomped on King's chest, and other officers struck and kicked King as he lay on the ground. A full minute passed from the time Koon reached for his handcuffs and when King was restrained. Throughout that period, the officers were beating and kicking King.[11]

Initially, criminal charges were filed against the police officers. Their trial took place in rural Simi Valley, California, before an all-white jury. The case focused attention on racial tensions in Los Angeles. Many African-Americans felt King was treated brutally simply because he was black. When the Simi Valley jury returned a "not guilty" verdict, South Central Los Angeles erupted in violence.

Soon after, federal criminal charges were filed against the officers. The indictment accused the police officers of violating King's civil rights, a criminal offense under federal law. Koon and Powell were convicted; Wind and Briseno were acquitted. Koon and Powell were sentenced to 30 months in jail.

This was not the first time that defendants have been prosecuted on federal charges for the same behavior they had previously been acquitted of at the state level. Although the practice dates back to the 1920s, prosecuting at the federal level was a popular tactic during the civil rights movement of the 1950s and 1960s, when it became obvious that local juries were intimidated into acquitting white supremacists who carried out violent attacks on civil rights activists. The most famous case from that period was the murder of three civil rights workers in Philadelphia, Mississippi, with the complicity of local law enforcement officers. When a local jury acquitted them, federal civil rights charges were filed, and the culprits were convicted in the federal trial.[12]

The legal doctrine that allows this prosecution is called **dual sovereignty**.[13] Under dual sovereignty, persons may be prosecuted by the different "sovereigns" without violating the double jeopardy provisions of the Constitution's Fifth Amendment.

HISTORICAL HIGHLIGHT
Heart of Atlanta Motel v. United States,
379 U.S. 241 (1964)

Facts: The Civil Rights Act of 1964 was passed pursuant to Congress' power to regulate interstate commerce. The Act provides that "all persons shall be entitled to the full and equal enjoyment of the goods, services, facilities, privileges, advantages, and accommodations of any place of public accommodation ... without discrimination or segregation on the ground of race, color, religion, or national origin." The Heart of Atlanta Motel was a 216-room motel located in downtown Atlanta. It was easily accessible from several interstate highways. The motel advertised nationally in magazines and on billboards along interstate highways in the South. About 75 percent of its guests were from out of state. The Heart of Atlanta Motel had a policy of refusing to rent rooms to African-Americans. After the Civil Rights Act passed, the motel sued the United States. The owner said he was denied the right to choose with whom he wanted to associate and sought to have the law declared invalid.

Supremacy Clause

The clause in the U.S. Constitution that states that the Constitution, federal law, and treaties are the supreme law of the land; Article VI, Section 2.

Preemption Doctrine

The concept that federal law must take precedence over state and local law.

The people made the Constitution, and the people can unmake it. It is the creature of their own will, and lives only by their will.
John Marshall, *Cohens v. Virginia* (1821)

Interstate Commerce

Commerce that occurs between states as opposed to strictly within a state's borders.

Commerce Clause

The clause of the U.S. Constitution that gives the federal government the right to regulate interstate commerce; Article I, Section 8, Clause 3.

Dual Sovereignty
The legal doctrine that allows a person to be prosecuted by different sovereigns or governmental entities for the same action or set of actions; most commonly prosecution by both the federal and state government for the same action.

When the Supreme Court heard the case, they addressed the question of whether Congress had the power under the Commerce Clause to dictate to whom a Georgia motel rented rooms. The court ruled the motel's refusal to rent to African-Americans affected interstate commerce. Therefore, Congress had the right to regulate it. The court reasoned that lack of lodging along interstate highways made it difficult for African-Americans to travel, and refusal to rent to African-Americans effectively prevented many from traveling across state lines and spending money on lodging, meals, and other attractions throughout the South. Therefore, the enactment of the Civil Rights Act was a valid exercise of the Commerce Clause.

auto theft. Interstate flight problems became so large that a federal law enforcement body was needed. This organization eventually became the Federal Bureau of Investigation (FBI).

POLICE POWER

What does it mean when we say a government has the right to regulate an activity? We mean that a government has the power to enforce existing laws and punish those who break them. This is commonly referred to as the government's exercise of its **police power.** A state's police power allows it to regulate the health, safety, morals, and general welfare of its citizens.

Most states have an extensive system of laws and regulations that govern how business is done within the state. The police powers are also exercised through the enactment of criminal laws to protect the public. Whereas federal laws cover crimes affecting interstate

Police Power
The power of a government to enforce laws and regulate the health, safety, morals, and welfare of the population.

HISTORICAL HIGHLIGHT
Birth of a National Police Force

Until 1908, there was no national law enforcement agency. States and cities all had their own police forces. But as travel became easier, crime became more mobile. Criminals could now easily cross state lines and elude prosecution. Local police departments often lacked training and were unable to coordinate investigations that crossed county and state lines. In some cases, police corruption also interfered with the ability to effectively control crime.

President Theodore Roosevelt and his Attorney General, Charles Bonaparte (a descendant of Napoleon I), realized the need for a law enforcement body that could cross state lines to apprehend criminals, coordinate the investigations of local police forces, and do it in a professional way with no trace of corruption. Bonaparte created a corp of special agents who were chosen strictly on the basis of their qualifications.

The force was small and tightly controlled by Congress. The idea of a national police force was very controversial. States were wary of this federal intrusion into an area that was traditionally the purview of states, counties, and municipalities. Many feared a national police force as a first step toward widespread federal control of state affairs.

Gradually, events led to a widening of the special agents' jurisdiction. In 1910, the Mann Act was passed into federal law. It is also known as the White Slave Act. White slavery refers to the practice of abducting or luring away rural southern girls and forcing them into prostitution in northern cities. Since white slavery abductions took place across state lines, local police forces were ill-equipped to stop these lucrative operations. Special agents became adept at investigating the trade in young girls.[14]

During World War I, the force was again expanded and charged with investigating violations of the Espionage, Selective Service, and Sabotage Acts. After the war, a series of bombings highlighted the need for the Bureau of Investigation, as the agency was now called. On the evening of June 2, 1919, U.S. Attorney General A. Mitchell Palmer heard a thud at his front door as he was going upstairs to bed. A second later an explosion ripped through the front of his house. No one in the Palmer household was injured, but the bomber was killed. The explosion scattered the anarchist political leaflets the bomber was carrying throughout the neighborhood. America's first "red scare" was on.

The explosion was the first in a series of bombings to take place across the country. The Bureau of Investigation began large-scale arrests of immigrants believed to be communists. These mass arrests became known as Palmer Raids. The Palmer Raids were organized and carried out by an ambitious law school graduate, J. Edgar Hoover.

Hoover would rise very quickly to assume control of the Bureau in 1926. Until his death in 1972, Hoover would run the FBI with the shrewd ability to manipulate, cajole, and influence Congress and the White House to gain increased funding and greater power. Although some of his methods have been criticized, he managed to build a law enforcement agency that has garnered national and international respect and praise. Today the FBI remains a vital part of the nation's policing forces and an integral part of the nation's homeland security.

---

commerce or interfering with the civil rights given all citizens in the Constitution, state criminal laws cover **intrastate** crime, or crime that occurs within the state's borders.

States are also free to delegate some of their police powers to local governments such as counties and municipalities. Local governments can then pass laws, usually called ordinances, to protect health, safety, morals, and general welfare of people in the county or municipality. Ordinances are sometimes classified as criminal laws. For example, it is fairly common for cities to have in place extensive building codes. Violating these may be a summary offense.

Intrastate

Occurring within a state's border.

THE CRIMINAL TRIAL PROCESS

The criminal trial process is a carefully orchestrated journey from suspicion to trial and possibly conviction or appeal. Convicted defendants may serve their sentence in full or be granted early release or parole after serving just part of the sentence. They may go through a lengthy period of postrelease supervision. In addition, convicts frequently must pay fines and penalties and make restitution to victims. This is where theory meets practice, where concepts of punishment, rehabilitation, and restorative justice come together.

Whether you are a paralegal working in the district attorney's office, a parole officer working for the county, or an investigator working with defense attorneys, you will be dealing with people who are facing some of the darkest hours of their lives. Those who haven't "been in trouble with the law" before may be very frightened. For the first time in their lives, they are staring at the power of the state. The process awes even the rich and famous. Before her trial on charges she lied about her sale of Imclone stock, Martha Stewart told Larry King on his show *Larry King Live* that "no one is ever strong enough for such a thing . . . you have no idea how much worry and sadness and grief it causes."

Others who are more experienced may seem nonchalant or even unconcerned about the criminal process. In either way, as a legal professional, you may be one of the few sources of reliable information for defendants facing criminal charges. How you handle questions about the process may help reduce anxiety and let the defendant better help in his or her defense.

The criminal process falls into four distinct phases. They are:

- Investigation, arrest, and pretrial
- Trial
- Appeal
- Serving the sentence

INVESTIGATION, ARREST, AND PRETRIAL

The criminal process begins when authorities are alerted to the possibility that a crime has taken place. This may be something as simple as a police officer observing an illegal act or as complicated as an auditor questioning a company's financial transactions and alerting appropriate authorities. In either way, the criminal process begins.

Once the government authority responsible for enforcing the law for the type of offense has enough information to institute criminal proceedings, an arrest may be made. In the case of an officer observing an illegal act, the arrest may take place immediately. Because probable cause must be present for all arrests, the officer will have to justify his decision with a sworn statement or complaint after the fact. The officer need not, however, wait for a magistrate to authorize the arrest. This is based on the practical reality that the offender might be long gone before a magistrate's permission could be obtained.

Arrest Warrant
Document approved by a magistrate or judge attesting that there is probable cause to believe that someone has committed a specific crime and authorizing that person's arrest.

A police officer may also issue a citation if the offense is minor. If you've ever been caught speeding or running a stop sign, you were probably issued a citation. Citations usually allow the defendant to plead guilty and send in a fine or elect to have a hearing before a district justice or magistrate. If the officer finds illegal narcotics or the driver fails a sobriety check, it's more likely that the driver will be arrested on the spot rather than cited, given the more serious nature of the offense.

Naturally, police officers don't catch every defendant red-handed so that an immediate arrest or citation is possible. Sometimes an arrest is made only after a long investigation, weeks or months after the offense was allegedly committed. In that case, the arrest is usually carried out by the use of an **arrest warrant.** To get an arrest warrant, a police

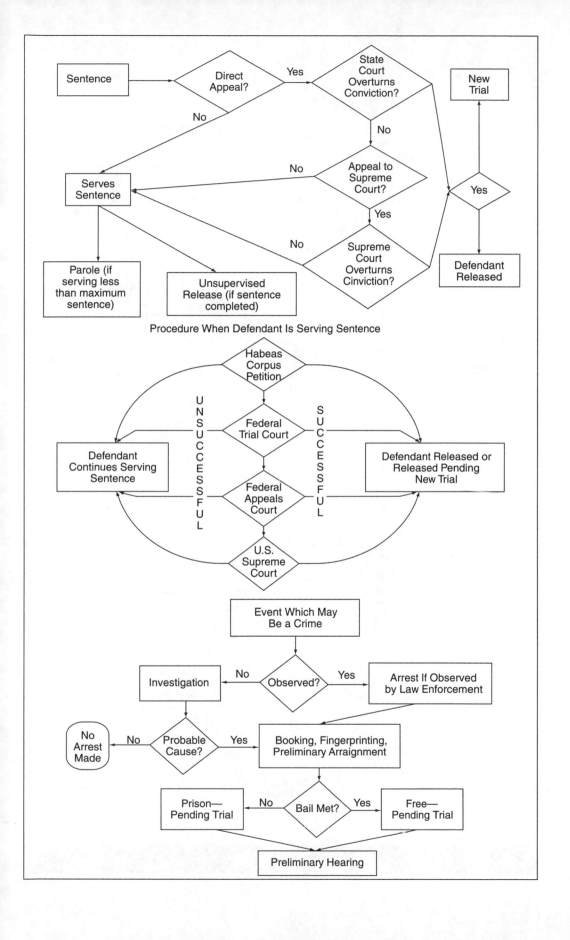

Procedure When Defendant Is Serving Sentence

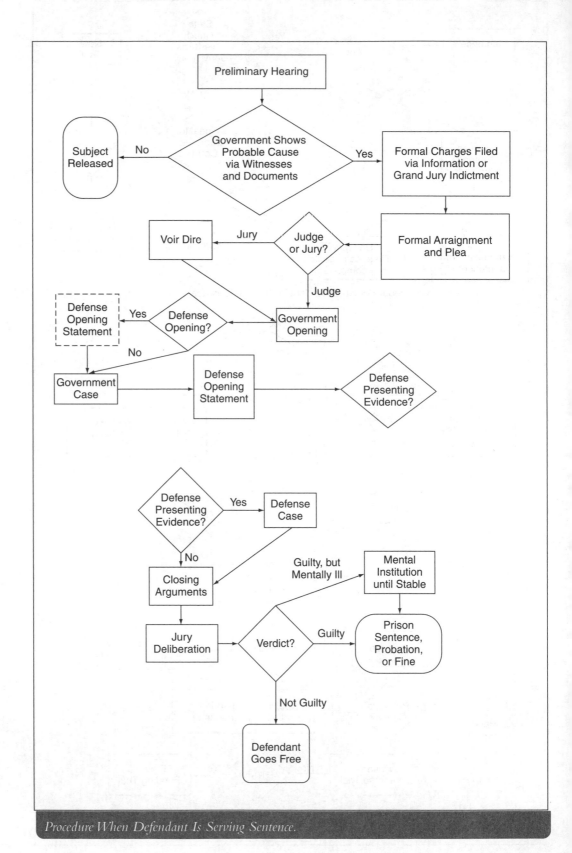

Procedure When Defendant Is Serving Sentence.

officer must apply for one with the local judiciary—usually a district magistrate or other judge assigned to oversee arrest warrants. The application includes a police officer or investigator's sworn statement or affidavit about what he or she believes happened and who committed the offense. Before an arrest warrant is issued, the magistrate or judge must be convinced that there is probable cause to believe the offense took place and the defendant committed it based on what the officer alleges in the affidavit or statement.

Armed with a signed arrest warrant, police officers can arrest the defendant and bring him or her to a central processing center, usually located at the police station, municipal building, or local jail. There, the defendant is held temporarily while being processed. Processing may include fingerprinting and a thorough search. If the police officers haven't already done so, they will now read the defendant the *Miranda* **warning.** (For a more thorough discussion of *Miranda* warnings, see Chapter 10.) The officers may then also question the defendant—who is free to refuse to answer or to demand an attorney be present during questioning.

In most jurisdictions, the defendant will be brought before a magistrate soon after arrest at a **preliminary arraignment.** At that point, the magistrate may rule on whether bail should be granted. Whether and how much bail is set depends on the seriousness of the charges and the likelihood that the defendant will appear for trial if he is released. The more serious the offense, the less likely bail will be granted and the higher bail is likely to be. In some cases, bail may be nothing more than the defendant's promise to appear for trial. This is usually referred to as being released on one's own recognizance. Defendants with close ties to the community and no prior criminal convictions are most likely to be released on bail or their own recognizance. Sometimes conditions are attached to bail, such as surrendering a passport to prevent flight to another country.

The next legal proceeding the defendant will face is the **preliminary hearing.** The preliminary hearing is the first stage in the criminal process in which the government is required to present actual evidence. In most cases, the state is represented by the arresting police officer. He or she will act as the government's representative and call any witnesses needed to prove that there is probable cause to hold the defendant over for trial. Sometimes, especially in cases where the defendant is mounting an aggressive defense, the district attorney or prosecutor will handle the preliminary hearing for the government.

In high-profile cases, preliminary hearings may become something akin to a minitrial. For the defense, the preliminary hearing may be a good opportunity to look at the evidence the state has against a client. The defense can also gauge how well a witness handles being on the witness stand. At this point, the defense gets a transcript of the witnesses' statements to use later if the witness' story changes later. The defense usually does not present any evidence at the preliminary hearing. If the government's case is weak, the case may even be dismissed after the preliminary hearing.

The evidentiary standard the government needs to meet at the preliminary hearing is simply that there is **probable cause.** Put succinctly, the government needs to prove that it is more likely than not that an offense took place and that it was the defendant who committed it. If the magistrate or district justice hearing the case believes the government has met those standards, the defendant will be ordered bound over for trial.

Even after the preliminary hearing, the defendant has not been officially charged with a crime. The government must jump yet another hurdle—it must either convince a **grand jury** that the defendant committed a crime, or it must persuade the prosecutor of the

Miranda **Warning**
The warning given suspects upon arrest informing of their constitutional rights.

Preliminary Arraignment

An accused's first official notification of the charges against him or her; preliminary arraignment generally occurs shortly after arrest.

Preliminary Hearing

A formal hearing that is the first occasion at which the government must produce evidence against the defendant; the prosecutor must convince the judge or magistrate hearing the case that it is more likely than not that the defendant committed the crime with which he or she is charged.

Probable Cause

A low standard of proof in a criminal case used to justify an arrest or hold a defendant over for trial after a preliminary hearing; the standard requires that there be sufficient proof to convince a reasonable person that it is more likely than not that he or she committed the crime charged. The amount of proof required before an officer can obtain a search warrant, stop a suspect, or make an arrest; enough evidence from which a reasonable person could conclude that the facts alleged are probably true.

Grand Jury

A body of citizens, usually 23, whose job it is to determine if a crime has been committed and if a person should be charged with that crime based on probable cause.

Information

A formal document signed and filed by a district attorney or prosecutor that charges an individual with a specific crime.

same. A grand jury is a body of citizens whose job it is to determine if a crime has been committed and if a person should be charged with that crime based on probable cause. In many jurisdictions, the decision to formally charge a defendant with a crime is left to the district attorney or state attorney. He or she has the authority to file an **information,** which formally charges the defendant with a crime and begins the next phase of the process—the actual trial phase. The information is very specific and names the penal sections of the law that the defendant is accused of violating. Very often it will include the most serious crimes the defendant is charged with as well as any other lesser included offenses. For example, a defendant may be charged with rape, indecent assault, aggravated assault, and simple assault. If the prosecution is unable to prove the more serious crime, he or she may still get a conviction for one of the lesser offenses. In addition, the inclusion of the lesser offenses allow some room for maneuvering if the prosecution and the defense decide to engage in **plea bargaining.** Plea bargaining is the practice of negotiating with a defendant and his attorney concerning the terms of a guilty plea. For example, a defendant might be persuaded to plead guilty to indecent assault but not rape because he knows that if he is convicted of rape he faces a much longer sentence than if he is sentenced on the indecent assault charge.

If the jurisdiction uses a grand jury to commence criminal trials, the charging document is referred to as an **indictment.** There is great flexibility in whether a defendant is charged with a crime. A district attorney has the discretion to decline to prosecute cases in most jurisdictions. The district attorney also typically can drop a case at any stage if he or she believes that would be in the interest of justice. This is done with a *nol pros* motion, which stands for the Latin *nolle prosequi,* translated loosely as no prosecution. Requiring an indictment or an information before people can be tried for a crime is another way to assure that innocent persons are not subjected to the power of the state without good reason. It is another check and balance on the power of the state over its citizens.

After the defendant is formally charged by indictment or information, he or she is then formally arraigned. At **arraignment,** the formal charges are read to the defendant, and he or she must enter a formal response to the charges, or a **plea.** The plea may be not guilty, guilty, *nolo contendere,* or not guilty by reason of insanity.

All jurisdictions have strict time limits requiring the government to move the criminal process forward in a timely fashion. Those limits are designed to prevent the government from holding defendants for extended periods of time without having the opportunity for a trial on the charges. For example, in many states, defendants must be brought to trial within 180 days of being charged, if imprisoned, or 360 days, if free on bail. Any continuance requested by the defendant is excluded from the count. If the case isn't brought in a timely fashion, the government must dismiss the charges.

There are some exceptions, most notably for those who have been detained on the battlefield in Afghanistan in the War on Terror or are suspected terrorists picked up elsewhere in the world, such as the battlefields of Iraq, and held at Guantanamo Bay in Cuba. In addition, Americans suspected of terrorist activities and picked up on the battlefield or even in the United States have been designated as enemy combatants by the president of the United States before being transferred to civilian authorities for trial. (For a more detailed discussion of the developing wartime criminal justice system put in place after the September 11 attacks, including the treatment of terror suspects, see Chapter 6.)

TRIAL

As a practical matter, most criminal cases never make it to trial. Most cases are disposed of by guilty pleas through plea bargaining. Plea bargaining in one form or another takes place in every jurisdiction. If the defendant doesn't plead guilty or no plea bargain is entered into, the case will proceed to trial.

Most jurisdictions hold special sessions of criminal court. Defendants who want a trial may select either trial by judge or trial by jury. Which a defendant chooses depends on many factors such as the reputation of the judge who would hear the case and the type of crime with which the defendant has been charged. A separate jury pool is called from the community for each criminal session with jurors for individual cases selected from the pool. Jurors called to jury duty may hear several cases.

If the defendant chooses a jury trial, he or she may assist in the selection of jurors from the jury pool. Sometimes the defense will even hire jury consultants, who are specially trained psychologists or sociologists well versed in human psychology who predict which jurors may favor one side over the other and who understand group dynamics.

The process of selecting jurors starts with ***voir dire,*** which involves asking potential jurors questions to determine whether they can judge the case fairly and impartially. *Voir dire* also helps to eliminate jurors who know too much about the case or who are related to the defendant, the victim, or any of the witnesses, attorneys, or police officers involved in the case.

Both the prosecution and the defense help choose the jurors. Either side may challenge the selection of a juror. The attorneys can reject an unlimited number of jurors *for cause.* For example, a juror who admits he has followed the case closely in the press and has already concluded that the defendant is guilty will be dismissed for cause. Attorneys can also reject potential jurors using a **peremptory challenge.** Peremptory challenges are essentially wild cards available to either side. When used, the attorney need not state a specific reason. Usually, there are a set number of peremptory challenges allowed. For more information on the jury process, see Chapter 12.

After a jury has been selected, the prosecution and the defense address the jury through **opening statements.** Because the government has the burden of proof to show the defendant is guilty beyond a reasonable doubt, the government makes its opening statement first. The government's opening statement usually outlines what the prosecutor expects to prove and whom the jurors can expect to hear testify for the prosecution. Essentially, the government tries to orient the jury by giving them a road map of the case.

The defense may make its opening statement next, or it may choose to wait until after the prosecution has rested its entire case. Many defense attorneys think it's better to wait until later, when they have already heard the government's witnesses and evidence. They can then tailor their opening to the weaknesses in the government's case.

After opening, the government presents its witnesses for **direct examination,** and the defense **cross-examines** them. Either party may then ask questions again by **redirect examination** and **recross examination**. Redirect and recross questions are limited to subject matter raised in the last cross or redirect exam.

Because the government has the burden of proof and the defendant is considered innocent until proven guilty, the government must prove each element of the crime charged. That is, they must prove beyond a reasonable doubt that the defendant intentionally committed the act charged. Many prosecutors use a checklist of the elements of the crime

Plea Bargaining

The process of negotiating the settlement of criminal charges without a trial.

Indictment

A written accusation claiming that a specific person committed a specific crime or crimes; prosecutors present indictments to grand juries so the jury can vote on whether the indictment is a true bill.

Arraignment

The stage of a criminal case at which the defendant is first formally charged with a specific crime.

Plea

A formal response to criminal charges; a plea may be not guilty, guilty, *nolo contendere*, or not guilty by reason of insanity.

Nolo Contendere

Latin for "I will not contest this,"; a plea entered that admits no wrongdoing but allows the court to sentence the defendant as if guilty.

Voir Dire

From the French meaning "to speak the truth," it refers to the examination of citizens to ascertain their fitness for serving on a jury; during the voir dire phase of a criminal trial, the attorneys or the judge ask questions of the jury pool. These are designed to ferret out those jurors who can't be impartial or who can't serve on the jury because of illnes or other obligations and to help the attorneys in the case decide where and when to use available peremeptory challenges.

Peremptory Challenge

Challenge to seating a juror that cannot be challenged. Generally each side is allowed a fixed number of peremptory challenges.

Opening Statements

The statements made by prosecuting or defense attorneys at the beginning of a trial outlining what the lawyer hopes to prove during the trial.

charged and cross off each element as the evidence is presented. For example, in a theft case, the prosecutor would have to present evidence of who owned the stolen goods and that the item was taken without the owner's permission. Finally, the prosecution would have to show that it was the defendant who physically took the owner's property, intending to permanently deprive the owner of it.

At the end of the prosecution's case, the government rests. If the defense thinks that the prosecution failed to prove an element of its case, it may ask for the charges to be dismissed. If the motion is denied, the defense may present its case. It is not required to do so, since the burden is on the prosecution to prove the case beyond a reasonable doubt. If the defense does present evidence or witnesses, the prosecution has a chance to cross-examine them. The defendant is not required to testify against himself and therefore may not testify. The jury will be instructed that it cannot consider the defendant's decision not to testify as evidence of guilt. The decision to testify or remain silent depends on the case and on the defendant. If his or her testimony is likely to be sympathetic, it may be best to testify. If not, the best option may be to stay silent. If the defense does have witnesses testify, the prosecution may present rebuttal evidence to disprove the evidence.

Once the prosecution has presented its case, the defense may make a motion for a judgment of acquittal. Under the *Federal Rules for Criminal Procedure*, a judge must "enter a judgment of acquittal for any offense for which the evidence is insufficient to sustain a conviction."[15] Most states have similar provisions. Judges have the option of waiting until the jury has rendered a verdict until ruling on the motion.

Finally, the attorneys present closing arguments. The prosecution goes first, usually outlining what it believes its evidence has proven. The defense then closes. In some jurisdictions, the prosecution may again address the jury to rebut issues made by the defense.

The jury then retires to the jury room and elects a foreperson to help direct its deliberations. In high-profile cases, the jury may be sequestered both during trial and deliberations to avoid tainting their process with outside news or opinions. If the jury is unable to reach a decision, the jury is said to be **hung**. The jury can judge the defendant guilty or not guilty. Its decision is the **verdict.** In a case in which the defendant has raised insanity as a defense, the jury can also find the defendant not guilty by reason of insanity. In some states, they can also find the defendant guilty but mentally ill. For more on the insanity defense, see Chapter 9, Common Law Defenses.

After the jury renders a verdict, the court will enter the judgment in the record. In those cases where the judge is deciding the case, he or she will announce the verdict and enter judgment.

The defendant may be sentenced immediately or after presentence investigation and recommendations. There may be sentence guidelines or mandatory sentences. In the case of a capital crime tried by a jury, there will be a sentencing phase of the trial.

APPEAL

Every defendant is entitled to an appeal of some sort. In state criminal cases, those appeals go through the state system and may include a trip to the state's highest court or even the U.S. Supreme Court. Except in very rare circumstances and only before the defendant has "been placed in jeopardy" (i.e., brought to trial), the prosecution may not appeal.

If the jury concludes that the defendant is not guilty, that is the end of the matter. Appeals generally must be filed within 30 days of sentencing, though some states set a shorter appeal period.

The defendant's appeal may attack any defect in the trial or evidence. Generally, the issue appealed must have been preserved during the trial by an objection on the record. For example, if the defense believes a piece of evidence should not have been admitted, it must have challenged the admission at the time to preserve the issue on appeal.

Once all direct appeals are exhausted, the defendant may still have an opportunity to be heard. He or she can do so through a process called *habeas corpus.* A *writ of habeas corpus* is an order by federal court to "bring the body" of the prisoner to the court. It is an old right designed to protect citizens from abusive government practices. A writ of habeas corpus may be filed years into a defendant's sentence and raise issues that weren't raised earlier such as ineffective counsel. It may also be raised if there is new evidence of innocence such as a DNA test that clears the defendant or proof of some form of corruption during the trial.

SERVING THE SENTENCE

The defendant may begin serving the sentence immediately after trial or may be free pending appeal. Once direct appeals are over, the defendant will have to start his sentence. He or she will get credit for any time already served while awaiting trial.

Most defendants will serve a minimum sentence (generally half of the bottom range of the sentence). In some cases, no deviation from the sentence range is permitted. Parole boards generally rule on when the defendant may be released. Defendants may also ask the parole board or the governor (or president) for a pardon under limited circumstances.

Once parole is granted or the defendant has served his sentence, the defendant is released. In the case of parole, he or she will be supervised for as long as the maximum sentence would have been. If he or she has served the maximum sentence, there is no additional supervision unless he or she is a sexual predator as defined under that state's laws.

SOURCES OF LAW

As you have already learned, the Constitution and the laws Congress passes pursuant to its powers are the supreme law of the land. But they aren't the only source of law in the United States. Law is also created by treaties signed with foreign governments, laws enacted by state and local legislatures, regulations of administrative agencies, executive orders, and judicial decisions.

CONSTITUTIONAL AMENDMENTS AND THE BILL OF RIGHTS

The original Constitution provided little to safeguard civil rights. Anti-Federalists, the group opposed to ratifying the Constitution, feared the new U.S. Constitution would create too strong a federal government and the freedom gained by overthrowing British rule would be lost. To address these fears, Federalists agreed to ten amendments to the constitution known as the Bill of Rights.

Direct Examination
The initial questioning of one's own witness.

Cross-Examination
Questioning of a witness put on the stand by the other side following direct examination.

Redirect Examination
Questioning of one's own witness following cross-examination.

Recross Examination
Questioning of a witness called by the other side following redirect examination.

Hung Jury
A jury that is unable to reach.

Verdict
A judge or jury's decision at the end of a trial; the verdict in a civil case must be by at least a preponderance of the evidence, while the verdict in a criminal case must be beyond a reasonable doubt.

Habeas Corpus
Literally meaning "you have the body," a judicial process for determining the legality of a particular person's custody. The "Great Writ," which orders another authority to bring a person held to the court. It was originally used to prevent kings from simply making enemies disappear.

The Bill of Rights provides protections for:

- Freedom of Religion
- Freedom of Speech
- Freedom of the Press
- The right against self-incrimination
- The right to be free from cruel and unusual punishment
- The right to due process and others

Subsequent constitutional amendments abolished slavery, provided women the right to vote, and legalized federal income tax. Clearly, some amendments are better than others.

HISTORICAL HIGHLIGHT
The English Civil War and the English Bill of Rights

The U.S. Bill of Rights owes much to the English Bill of Rights adopted 100 years before in 1689. By the seventeenth century, England had been using the concept of common law for over 400 years. But the first kings to sit on the throne in the seventeenth century believed in the "divine right of kings." In other words, kings ruled through a god-given mandate without regard to the rule of law.

Tensions grew until a long, bloody civil war broke out in 1642. Charles I was executed and replaced by Oliver Cromwell, who trampled English rights as effectively as the kings had done. Ultimately, Parliament agreed to restore the monarchy putting Charles II, a Protestant who did not believe in the divine right of kings, on the throne. Charles II agreed to many limits on his power.

Charles II died in 1685, and his brother James II, a Roman Catholic, became king. James II also believed in the divine right of kings, and England once again seemed poised for internal strife. The English did not want another civil war and tolerated James. The Protestant majority in England placed their hope for peaceful transition in James' daughter, Mary, who was a Protestant. But then James had a son, and Mary was no longer next in line for the throne under the laws of **primogeniture**

Parliament invited Mary and her husband, William of Orange, the ruler of the Netherlands, to invade England with an army and assume the throne. When William and Mary invaded, James left the country without a drop of blood being spilled. Because the change in monarchs happened without violence, it is referred to as the Glorious Revolution.

Parliament, however, did not intend to import an absolute ruler. Part of the deal was that William and Mary had to agree to a Bill of Rights. The **English Bill of Rights** of 1689 would prove to be a very influential document in the evolution of the U.S. legal system.

The English Bill of Rights reiterated the king's subservience to the law and the limited role of Parliament. Because monarchs had frequently abused the judicial system to silence political foes, Parliament inserted the following provisions to protect those accused of a crime:

Primogeniture
The ancient common law of descent where all the father's property went to the oldest son. Also the law of succession to the English throne.

English Bill of Rights
A precursor to the U.S. Bill of Rights, it guarantees due process and bars cruel and unusual punishment.

- That excessive bail ought not be required, nor excessive fines imposed; nor cruel and unusual punishments inflicted.
- That jurors ought to be duly empaneled and returned, and jurors which pass upon men in trials of high treason ought to be freeholders.
- That all grants and promises of fines and forfeitures of particular persons before conviction are illegal and void.

The provision about excessive bail became the Eighth Amendment to the U.S. Constitution. The provision about jurors carried over into U.S. law as well. The fines and forfeitures provision refers to the accused being innocent until proven guilty. No fine is due until the person has been convicted of a crime. You will learn more about these and other important Constitutional protections provided to persons accused of a crime in later chapters.[16]

TREATIES

Treaties with foreign governments have the force of law. Any treaty negotiated by the president or his representatives must be ratified by the U.S. Senate to become law. This is part of the Senate's **advise and consent** duty under the Constitution. The most common way treaties affect criminal law is through the power of **extradition.** Countries with an extradition treaty with the United States have agreed to send an accused criminal to the United States, where he or she can be charged with a crime and tried. Likewise, the United States is the signatory to many treaties that obligate it to return persons accused of a crime in another country to that country for trial. Not all countries have extradition treaties with the United States.

Extradition treaties may be limited in scope. For instance, since the European Union has no death penalty, it will not extradite an accused person facing a death sentence to any country, including the United States.

THE NAPOLEONIC CODE

Most of our discussion has centered on the tradition of English common law. However, there is another major influence on current U.S. criminal law—the French system of civil law based on the **Napoleonic Code.**

The Napoleonic Code was written under Napoleon I. The goals of the Napoleonic Code were to make criminal penalties more consistent and to bring the French government under the rule of law in much the same way the Charter of Liberties, Magna Carta, and other notable English documents made the English government accountable to the people.

Napoleon had seized power in the aftermath of the French Revolution. The French Revolution had taken place in large part in response to the excesses of the French monarchy. Under the French monarchy, an influential person could issue a *lettre de cachet*—a document that directed that a person be imprisoned indefinitely without trial or even without ever being charged with a crime. Following the French Revolution, there was the Reign of Terror during which many French nobles and members of the middle class were beheaded. After reeling between the extremes of royal tyranny on one hand and mob terror on the other, the need for an open and fair legal code was obvious.[17]

Governments . . . deriv(e) their just powers from the consent of the governed.
Thomas Jefferson, Declaration of Independence (July 4, 1776)

Advise and Consent
The constitutional relationship of the Senate to the president regarding the selection of federal judges and other duties.

Extradition
The process of returning an accused criminal to the jurisdiction in which he or she is charged.

Napoleonic Code
The French system of laws developed by Napoleon I, it is the basis of Louisiana law.

In the United States, only Louisiana relies heavily on the Napoleonic Code tradition. In 1803, the U.S. government purchased Louisiana. Its customs and laws were much more influenced by the French and Spanish than the English.

DIFFERENCES BETWEEN THE NAPOLEONIC CODE AND ENGLISH COMMON LAW

The way courtrooms are organized and run are very different under the two systems. Under the Napoleonic Code or civil law, criminal trials resemble boards of inquiry rather than the adversarial arrangement with which we are familiar. Judges in civil law cases may cross-examine witnesses to gather facts. In contrast to the English system, plea bargaining is unknown. The judge does not ratify deals made between the prosecution and defense attorneys. Rather the judge's duty is to conduct an investigation into the circumstances surrounding a crime and render a just verdict.[18]

Many of the legal maneuvers in U.S. criminal trials are designed to balance the rights of the accused and the state. Our system attempts to balance the rights of the individual and the state in an adversarial setting. The civil law system seeks to discover the truth about a crime with all parties participating in the search. Critics of the civil law system charge that it does not offer the same safeguards of individual rights that the English system provides. This may be why so many Louisiana criminal cases reach the highest court of the land, the U.S. Supreme Court. (For example, see Chapter 4 on the right to trial by jury.) The Napoleonic Code tradition is at odds with the English tradition of trial by jury and the right against self-incrimination.

CODIFIED LAWS

Codified laws are laws passed by either a federal or state legislature. These laws are collected and classified by topic. Laws passed by the U.S. Congress become part of the U.S. Code. State laws are published in the various state codes. Local governments are said to be "creatures of the state" in that they draw their power from state governments. They may pass local laws or ordinances within the bounds of their charters.

REGULATIONS

Regulations are written by administrative agencies. At the national level, these become part of the *Code of Federal Regulations* (CFR). When Congress passes a law, it often instructs an appropriate administrative agency to develop regulations to give guidance on how the law should be enforced. For instance, regulations dealing with counterfeiting are developed by the Department of the Treasury, the agency that is responsible for the legitimate printing of bills and coinage. Regulations that are consistent with the law under which they are promulgated are also law.

Model Penal Code and Commentaries
Code that attempts to unify state penal codes. Legislatures often look to it when drafting legislation.

MODEL PENAL CODE

Although not a law, the **Model Penal Code and Commentaries** is an attempt to standardize conflicting penal codes among the states. The code was developed in 1961 and

YOU MAKE THE CALL

TREATY OBLIGATIONS AND CRIMINAL LAW

Under the U.S. Constitution, ratified treaties have the same force of law as the Constitution, meaning that theoretically treaty provisions should have priority over state laws. But states have seldom been willing to abide by treaties to which they were not a party.

A case in point is the execution of a Paraguayan national by the name of Angel Francisco Breard. Breard was arrested for the stabbing death and sexual assault of Ruth Dickie, his neighbor. Under the Vienna Convention, an international treaty signed by 130 nations including the United States and Paraguay, police are required to notify the consular office of a nation if they arrest a foreign national. Virginia police never did so.

Mr. Breard confessed to the crime but claimed that the reason he committed the stabbing was that his father-in-law had put a satanic curse on him. Breard had the benefit of court-appointed attorneys who advised him not to testify at his trial and probably didn't endorse the satanic curse defense. Breard testified anyway and was sentenced to death. The government of Paraguay sued Virginia officials in federal court, complaining that Breard had been denied his rights under the Vienna Convention.

The case worked its way through to the U.S. Supreme Court. The Court ruled in a 6–3 decision that because Breard had not raised the Vienna Convention violation in his initial defense, he could not raise it now. Paraguay presented the case to the International Court of Justice. The International Court of Justice hears cases involving international treaties. It is also known as the World Court and is a part of the United Nations. The International Court of Justice agreed to hear the case and scheduled argument for fall 1998, well after Breard's date with the executioner.

Secretary of State Madeline Albright personally requested that Virginia authorities delay Breard's execution until the International Court of Justice could hear the case. She cited possible repercussions for Americans charged with crimes overseas. After all, if the United States refused to comply with the treaty, why should other signatory nations? Virginia refused and executed Breard on April 14, hours after the U.S. Supreme Court denied his final appeal for a stay of execution.[19] Eventually, Paraguay dropped the case, and no final decision was ever rendered by the International Court of Justice.

You make the call: If you were the Governor of Virginia, would you have stayed the execution until the International Court of Justice had a chance to rule? What would the political fallout have been for doing so?

provides commentary and advice to state legislatures, judges, and students of the law. State legislatures commonly refer to the Model Penal Code when drafting new legislation.

EXECUTIVE ORDERS

The president and the governors of the states have the power to issue executive orders. The power to issue executive orders comes from the power delegated by legislatures to the executive branch to enforce the laws. Examples of executive orders include George W.

Diplomatic Immunity

The courtesy afforded all diplomats while in foreign countries that allow them to be immune from prosecution for crimes they commit.

HISTORICAL HIGHLIGHT
Waiving Diplomatic Immunity

Foreign diplomats working or traveling in the United States are protected from arrest and imprisonment by diplomatic immunity. Some large U.S. cities have a continuous problem with foreign diplomats who exercise their right to diplomatic immunity. The problem is particularly big in New York City, home to the headquarters of the United Nations, and Washington, D.C., home to over one hundred foreign embassies. For example, in New York City, diplomats from Belarus managed to amass over $41,000 in overdue traffic fines during the first half of 1996. Overdue parking tickets may be frustrating to city officials in major cities where parking is hard to come by, but diplomatic immunity creates greater problems when diplomats commit crimes. In some cases, a foreign government will waive immunity and allow its consular employees to be prosecuted and imprisoned.

On January 3, 1997, 16-year-old Joviane Waltrick was killed in a five-car crash along Diplomat Row in Washington, D.C. Gueorgui Makharadze, a high-ranking diplomat of the Republic of Georgia, caused the accident. He was driving under the influence of alcohol and weaving through cars while traveling at a speed of nearly 85 miles per hour through crowded city streets. The Republic of Georgia waived diplomatic immunity for the criminal charges, but not the civil charges. Makharadze pleaded guilty to involuntary manslaughter and four counts of aggravated assault, but relatives of the victims could not recover civil damages in court.[20] Makharadze is now serving his sentence in a U.S. jail.[21]

Another instance in which diplomatic immunity was waived occurred in 1989, when a Belgian army sergeant was charged with murdering two homosexual men in Fort Lauderdale, Florida. Belgium agreed to waive immunity after the prosecutors pledged not to seek the death penalty. The sergeant is now serving two 25-year sentences.

The United States has not been quick to waive diplomatic immunity for its diplomats. In 1993, a U.S. envoy stationed in Moscow killed a pedestrian while driving down a dark street. He was accused of driving drunk, but U.S. officials insisted the accusation was false. The United States refused to waive diplomatic immunity and instead sent the diplomat home.

Bush's Executive Order of February 14, 2007, establishing "military commissions to try alien unlawful enemy combatants."

JUDICIAL DECISIONS

As you learned earlier in this chapter, the doctrine of *stare decisis* is employed by judges to create common law. Much of U.S. common law can be traced back to English common law.

Stare decisis lends uniformity and consistency to legal decisions, at least within a state. A court is bound to follow a precedent of a higher court in its system. For example, a state trial court is bound to follow the decision of that state's supreme court. But a state does not have to follow the precedence of another state's highest court. Thus, *stare decisis* promotes uniformity within a jurisdiction, but not necessarily across different jurisdictions.

PRIORITY OF LAW

The U.S. Constitution is the supreme law of the land. Any treaty ratified by the Senate carries the same weight as the Constitution. Federal statutes take precedence over federal regulations. Federal law takes precedence over state law.

Most state legal systems are a mirror image of the federal structure. The state constitution is the highest state law. State statutes supersede state regulations, and state laws take precedence over local laws and ordinances. Most state court systems also mirror the federal judicial system. Each state has a set of courts that are responsible for trials and another set that handles intermediate appeals. All 50 states also have a state supreme court, although it may go by another name.

CHAPTER SUMMARY

Every society has a body of laws. Laws govern the behavior of members of society. Laws are created and enforced by government. The United States has a system of law derived from English common law.

Common law relies on *stare decisis* and precedent to decide cases. Courts must follow earlier decisions when faced with a new case. This makes the legal system predictable and stable.

Jurisprudence is the study of law. There are many theories of law, or schools of jurisprudence. The consensus theory holds that society decides what is a crime and what isn't. The ruling class theory and the Command School theory posit that the ruling classes decide what is legal and what is illegal. Blackstone classified crime into two types: those that are *mala in se*, or inherently evil, and those that are *mala prohibita*, or illegal because society decides they are. The Natural Law School believes that people have natural, inherent rights and that laws are based on what is right. The Historical School sees laws as changing to accommodate changes in society. The Analytical School relies on logic. The Sociological School, or the realists, believe that law should be created to shape societal behavior. Finally, the Critical Legal Studies School and the Fem-Crits believe that laws are arbitrary rules to enforce the status quo and oppress and control those not in power.

A crime is a wrong against society. Criminal law differs from civil law in several important ways. First, criminal law seeks to protect all of society from lawbreakers, while civil law deals with vindication of individual, private rights. Secondly, criminal cases are always brought in the name of the people by a representative of the government, while litigants' private representatives bring civil cases. Third, in order to win a criminal case, the prosecutor must prove the case beyond a reasonable doubt, a very high standard. Private plaintiffs need only prove their case by a preponderance of the evidence, a much lighter burden of proof.

Crimes are classified in order of their relative seriousness. Summary offenses are minor violations, usually punishable by either a short period of imprisonment or a fine.

Misdemeanors are more serious offenses and carry a penalty of up to one year in prison. Felony offenses are the most serious and are punishable by a long prison sentence or death.

The U.S. judicial system is part of a federal system of government. The United States has a national government, 50 state governments, and numerous local governments. The framework for our federal system is found in the U.S. Constitution. It established three branches of government: the legislative to make laws, the executive to enforce laws, and the judicial to interpret laws. Each of the three branches serves as a check and balance on the others.

The U.S. Supreme Court, federal laws, and treaties are the supreme law of the land. The U.S. Supreme Court heads the federal judiciary. The system is divided into 13 circuits. Each circuit has trial courts called U.S. District Courts and an intermediate appellate court called the U.S. Court of Appeals. Justices of the U.S. Supreme Court and other federal judges serve for life. They may only be removed by impeachment. Federal courts have exclusive jurisdiction over some subject matter and concurrent jurisdiction with the states over other matters. Some areas of exclusive jurisdiction include patents and federal tax cases.

State court systems parallel the federal judicial system in many ways. Each has a trial court, at least one intermediate appellate court, and a supreme court. State courts follow the same hierarchy as federal courts. That is, the lower courts must follow the decisions previously handed down by the States highest court and the intermediate appellate court. The intermediate appellate court must follow the state highest court decisions. All state courts must abide by decisions made by the U.S. Supreme Court.

The Constitutions Supremacy Clause establishes that federal law takes precedence over state and local law. The Commerce Clause allows the federal government to pass laws that regulate interstate commerce. Both the federal government and state and local governments have police powers. Through its exercise of police powers, government can regulate the health, safety, morals, and welfare of its citizens.

The legal system provides many safeguards for persons accused of having committed a crime. These safeguards exist at every level of the criminal process. For example, persons may only be arrested for a crime if a law enforcement officer has either observed the accused committing the crime or has probable cause that the accused committed the crime to convince a magistrate or judge to issue a warrant. The defendant must then be formally charged with the crime and be given an opportunity early on to defend against the charges.

A defendant is entitled to a trial at which the prosecution must prove beyond a reasonable doubt that he or she has committed the crime. The convicted defendant may then appeal the verdict. He or she can also challenge the verdict later under some circumstances such as newly discovered evidence.

There are many sources of law. The Constitution is one source. Others include treaties, codified laws, regulations, ordinances, executive orders, and judicial decisions.

KEY TERMS

Advise and Consent	Bourgeoisie	Concurrent Jurisdiction
Analytical School	Burden of Proof	Confirmation
Arraignment	Checks and Balances	Consensus theory
Arrest Warrant	Command School	Crime
Beyond a Reasonable Doubt	Commerce Clause	Crits
	Common Law	Cross-Examines

Defendant

Diplomatic
 Immunity

Direct Examination

Dual Sovereignty

Elite or Ruling Class
 Theory

English Bill of Rights

Enumerated Powers

Exclusive Jurisdiction

Executive

Extradition

Federal Circuits

Federal System

Felonies

Fem-Crits

Grand Jury

Habeas Corpus

Historical School

Hung Jury

Impeachment

Indictment

Information

Interstate Commerce

Intrastate

Judicial

Jurisdiction

Jurisprudence

Law

Legislative

Mala In Se

Mala Prohibita

Miranda Warning

Misdemeanors

Model Penal Code and
 Commentaries

Moral Theory of Law

Napoleonic Code

Natural Law School

Nolo Contendere

Opening Statements

Peremptory Challenge

Petition for Certiorari

Plaintiff

Plea

Plea Bargaining

Police Power

Precedent

Preemption Doctrine

Preliminary
 Arraignment

Preliminary Hearing

Preponderance of the
 Evidence

Primogeniture

Probable Cause

Proletariat

Realists

Recross Examination

Redirect Examination

Sociological School

Stare Decisis

Summary Offenses

Supremacy Clause

Tort

Tort Feasor

U.S. Courts of Appeals

U.S. District Courts

U.S. Supreme Court

Verdict

Voir Dire

War on Terror

Writ of Certiorari

EXERCISE

Throughout the textbook, you will find several extended exercises designed to help you apply the information you are learning. The scenarios may sound familiar since they are based on events widely reported in the media. You will also find some of the underlying court documents reproduced there and in some of the exercises. Similar to the You Make the Call exercises presented elsewhere in the textbook, the material is designed to present you with common problems encountered in the criminal justice system by victims, defendants, law enforcement officials, and others and demonstrate the relevance the material has to the day-to-day operation of the criminal justice system.

1. **Scenario:** A 27-year old female college student, who works as an exotic dancer, is hired to perform at an off-campus party by members of a neighboring university's sports team. The dancer later reported to the police that she had been sexually assaulted by three of the team members at some time during the evening. The female is black, and the accused members of the team are white. Almost immediately, the press descends on the college town, and the tabloids print lurid headlines. Not

long after, the local district attorney announces that he had no doubt that the dancer was raped and begins a long investigation into the matter. Based on what you have learned so far in this course, answer the following questions about the case:

a. You work as a paralegal in the law firm that has been hired to represent the victim in a possible civil action. What considerations come into play should the district attorney file charges against the team members? How does what the district attorney must prove differ from what a lawyer filing a civil lawsuit must prove?

b. You work as a law clerk for the attorney hired to represent one of the team players. You and she will be meeting with the client to explain what will likely occur if he is charged. What will the two of you tell the client about the process he is about to experience?

DISCUSSION QUESTIONS

1. What do you see as the advantages and disadvantages of a Common Law system?
2. Durkheim felt that laws were agreed upon standards of a society, but Marx felt that laws were put in place by a society's elite to serve the elite's interest. Which do you think is closer to the truth and why?
3. What are the major differences between criminal law and civil law?
4. In what ways do the legislative and executive branches restrain the judiciary? What power does the judiciary have to restrain the other branches?
5. What is police power? Can you think of ways that states have abused police power? What is it that makes police power legitimate?
6. Does the U.S. policy of giving ratified treaties the force of law put the United States at a disadvantage internationally?
7. What do you think has been the impact of the U.S. Supreme Court's decision on African-Americans who choose to travel through several states?

FOR FURTHER READING

1. Hamilton, J., Madison, J., & Jay, J. *The Federalist Papers*. For the student who wants to develop an understanding of the Constitution as the founding fathers saw it, this classic work is essential reading. Written by Alexander Hamilton, James Madison, and John Jay, the work was originally circulated to argue for the ratification of the Constitution.
2. Young, A. (ed.). (1976). *The American Revolution: Explorations in the History of American Radicalism*. Dekalb, IL: Northern Illinois University Press. This collection of essays by historians explores the ideologies of the men who created the American Revolution.
3. DeTocqueville, A. (1969). *Democracy in America* (rev. ed.). New York: HarperCollins. This classic study of what makes U.S. democracy unique was first published in the 1800s by a Frenchman who traveled extensively through the new United States. His observations on U.S. democracy are regarded as some of the most insightful ever made.
4. Maier, P. (1997). *American Scripture*. New York: Alfred A. Knopf. This work analyzes the Declaration of Independence and the attitudes that shaped its framers' thoughts.

5. Burger, W. (1995). *It Is So Ordered: A Constitution Unfolds.* New York: William Morrow. Written by former chief justice of the U.S. Supreme Court Warren E. Burger, this book analyzes some of the most important cases to have been decided by the Supreme Court in layperson's terms.

ENDNOTES

1. E. Durkheim, *The Division of Labor in Society* (New York: Free Press, 1933; original work published 1893).

2. K. Marx and F. Engels, *The Communist Manifesto: A Modern Edition* (New York: Verso, 1998; original work published 1848; original English version 1888).

3. D. R. Coquillette, *Ideology and Incorporation III: Reason Regulated—The Post-Restoration English Civilians, 1653–1735+*, 67 B. U. L. Rev. 289 (1987).

4. W. Blackstone, *Commentaries on the Laws of England*, ed. Cooley (London: Callaghan and Company, 1899).

5. Coquillette, *Ideology and Incorporation III.*

6. Ibid.

7. Ibid.

8. Ibid.

9. D. L. Rhode, *Feminist Critical Theories*, 42 Stan. L. Rev. 617 (1990).

10. Cable News Network, *The Murder* (1995), *http://www.cnn.com/US/OJ/murder/index.html.*

11. *United States v. Koon, Powell, Wind, and Briseno*, 833 F. Supp. 769 (C. D. Cal, 1993).

12. *United States v. Price, et al.*, 383 U.S. 787 (1966).

13. *United States v. Lanza*, 260 U.S. 377 (1922).

14. Federal Bureau of Investigation, *A Short History of the Federal Bureau of Investigation* (Washington, DC, 1998), *http://www.fbi.gov/history/hist.htm.*

15. Federal Rules of Criminal Procedure, Rule 29(b).

16. W. Churchill, *History of the English-Speaking Peoples* (rev. ed.) (New York: Random House, 1965).

17. E. A. Tomlinson, *Symposium: Comparative Criminal Justice Issues in the United States, West Germany, England, and France: Nonadversarial Justice: The French Experience*, 42 Md. L. Rev. 131 (1983).

18. Ibid.

19. J. R. Schmertz Jr., and M. Meier, Despite requests for stay of execution from International Court of Justice, U.S. Supreme Court denies habeas corpus relief to convicted Paraguayan citizen for citizen's failure to raise violation of Consular Convention before Virginia Courts, *International Law Update*, Vol. 4, no. 4 (April, 1998).

20. "Georgian Diplomat Wins Immunity Claim," *Legal Times*, June 8, 1998, Update Section, page 12, American Lawyer Newspapers Group Inc.

21. "Georgian Diplomat Gets Up to 21 Years in Fatal Crash," *The Daily Record* (Baltimore, MD), December 22, 1997, page 17.

CHAPTER 2

What Is a Crime?

CHAPTER CONTENTS

Laws too gentle are seldom obeyed; too severe, seldom executed.

Benjamin Franklin, **Poor Richard's Almanac**

CHAPTER OBJECTIVES

After studying this chapter, you should be able to:

- Explain what makes an act or omission a crime.
- Explain *corpus delicti*.
- Explain the role of confessions in crime.
- Explain *mens rea*.
- List and explain the different types of liability.
- Explain how to prove *mens rea*.
- List and explain the different types of intent.
- Explain the difference between *mens rea* and intent.
- Explain *actus reus*.
- Explain possession.
- Explain omission.
- Explain harm.
- Explain causation.

INTRODUCTION AND HISTORICAL BACKGROUND

WHAT IS A CRIME?

Crime

A wrong against society or the public interest.

Corpus Delicti

Literally, "the body of the crime;" the fact that a crime has been committed.

A **crime** is a wrong against society or the public interest. It is typically punishable by imprisonment or death and sometimes an additional fine. Generally speaking, criminal law is designed to protect and vindicate public rights. Criminal law seeks to protect society as a whole from the aberrant (as defined by the law) behavior of some members of that society.

Before prosecuting anyone for a crime, the first work of the state is to establish that a crime has been committed. To do so, the state relies on a concept called **corpus delicti,** or the "body of the crime." It is tempting to take this to mean the body of the fallen victim lying outlined in tape on the floor of a crime scene, but corpus delicti means something more complex. It requires two things: one, a result or harm. For example, since we began with a body, imagine an investigator finding a body on the sidewalk in front of a high-rise apartment building, as happened in Harrisburg, Pennsylvania, on February 25, 2006. The woman, later identified as 23-year-old Rachel Kozlusky, was dressed in underwear and a sweater and had massive injuries indicating a fall from a great height. Above her, a hole in the skylight of a portico indicated a fall, likely from one of the balconies or windows overhead. The investigator had a dead body and harm a plenty, but no crime. Corpus delicti requires a second element: the harm must result from someone's criminal act. The investigator needed evidence to indicate that the woman's fall was more than an accident.

In this case, the state quickly found that evidence in an apartment on the 23rd floor of the building, from which Rachel Kozlusky's boyfriend, Kevin Eckenrode, exited and took the elevator down, "distraught and extremely inebriated." The boyfriend later told authorities that he had taken Kozlusky by the wrists and dangled her over the balcony as a game and accidentally let go. The incident followed a bout of heavy drinking and partying, ostensibly to celebrate their engagement.

Accident or crime? The state had to establish corpus delicti. "Obviously it's an unusual scenario," Dauphin County District Attorney Ed Marsico, Jr. told the press shortly after the accident. "Even if [Eckenrode's] version is true, to be holding someone out on a 23rd-story window is beyond ridiculous. It's as reckless an act as I can imagine, if not malicious."[1] The man's actions were not mere accident; they were at the very least criminally reckless. The state had corpus delicti and merely had to move on to prove which crime had occurred—murder or manslaughter. Eckenrode was eventually found guilty of involuntary manslaughter and sentenced to 11½ to 23 months in the county prison after a jury rejected third degree murder charges. His attorney had argued the whole thing was an unfortunate accident.[2]

Before prosecuting any crime, the state usually must show corpus delicti beyond a reasonable doubt. The state does not have to have a suspect or precise explanation of the crime, but it must establish that a crime has taken place. Sometimes, the suspects and circumstances strongly suggest a crime, but prosecution is impossible because corpus delicti cannot be confirmed. This would apply to cases for which truly accidental explanations are feasible. For example, say that in the Kozlusky case, the boyfriend claimed his girlfriend climbed out on the ledge to rescue their cat. When she began to fall, he grabbed her arms but lost his grip. In the absence of further evidence, the state might not have been able to establish that a crime had been committed.

Corpus delicti prevents a confession of a crime, unaccompanied by other evidence of either the crime or tying the confessor to the crime, to be used to convict the confessor of the crime he alleges to have committed. The state cannot convict someone of a crime if it cannot show that the crime took place or that the confessor was tied somehow to the criminal act. Otherwise, any person willing to confess could be convicted.

Why would anyone confess to a crime they did not commit? That is a question we will leave to the psychology experts. However, police officers and others who work in the criminal justice system are familiar with an odd, but fairly common occurrence—that of the false confession uttered by someone completely unconnected with the crime being investigated. For this reason officials often withhold a crucial piece of evidence from the media and the public—a piece of evidence that the real perpetrator would, but of which a bogus confessor would have know not.

Corpus delicti is often confused with the elements of a crime, which are examined following. While similar, the elements of a crime establish the precise nature of the crime. Corpus delicti merely establishes beyond a reasonable doubt that a crime has taken place. In the Eckenrode case, the body and Eckenrode's confession (which placed him at the scene and showed he was involved in the incident that led to the harm) established the crime, but the elements would determine more specifically whether he should be charged with manslaughter, voluntary or involuntary, or murder.

Sometimes corpus delicti determines where a case is tried. In cases where a crime crosses territorial boundaries, the courts will often try the case where the corpus delicti was found.

Federal courts and some state courts have moved away from applying corpus delicti because some crimes that do not necessarily produce physical evidence, such as conspiracy and fraud, do not fit the requirements well.

> I don't think there was any rush to judgment.
> Linda Fairstein, best-selling author and former prosecutor on her role in the Central Park Jogger confessions she oversaw

YOU MAKE THE CALL

THE DUKE RAPE CASE: WAS A CRIME COMMITTED?

On Saturday night, March 13, 2006, the Duke University lacrosse team held a party. For entertainment, the team had booked a stripper, an African-American student from nearby North Carolina Central University. By the end of the evening, the stripper told police that several Duke team members cornered her in a bathroom, sexually assaulted her, and raped her.

The accusations sent shock waves through the Durham, North Carolina, community. The image of privileged white athletes raping a struggling African-American student struck raw nerves and highlighted race and class divisions, politicizing what was at heart a criminal investigation. Newspapers criticized the university for not responding fast enough, insinuating that had the alleged victim been white the school's reaction would have been different. School apologists claimed the university did not know the stripper's race until March 24,[3] nearly two weeks after the incident.

Community tensions were heightened when police alleged that one of the players had written in an e-mail that he wanted to "invite strippers to his dorm room, kill them, and skin them."[4] But the players denied that any sexual activity took place at the party.

The situation was further complicated when district attorney Michael Nifong chose to handle the case himself instead of delegating it to a subordinate. Many

Actus Reus

A wrongful action.

Mens Rea

A wrongful mind.

Harm

Injury or damage.

Causation

The requirement that the act must cause the harm.

Principle of Legality

The theory that an action is not a crime unless it is prohibited by law and assigned a punishment by the state.

It may be true that the law cannot make a man love me, but it can keep him from lynching me, and I think that's pretty important.
Martin Luther King, Jr., 1962

Strict Liability

The legal responsibility for damage or injury, even if you are not at fault or negligent.

observers felt Nifong wanted to make the case an issue in his November 2006 reelection campaign.

Race, class, sex, and politics under intense media scrutiny, the Duke rape case seemed to have it all. Throughout the book, different aspects of the case will be reviewed to show what went right and what went wrong in the pursuit of justice. But the first question is: Was a crime committed? Based on what you know from this section, can you answer that question, or do you think more investigation is needed?

ELEMENTS OF A CRIME

The three main elements of a crime are a wrongful action, or **actus reus,** caused by a wrongful mind, **mens rea,** resulting in damage or **harm**. Some scholars include **causation,** the requirement that the act must cause the harm, as a separate element. Others substitute concurrence, or the coexistence of actus reus and mens rea, for causation. Still others have suggested that the **principle of legality,** which says that an action is not a crime unless it is prohibited by law and assigned a punishment by the state, is a separate element.

To successfully prosecute most crimes, a prosecutor usually must prove all the elements of the crime: mens rea, actus reus, and resultant harm. There are classes of crime that do not require all three elements, which we will examine following, but most crimes require those three elements.

MENS REA

Mens rea describes a person's intent while performing a criminal act and is critical to establishing the nature and degree of a crime. Take the case of a person fatally shooting someone in the chest. If the person is a child playing with a gun, that is not a crime. The child did not intend to harm anyone. If someone picks up a gun, believing it is unloaded, and accidentally fires it, hitting someone in the chest, that is usually not a crime. If a person awakened by an intruder in her room takes a gun from the nightstand in the dark and fires, the action and resulting harm are, again, the same, but the shooter's intent, stopping the intruder, would likely protect against criminal charges. On the other hand, a person who shoots a convenience store clerk and then empties the cash register, will likely face murder charges because the shooter fired with the intent to kill.

Since a person's state of mind is not visible, mens rea is generally deduced from surrounding circumstances. It is up to the jury or a judge, if the defendant elects to be tried without a jury, to decide whether the prosecution has proven the element of mens rea.

STRICT LIABILITY

For some crimes, intent, or mens rea, is irrelevant. **Strict liability** crimes require only a wrongful act to occur. Speeding and other traffic violations are an example of strict liability violations—it does not matter what is going through the driver's mind or whether the driver knows the speed limit. The only thing that matters is the car's speed. Strict liability imposes a duty on a person, such as a speed limit, and exacts penalties from those who do not uphold that duty, regardless of their intentions.

Generally, crimes mala prohibita are strict liability, while mala in se crimes require intent. (See Chapter 1 for more on these.)

VICARIOUS LIABILITY

Another set of crimes that do not require mens rea are **vicarious liability** violations, in which one person is held responsible for someone else's actions. For example, under **corporate liability,** employers may be charged with a crime because of the actions of employees who are carrying out their business. Corporate liability is based on the legal principle of **respondeat superior,** or "let the superior reply," borrowed from civil law. The employer does not have to be aware of the employee's actions to be held criminally liable; the liability comes from the employment relationship and the control that it gives the employer, or superior, over the employee.

> Men are not hanged for stealing horses, but that horses may not be stolen.
> 1st Marquess of Halifax, 1750

Vicarious Liability
Where one person is held responsible for someone else's actions.

Corporate Liability
The legal concept that allows employers to be charged with a crime resulting from their employees' actions while carrying out corporate business.

Respondeat Superior
A term literally meaning "let the superior respond" it refers most commonly to employer liability for employee action when the employee is acting as an agent of the employer.

HISTORICAL HIGHLIGHT
Nick Leeson and Barings Bank

Nick Leeson had a problem in early 1995. The Singapore-based investment banker had lost millions of his employer's money in bad trades. So far he had successfully hidden the losses from Barings Bank's administrators. He thought it was only temporary. He would guess right on one big trade and return all the funds. But when the Japanese stock market tanked, Leeson's hope of making amends went down with it.[5]

Leeson's fall took Barings, a firm that had been in business for 230 years, with him. Barings was bailed out by the Dutch firm ING, who bought Barings for one pound sterling. Although Leeson's guilt was clear, the company's liability soon came into question. Had the company supervised Leeson closely enough? The Singapore stock exchange was so alarmed by his trades that it hired retired policemen to monitor Barings' trades and end-of-day position. When the stock exchange approached Barings with their concerns, Barings told them the bank had enough in reserve to cover any anticipated shortfall. But Barings was working from Leeson's bogus figures. Some critics argue Barings did not do enough to protect investor's rights. With ING coming to the rescue, Barings eluded some of the more difficult questions. But what should their liability have been?

Parental Liability

The responsibility parents have for the actions of their minor children.

In Loco Parentis

Acting in the role of parents.

Another type of vicarious liability is **parental liability,** which holds parents or adults **in loco parentis,** responsible for their minor children's actions.

HISTORICAL HIGHLIGHT
Responsibility Follows the Bullet,
the Kayla Rolland Murder

Kayla Rolland did not want to go to school on February 29, 2000. The six-year-old did not explain why she was kicking and screaming that morning. By that afternoon, her mother was piecing together why Kayla fought so violently.

The day before a boy in her class had tried to kiss her. She slapped him, and the two got into an argument. The boy had a history of violent behavior, and Kayla must have sensed the argument was not over.

While Kayla was trying to avoid school, the boy was packing his uncle's gun in his backpack. When the two got to school, the day began normally. But their teacher had to escort two other students to another class. In the few minutes the teacher was gone, the boy pulled the gun and shot Kayla dead.

The courts were now faced with the question of how to punish a 6-year-old for an adult crime. The boy was taken from his family and became a ward of the state. The uncle and two other family members were charged on weapon's charges for their negligence in allowing the young boy access to the weapon. Although neither the uncle nor the two other relatives fired the gun, they went to jail for the girl's shooting.[6]

Instead of the criminal offender's intent, which forms the basis of strict liability, vicarious liability generally relies on the standard of what the superior in the relationship, parents or employers, allow or permit the person under their control to do.

Degree

A measure of severity for crimes with first degree crimes being the most severe and warranting stronger punishments.

First Degree

Under the Model Penal Code, crimes that are committed willfully.

PROVING MENS REA

Mens rea is the thorniest part of any criminal case because it cannot be measured or proven, but only inferred from circumstances. The convenience store robber cited previously may have acted out of fear, may have fired unintentionally, may have felt angry or hostile, or may have made a calculated, cold-blooded decision to terminate a potential witness. Even with a surveillance tape, none of those mental states would be easy to discern. Still, establishing mens rea is critical to strict liability cases, which also tend to be the most severe. Model Penal Code § 2.02 defines four levels of intent, or mens rea, which determine the **degree** of a crime.

"Purposely" committed crimes are crimes committed with the intent to accomplish a particular result. Purposeful acts, also frequently called wanton or willful acts, are designated **first degree** and carry the highest penalties. The next serious are crimes committed "knowingly," which the state defines as knowing a specific conduct will almost certainly bring about a particular result, but without necessarily intending that result. These crimes are **second degree.** Following that are crimes committed "recklessly," meaning with knowledge that there is a substantial and unjustifiable risk that the conduct might cause a particular result. Such crimes are **third-degree** offenses. Finally, crimes committed "negligently" are **fourth-degree** offenses. Negligence means thoughtlessly or carelessly creating a significant unjustifiable risk of harm without realizing the risk has been created or without intending to create it.

Establishing mens rea in second-, third-, and fourth-degree crimes is particularly challenging because it is based on the notion of "unjustifiable" risk, a term which means something different to every person. One person might not even consider it a risk to go 10 miles over the speed limit with a baby in the car, while others might consider that unacceptable. The state tries to define "justifiable" by weighing what the offender's conscious intentions were at the time of the crime, or her **subjective intent,** against what a reasonable person should have known or thought at the time of the event, the legal standard of **objective intent.** For example, it is clear that a reasonable person would understand that driving 110 miles per hour with a baby in the car puts the child at serious risk of harm; that objective standard is imposed on the offender whether the offender had the sense to perceive the risk or not.

The law also distinguishes mens rea based on the particular consequences intended by a person committing a crime. If a person does something with intent to cause a specific criminal result, then the person possessed **specific intent.** If a person intended an action only and not the results of the action, that person possessed **general intent.** For example, a person sets fire to a building, merely intending to burn it down. That person has specific intent to commit arson. If people die as a result of the fire, the state might assign general intent for their deaths to the arsonist. Of course, if the individual set the fire with the specific intent to kill someone inside the building and succeeds, the crime would be first degree murder and an example of specific intent. Crimes committed with general intent are generally third- or fourth-degree offenses. These classifications overlap with degrees of crime. First degree crimes are crimes of specific intent, second degree crimes may be one or the other, and third and fourth degree crimes are crimes of general intent.

Sometimes to prove specific intent, the state must show that the offender knew a certain fact or understood the law being broken. That requirement is known as **scienter.** For certain crimes, scienter is required. Drug possession is an example of a crime requiring scienter. If a drugrunner on the lam slips a stash of drugs into the knapsack of a hapless tourist, as frequently happens in the movies, the tourist is not guilty of drug possession. Receiving stolen property also requires scienter; the person receiving the goods has to know they are stolen to be guilty of the crime. But that knowledge does not have to be direct—it can be inferred from the circumstances. For example, if you were to purchase a television from a national retailer and it turned out the set was part of a lot of televisions stolen from a competitor, you would most likely not be aware of that underlying fact; there would be no scienter. On the other hand, if you bought the television in a back alley for $35, scienter probably would be present, since you know new televisions usually are not sold at such a deep discount and certainly not in a dark alley at night. But what if the set was bought at an online auction site such as eBay? That would be a murkier matter.

A small group of crimes include a scienter requirement that the people committing them know their actions are illegal. Such laws are the exception that make the often

Second Degree

Under the Model Penal Code, crimes that are committed knowingly.

Third Degree

Under the Model Penal Code, crimes that are committed recklessly.

Fourth Degree

Under the Model Penal Code, crimes that are committed negligently.

Subjective Intent

The offender's conscious intentions at the time of the crime.

Objective Intent

What a reasonable person should have known or thought at the time of the event.

Specific Intent

The type of intent where the person commits an act designed to cause a specific criminal result.

General Intent

The type of intent where the person intended an action only and not the results of the action.

Scienter

A necessary element to prove in some crimes where the offender knew a certain fact or understood the law being broken.

Transferred Intent

The type of intent where a person tries to harm one person and as a result harms someone else.

Constructive Intent

The concept that some actions are so likely to cause a specific result that the law treats that result as intended, whether the person meant to cause it or not.

Motive

The reason a person commits a crime.

quoted rule, "ignorance of the law is no excuse." In certain, very specialized cases, it is. Scienter requirements protect people from truly innocent errors.

Another type of intent is **transferred intent,** in which a person tries to harm one person and as a result harms someone else. For example, a person might shoot with intent to murder one person and wind up inadvertently killing another. In such cases, the shooter's intention toward the intended victim transfers to the bystander. The shooter did not intend to murder the bystander but may be charged with murder nonetheless, because the shooter's intentions toward his intended victim transfer to his actual victims.

Some actions are so likely to cause a specific result that the law treats that result as intended, whether the person meant to cause it or not. This is known as **constructive intent.** For example, shooting someone in the chest is so likely fatal that a person might be charged with murder even if it could be shown that the shooter only meant to injure the victim.

MOTIVE

Motive is the reason a person commits a crime. Mens rea is the intent; motive is the reason behind that intent. For example, a woman who kills her husband's lover has the intent of committing murder. Her motives are jealousy and revenge. Motive is not an element of a crime and therefore does not have to be proven to successfully prosecute a crime, but it often influences the severity of the punishment levied. For example, the true motive behind a crime such as serial killing may not even be clear to the perpetrator, but the killer can be prosecuted regardless. The mens rea of a serial killer, however, is an element of the crime; to establish it, the prosecution need only show that the killer intended to kill the victims.

ACTUS REUS

Actus reus is the action that causes the harm. Actus reus must be voluntary. It must also be active. For example, thoughts cannot be proven and cannot, by themselves, do harm. They cannot be considered a crime until they are acted on. Finally, it must be "wrong," or illegal. For example, shooting guns is not a crime. Firing a gun at a target range or in military training does not constitute an actus reus. Shooting a gun in a shopping mall, however, is an actus reus.

VOLUNTARY ACTS

Voluntary Act
The actus reus element of a crime; a crimes must be a voluntary act.

A crime must be a **voluntary act.** Reflex actions or actions committed under coercion or while unconscious are generally not crimes. Mere accidents are generally not criminal acts. There are exceptions, however, when people commit involuntary harm, as a result of voluntary decisions. For example, people who drive drunk are held criminally liable for their actions, even though the alcohol impairs their ability to control their actions. A person who suffers seizures and chooses to drive anyway may be similarly held accountable for harm resulting from accidents.

YOU MAKE THE CALL

SLEEP DRIVING

When Washington, DC police arrived at the scene of an accident in the early morning hours one May day in 2006, they discovered Representative Patrick Kennedy (D-RI) at the wheel. The politician claimed he had gone home the evening before and taken prescription medications, including a sleep aid.[7] He claimed to have no memory of getting in his car, although he vaguely reported that he thought he had to get back to the Capitol for an important vote. Later, the Food and Drug Administration issued a warning about certain sleep drugs, which apparently can cause something the FDA dubbed "Sleep Driving." Victims of the syndrome may get in their automobiles and drive off, all with no awareness that they are doing so. They may even make phone calls and prepare meals while technically asleep.[8]

Assuming a defendant can show he or she was taking one of the sleep medications for which the FDA requires a warning label, what would you argue if the defendant is charged with a crime such as vehicular homicide? What element of a crime would you argue was missing?

Personal Status as an Act   One's **personal status,** like one's thoughts, is not an action and generally cannot constitute a crime. This has not always been the case, however. In the past, laws prescribed severe criminal penalties for homosexuality, alcoholism, witchcraft, and homelessness. While it may not be a crime to be homeless, there remain some remnants of status crimes on the books. For example, vagrancy and loitering laws may be used to target the homeless and get them off the streets. But it is not the status as "homeless" that constitutes an element of the crime. Rather, it is an act—such as remaining on a public park bench past the park's stated closing time—that forms the basis of the crime.

Most status crimes have disappeared from the U.S. legal landscape. One notable exception remains—that of the illegal immigrant. He or she committed a crime by entering the country illegally, and his or her presence within our borders is also regarded as a criminal act by some. Thus, being an illegal immigrant (status) means that one is also committing a crime (overstaying a visa or being illegally present in the country).

TYPES OF ACTS

Possession   **Possession** is dominion or control over property, although it can be a passive act of failing to get rid of something one should not have. **Actual possession** means physically having the item on one's person, directly under physical control, or within reach. Most jurisdictions divide actual possession into **knowing possession,** which implies that a person possessed and held onto the item on purpose, and **mere possession,** which means the person possesses the item unawares. If a house guest hides cocaine in a spare bedroom, the homeowner might be guilty of mere possession. If the homeowner learns of the illegal items in the house and fails to remove them, the homeowner is guilty of criminal possession. In most jurisdictions, criminal possession implies knowledge of the presence of an illegal item long enough to get rid of it.

Personal Status

Generally current laws do not view personal status as an act, but historically personal status has been seen as a criminal act.

Possession

Dominion or control over property.

Actual Possession

Physically having the item on one's person, directly under physical control, or within reach.

Knowing Possession

The condition existing when a person possesses and holds onto an item intentionally.

Mere Possession

The condition occurring when a person possesses an item unawares.

Constructive Possession

The concept that extends liability to people who have some control over an item without possessing it.

Omission

The failure to perform a duty.

Duty

An obligation to perform an action.

Duty by Statute

A duty imposed by law.

Duty by Contract

A duty voluntarily assumed through an agreement.

Duty by Relationship

A duty expected of certain people, such as parents, by virtue of their connection with the person owed the duty, such as the parents' children.

Constructive possession extends liability to people who have some control over an item without possessing it. For example, a person may be convicted for possession of drugs found in the trunk of the person's car or in the person's attic, even though it is never on the defendant. A person may be guilty of possession of legal as well as illegal items. In the case of legal items, criminal intention must be shown. For example, a person carrying a box cutter into an airport is carrying something legal. If that person is a postal worker who carries the box cutter routinely, merely possessing it is not a criminal act. If the person intended to do harm with it, however, the person is guilty of criminal possession.

Omission Sometimes a failure to act is a crime known as an **omission.** An omission can occur only when someone has a **duty** or obligation to do something, which can arise by several means. The law may impose a **duty by statute,** an obligation to perform certain acts imposed by the state. The legal requirement for drivers to stay after an accident and render aid is a common statutory duty. Some laws require people to report child abuse or other crimes. Filing and paying taxes are duties imposed by statute. Failure to do so is a criminal omission.

Contracts are another means of imposing a duty. A **duty by contract** would require a lifeguard to save a drowning swimmer. A doctor working in a hospital emergency room is legally required to act to save patients; standing by while a patient died could be criminal homicide. On the other hand, a doctor who happens on a crime scene and does not help the victim probably would not be liable for either a crime or a civil wrong. He or she has no duty to render assistance.[9]

Sometimes a duty exists just by virtue of someone's relationship to another. A **duty by relationship** imposes on parents a duty to care for their children. For example, a parent who leaves a child out by the swimming pool unsupervised might be held criminally liable if the child drowns. No contract or specific law is required; the duty arises out of the relationship itself.

Finally, people can assume a legal duty simply by saying they will perform an action. A person who offers to watch the neighbor's children assumes the duty of their care and the liabilities that go along with it. If a group of people is witnessing someone struggling in the water and one person offers to swim out and save the victim, that person is legally obligated to follow through. If the rescuer decides to instead sit back and watch the victim drown, that person might be held criminally liable, since his assumption of that duty prevented others from helping. People also assume a duty to render aid to anyone they endanger. For example, an intoxicated individual who causes an automobile accident cannot walk away without making reasonable efforts to aid those injured by her actions—she must take reasonable steps to mitigate the harm she has caused.

Harm Most crimes result in harm. The seriousness of the harm usually dictates the severity of the punishment. Crime results in five categories of harm: crimes against life, including murder, kidnapping, and battery; crimes against habitation, which include burglary and arson; crimes against property, including theft; crimes against the public order, such as traffic violations; and crimes against public morality, such as prostitution and drug use.

Certain actions are criminal even though they do not harm anyone. Attempted crimes can be prosecuted even though the person never committed the harmful act. For example, if a group of Internet hackers breaks into a bank Web site and tries to download information but is caught in the act, the perpetrators will be charged with attempted theft as well as numerous computer law violations, even though they never downloaded or used the information or harmed their intended victims. Conspiracy and possession are examples of crimes that do not require harm to be successfully prosecuted; the mere act of conspiring to commit a crime is a crime.

To establish an attempted crime, the state must be able to show more than mere preparation. The Model Penal Code requires that a defendant must have completed a "substantial step in the course of conduct planned to culminate in his commission of the crime," § 5.01(1)(c). Courts use various tests to decide whether the steps a defendant has taken are substantial enough to constitute an attempted crime. Some examples of substantial steps are listed in § 5.01 (2)(a–g):

- Lying in wait, seeking or following the victim
- Luring the victim to the contemplated place of the crime
- Reconnoitering the contemplated place of the crime
- Unlawful entry of the contemplated place of the crime
- Possession of materials to commit the crime designed for unlawful use
- Soliciting an agent to participate in the crime

CAUSATION

Causation is the link between the actus rea and the harm. The state must be able to show that the criminal conduct, or actus reus, directly caused the harm. To do this, the courts rely on the concept of the **but for rule**—but for the defendant's actions, the harm would not have occurred. Another name for this is **sine qua non,** which means "without which, not."

Sine qua non establishes causation. Usually, however, causation is more complex. If there is a clear link between the criminal act and the effect, then the act is the **direct cause** of the harm. A person carjacks an elderly woman. This is a case of direct cause—the carjacking directly caused the harm, which is car theft. But what if the woman suffers a heart attack as the carjacker speeds away, falls to the pavement, and dies? The carjacking is the indirect cause of the woman's death. This is called **proximate cause.** Proximate cause is an act that sets in motion a chain of events leading to the harm. Complications often arise between a criminal act and all of its consequences. These are known as superceding or **intervening causes.** Proximate cause allows the state to hold people responsible for all the damages that result from their crimes.

To establish proximate cause, prosecutors rely on the concept of foreseeable consequences. Shooting a gun is an act with clearly foreseeable consequences; bystanders may be shot. If someone hits a pedestrian while leading police on a high-speed chase through busy streets, prosecutors will try to show that injuring pedestrians is a reasonably foreseeable outcome.

But For Rule

The rule that states but for the defendant's actions, the harm would not have occurred.

Sine Qua Non

Literally, without which, not; the Latin term for the "but for rule."

Direct Cause

The case where there is a clear link between the criminal act and the effect.

Proximate Cause

An act that sets in motion a chain of events leading to harm.

Intervening Causes

Complications that arise between a criminal act and all of its consequences.

> ## PRACTICE POINTERS
>
> After reading this chapter, you should have a pretty good idea of what makes an act or admission a crime. If you are called in your professional life to help in the prosecution or defense of an alleged crime, you should also have a pretty good idea of the traps and pitfalls that can befall either the prosecution or the defense.
>
> If your role is to assist the prosecution in bringing charges, you now understand that it takes more than an accusation to begin a criminal case. You understand that before charges are brought, a responsible prosecutor will analyze the evidence to assure that the elements of the crime that is alleged to have taken place are present. You may even find it helpful to develop a checklist of what the prosecution needs to show as a way of making sure the case is sound. That checklist may look something like this:
>
> - What are the elements of the crime charged, and are they all present (mens rea, actus rea, etc.)?
> - Has a suspect been identified?
> - Has that suspect confessed or given an account of his or her activities connecting him or her to the alleged crime?
> - Is there some independent evidence actually tying the defendant to the alleged crime, such as DNA or other physical evidence or witness testimony (corpus delicti)?
>
> If you are assisting the defense, you can use a similar list to test the prosecution's case.

CHAPTER SUMMARY

A crime is a wrong against society or the public interest typically punishable by imprisonment or death and sometimes an additional fine. Criminal law is designed to protect and vindicate public rights.

Before prosecuting anyone for a crime, the first work of the state is to establish that a crime has been committed. To do so, the state relies on a concept called corpus delicti, or the "body of the crime." The state usually must show corpus delicti beyond a reasonable doubt. The state does not have to have a suspect or precise explanation of the crime, but it must establish that a crime has taken place.

Corpus delicti prevents a confession of a crime, unaccompanied by other evidence of either the crime or tying the confessor to the crime, to be used to convict the confessor of the crime he alleges to have committed.

The elements of a crime establish the crime's precise nature. Sometimes corpus delicti determines where a case is tried. In cases where a crime crosses territorial boundaries, the courts will often try the case where the corpus delicti was found.

Federal courts and some state courts have moved away from applying corpus delicti because some crimes that do not necessarily produce physical evidence, such as conspiracy and fraud, do not fit the requirements well.

The three main elements of a crime are a wrongful action, or actus reus, caused by a wrongful mind, mens rea, resulting in damage or harm. To successfully prosecute most crimes, a prosecutor usually must prove all the elements of the crime: mens rea, actus reus, and resultant harm.

Mens rea describes a person's intent while performing a criminal act and is critical to establishing the nature and degree of a crime. Since a person's state of mind is not visible, mens rea is generally deduced from surrounding circumstances.

For some crimes, intent, or mens rea, is irrelevant. Strict liability crimes require only a wrongful act to occur. Strict liability imposes a duty on a person and exacts penalties from those who do not uphold that duty, regardless of their intentions. Generally, crimes mala prohibita are strict liability, while mala in se crimes require intent.

Another set of crimes that do not not require mens rea are vicarious liability violations, in which one person is held responsible for someone else's actions. Vicarious liability generally relies on the standard of what the superior in the relationship, parents or employers, allow or permit the person under their control to do.

Mens rea is the thorniest part of any criminal case because it cannot be measured or proven, but only inferred from circumstances. The Model Penal Code defines four levels of intent, or mens rea, which determine the degree of a crime.

Purposeful acts, also frequently called wanton or willful acts, are designated first degree crimes and carry the highest penalties. Knowingly committed acts are second degree crimes. Recklessly committed crimes where there is a substantial and unjustifiable risk that the conduct might cause a particular result are third degree offenses. Negligently committed crimes are fourth degree offenses. Negligence means thoughtlessly or carelessly creating a significant unjustifiable risk of harm without realizing the risk has been created or without intending to create it.

Establishing mens rea in second-, third-, and fourth-degree crimes is particularly challenging because it is based on the notion of unjustifiable risk, a term which means something different to every person. The state tries to define justifiable by weighing what the offender's conscious intentions were at the time of the crime, or her subjective intent, against what a reasonable person should have known or thought at the time of the event, the legal standard of objective intent.

If a person does something with intent to cause a specific criminal result, then the person possessed specific intent. If a person intended an action only and not the results of the action, that person possessed general intent.

Sometimes to prove specific intent, the state must show that the offender knew a certain fact or understood the law being broken. That requirement is known as scienter.

Transferred intent is where a person tries to harm one person and as a result harms someone else. Some actions are so likely to cause a specific result that the law treats that result as intended, whether the person meant to cause it or not. This is known as constructive intent.

Motive is the reason a person commits a crime. Motive is not an element of a crime and therefore does not have to be proven to successfully prosecute a crime, but it often influences the severity of the punishment levied.

Actus reus is the action that causes the harm. It must be voluntary, active, and illegal.

A crime must be voluntary. One's personal status is not an action and generally cannot constitute a crime.

Possession is dominion or control over property. Actual possession means physically having the item on one's person, directly under physical control, or within reach. Most jurisdictions divide actual possession into knowing possession, which implies that a person possessed and held onto the item on purpose, and mere possession, which means the person possesses the item unawares.

Constructive possession extends liability to people who have some control over an item without possessing it. Sometimes a failure to act is a crime known as an omission. An omission can occur only when someone has a duty or obligation to do something. The law may impose a duty by statute. A duty by contract most often occurs when a person's job or skills obligates them to assist individuals in ways people holding different jobs are not.

A duty by relationship imposes on parents a duty to care for their children. No contract or specific law is required; the duty arises out of the relationship itself. Finally, people can assume a legal duty simply by saying they will perform an action.

Crime results in five categories of harm: crimes against life, including murder, kidnapping, and battery; crimes against habitation, which include burglary and arson; crimes against property, including theft; crimes against the public order, such as traffic violations; and crimes against public morality, such as prostitution and drug use.

Certain actions are criminal even though they do not harm anyone. Attempted crimes can be prosecuted even though the person never committed the harmful act. Conspiracy and possession are examples of crimes that do not require harm to be successfully prosecuted. The Model Penal Code requires that a defendant must have completed a "substantial step in the course of conduct planned to culminate in his commission of the crime."

Causation is the link between the actus rea and the harm. The state must be able to show that the criminal conduct, or actus reus, directly caused the harm. To do this, the courts rely on the concept of the but for rule or sine qua non. If there is a clear link between the criminal act and the effect, then the act is the direct cause of the harm. Proximate cause is an act that sets in motion a chain of events leading to the harm.

KEY TERMS

Actual Possession	First Degree	Principle of Legality
Actus Reus	Fourth Degree	Proximate Cause
But For Rule	General Intent	Respondeat Superior
Causation	Harm	Scienter
Constructive Intent	In Loco Parentis	Second Degree
Constructive Possession	Intervening Causes	Sine Qua Non
Corporate Liability	Knowing Possession	Specific Intent
Corpus Delicti	Mens Rea	Strict Liability
Crime	Mere Possession	Subjective Intent
Degree	Motive	Third Degree
Direct Cause	Objective Intent	Transferred Intent
Duty	Omission	Vicarious Liability
Duty by Contract	Parental Liability	Voluntary Act
Duty by Relationship	Personal Status	
Duty by Statute	Possession	

EXERCISES

1. **Consider the Following Scenario.** You may recall the recent bizarre confession in the JonBenet Ramsey case, in which a six-year-old child beauty queen was murdered by an unknown assailant or assailants in 1996. JonBenet was found bound and dead in the basement of her family's Colorado home over the Christmas holiday. The police were unable to identify a suspect who might have been able to enter the locked home and murder JonBenet. But in 2006, John Mark Karr told authorities in Bangkok, Thailand, that it was he who had killed the little girl accidentally and that "I loved JonBenet."[10] Karr reportedly told Thai police that he wanted to kidnap the little girl for ransom but strangled her when things did not go according to plan.[11] He also claimed to have been sexually involved with the child and that she had died during a sexual encounter.

   DNA evidence taken from the body had been preserved, and prosecutors got a DNA sample from Karr. Karr's family, despite his insistence that he had been in Colorado, told investigators that Karr had been with them during the Christmas holiday period. DNA tests showed that Karr was not the source of the DNA on JonBenet.

   Could prosecutors charge Karr with either sexual assault or murder? Why or why not?

   To see what decision the prosecutors made and read more details on the case, see the Appendix.

2. **Consider the Following Scenario.** A woman goes for a jog in New York City's Central Park and is brutally attacked and raped. Five black males were interrogated for 40 hours and confessed to the rape and beating, providing graphic details about the event. They were convicted. There was no DNA evidence connecting the teens to the crime. The crime was prosecuted by an aggressive female prosecutor who also happens to have been the best-selling author of police procedurals. Linda Fairstein, author of such best sellers as *Bad Blood, Entombed*, and *Cold Hit*, has since been criticized for her handling of the case.[12]

   What arguments would you make if one of the males now says he had nothing to do with the alleged crime and another man has confessed? Would your answer change if the other man's DNA matched that found at the scene?

   To see what decision the prosecutors and judge made and read more details on the case, see the Appendix.

DISCUSSION QUESTIONS

1. Can you think of any reasons that someone might be inclined to confess to a crime they did not commit?
2. Has your understanding of what constitutes a crime changed after reading this chapter?
3. Should parents be held liable for the criminal actions of their minor children? Why or why not?

FOR FURTHER READING AND VIEWING

1. Forster, E. M. *A Passage to India.* This classic English novel, also made into a movie starring Alec Guinness, revolves around false rape accusations made by a British tourist visiting India for the first time.

2. Leeson, N. *Rogue Trader.* Little, Brown (1996). Leeson tells his side of the story, after being released from jail in Singapore and relocating to Galway, Ireland. The book was also made into a movie, *Rogue Trader,* starring Ewan McGregor as Leeson. Leeson has his own Web page and can be booked for dinner speeches. For a look at the new, reformed Leeson, check out *www.nickleeson.com*. Ironically, two other books written about the scandal are out of print, while Leeson's book is still available in both hardback and paperback. Crime does not pay?

3. *Minority Report* is a 2002 Steven Spielberg film starring Tom Cruise in which police are able to prevent crimes by looking into the minds of citizens to determine their intent (mens rea) before they ever take a step toward committing that crime. Citizens are punished for the crime the police determine they will commit. The movie is based on a 1956 short story by Philip Dick.

4. Westervelt, S. *Wrongly Convicted.* Rutgers University Press (2001). A collection of essays exploring, among other things, why someone would confess to a crime they did not commit.

5. Sullivan, T. *Unequal Verdicts: The Central Park Jogger Trials.* Simon & Schuster (1992). An exploration of the role of coerced confessions in an infamous rape case.

ENDNOTES

1. "Woman Who Fell from High-rise, Boyfriend Were Drinking," *The Pocono Record* (Stroudsburg, PA), February 27, 2006.

2. Michael, Race "Eckenrode Sentenced," *The Times Tribune* (Scranton, PA), February 21, 2007.

3. Karen Arenson, "Duke Failed to See Gravity of Rape Case Report Says," *New York Times*, May 9, 2006.

4. Duff Wilson, "Blacks Call for Calm in Duke Rape Case," *New York Times,* April 7, 2006. Note that the e-mail language was later revealed to have come from the book *American Psycho* by Bret Easton Ellis, which features a serial killer. It was made into a movie.

5. Dara Doyle and James Ludden, "Leeson, Who Ruined Barings, May Return to Trading," *Bloomberg News,* March 7, 2007.

6. Ken Palmer, "A Mom's Crusade; Veronica McQueen Presses on in Daughter's Memory," *The Flint Journal*, (Flint Michigan), February 19, 2006.

7. Andrew Miga, "Kennedy Blames Accident on Sleep Medicine," *Washington Post*, May 4, 2006.

8. FDA Requests Label Change for All Sleep Disorder Drug Products, FDA Press Release P07-45, March 14, 2007.

9. The author was shocked when, after a shooting occurred outside her home, a neighbor who happened to be a skilled surgeon stood and watched as the victim lay bleeding from a head wound. The surgeon made no move to assist. Technically, he had no duty to do so.
10. "Questions swirl around Karr's admissions," CNN online, August 17, 2006.
11. "Much work ahead despite JonBenet arrest, prosecutor warns," CBC News, August 17, 2006.
12. Benjamin Smith and Linda Fairstein changed the way rape is prosecuted by reconciling feminist ideals with the dirty work of investigating sex crimes. But will she be remembered for her pragmatism or her bad publicity? *Legal Affairs,* September/October 2003.

APPENDIX

This report includes graphic content.

DISTRICT COURT, BOULDER COUNTY, COLORADO Court Address: 1777 Sixth Street Boulder, Colorado 80302 Court Phone: (303) 441-3750	
PEOPLE OF THE STATE OF COLORADO vs. JOHN MARK KARR, Defendant(s)	▲COURT USE ONLY▲
Attorney Name: Mary T. Lacy District Attorney P.O. Box 471 Boulder, Colorado 80306 Attorney Phone: (303) 441-3700 Attorney Fax: (303) 441-4703 Attorney E-mail: mlacy@co.boulder.co.us Attorney Reg: # 15091	Case No: 2006 CR 1244 Division: 13
PEOPLE'S MOTION TO QUASH ARREST WARRANT	

The People, through Mary T. Lacy, District Attorney for the Twentieth Judicial District, move to quash the arrest warrant for John Mark Karr, to vacate the scheduled first appearance, to dismiss these proceedings, and to vacate all orders to seal documents previously entered in this matter, except for redaction of names of live children mentioned therein, on the following grounds:

1.   The People sought the arrest warrant for John Mark Karr after he had been identified as the writer of a series of anonymous e-mails sent to Professor Michael Tracey starting in 2002. The writer at first signed his e-mails as "D" and later as "Daxis." The e-mails were sent through a service that masked the identity and location of the sender.

2.   Until April 2006, the anonymous e-mails were not of substantial interest to the District Attorney's Office because they merely demonstrated that the writer had an intense interest in the JonBenet Ramsey case.

3.   Starting in April 2006, the writer began to claim more personal knowledge about the death of JonBenet Ramsey and to demonstrate a more personal interest in JonBenet Ramsey and in Mrs. Patsy Ramsey, the victim's mother. Although at first he claimed to know two people who participated in the crime, he later admitted personal responsibility for the death.

4.   The anonymous writer described the crime in terms of his love for JonBenet Ramsey. Over time, he provided increasing detail about his "recollection" of the night of the crime. But he refused to provide any detail that he thought might lead to his identification.

5.   Not only did the writer keep his identity secret, but he also kept his whereabouts secret. He did admit to traveling extensively after leaving the United States because he had been investigated in connection with the abduction and/or murder of other young children and that he could not return to the United States because of an active warrant for his arrest.

6.   The writer also showed an intense personal desire to communicate with Mrs. Patsy Ramsey and expressed an identification with her through what he perceived to be their common love for JonBenet.

7.   The writer expressed great concern and sympathy for Mrs. Ramsey because of her deteriorating condition due to cancer. He wrote a message that he wanted forwarded to Mr. and Mrs. Ramsey in an effort to make contact with them so that he could explain his relationship to their daughter and her death.

8.   Mr. Tracey convinced the writer to make telephone contact with the Ramseys. Law enforcement agencies cooperated in an unsuccessful effort to trace that call.

9.   In a further effort to identify and locate the anonymous writer, Mr. Tracey arranged to exchange telephone calls with the writer, who was by then identifying himself as "Daxis." In those calls, Daxis repeated his admissions about his involvement in and responsibility for the death of JonBenet Ramsey, but he continued to refuse to provide information that would help identify him.

10.   Daxis took part in eleven phone conversations with Mr. Tracey. He also continued to send daily e-mails. In the e-mails and phone conversation he expressed a fascination with not only JonBenet Ramsey but with the sexuality of young girls in general. He claimed to have been involved romantically and sexually with a number of young girls and expressed a preference for girls about six years of age.

11.   Daxis revealed that he had taught young girls in various schools and has also tutored, cared for, or otherwise had responsibility for young girls during his travels. He also revealed that he was currently teaching young girls.

12.   Daxis then began to provide his story in narrative form, which he wanted to be included in a book Mr. Tracey was planning to publish. He provided Tracey with several sections of this manuscript in which he gave descriptions of his own background and development, his fascination with the sexuality with young girls, and his involvement with the death of JonBenet Ramsey.

13.   Daxis provided details of his "recollection" of how JonBenet died in a way that supported the conclusion that he firmly believed that he loved JonBenet Ramsey, that he had involved her in sexual activities that included temporarily asphyxiating her, and that he had "accidentally" killed her by becoming so sexually involved that he lost track of time so that the asphyxiation lasted longer than he intended, causing her severe injury and leading him to inflict a severe blow to her head. His rationale for these events supported the conclusion that he still believed that it was proper for an adult such as himself to be sexually involved with six-year-old girls in the ways he described, and that JonBenet had died only because of a tragic "mistake" in what was intentional sexual behavior on his part.

14.   It was apparent from Daxis' emails, his manuscript, and from his phone conversations (1) that he believed his narrative of his responsibility for the death of JonBenet and (2) he believed his narrative about the sexuality of young girls and his ability to have a loving relationship with young girls, similar to the one he believed he had had with JonBenet Ramsey.

15.   After the death of Mrs. Ramsey, Daxis became more intense about his desire to publish his explanation about himself and his responsibility for the death of JonBenet, but to also keep his identity secret. He also began to express sexual interest in specific young girls he said he had met in the new school at which he had recently been hired and at which he was to teach when school began in mid-August. He began to describe his interest in several girls in much the same terms that he had described his interest in JonBenet Ramsey.

16.   The District Attorney's investigators informed authorities of the United States and Thailand about what had been learned and worked with those authorities and others in the effort to locate and identify Daxis.

17.   In the course of the numerous phone calls between Daxis and Mr. Tracey and through other means, the authorities were able to trace the calls and to locate him in Thailand. They then were able to identify him as John Mark Karr and ultimately to confirm that he was about to begin to teach young children in the new school he had described. They also were able to confirm that he was having personal involvement with at least one of the girls he had previously identified as the target of his personal and sexual interest.

18.   Until Mr. Karr was identified there was no way to try to confirm or disprove his admissions related to causing the death of JonBenet Ramsey. Until he was detained, there was great risk that he might disappear if he became aware that people from his past were being interviewed about his admissions.

19.   Because Mr. Karr's description of his sexual involvement with the victim during the events leading to her death included oral sex and tasting her blood after he caused her vagina to bleed, it was apparent that the DNA found in blood spots in her underwear would be crucial to confirming his account of his involvement.

20.   Although investigators in Thailand obtained swabs from several items touched by Mr. Karr in an effort to obtain his DNA, our expert who would be responsible for the DNA testing, Greggory S. LaBerge, informed us that because of the mixture of DNA involved in the sample from the underwear, it would be necessary to obtain an untainted sample through use of a buccal swab from Mr. Karr to provide a definitive comparison. There was no way to obtain a buccal swab without alerting Mr. Karr to the fact that he was being investigated, creating an unacceptable risk that he would flee unless he were detained when the buccal swab was obtained.

21.   After it was confirmed that Mr. Karr was indeed teaching young children and that the school year had begun, we obtained approval from the Court for an arrest warrant. Thai officials then revoked his work visa and American officials revoked his passport.

22.   After he was detained in Thailand, Mr. Karr refused to provide buccal swabs on two occasions. Although he later did consent to submit to such a swab, he did so when investigators were not expecting it and when they did not have the necessary kit available.

23.   Once Mr. Karr was detained, investigators from the Boulder District Attorney's office and detectives from the Boulder Police Department made extensive efforts to interview people who might have information about Mr. Karr's past and to investigate data banks that might have information about Mr. Karr's financial records in an effort to learn where he was on December 25–26, 1996. Although they could not positively place him anywhere in particular at the time of the crime, Mr. Karr's family provided strong circumstantial support for their firm belief that he was with them in Georgia at the time of the crime. In addition, no convincing evidence could be found that placed him in or near Boulder at that time of the murder.

24.   Immediately upon the return of Mr. Karr to Boulder County on August 24, 2006, investigators executed a search warrant to obtain a buccal swab from Mr. Karr. That sample from Mr. Karr was taken to Dr. LaBerge on August 25, 2006. He and his staff immediately began the process of testing that swab to identify Mr. Karr's DNA profile and to compare it with DNA previously identified from the scene of the crime. Dr. Leberge completed the testing and analysis and concluded on August 26, 2006, that Mr. Karr was not the source of the DNA found in the underwear of JonBenet Ramsey. This information is critical because, as mentioned above, if Mr. Karr's account of his sexual involvement with the victim were accurate, it would have been highly likely that his saliva would have been mixed with the blood in the underwear.

WHEREFORE because no evidence has developed, other than his own repeated admissions, to place Mr. Karr at the scene of the crime and, in particular, because his DNA does not match that found in the victim's blood in her underwear, the People would not be able to establish that Mr. Karr committed this crime despite his repeated insistence that he did.

The People therefore request that the Court quash the arrest warrant, dismiss this proceeding, and vacate the orders sealing arrest and search warrant documents involving Mr. Karr subject only to redaction of the names of live children referred to above.

Dated: August 28, 2006

Respectfully submitted,

By: _____
MARY T. LACY, DISTRICT ATTORNEY
Twentieth Judicial District

SUPREME COURT OF THE STATE OF NEW YORK
COUNTY OF NEW YORK—PART 58
-- x
THE PEOPLE OF THE STATE OF NEW YORK :

            -against-   :

KHAREY WISE, KEVIN RICHARDSON, :
ANTRON MCCRAY, YUSEF SALAAM, and :
RAYMOND SANTANA,   :

                Defendants. :
-- x

**AFFIRMATION IN RESPONSE
TO MOTION TO VACATE
JUDGMENT OF CONVICTION**

INDICTMENT NO. 4762/89

NANCY E. RYAN, an attorney duly admitted to practice in the State of New York and an Assistant District Attorney in and for the County of New York, hereby affirms under penalty of perjury that:

1. I am the Assistant District Attorney in charge of the above-captioned case, and as such I am fully familiar with the facts and circumstances herein.

2. This affirmation is based upon information and belief, the sources of said information and belief being transcripts of prior proceedings held in connection with the above-captioned indictment; files, records, briefs, notes, and videotapes maintained by the New York County District Attorney's Office, the New York City Police Department, the Federal Bureau of Investigation, and the City and State Departments of Corrections; interviews with police, civilian, and expert witnesses; and conversations with Assistant District Attorneys.

3. I make this affirmation in response to motions submitted by the defendants Kevin Richardson, Antron McCray, Raymond Santana, Yusef Salaam, and Kharey Wise, all of whom were convicted after trial of various charges contained in New York County Supreme Court Indictment Number 4762/89. The motions have been made pursuant to Criminal Procedure Law Section 440.10(1)(g). Each motion requests that guilty verdicts rendered against the defendants in connection with the above-captioned indictment be vacated and set aside based upon newly discovered evidence, and that the court grant whatever further relief may be just and proper.

4. The defendants were all convicted of charges relating to the April 19, 1989, assault and rape of a female jogger. Additionally, defendants Richardson, McCray, Salaam, and Santana were convicted of charges relating to the assault and robbery of a second, male jogger on the same date. Finally, defendant Wise was convicted of a riot charge in connection with a series of events that encompassed both those criminal incidents. The newly discovered evidence relied upon by all the defendants consists of an affidavit by Matias Reyes, in which he swears that he alone committed the attack on the female jogger of which each stands convicted.

5. Based on the facts and for the reasons set forth below, the People consent to the defendants' motions to set aside the verdicts on all the charges of which they were convicted.

6. This affirmation does not describe the full scope of the review, reinvestigation, and reevaluation of the evidence undertaken by the Office of the District Attorney in connection with this matter. It outlines the principal issues considered by the People in responding to the defendants' legal motions, summarizes some of the facts relevant to those issues, and explains the analysis undertaken to resolve them. In short, it deals with the specific legal issue presented by the defendants' motions: whether the newly discovered evidence in this matter creates a probability that, if the evidence had been received at trial, it would have resulted in a verdict more favorable to the defendants on one or more charges.

HISTORY OF THE PROSECUTION

7. On the night of April 19, 1989, a series of violent incidents occurred in Central Park, involving members of a group of more than 30 teenagers. The incidents resulted in the arrests and convictions of ten young men, including the above-named defendants. At approximately 9:05 p.m. Michael Vigna, a racing biker, was accosted by a band of youths on the East Drive, just north of the 102nd Street transverse. A few minutes later, Antonio Diaz was assaulted and robbed, also on the East Drive, at about the level of 102nd Street. He was left unconscious. At roughly 9:12 to 9:15 p.m., a couple on a tandem bicycle was menaced on the drive just south of the 102nd Street entrance to the park. Moments later, slightly south of that, a taxi driver had rocks hurled at his cab, and was threatened by a group of teenagers when he got out of the car to investigate. And, beginning at about 9:24 p.m. and continuing until roughly 9:45, a series of four male joggers were set upon on the jogging path at the northern end of the Central Park Reservoir. Two of the male joggers escaped essentially unharmed, but two, Robert Garner and John Loughlin, were assaulted. Garner was not seriously hurt. Loughlin, however, was knocked to the ground, kicked, punched, and beaten with a pipe and stick. He was knocked unconscious, and sustained significant but not life-threatening injuries.

8. At approximately 1:30 a.m., an unconscious woman was found by two men walking on a footpath through Central Park. She lay at the edge of a wooded area, roughly 300 feet north of the 102nd Street transverse road, which runs in an "s"-shaped curve connecting the East and West Drives of the park. Police and medical personnel were summoned. The victim, a twenty-nine year old white woman who came to be known as the "Central Park jogger," was removed to the hospital. She had been badly beaten about

the head, and suffered numerous bruises, scratches, and abrasions elsewhere on her body. Her t-shirt had been rolled into a ligature and used to tie her in a distinctive fashion.* Subsequent investigation revealed that she had left her apartment on East 83rd Street at roughly 8:55 p.m. to go jogging in the park, and that her expected route would have taken her across the transverse road. The investigation also revealed that she had been raped, and that her radio headset and keys were missing.

9. Raymond Santana and Kevin Richardson, as well as a number of other youths, were apprehended at approximately 10:15 p.m. on April 19, after police officers responding to reports concerning some of the incidents spotted them on the western outskirts of the park. Antron McCray, Yusef Salaam, and Kharey Wise were brought in for questioning on April 20, 1989, after they had been identified by other youths as having been present at or participants in some of the events in the park.

10. Each of the defendants was questioned by detectives and made one or more statements. All five of the defendants implicated themselves in a number of the crimes which had occurred in the park. None of them admitted actually raping the Central Park jogger, but each gave an account of events in which he made himself an accomplice to the crime. Kharey Wise was 16 years old at the time; Yusef Salaam and Antron McCray were 15; and Kevin Richardson and Raymond Santana were 14.

11. On May 4, 1989, Indictment Number 4762/1989 was filed charging each of the defendants with Attempted Murder in the Second Degree (Penal Law Section 110/125.25(1)), Rape in the First Degree (Penal Law Section 130.35(1)), Sodomy in the First Degree (Penal Law Section 130.50(1)), Sexual Abuse in the First Degree (Penal Law Section 130.65(1)), and two counts of Assault in the First Degree (Penal Law Sections 120.10(1) and (3)), with respect to the Central Park jogger. In addition, the indictment charged each of them with Robbery in the First Degree (Penal Law Section 160.15(3)), two counts of Robbery in the Second Degree (Penal Law Sections 160.10(1) and (2) (a)), and two counts of Assault in the Second Degree (Penal Law Sections 120.05(2) and (6)) in connection with the attack on John Loughlin, and with Assault in the Second Degree (Penal Law Section 120.05(6)) with respect to jogger David Lewis. All of the defendants were also charged with Riot in the First Degree (Penal Law Section 240.06).

12. Steven Lopez, 15, was also indicted in connection with the attack on the jogger. Lopez was named by Kevin Richardson, Raymond Santana, and Kharey Wise as having participated in the crime, although they varied greatly in their descriptions of his conduct. Lopez was interviewed and made a videotaped statement following his arrest on April 19, and denied any knowledge of an incident involving a female jogger. However, in subsequent forensic testing, a single hair taken from his clothing was found to be "consistent with" the jogger's hair, based upon a microscopic analysis. Lopez was charged in the same indictment as the five other defendants. On January 30, 1991, he pled guilty to Robbery in the First Degree in connection with the assault on John Loughlin, and on March 13, 1991, he received a sentence of one and one-half to four and one-half years.

13. Charges were also filed against five other defendants who were involved in the incidents which took place on April 19.

14. Michael Briscoe, 17, was named by Kevin Richardson as a participant in the assault on the female jogger; he was also named by Kharey Wise, in one of two videotaped statements Wise made. None of the other defendants mentioned him, at least by name. He was interviewed by investigators and made a videotaped statement. He denied knowledge of or culpability in the incident. Briscoe was initially charged in connection with the crime in a Criminal Court complaint, but was never indicted on those charges. On May 4, 1989, he was indicted for Riot in the First Degree (Penal Law Section 240.06) and Assault in the Second Degree (Penal Law Section 120.05(6)), in connection with the attack on jogger David Lewis. Briscoe pled guilty to the assault charge on May 31, 1990, and received a sentence of one year to run concurrently with a sentence imposed on an unrelated case.

15. Jermaine Robinson, 15, was also indicted on May 4, 1989, charged with Robbery in the First Degree (Penal Law Section 160.15(3), two counts of Robbery in the Second Degree (Penal Law Section (2) (a) and (1)), three counts of Assault in the Second Degree (Penal Law Section 120.05(2) and (6)), and Riot in the First Degree (Penal Law Section 240.06). The charges pertained to the assaults on John Loughlin and David Lewis. Robinson had not been identified by any of the defendants as a participant in the attack on the female jogger, and he denied knowing anything about such an attack in his interviews. On October 5, 1989, Robinson pled guilty to Robbery in the First Degree in connection with the incident involving John Loughlin. He also entered into a plea agreement that required him to testify for the prosecution if called upon to do so. Robinson was not called as a witness in the subsequent trials of the defendants, and he was sentenced to one year on April 4, 1991, and granted Youthful Offender treatment.

16. On January 10, 1990, Antonio Montalvo, 18, was charged under Indictment Number 0009/90 with two counts of Robbery in the Second Degree (Penal Law Section 160.10(2) (a) and (1)), one count of Assault in the Second Degree (Penal Law Section 120.05(2)), and Riot in the First Degree (Penal Law Section 240.06), in connection with the assault on Antonio Diaz. Montalvo, known as "Tony", had been named as a participant, though not a rapist, in Antron McCray's statement about the jogger attack.** None of the other defendants had named him. Montalvo was interviewed by investigators about the events in the park, and made a videotaped statement to an Assistant District Attorney. He denied any knowledge of an attack on a female jogger, and was never charged in connection with the crime. On January 29, 1991, he pled guilty to Robbery in the Second Degree. He received a sentence of one year.

---

*The shirt was placed behind her head, crisscrossed over and through her mouth, and then used to tie her hands and wrists up in front of her face.
**Montalvo's identity as the person McCray was referring to is firmly established by analyzing McCray's statement and a number of others made during the 1989 investigation. McCray identified "Tony" as a participant in the assault on Antonio Diaz, and the person who took his food and ate some of it. Four others said the same thing. Raymond Santana stated that Montalvo admitted to him that he was the person who had taken and eaten the food. In statements made to the police at the time, Montalvo acknowledged having done so. Finally, Kevin Richardson stated that a person named "Tony" participated in the assault on Diaz, and said that he lived in the Lehman Projects. That was Montalvo's residence at the time.

17. Orlando Escobar, 16, was also indicted on January 10 of 1990, for Robbery in the First Degree (Penal Law Section 160.15(3)), two counts of Robbery in the Second Degree (Penal Law Sections 160.10(2) (a) and (1)), two counts of Assault in the Second Degree (Penal Law Sections 120.05(2) and (6)), and Riot in the First Degree (Penal Law Section 240.06). The charges pertained to the assault on John Loughlin. Antron McCray had stated that a "Puerto Rican kid with a hoodie" had raped the jogger, and Escobar may have been the person he was referring to.* None of the other defendants mentioned him in their statements. Escobar was interviewed, denied any knowledge of the attack, and was never charged in connection with it. On March 14, 1991, he pled guilty to Attempted Robbery in the Second Degree. He was sentenced to six months incarceration and four and one-half years probation.

18. On April 21, 1989, Clarence Thomas, 14, was charged in a Criminal Court complaint with Rape in the First Degree (Penal Law Section 130.35(1)), Attempted Murder in the Second Degree (Penal Law Section 110/125.25(1)), and Assault in the First Degree (Penal Law Section 120.10(1) in connection with the attack on the Central Park jogger. Antron McCray had named Thomas as one of the people who actually raped the jogger; police notes reflect that Kevin Richardson had also placed him at the scene, though Richardson did not repeat the allegation in his written or recorded statements. None of the other defendants named him. Thomas was interviewed and made a videotaped statement. He denied that he played any part in an attack on a female jogger. Subsequently, additional charges were filed against him in Criminal Court in connection with the attacks on Loughlin and other joggers at the reservoir. Thomas was never indicted, and all charges against him were dismissed on October 31, 1989.

19. Pursuant to motions to suppress their statements filed by each defendant, a joint *Huntley* hearing was held before Justice Thomas Galligan from October 10 to November 29, 1989. On February 23, 1990, the court issued an opinion denying the defendants' motions, with the exception of a single oral statement made by Raymond Santana.

20. On June 25, 1990, Antron McCray, Yusef Salaam, and Raymond Santana proceeded to a joint trial before the Honorable Thomas Galligan. On August 18, 1990, after ten days of deliberations, the jury convicted each defendant of one count of Assault in the First Degree and Rape in the First Degree for the attack on the Central Park jogger; Robbery in the First Degree and three assault charges for the attack on John Loughlin; Assault in the Second Degree for the attack on David Lewis; and Riot in the First Degree. It acquitted each defendant of Attempted Murder and Sodomy as to the female jogger, and was instructed by the judge not to consider the other, lesser included counts. Since each was under 16 years of age, the court, on September 11, 1990, set aside all their convictions except those for First Degree Robbery and Rape, and then sentenced each of them, as juveniles, to consecutive prison terms of from three and one-third to ten years on each count. This resulted in an aggregate term of from five to ten years pursuant to Penal Law Section 70.30(1) (d).

21. Kevin Richardson and Kharey Wise were tried jointly, also before Judge Galligan, from October 22, 1990, to December 11, 1990. The jury deliberated for eleven days before reaching a verdict. Richardson was found guilty of each count of the indictment. Wise was convicted of Assault in the First Degree and Sexual Abuse in the First Degree with respect to the attack on the Central Park jogger, and of Riot in the First Degree. He was acquitted of the remaining charges. Because of Richardson's age, Justice Galligan set aside all of Richardson's convictions except for those for Attempted Murder in the Second Degree and First Degree Robbery, Rape, and Sodomy. The court sentenced Richardson, as a juvenile, to consecutive prison terms of from three and one-third to ten years on each count, resulting in an aggregate term of from five to ten years. Wise was sentenced to terms of imprisonment of five to fifteen years for Assault in the First Degree, two and one-third to seven years for Sexual Abuse in the First Degree, and one to three years for Riot. The sentences were imposed concurrently, for an aggregate term of five to fifteen years.

22. Yusef Salaam's conviction was affirmed by the Appellate Division (187 A.D.2d 363) and by the Court of Appeals (83 N.Y. 2d 51). Antron McCray's conviction was also affirmed by the Appellate Division (198 A.D.2d 200), and the Court of Appeals denied leave to appeal. The same is true of the conviction of Kharey Wise (204 A.D.2d 133). Kevin Richardson's conviction was affirmed by the Appellate Division (202 A.D.2d 207). Raymond Santana never perfected an appeal.

EVIDENCE AGAINST THE DEFENDANTS AT TRIAL

23. A thorough and extensive investigation was undertaken at the time of the original proceedings in an effort to develop additional evidence. Nevertheless, the People's case at both trials rested almost entirely on the statements made by defendants.**

---

*That conclusion is based upon an analysis of the contents of McCray's statement and others. In the course of his videotaped statement, McCray mentioned ultimately leaving the park with another youngster. He did not know the person well, and could not immediately recall his name. Later in the statement, he remembered that his name was Orlando. In Escobar's own statements, he made it clear that he had played a role in the incidents involving Diaz, the tandem bicyclists, and the joggers at the reservoir, but that he was not well known to the others in the group. In an interview with another individual conducted in 1989, that individual said that he saw McCray and Orlando Escobar when they returned to their apartment complex, and that both were wearing black hoods.

**Kevin Richardson and Antron McCray each made one written and one videotaped statement. Raymond Santana made two written statements, with a supplement to one of them, and a videotaped statement. Yusef Salaam made one oral, unrecorded, unsigned statement. Kharey Wise made two written and two videotaped statements.

24. In addition to the defendants themselves, twenty-four young men who were in Central Park on the night of April 19 were interviewed, some repeatedly, as were a number of the defendants' other associates. However, only one associate of one defendant, Kharey Wise, testified at trial. Her testimony related to a single inculpatory statement she said Wise had made to her, after he had been indicted.*

25. The crime scene, the victim, the defendants, and their personal effects were all examined for forensic evidence. Those examinations resulted in the collection of blood, semen, and hair evidence which was tested using the technologies in existence at the time.

26. The crime scene covered a wide area, and comprised five separate sites at which relevant evidence was recovered. All of the sites were on or north of the 102nd Street transverse. Two substantial bloodstains, each roughly two inches in diameter, were located on the transverse road itself, just north of the midline. Beginning at the edge of the roadway was a visible path of flattened vegetation, measuring from sixteen to eighteen inches wide, which extended to the treeline that began forty feet to the north. Within the wooded area where that vegetation ended, a trail continued to be visible for some distance in the dead leaves and other matter covering the ground.

27. Inside the treeline, approximately seventy-eight feet from the roadway, more bloodstains were discovered at a location where the ground—bare earth covered by leaves and twigs—appeared to have been disturbed. Blood samples were taken from leaves in the area, and a rock which appeared to have blood and several hairs on it was removed for testing. Approximately two hundred twenty-five feet beyond that, farther into the wooded area and down a slope, was another, larger area of disturbed ground with a considerably greater quantity of visible blood and a single hair. A trail of apparent blood spots was observed between the two sites. A white sock and the insole of a jogging shoe were found a short distance away from that second site, and a fragment of brick was also recovered. A second sock was found about forty feet away.

28. The jogger herself had been found at the bottom of the slope, near an unpaved path, forty-seven feet from the location of the disturbance above. On the opposite side of the path, scattered approximately thirty-two feet from where she lay, investigators recovered a pair of black jogging tights and two jogging shoes. One of the jogging shoes was untied, and the insole had been removed; the other shoe was tied.

29. Numerous items of physical evidence found at each of these locations were removed and tested for forensic evidence. For purposes of this motion, only two of the specific test results need be delineated.

30. The rock recovered from the disturbed site closest to the road was found to have human blood on it. The rock was sent to the F.B.I. for DNA testing, but no DNA profile could be created. It was, however, typed according to the far less discriminating ABO system, and certain proteins or antigens identified. The test results indicated that it was consistent with the jogger's blood type. The hair fragments found on the rock were also examined by the only means then available, a visual, microscopic comparison with samples taken from the jogger. The comparison yielded the conclusion that the hair on the rock was consistent with the jogger's—meaning that it had characteristics similar to her hair, and could have come from her.

31. Utilizing those results, testimony about the rock and the hairs that had been found on it was elicited at both trials. The microscopic analyst who had examined the hairs testified in the trial of Salaam, McCray, and Santana that the hair fragments on the rock were fragments of crushed and broken head hairs from the temporal area of the head. He further stated that in his opinion, they had been crushed and broken due to force from the rock. The expert went on to state that it was his belief that the rock could have been used to strike the head of the victim. In the trial of Richardson and Wise, he stated it as his opinion, to a reasonable degree of scientific certainty, that the victim had probably been struck on the side of the head with the rock.

32. DNA evidence was extracted from semen deposited on the jogger's sock, found near her at the crime scene. It did not match any of the defendants, or any other known sample.** The same was true of DNA evidence extracted from a cervical swab; it did not match the defendants or any other known sample. Expert testimony at trial, however, established that the DNA from both the victim and the sock appeared to have come from the same source. Testimony also established that the DNA was not a mixture; it was from a single source, meaning that only one individual had ejaculated. A pubic hair found on the sock was also examined microscopically. It was likewise found to be inconsistent with the defendants and every other known source. The known samples included samples from all of the individuals whom the defendants had specifically named as rapists.

---

*That witness was Melody Jackson. Her brother, much younger than she, was a friend of Wise, and she herself had known Wise for years. She testified that on one occasion when she was in the family apartment where her brother lived, Wise had telephoned from jail. He called to speak with members of the family, as he often did. She testified that when she got on the telephone, she told him she could not believe what she was hearing about his having sex with "that woman." According to Jackson's testimony, Wise replied that he had not had sex with her, but had only held and fondled the victim's leg. Jackson never mentioned Wise's statement to anyone, including members of her own family, until the eve of trial, when her brother was being questioned about Wise by the police, and Jackson interjected with the information.

**In addition to samples taken from the defendants, the jogger, John Loughlin, Antonio Diaz, and the jogger's boyfriend, samples were also secured from Steven Lopez, Michael Briscoe, Antonio Montalvo, Jermaine Robinson, Clarence Thomas, and Lamont McCall, all of whom had been with the defendants in Central Park that night.

33. The People offered testimonial and photographic evidence about the nature and extent of the injuries sustained by the jogger. All of the relevant medical personnel were interviewed, and a number were called to testify, including an expert witness from the Medical Examiner's Office who described each of the jogger's injuries for the juries. The People were unable to offer medical testimony to the effect that the injuries the jogger had sustained could only have been inflicted by multiple perpetrators.*

34. Ultimately, there proved to be no physical or forensic evidence recovered at the scene or from the person or effects of the victim which connected the defendants to the attack on the jogger, or could establish how many perpetrators participated.

35. The only forensic evidence recovered which in any way connected the defendants to the crime consisted of three hairs found on Kevin Richardson's clothing and one hair found on Steven Lopez's clothing.** Richardson's clothing yielded nine human hairs, all of which were examined microscopically. Six were not consistent with the jogger. Three others, one from his underwear, one from his t-shirt, and one from his blue jeans, were found by the examiner to be consistent with the jogger's hair. A similar conclusion was reached with respect to one out of the twelve hairs recovered from Steven Lopez's clothing; that hair was found on his shirt. The examiner's report of his findings with respect to the hairs on Richardson and Lopez, as well as the hair fragments recovered from the crime scene, stated that they "could have originated" from the jogger.***

36. Testimony concerning the hairs found on Richardson was introduced at both trials. Testimony concerning the hair found on Lopez was introduced only at the trial of defendants Richardson and Wise.

NEWLY DISCOVERED EVIDENCE

The Evidence Provided by Matias Reyes

37. In early February of 2002, the District Attorney's Office was notified that an inmate had come forward with a claim that he had attacked and raped the Central Park jogger, and that he had committed the crime alone. The inmate, Matias Reyes, had informed a Corrections Officer of his claim. He had then been formally interviewed, on January 17, by an investigative supervisor from the Inspector General's Office. Following that, information about his contentions was forwarded to the District Attorney's Office.

38. Reyes, now 31, is serving sentences totalling thirty-three and one-third years to life imprisonment for three rape/robberies, one rape/murder, and one robbery**** that he committed between June 11 and August 5, 1989. The sentences were imposed on November 1, 1991, after Reyes admitted his guilt and entered pleas of guilty to the top counts in each case.

39. Reyes' 1991 prosecutions had rested in part on DNA evidence taken from his victims and from the scenes of his crimes, which matched the DNA in a sample taken from him. That evidence had been tested using the technology then in existence, RFLP, as were the samples in the Central Park jogger case. Immediately upon learning of Reyes' claims, efforts were undertaken to locate the evidence from both cases, and the FBI laboratories were asked to make a comparison. On May 8, 2002, the District Attorney's Office was notified that Reyes' DNA matched the DNA taken from the sock that had been found at the Central Park crime scene.

40. As soon as notification of the initial comparison was received from the FBI, steps were taken to bring Reyes to the District Attorney's Office for a further investigation of his account. Reyes was interviewed for the first time on May 23. He was interviewed again on May 28, when he was brought to Central Park, and on May 30. He has subsequently been questioned on a number of occasions. Reyes has also provided samples of his blood, head, and pubic hair, and signed consent forms allowing investigators access to his complete prison file and all of his mail. He has been interviewed extensively about the Central Park jogger case, about his criminal and personal history, about his motives in coming forward, and about his associations.

41. The information Reyes provided in each of those areas has been extensively investigated with a view toward either corroborating or refuting his statements. The investigation has included interviews with police officers, Corrections personnel, inmates, and civilians, as well as a review of all relevant records pertaining to Reyes' personal, criminal, and psychological history and the original investigation and prosecution of the attack on the Central Park jogger.

42. That investigation has led to the conclusion that Reyes' account of the attack and rape is corroborated by, consistent with, or explanatory of objective, independent evidence in a number of important respects. Further, investigators have been unable to find any evidence that, as of 1989, Reyes knew or associated with the defendants or any of the individuals known to have been

---

*As part of the 2002 reexamination of the case, Dr. Charles Hirsch, Chief Medical Examiner of the City of New York, reviewed the jogger's medical records and photographs. He has stated as his opinion that "Nothing about the distribution or severity of . . . [the victim's] injuries indicates or reveals the number of assailants, which could have been one or more."

**The value of the hairs found on Richardson's clothing was compromised by the fact that the clothing was spread on the precinct floor to be photographed before the hairs were removed. There was, therefore, a possibility of contamination.

***Two hairs were also removed from the clothing of Antron McCray, and ten from the clothing of Raymond Santana; they were not consistent with the jogger's hair. Kharey Wise's clothing was not taken because it had been laundered. Yusef Salaam's jacket was taken; no hairs were recovered.

****According to Reyes' 2002 statements, he intended to rape the victim, but was interrupted by neighbors before he could force her into her apartment from the hallway where he accosted her.

in the park with them on the night of April 19. In any event, in their statements, several of the defendants themselves named or otherwise identified the individuals they claimed raped the Central Park jogger; the evidence indicates that none of those individuals is Matias Reyes. In addition, Reyes has proven to be candid and accurate about other aspects of his life, associations, and history, both personal and criminal. A full review and investigation of that criminal history has revealed significant parallels with the jogger attack, and also resulted in the discovery of important additional evidence.

43. Reyes states that his decision to come forward with his confession was prompted by a chance encounter with Kharey Wise in Auburn Correctional Facility, and the resultant realization that Wise was still incarcerated in connection with the attack on the Central Park jogger. Reyes says that he feared Wise's reaction, and therefore disclosed nothing to him about his own culpability. However, he began seeking advice from different individuals in the prison system, telling them that he had committed a crime for which someone else had been convicted, and wanting to know how he could bring his information to the attention of appropriate authorities.

44. Corrections records reflect that Wise and Reyes were both imprisoned at Auburn during the relevant time period,* and interviews with prison officials have established that the encounter Reyes described could have taken place. Interviews with a number of Corrections employees, volunteers, and inmates have confirmed Reyes' assertion that he began seeking help with a problem in late 2001. He specifically told some of them that he had committed a crime for which another person had been convicted, and that he wanted to rectify the situation. Ultimately a Corrections Officer, observing that Reyes seemed very troubled, induced him to explain what was bothering him and set in motion the process by which he came to the District Attorney's Office.

45. Reyes' does not attribute his decision to come forward to having "found God," although he has stated that he has found religious services to be helpful. He has consistently explained himself in terms of his positive experiences in prison, the fact that people have treated him decently despite the nature of his criminal history, and his guilty reaction to seeing Wise.

46. Reyes motives cannot be objectively proven or disproven. However, an extensive investigation has revealed no evidence that the defendants themselves induced him to come forward. There is no evidence of any connection between the defendants and Reyes prior to their incarceration in 1989. Except for a brief period in 1990 when he and Kharey Wise were in the same jail, he has not been imprisoned with any of them.** Moreover, none of them appeared to know of Reyes' claim until many months after he first spoke with Corrections officials. In fact, Kharey Wise was still incarcerated when Reyes made his claim, and did not apply for conditional release until July 26, 2002. Further, the one assurance Reyes sought when he first spoke with a Corrections Officer was that he would receive protection. He stated that he feared what Wise might do when he learned that it was Reyes who committed the crime he was imprisoned for.

47. More important, information Reyes has provided about himself and his history has consistently proven to be reliable and accurate, both about matters related to the case and matters with no direct connection to it. Reyes has also been candid, even with respect to aspects of his history that might cast doubt on his credibility.

48. For example, Reyes volunteered that he used to commit robberies and larcenies on a regular basis, stealing jewelry, money, and Walkmans. He frequently committed such crimes in Central Park, often by the reservoir. He was able to recall the details of several of his larcenies, and described the patterns he followed with respect to robberies. Those activities were not reflected in his records. Reyes also said that he had been arrested on one occasion, for a robbery he committed with several acquaintances in 1988, but that the case never went to court.

49. This information proved to be accurate. Investigators were able to retrieve records reflecting the arrest Reyes spoke about. They were also able to identify and locate individuals who knew Reyes in the late 1980's, and who confirmed the truth of his admissions. A number of people observed him with stolen property, including both jewelry and Walkmans.

50. The investigation has uncovered no evidence that Reyes knew any of the defendants or the others who were with them in Central Park on the night of April 19. That fact has been established by proof coming from two directions—on the one hand, from interviews with people who knew Reyes; and on the other hand, from current and past interviews with the defendants and their associates.

51. In 1989, Reyes was living on his own, working on an informal basis in a bodega on 102nd Street, across from the 23rd Precinct. Much of the time, he slept in a van belonging to the bodega's owner; occasionally he stayed with a neighborhood family who felt badly for him. Investigators from the District Attorney's Office interviewed fourteen people who knew Reyes in 1989. A number of them saw him on a daily basis.

52. Many of those people describe Reyes as having been a loner, whom they never saw in association with any young people other than the two teenage sons of the family which occasionally helped him. However, Reyes himself said in interviews that he used to commit petty crimes, such as shoplifting, with some neighborhood acquaintances. A number of those

---

*Wise and Reyes had last been incarcerated in the same institution from February to June of 1990, when both were in the Adolescent Reception and Detention Center at Riker's Island.

**Reyes himself picked a photograph of Michael Briscoe and stated that he thought they might have been in the same jail early in his incarceration. As noted above, Briscoe was one of the individuals charged in connection with the incidents in the park. Reyes' information was correct: the two were in the Adolescent Reception and Detention Center at Riker's Island from March 5, 1990 to May 31, 1990, although at that point, Briscoe was there for an unrelated arrest.

acquaintances were located. All were from the 102nd Street area—in their own minds, a neighborhood distinct from the defendants'.* None knew the defendants or their associates, and none ever saw Reyes with the defendants or their associates. Two detectives from the 23rd Precinct who knew Reyes from the bodega where he worked and saw him regularly state that he appeared to be a "loner", and that they never saw him with anyone other than those who frequented the bodega.

53.   In the defendants' own 1989 statements, they listed those they knew who were in Central Park with them. None named Reyes' by his real name or a nickname.** The same is true of the twenty-four other individuals from the park who were interviewed at the time. Raymond Santana, Kevin Richardson, and Michael Briscoe were interviewed in 2002, before news had broken of Reyes' information. They were shown photographs which included a picture of Reyes, and evinced no recognition at all. The same is true of a number of other individuals, present in the park in 1989, who were reinterviewed in 2002.

54.   In any event, in their 1989 statements about the crime, three of the five defendants named or otherwise identified everyone they said raped the jogger. Based upon the evidence, it is a fair conclusion that none of the people they identified is Reyes.***

55. Reyes' convictions arose from crimes he committed on June 11, June 14, July 19, July 27, and August 5, 1989. The basic facts of those crimes are as follows:

(1) On June 11, 1989, Reyes stalked, raped, robbed, stabbed, and beat a twenty-four year old white woman in her apartment on 116th Street, between Park and Lexington Avenues. He used a knife he got from the victim's kitchen, and he stole, among other things, the victim's Walkman. The victim suffered a fractured nose, two black eyes, and multiple areas of bruising, some of them large, on her knees, her legs, her neck, and her flank. In addition, the victim had two superficial stab wounds on her thigh, one in her side, one on a finger, one near her left eyebrow, and one under each eye.

(2) On June 14, 1989, Reyes raped, robbed, and stabbed to death a twenty-four year old, light-skinned, blonde Hispanic woman in an apartment on 97th Street, between Madison and Park Avenues. Again, Reyes used a knife he procured from the victim's kitchen.

(3) On July 19, 1989, Reyes stalked, raped, robbed, and cut a twenty year old white woman inside an apartment on Madison Avenue, between 95th and 96th Streets. Reyes brought a knife with him. In addition to other property, Reyes took his victim's ATM card and PIN number. He then tied her with extension cords in a fashion which parallels the way the Central Park jogger was tied,**** so that he could go to the bank and withdraw money. Because he had bound his victim, Reyes called 911 to summon help for her. The victim suffered small, superficial cuts over one eye and under the other.

(4) On July 27, 1989, Reyes stalked, robbed, and punched a twenty-eight year old white woman in the hallway of her apartment building on Lexington Avenue, at the corner of 95th Street. Reyes was unarmed. The crime was interrupted by neighbors. In his 2002 interviews, Reyes stated that he intended to rape the woman.

(5) On August 5, 1989, Reyes stalked, raped, and robbed a twenty-four year old white woman in her apartment on East 91st Street, between Lexington and Third Avenues. Reyes was unarmed. He took the victim's bank card, and forced her to give him her PIN number. He intended to tie his victim, but she escaped before he could carry his plan out.

56.   In the course of his interviews, Reyes volunteered information about other sex crimes he had committed, for which he had never been arrested. One of the crimes he discussed was a sexual assault which he said he had committed in Central Park. His memory of the event was limited. He accurately recalled the exact location of the incident, and thought it had occurred in the daytime, but beyond that, he essentially knew only that he had accosted a woman with the intention of raping her, and that the crime had been interrupted by bystanders. He did not know when the crime had taken place, although he believed it occurred in 1989.

57.   The crime Reyes was describing was eventually identified, and the victim and witness located. Reyes had told the truth when he said that he committed the crime. He had in fact attacked, beaten, raped, and robbed a twenty-six year old white woman who had been exercising in the park near Lasker rink and pool, at roughly the level of 107th Street. Reyes was unarmed. A bystander intervened as the attack was ongoing, and Reyes left the park, calmly, taking the victim's property with him.

58.   Substantial circumstantial evidence establishes Reyes' identity as the perpetrator. Reyes knew, and in fact drew, the precise location where the crime occurred. There are no records of any other attack occurring there during the relevant time period. The victim stated that the attacker identified himself as "Tony." The victim and witness gave descriptions which are similar to Reyes as he appeared at the time. The victim picked a photograph resembling Reyes as a look alike in 1989. The witness recently identified a 1989 photograph of Reyes as looking "most like" the attacker. The victim described the attacker as having fresh stitches

---

*The defendants and their companions were from housing complexes located somewhat farther north.

**At the time of his arrest in 1989, Reyes told police that he liked to call himself "Tony." However, in interviews with a dozen people who knew him in 1989, all said that they knew his nickname to be "Checo," and that they never knew him to be called "Tony." In his 2002 interviews, Reyes said that "Tony" was an older boy he admired when he was younger. He liked the name, and occasionally called himself that.

***Raymond Santana claimed that he left the scene after Kevin Richardson had raped the jogger, while the crime was still ongoing. Yusef Salaam's statement was incomplete, and he spoke of two unidentified individuals having raped her.

****Reyes used extension cords to tie his victim. He bound her feet with one cord, used another to tie her hands, and a third to gag her by wrapping a cord around her head and crisscrossing it through her mouth. The cords were attached so that her hands were raised in front of her face.

in a cut on the right side of his chin, and medical records reflect that Reyes had received stitches in that location the day before the incident. Reyes is not clear about whether the incident he remembered was an attempted or completed rape, but that may be explained by the fact that, according to the victim, the apparently did not ejaculate.

59.   The incident occurred on April 17, 1989, in mid-afternoon, two days before the attack on the Central Park jogger. The victim was badly beaten about the head. She had a large hematoma on her forehead, abrasions to both knees, bite marks on her left upper arm and neck, scratches over her neck, face, knees, and back, and multiple bruises. In addition, her right ear was bruised and swollen, and her right eye was bruised and showed subconjunctival hemorrhages. She recalls that at some point her attacker had his foot on her head. The victim was treated and released, and the case was marked closed after initial efforts to contact the victim were unsuccessful.

60.   Reyes disclosed information about a second sexual assault which he said occurred in a church located at Fifth Avenue and 90th Street. Reyes remembered and described the scene accurately and in detail, but again, could remember little about the incident itself. In summary, he knew that he had accosted a woman inside the church, dragged her down a staircase with the intention of raping her, and then abandoned the sexual attack when she claimed to have some sort of disease. He took money and jewelry from the victim, and left. He did not know when the crime was committed, nor did he remember any other particulars of the attack itself.

61.   That incident, also, was eventually identified. It occurred in the Church of the Heavenly Rest, across from Central Park, on September 21, 1988. Again, Reyes' admission that he committed the crime proved to be truthful. Reyes attacked, choked, struck, robbed and intended to rape a twenty-seven year old white woman. He was armed with a small knife, and he forced the victim to disrobe, but was dissuaded from raping her when she told him she had an infection. The victim suffered multiple superficial scratches and bruises.* The complainant viewed photographs on file with the Police Department, and picked no one; Reyes' photograph was not on file. The case was then marked closed.

62.   Reyes was also questioned about some of the other crimes for which he was convicted. The degree of detail with which he could describe them varied: in some instances his recollections were extraordinarily complete, particularly with respect to the events leading up to and following his crimes, and the concrete details of locations, pathways, and proceeds; in others, his memories were more sketchy.

63.   The following summarizes the essentials of Reyes' account of his attack on the jogger:

(1) Reyes states that he left the bodega where he worked and headed for Central Park. It was likely he would commit some kind of crime, but not necessarily a rape. He entered the park at 102nd Street, and he first saw the jogger as she proceeded north on the East Drive, just south of the 102nd Street entrance to the park. She was running in the jogging lane on the east side of the road, wearing long black or navy blue jogging tights. They were tight, and Reyes says he was attracted to her partly because he could see her "butt."

(2) Reyes moved to the other side of the East Drive and began to follow the jogger, with the intention of raping her. He did not want her to sense or see him directly behind her, so he began "zig-zagging" on the side of the road. He was waiting to see whether she would take the long route around the park, heading north until the road looped around, or the short route, cutting across the 102nd Street transverse. She took the short route, moving to the north side of the transverse road and heading west. He crossed to the north side as well, still following her.

(3) Reyes states that he caught sight of a "stick" or branch lying on the ground to the north side of the road. (In diagrams and in a visit to the park Reyes has indicated the area he is talking about.) He picked up the stick. The stick was substantial; it required two hands to hold. Reyes then accelerated to catch up to his victim.

(4) The jogger was wearing a headset, and she seemed to be playing it loudly, as she did not hear his approach. Reyes came up behind her and struck a heavy blow to the back of her head. Reyes does not know exactly where or how he hit her. He is left-handed, but says he may well have struck her overhand, or from some other angle. The jogger fell forward. Her Walkman fell to the roadway. Reyes has diagrammed and shown investigators the approximate point on the road where he says he struck her.

(5) Reyes says the jogger was conscious but clearly stunned and incapable of fighting, and that he then dragged her off the road. Initially, he dragged her over ground that was grassy, with some grass "higher," and some grass "lower", into a "bushy" area. He explains that by a "bushy" area, he means an area among the trees, covered with dead leaves and sticks, which becomes more overgrown in the summer; it was not overgrown at the time of the incident. The area he dragged her into is to the north of the roadway.

(6) Reyes does not know how he dragged the jogger. He stopped when he reached a reasonably secluded spot. At that point, she appeared to be recuperating from the original blow to her head, because she was talking and protesting. He has repeatedly described her as holding her hand up to the right rear of her head, saying that she was bleeding. He states that he saw blood on the right shoulder of her t-shirt.

(7) Reyes' account of what then took place inside the wooded area is more fragmentary. He says that he cannot remember all the details of what took place, and therefore cannot give a complete narrative, but is positive about certain facts.

---

*The victim in the case was interviewed in 2002, but this description of the crime is based on her 1989 account of what occurred.

(8) Reyes states that he knows that he pulled off the jogger's tights and shoes, and raped her. At some point, which he believes was after he raped her, she broke away from him and ran; he says that he has an image of her running while naked from the waist down. Somehow he brought her down, possibly by pulling her shirt up over her head. Reyes had already beaten her in the spot they were in originally, but at that point the violence escalated. Reyes knows that he struck her in the face and head with a rock and other things. He cannot specify what other things he used. At some point in the course of the incident, he also used his hands on her. He does not know how many times he hit her with the rock, but knows that it was "more than a couple."

(9) Reyes says that he also knows that at some point, he found the jogger's keys; he believes she had two, and he knows they were in a black key case which zipped around and had Velcro on it. He describes the case as being the sort that can be attached to a belt, but says he does not recall where she wore it since she had no belt. Reyes says he is particularly clear about the keys because after he found them, he began demanding that the jogger tell him her address. His intention was to burglarize her apartment. She refused to give him the information. That, he says, angered him, and caused him to escalate the level of violence. He knows that the jogger had no money on her, although he does not specifically remember searching for money.

(10) Reyes states that he threw her clothes somewhere. However, he cannot remember what happened to her t-shirt. He says that he recalls there being "something on her face" when he left, and thinks somehow her t-shirt might have been over her head. He does not have any memory of tying or gagging her. At various times, Reyes has also said that he may have moved her, or may have turned her over.

(11) Reyes says that when he left the jogger, she was bloody and unconscious, but still alive. He could hear her breathing, making some kind of hard sound in her throat, as though something had been broken.

(12) Reyes says that he tossed the rock he used somewhere, but does not know where, or even whether it was in the immediate area. He then made his way out of the wooded area in the same way he had come in. When he reached the roadway, he saw that the stick he had used on the jogger was still there; he picked it up and threw it off to one side of the road or the other. He also saw the jogger's headset, still lying where it had fallen. He put it on, walked up onto the baseball fields to the south of the road, and headed out of the park. At some point he tossed the keys and case away. He is not sure when or where; it may have occurred as he was leaving the park, but could have happened earlier.

(13) Reyes came out at the 102nd Street entrance to the park, which intersects with the East Drive at a point south of the transverse road. There, he saw a detective he knew from the 23rd Precinct named "Blondie," who was just entering the park. "Blondie" was in a yellow cab with a partner whom Reyes did not know. "Blondie" questioned him briefly about a commotion in the park, and let him go on his way.

64. Reyes' version of events regarding the attack on the jogger is corroborated by, consistent with, or explanatory of objective, verifiable evidence in a number of important respects. The following sets forth some of the more significant points, in summary form:

(1) Reyes is accurate about the direction the jogger was coming from and the direction she was travelling in, and he correctly describes her jogging tights, which were tight, black, and ankle-length. He has also indicated that she may have been wearing a white t-shirt, which she was.

(2) Reyes' assertion that he began his attack by striking the jogger in the back of the head with a heavy branch is consistent with and explanatory of medical and crime scene evidence. The same is true of his description of the jogger's mental status after the attack, of his recollection of her holding her hand to the right rear of her head, and of his observation of blood on her right shoulder. The jogger had a depressed skull fracture, with a large, overlying laceration, in the right parietal/occipital region of her head—in other words, in the upper right rear of her head. According to Dr. Hirsch, that injury is fully consistent with a blow from a heavy branch, and with the rest of Reyes' observations.

(3) Reyes maintains that the jogger was wearing a Sony AM/FM headset, with colors on the dial. The jogger was in fact wearing a headset when she was attacked. The Walkman disappeared, and despite an extensive search, was never found. She does not recall the make, but believes it may have had colors on the dial.

(4) Reyes is accurate in his description of the location where the attack occurred, and of the terrain he covered in dragging the jogger into the woods. Crime scene photographs show a distinct path of flattened groundcover in vegetation that is a mixture of grasses and weeds of varying heights. The pathway is sixteen to eighteen inches wide, and appears to be more consistent with a single attacker dragging an inert form than with a group. Vegetation to the side of the flattened path shows some sign of being disturbed, but trial testimony established that was the result of crime scene personnel walking there. There are no other indications of trampling in the immediate area.

(5) Reyes says that he took the jogger's keys, which he found in a small, black case that zipped around and had Velcro on it. He believes there were two keys. It was known in April of 1989 that the jogger's keys were gone; their disappearance was unexplained. At the time, nothing was known about a case. In 2002, the jogger was asked about the possibility that she had a case. She stated that she was inclined to say that she carried her keys on a ring, but that she did own a dark green or black case with Velcro on it. She does not think that it had a zipper. It was the type of case that can be attached to a shoe. One of the jogger's shoes, found at the scene, was untied, as it would have been had a case been removed from it. The other shoe was still tied, as would be expected if it were pulled off in the course of a violent attack. The jogger also believes that she carried two keys.

(6) Reyes' recollection that he threw the jogger's clothes is consistent with the crime scene evidence. The location of her tights, shoes, and one sock indicate that they were in fact thrown.

(7) Reyes says that he beat the jogger in the head repeatedly with a rock. According to Dr. Hirsch, the medical evidence shows five lacerations and a skull fracture in the left temporal forehead area, all caused by blunt force trauma. He also states that when he left her, she was unconscious but not dead. He could hear her making a hard sound in her throat as she breathed. His description of her condition is consistent with the nature and extent of her injuries. The first officer on the scene testified that when he arrived at the scene, he could hear gurgling sounds coming from deep in her throat.

(8) Reyes maintains that he ran into "Blondie" on his way out of the park, and had a brief conversation with him. "Blondie" is a detective from the 23rd Precinct who knew Reyes. He used to see him regularly at the bodega where he worked. He does not remember whether he saw and spoke with Reyes in the park that night or not. Circumstantially, however, it is clear that Reyes did at least see "Blondie" on the night of the 19th. "Blondie" confirms that he did in fact enter the park, and that he did so at 102nd Street, in response to reports about criminal activities in the park. "Blondie" also confirms that he was in fact in a cab and was with someone who was not his regular partner. To the detective, Reyes was a harmless teenager. As he candidly reports, if he had seen Reyes and spoken to him, he would not have suspected him of criminal activity, and would have let him go. The fact that Reyes did see "Blondie" tends to confirm that he was not with the defendants. Given the nature of the criminal activities being reported, it seems likely that "Blondie" would have stopped a group of teenagers.

65. Reyes' account of events is the first that has suggested an explanation for the existence of two areas of the crime scene where it appeared that attacks took place. His specific recollection that the jogger broke away only after he had raped her is, however, probably not correct. The jogger's clothing was found below the second site where an attack appeared to have occurred. That pattern of evidence indicates that her jogging tights were undoubtedly not pulled off her until she was at that second location. A more plausible scenario than the one Reyes recounts is that she broke and ran from him before the rape. However, the inaccuracy of Reyes' account in that regard should be evaluated in light of the passage of thirteen years.

66. Moreover, in evaluating the weight a jury would be likely to place upon his testimony, his failure to recall all the details of the incident must be placed in the context of his memories of other events. It was Reyes who freely disclosed that he had committed other sexual assaults, and the investigation revealed that he was telling the truth in that regard. Yet when the facts of those cases were uncovered, his memories of those particular events proved to be incomplete.

67. Corroboration of Reyes' account of the crime is found both in the pattern of his other sexual attacks and in some of their specific facts. He consistently targeted and stalked Caucasian women, or women who appeared to be Caucasian. His crimes all involved conversation with his victims, either as a way of making initial contact or as a way of acquiring information that would enable him to steal more property.* Frequently, conversation or a search for property alternated with outbursts of physical or sexual violence. All of his rapes or attempted rapes also involved robbery. In particular, where a Walkman was available, he took it. His beatings often focused on the head. His claim that he demanded the jogger's address echoes the cases in which he forced his victims to give him their PIN numbers. And although he cannot remember doing it, it is clear that Reyes is the person who tied the jogger with her own t-shirt. The manner in which she was tied—behind the head, through the mouth, with the hands in front—is strikingly similar to the way he tied another of his victims.

68. One additional piece of physical evidence may also corroborate Reyes' account. The victim had an oddly shaped wound on her left cheek, resembling a cross, but with curved arms. Reyes owned a ring, taken from him at the time of his arrest and retained in the District Attorney's Office, on which the figure of Christ is raised on the flat surface of a cross. Reyes, who is left-handed, states that he used to wear the ring on his left hand. The ring and photographs of the wound were examined at the Office of the Chief Medical Examiner.** The number of variables involved makes an exact comparison with the wound impossible. However, in the opinion of Dr. Hirsch, "The patterned injury over the prominence of the victim's left cheek bone is consistent with a left fist blow, striking at an acute angle, partially imprinting the image of approximately half of the prominent parts of Mr. Reyes' ring on her skin."****

Forensic Evidence

69. After preliminary DNA results were received from the F.B.I. in May, the District Attorney's Office retained a private laboratory to conduct additional forensic testing.

70. The laboratory performed further tests in connection with those DNA samples which connected Reyes to the crime. The tests provide additional corroboration of Reyes' account. The private laboratory concurred with testimony given at the defendants' trials that the DNA on the sock found at the Central Park crime scene and the DNA on the cervical swab taken from the victim came from the same person. Thus, Reyes' DNA matched both.

71. Moreover, the laboratory found additional, untested semen on the sock, which it tested using technology not in existence in 1989. That test established that Reyes was the source of the DNA to a factor of one in 6,000,000,000 people. In addition, mitochondrial DNA testing established that Reyes was also the source of the pubic hair found on the sock in Central Park.****

---

*Reyes makes no claim that this incident was initiated with conversation, a fact explained by the circumstances in which he targeted his victim.

**No DNA could be recovered from the ring, which Reyes wore until August 5, 1989.

***The People introduced expert testimony in the original trial to the effect that the injury could have been caused by a rock or a brick.

****More technically, mitochondrial DNA tests only establish that a sample came from a particular person or someone else in his maternal line. In this case, for all practical purposes, the test established that Reyes was the source of the pubic hair.

In short, the DNA tests showed that Matias Reyes' claim that he raped the jogger was true, and confirmed that no one else's DNA was present in the samples taken from the victim or the evidence at the scene.

72. Efforts were also made to locate all of the physical evidence which had been gathered at the time of the original prosecution. Those efforts were partially successful, and every item which could be found was retested. For purposes of this motion, however, the relevant test results pertain to hairs found on Kevin Richardson and the bloody rock found at the scene of the attack, and to the blood found on that rock. The hair found on Steven Lopez could not be located.

73. The three hairs found on Kevin Richardson were reexamined following F.B.I. protocols for questioned hair samples. The hairs were first re-examined microscopically and then submitted for mitochondrial DNA testing. All had been mounted on slides for examination in 1989.

74. The microscopic analysis of the hairs was performed by Special Agent Douglas Deedrick, formerly Chief of the Hair and Fibers Unit and currently Unit Chief of the Information and Evidence section of the F.B.I. Agent Deedrick disagreed with the expert opinion offered at the original trials. His conclusion was that the hairs were not suitable for comparison, and could not be used to link Richardson to the jogger. In his opinion, they were too undifferentiated and had too few characteristics for a meaningful comparison to be possible. He also disagreed with a characterization of one of the hairs as a pubic hair. In his view, no determination could be made as to what type of hair it was.

75. DNA was extracted from all three of the hairs found on Richardson, and none of the DNA matched the victim's. However, the official finding with respect to each of the hairs is that the results are "inconclusive." The reasons differ.

(1) One hair was found to contain a mixture of DNA from two different people. The jogger's DNA sequence was inconsistent with any combination of that mixture. The opinion of the examiner is that one of the DNA sequences probably resulted from contamination at the time the hair was originally mounted on a slide. Laboratory protocols require that when a mixture of DNA is found, no conclusion will be drawn as to the source of the hair.

(2) A partial DNA sequence was extracted from a second hair and compared to the jogger's, and seven "base differences" were observed; only two base differences are required to declare an exclusion. However, laboratory protocols require that results of each test be verified in order to eliminate the possibility of contamination. The verification is accomplished by performing a second test in order to replicate the original results, before conclusively excluding a possible source of the DNA. There was insufficient DNA extracted from the second hair to permit such verification to take place.

(3) The third hair had an intact DNA sequence extracted from it, which showed one base difference from the jogger's mitochondrial DNA. Two base differences are required in order to exclude a source, because single differences have been observed in hairs taken from the same source. However, when such differences occur in hairs from the same person, they are usually seen in particular regions of the DNA known as "hot spots." The difference observed between the jogger's hair and the third hair tested did not occur in a "hot spot". Additional samples of the jogger's hair were tested in order to see if the same base difference appeared. It did not. Both those factors reduce the likelihood that the questioned hair originated with the jogger, but she cannot be excluded as a source to a reasonable degree of scientific certainty.

76. The bloody rock found at the scene was also submitted for examination, and a limited DNA profile was obtained. That profile showed that the blood was female human blood, but inconsistent with the jogger's DNA profile. However, contamination cannot be excluded as a possibility. The rock has been handled by a number of people, and has not been stored in a manner which would ensure the integrity of the original DNA. If the original DNA has degraded, the profile raised may be DNA from an unknown person deposited over the original DNA.

77. The hair fragments found on the rock were also submitted for testing. As with the hairs found on Richardson, they were first examined microscopically by Special Agent Deedrick. He found them unsuitable for comparison, describing them as fragmentary and of limited value. In any event, the original hair samples from the jogger could not be located. Because hair changes over time, samples taken thirteen years later do not provide a suitable basis for comparison, even against standards of high quality. Accordingly, no new microscopic comparison could be made between the jogger's hair and the evidence.

78. Only one of the hair fragments was suitable for testing. The other fragments were too small. The fragment tested yielded only a partial DNA sequence, with a number of differences from the jogger's DNA. However, the size of the sample once again precluded verification through an additional test, and as a consequence no conclusive result was provided.

THE NEWLY DISCOVERED EVIDENCE CLAIM

79. Under *Criminal Procedure Law* 440.10(1) (g) newly discovered evidence must meet six criteria in order to justify the vacatur of a conviction: (1) it must be such that it would probably have resulted in a verdict more favorable to the defendant if it had been received at trial; (2) it must have been discovered since the trial; (3) it must be such as could not have been discovered before the trial by the exercise of due diligence; (4) it must be material to the issue; (5) it must not be cumulative to the issue; and (6) it must not merely impeach or contradict the former evidence. *People v. Salemi*, 309 N.Y. 208, 216, quoting *People v. Priori*, 164 N.Y. 459, 472 (1900).

80.   The newly discovered evidence in this case consists of the account of events provided by Matias Reyes, who states that he alone attacked and raped the Central Park jogger; DNA test results which conclusively establish that Reyes was the sole source of semen found on a sock at the crime scene and a cervical swab taken from the victim, as well as of a pubic hair found on the same sock; the record of prior, similar attacks committed by Reyes, including an assault and rape committed in Central Park two days before the jogger attack; and scientific test results undermining the probative value of evidence introduced in the defendants' trials. All of that evidence meets the criteria set forth in the statute.*

81.   The vacatur of a conviction, however, requires not merely that new evidence exist, but that it be ". . . of such a character as to create a probability that had such evidence been received at the trial the verdict would have been more favorable to defendant." *Criminal Procedure Law* Section 440.10 (1) (g). In determining whether newly discovered evidence would probably change a verdict, the evidence is not evaluated in a vacuum, but in light of the evidence contained in the record on appeal. *See People v. Salemi*, 309 N.Y. at 218-19; *see also, People v. Maynard*, 183 A.D.2d 1099 (3d Dept. 1992).

82.   In other words, an assessment of the likely impact of newly discovered evidence requires an honest appraisal of the strength or weakness of the case originally presented by the People. The defendants' statements in this case were sufficiently persuasive to result in the convictions of all five defendants on at least some of the charges against them, and, for that matter, persuasive enough to bring about those convictions before two separate juries. However, the confessions also had serious weaknesses.

83.   Perhaps the most persuasive fact about the defendants' confessions is that they exist at all. While all of the defendants began by denying knowledge of the attack, each ultimately made himself an accomplice in a terrible crime.

84.   In that regard, it is important to note that, with the exception of the unrecorded statement made by Yusef Salaam, each of the statements cast the speaker in a relatively minor role, and none of the defendants admitted that he personally raped her. Kevin Richardson stated that he grabbed at the jogger, but equivocated about it and, at least on video, stopped short of saying that he did so to assist in an assault or rape. Antron McCray said that he kicked the jogger and lay on top of her, but did not penetrate her. Raymond Santana finally stated that he "felt her tits." And Kharey Wise eventually said that he held and fondled her leg. Yusef Salaam, in his unrecorded statement, went furthest in ascribing culpability to himself, by saying that he struck the jogger with a pipe at the inception of the incident.

85.   In and of itself, the fact that each defendant minimized his own involvement would not be startling or necessarily significant; defendants certainly lie, even when confessing. On the other hand, it arguably makes the claim that the defendants made false admissions more plausible, by adding weight to their contention that, for whatever reason, each spoke about the crime with a view toward becoming a witness rather than a defendant. In that sense, it is an aspect of the confessions to be considered here.

86.   The significant weaknesses in the defendants' statements lie in the details they provide in describing the attack on the jogger. Taking the statements individually, those details appear to give them power. But a comparison of the statements reveals troubling discrepancies. Using their videotaped statements as the point of comparison,** analysis shows that the accounts given by the five defendants differed from one another on the specific details of virtually every major aspect of the crime—who initiated the attack, who knocked the victim down, who undressed her, who struck her, who held her, who raped her, what weapons were used in the course of the assault, and when in the sequence of events the attack took place.

87.   Thus, for example, on the issue of who actually knocked the jogger to the ground, Kevin Richardson said Antron, Raymond, and Steve did it; Antron McCray said everyone charged her; Raymond Santana said Kevin did it; Yusef Salaam said he did it; and Kharey Wise first named Raymond, and then named Steve.

88.   Similarly, as to who struck the jogger in the course of the attack, Kevin Richardson alleged that only Michael Briscoe hit her, and that he hit her only with his fist, in the face. Raymond Santana said that Steve smacked her, and then struck her in the face with a brick. Antron McCray stated that everyone was hitting and stomping her, and that a tall, skinny, black male struck her in the ribs and head with a pipe. Yusef Salaam said that he himself hit her with a pipe, and that someone else used a brick. Kharey Wise first said that Steve slapped her in the face, that someone cut her legs with a knife, and that Kevin used a "handrock"; he then said that Steve slapped her, punched her in the face, and cut her legs with a knife, and that Kevin, Steve, and Raymond punched her in the face and hit her with bricks.

89.   Likewise, on the issue of who raped her, Richardson named Antron, Raymond, and Steve. McCray identified a tall, skinny black male, a Puerto Rican with a black hoodie, Clarence, and Kevin, and said that he himself simulated having sex with her. Santana claimed that Kevin raped her, after which Santana left the park. Salaam named Kevin, Kharey, and a couple of unknown males. And Kharey Wise named Steven, Raymond, and Kevin. Kevin Richardson's is the only name common to all the statements, with the exception of his own. It was, however, Richardson who first implicated members of the group in the rape, providing a possible motive for others to accuse him.

---

*As already noted, the People requested that the F.B.I. laboratory reexamine the hair evidence introduced at the defendants' trials before having it tested for mitochondrial DNA, and the F.B.I. examiner disagreed with the original technician's findings. However, his opinion does not qualify as newly discovered evidence within the meaning of *C.P.L.* Section 440.10 since counsel could, with due diligence, have sought a second microscopic analysis at the time of the original proceedings.

**Since Yusef Salaam made only one, unrecorded statement, that statement is used for this analysis.

90.   There are certainly portions of the statements made by the defendants that are consistent with the evidence presented at trial. There was, for example, testimony to the effect that certain of the jogger's injuries could have been caused by a pipe, a brick, or a rock, weapons that were named in some of the statements. The jogger had bruising which could have resulted from the kicking or blows some defendants described. Antron McCray accurately stated that the jogger wore a white shirt.

91.   That said, it is nonetheless true that in many other respects the defendants' statements were not corroborated by, consistent with, or explanatory of objective, independent evidence. And some of what they said was simply contrary to established fact.

92.   None of the defendants, for example, related where the jogger was coming from, what direction she was running in, or how they happened to catch sight of her. None offered specific or accurate descriptions of the area where she was attacked, the terrain, or the crime scene. Yusef Salaam stated that he struck the jogger on the head with a pipe. He did not say where on the head, but his statement could explain the bloodstains on the road and the injuries to the back of her head. None of the others, however, gave an account which would adequately explain either. Only Kharey Wise said anything that would explain the dispersal of physical evidence and the indications that attacks occurred at more than one site, and Wise had been taken to the scene prior to his videotaped statements. None of the defendants mentioned the jogger's Walkman, although several mentioned John Loughlin's Walkman in the statements they made about him. None said a word about her keys. None said anything about a search for money, although the insole pulled out of the victim's jogging shoe certainly suggests that someone looked for it.

93.   Some of what the defendants said is simply wrong. Kharey Wise, for instance, declared that the jogger's clothes had been cut off, and that her legs had been cut with a knife. Her clothes were not cut off, and there were no knife wounds on the jogger; in fact, the prosecution affirmatively elicited testimony to that effect at trial. Likewise, Kevin Richardson said that her bra was ripped off, whereas in fact it was still on her when she was found. Raymond Santana described her as being naked during the incident, and others said she was naked when they left, although she was found with her jogging bra still on and her t-shirt tied around her head.

94.   Other statements the defendants made are simply not corroborated. For example, several defendants spoke of a brick being used as a weapon in the attack. But the only brick actually removed from the crime scene had no blood or other forensic evidence that would confirm its use as a weapon.

95.   More importantly, the defendants' statements about the rape could not be corroborated by DNA evidence. Each defendant, in his statement, minimized his participation in the rape, and none acknowledged having had intercourse with the victim. However, all but Raymond Santana claimed to have seen multiple individuals raping her. Despite that, the DNA of only one person was found. That required the jury to believe that, in a gang of teenaged rapists, only one ejaculated.

96.   Moreover, although the prosecution argued that the DNA must have been left by one of the defendants' accomplices, that argument presented difficulties of its own. For example, Kevin Richardson and Kharey Wise purported to name everyone who had raped her, and none of the people they named proved to be a DNA match.

97.   Perhaps most significant, none of the defendants accurately described where the attack on the jogger took place. With the exception of Kharey Wise, who had been to the scene, statements by all of the defendants describe events in such a way as to place the attack at or near the reservoir, at varying points in the sequence of events that actually occurred there. The defendants were not similarly confused about the locations of the other crimes they described.

98.   An additional issue is raised by the other incidents which took place in the park. For while the nature and locations of those incidents made it seem logical to believe that the defendants had attacked the jogger, the timing of events made it hard to understand when they could have. Shortly after their initial entry into the park, the larger group of which the defendants were a part temporarily split up. As a result, not all of the defendants participated both in the incidents that occurred along the East Drive and in the attacks at the reservoir; but at least some of them did. Given the times when each of those events were estimated to have occurred, it is difficult to construct a scenario that would have allowed the defendants the time to interrupt their progression south, detour to the 102nd Street transverse, and commit a gang rape.

99.   All of these issues were apparent at the time of trial. Counsel had access to the same confessions, the same objective evidence, and the same timeline that the prosecution did, and were free to exploit the weaknesses in the People's case to whatever extent they were able to do so. It could be, and it was, credibly, honestly, and persuasively argued by the prosecution that in any gang attack, discrepancies among accounts and confusion about details are not unusual. Indeed, given the involvement of a number of people and the violence of the events at issue, some level of genuine confusion is probably inevitable. In this case in particular, those arguments were bolstered by the fact that the crimes occurred at night, that the lighting was poor, and that the defendants were involved in a number of incidents.

100.   Nonetheless, the fact that these weaknesses in the confessions exist gives added weight to the newly discovered evidence in this matter, and increases the probability that evidence would result in a different verdict.

101.   The probative value of the only forensic evidence that connected the defendants to the attack, the hairs found on Kevin Richardson, was, by its nature, weak to begin with. It has been diminished further by the tests performed in 2002. And the specific argument the prosecution made—that a particular rock found at the scene had been used in the attack—has also been undermined, although the most reasonable interpretation of the new blood evidence is probably contamination.

102.   The difficulties inherent in the passage of time and the small size of the hair samples in existence made it impossible to obtain definitive DNA results. But with respect to each of those samples that was large enough to test, a jury would hear expert testimony that the DNA which could be extracted from the evidence did not match the jogger. Those results do not exclude the

jogger as a source to a reasonable degree of scientific certainty. Their effect, however, would be to undermine the jury's confidence in the only evidence other than the defendants' statements which showed contact between the victim and her alleged rapists.

103.   Most important, the jurors who originally heard the evidence were presented with no persuasive alternative theory of the case to consider. Certainly, no one would have thought that as the defendants and their group were making their way through Central Park, a serial rapist was also at large. The newly discovered evidence provides incontrovertible proof that he was.

104.   A self-confessed and convicted serial rapist—who habitually stalked white women in their 20's; who attacked them, beat them, and raped them; who always robbed his victims, and frequently stole Walkmans; who tied one of his victims in a fashion much like the Central Park jogger; who lived on 102nd Street; who beat and raped a woman in Central Park two days before the attack on the transverse; whose DNA was the only DNA recovered inside and alongside the victim; whose narrative of events is corroborated in a number of significant ways; who had no connection to the defendants or their cohorts; and who committed all his sex crimes alone—has come forward to say that he alone stalked, attacked, beat, raped, and robbed a white woman in her 20's, who was set upon on the 102nd Street transverse, was missing her Walkman, and was left tied in a way that has never before been explained. Had this evidence been available, the defendants' attorneys would have had an arguably compelling alternative to the People's theory of the case.

105.   It is the People's position that, as to those verdicts which arose specifically from the attack on the Central Park jogger, the newly discovered evidence in this case meets the standard set forth in *Criminal Procedure Law* Section 440.10(1) (g): it ". . . is of such a character as to create a probability that had such evidence been received at trial the verdict would have been more favorable to defendant."

106.   The newly discovered evidence at issue here relates directly only to those charges which arose out of the attack on the jogger herself. Factually, it has no relationship to the other crimes—riot, robbery, and assault—which occurred in Central Park on the night of April 19, 1989. Nonetheless, all of the defendants use the newly discovered evidence provided by Matias Reyes as the basis for a request that the court vacate their other convictions as well.

107.   The papers submitted on behalf of Kharey Wise, Kevin Richardson, Antron McCray, and Raymond Santana do not specify a legal basis for that request. Yusef Salaam argues that the nature and gravity of the charges involving the female jogger prejudiced the defendants' ability to receive a fair and dispassionate trial on the other charges against him.

108.   Under the extraordinary circumstances presented by this case, the People are constrained to consent to the defendants' motions with respect to the other charges of which they were convicted.

109.   The other crimes committed on April 19 were grave and inexcusable—unprovoked attacks on strangers, apparently undertaken for the fun of it, which left some terrorized, two knocked into unconsciousness, and one seriously injured. Nevertheless, as the evidence was presented at trial, the attack on the female jogger was of a far greater order of seriousness. The People's theory was that she was set upon by a number of young men, gang-raped by two or more of them, kicked and pummeled by the group, and beaten about the head with a pipe, a brick, and a rock. Had she been discovered sooner, her injuries might well have been less serious in their effects; but she was not, and by the time she was found, she was close to death. The People introduced photographs depicting her injuries, called a pathologist to describe and characterize them one by one, and presented medical evidence fully describing her condition thereafter; she remained comatose for some time, endured a lengthy period of rehabilitation, and suffered permanent impairment as a result of the attack.

110.   It is commonplace for defendants to be charged in a single indictment with crimes of very different levels of gravity. The law permits it, and correctly presumes that juries can and will follow instructions requiring that they weigh evidence of guilt as to different counts separately. Thus, in and of itself, the relative seriousness of the jogger attack plainly would not merit setting aside the juries' verdicts as to other charges.

111.   In this case, however, other factors must also be weighed. The crimes the defendants were charged with were not widely separated by time or location, either from each other or from the attack on the jogger; all occurred within a single hour, at the northern end of Central Park. In effect, all were considered to be part of a single incident—a rampage in the park, as is reflected in the fact that the defendants were charged with Riot in the First Degree.

112.   In fact, the prosecutor argued to the jurors in the trial of Kharey Wise and Kevin Richardson that they should not lose sight of the "overall pattern of the behavior . . . [as] this group continued through the park for a period of approximately an hour attacking one after another after another person." This, it was fairly and convincingly argued, showed that the group acted with a joint purpose, that they were "an entire group acting together in one violent outburst of destruction, of beating, of assaulting." Similar references were made in summation in the earlier trial of McCray, Salaam, and Santana.

113.   It was logical for the People to suggest that the 'defendants' culpability and criminal intent could be inferred from the pattern of conduct engaged in by the group of which they were a part. This would have been an inescapable inference for the jurors in any event. But the new evidence detailed above would, if credited, call into question the defendants' involvement in the most horrific crime in the pattern of incidents in the park—and indeed, the involvement of the larger group as well. Accordingly, it would likely have had a significant bearing, in the jurors' minds, on the defendants' culpability for those other crimes as well.

114.   Moreover, the trial evidence as to the other charges, like the evidence as to the attack on the female jogger, consisted almost entirely of the defendants' statements. The distinctive logo on Kevin Richardson's jacket was described by one of the tandem bikers, and he and Santana were apprehended on the outskirts of the park; but the People's proof was limited by one fundamental fact: none of the victims could identify any of the defendants.

115. Just as the other incidents in the park cannot be considered separately from the rape of the jogger, neither can the defendants' statements about those events. In the case of at least two defendants, Richardson and Salaam, the process of questioning about the rape and the process of questioning about other crimes overlapped and intertwined. And with a single exception, all of the substantial written or recorded statements made by Richardson, McCray, Wise, and Santana concern the attack on the female jogger as well as the other crimes of that night. That lone exception involves Santana, whose first substantial written statement deals only with other events; but just an hour and twenty minutes after he signed it, after further, continuous questioning, an addendum described the jogger attack.

116. Thus, the admissions concerning the other crimes were contained in the same written and recorded statements as the admissions concerning the rape, and were largely obtained as part of the same process of questioning. As a consequence, the newly discovered evidence would probably raise questions about the reliability of those admissions similar to the questions raised about the defendants' confessions to rape. There is some testimony that, in certain instances, admissions about other criminal incidents were made substantially before and apart from any statements about the rape. But that testimony alone, absent independent corroboration, would not have been sufficient to allay concerns about the defendants' confessions raised by the newly discovered evidence.

117. In sum, there was no significant evidence at trial establishing the defendants' involvement in the other crimes of which they stand convicted that would not have been substantially and fatally weakened by the newly discovered evidence in this matter. In the original investigation, a number of individuals identified one or more of the defendants Richardson, McCray, Santana, and Salaam in connection with the attack on John Loughlin, and statements also placed Wise at the scene of earlier incidents. In interviews in 2002, both Richardson and Santana candidly acknowledged involvement in criminal incidents that occurred on April 19, while steadfastly asserting their innocence of rape. But none of this additional evidence was before the trial juries. Accordingly, it cannot be considered in evaluating the newly discovered evidence claim.

118. Assessing the newly discovered evidence, as we are required to, solely in light of the proof introduced at the earlier trials, we conclude that there is a probability that the new evidence, had it been available to the juries, would have resulted in verdicts more favorable to the defendants, not only on the charges arising from the attack on the female jogger, but on the other charges as well.

119. The final determination of this motion must, of course, be made by the Court. Should the Court, as requested by the parties, vacate the convictions, the People will move the Court to dismiss the indictments. Under all the circumstances, no purpose would be served by a retrial on any of the charges contained in the indictment.

WHEREFORE, for the reasons stated, the People consent to the relief requested and recommend that the Court vacate the defendants' convictions in their entirety.

DATED: New York, New York
   December 5, 2002

NANCY E. RYAN
Assistant District Attorney
Chief of the Trial Division

SUPREME COURT OF THE STATE OF NEW YORK
COUNTY OF NEW YORK: PART 58

THE PEOPLE OF THE STATE OF NEW YORK

-against-

KHAREY WISE, KEVIN RICHARDSON, ANTRON MCCRAY,
YUSEF SALAAM, and RAYMOND SANTANA,

Defendants.

**AFFIRMATION IN RESPONSE TO MOTION
TO VACATE JUDGMENT OF CONVICTION**

INDICTMENT NO. 4762/89

Robert M. Morgenthau
District Attorney
New York County
One Hogan Place
New York, New York 10013
(212) 335-9000

EXECUTIVE SUMMARY

To determine whether police policy or procedures needed to be changed as a result of the Central Park jogger case, the Police Commissioner asked our panel to review the events of April 19, 1989, and thereafter, that resulted in the convictions of Kharey Wise, Kevin Richardson, Antron McCray, Yusef Salaam and Raymond Santana (the "defendants"), for assault, robbery and riot in the course of attacks on various individuals, and for the rape and sexual abuse of a female jogger. Defendants moved to vacate and dismiss all of their convictions on the basis of a claim by an imprisoned serial rapist/killer named Matias Reyes that he raped the jogger that night, and that he committed the crime alone. New York County District Attorney Robert Morgenthau consented to the defendants' motions and, on December 19, 2002, the convictions were vacated and dismissed by Justice Charles Tejada.

Our task was to provide an overview for the investigation of these events, determine whether the new evidence indicated that police supervisors or officers acted improperly or incorrectly, identify any possible weaknesses in Police Department procedures and make recommendations to address any failures or weaknesses. The panel relied heavily upon police personnel assigned to assist in the review of this matter.

SUMMARY OF EVENTS OF APRIL 19, 1989

On the evening of April 19, 1989, shortly after 9:00 PM, approximately 40 African-American and Hispanic teenagers, mostly between the ages of 14 and 16, entered Central Park at 110th Street and 5th Avenue for the purpose, according to many of them, of assaulting and robbing people. Not all of the individuals in this group knew everyone else. Not every individual was present at each of the events that followed. They proceeded, at times together and at other times splitting up into smaller groups, to terrorize people through a large section of the park for almost an hour. The attacks by the group included:

- Accosting Michael Vigna, a racing biker, who escaped without physical injury;
- Assaulting and robbing Antonio Diaz, who was left on the side of a roadway unconscious;
- Menacing a couple on a tandem bicycle;
- Hurling rocks at and threatening a taxi driver;
- Threatening a male jogger, David Goode, who escaped without physical injury;
- Threatening a male jogger, Robert Garner, who escaped without physical injury;
- Assaulting a male jogger, David Lewis, who sustained physical injuries; and
- Assaulting a male jogger, John Loughlin, who sustained serious injuries from being knocked to the ground, kicked, punched, and beaten with a pipe and a stick.

The most significant event that occurred that evening was the brutal beating and rape of a 29 year old female jogger, whose bloody and almost lifeless body was found at about 1:30 AM on April 20, 1989. Later investigation showed that she had apparently been accosted and knocked down on a transverse road in the park at about 102nd Street, dragged into the woods where she was assaulted, and then dragged further into the woods, where the major attack upon her occurred. She was found about 200 feet further into the park, near a footpath. Although she survived, the jogger had no memory of any of the events that occurred that evening. This attack was the basis for the most serious charges against the defendants.

Police responded immediately to several 911 calls for help that resulted from the various attacks. Two of the defendants, Raymond Santana and Kevin Richardson, were arrested on the evening of April 19th in the vicinity of Central Park shortly after the attacks. Without being contacted by the police, Antron McCray voluntarily appeared at the precinct, in the company of his mother, and was not held. Because of statements made by the defendants and others implicating them, Kharey Wise and Yusef Salaam, as well as McCray, were contacted by the police the next day, and came to the precinct voluntarily.

Out of the approximately forty teenagers who entered Central Park that night, thirty-seven were interviewed. Ten were arrested and ultimately convicted of charges resulting from their activities. Five of these ten (the defendants) were charged with the assault and rape of the female jogger, the assault of John Loughlin, the assault on David Lewis, and a riot charge. All but Wise were convicted of assault, riot, robbery and rape. Wise was convicted of assault, riot and sexual abuse.

The other individuals who were arrested pled guilty to the assaults on Diaz, Loughlin or Lewis, but not to the assault of the female jogger. The defendants had implicated these other individuals in the assaults on the victims other than the female jogger.

Matias Reyes, then 18 years of age, was also in the park on the night of April 19, 1989. In 2002, he came forward to reveal that he had raped the female jogger and to claim that he did so alone.

FINDINGS REGARDING POLICE CONDUCT

Based on our review of the material related to this case and conversations with various witnesses and interested individuals, we conclude that there was no misconduct on the part of the New York City Police Department in the arrests and interrogations of the defendants. The police officers followed carefully the special statutory rules relating to the questioning of individuals less than 16 years of age, in particular rules pertaining to the participation of parents or guardians in such interviews. The New York County District Attorney and his senior staff have stated to us that they have found no evidence of coercion in the questioning of the defendants or others involved in the events of April 19, 1989, and they have no criticism of the interrogation or arrest techniques employed by the police. Our conclusion is also strongly supported by the opinion of Justice Thomas B. Galligan regarding the defendants' original motions to suppress their statements.

Justice Galligan's Opinion

In 1989, the defendants challenged the validity of their initial arrests by police, and the admissibility of the statements they made, including: allegations of failure to notify parents and have them present during questioning; improper trickery and/or deception; the use or threat of physical force; and deprivation of food and sleep. Following a six week pre-trial hearing into the admissibility of defendants' statements and other evidence, Justice Galligan carefully analyzed each claim raised by each defendant and found, with one exception,[1] that there was no constitutional or statutory violation by any of the officers or prosecutors involved and thus, no basis to suppress any of the statements or evidence made by or taken from the defendants.

In the course of considering the new evidence of Reyes's involvement in the attack on the jogger, some have focused anew on the defendants' statements. It should be noted that the inconsistencies and weaknesses of the defendants' statements were fully explored at the time of the defendants' pre-trial hearing and the Court's decision. The same inconsistencies and weaknesses were vigorously but unsuccessfully raised again at defendants' trials. It would seem that consistency would be a feature of planted rather than spontaneous information. We believe the inconsistencies contained in the various statements were not such as to destroy their reliability. All of the defendants were obviously attempting to minimize their own involvement and the stories they told necessarily included fabrications. On the other hand, there was a general consistency that ran through the defendants' descriptions of the attack on the female jogger. She was jogging; she was knocked down on the road; dragged into

---

[1]The only statement that was suppressed was made by Santana at the beginning stages of the booking process. A police officer made a remark to the defendants to the effect that they shouldn't be out beating people, but "should be out with your girlfriends." Santana then looked at a co-defendant, smiled and said, "I already got mines," and they both laughed. The Court suppressed this statement on the grounds that the officer's remarks were the equivalent of interrogation and should have been preceded by a waiver of Miranda rights.

the woods; hit and molested by several assailants; sexually abused by some while others held her arms and legs; and left semi-conscious in a state of undress, after an assault that covered a relatively short period of time. This general description was common to all or most of the defendants' statements, despite some differences in specifics.

It has been suggested that the police improperly coached or otherwise provided the defendants with facts which they later regurgitated in their confessions. However, although the defendants have complained of being "coerced" and have claimed that the police officers pressed them to confess, only one of them purported to explain how they got the factual details they gave in their statements. Defendant Wise was the only defendant to claim he had been "fed" answers. This contention was rejected in Justice Galligan's exhaustive opinion. The parents or family members of Santana, McCray and Richardson were present during all of their interrogations and the giving of written and video statements. In addition, Santana acknowledged both at a parole hearing in 1994 and when reinterviewed in 2002, that he assaulted a man but made up the story regarding the rape; he did not say the police gave him a story for him to adopt as his own.

Reyes's Claim That He Acted Alone

Because of Reyes's claim that he acted alone, some have analyzed the case as if there were only two possible scenarios—either Reyes acted alone or the defendants did. Another possibility that must be considered is that both Reyes and the defendants participated, to some degree, in attacking the jogger. At defendants' trials, the juries accepted the prosecution's theory that the defendants, together with an unknown attacker, committed the rape. We believe, however, that it is necessary, for the purposes of our inquiry, to complete the record by considering other scenarios that a jury might also accept. Our examination of the facts leads us to suggest that there is an alternative theory of the attack upon the jogger—that both the defendants and Reyes assaulted her, perhaps successively.

It may have been, as a former inmate-acquaintance claimed Reyes told him, that the attack on the jogger was already in progress when Reyes joined, attracted to the scene by the jogger's screams. Or, the defendants might have abandoned the jogger after mauling her in the hit-and-run style typical of their rampage and Reyes could then have come upon her and perpetrated a new attack, but in a much more brutal fashion. In either scenario, it would have been likely that Reyes, not the defendants, was guilty of the more vicious outrages inflicted upon the jogger, which would have been more characteristic of Reyes than of the behavior exhibited by the defendants. The defendants' lesser role would in fact be consistent with their confessions.

There is no corroboration for Reyes's claim that he acted alone. The only evidence to support the view that he acted by himself remains his own statement that he did so. This makes Reyes's general credibility a matter of considerable importance. Reyes's former attorney and defense psychologist have attested to his instability and lack of credibility. Even Justice Galligan, who also presided over Reyes's murder/rape trial in 1991, was quoted in the press as stating that "[I]f Reyes is a credible witness, then credibility has a new meaning." Reyes has been interviewed extensively by the staff of the District Attorney's office, for the most part without the direct participation of the Police Department, who were permitted to view one videotaped interview and one brief audio recording of an interview. No hearing was held with respect to defendants' motions to vacate their convictions, thus no opportunity was given to cross-examine Reyes in public under oath. We understand that he has not been subjected to a polygraph examination, perhaps because he is thought to be too unstable to allow for a meaningful test.

Central to a consideration of the truth of Reyes's claim that he raped the jogger by himself is an assessment of his motive for coming forward to make the claim. Was he simply moved to do the right thing by feelings of guilt and the "positive experiences" that he has had in prison? The District Attorney's office accepts Reyes's statement that his decision to come forward was motivated by a chance encounter with Wise in Auburn Correctional Facility, and the resultant realization that Wise was still incarcerated in connection with the attack on the jogger. There is however evidence to suggest that he came forward in response to threats, delivered through the underground prison communications system, and/or that he acted in order to get a desired change in prison assignment.

From the various accounts that Reyes has given in different interviews that we have been able to review, there have been significant problems or inconsistencies in his description of the details of the attack and subsequent events. In addition, several statements were made by witnesses to officers investigating the incident and by the defendants, speaking outside the formal interrogation process, which directly contradict Reyes's claim that he acted alone, and evidence the participation of the defendants. They include inculpatory statements by defendants Wise, Richardson and Santana both to police officers and to civilian witnesses who reported the statements to police. Santana and Richardson separately pointed out the location of the rape when brought to Central Park. When Wise was questioned, he made reference to a man named "Rudy" who took the jogger's Walkman; the description of the jogger's "Walkman pouch" was similar to Reyes's description of a "fanny pack." At the time of this interview, the police had no way of knowing that the jogger had a Walkman or that she carried it in a pouch. Wise also commented on the amount of blood at the spot where the rape occurred. When asked why he was so surprised by the amount of blood, he answered, "I knew she was bleeding but I didn't know how bad she was. It was really dark. I couldn't see how much blood there was at night."

Elaborate analyses of proposed timelines covering the various events on the evening the jogger was attacked have been proposed, with the conclusion that the defendants did not have the time to participate in the attack upon the jogger because they were busy, at specific times, with other assaults. This reasoning depends upon a selective analysis of the evidence from which various events are timed. In fact, no accurate timeline can be constructed because the evidence regarding the timing of the various events and the individuals who participated in them is not sufficiently precise to allow any exact conclusion. For example, a key time necessary to calculate when the defendants might have had the opportunity to rape the female jogger is the time of the attack upon jogger David Lewis. However, estimates of that time vary from 9:24 PM to 9:42 PM. Not even the time during which the jogger is assumed to have been attacked, between 9:15 PM and 9:30 PM, is free from doubt. We believe that no accurate timeline exists and none can be reliably constructed.

Finally, relevant forensic evidence concerning the presence of hair, blood and semen on some of the defendants' clothing was presented at trial and has not been refuted. In particular, hair "consistent" with the female jogger's hair was found on the clothing of Richardson and co-defendant Steven Lopez; blood stains were found on Santana's right sneaker, Salaam's jacket and on co-defendant Lopez's underwear, and semen stains were found on the underwear of McCray and Richardson, and on Santana's sweatshirt. This evidence is by no means dispositive, but it contradicts various reports that no blood was found on any of the defendants.

ASSAULTS ON OTHERS

In addition to their convictions for the rape and assault on the female jogger, the defendants were also convicted of crimes with respect to other attacks occurring that evening. Justice Tejada ruled, as the District Attorney recommended, that the convictions on these charges against the defendants, as well as those involving the female jogger, should be vacated, although the newly discovered evidence of Matias Reyes's rape of the female jogger related only to that event. We understand the legal position underlying Justice Tejada's ruling, that the existence of new evidence regarding the most significant charge against the defendants may have affected the juries' ability to consider evidence regarding the other charges. However, we believe that there is no reason, on the merits, to think that a jury fairly presented with the evidence against the defendants would come to a different conclusion than was reached before.

Some of the defendants have repeated their admissions of guilt. Santana testified at a parole hearing in 1994 and he was questioned about the crimes he committed on April 19th, 1989. He admitted that he and his friends planned to go to the park that night to rob and assault people. He stated that about seven or eight friends devised the plan. They were prepared to attack whoever they encountered that night in the park. Santana reiterated that they had let one, a couple, go because the man was with his girlfriend. Santana also admitted to beating a man. He denied only the rape.

When McCray went before the parole board in November 1994, he admitted all of his crimes except for the rape of the female jogger. Two of the defendants, Raymond Santana and Kevin Richardson, during interviews conducted by detectives in 2002, admitted their participation in the assaults that did not involve the jogger.

In the first major event, the assault on Antonio Diaz, a total of 23 people were named as participants or as being present. All five defendants were implicated by accomplices and two admitted participation. The second major event was harassment of a couple on a tandem bike. A total of 13 people were named participants or as being present; four of the defendants were implicated by accomplices and admitted participation. The third major event was crossing the 96th Street Transverse road to the reservoir. A total of 17 people were identified as having gone south towards the reservoir. All five defendants were implicated by accomplices and admitted going. The fourth major event was the assault on jogger David Lewis. A total of 11 people were identified as participants or as being present. Four of the defendants were implicated by accomplices and one admitted participation. The fifth major event was the assault on jogger John Loughlin, who was very badly beaten. A total of 19 people were identified as participants or as being present. All five defendants were implicated by accomplices and three admitted participation. Whatever conclusions may be reached regarding Matias Reyes's claim that he raped the female jogger alone, there seems to be no reason to believe that the defendants were innocent of the other crimes for which they were convicted.

CONCLUSION

The only new evidence that exists regarding the events in Central Park on the night of April 19, 1989 is the statement by serial rapist/killer Matias Reyes that he alone assaulted and raped the female jogger. DNA confirms that Reyes raped the jogger but we have nothing but his uncorroborated word that he did so alone. If Reyes's claim that he attacked the jogger by himself is true, it necessarily follows that the statements of the five defendants who were convicted of the crime, as well as those of the other witnesses who described it, were erroneous.

In that event, the question arises whether the statements were coerced or "suggested" by the interrogating officers. That question is, of course, central to our task of analyzing police behavior with respect to these events.

We believe that the issue of coercion was laid to rest authoritatively by the exhaustive opinion of Judge Galligan, following a lengthy Huntley hearing. Whether the defendants' statements were accurate or not, the methods used in obtaining them were examined by Judge Galligan with utmost care. We have not seen any evidence to suggest that Judge Galligan was in error and our review of available information confirms that police interrogations were conducted professionally and in accordance with applicable rules.

Affirming that neither the police nor the prosecutors engaged in outright coercion, the District Attorney has theorized that facts may have inadvertently been suggested to defendants and witnesses, enabling them to describe the attack on the jogger with sufficient particularity to make their statements credible. To determine whether this sort of thing went on, it is necessary to analyze the consistencies and inconsistencies in the various statements. The considerations are similar to those relevant to the basic question of whether Reyes is to be believed when he says he attacked the jogger alone. Those who believe Reyes emphasize the inconsistencies in the defendants' statements and those who do not believe him point to the statements' consistencies and to other supporting evidence.

The District Attorney, in responding to defendants' motions to dismiss the charges against them, laid out, in considerable detail, the arguments supporting the contention that Reyes was the sole attacker. Since the District Attorney had no reason to explore counter-arguments, we have done so.

We conclude that the various inconsistencies in defendants' statements, and the other recently revealed weaknesses in the evidence presented at trial, when viewed in light of Reyes's claim that he alone attacked the jogger, could afford a reasonable basis for maintaining that Reyes did, indeed, commit an attack on the jogger by himself.

However, the consistencies found in the defendants' statements, the informal remarks made by the defendants at various times, the corroborative testimony of other witnesses, the absence of a convincing motive for Reyes and suspicion of his general credibility, lead us to conclude that it is more likely than not that the defendants participated in an attack upon the jogger.

We adopt the view that the most likely scenario for the events of April 19,1989 was that the defendants came upon the jogger and subjected her to the same kind of attack, albeit with sexual overtones, that they inflicted upon other victims in the park that night. Perhaps attracted to the scene by the jogger's screams, Reyes either joined in the attack as it was ending or waited until the defendants had moved on to their next victims before descending upon her himself, raping her and inflicting upon her the brutal injuries that almost caused her death.

On this theory of the facts, there is no reason to believe that the defendants were prompted into making erroneous statements.

With respect to the other crimes for which the defendants were convicted, we are aware of no new evidence or reason to review the old evidence regarding those crimes. Two of the defendants reaffirmed their guilt for these crimes at parole hearings and one of these, together with a third, did so in 2002, after Reyes came forward to make his confession. Moreover, four other individuals who had pleaded guilty to the assaults, implicated the defendants in these crimes in their interrogations or recorded statements. We understand the technical legal position espoused by the District Attorney and adopted by the Court, vacating these convictions. However, we firmly believe that this legal ruling affords no basis for maintaining that the defendants were not involved in the other crimes for which they were convicted.

OBSERVATIONS AND LESSONS LEARNED

In addition to our factual conclusions, we offer the following observations:

- Early assignment of a senior commander
  Some early confusion in this complex case could have been avoided if procedures which would likely be used today in a similarly complex investigation were in effect then, namely: the establishment of 12-hour tours for the senior commanders overseeing the investigation; the establishment of a command center where all information related to the investigation could be received and correlated; and the establishment of regular briefings so that all personnel assigned to the case could be kept informed.

- Establishment of a Management Team

  A management team should have been established on the evening of April 19, 1989, for the purpose of overseeing all investigative steps and facilitating information-sharing among all investigative personnel. Had this occurred, factual accounts provided by the suspects that lacked clarity or needed additional exploration could have been identified and resolved prior to videotaping.

- Allocation of adequate space to conduct interview of minors

  There was inadequate space to conduct interviews of minors. This problem has only become worse with the passage of time. The Department should consider rehabilitating or constructing new precinct space to accommodate interviews of minors.

- Evidence accountability and control

  The then Manhattan Chief of Detectives brought home with him the only available copies of some Polaroid photos of the female jogger that had been taken by investigators, making them unavailable for use by the prosecutor during the videotaped questioning of the suspects. The Polaroid photos were eventually made available to the prosecutor but only during Kharey Wise's videotaped interrogation. This action could have exacerbated problems associated with the interrogations. It was obviously wrong for this to have occurred, but it does not appear to be a systemic problem and is unlikely to recur.

- Forensic management

  During the photographing of the pants of one of the defendants, the pants were placed on the precinct floor, creating a risk of potential evidence contamination and compromise of any trace evidence taken from them. Again, this error is unlikely to recur because of reforms implemented after the Department's crime scene unit was reorganized and its procedures were reviewed and modified in 1995.

- Case review and coordination

  It is now known that among the series of violent crimes that he committed, Matias Reyes also raped a woman in Central Park on April 17, 1989, just two days before the jogger attack. There has been some criticism directed at the Department for the failure to connect the April 17, 1989 rape to the April 19, 1989 attack on the jogger. Reyes was identified as a possible suspect in the April 17, 1989 rape, and was later arrested, in August, 1989, for another rape and murder to which he ultimately pleaded guilty. If, at the time, it had occurred to either the police or the prosecutors that the April 19th rape might have been committed by the same individual that had raped someone on April 17th, it would have been simple to compare the DNA recovered from the jogger against that of the defendant they now had in custody. But, the police and the District Attorney's office had a set of confessions and were satisfied that the defendants perpetrated the attack on the jogger. They had no cause to search for links to other cases until DNA tests in November, 1989 indicated that the semen from the jogger did not match any of the defendants. Today's case review methods would substantially increase the probability of identifying cases with seemingly very few similarities.

  Another factor that may have interfered with a realization that the April 17th and April 19th rapes were connected was the fact that one of them was investigated as a homicide case and the other as a sex crimes case. Under current procedures, information in cases like this is shared.

- Use of DNA

  In 1989, procedures were not in place to facilitate the comparison of DNA evidence in one case with that in another, particularly after the DNA test results were taken by the District Attorney's office to prepare for trial. This problem is unlikely to recur due to the creation in 1994 of a DNA databank. DNA is now routinely collected from defendants convicted of certain statutorily prescribed crimes and fed into a database to which both the Department and the District Attorney's office have access. Unidentified DNA evidence recovered from a crime scene is entered into the databank and stored for future comparisons.

INTRODUCTION

To determine whether police policy or procedures needed to be changed as a result of the Central Park jogger case, the Police Commissioner asked our panel to review the events of April 19, 1989 and thereafter, that resulted in the convictions of Kharey Wise, Kevin Richardson, Antron McCray, Yusef Salaam and Raymond Santana (the "defendants"), for assault, robbery and riot in the course of attacks on various individuals, and for the rape and sexual abuse of a female jogger. Defendants moved to vacate and dismiss all of their convictions on the basis of a claim by an imprisoned serial rapist/killer named Matias Reyes that he raped the jogger that night, and that he committed the crime alone. New York County District Attorney Robert Morgenthau consented to the defendants' motions and, on December 19, 2002, the convictions were vacated and dismissed by Justice Charles Tejada.

Our task was to provide an overview for the investigation of these events, determine whether the new evidence indicated that police supervisors or officers acted improperly or incorrectly, identify any possible weaknesses in Police Department procedures and make recommendations to address any failures or weaknesses.

Included in this review was an examination of:

- Written statements of the defendants;
- Videotaped statements given by the defendants, and transcripts thereof;
- Notes of detectives' interviews with defendants;
- Notes, videotapes and transcripts of interviews of other witnesses;
- [LG1] People's opposition papers to Defendant's Motions to Suppress Evidence;
- Relevant portions of the transcript of the pre-trial hearing held by the trial judge, Justice Thomas B. Galligan, on defendants' Motions to Suppress;
- The trial court's decision on the Motions to Suppress, issued February 23, 1990 (Exhibit A);
- Defendants' recent Motions to Vacate the Judgments against them pursuant to Criminal Procedure Law §440.10;
- Affirmation of Assistant District Attorney Nancy Ryan, dated December 5, 2002, submitted in response to Defendants' Motions to Vacate (Exhibit B);
- Justice Tejada's opinion granting defendants' motions (Exhibit C);
- 1989 crime scene photographs and a map of the area;
- The defendants' Parole Board Hearing transcripts; and
- Results of some of the recent forensic tests conducted by the FBI.

The following evidence was unavailable for us to review:

- results of additional forensic DNA tests recently performed by the FBI and a private laboratory under the direction of the District Attorney's office;
- forensic evidence from defendants' trials; and
- notes and transcripts of interviews with Matias Reyes by the District Attorney's office and correction officers.

In addition, we have been unable to accomplish the following:

- a complete interview of Matias Reyes
- interviews of several of Reyes's inmate-acquaintances, some of whom have indicated that he had said things to them that contradicted the story he told the District Attorney.

The panel relied heavily upon police personnel assigned to assist in the review of this matter. Attached as Exhibit D is a list of those who were assigned and assisted the panel. These members also accompanied the panel to visit the crime scene several times.

SUMMARY OF EVENTS OF APRIL 19, 1989

On the evening of April 19, 1989, shortly after 9:00 PM, approximately 40 African-American and Hispanic teenagers, mostly between the ages of 14 and 16, entered Central Park at 110th Street and 5th Avenue for the purpose, according to many of them, of assaulting and robbing people. Not all of the individuals in this group knew everyone else. Not every individual was present at each of the events that followed. They proceeded, at times together and at other times splitting up into smaller groups, to terrorize people through a large section of the park for almost an hour.

The hectic and violent activity of that evening is described, in large part, in Justice Galligan's pre-trial opinion (Exhibit A, pp. 3-9) and in the Ryan Affirmation (Exhibit B, pp. 3-5). The attacks by the group included:

- Accosting Michael Vigna, a racing biker, who escaped without physical injury;
- Assaulting and robbing Antonio Diaz, who was left on the side of a roadway unconscious;
- Menacing a couple on a tandem bicycle;

- Hurling rocks at and threatening a taxi driver;
- Threatening a male jogger, David Goode, who escaped without physical injury;
- Threatening a male jogger, Robert Garner, who escaped without physical injury;
- Assaulting a male jogger, David Lewis, who sustained physical injuries; and
- Assaulting a male jogger, John Loughlin, who sustained serious injuries from being knocked to the ground, kicked, punched, and beaten with a pipe and a stick.

The most significant event that occurred that evening was the brutal beating and rape of a 29 year old female jogger, whose bloody and almost lifeless body was found at about 1:30 AM on April 20, 1989. Later investigation showed that she had apparently been accosted and knocked down on a transverse road in the park at about 102nd Street, dragged into the woods where she was assaulted, and then dragged further into the woods, where the major attack upon her occurred. She was found about 200 feet further into the park, near a footpath. Although she survived, the jogger had no memory of any of the events that occurred that evening. This attack was the basis for the most serious charges against the defendants.

Police responded immediately to several 911 calls for help that resulted from the various attacks. Two of the defendants, Raymond Santana and Kevin Richardson, were arrested on the evening of April 19th in the vicinity of Central Park shortly after the attacks. Without being contacted by the police, Antron McCray voluntarily appeared at the precinct, in the company of his mother, and was not held. Because of statements made by the defendants and others implicating them; Kharey Wise and Yusef Salaam, as well as McCray, were contacted by the police the next day, and came to the precinct voluntarily.

Out of the approximately forty teenagers who entered Central Park that night, thirty-seven were interviewed. Ten were arrested and ultimately convicted of charges resulting from their activities. Five of these ten (the defendants) were charged with the assault and rape of the female jogger, the assault of John Loughlin, the assault on David Lewis, and a riot charge. All but Wise were convicted of assault, riot, robbery and rape. Wise was convicted of assault, riot and sexual abuse.

The other individuals who were arrested pled guilty to the assaults on Diaz, Loughlin or Lewis, but not to the assault of the female jogger. The defendants had implicated these other individuals in the assaults on the victims other than the female jogger.

Matias Reyes, then 18 years of age, was also in the park on the night of April 19, 1989. In 2002, he came forward to reveal that he had raped the female jogger and to claim that he did so alone.

FINDINGS REGARDING POLICE CONDUCT

General Observations

Based on our review of the material referred to above and conversations with various witnesses and interested individuals, including the New York County District Attorney and his staff, we conclude that there was no misconduct on the part of the New York City Police Department in the arrests and interrogations of the defendants. The police officers followed carefully the special statutory rules relating to the questioning of individuals less than 16 years of age, in particular rules pertaining to the participation of parents or guardians in such interviews.

The New York District Attorney and his senior staff have stated to us that they have found no evidence of coercion in the questioning of the defendants or others involved in the events of April 19, 1989, and they have no criticism of the interrogation or arrest techniques employed by the police.

Justice Galligan's Opinion

An authoritative analysis of the activities of the police leading up to and including the taking of statements from the defendants, including the parents' participation in that process, is set forth in Justice Galligan's opinion (Exhibit A), which followed a six-week pre-trial hearing into the admissibility of defendants' statements and other evidence. The hearing consisted of testimony from: twenty-nine prosecution witnesses; defendants Wise, Richardson, Santana and Salaam; an additional defendant Steven Lopez; and parents, siblings, relatives and friends of the defendants who were present or involved in their initial encounters with the police or at the time that oral, written and videotaped statements were made.

At the hearing, each defendant challenged the validity of his initial arrest by police and the admissibility of the statements he made.[2] In addition, defendants McCray, Wise and Salaam challenged the seizure of physical evidence from them. Some of their

---

[2]The Court held one hearing to address the claims of the seven original defendants which included two individuals, Steven Lopez and Michael Briscoe, who eventually pled guilty to charges not involving the attack upon the female jogger.

claims included allegations that they were stopped and arrested without reasonable suspicion or probable cause; that the Family Court Act and Criminal Procedure Law provisions mandating parental notification and presence during questioning were not followed; that statements were obtained by improper trickery and/or deception; that false promises were made that they would be released if they cooperated; that physical force was used and/or threatened to obtain statements; that they were deprived of food and sleep; and that arraignments were delayed unreasonably to deny due process and the attachment of right of counsel.

Justice Galligan, an experienced and highly regarded jurist, carefully analyzed each claim raised by each defendant and found, with one exception, that there was no constitutional or statutory violation by any of the officers or prosecutors involved and thus, no basis to suppress any of the statements or evidence taken from the defendants. The only statement made by any of the defendants that was suppressed by the Court was made by Raymond Santana shortly after his arrest. According to the Court, while in the beginning stages of the booking process, a police officer made a remark to the defendants to the effect that they shouldn't be out beating people, but "You should be out with your girlfriends." Santana then looked at Lopez, smiled and said, "I already got mines," and they both laughed. (Exhibit A, p. 14) The Court suppressed this statement on the grounds that the officer's remarks were the equivalent of interrogation and should have been preceded by a waiver of Miranda rights. (Exhibit A, p. 95)

The Court's findings as to each defendant are summarized below:

1. Probable Cause For Initial Arrests

   a. Raymond Santana and Kevin Richardson

Raymond Santana was initially stopped, along with Steven Lopez, by Police Officers Eric Reynolds and Robert Powers at approximately 10:30 PM following the discovery of the first two seriously injured victims of that night, and numerous radio reports of a large group of young male African-Americans and Hispanics committing violent acts in the park. Santana and Lopez were part of a large group of similarly described individuals who were observed by Officers Reynolds and Powers walking northbound on the east side of Central Park West near 102nd Street shortly after the radio reports of the second assault. When the group was approached by the officers, all but Santana and Lopez fled. According to Justice Galligan, Santana and Lopez were "wide-eyed and appeared in shock" when first stopped and denied being part of the larger group which Lopez falsely claimed was about to "jump" them (Exhibit A, p. 10). Both Santana and Lopez claimed to have just come from their girlfriends' houses. (People's Brief, Vol. 1, P.9)

Kevin Richardson was part of the group that fled. He was apprehended by Officer Powers after a chase through the park. He was transported to the precinct together with another individual from the group, Clarence Thomas. The Court stated:

> En route to 100th Street and Central Park West Clarence Thomas began to cry. Without being questioned, he stated, I know who did the murder. 'I know who did the murder. I know where he lives and I'll tell you his name.' Richardson said he also knew who did it and would tell them too. Then Thomas said that it was Antron McCray and that he lived at a particular address on 111th Street. Kevin Richardson concurred saying, 'Yeah. That's who did it.' (Exhibit A, pp. 11, 12).

The Court carefully reviewed all of the information that had been reported as the news of the events of that night began to unfold, including numerous 911 calls and reports of witnesses and victims concerning a large group of African-American and Hispanic youths rampaging through the northern end of Central Park. The Court found specifically that the initial detention of the defendants was legally justified. (Exhibit A, pp. 75-76) Justice Galligan held that under the circumstances, the officers had reasonable suspicion to stop and detain the defendants and, as to Santana and Lopez were "entitled, indeed duty bound to stop them and detain them for questioning." (Exhibit A, p. 76) Richardson's flight served to escalate the suspicion about him as well as the suspicion about Santana and Lopez.

Probable cause for their subsequent arrests was supported by the facts originally known by the officers, and in addition (1) as to Richardson, his unprompted statement following Thomas' statement and while en route to the precinct, that he too knew who committed "the murder" and would provide his identity (Exhibit A, p. 78) (People's Brief, Vol.1 P. 11) and (2) as to Santana and Lopez, additional statements by Richardson and others that Santana and Lopez were with them in the park. (Exhibit A, p. 79) In summarizing its findings concerning the initial investigation of this incident the Court said:

> [I]t is clear the police action, at every step of the escalating encounter, was properly related in scope to the surrounding circumstances (citation omitted). Neither the initial detention of Santana, Lopez or Richardson, nor their subsequent arrests were, in any respect, precipitous or unreasonable. No taint, therefore, can flow from it. (Exhibit A, p.79)

   b. Kharev Wise and Yusef Salaam

The first contact between Wise, Salaam and the police officers conducting this investigation occurred around 10:30 PM on the evening of April 20th, the day after the investigation of the events began, when several officers were sent to the home of Yusef Salaam to ask him to come to the stationhouse to answer some questions. Wise and Salaam were sought for questioning because a number of the others who had been detained had implicated Salaam and a youth named "Kharey" (Exhibit A, p. 41). Wise,

Salaam, and another individual were met by several detectives in the hallway of Wise's apartment building. All three voluntarily agreed to accompany the officers to the 20th Precinct. They were not handcuffed because there was no intention to arrest them, just to question them.

Wise and Salaam both asked the Court to suppress statements and physical evidence obtained from them on the grounds that the encounter in the hallway was effectively an arrest without probable cause. The Court rejected these arguments and refused to suppress any evidence, holding that the defendants agreed voluntarily to go to the precinct:

> [The officers] approached defendants Wise and Salaam in a non-threatening manner, and made brief inquiries of them as to their name and age. Salaam admitted that they knew the police were upstairs when they returned to his floor. . . . The record supports the conclusion that defendants' agreements to go to the precinct were voluntary and unconstrained. (Citations omitted) Therefore, probable cause was not required as a predicate for their presence, and their statements and physical evidence will not be suppressed on that ground. (Exhibit A, pp. 80-81)

c. Antron McCray

Antron McCray's first encounter with the investigation occurred when he appeared at the Central Park Precinct with his mother at around midnight on April 19. He was not previously contacted by police. When asked if he had been with the others earlier in the evening he admitted that he was, but he denied beating anyone. He was not arrested at that time and went home. By the next morning, he had been implicated in the attacks by other detainees. He was visited by detectives at his house and was asked to come back, to answer more questions. Both McCray and his father agreed to do so. Indeed, they even agreed, before leaving with the officers, to have McCray change back into the clothes he was wearing the night before, which when examined were found to be caked with mud and dirt.

The Court rejected McCray's arguments that he, too, was unlawfully arrested and did not go the precinct voluntarily:

> Defendant argues that a number of factors establishes his custodial status: that Antron was not a mere witness; rather the police believed they had probable cause to arrest him; the manner in which he was "picked up" at his apartment including the failure of the police to first telephone and the number of police; that the questioning took place at the police precinct instead of at his home; and Detective Rosario's statement to Mr. McCray that a parent "would have" to accompany Antron to the precinct because he was a juvenile.

> I find, however, that the presence of these factors either individually or in their totality, did not render Antron's status custodial . . . (Exhibit A, pp. 104-105) . . . and that the defendant, in the presence of his parents, voluntarily agreed to accompany the police to the precinct for the express purpose of questioning and that the circumstances of this questioning were not custodial in nature (citations Omitted). (Exhibit A, p. 106)

2. Admissibility of Statements

a. Kevins Richardson

As discussed above, Kevin Richardson made an incriminating statement to police within the first few minutes of his apprehension when he indicated that Antron McCray committed the "murder."

Richardson's later incriminating written, oral and videotaped statements were made in the presence of his mother initially, and later in the presence of his adult sister after his mother left the precinct. Richardson's father joined the interviews in time to review and sign the first written statement prepared by his son and remained with his son during the videotaped interview.

Although Richardson, with others, was held for a number of hours awaiting the arrival of parents, he was not interrogated during that time. Comments have been made in the press implying that defendants were "grilled" during the hours they were held awaiting formal interrogation. There is no evidence to support this argument. In fact, as Judge Galligan noted, the defendants spent the waiting period together, laughing and joking. At no time was Richardson questioned by anyone outside of the presence of his mother or his older sister. Similarly, no defendant, who the police were aware was under the age of sixteen, was interrogated without a parent or guardian being present.

In claiming that his statements should be suppressed, Richardson made the following arguments, all of which were rejected by the Court:

- The significance of the Miranda rights was not adequately explained to his mother and sister and his mother's frail and nervous condition rendered her incapable of issuing a valid waiver.
- The police deceived and misled his mother into believing that his detention was to be temporary and her waiver of his rights was obtained by a false promise that Kevin would be released to her after his statement.
- Statements made at the crime scene should be suppressed because Richardson's father's consent for him to go alone with the detectives to the scene was obtained by a disingenuous representation that no further questions would be asked of Richardson.

After noting case law that "special care must be taken to insure the rights of minors who are exposed to the criminal justice system," the Court stated:

> In this case, one aspect of the special care shown to juveniles is reflected in the proper notification of Richardson's mother by the police as required by statute. Mrs. Cuffee's (Richardson's mother) ability to respond to the circumstances is demonstrated by her prompt arrival at the precinct shortly after being notified of her son's situation. Indeed, she was the first parent to respond. Moreover, that she was not passive in the presence of the police is evidenced in her taking the initiative to see that Richardson's interview proceeded ahead of other defendants. Clearly, to whatever extent the events of the evening took a physical and emotional toll on her, that toll was itself in part the product of Mrs. Cuffee's comprehension of the gravity of the charges against her son. (Exhibit A, pp. 82-83)

As to Richardson's sister's participation in place of her mother the Court found that "contrary to the defendant's contention, his sister Angela Cuffee was capable of participating in a meaningful way." Moreover, following their testimony at the hearing the Justice noted that he was satisfied that Mrs. Cuffee and her daughter "possessed the intelligence to understand Kevin's rights and the ability to press them had they chosen to." (Exhibit A, p. 83)

As to Richardson himself the Court found that he, too, "understood his Miranda rights and possessed the emotional and intellectual capacity to waive them." According to the Court:

> His manner and poise reflected this. So too did his appreciation of the significance of the scratch on his face[3] Further, his reluctance to incriminate himself in the most serious of crimes demonstrated both an understanding of his right not to do so and a realistic sensitivity towards law and its consequences. (Exhibit A, p. 83)

On the issue of deception, the Court concluded that no misrepresentations were made to Richardson, his parents or his sister. (Exhibit A, p. 85)

On the waiver by Richardson's father of his right to accompany the detectives and his son to the crime scene the Court found:

> The clear thrust of Assistant District Attorney Fairstein's discussion with Paul Richardson, Kevin's father, was that he could accompany them if he chose, but that no new avenues or subjects of inquiry were to be pursued. This conclusion is supported not only by the testimony at the hearing but by the inherent illogic of taking a defendant to a crime scene for any reason except to question him about it.

> I find that in issuing this waiver, Mr. Richardson was aware of Kevin's rights because they had been read to Kevin in his presence shortly before leaving for the crime scene and at the videotaped interview earlier. (Exhibit A, p. 85-86)

b. Raymond Santana

Santana was one of the more talkative defendants and made a number of incriminating statements which were noted in the pre-trial decision. There was significant difficulty in procuring the presence of a parent or guardian for Santana's questioning. Indeed the judge, as discussed below, was particularly critical of the failure of Santana's father to make himself available during the early stages of the investigation. Santana's grandmother was present for his initial written statement and his father was present for the videotaped interview. As grounds for suppression, Santana argued a laundry list of reasons including:

- That violations of the Family Court Act and Criminal Procedure Law occurred regarding the parental notice requirement with respect to statements made outside his father's presence.
- That deceitful representations were made to his father.
- That his grandmother should have been provided a Spanish interpreter and that the translation to her of the Miranda warnings created confusion resulting in her not being fully advised.
- That the duration of his pre-arraignment detention rendered his statements involuntary and the delay in arraignment deprived him of his right to counsel.

Again, the Court rejected all of these arguments and found that the statements made by Santana were admissible.

On the Family Court Act issue the Court found that the investigators complied with all applicable notice requirements:

> The police contacted Mr. Santana promptly after their arrival at the Central Park Precinct on the evening of April 19, and made repeated efforts to obtain his presence throughout the following morning. Indeed, they sent a police car to the grandmother's residence in order to obtain her presence before they began to formally question Raymond. Raymond's father came with the grandmother.

---

[3]The scratch on Richardson's face, which he admitted was caused by the female jogger.

The facts further show that Mr. Santana, despite being fully advised with regard to his son's circumstances, left the Central Park Precinct on the morning of April 20 and went to work. During the day he never called to inquire about his son. He returned after work and after he went home. He arrived as Raymond had completed his statement. He again left the Central Park Precinct later that day after consenting to his son's speaking to Detective Hartigan alone. Clearly, the decision by Mr. Santana not to attend the questioning of his son is not attributable to any action or inaction by the police and could not operate to forestall the police inquiries of Raymond. (Exhibit A, p. 90)

The deceit argument was completely refuted at the hearing. According to the Court:

Santana's argument that Detective Sheehan made deceitful representations to his father, thereby obtaining the father's consent to take another statement is not founded in fact. The record shows, to the contrary, that the detectives delayed further questioning of Santana until the father was present and then commenced their interrogation only after fully and fairly advising the father as to what had previously occurred and as to what they intended to do and after he had an opportunity to speak to his son. (Exhibit A, p. 91)

Regarding the failure to fully advise Santana's grandmother the Justice noted:

I find that Santana's arguments addressed to his grandmother's understanding of the <u>Miranda</u> warnings are not sustained; in fact, they are undercut by Mrs. Colon's own testimony at the hearing in which she demonstrated an ability to understand English far beyond her willingness to admit it.

In any event, the Precautions that the detectives exercised vis-à-vis Mrs. Colon were the result of an abundance of caution and were not statutorily or constitutionally required since Santana's father had previously been notified of, but waived, his right to be present. His cavalier approach to his son's situation was reflected in his initial failure to show up at the precinct when called; his later arrival with his mother after the police sent a car for her and his departure for work before Santana's case was called; his failure to communicate with anyone concerning his son, while at work. Mr. Santana's (the father) itinerant conduct throughout this time and the fact that he left his mother Mrs. Colon to stand with her grandson speaks volumes about him and also belies the argument that she did not understand English. (Exhibit A, pp.92–93)

As to the length of Santana's pre-arraignment detention and its effect on the voluntariness of his statements the Court noted:

It was established that Santana slept; he was fed, and that repeated efforts were made by the police to provide him access to a member of his family. The extent to which such access was delayed was clearly a product of his family's behavior, and not that of the police.

Moreover, the alleged debilitating effect upon Santana from lack of food and sleep are belied by his raucous behavior in the cellblock, and his participation, with his co-defendants, in the lewd comments and exuberant laughter with which they accepted their incarceration. (Exhibit A, p. 91)

Again, it is important to emphasize that although Santana was held for hours, awaiting the arrival of a parent or relative, he was not questioned during this period.

c. <u>Antron McCray</u>

Antron McCray's admissions included an initial statement admitting to the rape of the female jogger and a later videotaped interview. His father was present for both statements. His mother also was with him but, as detailed in the Court's decision, she left the initial interview following a discussion with her husband because it was felt that Antron was unwilling to be truthful about raping the female jogger in her presence. McCray's arguments for suppression of his statements included the claim discussed above that he did not voluntarily accompany the officers to the precinct and was arrested without probable cause. He also alleged that he was not given and did not waive his Miranda rights prior to the initial questioning and that his eventual waiver of Miranda was involuntary because he had been misled by the police.

As to these issues the Court rejected once again the notion that the police had done something improper in their treatment of McCray and ruled that all of his incriminating admissions were validly obtained:

The testimony established that defendant was given his full <u>Miranda</u> warnings in the presence of both his mother and father and that he waived those rights prior to his interrogation at the 20th Precinct and his videotape at the 24th Precinct. Defendant's contention that his waiver was involuntary because his parents had been misled by the police is not substantiated. The basis for this alleged, misleading was the statements by Detective Rosario that Antron should "tell the truth, no matter how horrible" and two later conversations between the father and Detectives Hildebrandt, Gonzalez and McCabe outside Antron's presence, in which they discussed whether Antron was telling the truth. In both conversations Mr. McCray agreed with the detectives that the son was not being truthful and on one occasion he relayed that information to Antron and on the second occasion he asked his wife to leave. Contrary to defendant's theory, none of the detectives' statements "rise to the level of those promises or statements which create a substantial risk that defendant might falsely incriminate himself (citations omitted)."

Moreover, the record reflects that the direct result of the detective's second discussion with Mr. McCray was not a waiver by defendant of any right he had not previously waived, but only that his mother stepped out of the room, leaving Antron, with his father and the police. (Exhibit A, pp. 106–107)

d. Yusef Salaam

Salaam initially lied to the police about his age, claiming and showing documentary proof that he was 16 years old, not 15 as it was later determined. Initially, therefore, Salaam's parents were not notified that he was being questioned and were not present for his statements. However, his aunt and a family friend both came to the precinct after learning that Salaam was brought there. Salaam's mother also went to the precinct when she returned from work at about 10:45 that evening. Neither the aunt nor the family friend were allowed to see Salaam; the mother's request to see him was also turned down because it was believed he was sixteen. When his mother claimed that Salaam was only fifteen, the questioning was quickly ended and no further statements were taken from him.

In his suppression motion, Salaam attempted to take advantage of his misleading behavior arguing that because he was actually only fifteen, all of his statements should be suppressed. The Court rejected this argument finding that reliance by police on his misrepresentation was reasonable. The Court also stated that the "defendant should not derive a benefit from his deliberate falsification," and that "he is bound by the consequences of that falsehood." (Exhibit A, p. 111)

The Court also rejected arguments that Salaam was improperly denied access to his family and that he was tricked into making an admission when the detective questioning him claimed that others had already implicated him and that if his fingerprints were found on the jogger's clothing, he was "going down for the rape." (Exhibit A, p. 113)

e. Kharey Wise

Kharey Wise's parents were not present for his interview, because he was over the age of sixteen.

Wise made the following claims with respect to suppression of his statements:

- Physical force was used or threatened, thus rendering his admissions involuntary.
- He was falsely promised that he would be released if he talked.

On the use of physical force to obtain his statements, the Court was quite clear:

The record simply does not sustain that. I note that the video taken of Wise after the time of the alleged beating gave no indication of any bruises. (Exhibit A, p. 114)

Nor does the record support Wise's argument that his will was overborne by shouting, intimidation and the lack of rest, food and drink. Wise slept, ate and received milk when he asked for it. Further, his behavior while in the cell at the 24th Precinct, particularly his laughing and asking his codefendants if they had told the police allegedly humorous incidents involving joggers, belies his contention that he suffered from physical abuse or psychological duress. (Exhibit A, p. 114)

On the issue of false promises the Court was equally clear:

Wise argues that his statements must be suppressed because he was promised that, if he made them, he would be released. The only basis in the record for this proposition is defendant's own testimony, which I find incredible. His motion to suppress statements is in all respects denied. (Exhibit A, p. 115)

3. Additional Observations Regarding the Defendants' Statements

In reaching his conclusions, Justice Galligan had the benefit of analyzing the testimony and assessing the credibility of everyone involved, including defendants, victims and police personnel. He carefully considered and rejected all of the defendants' claims that their statements had been somehow coerced.

In the course of considering the new evidence of Reyes's involvement in the attack on the jogger, some have focused anew on the defendants' statements. It has been asserted by the press and others that the fact that there were numerous inconsistencies in the defendants' statements demonstrates that the statements were coerced. These assertions fail to account for the fact that the inconsistencies and weaknesses of the defendants' statements were fully explored at the time of the defendants' pre-trial hearing and the Court's decision. The same inconsistencies and weaknesses were vigorously but unsuccessfully raised again at defendants' trials.

The newly discovered evidence of Matias Reyes's involvement in the jogger's rape, upon which the dismissal of the defendants' cases was based, casts no new light on the question of whether the police interrogations were properly conducted. No evidence, old or new, has been found that in any way disturbs or even bears upon Justice Galligan's factual findings.

It has been argued that the many inconsistencies in the statements of the defendants and the others involved in the events of April 19, 1989 indicate that the facts in the statements were not true, but were provided, deliberately or inadvertently, by the questioning of police officers or prosecutors. But, it would seem that consistency would be a feature of planted rather than spontaneous information. We believe that the inconsistencies contained in the various statements were not such as to destroy their reliability. All of the defendants were obviously attempting to minimize their own involvement and the stories they told necessarily included fabrications. On the other hand, there was a general consistency that ran through the defendants' descriptions of the attack on the female jogger. She was jogging; she was knocked down on the road; dragged into the woods; hit and molested by several assailants; sexually abused by some while others held her arms and legs; and left semi-conscious in a state of undress, after an assault that covered a relatively short period of time. This general description was common to all or most of the defendants' statements, despite some differences in specifics. We find it unlikely that such similar descriptions could have been given spontaneously. The defendants would have to have been told by their interrogators the outline of what they were supposed to say. As discussed above, we concur with the District Attorney and Justice Galligan's opinion that no such deliberate planting of information occurred.

Another factor to be considered was the condition of the jogger at the time the interrogations were being conducted. None of the detectives could have foreseen that, should she survive, she would have no memory of the events. Even an unprincipled questioner, bent upon planting a story with the defendants, would hardly do so when there was every chance that the jogger would refute the story upon her recovery.

4. "Suggested" Confessions

It has been theorized by the New York County District Attorney's office that the defendants' confessions can perhaps be explained as the result of legitimate interrogation techniques employed by detectives operating under the erroneous but reasonable premise that the defendants and their friends were the only ones assaulting people in the park that night. A certain amount of pressure is inevitable in any interrogation. The device, for instance, of telling a potential defendant that his cohort has confessed and implicated him is a standard questioning technique that has been approved by the courts. In the case of the jogger's rape, it is argued, such pressure may have been employed by detectives who operated under the logical assumption that the jogger must have been assaulted and raped in the course of the rampage that was then going on. The detectives were not aware that Reyes, a vicious rapist, was roaming the park at the same time. Under those circumstances, they could have suggested facts to the teenagers they were questioning which were later regurgitated in their confessions.

However, although defendants have complained of being "coerced" and have claimed that the police officers pressed them to confess, only one of them purported to explain how they got the factual details they gave in their statements. Kharey Wise was the only defendant to claim he had been "fed" answers. This contention was rejected in Justice Galligan's exhaustive opinion, ruling on defendants' motions to suppress. As the prosecutor argued, apparently persuasively, in her summation at the trial of McCray, Salaam and Santana:

> Mr. McCray testified that the police said he should put himself in it, and that was all the information that was given to Antron McCray about what he was supposed to put in his statement. He was never given any statements that he was to admit to. People v. Antron McCray, Yusef Salaam and Raymond Santana, Trial Transcript, p. 5336,1. 16–20, 8/8/90.
>
> * * * *
>
> The detectives told Mr. McCray, according to his testimony, that Antron McCray should tell them what they want to hear, without ever telling him what it was they wanted to hear. Id., p. 5337, l. 6-9.

In this regard, at his parole hearing on February 9, 1994, Raymond Santana was asked about the events of April 19, 1989. He admitted assaulting a man, but claimed that he made up the story regarding the rape, and he just used the names of those arrested with him that night as his cohorts. Santana was also interviewed by an Assistant District Attorney and detectives in June 2002 at Downstate Correctional Facility. Santana again admitted the facts other than those relating to the female jogger. When asked why he said what he said in 1989 about his participation in the attack on the female jogger, he responded that two of the detectives "okey doked me with that good cop bad cop routine. One of the detectives told me that the others admitted raping the woman and said I was there and that if I did not admit it he couldn't help me. So I made up the story you see on the tape to satisfy them." (Emphasis added) By his own admissions in 1994 and again in 2002, Santana stated that he made up the story—he did not say the police fed him a story for him to adopt as his own. Had they done so, Santana would surely have said that when he reversed himself, rather than claiming, truthfully or falsely, that he made the story up himself.

It is important to note again that the parents or family members of Santana, McCray and Richardson were present during all of their interrogations and the giving of written and video statements.

THE NEW EVIDENCE–REYES'S CLAIM THAT HE ACTED ALONE

Some have analyzed the case as if there were only two possible scenarios—either Reyes acted alone or the defendants did. According to this reasoning, since DNA testing proves that Reyes attacked the jogger, then it follows that the defendants did not. Another possibility that must be considered is that both Reyes and the defendants participated, to some degree, in attacking the jogger.

1. Reyes's Claim

At defendants' trials, the juries accepted the prosecution's theory that the defendants, together with an unknown attacker, committed the rape. It was brought out at trial that semen was recovered belonging to an unknown missing assailant. Thirteen years after the event, Reyes revealed that the semen was his, but he also asserted that he had attacked the jogger by himself. Reyes's claim that he acted alone qualified as new evidence that the prosecutor and the Court correctly found to be sufficient to require vacating the convictions.

The District Attorney and Justice Tejada did not have to explore alternative scenarios in order to reach the conclusion that the trial verdict should be vacated. It was enough that one permissible scenario existed that exculpated the defendants and had not been heard by the juries that convicted them. It may well be that the juries would have accepted Reyes's contention and concluded that the defendants were not present when the jogger was attacked.

We believe, however, that it is necessary, for the purposes of our inquiry, to complete the record by considering other scenarios that a jury might also accept.

2. Alternative Scenarios

Our examination of the facts leads us to suggest that there is an alternative theory of the attack upon the jogger—that both the defendants and Reyes assaulted her, perhaps successively.

It may have been, as a former inmate-acquaintance claimed Reyes told him, that the attack on the jogger was already in progress when Reyes joined, attracted to the scene by the jogger's screams. Or, he may have been following her and held back, temporarily, when the defendants intercepted her. Or, the defendants may have abandoned the jogger after mauling her in the hit-and-run style typical of their rampage that night. Coming upon her just after the attack, Reyes could have perpetrated a new attack, but in a much more brutal fashion.

In any of these scenarios, it would have been likely that Reyes, not the defendants, was guilty of the more vicious outrages inflicted upon the jogger. The bloody and sustained beating, the tying of the jogger's hands in front of her face, and the rape itself (which apparently was anal as well as vaginal) were more characteristic of Reyes than of the behavior exhibited by the defendants and their friends during their rampage.

Under any such theory, the defendants' lesser role is consistent with their confessions. In describing what they knew of the incident, they may have considered that an assault with sexual aspects to it constituted "rape," without being aware that a brutal rape, in the full sense of the term, took place after they had left.

If Reyes and the defendants both attacked the jogger at overlapping or different times, the only aspect of Reyes's account that is necessarily at odds with the statements of the defendants is the one for which there is no corroboration—that he came upon her alone.

It must be emphasized that we do not contend that any such theory would affect the correctness of the decision to vacate the defendants' convictions. That decision rested on new exculpatory evidence, which is Reyes's claim that he acted alone. The jury should have heard this new evidence regardless of whether there also might be a possibly convincing explanation for that new evidence that placed the defendants at the scene, albeit in a lesser role.

3. Considerations Bearing on Reyes's Claim

In considering Reyes's claim, we have focused upon Reyes's credibility; Reyes's motive; Reyes's accounts of the attack; the defendants' statements; statements by other witnesses; the timing of the events; and forensic evidence.

   a. Reyes's Credibility

      (1) General Considerations

There is no corroboration for Reyes's claim that he acted alone. The only evidence to support the view that he acted by himself remains his own statement that he did so. This makes Reyes's general credibility a matter of considerable importance.

Recently, the presiding justice of the Central Park jogger case, Justice Galligan, who also presided over Reyes's murder/rape trial in 1991, was quoted in the press as stating, "[I]f Reyes is a credible witness, then credibility has a new meaning." [Newsday, December 20, 2002 p. 4 N.Y. Daily News, December 21, 2002 p. 4.] Reyes's former attorney, Richard Siracusa, in a recent interview stated that Reyes is a "classic psychopath who cannot separate fact from fancy." [Newsday, December 20, 2002 p. 4 N.Y. Daily News, December 21, 2002 p. 4.] Reyes's defense psychologist in 1991, Dr. Neftali Berrill, concluded that Reyes could not tell a consistent childhood history. Dr. Berrill described Reyes as "an infantile, impulsive individual prone to viewing the world in a peculiar fashion, marked by monsters, blood, dead animals. He is demanding, particularly with his need for respect and attention." [Newsday, December 20, 2002 p. 4 N.Y. Daily News, December 21, 2002 p. 4.] In a recent interview conducted on November 5, 2002 by Detective Robert Mooney, Dr. Berrill confirms his findings regarding Reyes's psychological condition. He further stated that Reyes is capable of any amount of violence when faced with a threatening position, e.g., a victim fighting back.

These assessments came from individuals with first-hand experience with Reyes. They reflect the common view that a history of committing felonies is generally thought to undermine a witness's credibility. The crimes for which Reyes has been convicted include rape, robbery and murder. In addition, he has confessed to the commission of a host of crimes for which he was never convicted, including the rape of the jogger as well as the rape of his own mother. [N.Y. Daily News, October 20, 2002; Reyes's Videotaped Statement to Assistant District Attorney Ryan on May 23, 2002.] Reyes admitted to Dr. Berrill in 1991 that he sexually assaulted his mother, referring to it as a tragedy. [N.Y. Daily News, October 20, 2002 (quoting portions of Dr. Berrill's evaluation report).] His specific behavior in committing these crimes is sufficiently deviant to cast even further doubt on the reliability of what must be described as a "twisted" mind.

The Ryan Affirmation points out that the candor with which Reyes has admitted responsibility for past crimes that had previously been unsolved and his accuracy in describing these misdeeds (all of which are beyond the statute of limitations), tends to bolster his credibility. In weighing Reyes's credibility, it is certainly necessary to balance the positive implications of his being able to describe his life accurately against the negative conclusions to be drawn from the life of horrific crime he is describing.

(2) Cross Examination

It is generally accepted that the best way to test a witness's credibility is to subject him or her to cross-examination. With respect to Reyes, his defense psychologist, Dr. Neftali Berrill suggested in his recent interview, that when Reyes is interrogated, it should be done with authority and control to get to the core of what he knows or thinks.

Reyes has been interviewed extensively by the staff of the District Attorney's office, for the most part without the direct participation of Department personnel, who were permitted to view one videotaped interview and one brief audio recording of an interview. No hearing was held with respect to defendants' motions to vacate their convictions, thus no opportunity was given to cross-examine Reyes in public, under oath.

It may be that the interviews of Reyes by the District Attorney's office have been sufficient to ensure his credibility. However, our lack of information precludes us from being adequately prepared to make that judgment.

In a related issue, we understand that Reyes has not been subjected to a polygraph examination. Perhaps he is thought to be too unstable to allow for a meaningful test. Such a judgment would hardly be a testimonial to his general credibility.

b. Reyes's Motive

Central to a consideration of the truth of Reyes's claim that he raped the jogger by himself is an assessment of his motive for coming forward to make the claim. Was he simply moved to do the right thing by feelings of guilt and the "positive experiences" that he has had in prison? Or is it possible, as has been suggested by some, that he came forward in response to threats, delivered through the underground prison communications system? Or did he act in order to get a desired change in prison assignment? Or did he have some other motive?

The District Attorney's office accepts Reyes's statement that "his decision to come forward with his confession was prompted by a chance encounter with Kharey Wise in Auburn Correctional facility, and the resultant realization that Wise was still incarcerated in connection with the attack of the Central Park jogger." (Exhibit B, p. 20.) Wise and Reyes were both at Auburn from August 2001 through January 2002. Experiencing a "guilty reaction to seeing Wise, [Reyes] began seeking advice from different individuals in the prison system telling them . . . that he had committed a crime for which another person had been convicted, and that he wanted to rectify the situation." (Exhibit B, p.20.) As a result, this information came to the attention of Corrections' officials and then the District Attorney's office. Acknowledging that "Reyes's motives cannot be objectively proven or disproven" (Exhibit B, p. 21), the District Attorney's office accepts his claimed motivation:

> He has consistently explained himself in terms of his positive experiences in prison, the fact that people have treated him decently despite the nature of his criminal history, and his guilty reaction to seeing Wise. (Exhibit B, p. 21.)

It is certainly correct that Reyes's motives cannot be objectively proven or disproven, but certain factors would seem to create doubt with respect to his stated motivation.

At the outset, his prior history is not one of selfless concern for others. On the contrary, he has led a life of vicious, self-indulgent crime. As long ago as 1991, he gave as a reason for his pleading guilty to three rape/robberies, one rape/murder and another robbery, his "positive experiences" in prison—the same words he now uses to describe what prompted him to come forward about the jogger. At that time, he had been imprisoned a short enough time to make it doubtful that he had accumulated many "positive experiences." It seems unlikely that he changed much thereafter. He is described in the Ryan Affirmation as a "loner" (Exhibit B, P.28) and his prison experience has included 19 substantial conflicts or infractions ranging from arson to fighting. In fact, Reyes had a fight with Kharey Wise when they met in prison at Riker's Island in 1990. The altercation was supposedly over the selection of a television channel. There seems to be little evidence that Reyes has undergone some sort of a moral transformation in the 13 years he has been in prison.

An alternative possible motive for Reyes coming forward is that he was threatened. If, as discussed above, Reyes may have come upon the defendants as they were completing their assault upon the jogger and remained, after they moved on, to commit the rape and vicious beating that occurred, it is possible that Kharey Wise caught sight of Reyes and remembered him when he encountered him in Riker's Island soon after Wise's conviction. Their fight could have been prompted, not, as claimed, by a difference of opinion over a television channel, but by Wise's understandable anger at being blamed for the particularly vicious acts that Reyes had committed after Wise and his friends had left the scene.

According to Corrections' personnel, Wise apparently became a member of the Bloods "gang." As such, Wise would have some influence within the prison system. Reyes, on the other hand, was apparently a loner and was, therefore, vulnerable to various forms of extortion. Since he had no alignment to any group, he had no "protection." If Wise learned in 2001 that Reyes was still incarcerated, it could have occurred to him that Reyes might afford a means of exonerating himself. In interviews which the Department investigators were able to conduct with inmates and correction officers, it appears that Wise may have indirectly communicated with Reyes, threatening him with violence if he did not sign an "affidavit" that Wise's lawyer was preparing.

Interviews of two inmates in particular indicate there may have been contacts between Reyes and Wise in jail through third parties. Although inmates cannot send mail to each other, they can send mail to third parties (non-inmates) who can in turn forward messages or mail to other inmates. According to inmates Pedro Hernandez and Angel Acevedo, Reyes had sent letters to inmate Martin Mejias' relatives, who in turn would mail them back to Mejias. In the letters, Mejias would send communications directed by Wise.[4] Hernandez and Acevedo also mentioned that inmates Martin Mejias and Troy Ortega could corroborate this information. Documents from State Corrections reveals that the same 5-6 common names were on the list of visitors, phone calls or commissary (receipt of packages or letters) for Mejias, Ortega and Reyes.

Hernandez and Acevedo were not housed in the same area during the time that each had separately met Reyes. Each was interviewed separately. Mejias and Ortega refused to be interviewed, informing Department staff that they were instructed by the New York County District Attorney's office not to talk to "FBI, CIA or the police."

There is also reason to question Reyes's claim that a chance meeting with Wise in the yard at Auburn in 2001 triggered the remorse that led to his confession. Corrections officers have checked the movement records of both Wise and Reyes in 2001 at Auburn and assert that it is not possible that Reyes and Wise were at any time together in the yard.

Reyes's descriptions of his contacts with Wise have been inconsistent. According to the Ryan Affirmation, when Reyes encountered Wise at Auburn in 2001, "he feared Wise's reaction and therefore disclosed nothing to him about his own culpability." (Exhibit B, p. 20.) On another occasion, he told an investigator that when he met Wise he apologized to him for the fight that had occurred in 1990 and added "we didn't get to speak much about the case" (implying that some discussion of the case took place).[5]

Later, in an interview on the television show PrimeTime, Reyes admitted meeting Wise in 1990 when they had a fight at Riker's Island, but indicated that he had not met Wise later, in 2001, saying that he specifically "avoided crossing paths with Wise so nobody would say that Wise forced him to confess."

---

[4]Of course, information coming from inmates must usually be regarded with considerable skepticism. Hernandez, for example, has been identified by at least two District Attorneys as an extremely unreliable source.

[5]This information was obtained by Department staff listening to an audio taped interview of Reyes at Auburn Correctional Facility by State Inspector General Investigator Vern Fonda in January 2002. The New York County District Attorney's office is in possession of this tape, and it has not been released to us to date.

Such scraps of information, some of them of highly dubious reliability, certainly do not add up to proof that Reyes was motivated in coming forward by fear of threats. However, the possibility cannot be discounted and seems at least as likely as Reyes experiencing a sudden attack of conscience.

Another simpler and less speculative motive for Reyes to have come forward to exculpate the defendants is that he won a favorable prison assignment by doing so. Purporting to fear Wise's reaction to his revelation, Reyes demanded protection at the time he came forward. (Exhibit B, p. 21.) Within a month, he was transferred to the Clinton Assessment Programs Prepared Unit ("APPU") at Clinton Correctional Facility. According to State Corrections personnel, this is considered the safest and one of the most desirable locations in the New York State correction system. As a 260-bed facility, it has the lowest correction officer/inmate ratio. Most of the inmates housed in this unit have some sort of notoriety (usually easy targets for inmate abuse or assault). The inmates housed in this facility are generally on their best behavior in order to prevent being transferred to a more hostile environment.

In 2001, Reyes had been transferred out of APPU for fighting, having spent nine of his thirteen years in prison in that facility. He was well aware of how relatively safe and desirable it was. Reyes knew that his confession to the rape of the jogger would be confirmed by DNA. He stood no risk by confessing to the crime and claiming that he had committed it alone, because the statute of limitations had long since run and, in any event, he was incarcerated for life. By claiming that he had committed the crime for which others were convicted and served time, he put himself in the position of needing protection from the defendants or their friends in prison. In this manner, he was able to be reassigned to the desirable prison location from which he had just been removed.

c. Reyes's Accounts of the Attack

We have been informed that Reyes was first interviewed on the subject of the jogger in November, 2001 by Corrections Officer Todd Clark at Auburn. His notes were reviewed by the District Attorney's office and the New York City Police Department. There was a subsequent interview conducted by State Inspector General Investigator Vern Fonda in January 2002. This interview was audiotaped. Reyes was interviewed for the first time by prosecutors from the New York County District Attorney's office on May 23, 2002. New York City Police Department Detective Robert Mooney began the interview and was replaced by Assistant District Attorney Nancy Ryan. This second portion of the interview was videotaped. On May 28, 2002 Reyes was taken to the crime scene by Assistant District Attorney Ryan, accompanied by State Department of Corrections personnel and other members of the District Attorney's office. No one from the New York City Police Department was present.

On May 30, 2002, Reyes was re-interviewed by Assistant District Attorney Ryan alone. Part of this interview was audio taped. At the beginning of the tape, Assistant District Attorney Ryan stated that an unrecorded interview had preceded the taped interview for approximately two hours. Five to ten minutes into the tape, the tape recorder was turned off.

Reyes's last known interview was aired in September 2002 on the television show Prime Time.

From the various accounts that Reyes has given in all of his interviews that we have been able to review, we list below some observations:

(1) Reyes alleged that he followed the jogger. (The jogger informed detectives she customarily ran at the rate of an 8-minute mile or less). He claimed to have zig-zagged behind her from one side of the path to the other, stopping along the way to pick up a "stick" so heavy that it required two hands to lift and hold.

    Department personnel recently attempted to simulate the manner in which Reyes claims to have approached and attacked the jogger. A female jogger ran across the 102nd Street transverse at a pace of less than an eight minute mile while five different individuals attempted to keep up with her zig-zagging behind her and stopping to pick up a large stick, as Reyes described. None of the five, police cadets who approximated Reyes's height and weight, could catch up to or overtake her. There are many variables that are impossible to duplicate thirteen years later. While we cannot state with certainty that Reyes's account is physically impossible, the test we conducted raises some questions about the feasibility of his claim.

(2) Reyes's description of the jogger's clothing varied from black shorts with a matching tank top (5/23/02 interview) to a white t-shirt with long, tight pants, black or blue (5/30/02 and later). She was actually wearing long tight black stirrup jogging pants with a long sleeved white shirt.

(3) Reyes described the case used to hold the victim's keys as black with a zipper and Velcro. According to the victim, she owned a small black pouch, with Velcro only, that attached to the laces of her sneakers, but she normally carried only her door key in her hand while jogging. Initially Reyes told the District Attorney's office that the key case was brown Velcro. Later, on the PrimeTime interview, he described it as resembling a fanny pack.

(4) Reyes claims to have run into a police officer he knew as "Blondie" while leaving the park, with whom he had a conversation about whether there was any commotion in the park. "Blondie" is Detective Charles Frietag of the 23rd Precinct Detective Squad, who was on duty and responded to Central Park on April 19,1989. Detective Frietag, who knew Reyes from the

bodega where Reyes worked, has no recollection of meeting Reyes that night. It seems likely that Reyes saw Detective Frietag, but unlikely that Detective Frietag saw him. Detective Frietag would certainly have noticed blood on Reyes, who described bashing the jogger with the rock causing so much blood spattering that he could "smell it on himself." According to the PrimeTime reporter, Reyes said that the lower part of his pants was "drenched" with blood.

(5) Reyes stated that after he raped the jogger, she got up and ran away, naked from the waist down, which would have meant that she was barefoot as she ran through rough underbrush strewn with sticks and rocks. However, the jogger had no marks on the bottoms of her feet. Further, the original crime scene detective, Detective Robert Honeyman, has stated that there were drag marks and some blood between the first tree where there was evidence of an assault and the second tree where the evidence indicated the major assault took place, indicating that the victim did not run but was dragged.

(6) Reyes asserts that he knew nothing about the assault except through first hand knowledge. However, Reyes obviously read about the assault since he stated that he felt bad about the victim because he read about everything she went through.

d. Additional Factors of Significance:

(1) Wise: Knowledge of Walkman

In his February 2002 statement to the inspector general, Reyes purported to have exclusive knowledge that the Central Park jogger had worn a Walkman on the night of her attack. Reyes said he stole the Walkman, and only he knew about it, thereby helping to establish that he was the sole attacker. This was the first time that anyone had reason to focus on the existence of a Walkman. In the course of our review, we uncovered notes from New York City Police Department Detective August Jonza that documented the fact that Kharey Wise knew about the Walkman on April 19, 1989.

When the Central Park jogger was found, there was no Walkman on her body. With the victim in a coma (she subsequently had no memory of the attack or events leading up to it), detectives had no way of knowing she had the Walkman on her at the time of the attack. Although it was her custom to wear a Walkman when jogging, the victim had no memory of whether she did so on that night. When she was informed in 2002 that Reyes had said that he took her Walkman, she told detectives that she owned two Walkmen and one was missing.

Kharey Wise was questioned at 4:50 AM on April 21, 1989 by Detective Jonza, whose notes list what Wise told him regarding "persons present when girl raped." (Exhibit E.) Included on the list is the reference "Rudy—played with tits/took Walkman." At the bottom of the page, it is noted, "female had pouch for Walkman on her belt." Wise's description of the walkman "pouch" is, therefore, similar to Reyes's description of a "fanny pack." At the time of this interview, neither Detective Jonza, nor anyone else investigating the events of the evening, had any way of knowing that the jogger had a Walkman, or a pouch. One would have had to encounter the jogger to have that information, a point that has been emphasized by some who have claimed that only Reyes did so. The name "Rudy" was never linked to anyone, and Wise's reference to the name could represent confusion on his part, or his understanding of the name by which Reyes introduced himself. In any event, whatever else Wise may or may not have known, the important fact is that he knew the jogger had a Walkman, and a "pouch" to put it in.

(2) Witnesses Ronald Williams and Shabazz Head

In the afternoon of April 20,1989, prior to being arrested, Kharey Wise made admissions to two acquaintances, Ronald Williams and Shabazz Head. They approached Wise at 110th Street and Fifth Avenue and Wise told them to get away from him because the police were after him. Williams and Head walked away. A short time later they encountered him again and asked why the police were after him. Wise replied, "You heard about that woman that was beat up and raped in the park last night. That was us!"

Both Williams and Head were re-interviewed in 2002. Head claimed to have no memory of what he said to the detectives in 1989. Williams gave the same statement that he did in 1989. In addition, he was asked to explain what the statement "that was us" meant to him. He said that he took that to mean that Wise and others had raped the woman in the park on the night of April 19, 1989.

(3) Witness Melody Jackson

Just before trial, in an effort to locate and interview additional witnesses, detectives asked Corey Jackson, a 15-year old friend of Kharey Wise, to come into the precinct to be interviewed. Jackson came into the 25th Precinct with his 27-year old sister Melody. During this interview, Melody Jackson made an unsolicited statement concerning a conversation she had with Kharey some time after the pre-trial hearing. She explained that she was at her sister's house when the phone rang. She answered the phone and it was Wise calling from Riker's Island. She said hello and then said to him that she couldn't believe that they "did that." Wise repeatedly stated that he didn't rape anyone, finally saying that he "only held her legs down while Kevin fucked her." Jackson seemingly thought her information would be helpful to Wise. She was subpoenaed by the District Attorney's office to testify at trial, and repeated what she had said. Melody Jackson's interview in 2002 re-confirmed her testimony. She also explained the negative effect her testimony has had on her life, once it became apparent that the testimony inculpated Wise.

(4) Richardson: Scratches

When Kevin Richardson was interrogated by Detective Gonzalez on the morning of April 20, 1989, he was asked to explain the scratches on his face. At first, Richardson said it was an injury he received when he fell. Following more questioning, Richardson stated that he got the scratches from the arresting officer. When told of the possibility that the officer would be asked to corroborate his story, Richardson admitted that he received the scratches from the female jogger while trying to stop the others from attacking her. In a later statement to a detective, Kevin Richardson explained that he lied about how he received the scratch on his face. Richardson said he received it when he tried to take the female jogger off of the road.

(5) Witness/Defendant Dennis Commedo

Dennis Commedo was interviewed in 1989 because he was suspected of being part of the large group who initially entered the park. He stated that on the night of April 19, 1989, while standing in a ball field in the park at about 100th Street, Kevin Richardson said to him "we just raped somebody." This statement was given to Detective Jonza on April 25, 1989 at 12:45 AM. This statement by Commedo was included with culpable admissions of his own behavior. In 2002 he claims to have no memory of the event.

(6) Witness/Defendant Orlando Escobar

Orlando Escobar was interviewed in 1989 and again in 2002. Escobar was also implicated as being part of the original group. On May 11, 1989, Escobar was interviewed by Detective John Hartigan and he stated that on the night of April 19, 1989, while standing in the area of the ball fields, he saw Raymond Santana, Steven Lopez, Kevin Richardson and Yusef Salaam, with others, coming over the hill from the 102nd Street transverse road into the baseball fields. Escobar was re-interviewed on October 29, 2002 by Detective Tony Rivera. In this interview, he gave the same statement as in 1989, except he omitted naming Yusef Salaam, and stated others were with Santana, Lopez and Richardson. He also specified that the group was coming from the direction of where the rape took place. In both the 1989 and 2002 statements he admitted his own culpability.

(7) Witness/Defendant Antonio Montalvo

Antonio Montalvo was interviewed in 1989 and gave considerable information about the events of April 19, 1989, including the assault on Diaz, in connection with which he pled guilty. He did not mention the attack on the female jogger. In 2002, when he was re-interviewed, Montalvo stated that he had seen Santana, McCray and five others coming over a hill from the direction of the 102nd Street transverse road on the night of April 19, 1989. He had not realized the significance of this observation until later when he saw a memorial that had been set up at the spot where the female jogger was attacked and realized that Santana, McCray and the others had come from the place where the attack occurred.

Commedo, Escobar and Montalvo were not together when they made these observations nor when they reported them to the police.

(8) Witness/Defendant Clarence Thomas

During Clarence Thomas' videotaped statement, Thomas stated he overheard Santana and Lopez laughing and talking about how they "made a woman bleed."

(9) Santana: "I already got mines"

While being processed at the Central Park Precinct and in response to a comment by Police Officer Powers that the group should be home with their girlfriends and not beating people, Santana looked at Steven Lopez, smiled and said "I already got mines." Santana and Lopez then both laughed. (This statement was suppressed at trial as given without a Miranda warning.)

(10) Santana: Admission of Contact

While being transported from the Central Park Precinct to the 20th precinct by Detective Sheehan, Santana said, not in response to any question, "I had nothing to do with the rape. All I did was feel the woman's tits."

(11) Santana: Location of Attack.

Following his videotaped interview, Santana and his father were driven home by Detective Michael Sheehan to get fresh clothing, stopping at the 102nd Street transverse road along the way. When asked where the attack occurred, Santana pointed north of the transverse road down towards the ravine. They walked into the woods and Santana said that it was too dark to find anything else.

(12) Richardson: Reference to Woman

While interviewed by P.O. Powers, on April 20, 1989 at 6:00 PM, the officer asked Richardson who he thought was hurt worse, the man or the woman. Richardson replied that he thought "the man looked worse than the woman."

(13) Richardson: Reference to "Getting Her"

After being brought back to the crime scene on the morning of April 20th, Richardson, while standing on the 102nd Street transverse, told Detective Sheehan that, "This is where we got her."

(14) Richardson: Scene

Later that morning on a second trip to the scene, Richardson accurately identified an area northwest of a large tree on the slope north of the transverse as the area where "the raping occurred."

(15) Wise: "That's a lot of blood"

After being brought back to the crime scene by Detective Sheehan and Assistant District Attorney Fairstein on the morning of April 20th, and while walking down towards the spot where the rape occurred, Wise was overheard muttering, "Damn, damn that's a lot of blood. Damn, this is really bad, that's a lot of blood." When asked why he was so surprised by the amount of blood, he answered, "I knew she was bleeding but I didn't know how bad she was. It was really dark. I couldn't see how much blood there was at night." (See Hearing Transcript pp. 4560-4561, 4569.)

(16) Wise: Reference to Rape—"We" and "They"

When asked if he was familiar with the area, Wise responded, "This is where we" and stopped and finished "they raped her." When asked what happened here, Wise says, "This is where they dragged her." Again he started to say "we" and changed to "they."

(17) Wise: Washed his clothes

Kharey Wise was asked to go to the precinct the day after the April 19, 1989 assaults in Central Park. During one of his interviews with Detective Hartigan at the precinct on April 20, 1989, Wise revealed that he washed his clothes when he got home the night before.

e. The Timeline of Events

The press and others have produced elaborate analyses of proposed timelines covering the various events on the evening the jogger was attacked. The public is asked to conclude that the defendants did not have the time to participate in the attack upon the jogger because they were busy, at specific times, with other assaults. It is said that a series of attacks took place on the east side of the park, ending at 9:15 PM and that the first of several attacks around the reservoir occurred at 9:25 PM, leaving a window of only ten minutes for the assault on the female jogger.

This reasoning depends upon a selective analysis of the evidence from which various events are timed. In fact, no accurate timeline can be constructed because the evidence regarding the timing of the various events and the individuals who participated in them is not sufficiently precise to allow any exact conclusion.

A key time, necessary to the "window of opportunity" theory is the time of the assault upon the first of the male joggers, David Lewis. That time must be fixed at 9:25 PM, in order to support the argument that a "window" of only ten minutes existed. However, the following are the various times given as the possible time of the attack on Mr. Lewis: in the original police report created April 19th, a detective recorded the time as 9:25 PM; another summary of the events by a police officer had the attack occurring at 9:42 PM; a detective's chronology summary has the attack also as occurring at 9:42 PM; the Manhattan District Attorney's office recorded it as 9:42 PM in their chronology created April 28, 1989; at the first trial no time was fixed for the assault, only the time that Mr. Lewis left his residence at 89th Street as 9:22 PM; at the second trial, testimony indicated that 9:24-9:28 PM was the time of this assault; in a 2002 interview, Mr. Lewis stated that he never knew an exact time for the assault, but in 1989 he had estimated that he left his house sometime between 9:10 and 9:15 PM based on what the prosecutors had told him. Attached is Exhibit F, which shows some different possible timelines based on the credible testimony of individuals at different parts of these proceedings.

Illustrative of the unreliability of constructing timelines in this case is the fact that not even the basic assumption upon which the "window of opportunity" theory is based—that the jogger was attacked sometime between 9:15 PM and 9:30 PM—is free from doubt. It has been assumed that the jogger was attacked at approximately 9:15 PM, before the attacks upon the male joggers at the reservoir. Not previously a hotly contested issue, the evidence establishing the time of the attack on the jogger has been accepted to be: that she left her apartment at approximately 8:55 after having a chat of unknown duration with a neighbor; that her normal jogging rate, over her normal route, would have put her at the scene of the attack at approximately 9:15 to 9:30; and that she expected to be back at her apartment at 10:00 to meet someone. The time estimate based on these elements is hardly precise. Perhaps the jogger arrived at the park later than estimated if she was held up by traffic, or traveled a different route than the normal one, or stopped to speak to someone or to browse in a store. Any of these, or numerous other possibilities, could have delayed her arrival at the point of attack in the park to 9:45 PM, with still plenty of time to get back to her apartment at about 10:00. In that event, she was assaulted after the male joggers, and the "window of opportunity" theory becomes irrelevant.

We believe that no accurate timeline exists and none can be reliably constructed.

District Attorney Morgenthau and senior staff members, in a meeting with us to discuss the case, agreed that it was impossible to fix times accurately enough to support any argument, one way or the other, about the possible involvement of the defendants in the rape of the jogger. No precise estimate is offered in the Ryan Affirmation as to when the jogger was attacked.

f. Forensic Evidence

In the publicity surrounding the motions by the defendants to vacate their convictions, a common theme has been that the District Attorney's investigation demonstrated, by new DNA evidence unavailable at the time of the trial, that all of the forensic evidence admitted at trial has now been discredited. This contention is inaccurate.

The most important new forensic evidence is, of course, the DNA tests proving that the previously unidentified semen and pubic hair belonged to Matias Reyes. This finding adds nothing to the evidence introduced at trial other than Reyes's identity. The proof in defendants' trials brought out the fact that the semen and pubic hair evidence was that of an unidentified person, other than the defendants. The new DNA evidence, therefore, does not assist in determining whether the defendants were present during the attack on the jogger.

Other evidence admitted at trial consisted of: three hairs, one pubic, found on Kevin Richardson's clothing that were "consistent" with the jogger's hair; one hair "consistent" with the jogger's found on Steven Lopez' clothing; a blood stain on Raymond Santana's sneaker; individual blood stains on Yusef Salaam's jacket and Steven Lopez's underwear; and semen stains on the underwear of Antron McCray and Kevin Richardson and the sweatshirt of Raymond Santana.

We have not been given access to all of the forensic test material.[6] Nevertheless, it is apparent, from the Ryan Affirmation, that no new DNA evidence contradicts any of the evidence introduced at trial. Experts have now been retained by the District Attorney to redo the same tests to which their experts testified at trial. They have, in some respects, disagreed with the previous testimony.

Tests described in the Ryan Affirmation concern hairs found on Kevin Richardson. At the original trial, testimony was presented that the hairs found on Richardson were "similar" to the jogger's hair. The new FBI microscopic analysis tests, however, conclude that the hairs found on Richardson were not suitable for comparison. In other words, no comparison could be done. New mitochondrial DNA tests conducted on these hairs were inconclusive, i.e., no conclusions could be drawn from the results.

According to the Ryan Affirmation, the hair found on Lopez's clothing cannot be found and, therefore, cannot be retested.

In addition, new tests were conducted on hair and blood found on a rock recovered at the crime scene. The new test results apparently concluded that: (1) no comparison could be done on the hair fiber because no suitable control was available; and (2) the blood on the rock was found to be female but inconsistent with the jogger's profile, however, contamination is noted as a possible reason for this inconsistency. These test results seem to have no bearing on the defendants' participation in the jogger attack.

The Ryan Affirmation makes no reference to the blood or semen evidence. This evidence was by no means dispositive at trial, but the fact that it exists is important. For instance, it contradicts various reports that no blood was found on any of the defendants.

In sum, the new test results establish that Matias Reyes is the previously unknown source of the semen found on the female jogger and her clothing. They do not prove that the defendants could not have participated in the attack.

ASSAULTS ON OTHERS

In addition to their convictions for the rape and assault on the female jogger, the defendants were also convicted of crimes with respect to other attacks occurring that evening; Kevin Richardson, Antron McCray, Raymond Santana and Yusef Salaam were convicted of riot, the robbery and assault of John Loughlin and the assault upon David Lewis. Kharey Wise was convicted of riot. Another defendant, Steven Lopez, who was a central defendant in the case of the female jogger, arranged a plea bargain whereby he pleaded guilty to the assault on Loughlin and received a sentence of 11/2 to 4 years. In addition, Michael Briscoe, Jermaine Robinson, Antonio Montalvo and Orlando Escobar pleaded guilty to various charges of riot, assault, robbery and attempted robbery with respect to the attacks upon Antonio Diaz, Loughlin and Lewis.

Justice Tejada ruled, as the District Attorney recommended, that the convictions on these charges against the defendants, as well as those involving the female jogger, should be vacated, although the newly discovered evidence of Matias Reyes's rape of the

---

[6]As part of the District Attorney's investigation of Reyes's claim, new forensic tests were conducted by the FBI and a private laboratory on some of the physical evidence that was presented at the original trials. As yet, we have not been provided with the lab reports from the private laboratory and have been able to obtain access to only some of the lab reports prepared by the FBI in connection with those tests. Thus, it is not clear precisely what evidence was re-tested or what were the results of those tests.

female jogger related only to that event. We understand the legal position underlying Justice Tejada's ruling, that the existence of new evidence regarding the most significant charge against the defendants may have affected the juries' ability to consider evidence regarding the other charges. However, we believe that there is no reason, on the merits, to think that a jury fairly presented with the evidence against the defendants would come to a different conclusion than was reached before.

In the first place, some of the defendants have repeated their admissions of guilt. Raymond Santana testified at a parole hearing on February 9, 1994 and he was questioned about the crimes he committed on April 19, 1989. He admitted that he and his friends planned to go to the park that night to rob and assault people. He stated that about seven or eight friends devised the plan. They were prepared to attack whoever they encountered that night in the park. Santana reiterated that they had let one, a couple, go because the man was with his girlfriend. Santana also admitted to beating a man. He denied only the rape. When Antron McCray went before the parole board in November 1994, he admitted all of his crimes except for the rape of the female jogger. Two of the defendants, Raymond Santana and Kevin Richardson, during interviews conducted by detectives in 2002, admitted their participation in the assaults that did not involve the jogger.

The District Attorney has pointed out that these post-trial admissions of guilt cannot be taken into consideration with respect to the defendants' motions to vacate their convictions, since that issue must be decided on the basis of evidence that could have been introduced at trial. However, there is no reason to ignore such statements when attempting to come to a conclusion as to what actually happened.

As with the case involving the female jogger, most of the evidence with respect to the other crimes comes from the statements of the participants in those crimes.

The following is a listing of some of the evidence regarding the five defendants' participation in the other assaults:

The assault on Antonio Diaz. A total of 23 people were named as participants or as being present:

- Richardson was implicated by 7 accomplices; he also admitted participation.
- Santana was implicated by 5 accomplices; he denied participating although he saw some kind of commotion from a distance.
- McCray was implicated by 6 accomplices; he admitted participation.
- Salaam was implicated by 3 accomplices; he did not admit or deny participation but was present.
- Wise was implicated by 5 accomplices; he acknowledged being present, but denied participation.

The harassment of the couple on the tandem bike. A total of 13 people were named as participants or as being present:

- Richardson was implicated by 3 accomplices; he also admitted participation.
- Santana was not implicated by anyone; he did not mention this incident at all.
- McCray was implicated by 1 accomplice; he admitted participation.
- Salaam was implicated by 2 accomplices; he admitted participation.
- Wise was implicated by 2 accomplices; he admitted participation.

The crossing of the 96th Street Transverse road to the reservoir. A total of 17 people were identified as having gone south towards the reservoir:

- Richardson was implicated by 2 accomplices; he admitted going.
- Santana was implicated by 5 accomplices; he admitted going.
- McCray was implicated by 4 accomplices; he admitted going.
- Salaam was implicated by 3 accomplices; he admitted going.
- Wise was implicated by 1 accomplice; he eventually admitted going.

The assault on the jogger David Lewis. A total of 11 people were identified as participants or as being present:

- Richardson was implicated by 1 accomplice; he denied participation.
- Santana was implicated by 2 accomplices; he admitted participation.
- McCray was implicated by 3 accomplices; he did not discuss this assault.
- Salaam was implicated by 1 accomplice; he did not discuss this assault.
- Wise was not implicated by anyone; he did not discuss this assault.

The assault on the jogger John Loughlin. A total of 19 people were identified as participants or as being present:

- Richardson was implicated by 5 accomplices; he denied participation.
- Santana was implicated by 6 accomplices; he admitted participation.
- McCray was implicated by 6 accomplices; he admitted participation.

- Salaam was implicated by 7 accomplices; he admitted participation.
- Wise was implicated by 2 accomplices; he did not discuss this assault.

Whatever conclusions may be reached regarding Matias Reyes's claim that he raped the female jogger alone, there seems to be no reason to believe that the defendants were innocent of the other crimes for which they were convicted.

CONCLUSION

The only new evidence that exists regarding the events in Central Park on the night of April 19, 1989 is the statement by serial rapist/killer Matias Reyes that he alone assaulted and raped the female jogger. DNA confirms that Reyes raped the jogger but we have nothing but his uncorroborated word that he did so alone. If Reyes's claim that he attacked the jogger by himself is true, it necessarily follows that the statements of the five defendants who were convicted of the crime, as well as those of the other witnesses who described it, were erroneous.

In that event, the question arises whether the statements were coerced or "suggested" by the interrogating officers. That question is, of course, central to our task of analyzing police behavior with respect to these events.

We believe that the issue of coercion was laid to rest authoritatively by the exhaustive opinion of Judge Galligan, following a lengthy Huntley hearing. Whether the defendants' statements were accurate or not, the methods used in obtaining them were examined by Judge Galligan with utmost care. We have not seen any evidence to suggest that Judge Galligan was in error and our review of available information confirms that police interrogations were conducted professionally and in accordance with applicable rules.

Affirming that neither the police nor the prosecutors engaged in outright coercion, the District Attorney has theorized that facts may have inadvertently been suggested to defendants and witnesses, enabling them to describe the attack on the jogger with sufficient particularity to make their statements credible. To determine whether this sort of thing went on, it is necessary to analyze the consistencies and inconsistencies in the various statements. The considerations are similar to those relevant to the basic question of whether Reyes is to be believed when he says he attacked the jogger alone. Those who believe Reyes emphasize the inconsistencies in the defendants' statements and those who do not believe him point to the statements' consistencies and to other supporting evidence.

The District Attorney, in responding to defendants' motions to dismiss the charges against them, laid out, in considerable detail, the arguments supporting the contention that Reyes was the sole attacker. Since the District Attorney had no reason to explore counter-arguments, we have done so, in order to complete the record.

We conclude that the various inconsistencies in defendants' statements, and the other recently revealed weaknesses in the evidence presented at trial, when viewed in light of Reyes's claim that he alone attacked the jogger, could afford a reasonable basis for maintaining that Reyes did, indeed, commit an attack on the jogger by himself.

However, the consistencies found in the defendants' statements, the informal remarks made by the defendants at various times, the corroborative testimony of other witnesses, the absence of a convincing motive for Reyes and suspicion of his general credibility, lead us to conclude that it is more likely than not that the defendants participated in an attack upon the jogger.

We adopt the view that the most likely scenario for the events of April 19, 1989 was that the defendants came upon the jogger and subjected her to the same kind of attack, albeit with sexual overtones, that they inflicted upon other victims in the park that night. Perhaps attracted to the scene by the jogger's screams, Reyes either joined in the attack as it was ending or waited until the defendants had moved on to their next victims before descending upon her himself, raping her and inflicting upon her the brutal injuries that almost caused her death.

On this theory of the facts, there is no reason to believe that the defendants were prompted into making erroneous statements.

With respect to the other crimes for which the defendants were convicted, we are aware of no new evidence or reason to review the old evidence regarding those crimes. Two of the defendants reaffirmed their guilt for these crimes at parole hearings and one of these, together with a third, did so in 2002, after Reyes came forward to make his confession. Moreover, four other individuals who had pleaded guilty to the assaults, implicated the defendants in these crimes in their interrogations or recorded statements. We understand the technical legal position espoused by the District Attorney and adopted by the Court, vacating these convictions. However, we firmly believe that this legal ruling affords no basis for maintaining that the defendants were not involved in the other crimes for which they were convicted.

OBSERVATIONS AND LESSONS LEARNED

In addition to our factual conclusions, we offer the following observations:

* Early assignment of a senior commander
  Some early confusion in this complex case could have been avoided if procedures which would likely be used today in a similarly complex investigation were in effect then, namely: the establishment of 12-hour tours for the senior commanders overseeing the investigation; the establishment of a command center where all information related to the investigation could be received and correlated; and the establishment of regular briefings so that all personnel assigned to the case could be kept informed.

* Establishment of a Management Team
  A management team should have been established on the evening of April 19, 1989, for the purpose of overseeing all investigative steps and facilitating information-sharing among all investigative personnel. Had this occurred, factual accounts provided by the suspects that lacked clarity or needed additional exploration could have been identified and resolved prior to videotaping.

* Allocation of adequate space to conduct interview of minors
  There was inadequate space to conduct interviews of minors. This problem has only become worse with the passage of time. The Department should consider rehabilitating or constructing new precinct space to accommodate interviews of minors.

* Evidence accountability and control
  The then Manhattan Chief of Detectives brought home with him the only available copies of some Polaroid photos of the female jogger that had been taken by investigators, making them unavailable for use by the prosecutor during the videotaped questioning of the suspects. The Polaroid photos were eventually made available to the prosecutor but only during Kharey Wise's videotaped interrogation. This action could have exacerbated problems associated with the interrogations. It was obviously wrong for this to have occurred, but it does not appear to be a systemic problem and is unlikely to recur.

* Forensic management
  During the photographing of the pants of one of the defendants, the pants were placed on the precinct floor, creating a risk of potential evidence contamination and compromise of any trace evidence taken from them. Again, this error is unlikely to recur because of reforms implemented after the Department's crime scene unit was reorganized and its procedures were reviewed and modified in 1995.

* Case review and coordination
  It is now known that among the series of violent crimes that he committed, Matias Reyes also raped a woman in Central Park on April 17, 1989, just two days before the jogger attack. There has been some criticism directed at the Department for the failure to connect the April 17, 1989 rape to the April 19, 1989 attack on the jogger. Reyes was identified as a possible suspect in the April 17, 1989 rape, and was later arrested, in August, 1989, for another rape and murder to which he ultimately pleaded guilty. If, at the time, it had occurred to either the police or the prosecutors that the April 19th rape might have been committed by the same individual that had raped someone on April 17th, it would have been simple to compare the DNA recovered from the jogger against that of the defendant they now had in custody. But, the police and the District Attorney's office had a set of confessions and were satisfied that the defendants perpetrated the attack on the jogger. They had no cause to search for links to other cases until DNA tests in November, 1989 indicated that the semen from the jogger did not match any of the defendants. Today's case review methods would substantially increase the probability of identifying cases with seemingly very few similarities.

  Another factor that may have interfered with a realization that the April 17th and April 19th rapes were connected was the fact that one of them was investigated as a homicide case and the other as a sex crimes case. Under current procedures, information in cases like this is shared.

* Use of DNA
  In 1989, procedures were not in place to facilitate the comparison of DNA evidence in one case with that in another, particularly after the DNA test results were taken by the District Attorney's office to prepare for trial. This problem is unlikely to recur due to the creation in 1994 of a DNA databank. DNA is now routinely collected from defendants convicted of certain statutorily prescribed crimes and fed into a database to which both the Department and the District Attorney's office have access. Unidentified DNA evidence recovered from a crime scene is entered into the databank and stored for future comparisons.

Respectfully submitted,

Michael F. Armstrong, Esq.

Stephen L. Hammerman, Esq.

Jules Martin, Esq.

CHAPTER 3

Crimes against the Person: Murder

CHAPTER CONTENTS

And it came about when they were in the field, that Cain rose up against Abel his brother and killed him.

Genesis 4:8

CHAPTER OBJECTIVES

After studying this chapter you should be able to:

- Define murder.
- Distinguish between degrees of murder.
- Define conspiracy.
- Explain the felony murder rule as it applies to criminal conspiracies to commit a felony.

- Define infanticide.
- Distinguish between voluntary and involuntary manslaughter.
- Explain when killings are not crimes and when they are.
- Explain the assisted suicide movement.

O, my offence is rank, it smells to heaven; It hath the primal eldest curse upon 't, A brother's murder. Shakespeare, *Hamlet,* Act 3, Scene 3

Homicide

The killing of a human being.

Criminal Homicide

A killing that breaks the law, designated as either murder or manslaughter.

Wergild

Compensation paid to a family group if a member of that family was killed or suffered severe injury.

Bot

Compensation paid for minor injuries.

Wite

A public fine payable to a lord or tribal chieftain.

INTRODUCTION AND HISTORICAL BACKGROUND

The biblical story of Cain and Abel illustrates a second fall of humans from grace following expulsion from the Garden of Eden. Cain was sent to cultivate the ground and be a "vagrant and wanderer on the earth."[1] Cultivating the land is generally regarded as the beginning of modern civilization. Cain's exile to hard labor was both the first punishment for murder and symbolically the start of civilized society's struggle with violence.

As civilized populations increased, so did the number of murders or **homicides.** Traditions arose in each society as to how to treat those who took another's life. Under English Common Law, homicides were divided into three categories, criminal (or felonious), justifiable, and excusable. Attorneys most often deal with **criminal homicide,** which is when a person unlawfully and knowingly, recklessly, or negligently causes the death of another human being.[2] Depending on the circumstances, criminal homicide can be one of several crimes. Most commonly, homicides are categorized as murders or manslaughter. Murder may be premeditated or felony murder. Some states have distinctions such as first- or second-degree murder. Check the laws in your state to understand the distinctions. Manslaughter is a lesser crime usually classified as voluntary or involuntary.

HISTORICAL HIGHLIGHT
Murder in Tribal England

England in the first millennium A.D. was a savage place. Fierce warring tribes competed for dominance during a period punctuated by a series of invasions. Each onslaught brought refinements to the English legal system as the conquerors assimilated into the conquered.

Although tribal customs varied, criminal practices generally followed a fairly set practice. The victim or his family filed the complaint and often physically brought the accused to court. While this may seem unusual to us in modern times, it is important to bear in mind that these were very close-knit tribal communities. If a person attempted to flee, there simply was nowhere to go. He couldn't lose himself in the anonymity of a large urban area. Each person's ability to make a living and perhaps his entire life was tied up in the tribal community.

A criminal who was convicted of a crime was never imprisoned in tribal England because prisons didn't exist yet. He could be executed for particularly heinous crimes, he could be tortured, or more likely he would simply have to compensate the victims. This compensation fell into three categories, *wergild, bot,* and *wite. Wergild* was compensation paid to a family group if a member of that family was killed or suffered severe injury. In murder cases, the amount was determined by the social standing of the person murdered. The cause or circumstances of the crime were irrelevant. *Bot* was compensation paid for minor injuries. *Wite* was a public fine payable to a lord or tribal chieftain. This was then used for the benefit of the entire tribe. If the offender were too poor to pay, the fine would be assessed in livestock.[3]

MURDER

The first job of a prosecutor in a murder case is to prove a crime was committed. Proving a crime is committed is called establishing corpus delicti, or the body of the crime. Corpus delicti must be established beyond a reasonable doubt. If the state cannot prove a crime was committed, they may not prosecute anyone for its commission. Don't confuse corpus delicti with the actual body in a homicide. As you will see below, a body may make murder easier to prove but is not essential to a successful murder prosecution.

Cases where the victim's body cannot be found present problems for prosecutors. Evidence of violence, witnesses to a struggle, and various pieces of forensic evidence can be pieced together to provide evidence of a crime. Although evidence like this is circumstantial, it still may be used as evidence of a crime, if the whole body of evidence establishes beyond a reasonable doubt that a crime was committed.

PREMEDITATED MURDER

The first recorded murder in Colonial America was committed by one of the original Pilgrims from the *Mayflower*. Ten years after the Pilgrims landed, John Billington shot his neighbor with a blunderbuss. The punishment for murder was hanging. Billington was convicted and hanged.[4]

At the time, English Common law made no distinction between the types of murder. But this one-punishment-fits-all approach was soon to change. After the Revolution, state legislatures created various classifications of murders by statute. It probably occurred to them that it wasn't practical to kill every murderer. Clearly, different circumstances dictated different responses.

Premeditated murder is virtually always classified as **first-degree murder.** Second-degree murder is always a lesser charge, but the elements that comprise second-degree murder vary widely from state to state.

By definition, a person committing first-degree murder must form the **intent to kill** his victim. The law requires the person to have **malice aforethought.** In other words, the defendant must have an angry mental state toward the victim that allowed him to plan the victim's murder. This malice need not be of long duration. Even if the intent to kill was formed just prior to the act, the person can be convicted of first-degree murder.[5]

Since we cannot read a killer's mind, intent is very hard to prove. However, there are some Common Law doctrines that have traditionally been held to establish intent.

First is the **deadly weapon doctrine.** Under this doctrine, if the defendant points a loaded gun at the victim and pulls the trigger, he intended to kill the person. In other words, the defendant believed that the natural and probable consequences of his action would occur.

Deadly weapons do not have to be guns or knives. Fists, scarves, handkerchiefs, rocks, and other common items used as weapons have been held to be deadly weapons in murder trials. Juries must determine the presence of a deadly weapon on a case-by-case basis.

In films, murders are always very clean. I show how difficult it is and what a messy thing it is to kill a man.
Alfred Hitchcock

First-degree Murder

Murder committed deliberately with malice aforethought, that is, with premeditation.

Intent to Kill

The plan, course, or means a person conceives to take another life.

Malice Aforethought

Intent to kill or injure, or the deliberate commission of a dangerous or deadly act.

Deadly Weapon Doctrine

Use of a deadly weapon is proof of intent to kill.

Transferred Intent

The doctrine that if a defendant who intends to injure one person unintentionally harms another, the intent is transferred to the person who is unintentionally harmed.

Intent can be transferred to a party to whom the defendant bore no malice. **Transferred intent** can occur when the victim is not the one the defendant meant to kill. A person shooting at one person and accidentally hitting another is guilty of both the crime of murder and bad aim. Once the shot is fired with intent to kill and kills someone, the shooter is guilty regardless of who is killed.

HISTORICAL HIGHLIGHT
Intent Follows the Bullet . . . or the Flame

Kenneth Richey was mad. His girlfriend had left him and moved in with another man. Richey was going to get even. He set fire to the apartment building where his estranged girlfriend and new love now lived. But things went terribly wrong. The girl and her boyfriend escaped the flames, but a two-year-old girl upstairs from the couple did not.

Police soon arrested Richey and charged him with aggravated felony murder under Ohio law using the transferred intent theory. Even Richey's forensic expert testified the fire was the result of arson. Richey was convicted and sentenced to death.

Richey hired a new lawyer and appealed. He argued that the transferred intent theory did not apply to Ohio's aggravated felony murder law, and since the prosecution could not prove he intended to kill the two-year-old girl, the conviction should be overturned. The Sixth Circuit Court of Appeals agreed, and prosecutors appealed to the U.S. Supreme Court.

In a unanimous decision, the High Court ruled that prosecutors had directly proved Richey's intent to kill and because the transferred intent theory did apply to the law, the conviction should stand.[6]

LESSER DEGREES OF MURDER

Intent to Do Serious Bodily Harm

A defendant's plan to injure another.

Murder begins where self-defense ends.
Georg Buchner

Defendants who only intended to "rough someone up" but killed him or her by mistake may lack the intent to kill necessary for first-degree murder. Nevertheless, they are responsible for the person's death. In cases like this, defendants are said to possess an **intent to do serious bodily harm.** These murders may result in a conviction of second-degree murder or even manslaughter depending on the definitions in the state.

Some cases involve people who have no intent to cause bodily harm but are reckless in their behavior. Drunk driving is the most common example. When people behave in a way that endangers others resulting in the death of another person, the person may be charged with a lesser degree of murder or manslaughter depending on the fact situation.

YOU MAKE THE CALL

SHOULD CULTURAL DEFENSES BE PERMITTED IN MURDER CASES?

Spend enough time in a courtroom and you will hear many far-fetched explanations for crimes. But are they far-fetched or just the product of your cultural prejudice? Foreign-born murder defendants have raised cultural defenses to show that their murderous behavior would have been justified, or at least not as unusual in their native culture. Consider these examples:

- New York, 1987—After Chinese-born Dong Lu Chen's wife admits having an affair, he beats her to death with a hammer. At trial, a cultural anthropologist explains the deep humiliation and loss of manhood that befalls cuckolds in Chinese culture. Dong is convicted of manslaughter and sentenced to five years probation.
- Chicago, 1992—Celerina Galicia, an illegal alien from Mexico, stabs his girlfriend Roberta Martinez 44 times with a six-inch steak knife. At his murder trial, he explains his belief in *curanderismo*, a Mexican belief in folk healing and spirits. He was convinced that Martinez was a *bruja*, or witch, who had cast spells on him. When he could not find a healer to perform the ritual cleansing to remove the spells, he saw no option but to kill her.

  The judge in the case allowed some testimony about his beliefs but refused to let a letter from Galicia's aunt telling him that Martinez was a *bruja* into evidence. Galicia was convicted of first-degree murder and sentenced to 15 to 50 years in prison.
- Oakland, CA, 1993—An Ethiopian man who shot his girlfriend claimed she was a witch who cast spells on him. The charge was reduced from murder to assault.

One of the elements of a crime is intent. Can judges or juries properly ascertain the defendant's state of mind without understanding the defendant's culture? Cultures vary in relevant areas such as trust of the police, attitudes toward women, and comfort with the use of violence to settle disputes.

The late Johnnie Cochran, who defended O.J. Simpson, was a big proponent of cultural defenses. He once told an American Bar Association symposium that when cultural issues are involved, "You are committing malpractice if you do not avail yourself of the appropriate defense."[7]

On the other side of the argument, DePaul law professor John F. Decker argues that cultural defenses are just variations on the insanity defense and are "invariably rejected by judges and juries."[8] But the preceding examples show that may not always be the case.

For instance, an African-born father carried on his culture's custom of celebrating the birth of a son by kissing the newborn's penis. However, a neighbor reported the man for sexual abuse. Is this just a case of cultural misunderstanding or a real crime? What if the father had circumcised his daughter in accordance with African traditions? Would that be a crime? What if someone from a different culture committed the same act? Would that be a crime? You make the call.

FELONY MURDER

Felony Murder Rule

The rule that a death occurring by accident or chance during the course of the commission of a felony is first-degree murder.

A person can be held responsible for murder even if that person wasn't directly involved in the killing. This is known as the **felony murder rule.** Generally, the rule applies to those who agree to act with others to commit a criminal act. If one of the parties to the criminal enterprise commits the murder, all are held to be equally culpable under the felony murder rule. For example, assume two defendants conspire to commit a bank robbery. One defendant drives the getaway car while the other robs the bank and shoots a security guard in the process. The security guard dies. Both can be charged with murder, regardless of who pulled the trigger. In fact, under some circumstances the driver can even be executed.[9]

"Felony murder is committed when a person, acting alone or in concert with others, commits or attempts to commit one of nine predicate felonies, . . ." and "in the furtherance of such crime or of immediate flight therefrom, he, or another participant, if there be any, causes the death of a person other than one of the participants."[10] But, exactly what does "in furtherance of a crime or . . . flight therefrom" mean? Most jurisdictions follow the **res gestae theory** which states that if the "killing was committed in, about, or as part of the underlying transaction" that all conspirators were guilty of the murder.

Res Gestae Theory

Literally "the acts of the thing"; the acts or words through which an event speaks.

Clearly, the felony murder rule can be very broad in its application. A person who conspires to commit a felony may be charged with felony murder if his accomplice committed the murder. A **conspiracy** is an agreement between two or more persons to engage in a criminal act. It is one of a class of criminal offenses referred to as **inchoate** or incomplete crime. Other inchoate crimes are criminal solicitation and criminal intent. Conspiracy requires that at least one of the participants take a step toward the commission of the crime the parties agreed to commit, whether they actually manage to commit the crime. In other words, one of the conspirators must take an overt action toward the accomplishment of the criminal goal. Inchoate crimes like conspiracy are punished as if the crime had been completed. For example, if two people conspire to commit armed robbery and they are stopped before they can rob the target bank, they can be sentenced as if they actually robbed the bank.

Conspiracy

An agreement between two or more persons to engage in a criminal act; it requires at least one overt act and is punished as if the parties accomplished the objective of their agreement.

Some courts have moved to limit the felony murder rule. For instance, England abolished the felony murder rule in 1957. It is not universally recognized in the United States.[11]

However, in jurisdictions that still have felony murder laws, defendants can possibly face the death penalty. In *Tison v. Arizona*, the U.S. Supreme Court ruled that defendants may be executed even if they never "intended to kill the victims nor inflicted the fatal wounds" as long as they "had the culpable mental state of reckless indifference to human life."[12] However, the same set of facts in a jurisdiction lacking a felony murder law will only yield a conviction for the underlying felony.

Many states have limited felony murder laws. Limitations may include one or more of the following:

Inchoate

Incomplete.

- The felony that was attempted or committed must be one that is dangerous to life.
- There must be a direct causal connection between the felony and the death that occurred.
- The act that caused the death must have occurred while the felony was in progress.
- The felony must be *mala in se*.
- The act must be a Common Law felony.

MANSLAUGHTER

Manslaughter is a classification of criminal homicide that is less than murder. Manslaughter can either be voluntary or involuntary. The main difference between murder and manslaughter is that often manslaughter is the result of conflict between the defendant and the victim where the victim contributed to the conflict. Manslaughter can also be a catchall type of homicide where mitigating circumstances make the defendant's behavior understandable, but not excusable.

Voluntary manslaughter is where the defendant acted willfully but was somewhat justified in his actions. For instance, a child who kills an abusive parent when he feels no other avenue is open to him would be an example of voluntary manslaughter. Sentences for manslaughter are far less than those for murder.

Manslaughter also comes into play in plea-bargaining arrangements. Defendants may agree to take a manslaughter conviction instead of going to trial and risking a murder conviction.

Murder charges may be reduced to manslaughter charges if the court believes the crime occurred in the **heat of passion** as long as other elements are present. In addition to heat of passion:

- There must be adequate provocation.
- There must have been no opportunity to cool off.
- There must be a causal connection between the provocation, the rage, the anger, and the fatal act.

Adequate provocation is weighed on a case-by-case basis, but there are some absolutes. Words and gestures are insufficient provocation to reduce charges from murder to manslaughter.[13] Generally, a person who kills in response to physical attack or fear for the safety of his family will be charged with manslaughter. A person catching a spouse committing adultery will probably get manslaughter, but that rule does not necessarily apply to unmarried partners.

Often the homicide investigation will explore whether the defendant had time to "cool off" between the provocation and the crime. Generally, if there was time to cool off and the defendant killed anyway, juries will more likely convict for murder than manslaughter.

The killing must be in reaction to the provocation. This deals with both the reason and the time frame of the act. A defendant cannot kill someone for an act that occurred several years ago and argue manslaughter.

Juries must decide heat of passion issues in light of the reasonable person test. How much provocation could a reasonable person withstand without retaliating? The defendant's tolerance threshold is not an issue. If the defendant was less restrained than the jury believes a reasonable person would be, then the verdict will be murder, not manslaughter.

In many manslaughter trials, defendants claim they acted in self-defense. If the jury finds the defendant's actions reasonable in light of the circumstances, the defendant may be acquitted.

Involuntary manslaughter refers to two types of homicides, **criminal negligence manslaughter** and **unlawful act manslaughter.** Criminal negligence manslaughter is the crime of causing the death of a person by negligent or reckless conduct. For instance, the crime of a person who leaves a campfire burning that later burns down a home killing the occupant would be considered criminally negligent manslaughter. Unlawful act

Voluntary Manslaughter

A homicide committed with the intent to kill, but without deliberation, premeditation, or malice.

Heat of Passion

The expression for a mental state on the part of a criminal defendant adequate in law to reduce the crime from murder to manslaughter.

Involuntary Manslaughter

The unintentional killing of a human being by a person engaged in doing some unlawful act not amounting to a felony, or in doing some lawful act in a manner tending to cause death or great bodily injury.

Criminal Negligence Manslaughter

The crime of causing the death of a person by negligent or reckless conduct.

Unlawful Act Manslaughter

Where the defendant committed a crime that resulted in the death of a person.

manslaughter is where the defendant committed a crime that resulted in the death of a person. Many traffic deaths fall into this category, although some states have a special category of homicide entitled **homicide by vehicle.** Homicides by vehicle are not considered to be premeditated, but often the defendant broke one or more traffic ordinances in the process of causing the fatal accident.

Homicide by Vehicle

A form of criminal negligence manslaughter reserved for a person operating a motor vehicle.

Euthanasia

The act of causing death to end pain and distress; also called mercy killing.

EUTHANASIA

An irony of advances in medicine is that many terminally ill people are alive today who would not have been decades ago. As a result, a **euthanasia,** or mercy killing, movement has grown steadily since the 1970s. Advocates of euthanasia claim it gives people the right to end their life on their own terms. They say this gives the individual death with dignity.

Often, however, seriously ill patients are unable to end their own lives. They must be assisted to do so. When someone assists another person to commit suicide, it is sometimes hard to distinguish this act from murder.

The debate rages within the medical community as well. Doctors are pledged to provide care as long as there is any hope of recovery. Even when the patient is terminal, doctors are sworn to make the patient as comfortable as possible. Some have argued that patients who request their doctors provide them with drugs to end their life should have their wish granted under certain conditions. Some states have even passed "doctor-assisted suicide" laws.

HISTORICAL HIGHLIGHT
Oregon's Assisted Suicide Law—Death with Dignity or Murder?

In 1997, Oregon's Death with Dignity Act took effect. It allows doctors to provide a terminally ill patient with the means to end his or her life. Under the law, two Oregon doctors must agree that the patient has less than six months to live, has freely chosen to die, and is able to make critical health decisions. The law only applies to Oregon residents.

The law was enacted through a statewide referendum. Another referendum seeking to repeal the law failed. The U.S. Supreme Court has never addressed the law's constitutionality; however, the Court has upheld bans on assisted suicide in New York and Washington states. More to the point, in each of those cases, the Court ruled that states had the right to decide the issue themselves.

In November 2002, Attorney General John Ashcroft authorized federal drug enforcement agents to revoke the licenses of doctors who assist patients in committing suicide using federally regulated medications under the federal Controlled Substances Act (CSA). Earlier, in April 2002, U.S. District Judge Robert Jones ruled that states' rights to determine what constitutes legitimate medical practices couldn't be overridden by the CSA. The Ninth Circuit Court of Appeals agreed with Oregon, setting up a showdown before the U.S. Supreme

Court. The Court ruled in a 6–3 decision that the Controlled Substances Act did not trump Oregon's right to regulate doctors.[14]

Feelings run strong on both sides of the issue. Pro-life conservatives, who view assisted suicide in light of the abortion issue, fear that assisted suicide laws erode legal safeguards protecting life. Pro-choice activists claim to be protecting the right of the individual to choose the time and manner of his or her own death. They view assisted suicide as a reprieve from months of unwanted suffering. Like the abortion issue, assisted suicide is an issue that will be with us for many years to come. Others see the issue simply as one of states' rights.

How far can doctors and family members go to assist a suicide? The answer obviously varies from state to state. Generally speaking, without assisted suicide laws in place, it is criminal to aid in someone's suicide.

Doctors also confront the problem of how long to leave someone on artificial life support systems. Some patients leave doctors **living wills** that spell out clearly what steps should be taken to revive them and under what circumstances. Living wills should be notarized documents signed freely by an individual of sound mind. Unfortunately, older people are sometimes pressured by family members and doctors to sign documents they might not normally sign. A living will signed under duress is not a valid document.

Living Will
A document in which a person sets forth directions regarding medical treatment to be given if he or she becomes unable to participate in decisions regarding his or her health care.

YOU MAKE THE CALL

MURDER OR MERCY: THE TERRI SCHIAVO CASE

Terri Schiavo was a healthy 26-year-old woman in 1990. But one day she collapsed. By the time doctors stabilized her at the hospital, she had suffered irreversible brain damage. Doctors diagnosed her as being in a "persistent vegetative state." No amount of therapy would resurrect any lost brain function. For nine years, Terri's husband, Michael, and her parents, Bob and Mary Shindler, took care of Terri.

Finally, Michael decided it was time to take Terri off the feeding tube. The legal battles soon began. The Schindlers filed for custody to stop Michael, arguing he was only withdrawing the tube to collect her life insurance. Michael countered that removing the tube was the humane thing to do in the case.

The Schindlers countered with abuse allegations. The courts consistently sided with Michael. The Schiavo controversy hit the national news just before the 2004 presidential election. Many pro-life voters saw the issue as intricately linked with the abortion debate. Stirred by election fever, Congress passed a law specifically crafted to allow the Schindlers another appeal in court. The U.S. Supreme Court refused to hear an appeal, and Terri's feeding tube was removed in early 2005. She died thirteen days later.

The autopsy results fueled both sides of the argument. The medical examiner found no signs of abuse and noted that the brain was completely atrophied. Terri would never have recovered. But they also noted that had she been fed, she could have lived another ten years until infection or other maladies that normally affect the bedridden took their toll.

Some would say Terri Schiavo was murdered; others would say that she was allowed to die. Michael Schiavo acted under court order when he withdrew her feeding tube, but some feel the law should not have allowed it to happen. What do you think?[15]

Infanticide

The murder of a newborn or very young child.

Justifiable Homicides

Those killings committed out of duty with no criminal intent.

Sovereign Immunity

The protection from lawsuits government agencies enjoy.

Military Actions

Actions carried out by members of the armed services under the direction of appropriate civilian authorities.

To my mind to kill in war is not a whit better than to commit ordinary murder.
Albert Einstein

If we believe that murder is wrong and not admissible in our society, then it has to be wrong for everyone, not just individuals but governments as well.
Helen Prejean

INFANTICIDE

Infanticide is the murder of a newborn or very young child. Although some cultures condone or at least tacitly permit infanticide, Anglo-American jurisprudence has traditionally held it to be a crime.

Infanticide is different from abortion in that the child has been born. In fact, the live birth of the child is one element the prosecution must prove in an infanticide case. Many infanticides are accomplished by simply abandoning the baby in an area where it would die from exposure and dehydration. Often when children are found still alive, the charge of reckless endangerment or attempted murder is brought against the mother, if she can be located.

SUICIDE

Western culture has traditionally discouraged suicide. Under English Common Law, suicide was a crime punishable by forfeiture of property to the king. In early America, attempted suicide was a misdemeanor.

Suicide is no longer a crime, but most states interpret suicide attempts as signs of mental illness. Those who survive the attempts are often committed to mental hospitals under civil psychiatric commitment laws in hope of treating the underlying mental illness.

KILLINGS THAT ARE NOT CRIMES

Justifiable homicides are those killings committed out of duty with no criminal intent. When the state executes a person who has been duly convicted, the killing is not a murder. In fact, even if evidence that the person was denied due process comes to light later; the state operates under the color of **sovereign immunity.** Sovereign immunity is a holdover from the English legal system. The king could do no wrong and to a large extent was above the law.

Military actions are not murders. The need for the state to protect itself supersedes criminal law. For the most part, members of the military on active duty operate under the Uniform Code of Military Justice (UCMJ). The UCMJ proscribes appropriate behavior for active duty personnel. The UCMJ must conform to the Constitution. Of course, the military must be subject to the civilian authorities.

Killings done in self-defense are not murders. For a full discussion of self-defense, see Chapter 9, Common Law Defenses.

Finally, executions carried out by lawful authorities are not murder.

PRACTICE POINTERS

The consequences for those convicted of murder or any of the related offenses are so serious that these cases deserve great attention, regardless of what side of the case you are working for. Capital cases in particular have been in the spotlight and will continue to receive media and academic attention. Sloppy handling of these cases can result in grave injustices, destroyed careers, and the potential breakdown of the justice system. Representation of a capital defendant should not be taken lightly. It is an awesome responsibility, whether you are part of the prosecution or the defense.

HISTORICAL HIGHLIGHT
Dr. Death Gets "Life"

Dr. Jack Kevorkian earned the nickname Dr. Death for his role in 130 assisted suicides. Kevorkian was the most outspoken and flamboyant advocate of assisted suicide during the late 1980s and early 1990s. He developed a "death machine" that allowed terminally ill patients or a family member to easily administer a lethal injection.

Kevorkian was charged with murder five times but was acquitted the first four times. He was known for his moving testimony that persuaded jurors not to convict. In each of the first four cases, Kevorkian had merely been present when the patient had committed suicide. But the fifth trial was different.

By now, Kevorkian was no longer licensed to practice medicine. His license had been revoked after he botched a surgical procedure on a recently deceased patient. Kevorkian attempted to remove organs for transplant while performing surgery on a kitchen table. Surgeons noted that the organs were so poorly handled that they were useless for transplants.

In this case, Kevorkian went further than just assisting a patient. He gave Thomas Youk, a man suffering from Lou Gehrig's disease, a lethal injection. To erase any doubt, he videotaped the procedure. Kevorkian gave the tape to the popular television magazine *60 Minutes*, which broadcast it.

The tape was used as evidence at trial. This time the jury convicted Kevorkian of second-degree murder and sentenced him to 10 to 25 years in prison. In September 2000, at age 72, Kevorkian requested to be released on bail while he appealed his conviction. The request was denied. He asked again in 2003, but the request was again rejected. Finally, in late 2006, his request for parole was granted, and he was released on June 1, 2007, on condition he assist no one else in seeking death.

There are resources available today that were not available a few years ago. These include national and state bar associations, and professional associations such as the following:

- National Association of Legal Investigators, *www.nali.com*
- National Legal Aid and Defender Association, *www.nlada.org*
- National District Attorneys' Association, *www.ndaa.org*
- National Association of Attorneys General, *www.naag.org*
- National Association of Criminal Defense Lawyers, *www.criminaljustice.org*
- American Bar Association's Criminal Justice Section, *www.abanet.org/crimjust*
- National Criminal Justice Reference Service, *www.ncjrs.org*

Resources, especially research, at local colleges and universities with criminal justice programs or journalism programs are also available. In addition, many law schools operate law clinics that may be of assistance for research, investigation, and planning for a murder trial.

HISTORICAL HIGHLIGHT
Infanticide in the Suburbs: The Peterson/Grossberg Case

Brian Peterson and Amy Grossberg were high school sweethearts from the affluent New York suburb of Wyckoff, New Jersey. They attended different colleges—he at Gettysburg College in Pennsylvania and she at the University of Delaware—but they continued to see each other.

Amy became pregnant in early 1996. Amy claimed not to know she was pregnant, and even a doctor who treated her in July 1996 noted in his medical records that she did not appear to be pregnant. Nevertheless, in November she delivered a full-term baby boy.

Amy's boyfriend Brian delivered the baby in a Newark, Delaware, motel room. Brian threw the child into a nearby dumpster. The child died from multiple skull fractures and trauma from shaking. Police soon identified the child as belonging to Brian and Amy. Delaware prosecutors at first stated that they would seek the death penalty in the case.

The prosecutors played Brian against Amy. At first, neither would talk about the incident. However, once Brian's attorneys negotiated a manslaughter charge for him, he agreed to testify against Amy. Amy then negotiated a manslaughter plea and was sentenced to two and one-half years. A first-degree murder conviction for either of the two could have carried the death penalty or a life imprisonment sentence. Both were released early for good behavior, after serving half their sentence. Amy went on to counsel pregnant women as part of her parole.[16]

The case raised disturbing questions. First, how could two seemingly affluent, "all-American" kids murder their child? Second, several questions arose concerning fairness:

- Did these two get lighter sentences because they were affluent and could afford top-flight lawyers?
- Amy claimed not to know she had delivered a baby. If that is true, was she forced to plea to a manslaughter charge because her boyfriend lied to avoid a first-degree murder charge?
- Does this case illustrate the way that plea-bargaining skews justice? Does the first one to enter a plea get the better deal? If so, does that encourage the most culpable person to cooperate, resulting in a harsher sentence for others involved?

CHAPTER SUMMARY

Prosecutors in murder cases must prove that a crime was committed or establish a corpus delicti beyond a reasonable doubt. Where investigators cannot produce a body, circumstantial evidence such as evidence of violence, witnesses to a struggle, and various pieces of forensic evidence can be pieced together to provide evidence of a crime.

A person committing first-degree murder must form the intent to kill his victim. The law requires the person to have malice aforethought. The deadly weapon doctrine is used to establish intent to kill. If the defendant uses a deadly weapon to kill a person, it is assumed the requisite intent was present. Transferred intent can occur when the victim is not the one the defendant meant to kill.

Defendants who possess intent to do serious bodily harm are frequently convicted of second-degree murder. Cases involving people who have no intent to cause bodily harm but are reckless in their behavior generally result in manslaughter charges.

The felony murder rule states: "Felony murder is committed when a person, acting alone or in concert with others, commits or attempts to commit one of nine predicate felonies, . . ." and "in the furtherance of such crime or of immediate flight therefrom, he or another participant, if there be any, causes the death of a person other than one of the participants." In jurisdictions that still have felony murder laws, defendants can possibly face the death penalty if they "had the culpable mental state of reckless indifference to human life."

Manslaughter is a classification of criminal homicide that is less than murder. Manslaughter can either be voluntary or involuntary. Voluntary manslaughter is where the defendant acted willfully but was somewhat justified in his actions. Sentences for manslaughter are far less than those for murder.

Murder charges may be reduced to manslaughter charges if the court believes the crime occurred in the heat of passion as long as other elements are present.

Involuntary manslaughter refers to two types of homicides—criminal negligence manslaughter, which is the crime of causing the death of a person by negligent or reckless conduct, and unlawful act manslaughter, which is when the defendant committed a crime that resulted in the death of a person.

Euthanasia is mercy killing. When someone assists another person to commit suicide, it is sometimes hard to distinguish this act from murder. Some states have passed "doctor-assisted suicide" laws.

Infanticide is the murder of a newborn or very young child. Prosecutors must establish that the child was born alive to prosecute an infanticide case. Suicide is no longer a crime but may lead to civil commitment.

Justifiable homicides are those killings committed out of duty with no criminal intent. Executions are killings that are not murders, as are military actions. Killings done in self-defense are not murders.

KEY TERMS

Bot

Conspiracy

Criminal Homicide

Criminal Negligence Manslaughter

Deadly Weapon Doctrine

Euthanasia

Felony Murder Rule

First-degree Murder

Heat of Passion	Involuntary	Transferred Intent
Homicide by Vehicle	Manslaughter	Unlawful Act
Homicide	Justifiable Homicides	Manslaughter
Inchoate	Living Wills	Voluntary Manslaughter
Infanticide	Malice Aforethought	Wergild
Intent to Do Serious	Military Actions	Wite
Bodily Harm	Res Gestae Theory	
Intent to Kill	Sovereign Immunity	

EXERCISES

1. Mary Winkler, a petite young mother of three girls, was stopped on the Gulf Coast in a minivan shortly after church members found her husband's body at the family home in Selmer, Tennessee. Mary had rented a beach condo for her and the girls and was arrested as she left a restaurant with her children.

    Matthew and Mary Winkler had been married for over 10 years, and Matthew was a popular and charismatic preacher. When he was discovered, it was apparent he had been murdered. He had been shot at close range and had a single gunshot wound to the back.

    a. Mary quickly confessed. She has been charged with first-degree murder. How would you go about preparing the case for trial? What possible defenses do you see? How would you approach the case if you were prosecuting it?

    b. Would your approach change if you learned that Mary claimed her husband had abused her, made her watch pornography, and demanded she participate in sexual activities Mary considered "unnatural"?

    c. If you learned that Mary's confession included her statement that as he lay dying Matthew asked "Why" and Mary answered, "I'm sorry" and "I love you," would your approach change?

    d. Would your approach change if you learned that Mary managed the family's finances and had been moving money between accounts to prevent checks from bouncing and that she was short of money because she had been caught up in a so-called Nigerian scam, in which victims are promised a large reward for allowing a bank account to be used by strangers overseas? Of course, there is no reward, and the victim's money is simply drained from the account.

    e. Finally, check your approach against what really happened by researching the matter. Both Findlaw (www.findlaw.com) and Court TV (www.courttv.com) have extensive coverage of the case, including court documents. Then, discuss whether the verdict and sentence seems just and reasonable.

DISCUSSION QUESTIONS

1. In your opinion, when is the killing of a human being justified?
2. Should states outlaw assisted suicide?

3. Research the felony murder rule in your jurisdiction. If it has one, what underlying felonies are included?
4. Should drivers who drive drunk and kill be charged with murder?
5. Under what circumstances should heat of passion be a defense to murder?

FOR FURTHER READING

1. Scottoline, L. (2001). *The Vendetta Defense*. HarperCollins. This legal thriller by a former Philadelphia attorney explores a very delayed vendetta as defense to a murder committed by a senior citizen for wrongs long ago.
2. Berendt, J. (1994). *Midnight in the Garden of Good and Evil*. Random House. Nonfiction account of a Savannah, Georgia, murder trial; later made into a movie starring Kevin Spacey.
3. Capote, T. (1994 ed.). *In Cold Blood*: *A True Account of Multiple Murder and Its Consequences*. Vintage Books. Classic true crime nonfiction, made into an award-winning movie.

ENDNOTES

1. Genesis 4:12.
2. T. J. Gardner, *Criminal Law: Principles and Cases,* 3rd ed. (West Publishing Co., 1985).
3. J. A. Sigler, *An Introduction to the Legal System* (Homewood, IL: Dorsey Press, 1968).
4. J. R. Nash, *Bloodletters and Badmen: A Narrative Encyclopedia of the American Criminals from the Pilgrims to the Present* (New York: M. Evans & Co, 1974).
5. *State v. Neumann,* 262 N.W.2d 426 (1978).
6. *Bradshaw v. Richey,* 546 U.S. 74 (2005).
7. J. Gibeaut, *Troubling Translations: Cultural Defenses Tactic Raises Issues of Fairness,* 85 A.B.A.J. 93.
8. A. Drell, *Witchcraft Murder Defense Fails: Judge Bars Expert Testimony on Defendant's Belief in Victim's Supernatural Powers,* 79 A.B.A.J. 40.
9. *Hopkins v. Reeves*, 525 U.S. 88 (1998).
10. *New York v. Glandman*, 41 N.Y.2d 123 (1976).
11. *Commonwealth v. Matchett*, 436 N.E.2d 400 (1982).
12. *Tison v. Arizona*, 481 U.S. 137 at 147 (1987).
13. *Allen v. United States,* 157 U.S. 675 (1895).
14. *Gonzales v. Oregon,* 546 U.S. 243 (2006).
15. R. Phillips, Autopsy: No sign Schiavo was abused, *http://www.cnn.com/2005/HEALTH/06/15/schiavo.autopsy/index.html.*
16. Baby-slay mom returns to NJ, *Daily News* (New York), May 11, 2000.

CHAPTER 4

Crimes against the Person: Violence

CHAPTER CONTENTS

> *Women have got to make the world safe for men since men have made it
> so darned unsafe for women.*
>
> *Lady Nancy Astor*

CHAPTER OBJECTIVES

After studying this chapter, you should be able to:

- Explain the Common Law concepts of assault and battery.
- Explain the modern criminal law concept of assault and list some common variations of assault.
- Define Common Law rape and explain how modern rape statutes differ from the Common Law definition.
- Understand rape shield laws and the type of evidence they exclude and allow.

- Define domestic violence and describe federal efforts to reduce its occurrence.
- Define hate crime and explain the U.S. Supreme Court's major hate crime decisions.
- Define kidnapping and abduction.
- Explain the tension between the right of parents to raise their children and the right of the state to punish parent behavior it deems to be child abuse.

INTRODUCTION

In this chapter we consider crimes of violence against the person that do not necessarily result in loss of life. As you will see, a great many of these crimes are directed against women and children. Rape, indecent assault, domestic violence, abduction, and child abuse strike women and children with greater frequency than men. Old attitudes die hard, and in the Common Law system, women and children were frequently regarded as nothing more than chattel, or property. Domestic violence and child abuse may be remnants of the old system of laws that gave women little power over their lives and vested responsibility for the family in the male head of household.

Violence against women is a major problem in the United States today. Some estimates set the probability that a woman will be the victim of a violent crime during her lifetime at 75 percent.[1] Other studies suggest that violence is the leading cause of injuries to women ages 15 to 44.[2] Clearly, violent crime strikes women early and often.

That's not to say that men are never victimized. Indeed, there is ample evidence that males are more likely overall to experience violent crimes against the person. According to the Department of Justice, males experienced higher victimization rates than females for *all* types of violent crime except rape and sexual assault.[3]

To put crime into the proper perspective, consider these statistics from the U.S. Department of Justice, Bureau of Justice Statistics, National Crime Victimization Survey 2005.

U.S. residents age 12 or older experienced:

- 23 million crimes
- 77 percent (18.0 million) were property crimes.
- 22 percent (5.2 million) were crimes of violence.

For every 1,000 persons age 12 or older:

- There was one rape or sexual assault.
- There was one assault with injury.
- There were three robberies.

It is but reasonable that, among crimes of different natures, those should be most severely punished which are the most destructive of the public safety and happiness.
Blackstone, *Commentaries on the Laws of England*

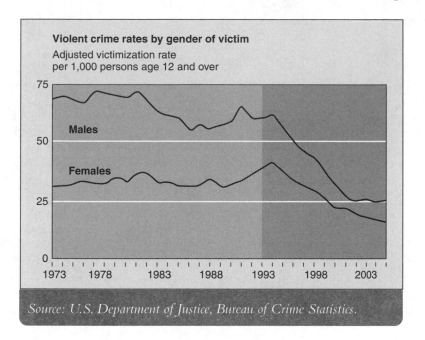

Violent crime rates by gender of victim
Adjusted victimization rate
per 1,000 persons age 12 and over

Males

Females

Source: U.S. Department of Justice, Bureau of Crime Statistics.

RAPE AND OTHER SEX CRIMES

Rape was traditionally defined as forced sexual intercourse with a woman, not one's wife. Rape was a serious Common Law offense, often punished harshly if the victim were high-born. Remedies included payment of wergild (see Chapter 3) to the family of the victim, presumably because the victim's value on the marriage market was decreased by the loss of her virtue.

Today, every state has amended its rape laws to reflect that both males and females can be victims of rape. Most have also amended the law to allow at least limited claims of marital rape. For example, a woman in Virginia, one of 32 states to exempt spouses from rape prosecution, could only have her husband charged with rape if the two were not living together or if she was physically harmed. However, in 2002, the Virginia legislature changed the law to allow prosecution for rape regardless of whether the couple was cohabitating or the victim suffered physical harm.[4]

Rape usually tops the sex crime hierarchy in each state's crime code. Other sex crimes include sexual assault short of rape (cases in which there is no penetration), **indecent assault or indecent touching** (in which there is groping or other offensive touching, but no sexual act is performed or attempted), **incest** (sexual activity between relatives within a prescribed degree of sanguinity or affinity), **statutory rape** (rape of a victim below the age of consent or otherwise defined by the statute as incapable of consenting due to physical or mental incapacity), and offenses such as public exposure. Because each state has a different set of sexual offenses on its books, practitioners must review the offenses in their jurisdiction. The elements the prosecution must prove vary greatly from state to state, as do the specific definitions of sexual acts covered.

Most rape statutes require prosecutors to prove three elements:

- Proof that a sex act took place, as defined in the particular statute. Generally, the sex act that constitutes rape is vaginal intercourse, but it can also include anal

Rape
Traditionally defined as forced sexual intercourse with a woman, not one's wife. Modern rape definitions don't distinguish between male or female victims and have expanded the types of sexual contact that are included in the definition. Most states also allow at least a limited right to bring rape charges against a spouse and no longer require the use of direct force or physical harm.

Indecent Assault or Indecent Touching
An attack on a person in which there is groping or other offensive touching, but no sexual act is performed or attempted.

Incest
Sexual activity between relatives within a prescribed degree of sanguinity or affinity.

YOU MAKE THE CALL

INCEST OR LOVE?

Woody Allen and Mia Farrow, both well-known Hollywood movie stars, had a long-term romantic relationship from 1980 to 1992. They had one biological child together and adopted two other children while together. They never lived in the same household or married, but Allen had a close relationship with their children and several other children from Ms. Farrow's previous relationships.

One of those children was South Korean-born Soon-Yi Previn.

In 1992, Farrow discovered that Allen was having a relationship with 21-year old Soon-Yi.

Both Allen and Previn denied that Allen was—technically at least—her step-father. Had he been, (that is, had Farrow and Allen been legally married), the relationship would have been illegal in many states since incest is based on legal affinity. No criminal charges were ever brought, and Previn married Allen in 1997.[5]

You make the call. Should the relationship between Allen and Previn be classified as an incestuous one?

Statutory Rape

Sexual intercourse with a victim below the age of consent or unable to consent due to a physical or mental impairment. The crime is commonly referred to as statutory rape because it is the statute that defines what may otherwise seem to be a consensual act as a crime. The legislative presumption is that some persons cannot give meaningful consent.

intercourse for both male and female victims as well as oral sex acts. Many state statutes require proof that there was penetration of the vagina or anus by the defendant's penis. Ejaculation is not required to prove rape.

- Proof that the charged sex act took place by force or threat of force. Most modern rape statutes don't require that there be physical evidence of force. The victim's testimony that he or she was forced or was afraid is enough. The victim need not risk physical harm by fighting back.
- Proof that the sex act performed by force or threat of force was without consent or under circumstances that made consent either invalid (as in statutory rape) or impossible to get (as when the victim is too intoxicated to validly consent or is incapacitated in some way that impairs the victim's ability to freely consent).

THE ROLE OF PHYSICAL EVIDENCE IN RAPE CASES

Physical evidence plays a major role in rape cases. In particular, the presence of semen and saliva can be powerful evidence that, at the very least, sexual activity took place. With the advances made in DNA analysis, identifying whose semen or saliva is present on the victim has become a routine matter. Experts can now state with virtual certainty what individual left biological material at the scene or on the victim. For more on the use of DNA evidence, see Chapter 11.

In a sexual assault case, it's crucial that evidence be promptly gathered and preserved. Unfortunately, far too few rape victims report the crime immediately. Many feel angry and upset or are in a state of shock after the attack. However, prompt reporting and immediate medical attention are vital to a successful prosecution. Today, most police departments have available specially trained counselors who can work with rape victims and help gather the necessary evidence as soon as possible. Special rape kits are generally used to gather evidence and assure that the appropriate chain of custody for the evidence is followed. Most local governments also have a victim assistance program to help victims through the many stages of a criminal prosecution.

Of course, there are also cases in which the victim is unaware that an assault has occurred. For example, children may delay reporting a sexual assault or attempted assault for months or even years. Victims who have been incapacitated before the attack may not recall exactly what happened or even that they were attacked. Such cases are more difficult to prosecute than other cases, but certainly not impossible.

DEFENSE TO RAPE

The most common defense to a rape charge is that the victim consented to sexual activity. Consent is a valid defense in most rape cases, but not against statutory rape charges. Defendants are charged with statutory rape when the victim was incapable of consenting because of age or because consent was obtained through trickery or coercion.

In a rape case, the prosecution must prove as an essential element of the crime that a sexual act took place and that the victim did not consent. Sexual activity and lack of consent can be proven directly by the victim's testimony and indirectly through evidence such as bruises, medical damage, ripped clothing, and other signs of a struggle or that physical force had been used. The defense may question the victim about the physical aspects of the attack and ask her if she consented.

Once the prosecution has rested its case, the defense may again raise consent by having the defendant testify. He can also present circumstantial evidence to bolster his claim, such as evidence that the victim freely entered his apartment or bedroom or that the two had sexual relations in the past. This tactic is very likely when the victim and the defendant have known each other for a time.

If the rape case involves a stranger and there was no biological evidence obtained from the victim (as could happen if there is a delay in reporting the crime, or the assailant used a condom, or the act was not completed, or the victim showered before reporting the crime), a common tactic is to claim the victim has misidentified her assailant. This defense typically involves casting doubt on the victim's state of mind and ability to make a positive identification. Given the trauma associated with an attack and that most attacks aren't witnessed, a claim of mistaken identity can be an effective defense.

YOU MAKE THE CALL

KOBE BRYANT: MINING THE VICTIM'S PAST

Basketball star Kobe Bryant visited Vail, Colorado, on June 30, 2003, in preparation for knee surgery. After checking in, Bryant met a 19-year-old college student who worked at the hotel. What happened next is a matter of conjecture, but evidence shows the two had sex. She claimed Bryant raped her and reported the assault to the police. Bryant was later charged with sexual assault and bound over for trial. In a television appearance, Kobe tearfully admitted to adultery, but not rape.

At a pretrial hearing, Bryant's lawyer, Pamela Mackey, mentioned the accuser's name, thus putting it in the court record. After being warned by the judge, she mentioned it five more times.[6] In fact, concealing the alleged victim's identity was a problem in the run-up to the trial. Several Web sites published the woman's name, picture, and address. A Los Angeles disk jockey broadcast her name, and one Web site offered her likeness on a T-shirt with the caption "lying bitch" under it.

Bryant's legal team sought to have the woman's mental health and sexual history brought in as evidence.[7] Ultimately, both sides worked out a deal.

Bryant made a statement in court that he may have not understood the young woman was saying no. The Eagle County district attorney dropped the charges. Bryant later paid his accuser an undisclosed sum.

If you had been the judge in the case and the case had gone to trial, would you have let the defense bring in the accuser's mental health history? Victim advocates say doing so puts the accuser on trial and virtually strips anyone with a mental health history of legal protection against rape. The defense argued revealing her mental health history would help the jury decide on her credibility. You make the call.

For a look at some of the court documents in the case, visit Findlaw's document archive at *http://news.findlaw.com/legalnews/documents/archive_b.html*.

RAPE SHIELD LAWS

Before rape shield laws were enacted, defendants frequently attempted to show their victims were less than chaste by presenting evidence the victims were sexually experienced. The tactic effectively discouraged many victims from coming forward. As a result, many rapes went unreported or unprosecuted.

Rape Shield Law
Codified rule of evidence that provides for the exclusion of a rape victim's sexual history unless it is directly relevant to his or her consent or other evidence in the case.

In response to pressure for fair treatment in sexual assault cases, states began passing rape shield laws. **Rape shield laws** are codified rules of evidence that exclude a rape victim's sexual history unless it is directly relevant to evidence in the case. The laws are based on the premise that evidence of past sexual conduct with others simply aren't relevant to the question of whether the victim consented to sex with the defendant in this case.

A typical rape shield law from Virginia provides that:

> evidence of the complaining witness's unchaste character or prior sexual conduct shall not be admitted. Unless the complaining witness voluntarily agrees otherwise, evidence of specific instances of his or her prior sexual conduct shall be admitted only if it is relevant and is . . . [e]vidence offered to provide an alternative explanation for physical evidence of the offense charged which is introduced by the prosecution, limited to evidence designed to explain the presence of semen, pregnancy, disease, or physical injury to the complaining witness's intimate parts.[8]

Evidence that the victim discussed wishing to have a sexual relationship with the defendant before the alleged rape, even if that evidence reveals prior sex acts with others, may also be admissible. In general, rape shield laws only exclude evidence of unchaste character. A prostitute's sexual history would be excluded in most cases, although evidence that she had sex for money with the defendant before may be admitted to show that she consented this time also.

HISTORICAL HIGHLIGHT
I Love My Calendar Girl . . . A Tale of Date Rape

What if a rapist could pick his victim, sedate her secretly, violate her sexually, and walk away knowing she would not remember a thing? Far from being the fantasy of a sociopath, the scenario plays out every day, especially on college campuses. A woman whose new acquaintance hands her a drink may very well wake hours later, not realizing she has been raped, thanks to a drug known chemically as flunitrazapam and by the brand name Rohypnol. The drug is manufactured by Hoffman-LaRoche as a sleeping aid for insomnia and to quiet psychotic patients but hasn't been approved in the United States. The drug reduces inhibitions and more. Those who take it have no memory of what happens while they are under its influence. The drug is popularly known as the date rape drug and can be combined with other drugs common on the college scene such as GHB, or gamma hydroxybutyrate, another unapproved drug. Both drugs are colorless and odorless when slipped into a drink, although they may have a salty flavor.[9]

According to court testimony, Jeffrey Marsalis of Philadelphia knew a thing or two about date rape drugs. He was a paramedic who had access to syringes and various drugs on his job. Marsalis allegedly sought out victims through the online dating service Match.com.[10] Each of the seven women Marsalis dated complained of "blacking out" or feeling "foggy" during their time with him. Experts testified in court that the women behaved as if they had consumed five times the amount of alcohol they claim to have while with Marsalis.

A search of Marsalis' apartment revealed a syringe filled with diphenhydramine HCI, an ingredient found in many over-the-counter cold remedies. But the liquid form, when mixed with alcohol acts as a potent central nervous system depressant. In effect, date rape on the cheap.

Marsalis kept a file he called "the yearly calendar of women" on his laptop computer for the years 2003, 2004, and 2005. The names of the seven women who accused him of rape appear in the calendar in the months the rapes allegedly occurred. Marsalis' attorneys maintain the drugs and syringes are just part of his job, and the calendar merely indicated his dates from Match.com. He was convicted on two accounts of rape and one of unlawful imprisonment and sentenced to the maximum sentence, 10 to 20 years in state prison.

Some evidence can still be admitted. Evidence that the victim had consensual sex with the defendant before is admissible if the court finds it relevant to the question of whether the victim consented this time. Evidence that the victim had sex with someone else in the hours or days preceding the alleged rape, if there is physical evidence of sexual activity (such as evidence of injury, but no biological evidence tying the victim to the defendant), is also admissible. In that case, prior sexual contact that could have caused the injury is relevant to showing that it was someone else other than the defendant who did the damage.

HISTORICAL HIGHLIGHT
Rape Shield Law Can't Exclude Victim's Sexually Explicit E-mail Addressed to Alleged Assailant

It began with a dinner date in November 1996. Oliver Jovanovic was a Columbia University doctoral student close to completing a Ph.D. in molecular biology when he arranged a dinner date with a Barnard College coed he had met in an Internet chat room. The two had exchanged a series of steamy e-mail messages where the coed identified herself as a submissive partner dating a sadomasochist.

After dinner the two went to Jovanovic's apartment. What happened next is unclear. The Barnard student claimed that Jovanovic tied her up, bit her, molested her with a baton, dripped hot wax on her, and held her captive for 20 hours, all against her will. Jovanovic claimed the activities were consensual.[11] At the ensuing trial, the defense sought to introduce the e-mail messages from the alleged victim and to question her about any prior sadomasochistic sexual activity. The trial judge ruled the evidence inadmissible under New York State's rape shield laws, and a jury convicted him. He was sentenced to at least 15 years.[12]

Jovanovic appealed and the conviction was overturned. The appeals court ruled that New York's Rape Shield Law wasn't meant to exclude evidence of the victim's interest in sadomasochistic sexual activity when her consent to such activity was at the heart of the case. The e-mail can be used to show the victim's state of mind about consent as well as the defendant's reasonable belief about the victim's intentions. The case was scheduled for a second trial in November 2001, but was dismissed when the victim declined to testify a second time.[13]

CHILD ABUSE AND NEGLECT

Parens Patriae

Common Law rule that requires that the Crown protect those most vulnerable in society when they cannot protect themselves.

When children are concerned, government plays an important role. Since Elizabethan days, government (whether king or state or federal jurisdiction) has served in the role of *parens patriae*. That role has required government to protect the interests of those who cannot protect themselves. As early as 1890, the U.S. Supreme Court held that the *parens patriae* theory was inherent in the power of the state to regulate the treatment of children.[14] In addition, states have rights under their general police powers to regulate the treatment of children within their jurisdictions.

On the other end of the spectrum are parents' rights to regulate family life in accordance with their personal, religious, and ethical belief systems. These constitutionally derived rights sometimes conflict with the government's *parens patriae* and police powers. For example, the state may intervene when a religious belief may harm children. Parents cannot in most cases deny lifesaving treatment to their children on the basis of religious belief in the power of prayer to heal without risking criminal child endangerment charges. Likewise, harsh punishments meted out on the religious theory that sparing the rod spoils the child may result in criminal charges of assault. Should death result, the parent may be charged with manslaughter or murder.

HISTORICAL HIGHLIGHT
AMBER Alert System Helps Recover Abducted Children

The first few hours following a child's abduction are crucial for the safe return of the child. The more time that passes, the less likely the child will return home safely. According to the Department of Justice, 74 percent of children who are kidnapped and later found murdered are killed within three hours of being abducted.[15] The AMBER (America's Missing Broadcast Emergency Response) Alert system was created to shorten response time in child abductions.

According to the national AMBER Alert Web site at *http://www.amberalert.gov*, as of June 2007, the AMBER Alert system has helped rescue more than 324 children nationwide. The AMBER Alert system began in 1996 in Texas and is named for Amber Hagerman, a young child who was abducted while riding her bike and brutally murdered. Since then, AMBER Alert has evolved into a program that includes news flashes and broadcasting information along electronic signs on the nation's highways. In 2002, the system went national, with many states coordinating their systems. In addition, AMBER Alerts are now available online and via pagers, cell phones, and other wireless devices.

CORPORAL PUNISHMENT AND CHILD ABUSE

Corporal punishment is another area where criminal law and parental authority conflict. Were an adult to slap another adult across the face, there would be no doubt that the act could be prosecuted as an assault. But if the same adult slaps his child, that may be seen as appropriate punishment in some jurisdictions, but as **child abuse** in another. Most state criminal assault statutes provide a defense for acts of reasonable corporal punishment. For example, Pennsylvania provides that the use of force on another person is justifiable if:

> The actor is the parent or guardian or other person similarly responsible for the general care and supervision of a minor or a person acting at the request of such parent, guardian, or other responsible person and:
>
> 1. The force is used for the purpose of safeguarding or promoting the welfare of the minor, including the prevention or punishment of his misconduct; and
> 2. The force used is not designed to cause or known to create a substantial risk of causing death, serious bodily injury, disfigurement, extreme pain or mental distress or gross degradation.[16]

Slapping a child on the rear as you stop him from running into the street is probably allowable under this statute, while slapping the child until he bruises probably is not. But the reality is that with corporal punishment as a defense, few children on whom the rod is not spared will find their parents prosecuted. The defense allows for a considerable amount of leeway for parents.

Child Abuse
Child abuse is the label given to crimes that are either committed against minors or crimes created to protect children who cannot act in their own best interest. Examples include statutory rape, incest, and child medical neglect.

HISTORICAL HIGHLIGHT
Child Wins Lawsuit Against Spanking Guardian

In countries bound by the rules of the European Union, parents who want to spank their children may find the wrath of the high court come down on them instead. The EU Treaty contains protections for children and encourages member states to ban corporal punishment for children. Sixteen EU nations have banned the practice.

One of the the last holdouts was the United Kingdom, which had an exception similar to the one common in the United States that allowed parents or guardians to use reasonable corporal punishment. The United Kingdom was forced to conform its laws to those of the rest of the members of the European Union when the European Court of Human Rights awarded £10,000 in damages and £20,000 in legal fees to a 14-year-old boy who claimed that a beating from his stepfather contravened the European convention on human rights. The court ruled in 1998 that "no one shall be subjected to torture or to inhuman or degrading treatment or punishment" and found that the corporal punishment meted out by the stepfather violated that rule. The United Kingdom's highest court had already ruled that the punishment given the boy did not violate English law.[17] The United Kingdom recently enacted a ban on spanking to comply with the European Union rules.

Child Molestation or Child Sexual Abuse

the engaging of a child in sexual activities that the child cannot comprehend, for which the child is developmentally unprepared and cannot give informed consent, and/or that violate the social and legal taboos of society. The sexual activity may include all forms of oral genital, genital, or anal contact by or to the child, or non-touching abuses, such as exhibitionism, voyeurism, or using the child in the production of pornography.

CHILD MOLESTATION

Child molestation or **child sexual abuse** is defined very broadly as "the engaging of a child in sexual activities that the child cannot comprehend, for which the child is developmentally unprepared and cannot give informed consent, and/or that violate the social and legal taboos of society. The sexual activity may include all forms of oral genital, genital, or anal contact by or to the child, or non-touching abuses, such as exhibitionism, voyeurism, or using the child in the production of pornography."[18]

Generally, if the parent or guardian's conduct goes beyond the corporal punishment defense, he or she can be charged with assault. Of course, a stranger committing the same act as a parent or guardian may be privileged to commit cannot use the defense. Many states apply ordinary criminal prohibitions against physical harm done to children and provide for a greater sentence when the victim is a child.

OTHER DEFENSES

Because child abuse and neglect laws must balance the state's interest in protecting children and parents' rights to raise their offspring as they see fit, child abuse laws are often written in a way that opens them to varying interpretations. As a result, those charged under the statutes can sometimes successfully claim that the law is so vague as to be unconstitutional.

HISTORICAL HIGHLIGHT
Child's Abduction and Murder Gives Birth to America's Most Wanted Television Program

On July 27, 1981, 6-year-old Adam Walsh was abducted and murdered. His head was found floating in a Florida river, but his body was never found. During the frantic search for Adam, his father, John Walsh, discovered there was little coordination between police departments when a child is reported missing and no centralized agency to coordinate the search. As the result of his lobbying, Congress passed the Missing Children Act of 1982 and the Missing Children's Assistance Act of 1984. Those laws led to the creation of the National Center for Missing and Exploited Children. The center maintains a toll-free line to report missing children or the sighting of one. John Walsh also went on to host the television show *America's Most Wanted*, which introduces the nation to unsolved crimes and serves as a clearinghouse for tips. Leads garnered through the program have resulted in the capture of over 943 suspects as of June 2007.

The U.S. Supreme Court has ruled on a number of occasions that a criminal law must "define the criminal offense with sufficient definiteness that ordinary people can understand what it prohibits and in a manner that does not encourage arbitrary and discriminatory enforcement."[19] The challenge can be that the statute overall is so vague or overbroad that it has no validity in any case. Defense counsel can also allege that as applied to the conduct a particular defendant is charged with, the statute is arbitrary and vague.

Sexual abuse's medical definition encompasses a long list of potential criminal charges, including rape, indecent assault, statutory rape, incest, and sexual assault. Although medically it is all sexual abuse, criminally, each act is a separate and distinct offense. For example, in Wisconsin a defendant commits a first-degree sexual assault when the defendant has had "sexual contact or sexual intercourse with a person who had not attained the age of 13 years," while she commits a second-degree sexual assault if the contact is with a person who is younger than 16 years.[20] In Pennsylvania, "a person commits a felony of the second degree when that person engages in sexual intercourse with a complainant under the age of 16 years and that person is four or more years older than the complainant and the complainant and the person are not married to each other."[21]

Depending on the jurisdiction, the fact that the defendant believed a consenting sex partner was over the age of consent in the jurisdiction may or may not be a defense. For example, Pennsylvania law proclaims it is not a defense that the defendant thought the victim was older than 14, when the child was 13. However, it is a defense that the defendant thought the child was older than 14, if in fact he or she was between the age of 14 and 16.[22] The defendant would have to prove to the court by a preponderance of the evidence that he reasonably thought the victim was older than 14.

Although most child sexual abuse cases are prosecuted on the state level, there are several federal statutes that may impact a particular case and lead to a federal rather than state prosecution. For example, it is a federal offense to cross state lines with the intent to engage in a sexual act with a child under 12 or to transport a child across state lines in order to engage in criminal sexual activity with that child.[23]

CHILD PORN PRODUCTION

For decades, pornography sat on the front lines of the culture wars. Government's attempts to regulate pornography often led to litigation filed by free speech advocates concerned that government restrictions were censoring art and strangling free expression. The problem lay in the definition of pornography. At one time, Justice Byron White is said to have remarked that he "knew it when he saw it." But that standard was hardly helpful to lower courts when they ruled on specific cases.

The matter was largely settled when the U.S. Supreme Court handed down its ruling in *Miller v. California.* The court gave three criteria to identify pornography that have come to be known as the *Miller* test.

1. Whether the average person, applying "contemporary community standards" would find that the work, taken as a whole, appeals to prurient interest.
2. Whether the work displays or describes, in a patently offensive way, sexual contact specifically defined by a state statute.
3. Whether the work, again taken as a whole, lacks serious literary, artistic, political, or scientific value.[24]

The *Miller* Test raises many questions but clarifies some aspects of the debate. First, obscenity can only involve sexual activity. Violence absent sexual content cannot be legally obscene. The law does not define "community" or "community standards."

At the time *Miller* was decided in 1973, child pornography was relatively virtually legislated out of existence. But the birth of the Internet allowed pornographic images to move around the world freely. With the burgeoning online market for pornography, many suppliers got into the act. Most operate overseas where U.S. laws cannot touch them.

The *Miller* test is irrelevant to child pornography. All states have enacted laws against producing, possessing, or distributing child pornography. Child pornography has been defined in the *United States v. Dost* where the U.S. Supreme Court said child pornography is a "visual depiction . . . of explicit sexual conduct" through "lascivious exhibition of the genitals or pubic area" where the:

- focal point of the visual depiction is on the child's genitalia or pubic area;
- setting of the visual depiction is sexually suggestive (i.e., in a place or pose generally associated with sexual activity);
- child is depicted in an unnatural pose, or in inappropriate attire, considering the age of the child;
- child is partially clothed or nude;
- visual depiction suggests sexual coyness or a willingness to engage in sexual activity; or
- visual depiction is intended or designed to elicit a sexual response in the viewer.[25]

The difference between adult and child pornography goes to the issue of consent. Children simply lack the legal capacity to consent to sexual acts, simulated sexual acts, or sexual exposure. Courts have consistently recognized the state's interest in protecting children by aggressively attacking both the supply and demand for child pornography.

ASSAULT

Assault is an act of force or threat of force intended to inflict harm upon a person or to put the person in fear that harm is imminent. Rape and the related offenses discussed earlier are specific forms of assault. At Common Law, assault did not involve the infliction of physical force. Rather, it was an act by the perpetrator that placed the victim in fear that bodily harm was imminent. Battery was the actual physical harm. Today, most crime codes combine the two into the crime of assault. States often create categories of assault, grading the crime in accordance with its seriousness. For example, possible criminal charges stemming from a bar brawl could include simple assault, aggravated assault, assault with a deadly weapon (if one is used), or assault with intent to kill, depending on the seriousness of the harm inflicted.

Other modern offenses more akin to the Common Law concept of assault as an act placing the victim in fear of imminent harm include ethnic intimidation, terroristic threats, harassment, stalking, and bomb threats. Each has its own set of unique elements that the prosecution must prove beyond a reasonable doubt. For example, in Pennsylvania the Commonwealth must prove that someone it charges with stalking engaged in "a course of conduct or repeatedly commits acts toward another person, including following the person without proper authority, under circumstances which demonstrate . . . an intent to place the person in reasonable fear of bodily injury or an intent to cause substantial emotional distress to the person."[26] Always check the law in your jurisdiction for guidance on the specific elements that must be proven in a particular case.

Some states have enacted statutes that create a special class of assault for the unauthorized administration of an intoxicant. These are generally meant to punish drugging a victim, particularly when the intent is to get the victim in a vulnerable position in order to do him or her harm. For example, in Pennsylvania it is a third-degree felony to "substantially impair [the victim's] power to appraise or control his or her conduct by administering, without the knowledge of the complainant, drugs or other intoxicants," when the defendant does so in order to facilitate a sexual assault. The law is meant to punish those who slip their victims drugs such as Rohypnol and other date rape drugs. Doing so can result in the imposition of an additional 10-year sentence on top of the sentence for the underlying sexual assault.[27]

Assault
An act of force or threat of force intended to inflict harm upon a person or to put the person in fear that such harm is imminent.

ESSENTIAL ELEMENTS OF ASSAULT

As you have seen in the previous discussion, each type of assault has its own specific proof requirements. It is impossible to provide a general list of elements of assault that would cover the wide variety of crimes that fall under the umbrella of assault. However, the following example of a state assault statute serves as a starting point for analyzing the essential elements of assault:

The defendant commits assault if he or she:

- attempts to cause or knowingly, recklessly, or intentionally causes bodily injury to another; or
- negligently causes bodily injury to another with a deadly weapon; or
- attempts by physical menace to place another in fear of imminent serious bodily injury.[28]

The statute defines bodily injury as "impairment of physical condition or substantial pain" and serious bodily injury as "bodily injury which creates a substantial risk of death or which causes serious, permanent disfigurement, or protracted loss or impairment of the function of any bodily member or organ." Deadly weapon is defined as "any firearm, whether loaded or unloaded, or any device designed as a weapon and capable of producing death or serious bodily injury, or any other device or instrumentality which, in the manner in which it is used or intended to be used, is calculated or likely to produce death or serious bodily injury."[29]

As you can see, the preceding simple assault statute allows room for charging a defendant with assault for a number of acts, including injuring someone in an automobile accident, leaving a gun unlocked and unattended leading to an injury, or threatening people in such a way that they fear for their life. Depending on which subsection the defendant is charged with, the prosecution must prove there was bodily injury or serious bodily injury as that term is defined in the statute. Because so many acts can constitute assault and there are so many definitions to consider, proving assault can be challenging. Many prosecutors use a simple checklist during the presentation to make sure each element has been proven.

Generally, aggravated assault can be charged if the state can prove that the defendant attempted to cause or caused serious bodily injury to the victim under circumstances manifesting extreme indifference to the value of human life. In some jurisdictions, simple assault is charged as aggravated assault if the victim belongs to a class of specially protected persons such as police, firefighting personnel, teachers, and public officials.[30] Simple assault is often graded as a misdemeanor, while aggravated assault is generally graded as a felony of the first or second degree.

DOMESTIC VIOLENCE

Domestic Violence

Assault, battery, aggravated assault, harassment, stalking, and other crimes involving physical or mental injury to a victim when perpetrated by the victim's partner.

Domestic violence in this country is overwhelmingly directed at women by men. According to the Department of Justice, 85 percent of all domestic violence incidents involve men directing violence at women.[31] The death toll is high. In 2000, 33 percent of all female murder victims in the United States were killed by their husbands or boyfriends.[32] For the 20-year period from 1976 to 1996, the total toll of women murdered by their husbands or boyfriends stood at over 31,000 women.[33]

Most states do not make domestic violence a specific crime. Rather, battery, assault, aggravated assault, harassment, stalking, and other crimes involving physical or mental injury to a victim when perpetrated by the victim's partner are characterized as domestic violence. The best way to look at domestic violence may be to view it as a syndrome, consisting of a series of criminal acts perpetrated against a spouse or paramour rather than as a specific crime.

Until recently, enforcement of criminal laws when the victim was the perpetrator's partner was spotty. Many in law enforcement viewed cases of domestic violence as nuisance cases, and sometimes even refused to respond to calls or arrest the perpetrator. In cases where law enforcement did respond, often the matter was dropped when the victim refused to press charges or to cooperate with police. It has only been in the last few decades that the psychological forces at play in domestic violence have begun to be understood. A victim with no or few economic resources, no place to go, and fear of the perpetrator often saw no way out but to reconcile and drop the charges.

With the advent of more shelters for victims and their families, the availability of educational and job opportunities, and the increasing recognition that acts of violence, no matter who the victim is, should be punished, more victims are cooperating with law enforcement. As a result, today there are far more successful prosecutions than in decades past.

HISTORICAL HIGHLIGHT
*Victims of Domestic Violence Win Right
to New Identity*

One of the most pressing concerns victims of domestic violence may have when leaving their abusers is that the abuser will simply follow them. Moving to another address, finding a new job, and starting a new life are difficult for anyone, especially someone fleeing physical danger. Disappearing isn't easy, especially in a time when access to public and private databases has become relatively available and inexpensive.

Consider how easy it would be to track a victim's whereabouts with just one piece of information—the victim's Social Security number. If the victim was married to her abuser, he certainly had access to her Social Security number since it appears on their joint tax return. Social Security numbers, because they are unique to each holder, are commonly used on credit reports and on medical, insurance, and school records. Today, anyone who can provide basic information such as a Social Security number and a credit card account number can get a credit report online in minutes. That credit report contains current addresses, phone numbers, and name of employer. Although it is a violation of federal law to access credit information for someone else without that person's permission, that's unlikely to stop an abuser who is intent on locating the victim.

To help domestic abuse victims establish new identities and avoid being tracked, the Social Security Administration now will issue new Social Security numbers to victims of domestic abuse and harassment. The policy went into effect in 1998 and allows victims to start new lives in relative anonymity. The Social Security Administration will cross-reference the numbers on earnings records to assure that victims later receive the retirement or disability payments to which they are entitled.

FEDERAL EFFORTS TO COMBAT DOMESTIC VIOLENCE

Recent years have seen an increase in federal involvement in domestic violence issues. Because it saw domestic violence as a problem affecting not just families and communities but the economy as a whole, Congress passed the **Violence Against Women Act (VAWA)** in 1994 and declared "all persons within the United States shall have the right to be free from crimes of violence motivated by gender."[34]

VAWA was enacted under the authority of the Commerce Clause of the U.S. Constitution and sought to end the cycle of violence and draw more women into the workplace and economy by strengthening state efforts to control domestic violence and by enacting federal crimes related to domestic violence.

Violence Against Women Act (VAWA)

The Violence Against Women Act, a federal law criminalizing interstate acts of domestic violence and funding research and education programs.

One provision that received widespread attention was Section 13981(c), which declared that:

> A person (including a person who acts under color of any statute, ordinance, regulation, custom, or usage of any State) who commits a crime of violence motivated by gender and thus deprives another of the right declared in subsection (b) of this section [to be free of crimes of violence motivated by gender] shall be liable to the party injured, in an action for the recovery of compensatory and punitive damages, injunctive and declaratory relief, and such other relief as a court may deem appropriate.

Essentially, VAWA gave victims of domestic or sexual violence a federal private right of action against the assailant for damages. The first test of the statute came when a student at Virginia Tech claimed she had been forcibly raped by two varsity football team members. She was unsatisfied with the administrative punishments meted out by the university and sued the university and the students in federal court for damages, as provided for in VAWA. The defendants raised the Constitution as a bar to the lawsuit, claiming that Congress exceeded its authority under the Commerce Clause when it enacted the law. The U.S. Supreme Court heard the case, *United States v. Morrison*, and concluded Congress didn't have the authority to "regulate non-economic, violent criminal conduct based solely on that conduct's aggregate effect on interstate commerce."[35]

The U.S. Supreme Court decision has wider implications for Congressional efforts to enact civil and criminal penalties for crimes that occur within state boundaries and most likely will mean Congress will not set up a parallel federal criminal and tort law system.

In response to the *Morrison* decision, VAWA was amended in 2000. Rather than relying on the economic impact domestic and sexual violence had on women, Congress focused on providing criminal penalties that punish behavior that crosses state lines, a traditional authority used to enact federal criminal laws. The major criminal provisions that survived in the original VAWA and were added in VAWA II are:

- *18 U.S.C. § 2261 (a): Interstate Domestic Violence:* Makes it a federal crime for anyone to cross a state line with the intent to injure, harass, or intimidate an intimate partner if, in the course of or as a result of such travel, the perpetrator intentionally commits a violent crime that causes bodily harm to his or her partner.
- *18 U.S.C. § 2261 (a) (2): Coercing Across State Lines:* Makes it a federal crime to cause an intimate partner to cross a state line by force, coercion, duress, or fraud and, in the course or as a result of that conduct, intentionally committing a crime of violence and thereby causes bodily injury to the intimate partner.
- *18 U.S.C. § 2262 (a) (1) and (2): Interstate Violation of a Protective Order:* Makes it a federal crime for anyone to cross a state line or force an intimate partner to cross a state line with the intent to engage in conduct that violates a state protection from abuse order already in place.
- *18 U.S.C. § 2261A: Interstate Stalking:* Makes it a federal crime to cross a state line intending to injure or harass another person and then placing that person in reasonable fear of death or serious bodily injury or reasonable fear of death or serious bodily injury to his or her immediate family.

- *18 U.S.C. § 922 (g) (1), (8), and (9): Possession of Firearm:* Makes it a federal crime for anyone who is subject to a state protection from abuse order, or has been convicted of a misdemeanor crime of domestic violence, or who has been convicted of a crime punishable by a year or more in prison to possess, transport, or receive a firearm or ammunition that has been in interstate or foreign commerce.

HATE CRIMES

In recent years there has been an increase in the number of state and local governments that have enacted what are popularly known as **hate crimes.** The U.S. Department of Justice defines hate or bias-motivated crimes as "offenses motivated by hatred against a victim based on his or her race, religion, sexual orientation, handicap, ethnicity or national origin."[36]

Hate Crimes
Offenses motivated by hatred against a victim based on his or her race, religion, sexual orientation, handicap, ethnicity, or national origin.

Generally, hate crimes consist of enhanced punishment for crimes that are motivated by hate or bias against a group, ethnicity, or religion. The Department of Justice, in accordance with a federal law requiring collecting data nationwide on the prevalence of hate crimes, conducted a pilot study of hate crimes in twelve states in the years 1997–1999. The agency analyzed over 3,000 reported hate crimes and found that of those victims, 3 were murdered, 4 abducted or kidnapped, 17 sexually assaulted, 42 robbed, and 2,138 assaulted. The most prevalent motivation was racial bias (61 percent), religious bigotry (14 percent), sexual orientation (13 percent), ethnicity (11 percent), and mental or physical disability (less than 1 percent).[37]

Today, there is hate crime legislation covering a wide range of bias, including:

- Race, ethnicity, and religion
- Sexual orientation
- Gender
- Institutional vandalism and interference with religious practices
- Mental and physical disability
- Age
- Political affiliation

The first model hate crime statute was developed by the Anti-Defamation League. The model language provides that "a person commits a Bias-Motivated Crime if, by reason of the actual or perceived race, color, religion, national origin, sexual orientation or gender of another individual or group of individuals" he violated the state's criminal laws such as murder, assault, battery, or the like. The model provision calls for bias-motivated crimes to be punished at least one degree greater than the underlying offense.

ESSENTIAL ELEMENTS OF A HATE CRIME

To obtain a conviction for a hate crime, the prosecution must prove the underlying criminal offense such as murder, rape, assault, battery, or harassment and also prove that the defendant was motivated to commit the crime by bias against a group or category covered by the specific hate crime law in the jurisdiction. That bias is an additional essential element of the offense. The U.S. Supreme Court has upheld enhanced penalties for hate crimes in face of a challenge that such laws violate the First Amendment because they punish speech in the form of intent to commit a crime based on prejudice, and not just the underlying crime.

Proving bias may be difficult in some cases. For example, belonging to a hate group or espousing racist or religiously bigoted views are generally considered free speech and free association privileges protected by the First Amendment. But even though expression of unpopular views may be protected, acting on those views is not. Thus, if a prosecutor has evidence that a defendant declared his intent to commit a crime against a member of a class protected by a hate law and then took action that is not protected. The closer in time to the crime statements showing the defendant's state of mind occur, the more likely that the evidence can be introduced to show intent.

In *Wisconsin v. Mitchell*, 508 U.S. 476 (1993), the U.S. Supreme Court considered Wisconsin's hate crime statute. The case involved a young black defendant who was convicted of selecting a white youth as a target for a beating. A group of young black men had gathered at an apartment complex and talk turned to a scene in the film *Mississippi Burning* in which a white youth beat a black youth praying. Mitchell suggested the group beat a white youth, stating "there goes a white boy; go get him." The group chased the white boy down and beat him so severely he spent four days in a coma.

After a jury trial, Mitchell was found guilty beyond a reasonable doubt. The same jury concluded that Mitchell had been motivated by racial bias. As a result, Mitchell was sentenced to seven years in prison rather than the maximum two-year sentence for the underlying crime. He appealed arguing that the hate crime statute that led to his lengthy sentence violated the First Amendment. The Wisconsin Supreme Court agreed and ruled that the law effectively punished offensive thoughts.

On appeal to the U.S. Supreme Court, the state argued that the statute only punished offensive conduct, not thought (i.e., the offensive conduct of selecting a victim on the basis of race rather than the offensive thought of wanting to select a victim because of his race). The court concluded that the use of speech as evidence of intent in a criminal prosecution does not violate the Constitution.

However, if the state statute doesn't require that the prosecution prove beyond a reasonable doubt as part of its case in chief that bias was the motivating factor for the crime, the enhanced sentence may not be constitutional. That is the issue that faced the U.S. Supreme Court in *Apprendi v. New Jersey*, 530 U.S. 466 (2000). In 1994, a few days before Christmas, Apprendi, a white resident of the suburb of Vineland, New Jersey, shot several .22-caliber bullets into the home of an African-American family who had recently moved into the previously all-white neighborhood. Apprendi was promptly arrested and told police he had fired into the home because he didn't want African-Americans in the neighborhood. He was charged under New Jersey law with various offenses, none of which laid out a bias motivation. Apprendi plead guilty to one weapon charge, and the plea was accepted on condition that at sentencing the state could argue for an enhanced sentence due to the alleged racial motivation for the shooting. Apprendi agreed on condition he could raise the constitutionality of the enhanced sentence on appeal.

At the sentencing hearing, the prosecution presented evidence of bias, and the judge found by a preponderance of the evidence that racial bias was the motive for the shooting. The judge then enhanced the sentence as New Jersey's hate crime legislation allowed. He appealed, arguing that the due process clause of the Constitution required that a jury, not a judge, decide whether bias was the motive for the crime and that the appropriate standard of proof was beyond a reasonable doubt. When the case reached the U.S. Supreme Court, a majority of the justices agreed. The court held that "the Constitution requires that any fact that increases the penalty for a crime beyond the prescribed statutory maximum, other than the fact of a prior conviction, must be submitted to a jury and proved beyond a reasonable doubt."[38]

In 2003, the U.S. Supreme Court ruled that states can make it a crime to burn a cross. Virginia's legislature had passed a law that created a presumption that burning a cross was racially motivated and made it a crime to do so. The U.S. Supreme Court struck the presumption but ruled that the state can charge and convict citizens who burn crosses with the intent to intimidate. Criminalizing cross burning does not violate the First Amendment.[39]

CYBER CRIMES—SOLICITATION, HATE SPEECH, AND INCITING TERRORISM

The computer and, more specifically, the Internet have created massive opportunities for business and criminals. Internet communications can be accomplished anonymously or operate under the privacy protections provided by Internet Service Providers (ISP), many of whom operate overseas far from the reach of U.S. law enforcement. Additionally, the sheer volume of Internet traffic makes finding any particular message difficult.

Law enforcement officials may have been slow to realize the threat posed by cyber criminals, but now computer-based crimes occupy a significant portion of law enforcement efforts. Most cyber crimes are property-based, where the perpetrator is trying to steal an unwitting person's money, identity, or other property. But the computer can be an entrée into violent crime when it becomes the medium to:

- solicit others to commit violent acts;
- agitate for racial, religious, or gender-based violence; or
- facilitate acts of terror.

Law enforcement officials thus far have been reluctant to name computer-based crimes differently from the same crime committed without a computer. They fear tying any legal definition to a specific technology when technology changes so quickly.

SOLICITATION

Criminal solicitation under Common Law occurs when one person requests or encourages another to perform a criminal act. The charge is the same whether the solicitation occurs in person, through the mail, on the phone, or over the Internet. But Internet solicitation is particularly harmful because it can reach large numbers of people easily and is more likely to involve minors.

Some studies have suggested that one in five children receives an unwanted sexual solicitation online each year and that 50,000 sexual predators prowl the Internet for child victims at any given time.[40]

In any solicitation scenario, the crime is committed when the perpetrator makes an offer or suggestion that the other person or persons commit a crime. Whether the person to

Criminal Solicitation

The act of when one person requests or encourages another to perform a criminal act.

whom the suggestion is made commits the crime is irrelevant. To convict a person of solicitation, the prosecutor must prove that the solicitation was made and that the person soliciting the crime sought to induce the person hearing the solicitation to commit the crime.

The soliciting individual need only attempt to communicate with the person he hopes to induce to commit a crime. In cyberspace, that means that a person soliciting a child to have sex with him is guilty of the crime even if the child's e-mail filter moves the e-mail message to the trash bin.

HATE SPEECH

Threatening e-mails directed at particular people because of their race, religion, or sexual orientation may run afoul of state hate speech laws. Hate speech laws make it a crime to "under . . . threat of force, willfully injure, intimidate, interfere with, oppress, or threaten any other person in the free exercise or enjoyment of any right or privilege secured to him or her by the Constitution or laws . . . of the United States because of the other person's race, color, religion, ancestry, national origin, disability, gender, or sexual orientation."[41]

Like other hate crime laws, hate speech, if proven, is used to increase the sentence given to the person convicted of the crime. E-mailed threats of violence would probably bring a charge of "making terroristic threats," but if the e-mail indicated the motivating reason for the threat was the recipient's race, color, religion, ancestry, national origin, disability, gender, or sexual orientation, then the crime could be considered a hate crime warranting a longer sentence.

TERRORISM

In addition to providing an outlet for pedophiles and racists, the Internet has created safe forms of communication for terrorists residing in different countries around the world. Some communications between some of the 9/11 hijackers consisted of computer code embedded in an image on a Web site. A Canadian woman of Iranian descent testified that she was part of a group who jointly accessed an e-mail account. Each member would write a message and save it as a draft of an e-mail. No e-mail was actually transmitted across the Internet. Group members could access the site and communicate by reading and writing drafts.

Currently, Internet Service Providers are not required to preserve e-mails for any specific period of time. However, law enforcement officials may ask ISPs to preserve e-mails they may find relevant to a criminal investigation. ISPs are not required to do so unless required to do so by a court order.

ABDUCTION AND KIDNAPPING

Perhaps no crime sends more chills down a parent's back than the thought of a child being abducted. Yet children disappear at an alarming rate every year. For example, the Federal Bureau of Investigation (FBI) reported that approximately 725,000 children disappeared in 2001. Of course, not all these cases were stranger abductions. Some were parental or other relative kidnappings, while other cases represent children and teens that have been reported as runaways or children who simply got lost or were the victims of accidents. However, of the total cases, stranger abduction cases (defined as missing in circumstances indicating that the disappearance was not voluntary) stood at 58,200. The figure includes children, teens, and adults.[42]

Because figures include all involuntary abductions, getting a clear picture of how many children really are taken by strangers and placed in grave danger or killed has been difficult. As a result, there has been a public perception that large numbers of young children are abducted and murdered every year. The U.S. Department of Justice has recently announced that it will begin tracking child abductions in a way more likely to paint an accurate picture of the pervasiveness of the problem. As of 2000, accurate data on a national level were being reported from 17 states, and that data indicated that abductions of children rarely result in death (only 1 out of 1,214 child kidnapping cases reported in 1997 from participating states).[43] Upon examination, the cases fell into three categories: parental kidnapping, acquaintance kidnapping, and stranger kidnapping. Parental kidnapping was least likely to result in physical harm to the victim, whereas acquaintance kidnapping carried the greatest risk of injury. The most likely victims of stranger kidnapping were young children, who were also most often taken from public places.[44]

Also in 2000, the Department of Justice began a large-scale study to finally get accurate figures for all categories of missing children, including those kidnapped and those who disappear for other reasons. The study is required by the Missing Children's Assistance Act and is ongoing.[45]

All 50 states as well as the federal government have laws in place criminalizing abduction, whether the victim is a child or an adult. In addition, removing a child from a custodial parent or guardian's care outside the parameters of a visitation order is a crime. Transporting a child across state lines in conjunction with a parental or other abduction violates federal law, as is transporting an abducted adult. But for a long time, there was very little coordination of efforts to recover missing children or adults since so many jurisdictions were involved. That all changed after several well-publicized cases involving the abduction and murder of children, including the abduction and murder of Adam Walsh and Polly Klaas. Adam was snatched from a store in Florida in 1981, and Polly was abducted from a slumber party in her California home in 1993 and later found murdered.

STATE STATUTES

Kidnapping is generally defined as the crime of taking and detaining a person against his will by force, intimidation, or fraud. **Abduction** is generally defined as the illegal carrying away, by force or deception, of a person. Kidnapping can occur when the person is held even momentarily, whereas abduction requires that the victim be moved from one place to another. Both crimes may involve the demand for a ransom and may be punished more severely when ransom is demanded.

Many states combine kidnapping and abduction into one offense and then create other offenses to cover situations outside the definition. A typical state kidnapping and abduction statute is Pennsylvania's. It provides that:

> A person is guilty of kidnapping if he unlawfully removes another a substantial distance under the circumstances from the place where he is found, or if he unlawfully confines

Kidnapping

The crime of taking and detaining a person against his will by force, intimidation, or fraud. Holding the victim for ransom is not required.

Abduction

The illegal carrying away of a person by force or coercion, generally with the intent to do harm to the victim. Today, the same criminal statute generally covers kidnapping and abduction.

another for a substantial period of time in a place of isolation, with any of the following intentions:

- To hold for ransom or reward, or as a shield or hostage;
- To facilitate the commission of a felony or flight thereafter;
- To inflict bodily injury on or to terrorize the victim or another;
- To interfere with the performance by public officials of any governmental or public function.

The Pennsylvania statute goes on to define confinement or removal as unlawful if "it is accomplished by force, threat or deception, or, in the case of a person who is under the age of 14 years or an incapacitated person, if it is accomplished without the consent of a parent, guardian or other person responsible for general supervision of his welfare."[46]

Pennsylvania also prohibits unlawful restraint,[47] false imprisonment,[48] interfering with custody of children,[49] interfering with custody of committed persons,[50] concealment of whereabouts of child,[51] and luring a child into a motor vehicle.[52] Each crime has its own elements and its own penalty. For example, the crime of luring a child into a motor vehicle does not require proof of the intent to harm that child, only proof that the child was persuaded or threatened and that there was no permission given by a guardian.[53]

HISTORICAL HIGHLIGHT
The Lindbergh Baby Abduction

The first federal kidnapping law was known as the Lindbergh Law and required that the victim be transported over a state line for federal jurisdiction to attach. Charles Lindbergh was the first man to fly a plane solo across the Atlantic, piloting the *Spirit of St. Louis* across the ocean on May 21, 1927. He would again attract national attention when his son was kidnapped and murdered.

The Lindbergh kidnapping began on March 1, 1932, when Charles Lindbergh's 20-month-old son disappeared from his crib at the family's Princeton, New Jersey, home.[54] A note left by the kidnappers demanded a ransom of $50,000. A baby believed to be the abducted child was found dead after the ransom was paid, and his suspected kidnapper was tried and executed. The FBI, which had no jurisdiction over kidnapping at the time, became involved because the ransom was paid in gold certificates, over which it did have jurisdiction. Its investigation eventually led to the suspect, Bruno Hauptmann, a carpenter who quit his job on the day the ransom was paid and began playing the stock market.

At the time, the trial was referred to as the "trial of the century."[55] When the Lindbergh baby was kidnapped, it was not yet a federal offense to take and hold a person for ransom, but almost immediately such a law was proposed.[56] The current federal kidnapping statute was originally named the Lindbergh Act. It greatly expanded the influence of the Federal Bureau of Investigation, which used the law to crack down on a nationwide rash of abductions for ransom.[57]

ESSENTIAL ELEMENTS OF KIDNAPPING AND ABDUCTION

To prove kidnapping, the government must show that the victim was taken or detained against his or her will. If the victim is competent to testify and survives and can testify, her testimony can establish that the defendant took or detained her against her will. Of course, witnesses to the event can also testify as to what they observed. In the case of a young victim who cannot be qualified to testify due to his tender years, a witness or circumstantial evidence can be used. For example, the elements can be established by showing that the child was recovered from the defendant's presence or custody and the defendant lacked the legal guardian's permission to take the child. Prosecutors can also present circumstantial evidence in cases where the victim doesn't survive.

Kidnapping doesn't require that the perpetrator demand a ransom. Since state laws differ, always check the specific statute in your jurisdiction for the essential elements the prosecutor must prove.

FEDERAL STATUTES

Federal law defines a kidnapper as someone who "unlawfully seizes, confines, inveigles, decoys, kidnaps, abducts, or carries away and holds for ransom or reward or otherwise any person" and transports that person "in interstate or foreign commerce, regardless of whether the person was alive when transported across a State boundary if the person was alive when the transportation began."[58] Kidnapping those under the age of 18 carries the potential for a longer sentence than if the victim is an adult. Likewise, if the young victim is subjected to life-threatening treatment or sexual or physical abuse, the penalty may be increased when the defendant's sentence is calculated under the federal Sentencing Guidelines.[59]

ELDER ABUSE

Elder abuse is the physical and mental abuse of an elderly person by someone responsible for his or her care. Law enforcement officials encounter many of the same problems addressing elder abuse crimes as they do with child spousal abuse. First, the crime is severely underreported because elderly victims are often afraid to complain fearing retribution by their abuser. Second, elderly victims may lack the mobility or mental acuity to contact law enforcement. Even if they did, those with mental health issues may not be credible witnesses.

Elder abuse usually occurs in one of two settings: at home or in an institution. Elderly people, whose caregiver is a family member or friend, often receive that care in their own home or the caregiver's home. If the caregiver is abusive, the elderly person becomes trapped in the home, unable to report the crime, or the victim may feel he or she has nowhere else to go and must accept the abuse.

Psychiatrists have labeled this syndrome as **Elder Abuse Syndrome.** The syndrome incorporates the learned helplessness concept of Battered Wife Syndrome and applies it to

Elder Abuse Syndrome

Similar to battered wife syndrome, it is a psychological condition where elder persons learn to accept the abuse they receive.

the elder abuse scenario. In both cases, the sufferer will be reluctant or unwilling to report the abuse to authorities.

Institutional elderly abuse is where paid caregivers abuse an elderly person in a nursing home or other similar institution. If the abuser is a licensed medical professional in the state, the abuse is also medical malpractice. In these cases, the abused victim could pursue civil damages from the abuser's malpractice insurance policy.

As a practical matter, insurance companies and other civil defendants opposing an elderly plaintiff may delay settling as long as possible with the cynical attitude that the victim will die before proceedings end.

Although elder abuse is another example of how society must protect its weakest citizens, the good news is that elderly Americans as a group are victimized less than the population as a whole. See the following chart.[60]

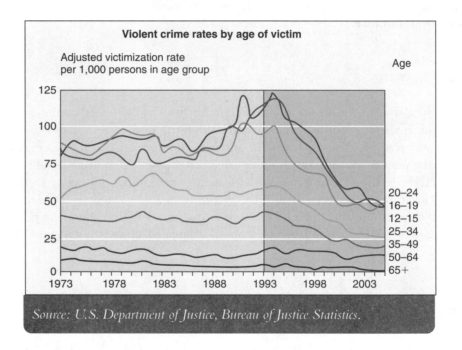

Source: U.S. Department of Justice, Bureau of Justice Statistics.

TRAFFICKING IN PERSONS

The Department of Justice defines trafficking in persons as a "form of modern-day slavery." Trafficking in persons or human trafficking occurs when individuals who have been lured or coerced into traveling to the United States are forced into servitude. The servitude comes in many forms. At its worst, women and children are forced into prostitution. In other cases, persons work as domestic servants or in factories colloquially called "sweat shops."

The crime is tied heavily to illegal immigration, and both the Department of Justice and the Department of Homeland Security enforce laws against human trafficking. Because human trafficking victims are often in the country illegally and/or are sending money home to their families, they are often reluctant to report their situation to authorities.

In response, the government, operating under a presidential executive order grants many victims of human trafficking refugee status. In some circumstances, minors may receive refugee status as well.[61]

When caught human traffickers are often charged with a variety of crimes including kidnapping, assault, immigration violations, and wage and hour violations.

Resources for those seeking information on missing or exploited children include:

- The National Center for Missing and Exploited Children, a nonprofit organization working in cooperation with the U.S. Department of Justice, serves as a national resource center and clearinghouse on missing child cases. The Center is linked with clearinghouses in all 50 states and can be reached at 1-800-843-5678 and online at *www.missingkids.org.*
- The Polly Klaas Foundation, dedicated to finding missing children and lobbying for laws protecting children from exploitation, can be reached at 1-800-587-4357 or online at *www.pollyklaas.org.*

HISTORICAL HIGHLIGHT
The Doctor's Maid

Wealthy Filipinos traditionally have maids to help with housework and child rearing. So when Jefferson and Elnora Calimlim needed help, they recruited Erma Martinez, a poor farmer's daughter, to travel from the Philippines to their home in Milwaukee, Wisconsin. The Calimlims were both doctors and had three children.[62]

Ms. Calimlim's father brought Erma to the United States on a tourist visa. He gave his daughter Ms. Martinez's passport to keep. Erma lived in the basement of the Calimlim's 8,000 square feet house, where she was hidden from all those outside the family. Erma believed she was only going to work for the Calimlims for five years, but she ended up in what amounted to modern slavery for almost two decades.

Erma cleaned, painted, washed laundry, and made grocery lists for the family. She was never allowed outside of the house and did not have a driver's license. The Calimlims paid her $150 per month for the first ten years she worked for them, and $400 per month after that. Erma sent money home to her family, providing money for clothes and education for her siblings.

In letters, her family pressed her for more money. Faced with demands from the Calimlims and her family, she kept working.

Only after the oldest Calimlim child divorced his wife did the scheme unravel. The scorned ex-wife phoned the Department of Justice with an anonymous tip. FBI and Immigration and Customs Enforcement agents raided the Calimlim home and found Erma hiding in her closet.

Erma testified at the Calimlim trial. Both Drs. Calimlim were sentenced to four years in prison after being convicted of forcing Erma to work as their domestic servant, harboring an illegal alien for 19 years, and using threats of serious harm and physical restraint against her. The oldest Calimlim son received a sentence of 120-days home confinement, three years supervised release, and a $5,000 fine.

Erma is also suing for back wages, which have been estimated at $704,635.[63]

> ## PRACTICE POINTERS
>
> Those representing the interests of domestic violence or sexual assault victims can find information on federal programs, grants, and laws at the Department of Justice's Violence Against Women Office, 810 7th Street, NW, Washington, DC 20531, (202) 307–6026. The Web site address is *http://www.ojp. usdoj.gov/vawo*. The agency offers a range of publications for those involved in the domestic violence field, including the *Toolkit to End Violence Against Women*, available at *http://toolkit.ncjrs.org*. Other helpful agencies and publications are:
>
> - National Domestic Violence Hotline: 1-800-799-SAFE (7233) and *http:// www.ndvh.org*.
> - Publications from the Office of Victims of Crime, Department of Justice, including *Understanding DNA Evidence: A Guide for Victim Service Providers*, available at *http://www.ojp.usdoj.gov/ovc/publications/bulletins/dna_4_2001/ welcome.html*.
> - National Institute of Justice's study, *Extent, Nature, and Consequences of Intimate Partner Violence: Findings From the National Violence Against Women Survey*, 2000, available at *http://www.ojp.usdoj.gov/nij/pubs-sum/181867.htm*.
> - National Institute of Justice's study, *The Sexual Victimization of College Women*, 2000, available at *http://www.ojp.usdoj.gov/nij/pubs-sum/182369.htm*.
> - National AMBER Alert System information can be accessed at *http://www. amberalert.gov*.
> - The National Sexual Assault Resource Center at *http://www.nsvrc.org* provides information on sexual assault.
> - Other specialized resources include the Battered Women's Justice Project at 1-800-903-0111, the Health Resource Center on Domestic Violence at 1-888-792-2873, and the Sacred Circle Center on Violence Against Native Women at 605-341-2050.
>
> Those working with victims of domestic abuse should guard against unrealistic expectations. Inevitably, advocates for the victim will be frustrated when a prosecution falls apart if the couple reconciles or the victim refuses to actively cooperate. Short of forcing victims to testify through subpoena and asking the victim to be held in contempt when he or she doesn't cooperate, there is little that can be done when the victim wants to drop the case.
>
> For those working in law enforcement investigating and prosecuting hate crimes, the Anti-Defamation League collects data on hate crime legislation, available at its Web site, *http://www.adl.org*.

- Families of missing children may find the booklet "When Your Child Is Missing: A Family Survival Guide" helpful. It is available from the Office of Juvenile Justice and Delinquency Prevention, the Department of Justice online at *www.ojjdp.ncjrs. org/pubs/childismissing,* or in pamphlet form from the Department of Justice. It was written by parents of missing and murdered children.

YOU MAKE THE CALL

FORGIVE ME, FATHER. THE CATHOLIC CHURCH'S CHILD SEXUAL ABUSE CRISIS

John Goeghan was found guilty of molesting a child in a swimming pool in January 2002. However, John Goeghan was not the average child molester—he was a well-respected priest in Boston. Over 130 people have accused him of child sexual abuse during his career at six different parishes over a 30-year span. He was eventually convicted and imprisoned, where he was brutally murdered by a fellow inmate. But how could one man have abused so many children over such a long period of time without getting caught?

Paul Shanley, also a priest in the Boston area, was arrested for similar allegations in May 2002. A month after his arrest, the Boston Archdiocese released internal documents that revealed that they had known about allegations of child sexual abuse against Shanley since 1967. Shanley's work records reflected that he had been moved by the Catholic Church from parish to parish as more allegations arose against him.

This practice of moving accused priests to new assignments seems to not have been an isolated incident. In March 2002, Bishop Anthony J. O'Connell resigned from the Diocese of Palm Beach, Florida, after admitting to sexually abusing a seminary student. Archbishop Rembert Weakland of Milwaukee, Wisconsin, resigned under similar allegations in May 2002. In June 2002, J. Kendrick Williams, also accused of child sexual assault, resigned from his post as bishop of the Diocese of Lexington, Kentucky. All three of these priests seem to have been shuffled from one assignment to another as victims came forward.

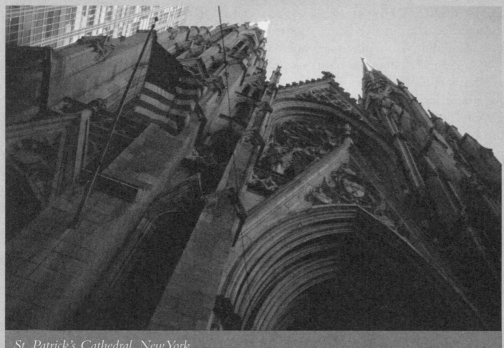

St. Patrick's Cathedral, New York.

> As these cases are being tried in both criminal and civil courts, many are beginning to speculate about the legal questions arising from them. Statutes of limitations may exist in many jurisdictions that would prevent criminal charges from being filed after a certain period of time has elapsed since the incidents occurred. Already, the U.S. Supreme Court has struck down an attempt by the California legislature to enact a new statute of limitations for childhood sexual abuse as a violation of the *ex post facto* rule.[64] California has had to release or drop charges against about 800 accused child molesters, including several Catholic priests, since the decision.[65] Has the Catholic Church used this method of moving accused priests from one place to the next as a strategy for exhausting these statutes of limitations so that criminal prosecutions can be avoided by the time the occurrences of child sexual abuse are revealed? Was the church simply moving priests away from their victims in hope they would reform in a new environment? You make the call.

CHAPTER SUMMARY

After reading this chapter, you should have a good understanding of the wide variety of crimes that exist outlawing injury to the person. The criminal law punishes a vast range of behavior considered morally repugnant by the majority as expressed through the laws enacted by their legal representatives. Many of the violent criminal offenses described in this chapter are in practice directed against women and children.

Traditionally defined as forced sexual intercourse with a woman, not one's wife, modern rape definitions don't distinguish between male or female victims and have expanded the types of sexual conduct that constitute rape. Most states also allow at least a limited right to bring rape charges against a spouse and no longer require the use of direct force or physical harm. The key elements of rape are that the statute's prohibited sexual activity took place and that there was no consent by the victim.

Consent is a defense to most charges of rape unless the victim is underage, drugged, or otherwise unable to give effective consent. Rape shield laws limit the type of evidence that can be introduced about the victim in a sexual assault case. Only evidence that is directly relevant to the case will be admitted, and testimony about the victim's prior sexual history is not admitted unless it directly relates to evidence in the case or to his or her consent to the sexual acts at the heart of the case.

Assault is an act of force or threat of force intended to inflict harm upon a person or to put the person in fear that such harm is imminent. Every state has its own set of rules about which acts constitute assault. To prove that an assault took place, the state must show that there was either an act that resulted in physical harm or a threat that resulted in the fear of imminent physical harm. Most states classify assault in accordance with the type of harm threatened or done and the type of weapon used to threaten or act. Thus, it is a more serious offense to threaten a victim with a gun (because it can cause serious bodily harm or death) than with a fist (which may cause less serious bodily harm unless the assailant is a boxer).

Domestic violence is assault, battery, aggravated assault, harassment, stalking, and other crimes involving physical or mental injury to a victim when perpetrated by the victim's partner. Domestic violence is a serious problem in the United States but has historically been ignored by many in law enforcement. Today, that is changing as shelters and educational opportunities open up for women (who are the overwhelming majority of domestic violence victims) and more charges are being filed. In addition, the federal government is funding research and programs to help victims of domestic violence start new lives through the authority given them in the Violence Against Women Act.

Hate crimes are offenses motivated by hatred against a victim based on his or her race, religion, sexual orientation, handicap, ethnicity, or national origin. Many states have enacted hate crime laws that enhance the sentence received for the commission of a crime if the motive for the criminal act was animus toward a protected class or member of a protected class. The U.S. Supreme Court has ruled that hate crime legislation is legal as long as proving that the motive for a crime's commission is an essential element of the crime and not a factor to be considered by the sentencing judge.

Kidnapping and abduction are crimes in which the perpetrator takes, holds, and sometimes carries away the victim through force or coercion. Neither kidnapping nor abduction requires that the perpetrator demand a ransom. Today, well over 28,000 children and adults disappear under circumstances that make it likely their disappearance wasn't voluntary. State laws regulate most cases of abduction unless there is evidence that the victim was taken across state lines.

Child abuse is the label given to crimes that are either committed against minors or crimes created to protect children who cannot act in their own best interest. The doctrine of *parens patriae* gives authority to government to protect the vulnerable, while police power give states the limited right to regulate the civil lives of its citizens. These two doctrines are the basis for special laws regarding children. Examples include statutory rape, incest, and child medical neglect. Some acts that would be crimes if committed against another adult are not crimes if the victim is a child and the perpetrator is a parent or guardian. For example, it would be a crime to spank a neighbor, but not to spank one's misbehaving child. It would also be a crime to spank a neighbor's child.

KEY TERMS

Abduction	Elder Abuse Syndrome	Rape
Assault	Hate Crimes	Rape Shield Laws
Child Abuse	Incest	Statutory Rape
Child Molestation or Child Sexual Abuse	Indecent Assault or Indecent Touching	Violence Against Women Act (VAWA)
Criminal Solicitation	Kidnapping	
Domestic Violence	Parens Patriae	

EXERCISES

1. The U.S. Department of Justice, Bureau of Justice Statistics collects an enormous amount of data on crimes and its victims. Its data collection is a rich source of information for anyone concerned about crime and its consequences. Visit the Bureau of Justice Statistics Web page at *http://www.ojp.usdoj.gov/bjs/abstract/cvusst.htm* and answer the following questions:

   a. By what type of crime are you most likely to become victimized? What about your parents? Your grandparents?

   b. Would the answer change if you were a member of the opposite sex? If your ethnicity was different? If your household income doubled? If you moved to another setting, that is, from the city to the suburbs or a rural area?

   c. Did your answers surprise you? Why or why not?

2. Let us return to the scenario we first discussed in the Chapter 1 Exercise. As you may recall, a 27-year-old female college student, who works as an exotic dancer, is hired to perform at an off-campus party by members of a neighboring university's sports team. The dancer later reported to the police that she had been sexually assaulted by three of the team members at some time during the evening. The female is black, and the accused members of the team are white.

Police and the attorneys representing the team members review 23 pages of medical reports, including the statement made by the sexual assault nurse who first spoke with the victim. The nurse described swelling of the victim's vaginal area and said the woman had undergone a traumatic experience.

Interviews with the victim reveal that she claimed none of the assailants used a condom during the assault.

Meanwhile, an article in a nationally known magazine reports that the victim's parents said the victim had reported another alleged gang rape 10 years earlier. At that time, she is reported to have told police that three young men beat and raped her three years earlier, when she was just 14 years old.

Based on what you have learned in this chapter, answer the following questions:

   a. If you represent the team members who have been accused of rape, what arguments will you make after reviewing the medical reports and reading the magazine article? What additional investigation will you do? If you get independent confirmation of the earlier rape allegations, what will you do with that information? What do you think the chances are you will be able to tell the jury that will hear the case about the victim's occupation? Sexual history? Past allegations? Sexual behavior in the days leading up to the party in question?

   b. If you represent the victim, what arguments will you make about the medical reports? About the admissibility of the victim's prior accusations? About her recent sexual contacts?

DISCUSSION QUESTIONS

1. Research your state's assault statutes and discuss how assault offenses in your state differ from those illustrated in this chapter. Select one assault offense in your jurisdiction and outline the elements of the offense. Then describe the evidence you would need to present in order to secure a conviction.

2. Research your state's rape and sexual assault laws. Outline the elements of your state's statutory rape and marital rape laws. Then describe the evidence you would need in order to secure a conviction. Next, outline the elements of your state's rape law and describe what evidence you would have to present to defend against a charge of rape.

3. Locate your state's rape shield law. What evidence of the victim's past sexual history does it allow into evidence and under what circumstances?

4. What is domestic violence, and what is your community doing to prevent it? Research the incident of domestic violence in your jurisdiction.

5. Should corporal punishment by parents and guardians be outlawed as it has been in the European Union?

6. Research the missing child emergency response system set up in your jurisdiction. Does it provide for immediate action, or does it require that parents wait before the police become involved in recovery efforts? If it requires a wait, how would you try to persuade local authorities to change their policy?

FOR FURTHER READING

1. Walsh, J. (1998). *Tears of Rage: From Grieving Father to Crusader for Justice*. Pocket Books.
   This book tells the story of Adam Walsh's kidnapping and murder through his father's perspective and chronicles John Walsh's efforts to make recovering lost and abducted children easier.

2. Those interested in historical materials from the FBI archives, which have been released to the public through the Freedom of Information Act, can visit the agency's Freedom of Information Act Electronic Reading Room. The archives include documents on the Lindbergh kidnapping and other high-profile cases. The Web site is *http://foia.fbi.gov*. The Department of Justice maintains a similar virtual reading room at *http://www.usdoj.gov/04foia/index.html*.

3. Temple-Raston, D. (2002). *A Death in Texas: A Story of Race, Murder, and a Small Town's Struggle for Redemption*. Henry Holt.
   Recounts the hate crime murder of James Byrd, Jr., in Jasper, Texas. The 49-year-old African-American man was tied to a pickup truck by three white men and dragged behind until he died.

4. Brownmiller, S. (1975). *Against Our Will: Men, Women, and Rape*. Simon & Schuster.
   Classic study of rape, its origins, and its effect on women.

5. Farrow, M. (1997). *What Falls Away*. Doubleday.
   Mia Farrow's memoir, including her account of her relationship with Allen and adopted daughter Previn.

6. Groth, N. (2006). *Men Who Rape: The Psychology of the Offender*. Basic Books.
   A comprehensive clinical profile of sexual offenders with extensive information on counseling, prevention, and psychiatric treatment.

ENDNOTES

1. U.S. Department of Justice, *Report to the Nation on Crime and Justice 29,* 2nd ed. (1988).

2. Surgeon General Antonia Novello, "From the Surgeon General," U.S. Public Health Services, 267 *JAMA* 3132 (1992).

3. Trends in violent victimization by gender, 1973–2005, Department of Justice, Bureau of Justice Statistics, Criminal Victimization in the United States, online at *http://www.ojp.usdoj.gov/bjs/cvict_v.htm*.

4. "Va. House Backs Bill to Outlaw Wife Rape," *Washington Post* (February 8, 2002) and Virginia Code Ann. § 18.2-61 (B).

5. Biskin, Peter, "Reconstructing Woody," *Vanity Fair,* December 2005.

6. "Lawyer may not see humor in 'SNL' skit; Bryant attorney flooded with calls after she's mocked on show," *Milwaukee Journal Sentinel*, October 15, 2003.

7. "Trial Judge Could Rule Our Testimony about Overdose," *The Denver Post* (July 22, 2003).

8. Virginia Code § 18.2-67.7.

9. Pennsylvania State Police, Bureau of Drug Law Enforcement, *Date Rape Drugs: Information You Need to Know*.

10. "FBI: Marsalis Had 7 Victims on a List," *Philadelphia Daily News* (June 6, 2007).

11. "Deal Proposed for Defendant in Net Sex Case," *New York Times* (November 22, 2000).

12. *Focus on New York's Rape Shield Law: Court Overturns Cybersex Torture Conviction,* Court TV Online (December 22, 1999).

13. "All Charges Dismissed by Judge in Columbia Sex Torture Case," *New York Times* (November 2, 2001).

14. *Mormon Church v. United States*, 136 U.S. 1 (1890).

15. Assistant Attorney General Deborah Daniels, National AMBER Alert coordinator.

16. 18 P.S. § 509.

17. "European Court Ruling Bans Corporal Punishment of UK Children," *The Guardian* (London) (September 23, 1998).

18. American Academy of Pediatrics, Guidelines for the Evaluation of Sexual Abuse of Children, 87 *Pediatrics* 254 (1991).

19. *Kolender v. Lawson*, 461 U.S. 352 (1983).

20. Wis. Stat. § 948.02 and 948.025.

21. 18 P.S. § 3122.1.

22. 18 P.S. § 3102. The defense reads "Whenever in this chapter the criminality of conduct depends on a child being below the age of 14 years, it is no defense that the defendant did not know the age of the child or reasonably believed the child to be the age of 14 years or older. When criminality depends on the child's being below a critical age older than 14 years, it is a defense for the defendant to prove by a preponderance of the evidence that he or she reasonably believed the child to be above the critical age."

23. 18 U.S.C. § 2241(c) and 2423.

24. 413 U.S. 915, 93 S. Ct. 2607, (1973).

25. 636 F. Supp. 828 (S.D. Cal.) 1986. *aff'd sub. nom.* United States v. Weigand, 812 F. 2d. 1239 (9th Cir.), *cert denied,* 484 U.S. 856 (1987*).

26. 18 P.S. § 2709(b).

27. 18 P.S. § 2714(a) and (b).

28. 18 P.S. § 2701(a).

29. 18 P.S. § 2301.

30. See, for example, Pennsylvania's aggravated assault statute at 18. P.S. § 2702, which affords protection to a long list of public officials including school board members, public defenders, district attorneys, and probation officers.

31. Bureau of Justice Statistics, U.S. Department of Justice, *Intimate Partner Violence, 1993–2001* (2003).

32. Ibid.

33. Bureau of Justice Statistics, U.S. Department of Justice, *Violence by Intimates: Analysis of Data on Crimes by Current or Former Spouses, Boyfriends and Girlfriends* (1998).

34. 42 U.S.C. § 13981(b).

35. *United States v. Morrison*, 529 U.S. 598 (2000).

36. Bureau of Justice Statistics, U.S. Department of Justice, Press Release, *Justice Department Releases 1997 to 1999 Hate Crime Statistics* (September 23, 2001).

37. Bureau of Justice Statistics, U.S. Department of Justice, *Hate Crimes Reported in NIBRS, 1997–99* (2001).

38. *Apprendi v. New Jersey*, 530 U.S. 466 (2000).

39. *Virginia v. Black*, 123 S. Ct. 1536 (2003).

40. U.S. Department of Justice News Release, *U.S. Department of Justice Announces Project Safe Childhood Initiative* (June 22, 2006).

41. California Penal Code, Section 422.6 (a).

42. U.S. Department of Justice, Office of Justice Progams, *National Incidence of Missing Abducted, Runaway, and Thrownaway Children,* October 2002.

43. U.S. Department of Justice, Juvenile Justice Bulletin, *Kidnapping of Juveniles: Patterns from NIBRS* (June 2000).

44. Ibid.

45. U.S. Department of Justice, Juvenile Justice Bulletin, *Second Comprehensive Study of Missing Children* (April 2000).

46. 18 P.S. § 2901.

47. 18 P.S. § 2902.

48. 18 P.S. § 2903.

49. 18 P.S. § 2904.

50. 18 P.S. § 2905.

51. 18 P.S. § 2909.

52. 18 P.S. § 2910.

53. *Commonwealth v. Nanorta*, 742 A.2d 176 (1999).

54. "Lindbergh Baby Kidnapped from Home of Parents on Farm near Princeton: Taken from His Crib; Wide Search On," *New York Times* (March 2, 1932).

55. "Haupthmann Guilty; Sentenced to Death for the Murder of Lindbergh Baby," *New York Times* (February 14, 1935).

56. "Federal Aid in Hunt Ordered by Hoover," *New York Times* (March 3, 1932).

57. Federal Bureau of Investigation, *History of the FBI*, online at *www.fbi.gov/fbinbrief/ historic/history/historymain.htm*.

58. 18 U.S.C. § 1201 (a).

59. 18 U.S.C. § 1201 (g).

60. Klaus, Patsy A., *Crimes Against Persons Age 65 or Older,* Bureau of Justice Statistics, Revised January 2000.

61. "What We Do: Fight Trafficking in Persons," U.S. Department of Justice, January 30, 2007.

62. Ortiz, V., "Maid Lived 20 Years in Quiet Struggle; Brookfield Family and Her Family in the Philippines Manipulated Her," *Milwaukee Journal Sentinel,* p. 1 (January 14, 2007).

63. Press release, U.S. Department of Justice, "Attorney General Alberto R. Gonzales announces creation of human trafficking prosecution unit within the civil rights division," (January 31, 2007).

64. *Stogner v. California,* 539 U.S. 607 (2003).

65. *High Court: California Can't Prosecute Long-ago Sex Crimes,* CNN online (June 27, 2003).

CHAPTER 5

Crimes against Property

CHAPTER CONTENTS

> *Nor shall any State deprive any person of life, liberty, or property without due process of law.*
>
> *U.S. Constitution, Amendment 14, Section 1*

CHAPTER OBJECTIVES

After studying this chapter, you should be able to:

- Understand what property is and the bundles of rights that accompany each type of property.
- Explain the terms **fee simple, joint tenants with right of survivorship, tenancy by the entireties,** and **tenant in common.**
- Define **theft** and name the different classifications of theft.
- List the essential elements required to prove theft.
- Differentiate embezzlement from other forms of theft.
- Define **robbery.**

- Define **burglary** and describe its Common Law origins.
- Define **arson** and explain why so few cases are cleared.
- Explain the most common methods of check fraud and forgery.
- Explain laws aimed at defacing property.
- Explain where graffiti fits as a property crime.
- Define identity theft.
- Explain how cyber crime fits into traditional concepts of crimes against property.
- Explain theft by deception.

Property

A bundle of rights, including the right to possess, use and enjoy, and dispose of something. It is not a material object itself, but a person's right to do what he or she wishes with that object, subject to limitations provided in the law.

Real Property

Consists of land and everything permanently attached to it. It includes land, subsurface rights, air rights, timbering and harvesting rights, and any buildings and structures permanently attached to the land.

INTRODUCTION

In order to have a true appreciation for crimes involving property, you must first understand what **property** is and is not. Implicit in any discussion of property is the premise that individuals can actually hold property. Some societies simply don't accept that premise. Under the Common Law tradition, the individual's right to own property is a bedrock concept underlying virtually every aspect of the rules governing society. In England and the United States, one of the most important rights accorded citizens is the protection of his or her right to property, both real and personal.

In the U.S. Common Law tradition, property consists of a bundle of rights, including the right to possess, use and enjoy, and dispose of something. It is not a material object itself, but a person's right to do what he or she wishes with that object, subject to limitations provided in the law.[1] Thus, the owner of a book has the right to possess it (perhaps put it on her bookshelf or nightstand), the right to use it (perhaps read it and make notes in the margins), and the right to dispose of it (perhaps by selling it or even burning it).

Understanding property law basics is essential to understanding crimes such as theft, burglary, forgery, and criminal trespass. Each of these crimes involves interference with another's property rights and requires that the prosecution prove ownership as well as interference with that ownership to convict the accused.

Property comes in two varieties. **Real property** is land and everything permanently attached to it. Land rights include the land itself, subsurface rights (i.e., the right to mine the land), air rights, timbering and harvesting rights (i.e., the right to farm, harvest, or log the land), and any buildings or structures permanently attached to the land (i.e., house, barn, silo, garage, and the like). Real property can be either private or public. Private property is property owned by a private individual, while public property is held by a state government or the federal government on behalf of us all. Examples of public real property are the national seashore and other national parks.

Personal property is everything else to which the law grants ownership rights. It is also known as **chattel.**[2] Personal property can be tangible, with a physical presence. For example, a car or a book is personal property. Personal property can also be intangible, without a physical presence. Examples include patents and copyrights. Personal property also includes domestic animals and livestock as well as wild animals that have either been domesticated or placed under control.

Property rights are not without limit. For example, real property is subject to seizure by governmental entities as part of the state's power of **eminent domain.** Eminent domain is the state's power to take private property for a public use or public purpose without the owner's consent.[3] A controversial 2005 U.S. Supreme Court decision allows governments to use eminent domain to condemn land and turn it over to a private developer under a state-devised economic development plan that provided more than "incidental or pretextual public benefits."[4]

Under the U.S. Constitution, any such taking must be after due process of law. Private property can't just be seized; some kind of a hearing is required. For example, when a criminal's ill-gotten gains from a criminal enterprise are seized in a drug raid, the state must still afford the defendant a hearing on that seizure before it becomes permanent. Typically, the state must show the court that there was some minimum nexus between the criminal activity and the acquisition of the property by the defendant.

Property can be owned outright. If it is, the owner is said to hold the property in **fee simple.** Fee simple is a legal term for ownership of the entire bundle of rights that go with a piece of property.[5] For example, you may own your house in fee simple. If you do, you have the right to use, possess, or dispose of the property during your lifetime and to pass it on to your heirs. You can dispose of some of your bundle of rights and keep the rest if you desire. For example, if you own a beach house in fee simple, you may periodically transfer your right to possess and enjoy the property to someone else by renting out the house to vacationers. While they rent the house, it is they who have the right to enjoy and possess it.

Ownership is not restricted to one person; many persons can own the same property together. For example, husbands and wives often own property as **tenants by the entireties.** Tenancy by the entirety is a legal joint ownership in which both spouses own an undivided interest in the whole property and in which neither spouse can sell his or her interest without the consent of the other.[6] Other forms of joint ownership are **tenancy in common** and **joint tenancy with right of survivorship.**[7] Tenants in common each own an undivided interest in the whole property. Neither tenant in common can exclude the other from the property, but any of the tenants can sell or will the property to another without the consent of the other joint tenants. If the owners hold property as joint tenants with right of survivorship, the survivor gets the property. However, if one joint tenant sells or gives away his interest before he dies, the property would no longer pass to the other joint tenant. Instead, the new owner would become a tenant in common.

Title to property can be acquired in several ways. Property rights can be bought for a price, inherited, acquired as a gift, or acquired by mere possession. Property rights are most commonly transferred through purchase or inheritance. Purchase of property is done by contract and involves the exchange of something of value. For example, if you purchase

Personal Property

All property other than real property.

Chattel

Personal property.

Eminent Domain

The state's power to take private property for a public use or public purpose without the owner's consent. The U.S. Constitution requires that property can only be taken after due process of law.

Fee Simple

The legal term for ownership of the entire bundle of rights that go with a piece of property.

Private property is held sacred in all good governments, and particularly in our own.
Andrew Jackson, 1815

Tenancy by the Entirety

The legal joint ownership in which both spouses own an undivided interest in the whole property and in which neither spouse can sell his or her interest without the consent of the other.

Tenancy in Common

Form of joint ownership in which each owns an undivided interest in the whole property.

Joint Tenancy with Right of Survivorship

Form of ownership in which the joint tenant receives the property should the other die. Either may sell their share before death, and the new owners then become tenants in common.

In no other country in the world is the love of property keener or more alert than in the United States, and nowhere else does the majority display less inclination toward doctrines which in any way threaten the way property is owned.
Alexis de Tocqueville, *Democracy in America,* 1840

a CD for $20, you have bought title to that CD. Acquiring property by gift or inheritance requires three things. First, the owner must intend to give the property away. Second, the gift must be delivered to the recipient. Third, the recipient must accept the gift. Property can also be acquired by possession. For example, a hunter who shoots a deer passing over his land becomes the owner of the deer when he takes possession of it. Before it was shot, the deer belonged to no one. After, it belongs to the hunter. Abandoned property can also be acquired by possession. For example, if a jogger spots a treasure sitting on the curb for garbage collection, she can take possession of it and becomes its owner.

In criminal law, ownership is important for several reasons. For example, a thief can only steal that which does not belong to him; he cannot steal his own property. Nor can he trespass against his own property. Thus, an estranged husband who breaks into the house he still owns jointly with his wife cannot be charged with criminal trespass, nor can he be charged with burglary if he removes personal articles that belong to the couple. Theft also requires that the prosecution prove beyond a reasonable doubt that the defendant intended to permanently deprive the owner of the property taken.

YOU MAKE THE CALL

ANIMAL RIGHTS ACTIVISTS SEEK ABOLITION OF PROPERTY STATUS OF ANIMALS

When Thomas Jefferson wrote that man had "inalienable rights" such as "life, liberty, and the pursuit of happiness," he was referring quite literally to men, specifically white, land-owning men. Women and people of color were not included. In fact, African-American slaves were considered property in the southern colonies. When the U.S. Constitution was drafted, their condition was upgraded only slightly; slaves were counted as three-fifths of a person for census purposes only.

Clearly, the perception of who is entitled to rights has changed over the last 200+ years. Today, some argue that children should have the right to "divorce" their parents. Gary Francione, a law and philosophy professor at Rutgers University School of Law in Newark, New Jersey, takes the concept further. Francione has developed an abolitionist theory of animal rights, which calls for "the incremental abolition of the property status of non-humans." On his Web site, Animal Rights: The Abolitionist Approach, online at *http://www.AbolitionistApproach.org*, Francione contends that "all sentient beings should have at least one right—the right not to be treated as property." Francione argues eating meat and using animal products must be abandoned. He writes that "it is important to recognize that just as an abolitionist with respect to human slavery cannot continue to be a slaveowner, an abolitionist with respect to animal slavery cannot continue to consume or use animal flesh or animal products."

Francione makes no claim to be part of mainstream thought, even among animal rights advocates. In fact, he rejects animal welfare groups that call for "humane" treatment in our use of animals. Francione joined Lee Hall, legal director for the advocacy group Fund For Animals, to write an op-ed in the *San Francisco Chronicle* criticizing such organizations. Francione and Hall wrote: "Who disagrees with the position that we ought to be 'kind' to animals? The problem is that as long as animals are our property, as long as we can buy them, sell them, kill them and eat them, it does not matter whether we call ourselves 'guardians' or how much we ramble about 'humane' treatment. In reality, we are still their masters and they are our slaves."[8]

He sees animals as the next beneficiaries of a civil rights movement. How do you view animal rights? Does your pet cat or gerbil have rights on a par with yours? Should they? Is it wrong and should it be illegal to own a fur coat? To eat meat? Drink milk from cows held in captivity on a dairy farm?

HISTORICAL HIGHLIGHT
Who Owns the Rights to Sunken Treasure?

On September 11, 1857, the steamship *Central America* was making the last leg of its journey from Panama to New York when it encountered a hurricane off the coast of South Carolina. The ship developed a leak that became worse as the storm went on. Eventually, water flooded the steam boilers, extinguishing the fire and leaving the ship at the mercy of the storm. A few passengers were set afloat in life boats and were safely picked up by another ship. The other 336 people on-board perished when the ship went down.

The *Central America* was a wooden-hulled luxury liner. Most of its passengers had found gold in California and were carrying it home to families on the East Coast. They had sailed from San Francisco to Panama, crossed the isthmus by train, and boarded the steamer on the Atlantic side. The ship was carrying gold for various companies as cargo, and many of the passengers had large personal amounts of gold. The newspaper reports of the day estimated the ship to be carrying $2 million of gold in 1857 dollars. Estimates of its modern-day equivalent ran as high as $1 billion.

As news of the sinking reached the United States, insurers paid the various claims for the lost gold. Because the ship sank in over two thousand feet of water, the insurers held no hope they would ever salvage the cargo.

In the late 1970s, ocean research scientist Thomas Thompson began studying newspaper accounts of the *Central America* sinking. He became convinced that modern ocean mapping and deep-sea exploration technology could make recovering the *Central America*'s treasure possible. Thompson began putting an investor syndicate together to fund the massive undertaking.

By 1987, Thompson had put together his syndicate, now called the Columbus-America Discovery Group, and began salvage operations. The group recovered one ton of gold bars and coins from the wreck. Insurance companies challenged Columbus-America's right to the treasure, claiming they had paid for the gold after the shipwreck in 1857. This claim would have been valid if the property were lost property.

However, Thompson and his group argued that it was abandoned property. In court, they showed that even after papers telling of the *Central America*'s location were published, insurers mounted no effort to salvage the gold. Further, no documentation existed from the 1857 claims.

Columbus-America won in federal district court where the judge ruled that conventional property laws applied and the property was abandoned and could be given to the first group to recover it. The Appeals Court saw things somewhat differently. Since the shipwreck was in international waters, maritime law applied. It sent the case back to the district court with instructions to apply maritime law.

Maritime law dates from the ancient city of Rhodes. The inhabitants of Rhodes instituted the first maritime code sometime around 900 B.C. When the Romans conquered Rhodes, they preserved the maritime code, and it came down through Anglo-American legal tradition. Maritime law has always held that salvors (those who salvage ships) are entitled to very liberal awards.

In this case, the district judge applied the maritime law and awarded the salvagers 90 percent of the market value of the treasure. Those few insurers whose claims survived would get the remainder. But dividing the spoils proved problematic. Columbus-America wanted to keep the treasure's full value and contents secret to increase its market value. The value of each item in the treasure was dependent on the value and contents of the entire find. Ultimately, a federal judge ordered Columbus-America to submit a full inventory and parcel out the insurers' shares. On June 17, 1998, after nearly a decade of legal wrangling, representatives from both sides met in a Brinks armored warehouse in Chesapeake, Virginia, where Columbus-America divided the treasure into 90 lots of equal value. Attorneys for each side took turn picking lots until the insurers had their share.

Thompson and his syndicate are still battling in court over claims to the treasure. In 2006, ten technicians from the recovery crew, including sonar operators and search-and-recovery experts, filed suit for their promised share of the booty. The group persuaded judges on the east and west coasts to allow them to seize $11.8 million in assets. Federal marshals, using a court order from U.S. District Court in Los Angeles, took six gold bars weighing a total of 115 pounds and a gold coin, which is being held by an armored-truck company while the lawsuit is tried. More than 161 partners who helped finance the expedition have divided into factions and filed suit over the treasure. Estimates of the treasure's full value run as high as $400 million.

HISTORICAL HIGHLIGHT
Telepossession: Laying Claim to Property in Outer Space

In deciding the fate of sunken treasure recovered from the *Central America*, the courts relied on the legal concept *pedis possessio*, Latin for "foothold," literally, "to walk on is to establish ownership."[9] According to this principle, the salvors of the

Columbus-America Discovery Group gained possession of the sunken treasure by establishing a live video link with the wreck site using telerobotic equipment. Richard Westfall, of Galactic Mining Industries, Inc., along with Declan O'Donnell PC, of United Societies in Space, Inc., and Gary Rodriguez, of sysRAND Corporation, all of Colorado, are trying to use that principle to establish title to asteroids, comets, moons, minerals, and even gravity wells and orbits. Relying on the *Central America* case, the group argues that "the telepresence of a research group can have legal standing to establish a priori domain over a property, and establish a form of legal possession." The group calls this remote-control claim on property "telepossession."[10]

The group proposes laying claim to objects in space using telerobotic probes, which can perform tasks such as assaying composition of the object, manipulating materials, and relaying information to Earth. The group also proposes planting RADAR transponders on them, which would transmit signals back to Earth. It might seem like a flight of fancy but consider the case of an abandoned satellite orbiting Earth. Remote technological links with the satellite could be used to establish salvage rights to it, just as Columbus-America claimed the wreckage of the *Central America*. Could the same logic be applied to real estate on the moon? Might the future colonization of space rely on the legal precedent set by the *Central America*?

THEFT OR LARCENY

The terms theft and larceny are interchangeable. Some jurisdictions call the crime theft, while others refer to it as larceny. We will use the term **theft** to refer to the crime. At Common Law, theft was defined as the taking and carrying away of another's personal property with the intent to deprive him or her of it permanently. There are many distinct acts that fit the definition of theft, and every state has its own list. Following are some common theft classifications.

Shoplifting or Retail Theft: More than $13 billion worth of goods, over $25 million per day, are stolen from U.S. retailers every year.[11] This form of theft includes concealing goods in stores to avoid paying for them or altering the price on an item in order to pay a lower price. Many states have escalating penalties for retail theft. The penalty varies according to the value of the merchandise stolen or the number of prior convictions the defendant has on record.

Purse Snatching: This form of theft involves a quick and usually observed taking of a purse, briefcase, or the like in a public place and then fleeing the scene.

Pickpocketing: This form of theft usually involves a secretive snatching of personal property such as a wallet or cash from another person's possession.

Looting: Looting is taking property from or near a building damaged or destroyed by a fire, riot, or natural disaster. Consider two recent examples of looting. Following Hurricane Katrina in 2005, looters floated garbage cans full of clothing and jewelry down the flooded streets of New Orleans. With much of the city underwater and law enforcement

Theft

The taking and carrying away of another's personal property with the intent to deprive him or her of it permanently.

organizations paralyzed, the city fell into chaos. A crowd of looters in a drug store near the French Quarter was interrupted by police, who came to seize drugs and water for sick residents of a nearby hotel. The police told the waiting crowd they would be out of their way as soon as they got the things they needed. In another incident a man, arms loaded with clothes, reportedly asked a policeman if he could borrow his car.[12]

One of the most famous examples of looting in recent history is the ransacking of Baghdad's Iraq Museum following the end of Saddam Hussein's regime in 2003. More than 15,000 objects, some more than 1,000 years old, were stolen or destroyed in a matter of days in the wake of the city's fall.

Library Theft: This type of theft is generally defined as theft of a circulating library item such as a book or record that is kept beyond its return date and after notification that the item must be returned. Library theft can also cover the concealing and taking of rare manuscripts from a library. A recent example of library theft involved a rare map dealer, Edward Forbes Smiley III, who pled guilty in July 2006 to stealing a circa 1578 Flemish map of the world, valued at about $150,000, from Yale's Beinecke Rare Book and Manuscript Library. As part of his plea agreement, Smiley confessed to removing an additional 96 maps from the Boston Public Library, the New York Public Library, and other institutions. The total value of the maps he stole is estimated between $1.8 million and $3 million.[13]

Theft by Deception: When a person commits theft by deception, he or she steals through surreptitious means such as fraud.

HISTORICAL HIGHLIGHT
Woman Faked Cancer, Stole Donations

In March 2001, Jeffrey Clark, special agent for the U.S. Drug Enforcement Agency (DEA) requested a medical-hardship transfer from Houston, Texas, to Utah so his wife Tania could undergo chemotherapy at the Huntsman Cancer Institute in Salt Lake City. "Over the past year and a half, I have had to exhaust my sick leave to care for Tania and my two sons during her ongoing illness," Clark wrote in his transfer request. "This has created a tremendous emotional and physical strain for me during these time periods." Clark included a letter from a Dr. Robert Bates at the University of Texas M. D. Anderson Cancer Center. He also included a letter from his wife, which said: "Our family has been crying, hugging, laughing, and healing since all this started."[14]

The DEA granted his request and paid nearly $48,000 to transfer the Clark family to Utah.

After moving to Utah, where Tania Clark's family lived, the couple told family, friends, neighbors, and other members of the community that she needed $62,000 for a bone marrow transplant. Members of her sons' hockey league, the Timpanogos Amateur Hockey Association, donated $1,000. Students at Oakcrest

Elementary School held a "Coins for Caring" drive, collecting more than $6,000 to help her. Neighbors gave the Clarks more than $5,000, and some offered to donate their bone marrow. The donations totaled more than $16,000.[15]

After an article about the Clarks' plight appeared in the *South Valley Journal*, Clark's sister e-mailed the newspaper saying her sister was not trustworthy. An investigation showed that Tania Clark had never been a patient at M. D. Anderson Cancer Center in Houston or the Huntsman Cancer Institute. No Robert Bates had ever practiced medicine at Anderson.[16] On February 16, 2005, Tania Clark confessed to a West Jordan detective that she had never had cancer.

In 2005, Tania Clark was sentenced by Third District Judge Paul Maughan to 30 days in jail. He ordered prison sentences of 1 to 15 years for theft by deception and up to 5 years for attempted theft by deception, but suspended the sentences. He placed Clark on 3 years probation instead and ordered her to perform 200 hours of community service and pay $5,378 in restitution. She also pleaded guilty to felony theft in neighboring Utah County, where she received probation and community service and was ordered to pay $5,800 in restitution.

Jeffrey Clark was also charged with theft by deception and forgery, but the charges were later dropped for lack of evidence that Mr. Clark knew of the scheme. He left his job under undisclosed circumstances. The DEA later filed suit against the couple, seeking restitution for the agency's moving expenses. In June 2007, the couple settled the lawsuit, agreeing to pay $60,000 in restitution to the DEA.[17]

Theft of Services: This form of theft is committed when someone obtains services such as cable television or other utilities by tapping into the source of those utilities with the intention not to pay for those services. Theft of services can also occur when someone uses false information to receive utility services.

Theft by Bailee or Trustee: This form of theft occurs when someone other than the true owner of property has custody of that property. For example, a jeweler who is going to repair a ring has temporary custody of the property. The owner of the ring has temporarily turned over the property for repair and safekeeping. If the jeweler keeps or sells the ring, she has committed theft. In some jurisdictions, this crime may be known as theft by failure to make required disposition of funds received. For example, a Lexington, Kentucky, lawyer and his secretary were indicted for taking $500,000 from a title company escrow account used for holding money during home sales and refinancing. The pair faced four counts of theft by failure to make a required disposition of property for failing to forward the funds to mortgage companies and other lenders.[18]

Auto Theft: One of the most costly property crimes in the United States is auto theft. The crime is costly because nearly every auto owner is insured for theft, so that most car thefts result in payment of the value of the car by an insurer. A car is stolen in the United States every 26 seconds, making the odds of a vehicle being stolen 1 in 190.[19]

The types of theft previously outlined are examples. Many jurisdictions have created other crimes of theft and will continue to do so as the need arises. For example, 50 years ago there was no need to define theft to include offenses such as stealing someone's credit profile and identity in order to apply for fraudulent credit cards. But all these crimes have the basic elements of theft in common. It is to these elements that we now turn.

TAKING AND CARRYING AWAY

The first element of the crime of theft is "taking and carrying away." The prosecution must prove that the defendant took possession of the object of the theft and carried it away. As you have seen in the discussion of specific types of theft, the taking can include keeping possession of something placed in the defendant's custody. But the essence of any theft is that the defendant takes personal property belonging to another and places it under his own control. For example, a customer who tries on a dress in a department store and then walks out with the dress on has taken and carried it away (and committed the crime of retail theft). The degree of carrying away can be slight. She would be guilty of retail theft even if she were caught before she got out of the store because she had taken possession of the dress and had begun to take it out of the store.

PERSONAL PROPERTY

Under the Common Law, the only type of property that could be stolen was tangible personal property. Real estate could not be stolen nor could other intangible things such as copyrights, stocks, or bonds. Now all jurisdictions have revised their theft statutes to include intangible personal property under their definitions of theft. That personal property can include such things as electric and cable service and intangible computer files. In addition, someone who forges a deed to real estate can also be charged with theft (by deception).

OF ANOTHER

The property stolen must belong to someone other than the defendant. The prosecution must therefore prove ownership of the property. Prosecutors need the cooperation of property owners in order to secure theft convictions. In order to constitute theft, the defendant must take the property without the consent of the owner. For example, it would not be theft to take your friend's ring if she gave it to you. But the prosecutor would have to put your friend on the stand to testify that she both owned the ring and did not give it to you in order for you to be convicted of theft.

Another very real problem is proving that the property the police found the defendant in possession of is actually the victim's property. For example, if the victim claims the defendant stole her diamond ring, she will have to identify the diamond as hers. If the ring is engraved, the victim can identify it. But what if the diamond has been removed from its setting (a common tactic used by gem thieves)? How will she identify the diamond as hers? Unless she has had the diamond marked, mapped, and registered (a service available for rare and high-end gems), she will be unable to tell her diamond from another, and the thief will walk away with the gem.

Because stolen property must be positively identified as belonging to the owner, it is crucial that owners keep careful track of serial numbers and other identifying characteristics of their property in case of theft. Without positive proof, the thief may very well walk away with his ill-gotten lot.

WITH THE INTENT TO PERMANENTLY DEPRIVE THE OWNER OF THE PROPERTY

The final element of the crime of theft involves intent. It is not enough that the defendant took possession of property belonging to another. He must also intend to permanently deprive the owner of the property. Intent may be proven with indirect or circumstantial evidence. Thus, a thief's actions may speak of his intent. For example, an art thief who steals a gallery's Monet painting and then displays it in his private study will likely find that a jury can be convinced that his actions indicate he intended to permanently deprive the gallery of the use and enjoyment of the painting. But what about a neighbor who takes a gas grill from down the block and is caught red-handed rolling the grill toward his house? Did he intend to permanently deprive the owner of the grill, or did he just borrow it?[20] Other cases where intent is less than clear are cases where absent-minded shoppers claim to have inadvertently placed merchandise in their pockets or bags and never intended to leave the store without paying. In such cases, credibility plays a major factor.

Embezzlement occurs when someone who has legal possession of property of another uses, converts, or retains that property for his own use or the use of someone other than the owner. It differs from other forms of theft because it does not require proof that the perpetrator took and carried away property of another. That is because the embezzler already lawfully possesses the property, albeit on behalf of the other. Many cases of embezzlement involve a trusted insider stealing from an employer.

Embezzlement
The use, conversion, or retention of property legally possessed by the perpetrator, but belonging to another.

Embezzlement tends to be a crime of opportunity and can often be avoided with proper oversight and financial controls. Take the case of a former Prothonotary and Clerk of Court for Mifflin County, Pennsylvania. Sue Ellen Saxton controlled thousands of dollars submitted to the court in fines, penalties, and other funds. Over the years she managed to divert over $800,000 of funds in her possession and control to her personal use. The funds were allegedly used to fund gambling expeditions to Las Vegas and Atlantic City. The embezzlement was accomplished by marking funds actually diverted to her personal account as having been returned to criminal defendants. She pled guilty to one count of conspiracy under federal law.[21]

In some cases, embezzlement can be a very subtle case of using resources inappropriately. For example, a retired professor at the University of North Texas pled guilty to embezzlement after an investigation revealed he had habitually used university staff, computers, and telephone systems to support a side business, Public Management Associates, while working at the university. From 1993 to 2006, the university estimated he used $463,000 in university resources to support his own business.[22]

In another case, Lawrence "Dale" and Christina Roberts, husband and wife, stole $386,000 from their employer, CheckFree Corporation, an electronic financial services provider headquartered in Norcross, Georgia. Dale Roberts handled payments to independent contractors working for CheckFree. He and wife Christina set up Harbor Consulting Group, a sole proprietorship, under her name and funneled all of CheckFree's payments to independent contractors through Harbor. They doubled all the contractors' fees and pocketed the difference and created bogus bills from fictitious contractors.

An investigation by the FBI's Atlanta Field Office led to the couple's arrest. Dale Roberts was sentenced to three years in federal prison, and Christina Roberts to one year and three months, and both were ordered to pay restitution.[23]

Had CheckFree looked, the company might have seen some warning signs. Harbor's address was a leased commercial mailbox, and its telephone line was a cell phone given to a neighbor acting as "president." Avoiding embezzlement requires putting in place an appropriate check to assure that no one can divert funds without notice. All businesses should assure that they have in place appropriate safeguards to prevent embezzlement.

HISTORICAL HIGHLIGHT
Bookkeeper Hid Her Double Life

When Angela Buckborough Platt first came to work as a temporary bookkeeper for J&J Materials of Rehoboth, Massachusetts, a landscaping and masonry supplier, owner John Ferreira was so impressed with her work that he paid a fee to the temp agency to hire her full-time. "Why isn't everybody like Angela?" Ferreira would ask others in the office. "She never leaves her office. She doesn't hang out at the copy machine and talk. She just works all day long."

Platt lived in an unassuming split level home in Cumberland, Rhode Island. Her only extravagance was a wild Halloween display, which grew so lavish after she joined the company that Ferreira's sister asked about the cost.

By 2004, the general manager of J&J's Nantucket Pavers plant became suspicious of the profit-and-loss reports Platt gave him every year. The company was not profiting as much as it should have been. In 2006, the manager brought in a second accountant, telling her: "We need to watch everything, cause we're getting robbed." The new bookkeeper was immediately suspicious and called vendors to verify three checks written out to them totaling about $74,000. None of the vendors had received the checks.

Ferreira sent his vice president to the bank to examine the checks, who called shortly after to say: "I'm looking at a check here for $44,000, and it's made out to Angela Buckborough."

Ferreira called Angela into his office that afternoon, where two Rehoboth police officers were waiting. He slid the $44,000 check across the table and asked if she knew anything about it. Angela replied, "Yes. I've been stealing money." When Ferreira asked how much, she said about $200,000. Ferreira asked Angela to get as much cash as she had in the bank, $60,000, and return it to him the following Tuesday, after a holiday weekend.

On Tuesday morning, Angela walked back into the conference room and told Ferreira and his lawyer, "I did some figuring over the weekend, and it was a little more than I thought." She slid a piece of paper over to Ferreira. It read $1,530,000, followed by a list of purchases.

When it was all said and done, her total take came to $6.9 million. "What, was she embezzling from the mob?" Ferreira asked. "That can't all be my money."[24]

Platt had been leading a double life. She owned a 104-acre ranch in West Haven, Vermont, with a heated saltwater swimming pool and two barns, one full of show horses, the other housing a commercial-caliber arcade. She owned time-shares in Florida and the Bahamas. She had assembled a fleet of motor vehicles, many vintage or unusual custom cars, including a 1937 Chevy panel car with a Bonnie and Clyde mural, faux bullet holes, and a portrait of Platt's husband dressed as a gangster on the rear tire compartment and a 1920s-era beer truck custom made from a toy model at a cost of $100,000. Platt had also purchased an unusual assortment of celebrity and cinema memorabilia, including six talking trees from the Wizard of Oz at $3,000 each, a 20-foot smoke-breathing dragon called "The Slayer," and a life-size ceramic statue of Al Capone, seated and smoking a cigar. She had hired Burt Bacharach to perform at her brother's wedding and planned a lavish party complete with $19,000 in fireworks.

She and her husband were known for going out to eat near their home in Vermont, picking up the tab for everyone in the restaurant, and giving $300 tips to the waitresses. When anyone asked where they got their money, the couple said they were CEOs of seven companies or that they had won the lottery.

Platt pleaded guilty to embezzling and was sentenced to four years in prison. She was also ordered to pay $4.48 million plus interest in restitution.[25]

How could Platt siphon off $6.9 million, seemingly right under her employer's nose? That's exactly how embezzlement happens. It's a crime committed in broad daylight, by a person entrusted with a position of power. Ferreira trusted Platt so much he put her in charge of a fortune and never looked over her shoulder. Many companies rely on the same people who write checks to audit the company's finances and do taxes and other accounting. This opens them up to abuse, as John Ferreira found out too late.

ROBBERY

Robbery is the taking of personal property from the person of another against his will, by either force or threat of force.[26] It is forcible stealing. To convict a defendant of robbery, the prosecution must prove that there was:

- A taking and carrying away of the property of another
- The intent to steal that property
- Property taken from the person or in the presence of the person
- The use of force or threat of the use of imminent force

Common acts of robbery include stopping someone and demanding his wallet when the demand is accompanied by the threat, either actual or implied, that the robber will harm the victim if he doesn't acquiesce and demanding a teller in a bank to hand over cash. What distinguishes robbery from other forms of theft is the element of threat to the person. Generally, states have two categories of robbery—simple robbery and armed robbery.

Robbery

The taking of personal property from the person of another against his will, by either force or threat of force.

Simple robbery is accomplished without weapons, while armed robbery is accomplished with the use of some sort of weapon such as a knife, gun, or other dangerous instrument. Armed robbery is punished more severely than simple robbery. In fact, many states mandate long prison terms for those who commit armed robbery.

CAUTION: FEDERAL LAW DIFFERS FROM COMMON LAW

There are also federal criminal laws prohibiting robbery. In some cases, federal laws do not parallel the common law of robbery. For example, if a banking institution is federally chartered, federal law defines a bank robber as:

> Whoever by force and violence, or by intimidation, takes, or attempts to take, from the person or presence of another, or obtains or attempts to obtain by extortion any property or money or any other thing of value belonging to, or in the care, custody, control, management, or possession of, any bank, credit union, or any savings and loan association.[27]

The Supreme Court has ruled that prosecutors seeking bank robbery convictions under this statute do not have to prove that the robber took or carried away the valuables he attempted to take.[28]

We now turn to the elements of the crime of robbery that differ from those of theft. Remember with most state statutes, the elements of the crime of theft must also be satisfied.

FROM THE PERSON OR IN THE PRESENCE OF THE PERSON

Robbery does not occur if force is neither threatened nor used. For example, if you have a party at your house and a guest picks up a ring you left by the sink, pockets it, and leaves, she has not committed robbery even if you saw her take the ring. However, if she pockets the ring while grabbing a steak knife and brandishes it threateningly toward you while she makes her exit, then she has committed robbery. The difference is in the fear she has inflicted on you. In the first example, she has committed theft, whereas in the second example she has committed robbery.

BY THE USE OF FORCE OR THREAT OF THE USE OF IMMINENT FORCE

Robbery must be committed with the aid of the use of force or the threat of the imminent use of force. A robbery can be committed when a defendant makes a threatening move toward the victim, if it seems to the victim that the defendant is capable of inflicting harm. A demand for "your money or your life" from an octogenarian weighing 100 pounds would probably not be robbery, but the same demand from a burly 25-year-old weight lifter probably would be.

Generally, if a weapon is displayed in the presence of a victim when a theft is attempted or takes place, the crime committed is armed robbery. A typical statute defines armed robbery as: "the crime of robbery while armed with a pistol, dirk, slingshot, metal knuckles, razor, or other deadly weapon."[29]

There is an interesting line of cases in which toy weapons were used. In most cases, the fact that a toy gun appears real is enough to sustain a charge of armed robbery. However, when the victim realizes the weapon used is fake, the crime committed is simple robbery.

Two Tampa, Florida, men were arrested and charged with multiple felonies for trying to rob a cab driver with a plastic gun. After arriving at their destination just after midnight, the men pulled the toy gun on the cabbie and demanded his van and all his property. The cab driver struggled with the men, drawing the attention of passing police, who arrested them.

Both men were charged with felony armed carjacking and felony attempted armed robbery. A sheriff's office spokeswoman said it didn't matter that the gun was plastic because it looked real and was used to commit a crime. The car driver said he "feared for his life" during the robbery.[30]

What if the defendant keeps a toy gun hidden during a robbery but it is discovered on him after the arrest? At least under federal law, that would not be armed robbery.[31]

What if the gun used in a bank robbery isn't loaded? Is that still the use of a dangerous weapon during the robbery of a federally chartered bank, qualifying the defendant for a longer sentence than if no weapon was used? According to the U.S. Supreme Court, the answer is "yes." The case involved two men who, both wearing stocking masks and gloves, entered a bank in Baltimore. One displayed a dark handgun and ordered everyone in the bank to put their hands up and not to move. While he remained in the lobby area holding the gun, his partner jumped over the counter and put $3,400 in a brown paper bag. The two were apprehended by a police officer as they left the bank. The officers discovered that the gun was unloaded. One defendant was convicted of using a dangerous weapon during a robbery. In a unanimous opinion, the Supreme Court reasoned that "the display of a gun instills fear in the average citizen; as a consequence, it creates an immediate danger that a violent response will ensue. Finally, a gun can cause harm when used as a bludgeon."[32]

Bank tellers robbed by a 76-year-old woman in West Mifflin, Pennsylvania, in March 2006, would agree. Marilyn Devine pointed an unloaded black 9 mm handgun at tellers in the National City Bank and gathered $5,960 in cash, stuffing it into a white trash bag. She was arrested after a low-speed chase. Devine was sentenced to 23 months of house arrest.[33]

Devine offered several explanations for the robbery, including that her son was suicidal over financial troubles and she wanted to help him. However, the tellers she robbed testified that they were harmed when Devine pointed her pistol at their faces. One of the tellers said she suffered nightmares. "You don't remember my face, but I'm haunted by yours," she said in court. In addition to the trauma Devine inflicted on her, the teller said she was upset by "the ridicule of people laughing that I got robbed by a grandmother."[34]

BURGLARY

At Common Law, **burglary** was the breaking and entering of the dwelling house of another at night with the intent to commit a felony inside. It was generally punishable by death. The crime required that the perpetrator secure entry by some use of force. That is, it was not burglary to enter an unlocked dwelling. Force must have been used, whether that meant pushing in a door or breaking a window. In addition, the entry had to be to a dwelling house. It was not burglary to break into a warehouse or other storage place.

The crime of burglary is complete when the entry with intent to commit a felony has taken place. It doesn't matter that the burglar doesn't actually commit a crime once inside. In fact, any crime committed once inside will be charged separately whether that crime is an assault, murder, or theft.

Burglary
At Common Law, the breaking and entering of the dwelling house of another at night with the intent to commit a felony inside. Today, burglary is the forcible entry into a structure with the intent to commit a felony once inside.

HISTORICAL HIGHLIGHT
Armed Robbery of LSAT Test Proves Costly

Law school may be a dream for many, but if you want to go, you have to have good grades and a good score on the Law School Admissions Test. Taking the standardized test is a ritual for all law school hopefuls. Some students are apparently so intent on getting a good score that they will resort to armed robbery.

During the February 8, 1997 exam, a student using fake identification to take the test at the University of California at Los Angeles walked out about 15 minutes into the test. When the proctor followed him onto the street and demanded the test back, the student pulled a switchblade knife, got in a car, and left. Shortly after, Danny Khatchaturian and Dikran Iskendarian, two students taking the test in Hawaii, began receiving the answers on their pagers. The time difference between Hawaii and California meant there was a 2-hour delay in the test.[35] In January 2001, the two were sentenced to 1 year of home detention and 5 years probation as well as to pay $97,000 in restitution to the LSAT.[36]

William Blackstone, the great English legal commentator, insisted that burglary could only occur at those times of the day when it was too dark to see a man's face without the aid of artificial light or moonlight. He wrote:

> The time must be by night, and not by day: for in the day time there is no burglary.... As to what is reckoned night, and what day, for this purpose: anciently the day was accounted to begin only at sun-rising, and to end immediately upon sun-set; but the better opinion seems to be, that if there be daylight or crepusculum enough, begun or left, to discern a man's face withal, it is no burglary. But this does not extend to moonlight; for then many midnight burglaries would go unpunished: and besides, the malignity of the offence does not so properly arise from its being done in the dark, as at the dead of night; when all the creation, except beasts of prey, are at rest; when sleep has disarmed the owner, and rendered his castle defenceless.[37]

Today, states have expanded the definition of burglary to cover just about any unauthorized entry into a structure, at any time of day or night. Some states simply retain the nighttime provision in their statutes and have added other sections to their crimes codes that also punish daytime break-ins. They distinguish between nighttime and daytime break-ins by punishing night activity more severely than the same crime committed in broad daytime. The most common definition today is that burglary is the unlawful entry of a structure to commit a felony or theft. For example, the criminal law of Pennsylvania provides that:

> A person is guilty of burglary if he enters a building or occupied structure, or separately secured or occupied portion thereof, with intent to commit a crime therein, unless the premises are at the time open to the public or the actor is licensed or privileged to enter.[38]

Pennsylvania grades the offense on the basis of how the building or occupied structure is used. If the building isn't set up for overnight accommodations (i.e., it isn't a residence or a hotel or inn) and no one is present during the burglary, the offense carries a lesser penalty than if the building is a home. A burglar who enters a jewelry store to steal the merchandise is subject to a lesser penalty than if the same burglar broke into a private home. However, if the same burglar broke into the jewelry store and the night watchman was there, he would face the higher penalty.

UNLAWFUL ENTRY INTO PREMISES

What does it mean to unlawfully enter premises? Does the burglar have to physically enter the premises with his whole body, or is it enough that he breaks a window and reaches in to help himself to another's belongings? Most states hold that reaching in is enough to constitute burglary. Most states still require that there must be at least some form of unauthorized entry into the premises. That is because the crime of burglary is based in part on the concept of the tort of trespass. Trespass is the unlawful and unprivileged entry or intrusion onto the property of another. If the building entered is normally open to the public and the defendant is legally present in the building, it is not burglary, just as his presence would not constitute the tort of trespass.

DWELLING HOUSE OF ANOTHER

The Common Law definition required that to constitute burglary, the unlawful entry must have been to a dwelling house of another. At Common Law, a dwelling house was a structure in which people lived and slept. States no longer limit burglary to dwelling houses and include just about any structure, occupied or unoccupied, in their definitions. Some states have expanded the definition to include unoccupied automobiles and even telephone booths. For example, California defines burglary so broadly as to include shoplifting and theft of goods from a locked but unoccupied automobile.[39]

The requirement that the building entered by a would-be burglar be "of another" is another reflection that the genesis of the crime of burglary is in the tort of trespass. Just as you cannot trespass on your own property, neither can you burglarize your own home. Although this may seem obvious, it is a fairly common problem, and courts must sometimes determine what is meant by "of another." For example, assume a husband and wife have separated, but the husband still is an owner of the marital home in which the wife continues to live. If the husband breaks the window and enters the house with the intent to steal property belonging to his wife, he cannot be charged with burglary. He has not entered the property of another. Of course, he could still be charged with theft, if he successfully made off with his wife's property.

In addition to proving that the defendant entered the dwelling house (or other building, depending on the definition used in your state's burglary statute), the prosecution must show that the defendant didn't have permission to be present in the structure. Clearly, a person present in a public place during normal business hours when the facility is open to the public has implied permission to be there. He was invited, and therefore isn't trespassing. The prosecution typically puts the property owner or a manager on the stand during trial to testify that the defendant didn't have permission to enter the building.

WITH INTENT TO COMMIT A FELONY

A defendant's entry into another's structure, no matter how violent or destructive that entry was, isn't burglary unless the defendant can be shown to have intended to commit a felony while inside. Many states have made proof even easier, since they have specified that the intent that must be shown is merely the intent to commit a crime once inside. That crime does not have to be theft-related. It would still be burglary to break into a home with the intent to kill or rape someone inside. In many cases, there will be direct evidence of intent—as happens when a defendant is caught leaving the site of the burglary with stolen goods.

Sometimes it's not clear whether the defendant formed the intent to commit a felony or other crime once inside. For example, a homeless person who seeks shelter in what appears to be an empty house but runs into the owner during his visit and then injures that owner may not be guilty of burglary. He may be guilty of a lesser offense such as unlawful entry or criminal trespass. He would also likely be guilty of assault, but not burglary.

Proving intent is generally not difficult in burglary cases even if the defendant isn't "caught in the act." Juries and judges rely on circumstantial evidence and common sense to prove intent. The fact that the defendant broke into a building containing personal property and was caught often leads to an inference that he intended to steal some of that property once inside. Unless the defendant testifies and comes up with a plausible explanation for his presence, judge or jury likely will consider his presence and the circumstances surrounding it as proof of intent.

ARSON

Arson

The intentional and malicious burning of a structure. At Common Law, it was the malicious burning of the dwelling house of another.

At Common Law, **arson** was the malicious burning of the dwelling house of another. The building burned had to be the dwelling of another, so that burning down a stable or other outbuilding was not arson. Nor was it a crime to burn down one's own building. In order to curtail insurance fraud (as might happen if an insured homeowner burned down his property and collected the insurance) and so-called spite arson (as might happen when an angry spouse burned down the home previously shared with a spouse and still jointly owned), most states expanded their definition of arson. Today, most states have changed their laws to define arson as the willful and malicious burning of a structure or building.

By setting the standard of intent as willful and malicious burning, arson statutes cover all the common motives for committing the crime. Possible motivation for committing arson include:

- *Arson for profit:* Arson committed in order to collect on insurance carried on the structure burned or by an owner who cannot sell the property and wants to move on. The latter can be a major problem in decaying urban areas with a large concentration of abandoned and boarded-up warehouses and businesses.
- *Arson for revenge:* Arson committed as payback for a failed love affair or marriage or in retaliation for an adverse employment decision.

- *Evidence destruction:* Arson committed to cover up another crime or destroy evidence, such as evidence that a victim in the structure was killed by fire rather than other means or as a means of eliminating documents sought in a criminal investigation.
- *Political act:* Arson to make a political statement, such as the firebombing of abortion clinics by antiabortion extremists.
- *Arson for thrill:* Some cases of arson are the work of thrill seekers who are frequently juveniles. These cases represent a high proportion of arson cases in which there is an arrest. Other fires may be set by perpetrators plagued by mental illness. Pyromaniacs may start fires as part of a quest for sexual or other excitement.[40]

Arson is a serious crime in the United States. Federal Bureau of Investigation data shows that 67,504 arson offenses were reported in 2005, causing more than $1 billion in damages and 315 civilian deaths. Unfortunately, the clearance rate for arson was only around 20 percent. A crime is defined as "cleared" in the FBI crime reports when a suspect is arrested and charged with the crime. That means a great many incidents of arson go unpunished every year.[41]

When arson is politically motivated, the arsonist is sometimes also charged under federal law. For example, Suzanne Nicole Savoie was sentenced under a federal terrorism law for her part in two Oregon arsons. Savoie, a member of "The Family," a secretive cell of the Environmental Liberation Front (ELF), pled guilty to serving as a lookout during an arson at Superior Lumber Co. in Glendale, which caused $1 million in damage. She also pled guilty to helping to plan and commit an arson that caused $994,000 in damage to Jefferson Poplar Farm in Clatskanie. U.S. District Judge Ann Aiken sentenced Savoie to four years and three months in prison. Judge Aiken ruled the tree farm arson a crime of terrorism because the conspirators' communications about the arsons ridiculed proposed legislation aimed at such crimes, making the government a target of the acts.[42]

YOU MAKE THE CALL

FREE SPEECH OR TERRORISM?

Gareth Groves, who lives in an affluent neighborhood near American University in Washington, DC, brought home a shiny new Hummer sports utility vehicle. Hummers have been the frequent target of anger among environmentalists, who criticize the car's dreadful gas mileage. He awoke one night after he bought the car to the sound of breaking glass. The noise was coming from the driveway, where Groves reportedly saw two masked men taking bats to the Hummer and spray painting "for the environment" on its side. They did $12,000 worth of damage.[43]

In a series of incidents in 2003, several California car dealerships who sold Hummers were vandalized. Police and the FBI suspected ELF, the Earth Liberation Front, as the source of the vandalism. Similar incidents have occurred at new home construction sites. In fact, the FBI estimates ELF has committed 1,100 criminal acts, including arson and vandalism, since 1976. In January 2006, the FBI indicted.

Are vandalism and arson justifiable as a way to call attention to the environment? Is it an exercise of free speech? Would you feel the same way if it were your property that was damaged? You make the call.

Essential Elements of Arson

The essential elements that the government must prove beyond a reasonable doubt in an arson case are:

- The fire was willfully and maliciously set by the defendant or someone else on his orders. Carelessness isn't enough.
- The fire set by the defendant caused damage. Merely scorching a building is not enough (although the offense charged might instead be attempted arson or criminal trespass and criminal mischief).

Arson cases are not easy to prove. First, the fire itself, if successful, destroys much of the evidence. Second, there are many fires that are accidental and not the result of intentional wrongdoing. Cigarettes left to smolder, careless cooking, faulty electrical systems, and lightning are frequent causes of fires. In addition, getting the appropriate evidence may sometimes be difficult. Fire officials who arrive on the scene can make a preliminary decision whether the fire was intentionally set or not and can seize any evidence in plain sight.

The U.S. Supreme Court has ruled that once a blaze has been extinguished and the firefighters have left the premises, a warrant is required to reenter the premises. The Fourth Amendment protects the owner of the premises from intrusion without probable cause that the fire was deliberately set. In order to get a warrant, a government official must show more than that a fire occurred. However, the firefighters who initially respond may seize evidence that is in plain view and investigate the cause of the fire as part of their efforts to contain it and make the area safe. That evidence can then be used to support an application for a warrant if it reached the level of probable cause. The case *Michigan v. Tyler*[44] involved a fire at a furniture store. When the fire chief arrived, the fire was still smoldering. Discovered in the embers were several plastic containers of flammable liquid, which aroused suspicion. Over the next few weeks, police and fire officials returned several times to gather evidence, all without a warrant. The testimony of fire experts and evidence obtained from the visits were introduced into evidence, and the store owners were convicted of arson. The Supreme Court reversed the convictions and ordered any evidence seized after the immediate exigency was over without a warrant be excluded in any retrial.

HISTORICAL HIGHLIGHT
How the FBI Began Collecting Crime Data

Early in the twentieth century, it became apparent to law enforcement officials that tracking the type and frequency of criminal activity was important to its containment. At the time, individual states seldom shared information about criminal activity within their borders with others in the union. In addition, each state had a unique set of criminal laws, and there were as many definitions of specific crimes as there were states.

In the late 1920s, the International Association of Chiefs of Police suggested the creation of a national database of crime and criminal activity. Voluntary data collection began in 1930, with information coming from state, county, and city law enforcement agencies. The information is now gathered at the Federal Bureau of Investigation. Law enforcement agencies use uniform definitions when deciding which crimes to report to help overcome differences in state laws. There are eight classifications of crimes reported to the FBI. These are:

1. Murder and nonnegligent manslaughter
2. Forcible rape
3. Robbery
4. Aggravated assault
5. Burglary
6. Larceny-theft
7. Motor vehicle theft
8. Arson

The FBI publishes an annual report of crime in the United States, which is available at the FBI Web site *www.fbi.gov*.

DEFACING PROPERTY AND GRAFFITI

Defacing property by damaging or writing on it, commonly known as graffiti, often falls under the catchall term, criminal or **malicious mischief.** Generally, malicious mischief is a lesser crime than arson but also results in the destruction of property. Primarily, malicious mischief involves a threat to property only. Arson has the potential to injure or kill people.

To prove malicious mischief, a prosecutor must prove that the defendant intended to destroy or harm property in a way that diminishes the property's value or dignity. Graffiti often involves diminishing the dignity of a piece of property. For example, spray painting satanic symbols on a church would be a crime even though the paint could probably be cleaned off. Plus, doing so might also be classified as a hate crime if the intent is to intimidate the worshippers.

Often malicious mischief involves clean-up costs for the property owner even if the property is not permanently damaged. For instance, pranksters putting soap into a public fountain in the hope the circulating water would create bubbles are guilty of malicious mischief. Usually, the amount of property damage determines whether the charge is a felony or misdemeanor. For instance, swinging a hammer to break a window is probably a misdemeanor; swinging a hammer to damage a Renaissance era sculpture is most likely a felony.

Malicious Mischief
Also known as criminal mischief, it is defined as the criminal offense of intentionally destroying another person's property.

FORGERY AND CHECK FRAUD

The number of checks written in the United States every year is staggering. Many of these checks are stolen and altered or counterfeited, resulting in a loss of more than $20 billion per year, according to the Payments Fraud and Control Survey of the Association of

Example of graffiti.

Forgery

The fraudulent making or altering of any writing in a way that alters the legal rights and liabilities of another.

Financial Professionals.[45] **Forgery** is the fraudulent making or altering of any writing in a way that alters the legal rights and liabilities of another. Although many types of documents can be forged, checks are the most common targets. Check fraud includes forgery and other forms of theft accomplished through the misuse of checks or the check processing system.

Check fraud and forgery can be committed in a number of creative ways. The most common forms of check fraud are:

- *Forged signatures:* Forged signature checks are legitimate checks with a forged signature. A thief may steal a checkbook from the owner or intercept an order of checks arriving in the mail and fill out the checks, supplying his signature for that of the account holder.
- *Forged endorsement:* In this form of check fraud, a thief steals an already-made-out check and forges the endorsement signature on the back and cashes or deposits the funds.
- *Altered checks:* In this form of check fraud, a thief alters a check to make it appear the check is made out to someone other than the intended payee or the amount to be drawn against the drawer's account is altered.
- *Check kiting:* In this form of check fraud, criminals deposit a check into one account, which is drawn on another bank's account, and then draws on the deposit knowing that the deposited check is no good.
- *Counterfeit checks:* This form of check fraud involves the creation of fake checks. Today, with the rapid development of computer technology and software, forging checks is easy. All a thief needs is a computer, a checking account number and bank routing number (found on every check), check writing software, and a printer. Software designed to allow consumers to print their own legitimate checks can churn out checks that look and seem indistinguishable from the real thing.

All states have criminal laws punishing check fraud and forgery, although the language varies from state to state. For example, in Minnesota, a person:

"is guilty of check forgery . . . if the person, with intent to defraud, does any of the following:

1. falsely makes or alters a check so that it purports to have been made by another or by the maker under an assumed or fictitious name, or at another time, or with different provisions, or by the authority of one who did not give authority; or

2. falsely endorses or alters a check so that it purports to have been endorsed by another."[46]

In addition, the United States Code has many provisions dealing with forged and counterfeited securities and other commercial documents.[47] Note also that the Uniform Commercial Code, which all states have adopted with some variation, has extensive provisions that govern liability of financial institutions and account holders when a check is forged or altered.

Most states also have laws that criminalize writing checks when there are insufficient funds in the account to cover the checks. Generally, these statutes provide that the maker of the check must be notified that the check has been dishonored and be given an opportunity to make the check good if the account was open. If he or she doesn't, criminal charges can be filed. For example, Pennsylvania provides that the drawer be notified that the check was dishonored within 30 days of presentment and that the drawer must make the check good within 10 days of notification. If he or she does not, the Commonwealth can rely on the presumption that the maker's intent was fraudulent.[48]

IDENTITY THEFT

Identity theft is a computer-era crime where the criminal uses another person's name, Social Security number, or other identifying information to represent that person for personal gain. Identity theft wreaks tremendous havoc on its victims, and law enforcement agencies are devoting increasingly more time to solving identity theft and similar cyber crimes.

Of course, identity theft can also be accomplished without the aid of computers. For example, thieves may go through garbage cans looking for discarded bills, tax returns, and other documents with indentification information. Armed with Social Security numbers, names, and addresses, they can apply for credit, order goods, or—as is becoming increasingly common—sell the information on the identity theft black market to the highest bidder.

HISTORICAL HIGHLIGHT
The Black Market for Stolen Data

Analysts say the nature of computer crime has changed over the past decade. Web-wide attacks by ingenious hackers have given way to targeted thefts by organized groups. "We're seeing rapid growth in cooperative attacks, where an insider works in concert with some sort of external source to make a financial gain," says Brian Contos, chief security officer at ArcSight and author of *Enemy at the Water Cooler*, a book analyzing computer crime trends. "It's not just hackers looking randomly for easy points of entry—these are attacks on specific companies."

Most companies today rely heavily on automated systems. Even tiny companies use computers to store data, and most use the World Wide Web. Access to corporate data is also more widespread than ever before, with a large share of employees in many companies working on personal computers. What once might have occupied a filing cabinet now fits in a tiny zip drive, smaller than a credit card, and can be broadcast at the touch of a button. In such an environment, it can be very difficult to keep data secure.

While access has increased, the black market for data has exploded. Social Security numbers, bank account information, mailing lists, customer lists, and even corporate secrets are readily bought and sold by individuals and organized groups. "There is a growing interest from organizations, like the Russian or Italian mafias, which basically just see stolen data as another revenue stream, like drugs or prostitution," says Chris Pierson, founder of the cybersecurity and cyberliability practice at Lewis and Roca LLP, a Phoenix law firm.

Thieves also use the Web to directly solicit information from unwary users. Phishers pose as banks or other financial concerns to try to get personal data directly from their customers. "You can buy a rootkit for $75 that will give you all of the advice, logos, and templates you need to execute a **phishing** attack," says Michael Rothschild, Director of Marketing at CounterStorm, maker of data security tools. The data goes pretty cheap. "You can get a hacked credit card on the Web for as little as $10," Rothschild says.[49]

Even Alcatel-Lucent, which helped develop data protection technology with Bell Labs and provides data protection services through its security division, suffered a serious security breach when a disk mailed to an insurer went missing in Somerset County, New Jersey, in April 2007. The disk contained names, addresses, Social Security numbers, salaries, and other personal information for all Lucent employees in the United States. Hewitt Associates in Bridgewater, which handles Lucent's health and pension benefits, prepared the disk and mailed it to insurer Aon Corporation on April 5. Aon reportedly received an empty envelope. Employees were dismayed to discover the data had not been encrypted.

The company hired a firm to provide free identity protection and credit monitoring for one year to the more than 200,000 affected employees and turned the case over to the Secret Service.[50]

Phishing

The attempt to obtain personal identifying information by posing as a bank or financial institution in an e-mail communication.

Identity theft is a crime of intent. Simply finding out someone's Social Security number is not a crime if you don't use it for personal gain. The Washington state code defines identity theft as follows:

1. No person may knowingly obtain, possess, use, or transfer a means of identification or financial information of another person, living or dead, with the intent to commit, or to aid or abet, any crime.

2. Violation of this section when the accused or an accomplice uses the victim's means of identification or financial information and obtains an aggregate total of credit, money, goods, services or anything else of value in excess of one thousand five hundred dollars in value shall constitute identity theft in the first degree. Identity theft in the first degree is a class B felony.

3. Violation of this section when the accused or an accomplice uses the victim's means of identification or financial information and obtains an aggregate total of credit, money, goods, services, or anything else of value that is less than one thousand five hundred dollars in value, or when no credit, money, goods, services, or anything of value is obtained shall constitute identity theft in the second degree. Identity theft in the second degree is a class C felony.

4. A person who violates this section is liable for civil damages of one thousand dollars or actual damages, whichever is greater, including costs to repair the victim's credit record, and reasonable attorneys' fees as determined by the court.

5. In a proceeding under this section, the crime will be considered to have been committed in any locality where the person whose means of identification or financial information was appropriated resides, or in which any part of the offense took place, regardless of whether the defendant was ever actually in that locality.

6. The provisions of this section do not apply to any person who obtains another person's driver's license or other form of identification for the sole purpose of misrepresenting his or her age.

7. In a proceeding under this section in which a person's means of identification or financial information was used without that person's authorization, and when there has been a conviction, the sentencing court may issue such orders as are necessary to correct a public record that contains false information resulting from a violation of this section.[51]

Because so much identity theft occurs via the computer, the perpetrator does not have to be near the victim. The preceding Washington state statute gives prosecutors wide geographic latitude in prosecuting identity thieves whereever they may be. Of course, there is only so long a reach. It is almost impossible to track down and prosecute some identity thieves, who may operate out of Internet cafes in Third World or other foreign countries.

CYBER CRIMES—THEFT, DECEPTION

Identity theft is not the only crime committed in cyberspace. The following were the seven most prevalent types of Internet fraud committed in 2006, according to Federal Bureau of Investigation statistics:

Auction Fraud Online auctions for goods that don't exist constitute 44.9 percent of fraud cases, averaging $602.50 per case, and was the fastest growing fraud category in 2006.

Non-Delivery Merchandise and services not delivered as promised accounted for 19 percent of cases, averaging $585 in losses per complaint.

Check Fraud 4.9 percent of cases involved check fraud, with losses averaging $3,744.

Credit and Debit Card Fraud 4.8 percent of fraud cases involved bankcard abuses, averaging $427.50 per complaint.

Confidence Fraud Frauds involving deception constituted 2.2 percent of the total, costing an average of $2,400 per case.

Identity Theft Identity theft comprised only 1.6 percent of fraud cases, but averaged $6,278 per case.

Investment Fraud Fraudulent investment schemes constituted 1.3 percent of fraud cases, and cost an average of $2,694.99.[52]

PRACTICE POINTERS

As with most criminal laws covered in this textbook, they are just guidelines and a starting point for research. Always check the exact wording of the criminal code of your state or the U.S. Code, if the case you are working on comes under federal jurisdiction. This is especially true of cases involving theft. State statutes vary greatly.

If the client has already been charged, read the statute carefully. This is especially true when the charge is robbery and the statute increases the sentence if the defendant used a dangerous weapon. The nature of the weapon used, especially if it was a fake or a toy, may give rise to an argument that the crime committed was at most simple robbery and be the basis for a plea bargain to a lesser offense.

If a client faces arson charges, be sure to examine the allegations and the evidence carefully. Evidence seized or observed without a warrant after the immediate exigency of the fire has passed may be inadmissible. If you are working for the prosecution, prepare as if defense counsel will raise the issue and determine what evidence was seized during or immediately after the fire and what was seized later. The earlier evidence may still be enough to allow an expert to conclude that the fire was set.

If you work for the defense, you may want to consider bringing in your own expert to determine if the evidence really indicates that the fire was deliberately set. Also examine the prosecution's indictment carefully. It will typically lay out the alleged motive the defendant had for torching his or another's property. Does the motive put forth by the prosecution make sense? For example, prosecutors will often suggest that insurance is the motivation. That may be logical if the policy was just issued or recently increased, but not if the policy is a long-standing one. Frank discussions should take place about the defendant's financial position. Heavy debt and a failing or underperforming business may be perceived as motivation for arson but can be countered with evidence that business was on the upswing or that alternative financing was in the works.

When defending a person accused of identity theft, make sure the prosecution proves all of the crime's elements. Merely possessing someone's personal information is not identity theft. The prosecution must prove the defendant obtained the information with the intent of personal gain. If the defendant took no action with the information, he has committed no crime in most jurisdictions.

Similarly, charges of theft or deception can be difficult to distinguish from simple misunderstandings. For that matter, locating and prosecuting the accused is often problematic. Most statutes give prosecutors long arms to go after perpetrators, but the global world of computing often puts cyber criminals beyond the law's reach.

Forgery and check fraud cases often depend heavily on expert testimony about the authenticity of a signature. Both the prosecution and the defense are likely to employ experts in document examination. When identifying an expert in arson or document examination, keep these guidelines in place:

- Examine each potential expert's resume and experience carefully. Note membership in relevant professional organizations and publications in juried or peer-reviewed journals. If the expert is affiliated with a major university or other well-respected organization, so much the better.
- Experts who only testify for the prosecution or only testify for the defense are suspect. At best, they appear less credible than those whose testimony has been more evenly spread. At worst, the expert will appear to be a hired gun or in the prosecutor's pocket.
- Check credentials carefully. In recent years, there has been a rash of cases involving erroneous or intentionally false testimony by forensic experts. Nothing will sink an expert's testimony faster than evidence that he or she faces professional negligence or even criminal charges arising out of testimony in other cases. This is an area where defense counsel have recently become more proactive, seeking out evidence that a particular laboratory or expert has lied or misled in other cases.
- When preparing the case, note any special rules in your jurisdiction about the exchange of expert testimony or notice of the intended use of an expert's opinion at trial.

CHAPTER SUMMARY

To understand crimes against property, you must first understand what property is. Property consists of a bundle of rights, including the right to possess, use and enjoy, and dispose of something. It is not a material object itself, but a person's right to do what he or she wishes with that object, subject to limitations provided in the law.

Real property is land and everything permanently attached to it. It includes land, subsurface rights, air rights, timbering and harvesting rights, and any buildings and structures permanently attached to the land. Personal property is everything else to which the law grants ownership rights. Property can be owned outright. If it is, the owner is said to hold the property in fee simple. Fee simple is a legal term for ownership of the entire bundle of rights that go with a piece of property.

Property can be held by one or jointly. Tenancy by the entirety is a legal joint ownership in which both spouses own an undivided interest in the whole property and in which neither spouse can sell his or her interest without the consent of the other. It only applies to married couples. Other forms of joint ownership are tenancy in common and joint tenancy with right of survivorship. Tenants in common each own an undivided interest in the whole property. If the owners hold property as joint tenants with right of survivorship, the survivor gets the property in the event of death of a joint tenant.

A basic understanding of the law of property is necessary in order to understand criminal laws that punish interference with property rights. Theft was defined at Common Law as the taking and carrying away of another's personal property with the intent to deprive him or her of it permanently. Laws that make theft a crime require that the person stealing the property intends to permanently deprive the owner of the use, possession, and enjoyment of that property.

Today, states and the federal government have passed many laws that build upon the Common Law definition of theft but apply to special situations. Theft offenses include theft by deception, embezzlement, library theft, shoplifting, auto theft, identity theft, and many others. Robbery is theft accomplished by the use of force or the threat of force. It differs from theft in that the victim is put in fear before surrendering the property sought by the robber. Robbery carried out with the use or brandishing of a weapon is a more serious offense than robbery without a weapon.

Burglary was defined at Common Law as breaking and entering of the dwelling house of another at night with the intent to commit a felony inside. Today the offense can occur at any time of day and does not require that a dwelling house be the target. A forcible entry into any structure with the intent to commit a felony once inside is all that is required.

Arson was the malicious burning of the dwelling house of another at Common Law. Today the definition has been expanded to cover the intentional and malicious burning of a structure. If the intention of the arsonist is to collect insurance proceeds, it does not matter that the property was his own. Arson is committed for many reasons, including insurance fraud, spite, as a political statement, and for thrill and excitement. Any of these motives are enough to establish that the fire was set intentionally and maliciously.

Identity theft occurs when someone appropriates another person's name, Social Security number, or other identifying information for the purposes of personal gain. Usually, identity theft occurs when computer information is breached or the victim is duped into providing information to the perpetrator. Cyber crimes also include theft or deception where victims are deprived of property or money through computer transactions.

Forgery is the fraudulent making or altering of any writing in a way that alters the legal rights and liabilities of another. Common forms of forgery involve check fraud. Check fraud includes forging the signature of another on a check, forging an endorsement on the back of a check, altering the amount of a check or to whom it is drawn, check kiting between accounts, and producing counterfeit checks. All are punishable under state laws. In addition, states often make it a crime to write a "bad" check. Once the maker is notified that the check was not honored, he or she generally has a short period of time to make it good before charges are filed.

KEY TERMS

Arson	Embezzlement	Forgery
Burglary	Eminent Domain	Joint Tenancy with
Chattel	Fee Simple	Right of Survivorship

Malicious Mischief	Real Property	Tenants by the
Personal Property	Robbery	Entireties
Phishing	Tenancy in Common	Theft
Property		

EXERCISE

Jose Lara was confused. An Arlington County, Virginia, bank sent him a check for almost $2,800, claiming it was an overpayment on his second mortgage. Jose was confused because he didn't have a second mortgage.

Jose did remember losing his wallet a few months before. He had reported his credit cards missing, but his wallet contained his Social Security card and other identifying information. The person who found it was Elizabeth Cabrera-Rivera. Elizabeth used Jose's information to obtain a mortgage from a predatory lender who never checked tax returns or income. Elizabeth bought a $419,000 townhouse in the Washington, DC suburb of Springfield, Virginia.

Unlike many identity thieves, she did not abscond with money. Instead, she refinanced the mortgage with a local bank and proceeded to make every payment. So despite the fact his identity was used, Jose's credit was not harmed, and he had not lost any money.

The bank was not happy though. They called Elizabeth and told her she had to come in to sign some additional paperwork. When she arrived, the police were waiting. Elizabeth was charged with credit card theft, identity fraud, and identity theft. No one lost any money (in fact, the "victim" actually got a check), so had she committed a crime? Look in the Chapter 5 Appendix to read how the Virginia Code defines the crimes with which Elizabeth was charged, and decide whether you think she is guilty or not.

DISCUSSION QUESTIONS

1. A community has enacted a law that requires residents to separate their garbage into recyclables and nonrecyclables. The recyclable items are placed in plastic containers marked "Property of the City of Ecology." The city collects the contents of the containers and sells it to a recycling facility, boosting the city budget by several hundred thousand dollars per year. Joe, a homeless man, makes the rounds on garbage day and selects metal cans from the recycling bins, which he crushes and sells to a recycling facility. He is arrested and charged with theft of city property. You have been asked to analyze the case on behalf of the public defender representing Joe. What is Joe's best defense to the theft charges?

2. What form of check fraud has occurred in each of the following factual scenarios?

    a. *Carla receives a birthday check from her grandmother and adds a "1" in front of the $10 and writes "One Hundred" in front of the Ten Dollars and no cents on the check.*

    b. *Sarah buys a copy of "Easy Check" software for her computer and uses the account number and bank routing number from her roommate's checks to print checks, which she then uses to pay her tuition bill.*

    c. *Jack finds a purse at a bus stop and takes a check from the checkbook he finds inside. He makes the check out to "cash" and signs the check with the account holder's name.*

    d. *Smitty maintains two checking accounts at two banks. He will be paid on Friday and has no funds in either account on Wednesday. Wednesday he writes a check for $100 to himself on account number one and deposits it in account number two. He then withdraws $100 from account number two. On Friday he deposits his paycheck in account number one to cover the check.*

3. Jessy decides to rob a bank. Jessy dresses up as a clown and carries a child's toy rifle, which has an orange tip. He approaches a teller and demands cash after brandishing the gun. He is caught a block from the bank as he trips on his clown shoes. Police charge him with armed robbery. How do you approach his defense?

4. Jerry is separated from his wife and still owns a house jointly with her. She has changed the keys to the house, and Jerry breaks a window to enter the house and retrieve personal belongings. He is charged with burglary. How do you defend him? Is your answer different if he takes his wife's possessions rather than his own?

5. Mary has been thinking about remodeling her kitchen. She has contacted several contractors and has received several estimates. She has also applied for a home equity loan to finance the project but has been turned down because she does not have enough equity in the home to qualify. Saturday night she fries some chicken and leaves the deep fryer full of oil on in the kitchen. She leaves for a walk. When she returns, she finds the firefighters dowsing a fire in her kitchen. Although the rest of the structure is saved, the kitchen is a total loss. Insurance covers the rebuilding. If you are the local prosecutor, how would you go about putting together a case against Mary? What evidence would you seek, and how would you obtain it?

FOR FURTHER READING

1. Morris, J. (1995). *DSM IV Made Easy.* The Guilford Press. This handbook helps demystify psychiatric diagnosis and is especially helpful for legal professionals working with psychiatric experts.

2. Faith, N. (2000). *Blaze: The Forensics of Fire.* St. Martin's Press. This book describes historic fires and the techniques used to determine their cause.

3. Bouquard, T. (2004). *Arson Investigation: The Step-by-Step Procedure,* 2nd edition. Charles C. Thomas Publisher. A guidebook for fire and arson investigators.

4. Shover, N. (1996). *Great Pretenders, Pursuits and Careers of Persistent Thieves.* Westview Press. This book looks at the career criminal who resumes a life of crime despite efforts to "go straight."

5. Cromwell, P. (Editor). (1998). *In Their Own Words: Criminals on Crime.* Roxbury. An anthology in which criminals explain their life of crime.

6. Berendt, J. (2005). *The City of Falling Angels.* Penguin Books. A story of the Venice Opera House arson in Venice, Italy, set among a rich cast of real-life characters.

7. Crichton, Michael. (2004). *State of Fear.* Harper Collins. A thriller involving ecoterrorism.

ENDNOTES

1. *Ballentine's Law Dictionary.*

2. Ibid.

3. Ibid.

4. *Kelo v. City of New London,* 545 U.S. 469.

5. Ibid.

6. Ibid.

7. Ibid.

8. "A deeply confused animal rights movement," Gary L. Francione and Lee Hall, *San Francisco Chronicle,* August 21, 2002, page A-21.

9. *Columbus-America Discovery Group v. Atlantic Mutual Insurance Company,* 974 F.2d 450 (4th Cir. 1992).

10. "Telepossession of Extraterrestrial Resources and Leveraged Financing of Outer Space Projects," Richard M. Westfall, Galactic Mining Industries, Inc., Denver, Colorado; Declan J. O'Donnell PC, United Societies in Space, Inc., Castle Rock, Colorado, and Gary Rodriguez, sysRAND Corporation, Parker, Colorado, from the Web site of Galactic Mining Industries, Inc., *www.angelfire.com/trek/galactic_mining/Telepossession.htm.*

11. National Association for Shoplifting Prevention (NASP), a nonprofit organization providing research-based shoplifting prevention initiatives including education, prevention, justice, and rehabilitation programs. Visit NASP at *www.shopliftingprevention.org.*

12. "Looters Strike New Orleans after Storm: 'It's Insane,' Says Tourist Watching Theft in French Quarter," Associated Press, MSNBC.com, August 30, 2005.

13. "Edward Forbes Smiley III Admits to Stealing 97 Rare Maps from US and UK Institutions," Laura Beach, *Antiques and the Arts Online,* (Newtown, CT), June 27, 2006.

14. "DEA Accuses Agent, Wife of Scheme," *Deseret News* (Salt Lake City, UT), October 1, 2006.

15. "Woman Guilty of Theft in Fake Cancer Scheme," Geoffrey Fattah, *Deseret Morning News* (Salt Lake City, UT), July 29, 2005.

16. "For Lying about Cancer, West Jordan Couple Must Pay the Feds $60,000," Pamela Manson, *The Salt Lake Tribune* (Salt Lake City, UT), June 16, 2007.

17. "'Fake Cancer' Couple Will Repay $60,000," Associated Press, KUTV.com, (Salt Lake City, UT), June 15, 2007.

18. Pair Charged with Theft from Title Fund Account," Brandon Ortiz, *Lexington Herald-Leader* (Lexington, KY), May 29, 2006, page A1.

19. Insurance Information Institute, Auto Theft Statistics, 2004, *www.iii.org.*

20. The author's first jury trial involved just such a case. The defendant, who represented himself, told the jury he was merely "borrowing" the grill and intended to return it after a backyard barbecue. He was acquitted.

21. Barasch, D. United States Attorney for the Middle District of Pennsylvania Press Release, February 20, 2001.

22. *Pegasus News*, University of North Texas (Denton, TX), June 25, 2007.

23. Department of Justice News Release, Patrick Crosby (Atlanta, GA), February 21, 2007.

24. "The Inside Job," Neil Swidey, *The Boston Globe*, September 17, 2006.

25. United States Department of Justice News Release, Samantha Martin (Boston, MA), February 12, 2007.

26. *Ballentine's Law Dictionary*.

27. 18 U.S.C. § 2113.

28. *Carter v. United States,* 530 U.S. 255 (2000).

29. S.C. Code Ann § 16–11–330.

30. "Two Men Arrested in Toy Gun Robbery," Andriy R. Pazuniak, *www.TBO.com*, July 5, 2007.

31. *United States v. Perry,* 991 F.2d 304 (6th Cir. 1993).

32. *McLaughlin v. United States,* 476 U.S. 16 (1986).

33. "Woman, 74, Charged in Bank Heist," Jonathan D. Silver and Lillian Thomas, *Pittsburgh Post-Gazette,* (Pittsburgh, PA), March 7, 2006.

34. "Woman, 76, Gets House Arrest for Robbery," Associated Press, July 5, 2007.

35. "LSAT Robbery Prompts Arrests," *The Daily Trojan* (UCLA), March 27, 1997.

36. "LSAT Cheaters Are Sentenced to Probation," *Corpus Christi Caller Times* (Corpus Christi, TX), January 28, 2000.

37. 4 W. Blackstone, Commentaries 224.

38. 18 P.S. § 3502.

39. 18 Cal. Penal Code Ann. § 459.

40. According to the American Psychiatric Association's *Diagnostic and Statistical Manual of Psychiatric Disorders,* Fourth Edition, patients with pyromania exhibit the following behavior: A patient must have set more than one fire, been tense or excited before setting the fire, have been fascinated by fire in the past, experienced pleasure, gratification, or relief after the fire or while watching it, and not had any of the other common reasons for setting the fire, such as revenge, political agenda, or profit motive.

41. United States Department of Justice, Federal Bureau of Investigation statistics, *Crime in the United States 2005, www.fbi.gov/ucr.htm*, September 2006.

42. "Two Women Sentenced to Prison in 'Operation Backfire' Arson Cases," Bill Bishop, *The Register-Guard,* (Eugene, OR), June 1, 2007.

43. Vandals Smash Man's Hummer, *Washington Post*, July 19, 2007.

44. 436 U.S. 499 (1978).

45. Payment Fraud and Control Survey, Association of Financial Professionals, March 2005, reported by *www.stopcheckfraud.com*.

46. Minn. Stat. § 609.631(2).

47. 18 U.S.C. § 470 et. seq.

48. 18 P.S. § 4105.

49. "Stolen Data's Black Market," *Dark Reading*, *www.darkreading.com*, Tim Wilson, September 7, 2006.

50. "Alcatel–Lucent Notifies Employees and Retirees of Former Lucent Technologies of Missing Computer Disk Containing Personal Information, Alcatel-Lucent News Release, *www.alcatel-lucent.com*, (Murray Hill, NJ), May 17, 2007.

51. Revised Code of Washington § 9.35.020.

52. Federal Bureau of Investigations Internet Crime Complaint Center (IC3) Annual Report, 2006.

APPENDIX

Elizabeth Cabrera-Rivera was charged with the following crimes as delineated in the Virginia Code.

§ 18.2-178. Obtaining money or signature, etc., by false pretense

A. If any person obtain, by any false pretense or token, from any person, with intent to defraud, money, a gift certificate or other property that may be the subject of larceny, he shall be deemed guilty of larceny thereof; or if he obtain, by any false pretense or token, with such intent, the signature of any person to a writing, the false making whereof would be forgery, he shall be guilty of a Class 4 felony.

B. Venue for the trial of any person charged with an offense under this section may be in the county or city in which (i) any act was performed in furtherance of the offense, or (ii) the person charged with the offense resided at the time of the offense.

§ 18.2-186.3. Identity theft; penalty; restitution; victim assistance

A. It shall be unlawful for any person, without the authorization or permission of the person or persons who are the subjects of the identifying information, with the intent to defraud, for his own use or the use of a third person, to:

   1. Obtain, record or access identifying information which is not available to the general public that would assist in accessing financial resources, obtaining identification documents, or obtaining benefits of such other person;

   2. Obtain goods or services through the use of identifying information of such other person;

   3. Obtain identification documents in such other person's name; or

   4. Obtain, record or access identifying information while impersonating a law-enforcement officer or an official of the government of the Commonwealth.

B. It shall be unlawful for any person without the authorization or permission of the person who is the subject of the identifying information, with the intent to sell or distribute the information to another to:

   1. Fraudulently obtain, record or access identifying information that is not available to the general public that would assist in accessing financial resources, obtaining identification documents, or obtaining benefits of such other person;

2. Obtain goods or services through the use of identifying information of such other person;

3. Obtain identification documents in such other person's name; or

4. Obtain, record or access identifying information while impersonating a law-enforcement officer or an official of the Commonwealth.

B1. It shall be unlawful for any person to use identification documents or identifying information of another person, whether that person is dead or alive, or of a false or fictitious person, to avoid summons, arrest, prosecution or to impede a criminal investigation.

C. As used in this section, "identifying information" shall include but not be limited to: (i) name; (ii) date of birth; (iii) social security number; (iv) driver's license number; (v) bank account numbers; (vi) credit or debit card numbers; (vii) personal identification numbers (PIN); (viii) electronic identification codes; (ix) automated or electronic signatures; (x) biometric data; (xi) fingerprints; (xii) passwords; or (xiii) any other numbers or information that can be used to access a person's financial resources, obtain identification, act as identification, or obtain goods or services.

D. Violations of this section shall be punishable as a Class 1 misdemeanor. Any violation resulting in financial loss of greater than $200 shall be punishable as a Class 6 felony. Any second or subsequent conviction shall be punishable as a Class 6 felony. Any violation of subsection B where five or more persons' identifying information has been obtained, recorded, or accessed in the same transaction or occurrence shall be punishable as a Class 6 felony. Any violation of subsection B where 50 or more persons' identifying information has been obtained, recorded, or accessed in the same transaction or occurrence shall be punishable as a Class 5 felony. Any violation resulting in the arrest and detention of the person whose identification documents or identifying information were used to avoid summons, arrest, prosecution, or to impede a criminal investigation shall be punishable as a Class 6 felony. In any proceeding brought pursuant to this section, the crime shall be considered to have been committed in any locality where the person whose identifying information was appropriated resides, or in which any part of the offense took place, regardless of whether the defendant was ever actually in such locality.

E. Upon conviction, in addition to any other punishment, a person found guilty of this offense shall be ordered by the court to make restitution as the court deems appropriate to any person whose identifying information was appropriated or to the estate of such person. Such restitution may include the person's or his estate's actual expenses associated with correcting inaccuracies or errors in his credit report or other identifying information.

F. Upon the request of a person whose identifying information was appropriated, the Attorney General may provide assistance to the victim in obtaining information necessary to correct inaccuracies or errors in his credit report or other identifying information; however, no legal representation shall be afforded such person.

§ 18.2-192. Credit card theft

(1) A person is guilty of credit card or credit card number theft when:

(a) He takes, obtains or withholds a credit card or credit card number from the person, possession, custody or control of another without the cardholder's consent or who, with knowledge that it has been so taken, obtained or withheld, receives the credit card or credit card number with intent to use it or sell it, or to transfer it to a person other than the issuer or the cardholder; or

(b) He receives a credit card or credit card number that he knows to have been lost, mislaid, or delivered under a mistake as to the identity or address of the cardholder, and who retains possession with intent to use, to sell or to transfer the credit card or credit card number to a person other than the issuer or the cardholder; or

(c) He, not being the issuer, sells a credit card or credit card number or buys a credit card or credit card number from a person other than the issuer; or

(d) He, not being the issuer, during any twelve-month period, receives credit cards or credit card numbers issued in the names of two or more persons which he has reason to know were taken or retained under circumstances which constitute a violation of § 18.2-194 and subdivision (1) (c) of this section.

CHAPTER 6

Treason, Terrorism, and Wartime Criminal Justice

CHAPTER CONTENTS

> *They that can give up essential liberty to obtain a little temporary safety deserve neither liberty nor safety.*
>
> *Benjamin Franklin*

> *The Congress shall have the power . . . to declare war, grant letters of marque and reprisal, and make rules concerning captures on land and water.*
>
> *U.S. Constitution, Article I, Section 8*

> *Treason against the United States, shall consist only in levying war against them, or in adhering to their enemies, giving them aid and comfort. No person shall be convicted of treason unless on the testimony of two witnesses to the same overt act, or on confession in open court.*
>
> *U.S. Constitution, Article III, Section 3*

CHAPTER OBJECTIVES

After studying this chapter, you should be able to:

- Explain the history of wartime criminal laws.
- List and explain the provisions in the U.S. Constitution that govern the powers of Congress and the president in time of war.
- Define treason and list and explain the provisions in the U.S. Constitution that apply to treason.

- Define the elements of **treason** and **sedition.**
- List two federal laws that define and punish terrorist acts.
- Understand the major provisions of the Patriot Act of 2001 as they apply to acts of terror directed against U.S. interests at home and abroad.
- Explain the history of presidential orders for military tribunals in time of war or armed conflict.

INTRODUCTION AND HISTORICAL BACKGROUND

Our history is full of contradictions when it comes to judging loyalty and putting out the welcome mat. On one hand, we are a country made up of a large population of immigrants. With the exception of those among us who can trace our ancestry to members of Native American tribes, we all descend from immigrants. The Statue of Liberty asks the world to "bring me your tired, your poor, your huddled masses yearning to breathe free."[1] On the other hand, as a nation we have been quick to judge and sometimes misjudge the loyalty of new arrivals, particularly in times of war or domestic turmoil.

Treason and sedition are crimes that punish the disloyalty of a country's citizens and resident aliens. All who reside in a country are assumed to owe it a duty of loyalty. Loyalty to one's nation is such an ingrained value that governments punish disloyalty reflexively. Similarly, espionage, whether for economic or ideological reasons, constitutes a breach of trust on both a personal and national level. Our discussion of treason, terrorism, and wartime criminal justice necessarily begins with a discussion of history. As you will see, what was done in the past is often prologue to the present. For example, when President George W. Bush issued an Executive Order on November 13, 2001, calling for secret military tribunals to try suspected terrorists, his supporters pointed to the trial of suspected World War II saboteurs by a military court as precedent for the order. At the time (early fall 2001), their story had all but been relegated to the dustbin of history. Their story, resurrected in support of the War on Terror, is now well-known.

One of the earliest examples of restrictions borne of doubts about loyalty were the Alien and Sedition Acts of 1798 signed into law by President John Adams. At the time, international tensions with France were high, and the President feared war was imminent. In particular, he eyed the many newly arrived French immigrants suspiciously. Their sheer number, an estimated 25,000 French immigrants lived in Philadelphia alone, looked like fertile recruiting ground for French spies. Additionally, newly arrived Irish refugees from the Irish Rebellion of 1798 represented another large Catholic population in the still largely Protestant country.

The Alien Act increased the time needed to qualify for citizenship from 5 to 14 years and gave the president the power to expel any foreigner he considered dangerous. The

Sedition Act made it a crime to either make "false, scandalous, and malicious" writings against the government or to stir up sedition among otherwise loyal Americans. The law was subsequently used to quiet troublesome newspaper editors.[2] Both laws remained in force for only a few years. In contrast, we are now more than half a decade post 9/11, and most of the restrictions put into place shortly after the attacks are still in force.

WARTIME POWER

As you have learned, the U.S. Constitution sets forth the framework for the U.S. system of justice. The arrangement relies heavily on all three branches of government having a say in running the country. Each branch has powers that serve as a check on the other branches lest any one branch become too powerful. The Constitution's framers wanted to avoid any possibility that a monarch or head of state could assume dictatorial powers.

The framers foresaw that there would inevitably be times when the country would face enemies, internal and external, as well as times of peace. To assure that our form of government would survive the inevitable challenges ahead, the Constitution provides for the **power to declare war.** Among the checks and balances found in the Constitution are power-sharing provisions for just such times. For example, the Constitution grants to Congress "the power . . . to declare war, grant letters of marque and reprisal, and make rules concerning captures on land and water."[3]

Letters of marque and reprisal are letters from a government formerly used to grant a private person the power to seize the subjects of a foreign state. The same clause of the Constitution also gives Congress the power:

- To raise and support armies
- To provide and maintain a navy
- To make rules for the government and regulation of the land and naval forces
- To call up the militia to execute the laws of the Union and suppress insurrections and repel invasions.

The president also plays a role in wartime. The Constitution provides that:

> The President shall be the Commander in Chief of the Army and Navy of the United States, and of the Militia of the several states when called into the actual Service of the United States.[4]

As you can see, it is Congress that has the power to declare war and the president who is in charge of planning, organizing, and executing that war. The limitation of the president's power in time of war has been tested several times, with the deciding vote coming from the judicial branch of government. Since 1973, the power to commit troops overseas had also been governed by the War Powers Resolution, passed by Congress. The legislation provides that the president may commit troops when Congress has declared war, when Congress has specifically authorized troops to be deployed, or when the United States has been attacked.

Both Congressional power and presidential power have been fine-tuned with the assistance of the U.S. Supreme Court. In times of turmoil, presidents sometimes issue orders citing as authority the inherent power of the president as commander in chief. That was the case during the Korean Conflict. Starting in 1950, North Korea, with the support of the People's

Power to Declare War

The power reserved by Congress in the U.S. Constitution. Congress can declare war on a belligerent, and then the Executive Branch conducts the war.

Letters of Marque and Reprisal

A letter from a government formerly used to grant a private person the power to seize the subjects of a foreign state.

I venture to say no war can be long carried on against the will of the people.
Edmund Burke

HISTORICAL HIGHLIGHT
Laws Restricting Freedom in Times of War or National Emergency

In times of war and national emergency, the federal government has historically enacted special legislation designed to protect the people from real or perceived danger. The most infamous of laws was the Executive Order authorizing the federal government to inter Japanese Americans in camps during World War II. Other examples include:

- ***The Alien and Sedition Acts of 1798.*** These laws gave the president the authority to exclude any alien he thought was dangerous and made it illegal to make false accusations against the government or to incite citizens to sedition.
- ***The Sedition Act of 1918.*** This law made it illegal to criticize the U.S. role in the war effort during World War I.
- ***Smith Act of 1940.*** This law made it a crime to "knowingly or willfully advocate, abet, advise, or teach the duty, necessity, desirability, or propriety of overthrowing any government in the U.S. by force or violence or to print, publish, edit, issue, circulate, sell, distribute, or publicly display any written or printed matter advocating, advising, or teaching the duty, necessity, desirability, or propriety of overthrowing governments."
- ***McCarren Act of 1950.*** Also known as the Internal Security Act, this federal law allowed for the establishment of internment camps for use in national emergencies.
- ***McCarren–Walter Act of 1952.*** This law, also known as the Immigration and Nationality Act, tightened restrictions on aliens and reduced immigration from nonwhite countries. It also legalized stripping naturalized citizens who were judged "subversive" of their citizenship and deporting them. In addition, the law allowed deportation of resident aliens engaged in political activity.

Republic of China and the Soviet Union, waged war against South Korea. It was a conflict widely viewed as an attempt by Communist forces to expand their influence. President Harry Truman bypassed Congress and did not ask for a declaration of war. Instead, he called the conflict a "police action" and worked with the United Nations in defending South Korea.

By 1952, the conflict in Korea was in full force, and at home steel workers were talking about going on strike. President Truman saw the steel industry as essential to a successful police action in Korea and, to avoid a shutdown, took decisive action. He issued an Executive Order that authorized the secretary of commerce to "take possession of all such plants, facilities, and other property ... as he may deem necessary in the interests of national defense."[5]

Within hours, the owners of the steel plants seized sought help from federal courts. The case came to the Supreme Court within weeks. The president argued that he had the power as commander in chief to take immediate action in an emergency. The Supreme Court disagreed. Justice Black concluded that "the founders of this Nation entrusted the law-making power to the Congress alone in both good and bad times," so that if the president wanted to nationalize an industry, he had better get Congress to pass legislation doing so.[6]

At times when Congress has declared war, the Supreme Court has been less reluctant to second-guess presidential Executive Orders. For example, after the Japanese bombed Pearl Harbor in a sneak attack and Congress declared war on Japan, people on the West Coast became concerned about the prospect of either a direct invasion by the Japanese or acts of internal sabotage by Japanese aliens and immigrants and even their American-born children. One of the first to call for the internment of Japanese Americans was the Republican congressman from Santa Monica, California, Leland M. Ford. Congressman Ford insisted that "all Japanese, whether citizens or not, be placed in inland concentration camps." His voice was joined by others, and soon the delegations from California, Oregon, and Washington were calling for internment.

Earl Warren was the California attorney general at the time. He ordered his staff to prepare maps detailing the location of all Japanese and Japanese American landowners in California. These maps revealed that people of Japanese ancestry owned land located near or around what could be considered strategic targets for sabotage, such as beaches, air and oil fields, and water reservoirs.

On February 19, 1942, President Roosevelt signed Executive Order 9066. The order authorized the military to clear sensitive areas of any and all persons and to restrict movement into and out of such areas. Excluded from many areas, the presence of Japanese Americans in communities could, according to Warren, "bring about race riots and prejudice and hysteria and excesses of all kinds." The solution was, allegedly for their own safety, that the displaced should be confined. By March 2, the military designated the western half of California, Oregon, and Washington as a military area and ordered those of Japanese heritage removed.[7]

Recently, the U.S. Census Bureau revealed that it provided the Justice Department and other federal agencies with the names and addresses of Japanese Americans. Individual information is confidential under normal circumstances, but the Second War Powers Act allowed federal agencies to share information. Similar information sharing was authorized under the USA Patriot Act. The Census Bureau provided numbers of Arab Americans by ZIP Code to the Justice Department but claims not to have turned over individual information.[8]

More than 110,000 people were confined to internment camps during World War II. The Supreme Court went on to uphold the evacuation and internment in *Korematsu v. United States.*[9] Many of the internees, most of whom were U.S. citizens, lost their homes and businesses. Although the internment of Japanese Americans is probably best known, the United States also interned Italian and German Americans and resident aliens from Italy, Germany, and Japan. Congress apologized decades later, and President Ronald Reagan signed the Civil Liberties Act of 1988. The Act was passed by Congress to provide a presidential apology and symbolic payment of $20,000 to the internees, evacuees, and persons of Japanese ancestry who lost liberty or property due to the forced internments. Earl Warren, who played such a pivotal role as California attorney general, went on to become chief justice of the Supreme Court. His decisions were to be known as some of the most liberal ever and included *Brown v. Board of Education* and *Miranda v. Arizona,* which integrated the nation's schools.

Hardships are part of war, and war is an aggregation of hardship.
Justice Black in *Korematsu v. United States*

We'd be in a bad way if we won the war and lost our civil liberties.
Earl Warren, on the dismissal of all Japanese-Americans for civil service positions after Pearl Harbor

HABEAS CORPUS IN WARTIME AND THE QUESTION OF MILITARY TRIBUNALS

You may recall that habeas corpus is a legal term that literally means "have the body." When a court exercises the writ of *habeas corpus,* or the "Great Writ," it literally orders another authority to bring a person held to the court. It was originally used to prevent kings from simply making enemies disappear. Today, *habeas corpus* petitions are commonly filed by prisoners in state systems who want a federal court to review whether the justice they are receiving at the hand of the state meets minimum constitutional standards. Thus, a state prisoner who believes the conditions in his prison cell amount to cruel and unusual punishment can have access to a federal court to hear that complaint by filing a *habeas corpus* petition.

The right of *habeas corpus* is an important one in both English and U.S. jurisprudence. It is seen as a pivotal right. For example, the great English legal scholar William Blackstone thought the right of *habeas corpus* as "the bulwark of the British Constitution." He wrote that the right to *habeas corpus* was even more important than the right to be free from the loss of property without due process of law because "confinement of the person, by secretly hurrying him to jail, where his sufferings are unknown or forgotten is a less public, a less striking, and therefore a more dangerous engine of arbitrary government."[10]

The U.S. Constitution provides that "the privilege of the Writ of Habeas Corpus shall not be suspended, unless when in cases of rebellion or invasion the public safety may require it."[11] The standard is a tough one. The presumption is that every person held under the control of an agent or unit of government is entitled to some means of judicial review of his confinement, conviction, or sentence. Even during World War II when the federal government tried suspected German saboteurs in a military tribunal, the prisoners had the right to have their case reviewed by courts.

Military Tribunal

A military court convened in times of emergency to try those accused of war-related crimes, such as terrorism, espionage, or treason.

The federal government has employed the use of **military tribunals** during time of war. For example, President Lincoln used a military court to try Lambdin P. Milligan during the Civil War. He was sentenced to hanging by a military tribunal for planning to form a secret military faction to free captured Confederate soldiers, rearm them, and invade Indiana. The case came before the U.S. Supreme Court on a petition for *habeas corpus,* even though President Lincoln had suspended *habeas corpus.* The Court wrote that only Congress had the authority to set up military tribunals, and then only in time of war. As long as the country's courts are open, concluded the Court, they were the proper venue for trial and reversed the conviction.[12]

MILITARY TRIBUNALS TODAY

In the aftermath of the terrorist attacks on September 11, 2001, President George W. Bush signed an Executive Order authorizing the detention and trial of noncitizens by military tribunals. This order cites as authority by Congress for authorization for use of military force. That authorization declared:

> That the President is authorized to use all necessary and appropriate force against those nations, organizations, or persons he determines planned, authorized, committed, or aided the terrorist attacks that occurred on September 11, 2001, or harbored such organizations or persons, in order to prevent any future acts of international terrorism against the United States by such nations, organizations or persons.

HISTORICAL HIGHLIGHT
Habeas Corpus *Lends Helping Hand to Imprisoned Student after September 11th Attacks*

Imagine that you are a 21-year-old student from Jordan who is being questioned after the attacks on the United States on September 11th. You are being asked hundreds of questions while strapped to a lie detector machine. Imagine further that, although you did not commit any crime and are not being charged with any crime, you might know a few things about what happened, making you a material witness. Would you be nervous or scared?

Osama Awadallah, a student at Grossmont College in El Cajon, California, was in just this situation. After being questioned by the Federal Bureau of Investigation (FBI) and being identified as a possible material witness for a grand jury, Awadallah was in maximum security prisons for the next three weeks, transported from Southern California, to Oklahoma, and then to Manhattan. During this time, he was shackled, strip-searched, and sometimes kept in solitary confinement. But Osama Awadallah had not been arrested for any crime; he was being held to testify before a grand jury.

Thanks to *habeas corpus,* Shira A. Scheindlin, a judge for the U.S. District Court for the Southern District of New York, was able to find that Awadallah was unlawfully detained and that "since 1789, no Congress has granted the government the authority to imprison an innocent person in order to guarantee that he will testify before a grand jury conducting a criminal investigation." Osama Awadallah was released, and his testimony to the grand jury was suppressed.[13]

President Bush's order called for some suspected terrorists to be tried by military tribunals and announced that the rules of evidence ordinarily applied to criminal cases tried in federal court would not be followed. The order covers noncitizens designated personally by the president for military tribunal trial after he concludes any of the following:

- If they are or were al Qaeda members
- If they engaged in, aided or abetted, or conspired to commit acts of international terrorism
- If they have harbored such individuals

The order also says the president can designate noncitizens for military trials if "it is in the best interest of the United States that such individual be subject to this order."

Those designated by the president for military trial will be tried either in the United States or abroad under the following conditions:

- The military commission sits as trier of fact and law; roles usually split between the jury and judge.
- The presiding officer can admit any evidence that has "probative value to a reasonable person."

- The secretary of defense designates the prosecutor, and the defendant may have an attorney.
- Conviction need not be unanimous, but can be by vote of two-thirds of the commission, and sentencing agreed upon by two-thirds of the commission.
- Any appeal goes to the president or the secretary of defense, and their decision is final. The order specifies that those tried by military tribunal can't appeal to any court in the United States, foreign country, or any international tribunal.

HISTORICAL HIGHLIGHT
FBI Rushes World War II Would-Be Saboteurs to Electric Chair

In 1942, after the United States declared war on Germany, eight would-be Nazi saboteurs left German-occupied France for America. Submarines dropped the two groups off along a Long Island, New York, beach and Ponte Vedra Beach in Florida. Seven were German citizens, but the eighth was a U.S. citizen. One declared to his partner that he intended to turn himself in rather than commit acts of sabotage. He did so and was questioned for eight days by the FBI. He told the FBI that the Germans were intent on landing others and engaging in a war of terror by leaving bombs in public places and blowing up vital industrial plants.[14]

The FBI arrested all eight men and turned them over to a military commission. They were tried under the Articles of War (military laws authorized by Congress earlier), convicted, and sentenced to death. While the trial was still underway, they filed a request for *habeas corpus* with the U.S. Supreme Court, relying on *Ex parte Milligan* to claim that the military tribunal had no jurisdiction and that state or federal courts should handle the case.

The Court agreed to hear the case. The Articles of Law previously enacted by Congress allowed a military commission to try those not ordinarily tried by court martial. Therefore, this time the Court upheld the military tribunal's convictions of spying, conspiracy, and violating the laws of war. It held that those who are unlawful combatants such as these men who entered the country secretly and did not wear uniforms or carry identification weren't prisoners of war and could be tried by a military commission when Congress has provided for such commissions in legislation. Within one month, all eight men were sentenced, and six of them were executed by electrocution in a Washington, D.C. jail.[15]

One problem with the president's order is that it may well interfere with efforts to extradite to the United States or otherwise put suspected terrorists in the hands of U.S. military tribunals. For example, the idea of secret hearings, few rights for the accused, and military officers serving as both judge and jury may violate treaties in force such as the 1950 European Convention on Human Rights. In addition, the European Union (EU) countries have all banned capital punishment and may refuse to extradite suspects without promises that they would not be executed if convicted. Even if an EU country did agree to extradite a suspect, he or she would have the right to appeal to the European Court of Human Rights, whose decision is binding on all EU member countries.

At the time of the writing of this textbook, it was unclear how many, if any, detainees have been tried or convicted. One individual, Australian David Hicks, entered into an agreement with the United States which released him into the custody of Australian authorities. A condition of his release was that he acknowledge U.S. authority to hold him for the five years he spent in detention at Guantanamo and that he not speak to the public about his case. The United States has released some of the other prisoners or returned them to their own countries, which will have to decide whether to detain or release them. According to the Pentagon, there have been quite a few hearings, with 38 out of 558 cases ending in a decision in favor of the detainee.[16]

Some members of Congress as well as civil rights organizations were questioning whether President Bush had the authority to call for tribunals without the express consent of Congress and whether any president or Congress had the authority to suspend the right of *habeas corpus* under the circumstances and in the manner the order purports.

Now that several years have passed since the events of 9/11, the legal community has begun looking more closely at the need for special tribunals and especially at the idea that "enemy combatants" can be detained indefinitely without charges being filed or their cases being adjudicated. In fact, the U.S. Supreme Court decided two so-called enemy combatant cases during 2004. Both involved U.S. citizens being held by the military as suspected terrorists.

The first case involves Yasir Esam Hamdi, a Saudi national who was born in Louisiana while his parents worked for an oil company. Because he was born in the United States, he is a U.S. citizen. Hamdi was captured on a battlefield in Afghanistan and eventually was moved to the detention center in Guantanamo, Cuba. When the U.S. military discovered he was a citizen, it transferred him to a naval brig in Virginia.

His parents filed a lawsuit, alleging that as a citizen he could not be held indefinitely. The Fourth Circuit Court of Appeals concluded that because he was caught on the battleground as an enemy, he could be held without charges.[17] His parents appealed, and the Supreme Court agreed to decide whether Hamdi was being legally held as an enemy combatant. The Department of Defense argued that Hamdi had been caught on the battlefield, that he was armed and ready to fight other U.S. citizens, and that he had been interrogated by our military. The government argued that interrogation gave him the opportunity to challenge his detention.

On the last day of the 2003–2004 term, the Court issued its opinion. It told the Bush administration that any U.S. citizen held as an enemy combatant without charges must be given a meaningful opportunity to challenge that designation before an independent and neutral decisionmaker. The Court wrote, "An interrogation by one's captor, however, effective as an intelligence-gathering tool, hardly constitutes a constitutionally adequate factfinding before a neutral decision-maker." The Court did not specify the mechanics of that review but instead sent the case back to the federal trial court.[18] The Court left open the possibility that a military tribunal like that authorized by the president shortly after 9/11 might be adequate but reiterated that any decision could be challenged in federal courts.

The government released Hamdi on October 11, 2004, and sent him home to Saudi Arabia. He agreed to renounce his U.S. citizenship, since the government was apparently not prepared to try him.

The second case involves Jose Padilla, a U.S. citizen from Chicago who was arrested in 2001, after returning on a flight from the Middle East. He was alleged to have been involved with al Qaeda plans to detonate a "dirty bomb" (a bomb capable of dispersing radiological material over a large area, but without a nuclear explosion) in the United States. Rather than charging him with any specific crime, President Bush designated him an "enemy combatant" and had him moved to the naval brig in Charleston, South Carolina.

An attorney eventually contacted to represent Padilla filed a petition to have him released or charged. On December 18, 2003, the Second Circuit Court of Appeals ordered that he be charged or released within 30 days. Solicitor General Theodore Olson (who lost his wife on 9/11—she was a passenger on the plane that hit the Pentagon) filed an appeal to the U.S. Supreme Court in order to halt Padilla's release. The Supreme Court accepted this case. It decided Padilla's case the same day it issued the *Hamdi* decision. But rather than decide the merits of the case, the Court sent it back to the trial court on the premise that Padilla had filed his case in the wrong federal circuit.[19] Padilla then refiled in the correct circuit, and the federal district court ruled he should be charged or released. The government appealed the decision, and it was overturned. Padilla appealed to the Supreme Court, but while the appeal was pending, the government transferred him to federal prison and filed charges.[20] A jury found Padilla guilty of far lesser charges than those originally made.[21] Based on a fingerprint found on an alleged "al Qaeda application" retrieved by the Central Intelligence Agency (CIA) in Afghanistan, he was convicted of "providing material support for terrorists" and two other related charges. The jury did not hear that he had been held in a military brig for more than three years or that he had originally been accused of plotting to detonate dirty bombs in U.S. cities. Padilla was sentenced to 17 years in federal prison.

The Supreme Court also took up the case of several noncitizens who challenged their internment at Guantanamo Bay, Cuba. They challenged the Bush administration's indefinite detention. The government argued that the facility they are held in is in Cuba and therefore outside federal court jurisdiction. The Court disagreed and ordered their cases to be heard by a federal district judge without expressing an opinion on whether they are entitled to a trial or can be held indefinitely.[22]

In response, President Bush asked Congress to pass legislation removing the detainees from federal jurisdiction. Congress enacted and the President signed the Detainee Treatment Act of 2005 which provides:

> "no court, justice, or judge" may exercise jurisdiction over
>
> 1. an application for a writ of habeas corpus filed by or on behalf of an alien detained by the Department of Defense at Guantanamo Bay, Cuba; or
> 2. any other action against the United States or its agents relating to any aspect of the detention by the Department of Defense of an alien at Guantanamo Bay, Cuba, who
>   a. is currently in military custody; or
>   b. has been determined by the United States Court of Appeals for the District of Columbia Circuit . . . to have been properly detained as an enemy combatant."[23]

The detainees' lawyers challenged the law in court. Ultimately, the Supreme Court ruled that the Detainee Treatment Act did not apply to detainees whose cases were already in the federal courts at the time the law was passed.[24] Congress then passed the Military Commissions Act of 2006, barring any federal judge from reviewing any case involving the detainees.[25]

In all its rulings, the Supreme Court has not definitively ruled whether the detainees at Guantanamo fall within federal court jurisdiction. Lower courts have consistently ruled they do not. One such case was *Boumediene, et al., v. Bush.* When the case was appealed to the Supreme Court in April 2007, the Court refused to hear it.[26] Just two months later, at the close of the term, the Court reversed itself and agreed to hear the case during the 2007–2008 term.[27] There are currently about 360 men (some who were young teens when first detained) still at Guantanamo awaiting hearings or some other action.

YOU MAKE THE CALL

FAIR PROCESS OR DENIAL OF DUE PROCESS?

During the 2007–2008 term, the U.S. Supreme Court will hear the cases of detainees Boumediene and Al Odah and several others who are being held at Guantanamo. At issue is whether the Detainee Treatment Act, passed by Congress on New Year's Eve 2005, and the Military Commissions Act are constitutional and allow the detention of enemy combatants without legal review in the federal court system.

Lakhdar Boumediene and several others were caught in Bosnia and transported to Guantanamo by U.S. forces. They are natives of Algeria, but citizens or permanent residents of Bosnia. In Cuba, they are confined to individual 8' by 6' cells made of concrete walls and steel mesh. Above each man's bunk a fluorescent light shines 24/7.

At some time in 2004, the U.S. military conducted a "Combatant Status Review Tribunal" at which none of the prisoners were represented by counsel or allowed to view any classified evidence relied on by the three-member review panel. Apparently, the panel ruled in the government's favor, and the detainees remained incarcerated. Meanwhile, their attorneys (hired by their families) sought court review of their detentions.

In the Al Odah case, lawyers represent 39 other Guantánamo Bay detainees, each of whom claims to never have picked up arms against the United States or otherwise been involved with any type of terrorist activity. In short, they claim to be entirely innocent and ask "a single remedy: a fair and impartial hearing before a neutral decision-maker to determine whether there is a reasonable basis in law and fact for detaining them."[28]

Just who are the prisoners at Guantanamo? According to the U.S. Department of Defense, about 5 percent were captured by U.S. military forces, while the rest were taken into custody by either Pakistani or Northern Alliance forces in Afghanistan or Pakistan. According to one attorney, who as a reservist was assigned to be a member of one of the panels set to decide whether detainees were indeed enemy combatants, the process was flawed, and panel members were asked to reconsider any case in which they decided the detainee should not be held. Stephen Abraham provided his account to the Supreme Court days before the Court took up the cases.[29]

Should the detainees get a fair and impartial hearing? Do the Military Commissions Act and the Detainee Treatment Act violate the Constitution and illegally strip the courts of jurisdiction? You make the call.

For more on the cases, including a look at the underlying court decisions, see the Appendix. There you will also find an example of a Combatant Status Review Tribunal decision, plus a transcript of a "high value detainee" hearing.

DEFINING TREASON AND SEDITION

Treason is the only crime that is specifically defined in the U.S. Constitution. The Constitution provides that "treason against the United States, shall consist only in levying war against them, or in adhering to their enemies, giving them aid and comfort."[30]

The Constitution also specifically singles out treason as a crime that requires the government to produce more evidence against the accused than any other crime. It provides that "no person shall be convicted of treason unless on the testimony of two witnesses to the same overt act, or on confession in open court."[31] Thus, treason requires very solid evidence or a confession in the courtroom before a conviction can be obtained. Why did the framers of the Constitution see fit to accord extraordinary protection to those charged with treason? Perhaps because they saw charges of treason as so serious that a wrongful conviction must be guarded against. Perhaps they feared that unless a confession was repeated in open court, it was susceptible to being obtained fraudulently or through the use of torture. Perhaps the framers simply wanted to avoid the possibility that government officials might prosecute political disagreements as treason without concrete evidence of disloyalty. Whatever the reason, treason was singled out for special attention.

The crime of treason is defined in the *U.S. Code* as a person "owing allegiance to the United States, levies war against them or adheres to their enemies, giving them aid and comfort within the United States or elsewhere."[32] Traditionally, treason has been viewed as the most serious crime.[33]

Treason is a breach of allegiance to the United States; therefore, only those whom the law defines as owing allegiance to the United States can be prosecuted for treason.[34] Allegiance can be either temporary or permanent. U.S. citizens, whether natural-born or naturalized, are viewed as having permanent allegiance to the United States, but aliens residing in the United States are perceived to have only temporary allegiance.[35]

Elements   There are two elements to the crime of treason:

- Adherence to the enemy
- Rendering the enemy aid and comfort

Adherence to the Enemy   Enemies of the United States are defined as any "party who was [a] subject of foreign power in state of open hostility with [the] United States." Adherence to the enemy can take the form of:

- Selling goods to an agent of an enemy of the United States[36]
- Statements praising the enemy[37]
- Residing in an enemy country[38]
- Delivery of prisoners to the enemy, unless under a death threat that was likely to be carried out[39]

Rendering the Enemy Aid and Comfort   Examples of rendering aid and comfort to the enemy are:

- A person who acted as an interpreter at a Japanese mine during World War II where U.S. soldiers were beaten in order to increase production[40]

Treason

Levying war against the United States, or in adhering to their enemies, giving them aid and comfort. Treason must be proven by the testimony of two witnesses to the same overt act, or the defendant's confession in open court; transferring loyalty or allegiance to the enemy.

Money is this man's god, and to get enough of it he would sacrifice his country.
Quote in a leaflet attacking Benedict Arnold

I would love to say that I did what I did out of some moral outrage over our country's acts of imperialism, or as a political statement or out of anger toward the CIA or even a love for the Soviet Union. But the sad truth is that I did what I did because of money . . .
Aldrich Ames, a CIA agent who spied for the Soviet Union

- Any act that strengthens the enemy or weakens the United States[41]
- Concealing a spy's identity or supplying him with funds and assistance[42]

In order to commit treason, a person must have not only the intent to commit the overt act in question, but also to betray the country by that act.[43] A person who commits no overt act but still sides with the enemy is not guilty of treason. A person who commits an overt act but without treasonous intent is also not guilty of treason.[44]

Defenses Various defenses are available to a person charged with treason. Some of them are:

- Duress
- First Amendment privilege
- Immunity from prosecution

Duress In order for this defense to succeed, the defendant must demonstrate that he or she was in immediate danger of loss of life or severe bodily harm.[45] Any assertion of duress must be substantiated by facts.[46]

First Amendment Privilege The First Amendment's guarantee of free speech does not apply to treasonous speech. The First Amendment defense was tried by a man who made shortwave radio broadcasts for the enemy during World War II. The U.S. Supreme Court ruled that this type of speech fell outside the protection of the First Amendment.[47] A similar fate awaited a man who made anti-American broadcasts on German radio during World War II.[48]

Immunity from Prosecution If the defendant can demonstrate that he or she is part of a class of people who have been granted immunity, he or she can avoid prosecution. The most notable case of this happening was the blanket amnesty given Confederate soldiers after the Civil War.[49]

Very few treason trials have actually taken place in the United States. One of the most significant treason trials in U.S. history is that of Aaron Burr. Aaron Burr served as vice president under Thomas Jefferson. During Jefferson's second term (and after Burr was no longer vice president), President Jefferson charged Burr with treason.[50] Burr faced the prospect of being put to the gallows or a firing squad for activities allegedly involving seeking foreign support for a new country in the western part of the American continent. Burr was caught with a flotilla of armed men and was accused of treason by Jefferson. During the trial, Jefferson was ordered to turn over private papers concerning his communications with the general who investigated the charges. It was the first time in our history that a president had been ordered to produce documents or appear in court. Justice Marshall, who heard the case, told the jurors that "levying war" meant more than making plans to go to war; it meant "the actual assembling of men for the treasonable purpose." In the end, the jury did not convict Burr, since there was no confession in court, nor evidence presented by two witnesses to the same act.[51]

More recently, the Department of Justice debated whether it should charge John Walker Lindh, the alleged "American Taliban" picked up in Afghanistan with other Taliban fighters, with treason. In the end, it elected not to charge him, most likely because Lindh probably would never confess in open court to acts of treason. In addition, it seems unlikely that two witnesses can be found willing to testify that he committed an act of treason. Instead, the "American Taliban" was charged with violating federal antiterrorism laws and pled guilty in a plea agreement.

HISTORICAL HIGHLIGHT

The Clash between Church and State: Henry II and Thomas Becket

Thomas Becket was the Paris-educated son of a former sheriff of London. Becket was admired for his administrative abilities. He was politically astute, well connected, universally admired, and respected. When introduced to King Henry II, the attraction was immediate. Henry recognized Becket's political skill and strong intellect. Henry would eventually appoint Becket to the position of chancellor.

Henry relied on Becket's advice and considered him an ally in his ongoing power struggle with the Church. When archbishop of Canterbury Theobald died in 1161, Henry appointed Becket to the post. Henry was sure that with Becket in the archbishop's chair, the Church would be subservient to him.

However, Becket underwent something of a religious conversion after assuming office. He saw his loyalty to the Church in religious terms. He could not, in good conscience, put his allegiance to Henry before his allegiance to God.

The Church in those days would try any clerics accused of wrongdoing in the ecclesiastical courts. Henry was determined that they should be tried in the king's court. The disagreement came to a head when a canon was accused of murder in 1163. The ecclesiastical court acquitted the cleric, and the public demanded justice. The king insisted on trying the cleric, but Becket protested. Henry relented in this particular case but proposed the Constitutions of Clarendon that would extend the king's jurisdiction over the clerics. Becket reluctantly agreed.

Henry began to see Becket as unreliable and disloyal. Henry summoned Becket to his castle at Northampton and demanded to know what he had done with the large sums of money he had handled when he was chancellor. Becket saw the trap set for him and fled to France. His exile lasted six years.

Even in exile, Becket agitated against the king. He excommunicated all clerics who supported the king. In 1170, Henry met with Becket in France, and it appeared the rift was healed. Becket returned to his post in Canterbury. Henry requested that Becket reinstate the excommunicated clerics, but Becket refused. While still in France, Henry is said to have flown into a rage, shouting: "What sluggards, what cowards have I brought up in my court, who care nothing for their allegiance to their lord. Who will rid me of this meddlesome priest?"

Four of the king's knights sailed to England and confronted Becket in Canterbury Cathedral. When Becket still refused to reinstate the excommunicated clerics, they drew their swords and struck his head repeatedly until the altar was splattered with his brains and blood. Allegedly the stains are still visible today. Henry was despondent when he heard the news. His momentary rage had led to the martyrdom of his nemesis.

Sculpture at Canterbury at the spot where Becket was killed.

Becket's reputation grew in death far beyond what it was in life. Miracles were said to have occurred at his tomb. Henry was forced to do penance four years later. He wore sackcloth in a procession to Becket's tomb while being flogged by 80 monks. He then spent the night at the tomb. Becket remained a cult figure for centuries. The pilgrimages made by the faithful to his tomb were immortalized in Chaucer's *Canterbury Tales*.

SEDITION

Sedition is a conspiracy "to overthrow, put down, or to destroy by force the Government of the United States, or levy war against them, or to oppose the authority thereof, or by force to prevent, hinder, or delay the execution of any law of the United States, or by force to seize, take, or possess any property of the United States contrary to the authority thereof."[52]

Sedition
Advocating the overthrow of the government by force or violence.

ELEMENTS

The elements of sedition are:

- Conspiracy
- Overthrow of the United States
- Oppose by force the authority of the United States
- Prevent, hinder, or delay execution of law
- Use of force

Conspiracy

An agreement between two or more persons to engage in a criminal act.

Conspiracy A **conspiracy** is an agreement between two or more persons to engage in a criminal act.[53] For purposes of sedition, the conspirators must agree among themselves to commit an act of sedition.[54]

Overthrow of the United States Any group who states that their goal is the overthrow of the government of the United States by unconstitutional means would possess this element. The Communist Party met this requirement in a 1922 case.[55]

Oppose by Force the Authority of the United States This element is satisfied if a person or persons attempts by force to prevent actual exercise of federal authority. Merely disobeying a law is not sufficient to satisfy this element.[56]

Prevent, Hinder, or Delay Execution of Law To satisfy this element, the person or persons involved must forcibly resist the government's execution of the law. As an example, when Chinese immigrants became the target of violence in the American West in the 1880s, the U.S. government entered into two treaties with China that obligated the U.S. government to protect Chinese citizens residing in the United States. Those who opposed the U.S. government's efforts to protect Chinese immigrants were charged with sedition. However, their actions were taken against the Chinese, but not in actual defiance of the civil authority; therefore, their actions did not constitute sedition.[57]

During World War I, draft resistors were prosecuted under the sedition statute.[58]

Use of Force Any seditious conspiracy must contemplate the use of force.[59] However, no overt act must necessarily take place for a sedition prosecution, merely the planning of one.

DEFINING TERRORISM

Espionage

Knowingly and willfully communicating, furnishing, transmitting, or otherwise making available to an unauthorized person, or publishing, or using in any manner prejudicial to the safety or interest of the United States, or for the benefit of any foreign government to the detriment of the United States, any classified information; spying.

Because treason is a crime singled out for special protection and can be hard to prove given the Constitution's restrictions, Congress has enacted other laws designed to punish activities that serve the same purpose as treasonous behavior, but fall short of fitting the definition of treason. Espionage, terrorism, and other subversive activities may amount to treason but are separate crimes. Here are some samples of acts that are federal crimes:

- **Espionage** includes: [w]hoever knowingly and willfully communicates, furnishes, transmits, or otherwise makes available to an unauthorized person, or publishes, or uses in any manner prejudicial to the safety or interest of the United States or for the benefit of any foreign government to the detriment of the United States any classified information.[60]

Rebellion or Insurrection

An attempt to overthrow the government by force or unconstitutional means.

- **Rebellion or insurrection** includes: Whoever incites, sets on foot, assists, or engages in any rebellion or insurrection against the authority of the United States or the laws thereof, or gives aid or comfort thereto.[61]

Advocating Overthrow of Government

Speaking in favor of rebellion or insurrection.

- **Advocating overthrow of government** includes: Whoever knowingly or willfully advocates, abets, advises, or teaches the duty, necessity, desirability, or propriety of overthrowing or destroying the government of the United States or the government of any State, Territory, District or Possession thereof, or the government of any political subdivision therein, by force or violence, or by the assassination of any officer of any such government.[62]

HISTORICAL HIGHLIGHT
Hanssen Betrays His Country

On July 6, 2001, former FBI agent Robert Hanssen pled guilty in federal court to 15 counts of espionage and conspiracy. He did so pursuant to a plea agreement with prosecutors that saved him from a potential death sentence. Hanssen, who worked for the FBI for 15 years, admitted to spying for the former Soviet Union and later for Russia between 1979 and 1999. Prosecutors alleged that the father of six and long-time FBI agent was paid about $1.4 million in cash and diamonds in exchange for intelligence information. The information included identities of U.S. spies, classified information about eavesdropping technology, and nuclear secrets. Hanssen was accused of compromising dozens of Soviet spies who were working for the United States, some of whom were executed.

Hanssen was caught after leaving a package under a wooden footbridge in a Virginia park, when the United States had been given the tip-off by an informant in Russian intelligence that the FBI had a double agent.

The plea agreement provided that in exchange for a guilty plea, Hanssen would receive a life sentence with no possibility of parole and would be required to cooperate with both the FBI and the CIA. He is currently serving his sentence in the supermax federal prison in Florence, Colorado. His wife will receive part of the pension he would have earned had he retired.

> What took you so long?
> Robert Hanssen, after his arrest

There are also federal laws against acts of **terrorism**, generally defined as the unlawful use or threat of violence especially against the state or the public as a politically motivated means of attack or coercion. We will examine both international and domestic terrorism, as those terms are defined in federal criminal laws.

Terrorism is not a new problem for the United States. In fact, terrorist acts have been the focus of law enforcement with some frequency in the last century and appears likely to continue well into the first decade of the new century.

For example, during the years 1919 and 1920, the nation found itself facing an internal security threat: anarchists who sought to destroy the U.S. government and a modern capitalist world. The most outward sign of this revolutionary fervor was a series of attempted bomb attacks on U.S. institutions and government officials. Beginning in the spring of 1919, government officials such as Supreme Court Justice Oliver Wendell Holmes and Attorney General A. Mitchell Palmer received bombs (which did not injure either man). A post office clerk discovered over 30 bombs awaiting delivery in the system in New York. Later the next year, a bomb did go off in the New York City financial district. It had been left in a horse-drawn wagon between a U.S. Treasury office and the J. P. Morgan & Company office.

Attorney General Palmer's response was to crack down on those perceived to be radicals. Recent immigrants from southern and eastern Europe were deported, and over 6,000 people were arrested in a roundup Attorney General Palmer alleged would prevent a large-scale terror attack. When no new terror attacks emerged, the crisis ended.[63]

Terrorism
The unlawful use or threat of violence, especially against the state or the public as a politically motivated means of attack or coercion.

International Terrorism

Activities that occur primarily outside U.S. jurisdiction and involve criminal acts dangerous to human life, including acts of mass destruction, intended to influence the policy of a government by intimidation or coercion or to affect the conduct of a government by assassination or kidnapping.

Domestic Terrorism

Activities that occur primarily within U.S. jurisdiction, that involve criminal acts dangerous to human life, and that appear to be intended to intimidate or coerce a civilian population, to influence government policy by intimidation or coercion, or to affect government conduct by mass destruction, assassination, or kidnapping.

Prior to 2001, the deadliest terror attack on the United States happened in Oklahoma City, Oklahoma. Timothy McVeigh, a disaffected former soldier who claimed to engage in terror as retaliation for alleged FBI wrongdoing, blew up the Alfred P. Murrah Federal Courthouse with a homemade fertilizer bomb. The explosion killed 168 people, including 19 children, and injured hundreds. McVeigh was tried under federal law and executed by lethal injection on June 11, 2001. He became the first federal prisoner executed since 1963.

On September 11, 2001, the United States faced the worst attack on its civilian population in its history. Quickly it became obvious that the hijacking of four airliners and their use as missiles to bring down the Twin Towers of the World Trade Center, destroy a portion of the Pentagon, and crash into a field in rural Pennsylvania was the work of international terrorists. As the identities of the hijackers became known, it became clear the terror acts were probably the work of Osama bin Laden and his al Qaeda terrorist network. Congress quickly authorized the president to take military action against the terrorists and the nation that provided them shelter, Taliban-ruled Afghanistan.

At the same time, Congress also passed tough new amendments to the Antiterrorism and Effective Death Penalty Act of 1996. The amendments are commonly referred to as the USA Patriot Act of 2001. The Act provides that:

- Wiretaps can be obtained to follow the persons whose conversations are sought, rather than being linked to a specific phone. This provision allows investigators to track the conversations of a suspect whether he is using his own phone, a cell phone, or another phone.
- Law enforcement officers, armed with a subpoena, are allowed to seize voice mail and other electronic communication and to obtain information about the means of payment and account numbers.
- Aliens may be detained for seven days without charges being filed.
- The federal criminal code is amended to: (1) revise the definition of **international terrorism** to include activities that appear to be intended to affect the conduct of government by mass destruction; and (2) define **domestic terrorism** as activities that occur primarily within U.S. jurisdiction, that involve criminal acts dangerous to human life, and that appear to be intended to intimidate or coerce a civilian population, to influence government policy by intimidation or coercion, or to affect government conduct by mass destruction, assassination, or kidnapping.
- Harboring any person knowing or having reasonable grounds to believe that such person has committed or is about to commit a terrorism offense is prohibited.
- There is no statute of limitations for terrorist offenses.

The federal penal code provisions dealing with terrorism are extensive and reach out beyond our borders. In most cases, criminal acts that involve the use of bombs or chemical, biological, or nuclear weapons against Americans abroad or in the United States and that kill those targets are punishable by death. The specific provisions and definitions are found in Title 18, Part I, Chapter 113B of the *U.S. Code.*

HISTORICAL HIGHLIGHT
Eric Rudolph Caught after Years on the Run

The strange tale of Eric Rudolph underscored that all terrorism isn't international, but very frequently is of the home-grown variety. Rudolph was a suspect in a string of abortion clinic and nightclub bombings and may have been involved in the bomb that went off in Atlanta during the 1996 Summer Olympic Games as well. The Olympic bombing killed one woman and injured many others. In one of the clinic bombings, an off-duty police officer was killed and a receptionist was badly injured. Not much is known about his political leanings.

Rudolph was on the run and believed to be hiding in the Nantahala National Forest in North Carolina. He was on the FBI's ten most wanted list, with a $1 million prize on his head. The last known sighting was in 1998, when Rudolph likely stole a pickup truck with 75 pounds of food and supplies in it, until he was caught May 31, 2003, by an off-duty police officer. Rudolph was caught while rooting through a dumpster.

He admitted his role in the bombings and was sentenced to life in prison at the federal supermax prison in Florence, Colorado.[64]

HISTORICAL HIGHLIGHT
Attorney General Listens in on Attorney-Client Conversations

On October 30, 2001, U.S. Attorney General John Ashcroft approved a Department of Justice rule that allows federal agents to listen in on some conversations between inmates in the federal prison system and their attorneys. The rule provides that in cases where the attorney general has certified that reasonable suspicion exists to believe that an inmate may use communications with attorneys or investigators to further or facilitate acts of violence or terrorism, those conversations may be monitored. The rule applies to anyone held in federal custody, including convicts, detainees, those awaiting trial, and anyone held as a material witness.

Critics point out that the rule is sure to stifle legitimate conversations between attorneys, support staff, and clients and that the rule may go too far insofar as it allows the executive branch with no judicial oversight to make the determination of who is monitored.[65]

The rule of law is essential to our American freedom.
Patrick Leahy, in a letter to former Attorney General John Ashcroft

PRACTICE POINTERS

Legal assistants and investigators who work for criminal defense attorneys, prosecutors, or public defenders probably will not see many terrorism cases in any given year. But if a client does face possible charges, those preparing the defense or prosecution should keep these statistics, prepared by the Transactional Records Access Clearinghouse of Syracuse University,[66] in mind:

- The FBI prosecuted 118 domestic and federal terrorism cases during federal fiscal year 2002. The numbers have fallen dramatically since then, down to just 19 during the first nine months of FFY 2006.
- Prosecutors elected not to bring charges in 87 percent of the terrorism cases referred to them for prosecution.
- The median prison term for terror-related convictions is less than 6 months.

The bottom line? Few cases are prosecuted, and convictions don't usually result in long sentences. Could it be that the most dangerous terrorists are housed at Guantanamo or have not yet been apprehended? Hard to tell.

Since few legal offices have much experience with cases involving either domestic or international terrorism, those who find themselves working on such cases will have to get up to speed quickly. That's equally true no matter for which side of the fence they work.

Legal professionals involved in interviewing or questioning defendants represented by their firms should be aware that conversations conducted in federal detention facilities may be monitored. Ordinarily, any conversation dealing with legal matters between an attorney and a client is considered confidential. The attorney-client privilege generally extends to conversations the client has with support staff also. Consult your supervising attorney about what to tell the client about confidentiality of conversations.

ASSISTANCE WITH CASES INVOLVING IMPORTANT PUBLIC POLICY QUESTIONS

Those who work at defending suspects accused of planning or committing terror acts or of aiding and abetting such acts may want to seek information or assistance from several groups interested in the larger issues raised by new enforcement realities such as the Patriot Act and the prospect of military tribunals. In addition to many state and local bar associations, help may be available from:

- Center for Constitutional Rights, a New York group initially organized to defend civil rights protesters in the 1960s, at *www.humanrightsnow.org*.
- The Cato Institute, a group known for championing "conservative" causes, at *www.cato.org*.
- People for the American Way, a Washington area group known for championing "liberal" causes, at *www.pfaw.org*.

- The American Civil Liberties Union at *www.aclu.org*.
- National Association of Criminal Defense Lawyers at *www.nacdl.org*.

CHAPTER SUMMARY

The U.S. Constitution provides the framework for much of the law that applies in times of war or domestic turmoil. First, the Constitution sets forth the power of both Congress and the president in time of war. It gives to Congress the power to make declarations of war and to the president the role of commander in chief. Once Congress has declared war, the president exercises his power as commander in chief to set, execute, and achieve war goals.

The power to conduct war has led presidents to order groups suspected of disloyalty into internment camps and suspected saboteurs tried by military commissions. In each of these two examples, the U.S. Supreme Court upheld the presidents' actions by finding that the procedures were authorized by Congressional legislation.

The Constitution also defines treason and sets strict standards required to find someone guilty of treason. Treason is levying war against the United States or in adhering to their enemies, giving them aid and comfort. Treason must be proven by the testimony of two witnesses to the same overt act or the defendant's confession in open court.

Congress has passed other laws designed to punish activities that fall short of treason, but that harm the security of the country or its citizens. Examples include criminal laws punishing the disclosure of classified information to unauthorized persons or foreign countries.

Congress has also passed federal criminal laws outlawing activities that may be crimes under state law but the commission of which has as an intention undermining governmental authority or intimidating the population. Thus, the bombing of abortion clinics by domestic terrorists, the leveling of a federal building in Oklahoma City, or the destruction of U.S. embassies overseas have been labeled as terrorist acts and prosecuted accordingly.

KEY TERMS

Advocating Overthrow of Government	International Terrorism	Rebellion or Insurrection
Conspiracy	Letters of Marque and Reprisal	Sedition
Domestic Terrorism	Military Tribunals	Terrorism
Espionage	Power to Declare War	Treason

EXERCISE

Consider the following case: Lynne Stewart is a former attorney (having been automatically disbarred following the conviction that is the subject of this exercise) who once represented Sheikh Omar Abdel-Rahman. The Sheikh is the so-called "blind cleric" who is imprisoned for his involvement in the first World Trade Center bombing. He is also reportedly the mastermind behind the 1997 murder of 58 tourists in Luxor, Egypt.

As a condition of her representation of the Sheikh, Stewart agreed to not pass any information or comments made by her client to the press. Apparently, the government feared that her client could direct further terror attacks from his cell and suspected that he might attempt to send coded messages through the media.

Unknown to Stewart, all her conversations with her client, which were conducted with the help of a translator, were recorded. Stewart and the translator were charged with giving material support to terrorists, based in part on a press release by Stewart that purportedly stated the Sheikh had withdrawn his support for a ceasefire in his home country of Egypt. This statement the government later said amounted to Stewart's passing on of a "fatwa" or religious order to commit terror acts against Americans and others.

A federal jury convicted Stewart of the charges, after they listened to hundreds of hours of taped conversations between Stewart and her client. The judge sentenced her to 28 months in prison but allowed her to remain free pending appeal.

Do you think attorneys should be allowed to speak freely with their clients without the fear that their conversations will be recorded? Is releasing a statement by a client to the press a criminal act? You make the call.

For more information on the Stewart cases, read the Department of Justice indictment announcement and Stewart's letter to the judge before he sentenced her, found in the chapter Appendix.

DISCUSSION QUESTIONS

1. Is it appropriate to subject noncitizens to military trials for acts allegedly carried out against U.S. interests at home or abroad?
2. Under what circumstances, if any, should subjects be tried and convicted with an evidentiary standard short of reasonable doubt?
3. Should civil liberties be restricted in time of war?
4. Why do you think the founding fathers set such high standards for conviction of treason?
5. Should a person be prosecuted for espionage if he or she is spying for one of our allies?

FOR FURTHER READING AND VIEWING

BOOKS AND PERIODICALS

1. Chapin, B. (1971). *American Law of Treason: Revolutionary and Early National Origins*. University of Washington Press.
2. Hurst, J. W. (1971). *The Law of Treason in the United States: Collected Essays (Contributions in American History, No. 12)*. Greenwood Publishing.
3. Vise, D. (2001). "The Bureau and the Mole: The Unmasking of Robert Philip Hanssen, the Most Dangerous Double Agent in FBI History," *Atlantic Monthly*.
4. Vidal, G. (2000). *Burr*. Vintage Books. Fictional account of the Burr affair.

5. Goldenberg, E. (1993). *The Spy Who Knew Too Much: The Government Plot to Silence Jonathan Pollard*. SPI Book. Another true spy-catching story.

6. Scottoline, L. (2004). *Killer Smile*. Harper Collins. Legal thriller set in 2004, but exploring what happened to an Italian immigrant interned during World War II. Ms. Scottoline's parents were required to register as alien enemies during WWII, even though they had made their home in Philadelphia for decades.

7. Dobbs, M. (2004). *Saboteurs: The Nazi Raid on America*. Alfred A. Knopf. This recent account of the Nazis tried by military tribunals during World War II includes recently unearthed material from the National Archives.

8. Otsuka, Julie. (2004). *When the Emperor Was Divine*. Penguin Books. This short novel tells the story of a Japanese American family sent to the camps during World War II.

FILMS

1. *The Wind and the Lion*. A 1975 film telling the story of an American woman and her children who were kidnapped by a Berber tribe in 1904 and rescued by the application of Teddy Roosevelt's Big Stick policy; stars Candice Bergen, Brian Keith, and Sean Connery.

2. *The Spy Who Came in From the Cold*. A 1965 classic Cold War thriller based on John LeCarre's book of the same name; stars Richard Burton.

3. *Black Sunday*. A 1976 thriller in which Palestinian terrorists try to wipe out the crowd at the Super Bowl; stars Robert Shaw and Bruce Dern.

4. *The Day of the Jackal*. A 1973 thriller that deals with an attempted assassination of Charles de Gaulle and is a chilling look at the cool composure of someone capable of terrorist acts.

5. *The Eye of the Needle*. Stars Donald Sunderland as a Nazi spy in England who must deliver information about Britain's military capacity directly to Hitler. This 1981 thriller has a surprise ending.

6. *The Year of Living Dangerously*. A 1983 Mel Gibson, Linda Hunt, and Sigourney Weaver film set in 1965 Jakarta during the political upheavals that were threatening to collapse the unstable government of President Sukarno.

7. *The Ugly American*. Featuring Marlon Brando, the film adaptation of Eugene Burdick's Cold War thriller based loosely on Vietnam.

8. *The Little Drummer Girl*. Stars Diane Keaton as a left-wing pro-Palestinian actress recruited to spy for Israel.

9. *Breach*. Starring Chris Cooper as FBI agent turned Soviet mole Robert Hanssen.

10. *The Good Shepherd*. Starring Matt Damon and Angelina Jolie in a fictionalized account of the founding of the Central Intelligence Agency and its early years.

ENDNOTES

1. The inscription was written by Emma Lazarus (1849–1887).

2. D. McCullough, *John Adams* (Simon & Schuster, 2001).

3. U.S. Constitution, Article I, Section 8.

4. U.S. Constitution, Article II, Section 2.

5. Executive Order No. 10340 (April 8, 1952).

6. *Youngstown Sheet & Tube Co. v. Sawyer*, 343 U.S. 579 (1952).

7. E. Cray, *Chief Justice. A Biography of Earl Warren* (Simon & Schuster, 1997).

8. H. El Nasser, "Papers Show Census Role in WWII Camps: Japanese-American's Data to ID Them for Round-ups," *USA Today,* March 30, 2007.

9. *Korematsu v. United States*, 323 U.S. 214 (1944).

10. W. Blackstone, *Commentaries on the Laws of England* (1765).

11. U.S. Constitution, Article I, Section 9.

12. *Ex parte Milligan*, 71 U.S. (4 Wall) 2 (1866).

13. *United States v. Awadallah*, 202 F. Supp. 2d 55 (2002).

14. J. Curt, *Edgar Hoover: The Man and the Secrets* (W. W. Norton & Company, 1991).

15. *Ex parte Quirin et al.,* 317 U.S. 1 (1942).

16. William Glaberson, "Unlikely Adversary Arises to Criticize Detainee Hearings," *New York Times,* July 23, 2007.

17. *Hamdi v. Rumsfeld*, 337 F.3d 335 (4th Cir. 2003).

18. *Hamdi v. Rumsfeld*, 124 S. Ct. 2633 (2004).

19. *Rumsfeld v. Padilla*, 124 S. Ct. 2711 (2004).

20. *Padilla V. Hanft*, No. 05–533, 547 U.S. 1062, 126 S. Ct. 1649.

21. Jury Finds Padilla Guilty on Terror Charges, CNN online August 16, 2007, available at *http://www.cnn.com/2007/US/08/16/padilla.verdict.*

22. *Rasul v. Bush*, 124 S. Ct. 2711 (2004).

23. Pub. L. No. 109-148, 119 Stat. 2680 (2005).

24. *Hamdan v. Rumsfeld*, 126 S. Ct. 2749, 165 L. Ed. 2d 723 (2006).

25. Pub. L. No. 109-366, 120 Stat. 2600 (2006).

26. *Boumediene v. Bush,* 127 S. Ct. 1478, 167 L. Ed. 2d 578, 2007 U.S. LEXIS 3783.

27. 2007 U.S. LEXIS 8757.

28. Petition for writ of certiorari, U.S. Supreme Court, *Al Odah, et al., v. United States, et al.*

29. William Glaberson, "Unlikely Adversary Arises to Criticize Detainee Hearings," *New York Times*, July 23, 2007.

30. U.S. Constitution, Article III, Section 3.

31. Ibid.

32. 18 U.S.C. § 2381.

33. *Stephan v. United States*, 133 F.2d 87 (6th Cir. 1943), *cert. denied,* 318 U.S. 781, *reh'g denied,* 319 U.S. 783 (1943).

34. *Young v. United States*, 97 U.S. 39 (1878).

35. *Carlisle v. United States*, 8 Ct. Cl. 153 (1872).

36. *Hanauer v. Doane*, 79 U.S. 342 (1871); *Carlisle v. United States,* 83 U.S. 147 (1873).

37. *Kawakita v. United States*, 343 U.S. 717 (1952).

38. *United States v. Chandler*, 72 F. Supp. 230 (D.C. Mass. 1947).

39. *United States v. Hodges*, F. Cas. No. 15374 (C.C. Md. 1815).

40. *Kawakita v. United States*, 343 U.S. 717 (1952).

41. *United States v. Haupt*, 47 F. Supp. 836 (D.C. Ill. 1942).

42. *United States v. Fricke*, 259 F. 673 (D.C. N.Y. 1919).

43. *Cramer v. United States*, 325 U.S. 1 (1945).

44. *Kawakita v. United States*, 343 U.S. 717 (1952).

45. *D'Aquino v. United States,* 1922 F.2d 338 (9th Cir. 1951), *cert. denied,* 343 U.S. 935 (1952).

46. *Miller v. The Ship Resolution* (1781, F C.C. Pa.) 2 U.S. 1, later Op. (F C.C. Pa.) 2 U.S. 19.

47. *United States v. Chandler*, 72 F. Supp. 230 (D.C. Mass. 1947).

48. *United States v. Burgman*, 87 F. Supp. 568 (D.C. 1949), *cert. denied,* 342 U.S. 838 (1950).

49. *Young v. United States*, 97 U.S. 39 (1878); *United States v. Morrison,* 30 F. Cas. No. 18270 (1869).

50. Burr was involved in another scandal as well. He killed Alexander Hamilton in a duel.

51. W. Burger, *It Is So Ordered: A Constitution Unfolds* (William Morrow and Company, 1995).

52. 18 U.S.C. § 2384.

53. *Ballentine's Law Dictionary.*

54. *Wright v. United States*, 108 F. 805 (5th Cir. 1901), *cert. denied,* 181 U.S. 620 (1901).

55. *Skeffinton v. Katzeff*, 277 F. 129 (1st Cir. 1922).

56. *Baldwin v. Franks*, 120 U.S. 678 (1887).

57. Ibid.

58. *Wells v. United States*, 257 F. 605 (9th Cir. 1919); *Enfield v. United States*, 261 F. 141 (8th Cir. 1919); *Orear v. United States*, 261 F. 257 (5th Cir. 1919).

59. *Hays v. American Defense Soc.*, 252 N.Y. 266, 169 N.E. 380 (1929).

60. 18 U.S.C. § 798.

61. 18 U.S.C. § 2383.

62. Ibid.

63. M. Sullivan and D. Rather, eds., *Our Times: America at the Birth of the 20th Century* (New York: Scribner, 1996).

64. Walker, T. "Five-year Hunt for a Killer Eric Rudolph Was Angry, But It Was Abortion That Fired His Passion," *Denver Post,* December 10, 2006.

65. "A Question of Confidentiality; Eavesdropping in the Lockup Poses a Potential Threat to Attorney-Client Privilege. Some Lawyers Fear the Post-Sept. 11 Climate May Further Erode Privacy Rights," *Los Angeles Times* (December 7, 2001).

66. The Transactional Records Access Clearinghouse is a nonprofit, nonpartisan group associated with Syracuse University. The information was gleaned from computer tapes released by the Justice Department after the group won a court order for the information under the Freedom of Information Act.

APPENDIX

No. 06-1196

In the Supreme Court of the United States

Khaled A. F. Al Odah, et al., Petitioners,

v.

United States of America, et al., Respondents.

ON PETITION FOR WRIT OF CERTIORARI TO THE UNITED STATES COURT OF APPEALS FOR THE DISTRICT OF COLUMBIA CIRCUIT

REPLY TO OPPOSITION TO PETITION FOR REHEARING

David J. Cynamon
Matthew J. MacLean
Osman Handoo
Pillsbury Winthrop Shaw Pittman llp
2300 N Street, N.W.
Washington, DC 20037
202-663-8000

Gitanjali Gutierrez
J. Wells Dixon
Shayana Kadidal
Center For Constitutional Rights
666 Broadway, 7th Floor
New York, NY 10012
212-614-6438

Thomas B. Wilner Counsel of Record
Neil H. Koslowe
Amanda E. Shafer
Sheri L. Shepherd
Shearman & Sterling llp
801 Pennsylvania Ave., N.W.
Washington, DC 20004
202-508-8000

George Brent Mickum IV
Spriggs & Hollingsworth
1350 "I" Street N.W.
Washington, DC 20005
202-898-5800

Counsel for Petitioners
Additional Counsel Listed on Inside Cover

Joseph Margulies
Macarthur Justice Center
Northwestern University Law School
357 East Chicago Avenue
Chicago, IL 60611
312-503-0890

Mark S. Sullivan
Christopher G. Karagheuzoff
Joshua Colangelo-Bryan
Dorsey & Whitney LLP
250 Park Avenue
New York, NY 10177
212-415-9200

David H. Remes
Covington & Burling
1201 Pennsylvania Ave., N.W.
Washington, DC 20004
202-662-5212

Scott Sullivan
Derek Jinks
University of Texas School of Law
Rule of Law in Wartime Program
727 E. Dean Keeton Street
Austin, TX 78705
512-471-5151

STEPHEN YAGMAN
723 Ocean Front Walk
Venice, CA 90291
(310) 452-3200

JOHN J. GIBBONS
LAWRENCE S. LUSTBERG
GIBBONS P.C.
One Gateway Center
Newark, NJ 07102
973-596-4500

BAHER AZMY
SETON HALL LAW SCHOOL
CENTER FOR SOCIAL JUSTICE
833 McCarter Highway
Newark, NJ 07102
973-642-8700

MARC D. FALKOFF
COLLEGE OF LAW
NORTHERN ILLINOIS UNIVERSITY
DeKalb, IL 60115
815-753-0660

ERWIN CHEMERINSKY
DUKE LAW SCHOOL
Science Drive & Towerview Rd.
Durham, NC 27708
919-613-7173

CLIVE STAFFORD SMITH
JUSTICE IN EXILE
636 Baronne Street
New Orleans, LA 70113
504-558-9867

Contrary to the government's claim (Opp. 1-2), events since the Court denied certiorari demonstrate that the Court should reconsider that decision and grant review.[1] Specifically, the government's subsequent filings confirm that the review provided under the Detainee Treatment Act of 2005 ("DTA") can *never* be an adequate substitute for habeas and that there is no reason to delay determining the important question of whether the Military Commissions Act (MCA) deprives the Guantanamo detainees of constitutionally-protected rights.

1. After the Court denied certiorari, the government finally conceded that DTA review—exhaustion of which the government says is "a principal reason" to deny certiorari here (Opp. 4)—is more limited than, and not the equivalent of, habeas review. In *Bismullah*,[2] a pending DTA case, the government filed a brief urging the court of appeals not to extend to counsel for the detainees the same access to Guantanamo that the district court granted to them under habeas. The government stated:

> [T]he district court habeas regime should not be recreated in this Court because it is not appropriate to this Court's limited review under the DTA. . . . [T]he review here is administrative in nature and is on the record of the CSRT [Combatant Status Review Tribunal]. Accordingly, factual development at Guantanamo will not be necessary in pursuing this action—the broad access to Guantanamo by private counsel under the Habeas Protective Order is therefore not necessary.[3]

Thus, the government now admits that, under the DTA, the detainees will *not* be able to develop, and the court of appeals will *not* be able to consider, plainly exculpatory evidence and other relevant facts outside the "record" of the CSRT that may determine the validity of their detention. The development and judicial consideration of such evidence and relevant facts, of course, is the *sine qua non* of habeas review.

2. The government also has conceded in its opposition to the petitions for rehearing that DTA review does not contemplate the judicial remedy of release from imprisonment, a remedy that is the hallmark of habeas. Instead, if the court of appeals concludes that the CSRT committed legal error and the detainee is not properly detained as an "enemy combatant," the government maintains that "a remand would be the appropriate remedy" (Opp. 7). The government speculates that such a remand "could" lead the CSRT to enter a finding that the detainee is not an "enemy combatant," and it says that, eventually, all detainees determined to be no longer enemy combatants have been released by the Defense Department (*Id.* 7–8).[4] However, the government does not suggest that, under the DTA, the court of appeals may order a release, even if it finds that there is *no* factual or legal basis for the detention.

Indeed, under the government's reading of the DTA, the Defense Department could hold a detainee forever, even where the court of appeals repeatedly invalidates a CSRT determination that a detainee is an "enemy combatant." Moreover, the government can avoid review by this Court through an endless loop of remands for further CSRT determinations followed by further DTA reviews, *ad infinitum*. This is the inverse of the habeas process, where release is a matter of legal right and not executive grace.

---

[1]"Opp." refers to the Brief for the Respondents in Opposition to the Petitions for Rehearing in No. 06-1195 and this case.
[2]*Bismullah v. Gates*, No. 06-1197 (D.C. Cir.).
[3]*Id.*, Resp. Br. Address. Pending Prelim. Mots. 32 (Apr. 9, 2007).
[4]In fact, detainees determined by CSRTs not to be properly detained as enemy combatants remained imprisoned at Guantanamo for months after the conclusion of the CSRT process before they were released by the Defense Department. *See http://www.defenselink. mil/Releases.Release.aspx?ReleaseID=10204.*

3.   In light of the government's concessions, if the detainees do have a right to habeas corpus protected by the Suspension Clause, as they maintain, then the review provided by the DTA can never be an adequate substitute for habeas and the revocation of their right to habeas by the MCA would appear to be unconstitutional. *See Sanders v. United States*, 373 U.S. 1, 14 (1963). The Court should grant certiorari to resolve this important question.

There is no reason to delay determination of whether the detainees have fundamental constitutional rights. The government, in its opposition, insists that, under the DTA, the court of appeals is authorized to consider petitioners' constitutional claims (Opp. 6). *See* DTA § 1005(e)(2)(C), 119 Stat. 2742. However, the court of appeals reiterated below (*Boumediene v. Bush*, 476 F.3d 981, 991-92 (D.C. Cir. 2007)), as it previously held in *Al Odah v. United States*, 321 F.3d 1134, 1140-41 (D.C. Cir. 2004), that, under its interpretation of *Johnson v. Eisentrager*, 339 U.S. 763 (1950), petitioners have no rights under the Constitution. Unless and until this Court reviews and reverses that erroneous holding, it is the unshakeable law of the circuit. *See Boumediene*, 476 F.3d at 1011 (Rogers, J., dissenting) ("Although in *Rasul* the Court cast doubt on the continuing vitality of *Eisentrager*, 542 U.S. at 475-79, absent an explicit statement by the Court that it intended to overrule *Eisentrager*'s constitutional holding, that holding is binding on this court").

Petitioners were accorded the right to the Great Writ three years ago in *Rasul v. Bush*, 542 U.S. 466 (2004). Now, in the *sixth year* of petitioners' unlawful detention under inhumane conditions of confinement, it would be nothing short of tragic to force petitioners to wait another year or more to first pursue a pointless remedy and receive another decision from the court of appeals that they have no constitutional rights before they can raise this critical issue in this Court. *See* 127 S. Ct. 1478 (statement of Stevens & Kennedy, JJ., respecting denial of certiorari) (habeas corpus "does not require the exhaustion of inadequate remedies"); *Wilwording v. Swenson*, 404 U.S. 249, 250 (1971). That issue is ripe for decision now.

4.   Finally, it is now clear that, not only is the remedy provided by the DTA inadequate, but also the underlying CSRT process was an irremediable sham. A courageous military officer, Lieutenant Colonel Stephen Abraham, United States Army Reserve, has come forward with a declaration responding to assertions about the adequacy of the CSRT process made on behalf of the government by Rear Admiral (Retired) James M. McGarrah in the *Bismullah* case. Based on his personal experience, first as a factual investigator and then as a member of a CSRT tribunal, Lieutenant Colonel Abraham avers that, in every phase, the CSRT process was infected with command influence and an illusion. *See* annexed Declaration of Stephen Abraham.

No review under the DTA can cure such a sham process. No remand by a court for such a process can be an adequate substitute for independent review by a habeas court. Therefore, no exhaustion of the DTA remedy should be required before certiorari is granted in this case.

CONCLUSION

The Court should grant the Petition for Rehearing from Denial of *Certiorari*.

Respectfully submitted,

DAVID J. CYNAMON
MATTHEW J. MACLEAN
OSMAN HANDOO
PILLSBURY WINTHROP
SHAW PITTMAN LLP
2300 N Street, N.W.
Washington, DC 20037
202-663-8000

GITANJALI GUTIERREZ
J. WELLS DIXON
SHAYANA KADIDAL
CENTER FOR CONSTITUTIONAL RIGHTS
666 Broadway, 7th Floor
New York, NY 10012
212-614-6438

THOMAS B. WILNER COUNSEL
 OF RECORD
NEIL H. KOSLOWE
AMANDA E. SHAFER
SHERI L. SHEPHERD
SHEARMAN & STERLING LLP
801 Pennsylvania Ave., N.W.
Washington, DC 20004
202-508-8000

GEORGE BRENT MICKUM IV
SPRIGGS & HOLLINGSWORTH
1350 "I" Street N.W.
Washington, DC 20005
202-898-5800

Counsel for Petitioners with Counsel Listed on Inside Cover

JUNE 22, 2007

Appendix

DECLARATION OF STEPHEN ABRAHAM
Lieutenant Colonel, United States Army Reserve

I, Stephen Abraham, hereby declare as follows:

1.   I am a lieutenant colonel in the United States Army Reserve, having been commissioned in 1981 as an officer in Intelligence Corps. I have served as an intelligence officer from 1982 to the present during periods of both reserve and active duty, including mobilization in 1990 ("Operation Desert Storm") and twice again following 9-11. In my civilian occupation, I am an attorney with the law firm Fink & Abraham LLP in Newport Beach, California.

2.   This declaration responds to certain statements in the Declaration of Rear Admiral (Retired) James M. McGarrah ("McGarrah Dec."), filed in *Bismullah v. Gates*, No. 06-1197 (D.C. Cir.). This declaration is limited to unclassified matters specifically related to the procedures employed by Office for the Administrative Review of the Detention of Enemy Combatants ("OARDEC") and the Combatant Status Review Tribunals ("CSRTs") rather than to any specific information gathered or used in a particular case, except as noted herein. The contents of this declaration are based solely on my personal observations and experiences as a member of OARDEC. Nothing in this declaration is intended to reflect or represent the official opinions of the Department of Defense or the Department of the Army.

3.   From September 11, 2004 to March 9, 2005, I was on active duty and assigned to OARDEC. Rear Admiral McGarrah served as the Director of OARDEC during the entirety of my assignment.

4.   While assigned to OARDEC, in addition to other duties, I worked as an agency liaison, responsible for coordinating with government agencies, including certain Department of Defense ("DoD") and non-DoD organizations, to gather or validate information relating to detainees for use in CSRTs. I also served as a member of a CSRT, and had the opportunity to observe and participate in the operation of the CSRT process.

5.   As stated in the McGarrah Dec., the information comprising the Government Information and the Government Evidence was not compiled personally by the CSRT Recorder, but by other individuals in OARDEC. The vast majority of the personnel assigned to OARDEC were reserve officers from the different branches of service (Army, Navy, Air Force, Marines) of varying grades and levels of general military experience. Few had any experience or training in the legal or intelligence fields.

6.   The Recorders of the tribunals were typically relatively junior officers with little training or experience in matters relating to the collection, processing, analyzing, and/or dissemination of intelligence material. In no instances known to me did any of the Recorders have any significant personal experience in the field of military intelligence. Similarly, I was unaware of any Recorder having any significant or relevant experience dealing with the agencies providing information to be used as a part of the CSRT process.

7.   The Recorders exercised little control over the process of accumulating information to be presented to the CSRT board members. Rather, the information was typically aggregated by individuals identified as case writers who, in most instances, had the same limited degree of knowledge and experience relating to the intelligence community and intelligence products. The case writers, and not the Recorders, were primarily responsible for accumulating documents, including assembling documents to be used in the drafting of an unclassified summary of the factual basis for the detainee's designation as an enemy combatant.

8.   The information used to prepare the files to be used by the Recorders frequently consisted of finished intelligence products of a generalized nature—often outdated, often "generic," rarely specifically relating to the individual subjects of the CSRTs or to the circumstances related to those individuals' status.

9.   Beyond "generic" information, the case writer would frequently rely upon information contained within the Joint Detainee Information Management System ("JDIMS"). The subset of that system available to the case writers was limited in terms of the scope of information, typically excluding information that was characterized as highly sensitive law enforcement information, highly classified information, or information not voluntarily released by the originating agency. In that regard, JDIMS did not constitute a complete repository, although this limitation was frequently not understood by individuals with access to or who relied upon the system as a source of information. Other databases available to the case writer were similarly deficient. The case writers and Recorders did not have access to numerous information sources generally available within the intelligence community.

10.   As one of only a few intelligence-trained and suitably cleared officers, I served as a liaison while assigned to OARDEC, acting as a go-between for OARDEC and various intelligence organizations. In that capacity, I was tasked to review and/or obtain information relating to individual subjects of the CSRTs. More specifically, I was asked to confirm and represent in a statement to be relied upon by the CSRT board members that the organizations did not possess "exculpatory information" relating to the subject of the CSRT.

11.   During my trips to the participating organizations, I was allowed only limited access to information, typically prescreened and filtered. I was not permitted to see any information other than that specifically prepared in advance of my visit. I was not permitted to request that further searches be performed. I was given no assurances that the information provided for my examination represented a complete compilation of information or that any summary of information constituted an accurate distillation of the body of available information relating to the subject.

12.   I was specifically told on a number of occasions that the information provided to me was all that I would be shown, but I was never told that the information that was provided constituted all available information. On those occasions when I asked that a representative of the organization provide a written statement that there was no exculpatory evidence, the requests were summarily denied.

13.   At one point, following a review of information, I asked the Office of General Counsel of the intelligence organization that I was visiting for a statement that no exculpatory information had been withheld. I explained that I was tasked to review all available materials and to reach a conclusion regarding the non-existence of exculpatory information, and that I could not do so without knowing that I had seen all information.

14.   The request was denied, coupled with a refusal even to acknowledge whether there existed additional information that I was not permitted to review. In short, based upon the selective review that I was permitted, I was left to "infer" from the absence of exculpatory information in the materials I was allowed to review that no such information existed in materials I was not allowed to review.

15.   Following that exchange, I communicated to Rear Admiral McGarrah and the OARDEC Deputy Director the fundamental limitations imposed upon my review of the organization's files and my inability to state conclusively that no exculpatory information existed relating to the CSRT subjects. It was not possible for me to certify or validate the non-existence of exculpatory evidence as related to any individual undergoing the CSRT process.

16.   The content of intelligence products, including databases, made available to case writers, Recorders, or liaison officers, was often left entirely to the discretion of the organizations providing the information. What information was not included in the bodies of intelligence products was typically unknown to the case writers and Recorders, as was the basis for limiting the information. In other words, the person preparing materials for use by the CSRT board members did not know whether they had examined all available information or even why they possessed some pieces of information but not others.

17.   Although OARDEC personnel often received large amounts of information, they often had no context for determining whether the information was relevant or probative and no basis for determining what additional information would be necessary to establish a basis for determining the reasonableness of any matter to be offered to the CSRT board members. Often, information that was gathered was discarded by the case writer or the Recorder because it was considered to be ambiguous, confusing, or poorly written. Such a determination was frequently the result of the case writer or Recorder's lack of training or experience with the types of information provided. In my observation, the case writer or Recorder, without proper experience or a basis for giving context to information, often rejected some information arbitrarily while accepting other information without any articulable rationale.

18.   The case writer's summaries were reviewed for quality assurance, a process that principally focused on format and grammar. The quality assurance review would not ordinarily check the accuracy of the information underlying the case writer's unclassified summary for the reason that the quality assurance reviewer typically had little more experience than the case writer and, again, no relevant or meaningful intelligence or legal experience, and therefore had no skills by which to critically assess the substantive portions of the summaries.

19.   Following the quality assurance process, the unclassified summary and the information assembled by the case writer in support of the summary would then be forwarded to the Recorder. It was very rare that a Recorder or a personal representative would seek additional information beyond that information provided by the case writer.

20.   It was not apparent to me how assignments to CSRT panels were made, nor was I personally involved in that process. Nevertheless, I discerned the determinations of who would be assigned to any particular position, whether as a member of a CSRT or to some other position, to be largely the product of ad hoc decisions by a relatively small group of individuals. All CSRT panel members were assigned to OARDEC and reported ultimately to Rear Admiral McGarrah. It was well known by the officers in OARDEC that any time a CSRT panel determined that a detainee was not properly classified as an enemy combatant, the panel members would have to explain their finding to the OARDEC Deputy Director. There would be intensive scrutiny of the finding by Rear Admiral McGarrah who would, in turn, have to explain the finding to his superiors, including the Under Secretary of the Navy.

21.   On one occasion, I was assigned to a CSRT panel with two other officers, an Air Force colonel and an Air Force major, the latter understood by me to be a judge advocate. We reviewed evidence presented to us regarding the recommended status of a detainee. All of us found the information presented to lack substance.

22.   What were purported to be specific statements of fact lacked even the most fundamental earmarks of objectively credible evidence. Statements allegedly made by percipient witnesses lacked detail. Reports presented generalized statements in indirect and passive forms without stating the source of the information or providing a basis for establishing the reliability or the credibility of the source. Statements of interrogators presented to the panel offered inferences from which we were expected to draw conclusions favoring a finding of "enemy combatant" but that, upon even limited questioning from the panel, yielded the response from the Recorder, "We'll have to get back to you." The personal representative did not participate in any meaningful way.

23.   On the basis of the paucity and weakness of the information provided both during and after the CSRT hearing, we determined that there was no factual basis for concluding that the individual should be classified as an enemy combatant. Rear Admiral McGarrah and the Deputy Director immediately questioned the validity of our findings. They directed us to write out the

specific questions that we had raised concerning the evidence to allow the Recorder an opportunity to provide further responses. We were then ordered to reopen the hearing to allow the Recorder to present further argument as to why the detainee should be classified as an enemy combatant. Ultimately, in the absence of any substantive response to the questions and no basis for concluding that additional information would be forthcoming, we did not change our determination that the detainee was not properly classified as an enemy combatant. OARDEC's response to the outcome was consistent with the few other instances in which a finding of "Not an Enemy Combatant" (NEC) had been reached by CSRT boards. In each of the meetings that I attended with OARDEC leadership following a finding of NEC, the focus of inquiry on the part of the leadership was "what went wrong."

24.   I was not assigned to another CSRT panel.

I hereby declare under the penalties of perjury based on my personal knowledge that the foregoing is true and accurate.

Stephen Abraham
Dated: June 15, 2007

IN THE UNITED STATES DISTRICT COURT
FOR THE DISTRICT OF COLUMBIA

LAKHDAR BOUMEDIENE,　　　　　　　　　)
　　　　　　　　　　et al.　　　　　　)
　　　　　　　　　　　　　　　　　　　)
　　　　Petitioners,　　　　　　　　　)
　　　　　　　　　　　　　　　　　　　)　　　Civil Action No. 04-CV-1166 (RJL)
　　　　v.　　　　　　　　　　　　　　)
　　　　　　　　　　　　　　　　　　　)
GEORGE W. BUSH,　　　　　　　　　　　)
　　　President of the United States, *et al.,*　)
　　　　　　Respondents.　　　　　　　　)
　　　　　　　　　　　　　　　　　　　)
_____)

DECLARATION OF JAMES R. CRISFIELD JR.

Pursuant to 28 U.S.C. § 1746,1, Commander James R. Crisfield Jr., Judge Advocate General's Corps, United States Navy, hereby state that to the best of my knowledge, information and belief, the following is true, accurate and correct:

1.　I am the Legal Advisor to the Combatant Status Review Tribunals. In that capacity I am the principal legal advisor to the Director, Combatant Status Review Tribunals, and provide advice to Tribunals on legal, evidentiary, procedural, and other matters. I also review the record of proceedings in each Tribunal for legal sufficiency in accordance with standards prescribed in the Combatant Status Review Tribunal establishment order and implementing directive.

2.　I hereby certify that the documents attached hereto constitute a true and accurate copy of the portions of the record of proceedings before the Combatant Status Review Tribunal related to petitioner Lakhdar Boumediene that are suitable for public release. The portions of the record that are classified or considered law enforcement sensitive are not attached hereto. I have redacted any information that would personally identify other detainees and certain U.S. Government personnel in order to protect the personal security of those individuals. I have also redacted internee serial numbers because certain combinations of internee serial numbers with other information become classified under applicable classification guidance.

I declare under penalty of perjury that the foregoing is true and correct.

Dated: <u>12 Oct 04</u>

James R. Crisfield Jr.
CDR, JAGC, USN

Department of Defense
Director, Combatant Status Review Tribunals

OARDEC/Ser: 0211
11 October 2004

FOR OFFICIAL USE ONLY

From: Director, Combatant Status Review Tribunal

Subj: REVIEW OF COMBATANT STATUS REVIEW TRIBUNAL FOR DETAINEE ISN #

Ref: (a) Deputy Secretary of Defense Order of 7 July 2004
      (b) Secretary of the Navy Order of 29 July 2004

1. I concur in the decision of the Combatant Status Review Tribunal that Detainee ISN #   meets the criteria for designation as an Enemy Combatant, in accordance with references (a) and (b).
    2. This case is now considered final, and the detainee will be scheduled for an Administrative Review Board.

J. M. McGARRAH
RADM, CEC, USN

Distribution:
NSC (Mr. John Bellinger)
DoS (Ambassador Prosper)
DASD-DA
JCS (J5)
SOUTHCOM (CoS)
COMJTFGTMO
OARDEC (Fwd)
CITF Ft Belvoir

FOR OFFICIAL USE ONLY

UNCLASSIFIED

11 Oct 04

MEMORANDUM

From: Legal Advisor

To: Director, Combatant Status Review Tribunal

Subj: LEGAL SUFFICIENCY REVIEW OF COMBATANT STATUS REVIEW TRIBUNAL FOR DETAINEE ISN #

Ref: (a) Deputy Secretary of Defense Order of 7 July 2004
(b) Secretary of the Navy Implementation Directive of 29 July 2004

Encl: (1) Appointing Order for Tribunal #6 of 13 September 2004
(2) Record of Tribunal Proceedings

1. Legal sufficiency review has been completed on the subject Combatant Status Review Tribunal in accordance with references (a) and (b). After reviewing the record of the Tribunal, I find that:

a. The detainee was properly notified of the Tribunal process and voluntarily elected not to participate.

b. The Tribunal was properly convened and constituted by enclosure (1).

c. The Tribunal complied with the provisions of references (a) and (b). Note that some information in exhibits R-3, R-4, and R-6 was redacted. The FBI properly certified in exhibit R-2 that the redacted information would not support a determination that the detainee is not an enemy combatant.

d. The detainee made no requests for witnesses or other evidence.

e. The Tribunal's decision that detainee #   is properly classified as an enemy combatant was unanimous.

f. The detainee's Personal Representative was given the opportunity to review the record of proceedings and declined to submit comments to the Tribunal.

2. The proceedings and decision of the Tribunal are legally sufficient and no corrective action is required.

3. I recommend that the decision of the Tribunal be approved and the case be considered final.

James R. Crisfield Jr.
CDR, JAGC, USN

Department of Defense
Director, Combatant Status Review Tribunals

13 Sep 04

From: Director, Combatant Status Review Tribunals

Subj: APPOINTMENT OF COMBATANT STATUS REVIEW TRIBUNAL #6

Ref: (a) Convening Authority Appointment Letter of 9 July 2004

By the authority given to me in reference (a), a Combatant Status Review Tribunal established by "Implementation of Combatant Status Review Tribunal Procedures for Enemy Combatants Detained at Guantanamo Bay Naval Base, Cuba" dated 29 July 2004 is hereby convened. It shall hear such cases as shall be brought before it without further action of referral or otherwise.

The following commissioned officers shall serve as members of the Tribunal:

MEMBERS.

　　　　,Colonel, US. Army, President

　　　　,Commander, JAGC, U.S. Navy; Member (JAG)

　　　　,Lieutenant Colonel, U.S. Marine Corps; Member

J. M. McGARRAH
Rear Admiral
Civil Engineer Corps
United States Naval Reserve

HEADQUARTERS, OARDEC FORWARD
GUANTANAMO BAY, CUBA
APO AE 09360

6 October 2004

MEMORANDUM FOR DIRECTOR, CSRT

FROM: OARDEC FORWARD Commander

SUBJECT: CSRT Record of Proceedings ICO ISN#

1. Pursuant to Enclosure (1), paragraph (I)(5) of the *Implementation of Combatant Status Review Tribunal Procedures for Enemy Combatants Detained at Guantanamo Bay Naval Base, Cuba* dated 29 July 2004, I am forwarding the Combatant Status Review Tribunal Decision Report for the above mentioned ISN for review and action.

2. If there are any questions regarding this package, point of contact on this matter is the undersigned at DSN 660-3088.

DAVID L. TAYLOR
Colonel, USAF

SECRET//N0FORN//X1

(U) Combatant Status Review Tribunal Decision Report Cover Sheet

(U) This Document is UNCLASSIFIED Upon Removal of Enclosures (2) and (3).

(U) TRIBUNAL PANEL: ____#6____

(U) ISN#: _____

Ref: (a) (U) Convening Order for Tribunal #6 of 13 September 2004 (U)
      (b) (U) CSRT Implementation Directive of 29 July 2004 (U)
      (c) (U) DEPSECDEF Memo of 7 July 2004 (U)

Encl: (1) (U) Unclassified Summary of Basis For Tribunal Decision (U)
      (2) (U) Classified Summary of Basis for Tribunal Decision (S/NF)
      (3) (U) Copies of Documentary Evidence Presented (S/NF)
      (4) (U) Personal Representative's Record Review (U)

1.   (U) This Tribunal was convened by references (a) and (b) to make a determination as to whether the detainee meets the criteria to be designated as an enemy combatant as defined in reference (c).

    2.   (U) On 1 October 2004, the Tribunal determined, by a preponderance of the evidence, that Detainee #   is properly designated as an enemy combatant as defined in reference (c).

    3.   (U) In particular, the Tribunal finds that this detainee is a member of, or affiliated with, Al Qaida forces, or associated forces that are engaged in hostilities against the United States or its coalition partners, as more fully discussed in the enclosures.

    4.   (U) Enclosure (1) provides an unclassified account of the basis for the Tribunal's decision. A detailed account of the evidence considered by the Tribunal and its findings of fact are contained in enclosures (1) and (2).

                                            _____
                                            Colonel, U.S. Army
                                            Tribunal President

DERV FM: Multiple Sources   **SECRET//NOFORN//X1**
DECLASS: XI

UNCLASSIFIED SUMMARY OF BASIS FOR TRIBUNAL DECISION

(Enclosure (1) to Combatant Status Review Tribunal Decision Report)

TRIBUNAL PANEL: ___#6___

ISN #: _____

1. Introduction

As the Combatant Status Review Tribunal (CSRT) Decision Report indicates, the Tribunal has determined that this detainee is properly classified as an enemy combatant and was part of or supporting Al Qaida forces, or associated forces that are engaged in hostilities against the United States or its coalition partners. In reaching its conclusions, the Tribunal considered both classified and unclassified information. The following is an account of the unclassified evidence considered by the Tribunal and other pertinent information. Classified evidence considered by the Tribunal is discussed in Enclosure (2) to the CSRT Decision Report.

2. Synopsis of Proceedings

The initial session of this Tribunal was held on 27 September 2004. The Recorder presented Exhibits R-1 and R-2 during the unclassified portion of the Tribunal. The Unclassified Summary of Evidence (Exhibit R-1) indicates, among other things, that the detainee is a supporter of Al Qaida and has on multiple occasions provided subsistence to   a known Al Qaida operative. The Unclassified Summary of Evidence also indicates the detainee admitted retaining and financing legal representation for a known Al Qaida operative after that operative's arrest for terrorist activities. The Recorder called no witnesses.

The detainee chose not to attend the Tribunal as reflected in the Detainee Election Form (Exhibit D-A), and the Personal Representative presented no evidence and called no witnesses.

During the classified session of the Tribunal, the Recorder presented Exhibits R-3 through R-14. The Personal Representative presented no classified evidence, and neither the Recorder nor the Personal Representative commented on the classified exhibits. After the Tribunal read all of the classified exhibits, the Tribunal requested additional information and recessed until the Recorder could obtain it.

The Tribunal reconvened on 1 October 2004. In response to the Tribunal's request, the Recorder offered into evidence additional classified Exhibits R-15 through R-24 after giving the Personal Representative an opportunity to review the documents. Neither the Recorder nor the Personal Representative had any comments on the additional documents. After considering the unclassified and the classified evidence, the Tribunal determined that the detainee is properly classified as an enemy combatant.

3. Evidence Considered by the Tribunal

The Tribunal considered the following evidence in reaching its conclusions:

     a. Exhibits: R-1 through R-24 and D-A.
     b. Testimony of the following persons: None.
     c. Statement of the detainee: None.

4. Rulings by the Tribunal on Detainee Requests for Evidence or Witnesses

The Detainee requested no witnesses.

The Detainee requested no additional evidence be produced.

5. Discussion of Unclassified Evidence

The Recorder offered Exhibits R-1 and R-2 into evidence during the unclassified portion of the proceeding. Exhibit R-1 is the Unclassified Summary of Evidence. While this summary is helpful in that it provides a broad outline of what the Tribunal can expect to see, it is not persuasive in that it provides conclusory statements without supporting unclassified evidence. Exhibit R-2, the FBI redaction certification, provided no usable evidence. Accordingly, the Tribunal had to look to the classified exhibits for support of the Unclassified Summary of Evidence. A discussion of the classified evidence is found in Enclosure (2) to the Combatant Status Review Tribunal Decision Report.

ISN#
Enclosure (1)
Page 1 of 2

6. Consultations with the CSRT Legal Advisor

No issues arose during the course of this hearing that required consultation with the CSRT Legal Advisor.

7. Conclusions of the Tribunal

Upon careful review of all the evidence presented in this matter, the Tribunal makes the following determinations:

a. The detainee chose not to participate in the Tribunal proceeding. No evidence was produced that caused the Tribunal to question whether the detainee was mentally and physically capable of participating in the proceeding, had he wanted to do so. Accordingly, no medical or mental health evaluation was requested or deemed necessary.

b. The Personal Representative informed the Tribunal that the detainee understood the Tribunal process, but chose not to participate, as indicated in Exhibit D-A.

c. The detainee is properly classified as an enemy combatant because he was part of or supporting Al Qaida forces, or associated forces that are engaged in hostilities against the United States or its coalition partners.

8. Dissenting Tribunal Member's report

None. The Tribunal reached a unanimous decision.

Respectfully submitted,

Colonel, U.S. Army
Tribunal President

ISN#
Enclosure (1)
Page 2 of 2

UNCLASSIFIED//FOUO

DETAINEE ELECTION FORM

Date: <u>24-Sep-04</u>
Start Time: <u>1830</u>
End Time: <u>1850</u>

ISN#: _____

Personal Representative: _____ <u>LCDR, USN</u> _____
(Name/Rank)

Translator Required? <u>YES</u>   Language? _____ **ARABIC** _____

CSRT Procedure Read to Detainee or Written Copy Read by Detainee? <u>YES</u> _____

Detainee Election:

☐   Wants to Participate in Tribunal

☒   Affirmatively Declines to Participate in Tribunal

☐   Uncooperative or Unresponsive

Personal Representative Comments:

Stated he would not participate in the tribunal or make any statements. _____

_____

_____

_____

_____

_____

_____

_____

_____

_____

_____

_____

_____

_____

_____

Personal Representative: _____ <u>LCDR, USN</u> _____

UNCLASSIFIED//FOUO   Exhibit <u>D-A</u>

UNCLASSIFIED

Combatant Status Review Board

TO: Tribunal Member

FROM: OIC, CSRT (21 September 04)

Subject: Summary of Evidence for Combatant Status Review Tribunal BOUMEDIENE, Lakhdar.

1.   Under the provisions of the Secretary of the Navy Memorandum, dated 29 July 2004, *Implementation of Combatant Status Review Tribunal Procedures for Enemy Combatants Detained at Guantanamo Bay Naval Base Cuba,* a Tribunal has been appointed to review the detainee's designation as an enemy combatant.

2.   An enemy combatant has been defined as "an individual who was part of or supporting the Taliban or al Qaida forces, or associated forces that are engaged in hostilities against the United States or its coalition partners. This includes any person who committed a belligerent act or has directly supported hostilities in aid of enemy armed forces."

3.   The United States Government has previously determined that the detainee is an enemy combatant. This determination is based on information possessed by the United States that indicates that he is an al Qaida supporter.

a. The detainee is a supporter of al Qaida:

1. The detainee is a native of Algeria who, since 1990, has repeatedly traveled to hotspots of regional conflict throughout the Middle East and Eastern Europe.
2. The detainee has on multiple occasions provided subsistence to   .
3.   is a known al Qaida operative.
4. The detainee has given conflicting statements as to the nature of his association with   .
5. The detainee admitted retaining and financing legal representation for a known al Qaida operative after that operative's arrest for terrorist activities.

4.   The detainee has the opportunity to contest his designation as an enemy combatant. The Tribunal will endeavor to arrange for the presence of any reasonably available witnesses or evidence that the detainee desires to call or introduce to prove that he is not an enemy combatant. The Tribunal President will determine the reasonable availability of evidence or witnesses.

UNCLASSIFIED

Exhibit R1

UNCLASSIFIED

Memorandum

To:	Department of Defense Office of Administrative Review for Detained Enemy Combatants, Col. David Taylor, OIC, CSRT	Date 09/17/2004
From:	FBI GTMO Counterterrorism Division, Office of General Counsel,	
Subject	REQUEST FOR REDACTION OF NATIONAL SECURITY INFORMATION ISN #	

Pursuant to the Secretary of the Navy Order of 29 July 2004, implementation of Combatant Review Tribunal Procedures for Enemy Combatants Detained at Guantanamo Bay Naval Base, Cuba, Section D, paragraph 2, the FBI requests redaction of the information herein marked.[1] The FBI makes this request on the basis that said information relates to the national security of the United States.[2] Inappropriate dissemination of said information could damage the national security of the United States and compromise ongoing FBI investigations.

CERTIFICATION THAT REDACTED INFORMATION DOES NOT SUPPORT A DETERMINATION THAT THE DETAINEE IS NOT AN ENEMY COMBATANT

The FBI certifies the aforementioned redaction contains no information that would support a determination that the detainee is not an enemy combatant.

The following documents relative to ISN #   have been redacted by the FBI and provided to the OARDEC, GTMO:

FD-302 dated 02/18/2002
FD-302 dated 03/07/2002
FD-302 dated 05/03/2002

Memorandum from   to Col. David Taylor
Re: REQUEST FOR REDACTION, 09/17/2004

If you need additional assistance, please contact Assistant General Counsel   or Intelligence Analyst

Personal Representative Review of the Record of Proceedings

I acknowledge that on 4 October 2004, I was provided the opportunity to review the record of proceedings for the Combatant Status Review Tribunal involving ISN #

____✓__ I have no comments.

_____ My comments are attached.

_____	04 oct 04
Name	Date

LCDR, USN
Signature

---

[1]Redactions are blackened out on the OARDEC provided FBI document.
[2]See Executive Order 12958

ISN#
Enclosure (4)

UNCLASSIFIED

Verbatim Transcript of Combatant Status Review Tribunal Hearing for ISN 10024

OPENING

REPORTER: On the record

RECORDER: All rise.

PRESIDENT: Remain seated and come to order. Go ahead. Recorder.

RECORDER: This Tribunal is being conducted at 1328 March 10, 2007 on board U.S. Naval
Base Guantanamo Bay, Cuba. The following personnel are present:
Captain [REDACTED], United States Navy, President
Lieutenant Colonel [REDACTED], United States Air Force. Member
Lieutenant Colonel [REDACTED], United States Marine Corps, Member
Lieutenant Colonel [REDACTED], United States Air Force, Personal Representative
Language Analysis [REDACTED]
Gunnery Sergeant [REDACTED], United States Marine Corps, Reporter
Lieutenant Colonel [REDACTED], United States Army, Recorder
Captain [REDACTED] is the Judge Advocate member of the Tribunal.

OATH SESSION 1

RECORDER: All Rise.

PRESIDENT: The Recorder will be sworn. Do you, Lieutenant Colonel [REDACTED] solemnly swear that you will faithfully
perform the duties as Recorder assigned in this Tribunal so help you God?

RECORDER: I do.

PRESIDENT: The Reporter will now be sworn. The Recorder will administer the oath.

RECORDER: Do you Gunnery Sergeant [DELETED] swear or affirm that you will faithfully discharge your duties as Reporter
assigned in this Tribunal so help you God?

REPORTER: I do.

PRESIDENT: The Translator will be sworn.

RECORDER: Do you swear or affirm that you will faithfully perform the duties of Translator in the case now in hearing so help
you God?

TRANSLATOR: I do.

PRESIDENT: We will take a brief recess now in order to bring Detainee into the room. Recorder note the date and time.

RECORDER: The time is 1:30 pm hours on 10 March 2007. This Tribunal is now in recess.
[The Tribunal recessed at 1330, 10 March 2007. The members withdrew from the hearing room.]

CONVENING AUTHORITY

RECORDER: All Rise.
[The Tribunal reconvened and the members entered the room at 1334, 10 March 2007.]

PRESIDENT: This hearing will come to order. Please be seated.

PRESIDENT: Before we begin, Khalid Sheikh Muhammad, I understand you speak and understand English. Is that correct?

DETAINEE: [Detainee nods his head in affirmative].

PRESIDENT: Alright. Are you comfortable in continuing in English or would you like everything translated in Arabic?

ISN #10024
Enclosure (3)
Page 1 of 15

UNCLASSIFIED

UNCLASSIFIED

DETAINEE:	Everything in English but if I have a problem the linguist will help me.
PRESIDENT:	We will proceed in English. If you indicate to me that you would like something translated we will go ahead and do that. Alright?
PRESIDENT:	This Tribunal is convened by order of the Director, Combatant Status Review Tribunals under the provisions of his Order of 22 February 2007.
PRESIDENT:	This Tribunal will determine whether Khalid Sheikh Muhammad meets the criteria to be designated as an enemy combatant against the United States or its coalition partners or otherwise meets the criteria to be designated as an enemy combatant.

OATH SESSION 2

PRESIDENT:	The members of this Tribunal shall now be sworn. All rise.
RECORDER:	Do you swear or affirm that you will faithfully perform your duties as a member of this Tribunal; that you will impartially examine and inquire into the matter now before you according to your conscience, and the laws and regulations provided; that you will make such findings of fact and conclusions as are supported by the evidence presented; that in determining those facts, you will use your professional knowledge, best judgment, and common sense; and that you will make such findings as are appropriate according to the best of your understanding of the rules, regulations, and laws governing this proceeding, and guided by your concept of justice so help you God?
TRIBUNAL:	I do.
PRESIDENT:	The Recorder will now administer the oath to the Personal Representative.
RECORDER:	Do you swear or affirm that you will faithfully perform the duties of Personal Representative in this Tribunal so help you God?
PERSONAL REPRESENTATIVE:	I do.
PRESIDENT:	Please be seated.
PRESIDENT:	The Recorder, Reporter, and Translator have previously been sworn.

EXPLANATION OF PROCEEDINGS

PRESIDENT:	Khalid Sheikh Muhammad, you are hereby advised that the following applies during this hearing:
PRESIDENT:	You may be present at all open sessions of the Tribunal. However, if you become disorderly, you will be removed from the hearing, and the Tribunal will continue to hear evidence in your absence.
PRESIDENT:	You may not be compelled to testify at this Tribunal. However, you may testify if you wish to do so. Your testimony can be under oath or unsworn.
PRESIDENT:	You may have the assistance of a Personal Representative at the hearing. Your assigned Personal Representative is present.
PRESIDENT:	You may present evidence to this Tribunal, including the testimony of witnesses who are reasonably available and whose testimony is relevant to this hearing. You may question witnesses testifying at the Tribunal.
PRESIDENT:	You may examine documents or statements offered into evidence other than classified information. However, certain documents may be partially masked for security reasons.
PRESIDENT:	Khalid Sheikh Muhammad, do you understand this process?
DETAINEE:	Yes. If I have question can I ask you?
PRESIDENT:	Yes, you may.
DETAINEE:	About the testimony which I ask about the witnesses.
PRESIDENT:	Yes, I'm going to address the witnesses shortly. So, if you will bear with us I will take that up in a few moments.

ISN #10024
Enclosure (3)
Page 2 of 15

UNCLASSIFIED

DETAINEE:	Okay.
PRESIDENT:	Do you have any questions concerning the Tribunal process?
DETAINEE:	Okay by me.

PRESENTATION OF UNCLASSIFIED INFORMATION

PRESIDENT:	Personal Representative, please provide the Tribunal with the Detainee Election Form.
PERSONAL REPRESENTATIVE:	I am handing the Tribunal the Detainee Election Form, which was previously marked as Exhibit D-a.
PRESIDENT:	Alright, the Tribunal has received Exhibit D-a that indicates the Detainee wants to participate in the Tribunal and wants the assistance of the Personal Representative.

RECORDER PRESENTS UNCLASSIFIED

PRESIDENT:	Recorder, please provide the Tribunal with the unclassified evidence.
RECORDER:	I am handing the Tribunal what has previously been marked as Exhibit R-1, the unclassified summary of the evidence that relates to this Detainee's status as an enemy combatant. A translated copy of this exhibit was provided to the Personal Representative in advance of this hearing for presentation to the Detainee. In addition, I am handing to the Tribunal the following unclassified exhibits, marked as Exhibit R-2. Copies of these Exhibits have previously been provided to the Personal Representative. [Documents presented to Tribunal]
PRESIDENT:	Recorder, please read the unclassified summary of evidence for the record. But before you proceed, Khalid Sheikh Muhammad, let me remind you that you must not comment on this evidence at this time. You will be provided with an opportunity shortly to provide any comments that you would like. Recorder, please proceed.
RECORDER:	The following facts support the determination that the Detainee is an enemy combatant:

Paragraph a. On the morning of 11 September 2001, four airliners traveling over the United States were hijacked. The flights hijacked were: American Airlines Flight 11, United Airlines Flight 175, American Airlines Flight 77, and United Airlines Flight 93. At approximately 8:46 a.m., American Airlines Flight 11 crashed into the North Tower of the World Trade Center, resulting in the collapse of the tower at approximately 10:25 a.m. At approximately 9:05 a.m., United Airlines Flight 175 crashed into the South Tower of the World Trade Center, resulting in the collapse of the tower at approximately 9:55 a.m. At approximately 9:37 a.m., American Airlines Flight 77 crashed into the southwest side of the Pentagon in Arlington, Virginia. At approximately 10:03 a.m., United Airlines Flight 93 crashed in Stoney Creek Township, Pennsylvania. These crashes and subsequent damage to the World Trade Center and the Pentagon resulted in the deaths of 2,972 persons in New York, Virginia, and Pennsylvania.

Paragraph b. The Detainee served as the head of the al Qaida military committee and was Usama bin Laden's principal al Qaida operative who directed the 11 September 2001 attacks in the United States.

Paragraph c. In an interview with an al Jazeera reporter in June 2002, the Detainee stated he was the head of the al Qaida military committee.

Paragraph d. A computer hard drive seized during the capture of the Detainee contained information about the four airplanes hijacked on 11 September 2001 including code names, airline company, flight number, target, pilot name and background information, and names of the hijackers.

Paragraph e. A computer hard drive seized during the capture of the Detainee contained photographs of 19 individuals identified as the 11 September 2001 hijackers.

Paragraph f. A computer hard drive seized during the capture of the Detainee contained a document that listed the pilot license fees for Mohammad Atta and biographies for some of the 11 September 2001 hijackers.

Paragraph g. A computer hard drive seized during the capture of the Detainee contained images of passports and an image of Mohammad Atta.

Paragraph h. A computer hard drive seized during the capture of the Detainee contained transcripts of chat sessions belonging to at least one of the 11 September 2001 hijackers.

Paragraph i. The Detainee directed an individual to travel to the United States to case targets for a second wave of attacks.

UNCLASSIFIED

Paragraph j. A computer hard drive seized during the capture of the Detainee contained three letters from Usama bin Laden.

Paragraph k. A computer hard drive seized during the capture of the Detainee contained spreadsheets that describe money assistance to families of known al Qaida members.

Paragraph l. The Detainee's name was on a list in a computer seized in connection with a threat to United States airlines, United States embassies and the Pope.

Paragraph m. The Detainee wrote the *bojinka plot,* the airline bomb plot which was later found on his nephew Ramzi Yousef's computer.

Paragraph n. The *Bojinka plot* is also known as the Manila air investigation.

Paragraph o. The Manila air investigation uncovered the Detainee conspired with others to plant explosive devices aboard American jetliners while those aircraft were scheduled to be airborne and loaded with passengers on their way to the United States.

Paragraph p. The Detainee was in charge of and funded an attack against United States military vessels heading to the port of Djibouti.

Paragraph q. A computer hard drive seized during the capture of the Detainee contained a letter to the United Arab Emirates threatening attack if their government continued to help the United States.

Paragraph r. During the capture of the Detainee, information used exclusively by al Qaida operational managers to communicate with operatives was found.

Paragraph s. The Detainee received funds from Kuwaiti-based Islamic extremist groups and delivered the funds to al Qaida members.

Paragraph t. A computer hard drive seized during the capture of the Detainee contained a document that summarized operational procedures and training requirements of an al Qaida cell.

Paragraph u. A computer hard drive seized during the capture of the Detainee contained a list of killed and wounded al Qaida martyrs.

And lastly, Paragraph v. Passport photographs of al Qaida operatives were seized during the capture of the Detainee.

RECORDER: Sir, this concludes the summary of unclassified evidence.

PRESIDENT: Very well.

PRESIDENT: Personal Representative, does the Detainee have any evidence to present to this Tribunal?

PERSONAL REPRESENTATIVE: Yes, sir. I am handing to the Tribunal the following unclassified exhibits marked as Exhibits D-b through D-d. Copies of these exhibits have been previously provided to the Recorder. [Documents presented to Tribunal]

PRESIDENT: Exhibit D-b appears to be a statement that the Detainee has provided.

PERSONAL REPRESENTATIVE: Yes, Sir.

PRESIDENT: Alright. And Exhibit D-c contains hand written notes that appear to be Arabic and English as well as the typed version of that. Is that correct?

PERSONAL REPRESENTATIVE: Yes, Sir.

PRESIDENT: Alright. And D-d is a written statement regarding alleged abuse or treatment that the Detainee received.

PERSONAL REPRESENTATIVE: Yes, Sir.

PRESIDENT: Alright. We will go into those shortly.

PRESIDENT: Khalid Sheikh Muhammad, you may now make an oral statement to the Tribunal, and you have the assistance of your Personal Representative in doing so. Do you wish to make an oral statement to this Tribunal?

DETAINEE: He will start, the Personal Representative; PR will read then later I will comment.

UNCLASSIFIED

PRESIDENT:	Very well, you may proeeed.
RECORDER:	Sir, would you hold one moment?
PRESIDENT:	Yes.
RECORDER:	Ah, before the Detainee makes a statement, ah, I'd like to ah.
PRESIDENT:	Question of the oath?
RECORDER:	Ah, no sir.
RECORDER:	Concerning classified evidence.
PRESIDENT:	Very well.
PRESIDENT:	Do you have any further evidence to present at this time, Recorder?
RECORDER:	Mr. President, I have no further unclassified evidence for the Tribunal but I respectfully request a closed Tribunal session at an appropriate time to present classified evidence relevant to this Detainee's status as an enemy combatant.
PRESIDENT:	Very well, your request for a closed session is granted and will be taken up in due course.
PRESIDENT:	You may proceed, PR.
PERSONAL REPRESENTATIVE:	The Detainee responds to the unclassified summary of evidence with the following key points.
PERSONAL REPRESENTATIVE:	"Some paragraphs under paragraph number 3, lead sentence are not related to the context or meaning of the aforementioned lead sentence. For example, paragraph 3-a is only information from news or a historical account of events on 11 September 2001, and note with no specific linkage being made in this paragraph to me or the definition of Enemy Combatant. As another example, sub-paragraph 3-n makes no linkage to me or to the definition of Enemy Combatant."
DETAINEE:	Are they following along?
PERSONAL REPRESENTATIVE:	Ah, they have that in front of them for reference.
PRESIDENT:	Yes.
DETAINEE:	Okay.
PERSONAL REPRESENTATIVE:	Second main point; "There are two false statements in the Summary of Evidence. Sub-paragraph 3 c is false. I never stated to the Al Jazeera reporter that I was the head of the al Qaida military committee. Also, sub-paragraph 3-s is false. I did not receive any funds from Kuwait."
PERSONAL REPRESENTATIVE:	Point number 3. 'There is an unfair 'stacking of evidence' in the way the Summary of Evidence is structured. In other words, there are several subparagraphs under parent-paragraph 3 which should be combined into one subparagraph to avoid creating the false perception that there are more allegations or statements against me specifically than there actually are. For example, subparagraphs 3-m through 3-o, which pertain to the *bojinka* plot should be combined into one paragraph, as should paragraphs 3-a through 3-h, which pertain to 9/11."
PERSONAL REPRESENTATIVE:	Lastly, my name is misspelled in the Summary of Evidence. It should be S-h-a-i-k-h or S-h-e-i-k-h, but not S-h-a-y-k-h, as it is in the subject line.
PRESIDENT:	Would you like to add anything to that, Khalid Sheikh Muhammad?
PERSONAL REPRESENTATIVE:	Final statement.
DETAINEE:	No, I just want to ask about witnesses.

ISN #10024
Enclosure (3)
Page 5 of 15

UNCLASSIFIED

UNCLASSIFIED

PRESIDENT:	Okay, ah, let's finish with these then I will get to the witnesses.
DETAINEE:	Okay.
PRESIDENT:	Try to keep it in order.
PRESIDENT:	You want to continue, PR? Do you have another statement?
PERSONAL REPRESENTATIVE:	That concludes this Detainee's response to the, ah, unclassified summary of evidence, sir.
PRESIDENT:	Oh.

CALLING OF WITNESSES

PRESIDENT:	We will now allow for the calling of witnesses. All witnesses called before this Tribunal may be questioned by the Detainee if present, the Personal Representative, the Recorder, and the Tribunal Members.
PRESIDENT:	Does the Recorder have any witnesses to present?
RECORDER:	No, sir.
PRESIDENT:	Alright.
PRESIDENT:	From the Detainee Election Form and I was informed earlier that the Detainee requested the presence of two witnesses to testify here today. Ramzi bin al-Shihh and Mustafa Hawsawi. The Detainee believes the witnesses can provide testimony related to the Detainee's actions specified in the unclassified summary of the evidence.
PRESIDENT:	I have had the opportunity to review the request for witnesses and I have made some findings and I'm going to place them on the record now and when I conclude that, Khalid Sheikh Muhammad, you may respond to that if you'd like.
PRESIDENT:	First the request for Ramzi bin al-Shib, the proffer of the testimony from the Detainee was that Ramzi is alleged to have been present during the al Jazeera interview in June 2002 during which it is said the Detainee claimed to be head of al Qaida Military Committee. The Detainee claims he never stated that, to be the head of the Military Committee, during the interview and states that Ramzi, if called, can confirm this.
PRESIDENT:	This witness is not relevant in the President's view for the following reasons. In the totality of the circumstances and given the nature and quality of the other unclassified evidence, the Detainee's alleged statements as reported in al Jazeera are of limited value and negligible relevancy to the issue of combatant status. As such, any corroboration or contradiction by the proffered witness is not relevant. The creditability determinations with regard to R-2, which is the al Jazeera article, can be made by the Tribunal without the proffered testimony. As such, the Detainee's request for the production of that witness is denied.
PRESIDENT:	As to the request for Mustafa Hawsawi, ah, it is proffered that Hawsawi, if called, could testify that the computer/hard drive referenced in the unclassified summary was not this Detainee's property and that the place of the Detainee's capture was not the house of the Detainee. In the President's view this testimony is not relevant to the issues regarding the Detainee's capture or his combatant status for the following reasons.
PRESIDENT:	Whether the Detainee had actual legal title or ownership of the computer/hard drive or the house where the capture took place is irrelevant to the determination of the Detainee's status as an enemy combatant. Based on the proffer, if true, Hawsawi's testimony will not provide relevant information. The issue of ownership, while of some interest, is not relevant to status. What is relevant is possession, usage, connection and presence. Hawsawi's testimony will not speak to any relevant information in regard to such points. As such, the request for the production of that witness is denied.
PRESIDENT:	If you would like to respond to that, I'll hear you.
DETAINEE:	Most of these facts which be written are related to this hard drive. And more than eleven of these facts are related to this computer. Other things are which is very old even nobody can bring any witnesses for that as you written here if it will be ah a value for you for the witness near by you will do it. This computer is not for me. Is for Hawsawi himself. So I'm saying I need Hawsawi because me and him we both been arrested day. Same way. So this computer is from him long time. And also the problem we are not in court and we are not judge and he is not my lawyer but the procedure has been written reported and the way has mostly as certain charged against me; tell him, [Arabic Phrase].

TRANSLATOR:	[Translating] They are only accusations.
DETAINEE:	So accusations. And the accusations, they are as you put for yourself ah definition for enemy combatant there are also many definitions for that accusation of fact or charges that has been written for any ah. [Arabic Phrase]
TRANSLATOR:	[Translating] Person is accused.
DETAINEE:	So, if I been accused then if you want to put facts against me also the definition for these facts. If you now read number N now what is written the *bojinka* plot. Is known many lead investigation it is not related to anything facts to be against me. So when I said computer hard drive/hard disk, same thing. All these point only one witness he can say yes or not cause he is this computer is under his possession him computer. And also specifically if he said Mohammad Atta picture been this hard drive. I don't think this should accepted. There are many 100 thousand Americans who have a lot of picture on their computer. You cannot say I find Muhammad Atta on your computer then you use this fact against you. Or you find any files in your computer to be what about it's mine, it's not my computer. If this witness, he will state that this known and here that has been ninety percent of what is written is wrong. And for Ramzi, for reporter in Jazeera, he claimed that I state this one and you know the media man. How they are fashionable. What they mean in their own way in a whole different way. They just wrote it so he say I state. But I never stated and I don't have any witnesses and witness are available here at Guantanamo. He is Detainee. He was with me. Which he been mostly in all my interview with him. Me and them, there was three person, me and Ramzi and this reporter. So if you not believe me, not believe him, believe my witness Ramzi. Then he's what he state the reporter most is false. I not denying that I'm not an enemy combatant about this war but I'm denying the report. It not being written in the proper way. Which is really facts and mostly just being gathered many information. General information that form in way of doing, to use in facts against me.
PRESIDENT:	I have heard and understood your argument. In order for me to make my determinations regarding the production of witnesses I first have to believe that they are relevant for the reasons that I have stated. For the reasons I have stated, I do not believe they are relevant. Whether or not they may be available here on Guantanamo, is a second decision to be made, but only if I decide they are relevant. I have heard your arguments. I noted them. However, my ruling stands.
PRESIDENT:	The Recorder has no witnesses, is that my understanding?
RECORDER:	No, sir.
PRESIDENT:	And there are no other approved witnesses to taken up. Ah, we will take a brief moment to review the unclassified evidence that we received so far and then we will pick back up in the proceeding.
MEMBER:	If I might ask a question real quick of the PR. This is the entire translation of the hand written notes?
PERSONAL REPRESENTATIVE:	Yeah. The hand written notes are the Detainee is on yellow.
MEMBER:	Yes.
PERSONAL REPRESENTATIVE:	and, then the next set of notes, hand written notes, are the Linguist's translation and then the final hard copy printed that's, ah, that . . .
MEMBER:	Type written.
PERSONAL REPRESENTATIVE:	Typed from Linguist's notes.
MEMBER:	Type from Linguist's translations. Okay.
PRESIDENT:	Khalid Sheikh Muhammad, I did not offer you an oath early because I was informed by the Personal Representative that you would be making some statement later on in these proceedings relevant to the truthfulness of your comments. So, if you would like to take an oath I would administer one to you but I did understand that you going to make a statement.
DETAINEE:	In the final statement, I will explain why then.
PRESIDENT:	Alright. Thank you. [Tribunal pauses to review D-a thru D-d]
MEMBER:	Seen those.

UNCLASSIFIED

TRANSLATOR:	Sir.
PRESIDENT:	Yes.
TRANSLATOR:	He wanted me to translate a Koranic verse on the spot.
PRESIDENT:	I will permit it.
TRANSLATOR:	Thank you.
TRANSLATOR:	Can I ask him for clarification?
PRESIDENT:	Yes.
PRESIDENT:	Do you need a few more moments, Translator?
TRANSLATOR:	Yes, sir, about thirty seconds.
PRESIDENT:	Go ahead and take your time.
TRANSLATOR:	Would you me to read the English translation after he read Arabic verse or would like him to read it.
PRESIDENT:	You want to save that for later?
TRANSLATOR:	[Nods head]
PRESIDENT:	Alright.
PRESIDENT:	Let me take up a few things that have come up as based on my review of these documents that have been provided to us so far. D-d, appears to be a written statement regarding certain treatment that you claim to have received at the hands of agents of the United Stated government as you indicated from the time of your capture in 2003 up until before coming here to Guantanamo in September 2006.
PRESIDENT:	Is that correct?
DETAINEE:	Yes.
PRESIDENT:	Alright.
PRESIDENT:	Now, I haven't seen any statements in the evidence we receive so far that claim to come from you other than acknowledging whether you were or not the head of the Military Committee. Were any statements that you made as the result of any of the treatment that you received during that time frame from 2003 to 2006? Did you make those statements because of the treatment you receive from these people?
DETAINEE:	Statement for whom?
PRESIDENT:	To any of these interrogators.
DETAINEE:	CIA peoples. Yes. At the beginning when they transferred me [REDACTED].
PRESIDENT:	What I'm trying to get at is any statement that you made was it because of this treatment, to use your word, you claim torture. Do you make any statements because of that?
TRANSLATOR:	Sir, for clarification.
PRESIDENT:	Can you translate it?
TRANSLATOR:	I will translate in Arabic.
PRESIDENT:	Yes.
TRANSLATOR:	[Translating above]
DETAINEE:	I ah cannot remember now [REDACTED] I'm senior man. Many people they know me which I don't them. I ask him even if he knew George Bush. He said, yes I do. He don't know you that not means its false. [REDACTED]. I said yes or not. This I said.
PRESIDENT:	Alright, I understand.

UNCLASSIFIED

PRESIDENT:	Is there anything you would like to correct, amend, modify or explain to us from what you said back then?
DETAINEE:	I want to just it is not related enemy combatant but I'm saying for you to be careful with people. That you have classified and unclassified facts. My opinion to be fair with people. Because when I say, I will not regret when I say I'm enemy combatant. I did or not I know there are other but there are many Detainees which you receive classified against them maybe, maybe not take away from me for many Detainees false witnesses. This only advice.
PRESIDENT:	So you are aware that other . . .
DETAINEE:	Yes.
PRESIDENT	People made false statement as a result of this?
DETAINEE:	I did also.
PRESIDENT:	Uh huh.
DETAINEE:	I told him, I know him yes. There are and they are. Not even you show me. This I don't know him I never met him at all. So, unclassified which is both classified and unclassified so this is you know him you don't know him. You have to be fair with people. There are many many people which they have never been part of the Taliban. Afghanistan there have been many people arrested for example people who have been arrested after October 2001 after make attack against Afghanistan many of them just arrive after they don't what has happen. When Russian came to Afghanistan they felt they went back but they did anything with Taliban and al Qaida then came after that. I don't know why it was younger people same thing for Afghanis people they show Afghanis people. I will give example one. His name is Sayed Habib. This I remember. [REDACTED]
PRESIDENT:	Alright.
PRESIDENT:	Now what.
DETAINEE:	For me nothing which was recorded. For which is written here is not related.
PRESIDENT:	I understand.
PRESIDENT:	I do note that in one of the exhibits you indicate you are not under any pressure or duress today. Is that correct?
DETAINEE:	That is about I'm hearing today. Yes.
PRESIDENT:	So anything.
DETAINEE:	Some of this information, I not state it to them.
PRESIDENT:	The information that you are telling us today, so we are clear. You do not believe you are under any pressure or threat or duress to speak to us today, is that correct?
DETAINEE:	Yes, that's correct.
PRESIDENT:	Alright.
PHESIDENT:	Now what you have told us about your previous treatment is on the record of these proceeding now and will be reported for any investigation that may be appropriate. Also, we will consider what you have told us in making our determination regarding your enemy combatant status.
DETAINEE:	I hope you will take care of other Detainees with what I said. It's up to you.
PRESIDENT:	I will do as I've said. I'll see to it that it is reported.
PRESIDENT:	Alright. At this point, we are going to go into the final statement but I do want to give the opportunity to the Recorder, PR, and Tribunal member to ask questions if they would like. So, what we'll do is proceed then to the Detainee's final statement and then I'll have a question and answer session following that. Alright just give me a moment.
PRESIDENT:	Alright.
PRESIDENT:	Khalid Sheikh Muhammad, this concludes the presentation of unclassified information to the Tribunal. We are about to conclude the unclassified portion of the hearing. Do you wish to now make any final statement to the Tribunal? You have the assistance of your PR.

ISN #10024
Enclosure (3)
Page 9 of 15

UNCLASSIFIED

UNCLASSIFIED

DETAINEE:	I make a two part. Maybe he will read then I will go also.
PRESIDENT:	Very well. You may continue.
PERSONAL REPRESENTATIVE:	Mr. President, the Detainee has asked me to read his final statement to the Tribunal with the understanding he may interject or add statements if he needs to, to correct what I say. According to the Detainee:

"I hereby admit and affirm without duress to the following:

1. I swore Bay' aat (i.e., allegiance) to Sheikh Usama Bin Laden to conduct Jihad of self and money, and also Hijrah (i.e., expatriation to any location in the world where Jihad is required).
2. I was a member of the Al Qaida Council.
3. I was the Media Operations Director for Al-Sahab, or 'The Clouds,' under Dr. Ayman Al-Zawahiri. Al-Sahab is the media outlet that provided Al-Qaida-sponsored information to Al Jazeera. Four."

DETAINEE:	[speaking inaudibly to Personal Representative]
PRESIDENT:	Please tell.
PERSONAL REPRESENTATIVE:	In other channels or other media outlets.
PRESIDENT:	Thank you.
PERSONAL REPRESENTATIVE:	[continuing] "4. I was the Operational Director for Sheikh Usama Bin Laden for the organizing, planning, follow-up, and execution of the 9/11 Operation under the Military Commander, Sheikh Abu Hafs Al-Masri Subhi Abu Sittah.

5. I was the Military Operational Commander for all foreign operations around the world under the direction of Sheikh Usama Bin Laden and Dr. Ayman Al-Zawahiri.
6. I was directly in charge, after the death of Sheikh Abu Hafs Al-Masri Subhi Abu Sittah, of managing and following up on the Cell for the Production of Biological Weapons, such as anthrax and others, and following up on Dirty Bomb Operations on American soil.
7. I was Emir (i.e., commander) of Beit Al Shuhada (i.e., the Martyrs' House) in the state of Kandahar, Afghanistan, which housed the 9/11 hijackers. There I was responsible for their training and readiness for the execution of the 9/11 Operation. Also, I hereby admit and affirm without duress that I was a responsible participant, principal planner, trainer, financier (via the Military Council Treasury), executor, and/or a personal participant in the following:
1. I was responsible for the 1993 World Trade Center Operation.
2. I was responsible for the 9/11 Operation, from A to Z.
3. I decapitated with my blessed right hand the head of the American Jew, Daniel Pearl, in the city of Karachi, Pakistan. For those who would like to confirm, there are pictures of me on the Internet holding his head.
4. I was responsible for the Shoe Bomber Operation to down two American airplanes.
5. I was responsible for the Filka Island Operation in Kuwait that killed two American soldiers.
6. I was responsible for the bombing of a nightclub in Bali, Indonesia, which was frequented by British and Australian nationals.
7. I was responsible for planning, training, surveying, and financing the New (or Second) Wave attacks against the following skyscrapers after 9/11:

    a. Library Tower, California.
    b. Sears Tower, Chicago,
    c. Plaza Bank, Washington state.
    d. The Empire State Building, New York City.

8. I was responsible for planning, financing, & follow-up of Operations to destroy American military vessels and oil tankers in the Straights of Hormuz, the Straights of Gibralter, and the Port of Singapore.

UNCLASSIFIED

9. I was responsible for planning, training, surveying, and financing for the Operation to bomb and destroy the Panama Canal.
10. I was responsible for surveying and financing for the assassination of several former American Presidents, including President Carter.
11. I was responsible for surveying, planning, and financing for the bombing of suspension bridges in New York.
12. I was responsible for planning to destroy the Sears Tower by burning a few fuel or oil tanker trucks beneath it or around it.
13. I was responsible for planning, surveying, and financing for the operation to destroy Heathrow Airport, the Canary Wharf Building, and Big Ben on British soil.
14. I was responsible for planning, surveying, and financing for the destruction of many night clubs frequented by American and British citizens on Thailand soil.
15. I was responsible for surveying and financing for the destruction of the New York Stock Exchange and other financial targets after 9/11.
16. I was responsible for planning, financing, and surveying for the destruction of buildings in the Israeli city of Elat by using airplanes leaving from Saudi Arabia.
17. I was responsible for planning, surveying, and financing for the destruction of American embassies in Indonesia, Australia, and Japan.
18. I was responsible for surveying and financing for the destruction of the Israeli embassy in India, Azerbaijan, the Philippines, and Australia.
19. I was responsible for surveying and financing for the destruction of an Israeli 'El-Al' Airlines flight on Thailand soil departing from Bangkok Airport.
20. I was responsible for sending several Mujahadeen into Israel to conduct surveillance to hit several strategic targets deep in Israel.
21. I was responsible for the bombing of the hotel in Mombasa that is frequented by Jewish travelers via El-Al airlines.
22. I was responsible for launching a Russian-made SA-7 surface-to-air missile on El-Al or other Jewish airliner departing from Mombasa.
23. I was responsible for planning and surveying to hit American targets in South Korea, such as American military bases and a few night clubs frequented by American soldiers.
24. I was responsible for financial, excuse me, I was responsible for providing financial support to hit American, Jewish, and British targets in Turkey.
25. I was responsible for surveillance needed to hit nuclear power plants that generate electricity in several U.S. states.
26. I was responsible for planning, surveying, and financing to hit NATO Headquarters in Europe.
27. I was responsible for the planning and surveying needed to execute the Bojinka Operation, which was designed to down twelve American airplanes full of passengers. I personally monitored a round-trip, Manila-to-Seoul, Pan Am flight.
28. I was responsible for the assassination attempt against President Clinton during his visit to the Philippines in 1994 or 1995.
29. I was responsible for the assassination attempt against Pope John Paul the second while he was visiting the Philippines."

| DETAINEE: | I was not responsible, but share. |
| PERSONAL REPRESENTATIVE: | I shared responsibility. I will restate number twenty nine. |

30. "I shared responsibility for the assassination attempt against Pope John Paul the second while he was visiting the Philippines.
31. I was responsible for the training and financing for the assassination of Pakistan's President Musharaf.
32. I was responsible for the attempt to destroy an American oil company owned by the Jewish former Secretary of State, Henry Kissinger, on the Island of Sumatra, Indonesia."

| PERSONAL REPRESENTATIVE: | Sir, that concludes the written portion of the Detainee's final statement and as he has alluded to earlier he has some additional comments he would like to make. |

ISN #10024
Enclosure (3)
Page 11 of 15

UNCLASSIFIED

PRESIDENT: Alright. Before you proceed, Khalid Sheikh Muhammad, the statement that was just read by the Personal Representative, were those your words?

BEGIN DETAINEE ORAL STATEMENT

DETAINEE: Yes. And I want to add some of this one just for some verification. It like some operations before I join al Qaida. Before I remember al Qaida which is related to *Bojinka Operation* I went to destination involve to us in 94, 95. Some Operations which means out of al Qaida. It's like beheading Daniel Pearl. It's not related to al Qaida. It was shared in Pakistani. Other group, Mujahadeen. The story of Daniel Pearl, because he stated for the Pakistanis, group that he was working with the both. His mission was in Pakistan to track about Richard Reed trip to Israel Richard Reed, do you have trip? You send it Israel to make set for targets in Israel. His mission in Pakistan from Israeli intelligence, Mosad, to make interview to ask about when he was there. Also, he mention to them he was both. He have relation with CIA people and were the Mosad. But he was not related to al Qaida at all or UBL. It is related to the Pakistan Mujahadeen group. Other operations mostly are some word I'm not accurate in saying. I'm responsible but if you read the heading history. The line there [Indicating to Personal Representative a place or Exhibit D-c].

PERSONAL
REPRESENTATIVE: [Reading] "Also, hereby admit and affirm without duress that I was a responsible participant, principle planner, trainer, financier."

DETAINEE: For this is not necessary as I responsible, responsible. But with in these things responsible participant in finances.

PRESIDENT: I understand. I want to be clear, though, is you that were the author of that document.

DETAINEE: That's right.

PRESIDENT: That it is true?

DETAINEE: That's true.

PRESIDENT: Alright. You may continue with your statement.

DETAINEE: Okay. I start in Arabic.

PRESIDENT: Please.

DETAINEE
(through translator): In the name of God the most compassionate, the most merciful, and if any fail to retaliation by way of charity and. I apologize. I will start again. And if any fail to judge by the light of Allah has revealed, they are no better than wrong doers, unbelievers, and the unjust.

DETAINEE: For this verse, I not take the oath, Take an oath is a part of your Tribunal and I'll not accept it. To be or accept the Tribunal as to be, I'll accept it. That I'm accepting American constitution, American law or whatever you are doing here. This is why religiously I cannot accept anything you do. Just to explain for this one, does not mean I'm not saying that I'm lying. When I not take oath does not mean I'm lying. You know very well peoples take oath and they will lie. You know the President he did this before he just makes his oath and he lied. So sometimes when I'm not making oath does not mean I'm lying.

PRESIDENT: I understand.

DETAINEE: Second thing. When I wrote this thing, I mean, the PR he told me that President may stop you at anytime and he don't like big mouth nor you to talk too much. To be within subject. So, I will try to be within the enemy combatant subject.

PRESIDENT: You can say whatever you'd like to say so long as it's relevant to what we are discussing here today.

DETAINEE: Okay, thanks.

DETAINEE:

What I wrote here, is not I'm making myself hero, when I said I was responsible for this or that. But your are military man. You know very well there are language for any war. So, there are, we are when I admitting these things I'm not saying I'm not did it. I did it but this the language of any war. If America they want to invade Iraq they will not send for Saddam roses or kisses they send for a bombardment. This is the best way if I want. If I'm fighting for anybody admit to them I'm American enemies. For sure, I'm American enemies. Usama bin Laden, he did his best press conference in American media. Mr. John Miller he been there when he made declaration against Jihad, against America. And he said it is not no need for me now to make explanation of what he said but mostly he said about American military presence in Arabian peninsula and aiding Israel and many things. So when we made any war against America we are jackals fighting in the nights. I consider myself, for what you are doing, a religious thing as you consider us fundamentalist. So, we derive from religious leading that we consider we and George Washington doing same thing. As consider George Washington as hero. Muslims many of them are considering Usama bin Laden. He is doing same thing. He is just fighting. He needs his independence. Even we think that, or not me only. Many Muslims, that al Qaida or Taliban they are doing. They have been oppressed by America. This is the feeling of the prophet. So when we say we are enemy combatant, that right. We are. But I'm asking you again to be fair with many Detainees which are not enemy combatant. Because many of them have been unjustly arrested. Many, not one or two or three. Cause the definition you which wrote even from my view it is not fair. Because if I was in the first Jihad times Russia. So I have to be Russian enemy. But America supported me in this because I'm their alliances when I was fighting Russia. Same job I'm doing. I'm fighting. I was fighting there Russia now I'm fighting America. So, many people who been in Afghanistan never live. Afghanistan stay in but they not share Taliban or al Qaida. They been Russian time and they cannot go back to their home with their corrupted government. They stayed there and when America invaded Afghanistan parliament. They had been arrest. They never have been with Taliban or the others. So many people consider them as enemy but they are not. Because definitions are very wide definition so people they came after October of 2002, 2001. When America invaded Afghanistan, they just arrive in Afghanistan cause the hear there enemy. They don't know what it means al Qaida or Usama bin Laden or Taliban. They don't care about these things. They heard they were enemy in Afghanistan they just arrived. As they heard first time Russian invade Afghanistan. They arrive they fought when back then they came. They don't know what's going on and Taliban they been head of government. You consider me even Taliban even the president of whole government. Many people they join Taliban because they are the government. When Karzai they came they join Karzai when come they join whatever public they don't know what is going on. So, many Taliban fight even the be fighters because they just because public. The government is Taliban then until now CIA don't have exactly definition well who is Taliban, who is al Qaida. Your Tribunal now are discussing he is enemy or not and that is one of your jobs. So this is why you find many Afghanis people, Pakistanis people even, they don't know what going on they just hear they are fighting and they help Muslim in Afghanistan. Then what. There are some infidels which they came here and they have to help them. But then there weren't any intend to do anything against America. Taliban themselves between Taliban they said Afghanistan which they never again against 9/11 operation. The rejection between senior of Taliban of what al Qaida are doing. Many of Taliban rejected what they are doing. Even many Taliban, they not agree about why we are in Afghanistan. Some of them they have been with us. Taliban never in their life at all before America invade them they intend to do anything against America. They never been with al Qaida. Does not mean we are here as American now. They gave political asylum for many countries. They gave for Chinese oppositions or a North Korean but that does not mean they are with them same thing many of Taliban, They harbor us as al Qaida does not mean we are together. So, this is why I'm asking you to be fair with Afghanis and Pakistanis and many Arabs which been in Afghanistan. Many of them been unjustly. The funny story they been Sunni government they sent some spies to assassinate UBL then we arrested them sent them to Afghanistan/Taliban. Taliban put them into prison. Americans they came and arrest them as enemy combatant. They brought them here. So, even if they are my enemy but not fair to be there with me. This is what I'm saying.

The way of the war, you know, very well, any country waging war against their enemy the language of the war are killing. If man and woman they be together as a marriage that is up to the kids, children. But if you and me, two nations, will be together in war the others are victims. This is the way of the language. You know 40 million people were killed in World War One. Ten million kill in World War. You know that two million four hundred thousand be killed in the Korean War. So this language of the war. Any people

UNCLASSIFIED

who, when Usama bin Laden say I'm waging war because such reason, now he declared it. But when you said I'm terrorist, I think it is deceiving peoples. Terrorists, enemy combatant. All these definitions as CIA you can make whatever you want. Now, you told me when I ask about the witnesses, I'm not convinced that this related to the matter. It is up to you. Maybe I'm convinced but your are head and he [gesturing to Personal Representative] is not responsible, the other, because your are head of the committee. So, finally it's your war but the problem is no definitions of many words. It would be widely definite that many people be oppressed. Because war, for sure, there will be victims. When I said I'm not happy that three thousand been killed in America. I feel sorry even. I don't like to kill children and the kids. Never Islam are, give me green light to kill peoples. Killing, as in the Christianity, Jews, and Islam, are prohibited. But there are exception of rule when you are killing people in Iraq. You said we have to do it. We don't like Saddam. But this is the way to deal with Saddam. Same thing you are saying. Same language you use, I use. When you are invading two-thirds of Mexican, you call your war manifest destiny. It up to you to call it what you want. But other side are calling you oppressors. If now George Washington. If now we were living in the Revolutionary War and George Washington he being arrested through Britain. For sure he, they would consider him enemy combatant. But American they consider him as hero. This right the any Revolutionary War they will be as George Washington or Britain. So we are considered American Army bases which we have from seventies in Iraq. Also, in the Saudi Arabian, Kuwait, Qatar, and Bahrain. This is kind of invasion, but I'm not here to convince you. Is not or not but mostly speech is ask you to be fair with people. I'm don't have anything to say that I'm not enemy. This is why the language of any war in the world is killing. I mean the language of the war is victims. I don't like to kill people. I feel very sorry they been killed kids in 9/11. What I will do? This is the language. Sometime I want to make great awakening between American to stop foreign policy in our land. I know American people are torturing us from seventies. [REDACTED] I know they talking about human rights. And I know it is against American Constitution, against American laws. But they said every law, they have exceptions, this is your bad luck you been part of the exception of our laws. They got have something to convince me but we are doing same language. But we are saying we have Sharia law, but we have Koran. What is enemy combatant in my language?

DETAINEE (through translator): Allah forbids you not with regards to those who fight you not for your faith nor drive you out of your homes from dealing kindly and justly with them. For Allah love those who are just. There is one more sentence. Allah only forbids you with regards to those who fight you for your faith and drive you out of your homes and support others in driving you out from turning to them for friendship and protection. It is such as turn to them in these circumstances that do wrong.

DETAINEE: So we are driving from whatever deed we do we ask about Koran or Hadith. We are not making up for us laws. When we need Fatwa from the religious we have to go back to see what they said scholar. To see what they said yes or not. Killing is prohibited in all what you call the people of the book, Jews, Judaism, Christianity, and Islam. You know the Ten Commandments very well. The Ten Commandments are shared between all of us. We all are serving one God. Then now kill you know it very well. But war language also we have language for the war. You have to kill. But you have to care if unintentionally or intentionally target if I have if I'm not at the Pentagon. I consider it is okay. If I target now when we target in USA we choose them military target, economical, and political. So, war central victims mostly means economical target. So if now American they know UBL. He is in this house they don't care about his kids and his. They will just bombard it. They will kill all of them and they did it. They kill wife of Dr. Ayman Zawahiri and his two daughters and his son in one bombardment. They receive a report that is his house be. He had not been there. They killed them. They arrested my kids intentionally. They are kids. They been arrested for four months they had been abused. So, for me I have patience. I know I'm not talk about what's come to me. The American have human right. So, enemy combatant itself, it flexible word. So I think God knows that many who been arrested, they been unjustly arrested. Otherwise, military throughout history know very well. They don't war will never stop. War start from Adam when Cain he killed Abel until now. It's never gonna stop killing of people. This is the way of the language. American start the Revolutionary War then they starts the Mexican then Spanish War then World War One, World War Two. You read the history. You know never stopping war. This is life. But if who is enemy combatant and who is not? Finally, I finish statement. I'm asking you to be fair with other people.

PRESIDENT: Does that conclude your statement, Khalid Sheikh Muhammad?

DETAINEE: Yes.
PRESIDENT: Alright.

UNCLASSIFIED

DETAINEE QUESTION & ANSWER

PRESIDENT: Does the Personal Representative have any questions for the Detainee based on his statement?

PERSONAL
REPRESENTATIVE: No, Sir.

PRESIDENT: Does the Recorder have any questions for the Detainee?

RECORDER: No, Sir.

PRESIDENT: Do either of the Tribunal members wish to question the Detainee?

MEMBERS: No, sir. Nothing further Sir.

PRESIDENT: Alright.

CLOSING UNCLASSIFIED SESSION

PRESIDENT: All unclassified evidence having been provided to the Tribunal, this concludes the open tribunal session.

PRESIDENT: Khalid Sheikh Muhammad, you shall be notified of the Tribunal decision upon completion of the review of these proceed by the Combatant Status Review Tribunal convening authority in Washington, D.C. If, the Tribunal determines that you should not be classified as an enemy combatant, you will be released to your home country as soon as arrangements can be made. If however, the Tribunal determines your classification as an enemy combatant you may be eligible for an Administrative Review Board hearing at a future date.

PRESIDENT: The Administrative Review Board will make an assessment of whether there is continued reason to believe that you pose a threat to the United States or its coalition partners in the ongoing armed conflict against terrorist organizations such as al Qaeda and its affiliates and supporters or whether there are other factors bearing upon the need for continued detention.

PRESIDENT: You will have the opportunity to be heard and to present relevant information to the Administrative Review Board. You can present information from your family and friends that might help you at that Board. You are encouraged to contact them as soon as possible to begin to gather information that may help you.

PRESIDENT: A military officer will be assigned at a later date to assist you in the Administrative Review Board process.

ADJOURN OPEN SESSION

PRESIDENT: The open session of this Tribunal hearing is adjourned.

RECORDER: The time is 2:43 pm. The date is 10 March 2007.

RECORDER: All Rise.

[The Tribunal withdrew from the hearing room]

AUTHENTICATION

I certify the material contained in this transcript is a true and accurate verbatim rendering of the testimony and English language translation of Detainee's words given during the open session of the Combatant Status Review Tribunal of ISN 10024.

[REDATED]

CAPT JAGC USN
Tribunal President

ISN #10024
Enclosure (3)
Page 15 of 15

UNCLASSIFIED

Department of Justice

FOR IMMEDIATE RELEASE   CRM
WEDNESDAY, NOVEMBER 19, 2003   (202) 514-2008
WWW.USDOJ.GOV   TDD (202) 514-1888

SUPERSEDING INDICTMENT ADDS NEW CHARGES AGAINST AHMED ABDEL SATTAR, LYNNE STEWART, AND MOHAMMED YOUSRY

WASHINGTON, D.C. – Attorney General John Ashcroft and U.S. Attorney James B. Comey of the Southern District of New York announced today that a federal grand jury in Manhattan has returned a superseding indictment adding new charges against Ahmed Abdel Sattar, defense attorney Lynne Stewart, and translator Mohammed Yousry. The new charges, like those originally brought against the defendants in April 2002, are based on their dealings with the imprisoned Sheik Omar Ahmad Ali Abdel Rahman, an influential and high-ranking member of terrorist organizations based in Egypt and elsewhere, who is serving a sentence of life in prison in the United States for conspiring to wage a war of urban terrorism against the United States.

"The government's decision to bring additional charges against the defendants in this case is justified by the evidence we obtained during our investigation, and reflects the seriousness of the conduct allegedly engaged in by the defendants," Ashcroft said. "The Department of Justice remains committed to identifying, investigating and prosecuting those who are alleged to have aided our terrorist enemies by providing their support and resources to terrorist causes."

"I commend the outstanding work of James Comey, United States Attorney for the Southern District of New York, and his office, Pasquale J. D'Amuro, the Assistant Director in Charge of the New York Office of the FBI, and all the members of the Joint Terrorism Task Force, particularly the NYPD, for their work on this case and their continued efforts to protect America from terrorism."

The new charges include a count against Sattar for his alleged participation in a conspiracy to kill and kidnap persons in a foreign country. The new charges also include allegations that Stewart and Yousry conspired to provide and conceal, and did provide and conceal, material support to terrorist activity, by making the imprisoned Abdel Rahman available as personnel to carry out the conspiracy to kill and kidnap persons in a foreign country, and by concealing Abdel Rahman's service as personnel preparing for and carrying out such a conspiracy. Stewart and Yousry did this by, among other things, passing and messages between Abdel Rahman and his co-conspirators (including Sattar), and by actively concealing that they were doing so.

In the original indictment unsealed on April 9, 2002, Stewart, Sattar and Yousry (and a fourth co-defendant, Yasser Al-Sirri, who is in England) were charged with, among other things, conspiring to provide, and providing, material support and resources to the Egypt-based terrorist organization known as the "Islamic Group," including by, among other things, passing and disseminating messages regarding Islamic Group activities to and from Abdel Rahman.

On July 22, 2003, United States District Judge John G. Koeltl dismissed the material-support charges against Stewart, Sattar and Yousry, based on the Court's finding that the statute under which the charges were brought, Section 2339B of Title 18 of the United States Code, was unconstitutionally vague as applied to the defendants' conduct. Following the dismissal of those charges, all three defendants remained charged with conspiring to defraud the United States in its administration of the Special Administrative Measures ("SAMs") imposed upon Abdel Rahman, which limited his access to the mail, the media, the telephone and visitors, in order to protect "persons against the risk of death or serious bodily injury" that might otherwise result.

Sattar also remained charged with soliciting crimes of violence in connection with his efforts to persuade others to engage in violent terrorist operations worldwide. Stewart also remained charged with making false statements to the Department of Justice in connection with her submission in May 2000 of an affirmation to the United States Attorney's Office for the Southern District of New York, in which she falsely stated that she would comply with the SAMs, only communicate with Abdel Rahman concerning legal matters, and not use meetings or phone calls with him to pass messages between him and third parties, including the media.

The superseding indictment charges that, "[a]fter Abdel Rahman's arrest, a coalition of terrorists, supporters, and followers, including leaders and associates of the Islamic Group, al Qaeda, the Egyptian Islamic Jihad, and the Abu Sayyaf terrorist group in the Philippines, threatened and committed acts of terrorism directed at obtaining the release of Abdel Rahman from prison."

According to the superseding indictment, after his arrest, Abdel Rahman himself "urged his followers to wage jihad to obtain his release from custody. For instance, in a message to his followers recorded while he was in prison, . . . Abdel Rahman stated that '. . . It is a duty upon all the Muslims around the world to come to free the Sheikh, and to rescue him from his jail.' Referring to the United States, Abdel Rahman implored, 'Muslims everywhere, dismember their nation, tear them apart, ruin their economy, provoke their corporations, destroy their embassies, attack their interests, sink their ships, and shoot down their planes, kill them on land, at sea, and in the air. Kill them wherever you find them.'"

The New Charge Against Sattar

The superseding indictment charges that Sattar, with Abdel Rahman and others, was a member of a conspiracy to kill and kidnap persons in a foreign country. The superseding indictment describes a series of acts committed by Sattar, Abdel Rahman, and their co-conspirators around the world. For example, in October 2000, according to the superseding indictment, Sattar and others wrote and published on the Internet a fatwah entitled "Fatwah Mandating the Killing of Israelis Everywhere," under Abdel Rahman's name, which called on "brother scholars everywhere in the Muslim world to do their part and issue a unanimous fatwah that urges the Muslim nation to fight the Jews and to kill them wherever they are," and stated that "the Muslim nation" should "fight the Jews by all possible means of Jihad, either by killing them as individuals or by targeting their interests, and the interests of those who support them, as much as they can."

A further example is Sattar's participation in communicating Abdel Rahman's withdrawal of support for a cease-fire to which Abdel Rahman's terrorist followers were adhering in Egypt. The superseding indictment alleges that, in 1999 and 2000, Sattar told leaders of the Islamic Group that Abdel Rahman had issued a statement calling for an end to the cease-fire.

The New Charges Against Stewart and Yousry

The superseding indictment charges Stewart and Yousry with conspiring to provide material support to the conspiracy to kill and kidnap persons in a foreign country, and with conspiring to conceal and disguise Abdel Rahman's service as personnel to prepare for and carry out that conspiracy. In addition to the conspiracy count, Stewart and Yousry are also charged with the substantive offense of providing and concealing material support to the conspiracy to kill and kidnap. The superseding indictment describes a series of acts committed by Stewart and Yousry. For example, according to the superseding indictment, during a May 2000 prison visit to Abdel Rahman by Stewart and Yousry, Yousry read communications to Abdel Rahman from Sattar and from terrorist followers of Abdel Rahman while Stewart actively concealed that fact from the prison guards. The superseding Indictment alleges that, "[a]t one point, Stewart and Yousry explicitly discussed the fact that the guards were patrolling close to the prison conference room and might notice that Stewart was not involved in the conversation between Yousry and Abdel Rahman. To conceal the fact that Stewart was not participating in the meeting, among other things, Stewart instructed Yousry to make it look as if Stewart were communicating with Abdel Rahman and Yousry were merely translating, by having Yousry look periodically at Stewart and Abdel Rahman in turn, even though Yousry was in fact reading. Stewart also pretended to be participating in the conversation with Abdel Rahman by making extraneous comments such as 'chocolate' and 'heart attack.' Stewart contemporaneously observed to Yousry that she could 'get an award for' her acts of concealment, and Yousry agreed that Stewart should 'get an award in acting.'"

The superseding indictment further charges that, during this May 2000 prison visit, "Abdel Rahman dictated letters to Yousry indicating that he did not support the cease-fire and calling for the Islamic Group to re-evaluate the cease-fire, while Stewart again actively concealed the conversation between Yousry and Abdel Rahman from the prison guards. Among other things, Stewart periodically interrupted the dictation with extraneous comments, and stated explicitly that she would do so from time to time in order to keep the guards from realizing that she was not participating in the conversation."

Also during the May 2000 prison visit, the superseding indictment alleges that Yousry told Abdel Rahman and Stewart about kidnappings by the Abu Sayyaf terrorist group in the Philippines and "Abu Sayyaf's demand to free Abdel Rahman, to which Stewart replied, 'Good for them.'"

The superseding indictment further alleges that, in June 2000, Stewart "released a statement to the press that quoted Abdel Rahman as stating that he 'is withdrawing his support for the cease-fire that currently exists.'" Another example involves Stewart and Yousry's alleged conduct during a July 2001 prison visit to Abdel Rahman. The superseding indictment charges that, during the July 2001 prison visit, "Yousry told Abdel Rahman that Sattar had been informed that the U.S.S. Cole was bombed on Abdel Rahman's behalf and that Sattar was asked to convey to the United States government that more terrorist acts would follow if the United States government did not free Abdel Rahman. While Yousry was informing Abdel Rahman about this scheme, Stewart actively concealed the conversation between Yousry and Abdel Rahman from the prison guards by, among other things, shaking a water jar and tapping on the table while stating that she was 'just doing covering noise.'"

The conspiracy to defraud charges against all three defendants in the superseding indictment rest on the same conduct underlying the charges that Sattar conspired to kill and kidnap persons in a foreign country and that Stewart and Yousry provided and concealed material support to that conspiracy. The charge that Sattar solicited crimes of violence rests on the same conduct underlying the charge that Sattar conspired to kill and kidnap persons in a foreign country.

U.S. Attorney James B. Comey noted that although the new material-support charges in the superseding indictment, like the material-support charges that were dismissed from the original indictment, are based on Stewart's and Yousry's dealings with Abdel Rahman, the new charges rest on a different legal foundation than the original charges. The new charges are based on Section 2339A of Title 18 of the United States Code, whereas the original charges were based on Section 2339B. Section 2339A makes it a crime to provide or conceal "material support or resources". . . "knowing or intending that they are to be used in preparation for, or in carrying out" a specified terrorist crime, "or in preparation for, or in carrying out, the concealment or an escape from the commission of any such" crime. The original material-support charges alleged that the defendants provided "communications equipment," and provided themselves and each other as "personnel" to the Islamic Group, which had been designated by the United States Secretary of State as a foreign terrorist organization. The new material support charges allege that Stewart and Yousry "provided" and "concealed" Abdel Rahman as "personnel" to a conspiracy to kill and kidnap people outside the United States. Thus, Comey said, the new charges do not raise the same concerns that prompted the Court's July 22, 2003 opinion.

The United States asked the grand jury to return the superseding Indictment adding these new charges against Sattar, Stewart and Yousry after a careful review of the Court's July 22, 2003, ruling and a further reexamination of the evidence gathered against all three defendants in light of that ruling. In the view of the United States, these new charges appropriately and adequately reflect the gravity of all three defendants' conduct and address the legal concerns articulated by the Court in its July 22, 2003, ruling, Comey said.

If convicted of the charges, Sattar faces maximum jail sentences ranging from five years to life imprisonment on the counts on which he is charged, and Stewart and Yousry face maximum jail sentences ranging from five years to 15 years on the counts on which they are charged.

The charges in the indictment are merely accusations, and the defendants are presumed innocent unless and until proven guilty.

Lynne F. Stewart
1676 8th Avenue
Brooklyn, New York 11215

Honorable John G. Koeltl
United States District Judge
Southern District of New York
United States Courthouse
500 Pearl Street
New York, New York 10007

September 26, 2006

Dear Judge Koeltl:

In the months since the verdict I have made a great effort, after solitary soul searching and long, intense discussions with my husband and children and long time friends and colleagues, to come to grips with my conduct that now brings me before Your Honor, to be sentenced. Hindsight and reflection, I hope, have afforded me a clarity that was not always present during my representation of Omar Abdel Rahman or even during my trial.

My only relationship to the Sheikh's case and his cause was as his lawyer. Throughout all the events, I believed I was acting as I should, as his lawyer. I violated my SAMs affirmation in that I permitted him to communicate publicly and these statements if misused may have allowed others to further their goals. These goals were not mine.

That said, I want to say as forthrightly as I can: I am not a traitor. The government's characterization of me and what occurred is inaccurate and untrue. It takes unfair advantage of the climate of urgency and hysteria that followed 9/11 and that was re-lived during the trial. I did not intentionally enter into any plot or conspiracy to aid a terrorist organization.

I inadvertently allowed those with other agendas to corrupt the most precious and inviolate basis of our profession—the attorney-client relationship. The acts in violation of my SAMs affirmation—speaking to a reporter and allowing prohibited communications—were committed intentionally. My only motive however was to serve my client as his lawyer. What might have been legitimately tolerated in 2000—2001, was after 9/11, interpreted differently and considered criminal. At the time I didn't see this. I see and understand it now.

Many who have written to you on my behalf, have characterized my actions as mistakes or lapses of judgment. I would add that I was also naive in the sense that I was overly optimistic about what I could and should accomplish as the Sheik's lawyer, and I was careless. I did not appreciate that representing this convicted terrorist was still uncharted territory in the years 1997-2001. A lawyer might need to tread lightly on this ground. I was busy and absorbed in my practice. I failed to appreciate that in seeking to represent the Sheik, as I understood I ought, my actions could be misinterpreted.

I ask that you see me as I was in 1999–2001. I had many criminal cases, all serious to the clients who relied on me. They required my full attention. I saw my job as caring for the whole client—not only the legal problems but also the circumstances from which those problems stemmed, be they poverty, anger, loss of a father at an early age or misguided loyalties. I tried their cases; and I also on occasion gave them money for food or their families. I visited them in jail on holidays on which they were alone, when only a lawyer could gain entry. I sent them Christmas cards. I came to know their families. As many of their letters attest, I as able to urge them to come to terms with their actions in face of the realities in which they found themselves.

Practicing law this way takes extraordinary amounts of time and energy. I can see that I became spread too thinly, so thinly that I failed to give sufficient attention to the possible repercussions or the gravity of my actions in how I represented Sheik Omar Abdel Rahman.

I think that Jo Ann Harris is correct when she wrote to you that the "time changed, Justice changed . . . ," but that I was still operating in the style of lawyering for which I was known by the government and others. To me, this was the essence of zealous advocacy. I also held the unrealistic belief that my stature in the legal community, and in particular with the prosecutors, excused me in their eyes. I was blind to the fact that by breaching the SAMs affirmation, even openly, the government could misunderstand and misinterpret my true purpose, which was to advocate for my client.

Some of the barbs of cross examination still haunt me. Why didn't I challenge the SAMs when they were imposed? Why didn't we mount a major conditions law suit and include issues regarding what his lawyers were allowed to do on his behalf? At the time of the press statement, could I have clarified my motivations and expectations and thus avoid the government's misperceptions? While there were financial and time and distance constraints on civil litigation, I was careless, secure in my belief that I was representing the Sheik in the best and most zealous way I knew how. Because I had done so for so long, I believed that the government would allow me to do what I thought appeared legally necessary.

The government disparages the idea of zealous advocacy because it has never practiced criminal defense law as I did, with heartfelt concern for my clients. I tested the limits of what the courts and law would allow for my clients because I believed I was, as criminal defense lawyers often say, "liberty's last champion." I had acted for my clients as this kind of lawyer for my entire career. Clients were extremely grateful, as were many judges, who called upon me to represent some of the most difficult clients to come before them. When Mattias Reyes, the true perpetrator of the attacks and rape of the Central Park jogger, wanted to come forward and confess to his crimes, he turned to me. He had learned that I was a lawyer who he could trust and who was also trusted by prosecutors and judges, and who would represent him with the integrity necessary to accomplish his purpose. This kind of lawyering is very difficult to comprehend for those who have not been in the trenches with poor and vilified defendants.

As I read the government's memorandum, I cringed at the characterization of my work as wholly lacking in the exercise of a lawyer's judgment and not within the realm of zealous advocacy. This is simply not true. As the many letters from colleagues state, perhaps better than I can, it may have been an excess of zeal that drove my actions, but it was entirely within the course of representing my client.

My greatest regret, more than any personal loss, is that my case—this prosecution—may bring new burdens to my fellow lawyers who already understand that to be intimidated by one's adversaries precludes being able to fully represent the client. Now, I fear that in addition to standing up to the power of the government, they will have to worry about whether their zealous advocacy will be misinterpreted by their adversaries.

The criminal defense bar has always had a narrow path to maneuver in making decisions for and with clients. It is fraught with peril; I fear that by allowing my actions representing the Sheik to be misunderstood, I and the government have made that path much more difficult. If it is the perception that something I have said or done has damaged the adversary system, that I demeaned rather than championed the notion of zealous advocacy, I am heartily sorry. I only hope that time and the appeal will vindicate me.

I also need and desire to clarify the intersection of my personal political beliefs with my practices as a lawyer, because the government would have you believe that the two were intertwined. Nothing I did in representing the Sheik was the result of my leftist politics. I personally have no alliance with and do not support either virtually or actually Sheik Abdel Rahman's political agenda. My actions were not intended to foster a revolution in Egypt; they were intended only to foster the possibility that my client might one day be able to return to Egypt, even as a prisoner of the current regime or one akin to it.

I have learned from history that politics are shifting constantly and sometimes in ways we can never predict. What seemed impossible 20, 30, 40 years ago now has happened or is in the foment of coming to be. When I was first visiting clients at the MCC in the early 80's, I met a young man named Joe Doherty who was the subject of a protracted extradition as a former terrorist, to Northern Ireland. He eventually lost, was extradited to Lang Kesh prison. Today he is a free citizen working and living in his native Ireland, all a result of change in the political postures of the combatants in that country. Nelson Mandela, imprisoned and after three decades was released to become the President of his country. Unlike other lawyers who may not practice with an eye toward international upheavals and changes, my early lessons in criminal defense were replete with models like these. I am not comparing South Africa or Ireland to Egypt. The point is that just as Doherty and Mandela were ultimately freed from prison, I believed it my job to foster diplomatic as well as other legal solutions for the Sheik to ultimately be returned to his country. I believed, as did Ramsey Clark, rightly or wrongly, that it might some day be possible for a treaty or diplomatic negotiations to return the Sheik to Egypt.

The government contends that I broke the rules in a most deceitful, underhanded manner. I can only say that my life as an officer of the court, as a lawyer, belies this. I have never had any desire to change the form of our adversary system; I've had an unblemished career as an advocate. I would eliminate the racism that exists there as well as in every other facet of our society. I would want to make certain that justice was not meted out based upon what a person could afford. However, I am a firm believer in adversarial justice, and I have spent my life in the quest to improve it. I am not an iconoclast who seeks to tear down for the sake of destruction. I have always been respectful of the sphere in which I have devoted my life's energies. A number of judges, both federal and state, would have shared with you their view of me as a practicing lawyer over the years in the courts, had the Code of Judicial Conduct not prevented them from comment. I believe they would have spoken of me as someone who operated by the rules, always, and who could be trusted. My word was my bond absolutely.

In the course of the trial I perhaps relied too greatly on what I believed were the ethics of the legal representation. The "bubble" was the inartful concept that I used to attempt to characterize what I believed was the government's posture toward my work, even under the SAMs. What I meant was that I was operating in the mind set I had developed over 30 years without any appreciation or understanding that a violation of the SAMs affirmation could be viewed as seriously as it was.

Perhaps the idea was presumptuous, but part of my overly optimistic naiveté was that it did not for a moment occur to me that I was venturing anywhere near breaking the law. That my actions would be interpreted as aiding or providing support to a dangerous or terrorist agenda was simply beyond anything I could possibly have imagined. I believed that the worst case scenario was that I would be barred from visiting my client. If that occurred, he would still be ably represented by others while I litigated this in New York.

The government wants to infer both intent and motive from the many newspaper articles that were found in my files during the search of my office. I had collected these as background for the Sheik's case and in representing other clients. I did not pay close attention to every name mentioned or the roles that the press ascribed to them. I repeat that I did not realize who Taha was until my trial. The government appreciated who Taha was in the worldwide terrorist picture; I did not.

Finally, and this was fully revealed to me in my discussions post-trial with Dr. Teich, if I have a tragic flaw it is that I care too much for my clients. I am soft hearted to the point of self-abnegation. When one reaches out to another human being, even a hated and despised defendant, the client is grateful, the lawyer is fulfilled and an emotional mutuality arises. The lawyer sees beyond the orange jumpsuit and the crime, to the defendant as a person; the heart responds. A deep human connection is established. I have always believed that when my clients are in distress, it is my duty as both a lawyer and a person to alleviate it.

When I visited the Sheik in May of 2000, he was so diminished. He appeared mentally undone and hallucinating. He had no one to speak to and no one to answer him. He could not escape into the pages of a book because of his blindness; he could not read Braille any longer because he had lost his sense of touch. I watched helplessly as his powerful intellect and fervent faith were replaced by imaginings and paranoia. Eight years of incarceration and three years under the SAMs were taking their intended toll. I found it unbearable. My training and my heart told me to stand between the Sheik and the government.

The government's contention that I don't care about the deaths of innocent civilians makes me gasp. I care too much. I do not distinguish between "us" and "them" in caring. Any loss of life seems a throwback to Neolithic times. In May 2000, my emotional response to the Sheik's conditions, my lifelong experiences all contributed to the circumstances that led me to talk to the Reuter's reporter on his behalf. That act has now become an ever present burden of self awareness and loss, worry and my own self chastisement. The distress it has all brought to those I love most is torment to me.

During this very difficult time I have been held in the love and concern that only a large and loving family can provide. I am not a person who acts alone or in secrecy in any part of my life. My husband, my children and grandchildren watched as I struggled toward understanding the fact and consequences of conviction; they watched and shared my fear when I was diagnosed with breast cancer; they shared with me in the effort to place this conviction, and the ensuing illness, in the context of the life in which they were raised, and which we continue to share. Those who know me best, as a mother, a family member and, a lawyer know that I am not a terrorist. As their letters attest, the mother and grandmother they know raised them but with a single mission in life—to help others. Their lives reflect this. I passed on to all of them what my father instilled in me from an early age. He wrote in my 8th grade graduation yearbook: your mission is to serve others.

The government asks you to give me 30 years in prison. I have given over 30 years service to my clients and the community. No one ever loved being a lawyer, a champion for those with no power or voice, more than I did. I had no plans to ever "retire" as long as there were people who requested my services. I had no pension plan. I fully intended to go out with my boots on, yellow pad in hand. To be deprived of this, the chance to continue to work is the worst punishment I can imagine. I cannot be near any courthouse at 9 o'clock in the forenoon and not have tears in my eyes. To have lost my career. To be looked at askance. This loss of my personhood is immeasurable to me. It is the worst sentence and it is immutable.

I am now before you for sentence. I ask for nothing more than justice, tempered with mercy.

Respectfully,

Lynne F. Stewart

CHAPTER 7

Crimes against the State

CHAPTER CONTENTS

> *A single witness shall not rise up against a man on account of any iniquity or any sin he has committed; on the evidence of two or three witnesses a matter shall be confirmed.*
>
> *Deuteronomy 19:15*

CHAPTER OBJECTIVES

After studying this chapter, you should be able to:

- Understand the significance of perjury.
- Explain the essential elements of obstruction of justice.
- Understand the different types of contempt.
- Know what constitutes bribery.

- Explain the ways that the government seeks to control corrupt organizations.
- Know the steps in the impeachment process.
- Appreciate the special problems that offenses against the state pose for society and the rule of law.

INTRODUCTION

Every system of government must establish laws that protect its own integrity. The U.S. system drew heavily on its English heritage to enact laws that preserve the public's trust in its institutions. Crimes such as perjury, obstruction of justice, and contempt are committed by those who seek to thwart our judicial system's proper operation. The system simply could not function if no steps were taken to counter these crimes. Simply put, our legal system cannot function if the people do not trust that it delivers fair and impartial judgments most of the time.

The natural law tradition that governments exist by the consent of the governed demands that political officials have a duty to the people. Bribery, the selling of an office, constitutes a betrayal of that duty. In addition, much of the proper functioning of government relies on the integrity of the people who work within it. When corrupt officials lack that integrity and refuse to leave office voluntarily, government must use its impeachment power to remove them and restore integrity to the system.

Corrupt organizations also pose a threat to government, often by seeking to usurp government's role. For example, organized crime operations may offer "protection" for businesses in exchange for a "contribution." Legitimate government's battle with organized crime has been a long and arduous one. We will examine some of the laws crafted to disrupt the operations of corrupt organizations and punish the operators.

Unfortunately, the very guarantees that undergird a free society sometimes create a refuge for criminals. When writing laws governing crimes against the state, the battle has always been to structure laws that prevent corruption and preserve liberty. As you will see, that means that those engaged in sophisticated criminal activities are sometimes difficult to catch and punish.

PERJURY

Perjury is defined as "giving false testimony in a judicial proceeding or an administrative proceeding, lying under oath as to a material fact, swearing to the truth of anything one knows or believes to be false."[1] Obviously telling the truth is vital to the judicial system's

---

But who is to guard the guard themselves?
Juvenal, in *Satires*

Perjury

Giving false testimony in a judicial or administrative proceeding; lying under oath as to a material fact; swearing to the truth of anything one knows or believes to be false.

integrity. Judges and juries often base decisions on witness testimony, and false testimony may mean unjust conviction. False convictions impair the integrity of the justice system and injure us all. Therefore, perjury is a very serious crime against the state.

Under federal law there are three types of perjury. The first type, often referred to as section 1621 perjury (for the section of the U.S. Code describing it—18 U.S.C. § 1621), is a general giving of false testimony. Section 1621 perjury is the broadest of the three types of perjury. It applies to all material statements or information provided under oath "to a competent tribunal, officer, or person, in any case in which a law of the United States authorizes an oath to be administered." It is not limited to testimony in court but includes any sworn statement to a government official or representative. For example, students seeking federal financial aid may commit perjury if they provide false or misleading information on the Free Application for Federal Student Aid (FAFSA).

The second type of perjury is section 1623 perjury (18 U.S.C. § 1623). Section 1623 perjury is false testimony given in court or before a grand jury. Unlike the general giving of false testimony, this type is limited to court and grand jury testimony.

The third type is subornation of perjury (18 U.S.C. § 1622). **Subornation of perjury** is defined as convincing or seeking to convince another person to commit perjury. In order to be convicted of subornation of perjury, a person must convince another to commit perjury, and that person must then actually perjure himself or herself.

Subornation of Perjury

Convincing or seeking to convince another person to commit perjury.

Every state has its own set of criminal laws punishing perjury and other forms of dishonest testimony or representation. For example, Pennsylvania has a criminal offense called "Unsworn Falsification to Authorities," which provides that a

> person commits a misdemeanor of the second degree if, with intent to mislead a public servant in performing his official function, he . . . makes any written false statement which he does not believe to be true.[2]

DIFFERENCES BETWEEN SECTION 1621 AND SECTION 1623 PERJURY

The Two-Witness Rule   Section 1621 perjury has its origins in Common Law concepts of perjury. Under Common Law, a person could not be convicted of perjury unless two people testified that the alleged perjurer's statements were not true. This is called the **two-witness rule.** Section 1621 carries on this Common Law tradition, but with some modifications. For example, physical evidence that corroborates testimony satisfies the two-witness rule. That is, if the prosecution presents one witness who testifies that the defendant lied and an additional piece of physical evidence that corroborated the testimony, the rule is satisfied.

Two-Witness Rule

The Common Law rule that requires two witnesses to testify to another's perjury in order for a conviction to take place.

Section 1623 requires that "proof beyond a reasonable doubt . . . is sufficient for conviction."[3] In other words, the proof may take any form—physical evidence, testimony, or any other type of proof. The standard of proof is thus lower than for section 1621 perjury. Stated another way, proving section 1621 perjury requires a stricter standard than is required for most other crimes. The two-witness rule specifically does not apply to section 1623 cases. You may recall from Chapter 2 that there is another crime that requires this higher level of proof for conviction—treason.

Another key difference between section 1621 and section 1623 is what occurs when a witness recants his or her testimony. **Recantation** is the retraction of testimony. Under

Recantation

The retraction of testimony.

section 1621, even if a witness recants his or her testimony, he or she can still be prosecuted for perjury.[4] However, under section 1623, a witness can recant testimony during the same proceeding as long as that testimony has not "substantially affected the proceeding."[5]

Another important difference comes into play when a witness contradicts himself or herself on the stand. Under section 1621, the government must prove which of the contradictory statements is false. However, section 1623 places no such burden on the prosecution. Contradictory statements are sufficient for conviction in and of themselves.[6]

Elements of Perjury   The elements of perjury are:

- An oath
- Intent
- Falsity
- Materiality

An Oath Perjury can only occur if a false statement is made under oath to speak truthfully. There is no standard wording for the oath, but a legally authorized person must administer the oath. The authority for administering the oath can be derived from law, rules, or regulation. Rules and regulations often govern administrative proceedings, but the oath is just as valid in these cases as it would be in a courtroom. Consequently, sworn false statements in administrative hearings can be prosecuted under perjury statutes.

Intent Under both sections 1621 and 1623, the person giving the false testimony must be aware that what he or she is saying is false and must intend to mislead by giving the false testimony.

Falsity In any perjury or subornation of perjury case, the falsity of the statement in question must be proved beyond a reasonable doubt in order to secure a conviction.

Materiality In order to qualify as perjury, a statement must be material to a case. Lying about something of no consequence is not a crime. A statement is material if it is likely that the case or matter in which the falsehood was presented was influenced by it. In other words, if the statement had the possibility of influencing the outcome of a proceeding, it is material. A witness who tells the court that he had scrambled eggs for breakfast, when he had pancakes, is not guilty of perjury unless what he had for breakfast is relevant to the case.

Defenses to Perjury   The defenses to perjury are:

- Recantation
- Assistance of counsel
- Double jeopardy
- The perjury trap
- Fifth Amendment

Recantation As noted earlier, recantation is the retraction of earlier testimony. Recantation traditionally has not done well as a defense but is most effective when the defendant uses recantation to demonstrate that there was no criminal intent in testifying falsely. In other words, recantation is used to clarify statements later discovered to have been misleading or in error. A defendant, in effect, explains away his or her earlier statements by "clarifying" them.

Assistance of Counsel Sometimes witnesses called to testify don't consult with an attorney before testifying and thus may never know that being less than truthful can be a crime. However, there is no requirement that a witness be told he or she can consult with an attorney. However, a witness can assert that he or she testified on the advice of counsel. In this case, the defendant eliminates the element of intent if he or she can prove the testimony was given in good faith on bad advice.

Double Jeopardy The double jeopardy defense can be raised when the defendant's acquittal in a criminal trial was based on the jury believing his or her untrue testimony.[7] Prosecutions for perjury after an acquittal sometimes give the appearance of being a vindictive prosecution. There is no blanket prohibition against prosecuting someone for perjury in a case where he or she was the defendant. As a practical matter, it seldom happens.

HISTORICAL HIGHLIGHT
The Anglo-Saxon Way to the Truth: Oath-Helpers and Trial by Ordeal

In the tribal society of Anglo-Saxon England, two very important things were a man's reputation and the perceived "will of God." A person's reputation was measured by the number of "oath-helpers" he could find to speak on his behalf when accused of a crime.

If a person was accused of a crime and maintained his innocence, he could bring in oath-helpers. They would take an oath swearing that the accused was telling the truth. The oath read: "In the name of Almighty God, so I stand here in true witness, unbidden and unbought, as I saw with my eyes and heard with my ears that which I pronounce with him." The oath-helper was not required to testify or present evidence; he merely stated that he believed the accused. In most cases, this was enough for charges to be dropped.

However, if the court still had reason to doubt the accused's innocence, it could employ trial by ordeal. The Church administered the trial by ordeal. It was seen as a way of determining the will of God. The trial began with three days of fasting and a mass. The accused had the opportunity to confess if he chose. If he insisted he was innocent, he was offered the choice between the water or iron ordeal.

The water ordeal came in two varieties, hot and cold. The cold water ordeal involved the accused drinking holy water and then being thrown into a river. If he floated, he was guilty. If he was innocent, he sank. With any luck, the innocent were fished out before they drowned.

The hot water ordeal involved the accused reaching into boiling water to retrieve a stone. In the iron ordeal, the accused had to carry a red-hot iron bar nine feet. In both cases, the accused's hands were bandaged, and if the wounds did not fester in three days, he was pronounced innocent. Contrary to popular belief, the trial by ordeal was not used to force confessions, but rather as a good faith attempt to ascertain divine truth. All in all, it was probably a good idea to avoid being accused of a crime in the first place.[8]

Trial by ordeal has fortunately disappeared from criminal courts, but the use of "oath-helpers" survives in the form of character witnesses.

The Perjury Trap Grand juries often serve an investigative function. They can call witnesses and seek out evidence in a case in order to decide whether there are grounds to charge someone with a crime. Zealous prosecutors may sometimes use the grand jury's power to attempt to force a witness to provide testimony contradicting what he or she told investigators. The witness is then caught in the **perjury trap.** If the witness tells the truth this time, it is the same as admitting the earlier testimony was a lie. If the witness lies again, the prosecutor may file additional charges. If the witness can prove that the prosecutor's main purpose in subpoenaing the witness was to force the witness into the perjury trap, the witness may be able to defend against any subsequent perjury prosecution.

Fifth Amendment As you learned earlier, the Fifth Amendment to the U.S. Constitution protects an accused person from self-incrimination. A witness may invoke Fifth Amendment immunity ("taking the Fifth") if testifying leaves the witness with the choice of committing perjury or proving the witness committed perjury earlier.

Perjury Trap

A situation where a grand jury subpoenas a witness for the sole purpose of obtaining perjured testimony.

OBSTRUCTION OF JUSTICE

Obstruction of Justice

The crime of impeding or hindering the administration of justice in any way.

Closely related to perjury is **obstruction of justice**. Obstruction of justice is defined as "the crime of impeding or hindering the administration of justice in any way." Obstruction of justice is a broad term that may apply to many different types of activities. Witness tampering or intimidation, jury tampering, or even suborning perjury can be forms of obstruction of justice. At the heart of the crime is interfering with the full and fair administration of justice. For example, prosecutors or police officers who hide, tamper with, or destroy evidence can be charged with obstruction of justice, as can defendants who threaten or bribe witnesses.

ELEMENTS

In order to prove the crime of obstruction of justice, the following elements must be satisfied:

- There is a pending judicial proceeding.
- The defendant knew of the proceeding.
- The defendant acted corruptly with the specific intent to obstruct or interfere with the proceeding or due administration of justice.[9]

Pending Proceedings A proceeding must be pending in order to charge obstruction of justice. A person believing that an investigation may begin can be convicted of obstruction of justice if he or she takes action that may destroy evidence. Consider this example. A police department is running out of space to keep evidence collected over the years, including evidence used in prior cases where all appeals have been exhausted. If the department decided to dispose of old evidence, they may do so. However, if the department has reason to believe the evidence in a particular case is tainted, has been tampered with, or will be needed in a pending appeal, it would be obstruction of justice to destroy it.

In recent years, there has been a dramatic improvement in the use of scientific evaluation of evidence. There have been cases in which new scientific tests on old evidence have either confirmed to a high degree of probability that the convicted individual was guilty or proven that he was innocent. These new tests have been performed on evidence that in some cases had been in storage for decades. Because of this, some legislatures have proposed extending the time that those holding evidence must store and maintain it.

Knowledge Very simply, the defendant must have known a judicial proceeding was pending in order to form the intent to obstruct justice—no knowledge, no intent, no crime.

Acting Corruptly with Intent to Obstruct Justice The defendant must intentionally commit an act designed to disrupt a judicial proceeding. The act must occur in a time frame that is consistent with that purpose. In order to act "corruptly," the act must be done with the intent of obstructing justice. The term corruptly means acting with an improper purpose, personally or by influencing another, including making a false or misleading statement or withholding, concealing, altering, or destroying a document or other information.[10]

The defendant need not succeed in obstructing justice, but only in attempting to. He or she must "endeavor" to obstruct justice.[11] Endeavor is loosely defined to mean any effort carried out with the intent of obstructing justice. It is not limited to any one or group of activities but applies generally to any attempt to obstruct justice.[12]

TYPES OF OBSTRUCTION

Obstruction of justice can take many forms, but the actions generally prosecuted under the federal statute fall into three groups. The first group involves hiding, changing, or destroying relevant documents such as court records, and the second is encouraging or giving false testimony. The third group is comprised of offenses involving intimidation, threats, or other harm to witnesses, jurors, judges, or others involved in legal proceedings or investigations in an attempt to prevent or shape their testimony or judgment. Examples of obstruction under federal law include:

18 U.S.C. § 1503. Influencing or Injuring Officer or Juror Generally
18 U.S.C. § 1504. Influencing Juror by Writing
18 U.S.C. § 1505. Obstruction of Proceedings Before Departments, Agencies
18 U.S.C. § 1506. Theft or Alteration of Record or Process
18 U.S.C. § 1509. Obstruction of Court Orders

18 U.S.C. § 1510. Obstruction of Criminal Investigations

18 U.S.C. § 1511. Obstruction of State or Local Law Enforcement

18 U.S.C. § 1512. Tampering with a Witness, Victim, or an Informant

18 U.S.C. § 1513. Retaliating Against a Witness, Victim, or an Informant

18 U.S.C. § 1516. Obstruction of Federal Audit

18 U.S.C. § 1517. Obstructing Examination of Financial Institution

18 U.S.C. § 1518. Obstruction of Criminal Investigations of Health Care Offenses

States have similar statutes in place that apply to state investigations and legal proceedings.

HISTORICAL HIGHLIGHT
Did Chemists Obstruct Justice?

The legal system depends on the integrity of the participants. This is especially true of those who are called to testify as experts about scientific evidence. In many criminal cases, the outcome of the case depends on the scientific analysis of bits of evidence found at the scene of the crime implicating the defendant. Take DNA evidence. Scientific analysis of hair, body fluids, and other organic matter can exclude or implicate the defendant. What happens if the presumably neutral scientists, who perform the tests and inform the jury of their conclusions, do sloppy and unreliable work? Or even worse, what if they actually lie?

For example, take the work of serologist Fred Zain. Mr. Zain has twice been tried by the state of West Virginia for defrauding the state and lying under oath in dozens of criminal cases. He headed up the serology unit of the West Virginia State Police crime lab. So far, no jury has convicted him. Both times, the jury was hung six-six on all charges. However, five men have had their convictions overturned because of errors in the tests Zain performed on evidence used to convict them. Many others are asking for new DNA testing of the evidence used to convict them.[13]

Then there is the mess in which Oklahoma had found itself. There, chemist Joyce Gilchrist is alleged to have falsified evidence reports in perhaps hundreds of cases before she was fired in September 2001. Reexamination of her work has freed a convicted rapist and a death row inmate, overturned another death sentence, and may call into question the guilt of one man who was executed. Malcolm Johnson was executed in January 2000 for the rape and murder of an Oklahoma City woman. He claimed that he was innocent, but Gilchrist had testified that semen found at the scene was consistent with Johnson's blood type. Later examination of the slides Gilchrist reviewed showed no semen present.[14]

Finally, there are the numerous cases handled by Pennsylvania State Police chemist Janice Roadcap.[15] In 1987, she testified at the trial of Barry Laughman who was accused of raping and murdering an elderly distant relative who lived nearby. Roadcap testified that the semen on the victim's body matched Laughman's blood type. When police claimed that Laughman, a mildly retarded man, confessed to the crime, it seemed like an open and shut case. In 1994, after DNA evidence gained credibility, Laughman's court-appointed attorney sent the semen sample to a Penn State professor for analysis. The professor asked for a comparative sample, but the court-appointed attorney never responded. Had he responded, the tests would have cleared Laughman and shown Roadcap's testimony to be wrong.

But Janice Roadcap had other skeletons in her laboratory. John Eddie Mitchell was 13 in 1970, when he was brutally murdered inside a garage belonging to Steven Crawford's family in Harrisburg, Pennsylvania. The garage was open, and many neighborhood children played there. Four years after the murder, the state police charged Crawford, who was a year older than Mitchell at the time of the murder, with bludgeoning the boy and stealing the $32 he had collected on his paper route.

The key prosecution theory was the blood splattered on handprints on a car in the garage. Everyone agreed the handprints belonged to Crawford. According to Roadcap's testimony, because the blood was only on the ridges of the palm prints, the blood must have been on Crawford's hands when he touched the car. This evidence was used to convict Crawford three times, in 1974, 1977, and 1978.

Chief investigator Walton Simpson kept Roadcap's notes even after he retired. Simpson died in 1994, and the notes became part of his estate. Two youths found the documents in 2001 and turned them over to Dauphin County prosecutors. The notes showed that Roadcap had found blood in the valleys of Crawford's handprints but testified otherwise at his trial. Crawford was released in 2002, and in 2006, Roadcap and the Pennsylvania Attorney General's office settled a federal lawsuit filed by Crawford.[16]

Because juries these days, fed on a steady diet of *CSI* and *Court TV,* put particular stock in forensic evidence, the reliability of that evidence is crucial to a fair trial. Tampering with, lying about, or otherwise misstating what forensic evidence means is a serious matter.

YOU MAKE THE CALL

THE DUKE RAPE CASE: DID THE DUKE PROSECUTOR OBSTRUCT JUSTICE?

District Attorney Richard Nifong used the alleged rape victim's eyewitness testimony to pursue three members of the Duke University lacrosse team. According to the African-American exotic dancer, the three white players, Reade Seligmann, Collin Finerty, and David Evans, cornered her in a bathroom after she had danced for the entire group and gang-raped her.

But her story changed repeatedly in subsequent interviews. As the racially charged case moved toward prosecution, Nifong needed physical evidence to back his waffling witness' account. But Nifong had a problem; the DNA recovered in the rape kit did not match any of the three lacrosse players.

Nifong made the contract technician agree not to disclose this fact to the lacrosse players' attorneys. Only under cross-examination in court does the technician reveal that no DNA linked the players to the alleged rape. The charges were dropped on December 22, 2006, eight months after Nifong knew of the DNA results.

You make the call. Did Nifong's refusal to turn over exculpatory evidence to the lacrosse players' attorneys constitute obstruction of justice? See some of the documents in the chapter Appendix to help you decide.

CIVIL DISOBEDIENCE, TRESPASS, AND PROTEST

The Bill of Rights prohibits government from limiting U.S. citizens' freedom of speech. Originally viewed as an individual right, large-scale political movements took legal cover under the First Amendment to produce mass demonstrations. Adherents of the Indian ascetic Mahatma Gandhi such as the Reverend Doctor Martin Luther King Jr. used nonviolent protests to focus national and international attention on the plight of African-Americans.

Gandhi and King advocated a protest form known as civil disobedience, which was popular among nineteenth century American transcendentalists. Civil disobedience was used to show that a particular law or practice was unconscionable and should be repealed. For instance, in 1957, buses in Montgomery, Alabama, were segregated by race. Black leaders arranged for Rosa Parks, an African-American woman, to refuse to give up her seat for a white rider as required by Alabama law. Ms. Parks was arrested, and Dr. King helped to arrange a boycott of Montgomery buses until the law was changed. Eventually, the U.S. Supreme Court ruled segregation on public transportation was illegal. Similar protests took place to highlight discriminatory laws that limited African-Americans' rights to vote, obtain housing, and jobs.

Civil disobedience has not always remained civil. Protesters challenging President Nixon's invasion of Cambodia in 1970 burned the campus ROTC building at Kent State University. Ohio's governor called in the National Guard, and when students began protesting the next day, the guardsmen opened fire killing four and wounding nine.

Civil disobedience often becomes criminal behavior by design. At a minimum, civil disobedience often involves trespass. In the 1960s, antiwar protesters would simply sit

Police confront antiwar protesters in front of U.S. Captial, January 2007.

down and refuse to leave various public buildings in what became known as sit-ins. These protesters were intentionally trespassing to occupy the buildings to generate publicity for their cause. In some cases, protesters damaged the property they were occupying, leaving them open to charges of vandalism.

Protest using civil disobedience tactics always attempts to portray law enforcement in a bad light. The more extreme law enforcement's reaction, the more sympathy the protesters generate for their cause when the videotape is played on the evening news. After arrest the protesters can also seek to generate publicity from their trial. For a textbook example of putting the system on trial by provoking police, see the Historical Highlight in the contempt section.

CONTEMPT

Contempt is defined as "conduct that brings the authority and administration of the law into disrespect or that embarrasses or obstructs the court's discharge of its duties."[17] Contempt is descended from English Common Law where disobedience to a writ under the king's seal was considered contempt. The federal rule on contempt states that:

> A court of the United States shall have power to punish by fine or imprisonment, at its discretion, such contempt of its authority, and none other, as—
>
> 1. Misbehavior of any person in its presence or so near thereto as to obstruct the administration of justice;
> 2. Misbehavior of any of its officers in their official transactions;
> 3. Disobedience or resistance to its lawful writ, process, order, rule, decree, or command.[18]

There are two forms of contempt—civil and criminal. Civil contempt findings can be issued on the spot by judges. In most cases, civil contempt cases involve a finding by the presiding judge that an individual is in contempt of court and the issuing of an order for the payment of a fine. The proof required is simple. The individual knew there was a court order directing him to do something, and he did not comply. For example, a witness who was served with a subpoena for records and does not bring those records can be held in contempt. Sometimes judges issue civil contempt orders to attorneys involved in a case who do not behave appropriately in the courtroom in accordance with the standards of decorum the judge has set. In those cases, the punishment is typically a fine.

Civil contempt orders can also order an individual to comply with a court order and impose incarceration until the person held in contempt complies with the order or demand. He or she can be jailed until he or she complies. In essence, civil contempt proceedings are remedial in nature, meant to force compliance with the court's will. The incarcerated individual holds the "keys to the jailhouse."

Persons charged with and convicted of criminal contempt, however, cannot purge themselves of that contempt by later complying. That is, criminal contempt is a separate crime for which the individual is being punished, rather than a mechanism to force someone to comply. Criminal contempt can be either a summary offense or a felony. Criminal contempt requires both a contemptuous act and a wrongful state of mind.[19]

Contempt

Conduct that brings the authority and administration of the law into disrespect or that embarrasses or obstructs the court's discharge of its duties.

Criminal contempt is reserved for obstinance and does not cover a good faith disagreement.[20] Judges can impose summary criminal contempt with no due process for charges of misconduct in open court in the presence of the judge which disturbs the court's business. Recall that the right to a jury trial in criminal cases does not apply in every case, only in those where the punishment includes a substantial prison term. Felony contempt would require a trial by jury and finding of guilt beyond a reasonable doubt since it could be punished by a substantial jail term.

DEFENSES

Some of the more popular defenses against contempt are:

- Absence of warning by court
- Attorney-client privilege
- Double jeopardy
- Reporter's privilege

Absence of Warning by Court While a warning by the court that certain behavior will result in a contempt citing is not absolutely necessary, the absence of a warning has been successfully used as a defense. The defense has worked on at least one occasion when the defendant claimed to have no idea the behavior in question would result in contempt.[21]

HISTORICAL HIGHLIGHT

The Chicago Eight Minus One: The Story of Bobby Seale

It was the last week of August in 1968. The United States was weary of the Vietnam War. The Democrats gathered in Chicago to nominate their candidate for president. Chicago was at the crossroads of epochs. The era of big-city boss politics was about to end, and the quintessential big-city boss, Richard Daley, was hosting the convention. He fully expected to have his man, Vice President Hubert Humphrey, nominated.

Outside the convention, a well-organized antiwar protest was taking place in Chicago's Grant Park. When the protesters attempted to leave the park and march to the convention center, the Chicago police reacted with reckless violence. They began beating the protesters with clubs, often attacking innocent bystanders and members of the press.

Despite the fact that a national study labeled the event a "police riot," eight demonstration organizers were charged with violating antiriot statutes. The eight were long-time liberal activist David Dellinger; two of the founders of the Students for a Democratic Society, Rennie Davis and Tom Hayden; the cofounders of the Youth International Party or Yippies, Abbie Hoffman and Jerry Rubin; student Lee Weiner; Professor John Froines; and Black Panther activist Bobby Seale.

In court, seven of the defendants were represented by activist attorney William Kunstler. Bobby Seale had retained the services of California attorney Charles Garry. But Garry had to have gallbladder surgery and asked for a six-week continuance. Judge Julius Hoffman denied the motion because local attorneys had put in appearances for Seale with the understanding they were only to help with the pretrial preparation. Judge Hoffman replied, "There was no such thing as a limited appearance in a criminal case."[22]

Hoffman's gruff demeanor and no-nonsense, old school attitude appeared right out of central casting, and the Chicago Eight decided to treat the trial like theater. In fact, they referred to their strategy as "guerilla theater," a confrontational style pioneered by defendant Jerry Rubin. Rubin had used it successfully when the House Un-American Activities Committee subpoenaed him. Rubin showed up to testify dressed in eighteenth-century colonial costume. The hearing adjourned, and Rubin's subpoena was forgotten.

The eight viewed the trial as an attempt by the Nixon administration to intimidate them. Their suspicion had some basis in fact. As the investigation of the Chicago riots concluded in the waning days of the Johnson administration, Attorney General Ramsey Clark felt that the eight should not be prosecuted. However, Clark left the decision to the new administration. Nixon's Attorney General John Mitchell wanted to prosecute.[23] He even went so far as to have the FBI monitor communications between the defendants and their lawyers.

At the trial, Seale repeatedly protested his not being allowed to have the counsel of his choice. Seale attempted to represent himself. The exchanges between Seale and Hoffman grew more heated. Seale, noting that all the white defendants had the counsel of their choice, called Hoffman a racist, fascist pig. Finally, Hoffman ordered Seale to be gagged and chained to his chair.

Eventually, Hoffman severed Seale's case from the others. When he severed the case, he cited Seale for 16 counts of contempt for which he was to serve three months each.

The Court of Appeals saw this as an abuse of power. Under the law at that time, a judge could not impose a contempt sentence for longer than six months without a jury trial. The appeals court saw Hoffman's action as an attempt to circumvent the law. Seale's case was remanded for a jury trial, but by then news of the FBI's monitoring of the attorney-client communications was public. The government elected to drop the charges rather than reveal the contents of the taped conversations.

Attorney-Client Privilege An attorney cannot be forced to reveal privileged information communicated to him or her by a client. In other words, an attorney can't be charged with contempt for refusing to disclose information he or she received while discussing a case with a client. However, for this defense to work, an attorney must provide independent evidence that the communications in question are attorney-client communications. The attorney's mere assertion that they are is not enough.[24]

Double Jeopardy Double jeopardy defenses for contempt seldom prevail. The defense has been raised when the same conduct resulted in both civil and criminal contempt charges, but was unsuccessful.[25] Courts are free to charge each incident of contemptuous behavior as a separate count of contempt.[26] Even acts that are punishable by other crimes can also be cited as contempt. For example, a defendant who assaulted the prosecutor in court was successfully charged with both assault on a federal officer and contempt.[27]

Reporter's Privilege Over the years, journalists seeking to protect sources have sometimes asserted that they cannot be forced to testify about those sources. Sometimes courts have held them in contempt for refusing to provide the information. For example, a *Los Angeles Herald-Examiner* reporter who refused to disclose his source of material related to the Charles Manson trial was jailed for 46 days in 1972.

In a federal criminal case or grand jury proceeding, the United States attorney general is required to review each subpoena for a journalist's testimony before it is sought. The regulations require that the Department of Justice, when reviewing the request, "strike the proper balance between the public's interest in the free dissemination of ideas and information and the public's interest in effective law enforcement and the fair administration of justice."[28]

HISTORICAL HIGHLIGHT

New York Times *Reporter Does 85 Days for Contempt*

Judith Miller knew all the players. The *New York Times* reporter met regularly with high-ranking Bush administration officials in the run-up to the Iraq war. Miller had the reputation of keeping confidential sources confidential. She would learn the price of such professionalism.

The Bush administration thought it had information tying Saddam Hussein to the 9/11 attacks. The intelligence never quite panned out. Then a report surfaced indicating Hussein was trying to buy "yellowcake" uranium from the African nation of Niger. The Central Intelligence Agency (CIA) wanted to verify the claim and asked its Weapons Intelligence, Non-Proliferation, and Arms Control (WINPAC) unit to check into it.

WINPAC operative Valerie Plame Wilson told her superiors that her husband Joseph C. Wilson IV was a former ambassador to Niger and knew the country well. The CIA sent Wilson to investigate. Wilson reported back that he could find no evidence that anyone had contacted Niger attempting to purchase uranium.[29]

CIA Director George Tenet convinced the White House to remove any reference to Niger and uranium from an upcoming presidential speech in October 2002.[30] But someone in the White House got the announcement back into a presidential speech, specifically the State of the Union speech where the

President said, "The British government has learned that Saddam Hussein recently sought significant quantities of uranium from Africa."

The president used this information to urge Congress to back an invasion of Iraq. Even though the United Nations labeled the documents supporting the Hussein-Niger connection as bogus, Congress gave the president the authority to invade. In July, Wilson criticized the administration in an op-ed piece for its rush to war using faulty intelligence.

Administration operatives allegedly started looking for ways to get even with Ambassador Wilson. After some investigation, I. "Scooter" Libby, who worked in the vice president's office, found that Valerie Plame was Wilson's wife. He leaked her name to Miller and *Time* magazine's Matthew Cooper.

When Plame's name was broadcast by CNN's Robert Novak, the CIA asked the Justice Department to investigate. By the end of the year, a special prosecutor had been appointed, and a grand jury convened. Miller and Cooper were subpoenaed, and both the *New York Times* and *Time* tried to quash the subpoenas.

When those efforts failed, both reporters were held in contempt. Libby released Cooper from his vow of confidentiality, and Cooper testified before the grand jury. But Libby did not release Miller, even though she never used the information he gave her in an article. Miller refused to testify and was sent to jail.

Eighty-five days later after her source "voluntarily and personally released [her] from [her] promise of confidentiality," Miller was released to testify before the grand jury. Libby was indicted for obstruction of justice and two counts each of making false statements and perjury.

Libby was later convicted on four of the five counts and sentenced to two and one-half years in jail. His sentence was commuted to time served by President Bush in June 2007.

BRIBERY

Bribery is defined as "the crime of giving something of value with the intention of influencing the action of a public official."[31]

ELEMENTS

The elements of bribery are:

- The recipient or target of the bribe must be a government official.
- A bribe in the form of money, goods, favors, or something of value was offered or given.
- The bribe was meant to induce an action or inaction.
- The person offering the bribe expects something in return.

A Recipient of the Bribe A bribe recipient can be any government official ranging from a congressman to a clerk issuing permits or licenses. For example, after the

Moral principle is a looser bond than pecuniary interest.
Abraham Lincoln

Bribery
The crime of giving something of value with the intention of influencing the action of a public official.

September 11 terror attacks, investigators discovered that a number of men of Middle Eastern heritage had received special permits allowing them to transport hazardous material via truck across the nation's highways. The licensees had not taken the special test required of applicants. Eventually, a clerk working in the Pennsylvania Department of Transportation was charged with accepting bribes in exchange for issuing the licenses without examinations. Though a low-level clerk, he held a government position and was in a position to take official action. In this case, he could issue or deny a license to applicants.

A Bribe The bribe itself is money or something of value that is given to the recipient in return for certain action or, in some cases, inaction. The crime of bribery is complete when the offeror expresses ability and desire to pay, assuming he intends the proffered payment will lead to a favorable decision by the offeree.[32] Therefore, the bribe doesn't have to be given directly to the government official. It can be given to someone else, if that's what the recipient wants. The bribe itself can be anything of value such as cash, paid vacations, jewelry, or anything else other than a fee charged to all. In fact, some states even regulate the type and value of gifts that can be given to government officials, such as holiday and appreciation gifts. The U.S. Postal Service prohibits gifts to carriers and others that are worth more than $20.

Action Meant to Result from the Bribe The action meant to result from the bribe need not be illegal in and of itself. The government must merely show that the receipt of the bribe influenced the decision. For example, it would still be bribery to offer a passport clerk a $500 "bonus" if he or she issues you a passport today instead of tomorrow.

Bribery can also be prosecuted despite the fact that the recipient lacks the authority to accomplish the action desired by the offeror. It also does not matter if the recipient of the bribe never delivers what he or she promises to do for the bribe.

State of Mind The person offering the bribe must intend that his offer will result in favorable action on the part of the recipient. As long as the bribe was intended as *quid pro quo* for a favor, the intent requirement has been met.

> The whole art of government consists in the art of being honest.
>
> Thomas Jefferson

DEFENSES

A frequently raised defense to bribery charges is:

- Entrapment or extortion by public official

Entrapment Entrapment can be claimed as a defense where it can be proven that the government agent initiated the bribery scheme and forced the defendant into a course of action he or she normally would not have taken. An entrapment defense has two elements: government inducement and the defendant's lack of predisposition to commit the crime.[33] Keep in mind that proving entrapment in any case is difficult; the defendant must prove that he or she wasn't predisposed to paying a bribe or was unaware that the requested payment was a bribe rather than the customary fee for a government service. Even in cases where a government official demands payment before carrying out official duties, the person from whom the bribe is being extorted has other avenues for recourse. For example, he or she can file a mandamus action, which is a lawsuit seeking to compel government to do something they are required to do. The target can also report the attempted extortion to police or other law enforcement.

What happens if a defendant pays money as a bribe and then raises entrapment as a defense? Does he get his money back? In at least one case, the answer was no, even though there was no bribery conviction.[34]

CORRUPT ORGANIZATIONS

For many years, government has sought to control and eliminate corrupt organizations. One of the most comprehensive pieces of legislation in this battle is the Organized Crime Control Act. Part of this act is the Racketeering Influenced and Corrupt Organizations Act or **RICO**, which was passed in 1970.[35] RICO was originally intended to prosecute organized crime but was drafted very broadly. The original intention was to provide a way to prosecute organized crime activities run through both illegitimate business enterprises and through legitimate-appearing businesses. Sometimes legitimate businesses serve as a shield for illegitimate activities or a way to funnel earnings from crime to make the profits appear legitimate. However, in recent years RICO has been applied to business activities far removed from organized crime syndicates.

Under RICO, it is a federal crime to acquire or maintain an interest in, use income from, or conduct or participate in the affairs of an "enterprise" through a pattern of "racketeering activity."

An enterprise can be:

- A corporation
- A partnership
- A sole proprietorship
- Any business or organization
- The government

Racketeering activity includes many crimes and activities such as:

- Bribery
- Embezzlement
- Gambling
- Arson
- Counterfeiting money, recordings, copyrighted materials, and computer programs
- Trafficking in contraband cigarettes
- Harboring illegal aliens

At least two acts must be committed by the organization being charged with racketeering within a 10-year period. In addition to fines and imprisonment, persons or organizations convicted under RICO are subject to seizure of property obtained with illegally acquired funds. For example, a partnership that used a pizza shop as a front for dealing in cigarettes on which the partnership hasn't paid cigarette taxes may find that the pizza shop will be seized and sold, with the proceeds going to the government.

RICO

The Racketeering Influenced and Corrupt Organizations Act is legislation that enables the government to prosecute individuals and organizations for a pattern of criminal activity; originally meant to target organized crime.

Because RICO is so broadly written, it has invited unique legal approaches to address problems far from what its authors envisioned. The U.S. Supreme Court recently ruled that pro-life protesters at abortion clinics do not violate RICO.[36] A Wyoming rancher alleged the U.S. government violated RICO through a pattern of harassment, but the Court decided the man had other avenues available to address individual government actions that he had not pursued and dismissed the case.[37] A New York retailer tried to take a competitor to court because the store did not charge New York State sales tax. The court ruled the charging retailer lacked standing to file a RICO suit, but it is likely New York State revenue agents will be checking the no-tax retailer's books very closely.[38]

One RICO case that may break new ground involves illegal immigration. Four North Georgia employees have filed suit against the Mohawk Carpet Company, alleging the company conspired with a temporary service company to bring in illegal aliens who will work for low wages. Mohawk had attempted to have the case dismissed, and the Eleventh Circuit Court of Appeals refused. Mohawk appealed to the Supreme Court, who was looking at the New York State RICO case at the time. The Court sent the case back to the Eleventh Circuit to decide in light of the New York decision. The Eleventh Circuit concluded the case could go to trial under the guiding Supreme Court opinion.[39]

IMPEACHMENT

Impeachment
An indictment of a public official that leads to a trial to determine whether he or she should be removed from office.

Impeachment is an indictment of a federal official charging him or her with "treason, bribery, and high crimes and misdemeanors."[40] Once an official is impeached, he or she is tried and, if found guilty, removed from office.

The form of impeachment outlined in the U.S. Constitution owes much to its English predecessor. Although impeachment is no longer used in the United Kingdom (all officials now serve at the pleasure of Parliament), in the days of a strong executive, in the form of a king, it was necessary to have a mechanism to remove corrupt royal appointees.

Impeachment articles are voted upon by the House of Representatives (House of Commons in England), and then a trial is held in the Senate (House of Lords in England). In order to be removed from office, the Senate must vote to convict by a two-thirds supermajority.

Impeachment was intended to be a seldom-used remedy. The standard of "high crimes and misdemeanors," while vague, does imply that the framers intended it to be a remedy for very serious infractions by public officials. The widened context of "treason, bribery, high crimes and misdemeanors" leads to the conclusion that the Founding Fathers were concerned about officials selling their office or betraying the citizens to whom they must ultimately answer.

One reason there have been few impeachment cases in our history is that in many cases public officials have simply been voted out when their term expired. There is one group of officials for whom impeachment is the only avenue for removal, absent death or voluntary retirement. Recall that federal judges are appointed for life. Thus, a federal judge can only be forced out of office by impeachment.

The most high-profile impeachment cases are those of presidents. Two U.S. presidents, Andrew Johnson and Bill Clinton, have been impeached, but neither was removed from office. A third president, Richard Nixon, lost an impeachment vote in the U.S. House of

Representatives Judiciary Committee, where the process begins, but resigned before the matter came before the full House of Representatives.

PROCEDURES

The procedures in an impeachment are not spelled out in the U.S. Constitution or U.S. Code. Congress can decide on procedures on an ad hoc basis. In modern times, Congress has initiated two presidential impeachment proceedings, against Presidents Nixon and Clinton.

When proceedings began against President Nixon, Congress found that the Constitution offered little guidance. The House Judiciary Committee developed rules of evidence and procedures for the impeachment proceedings. However, those rules only bound Congress for the duration of the Nixon impeachment process.

> The greater the power, the more dangerous the abuse.
> Edmund Burke

HISTORICAL HIGHLIGHT
Impeachment after Acquittal: The Story of Alcee Hastings

Alcee Hastings was a pioneer for African-Americans. He was the first black to be named United States District Judge for the Southern District of Florida. Unfortunately, he also became the first black federal official ever to be impeached. He was also the first federal official of any race to be impeached and removed from office after being acquitted in federal court on the same charges.

How this strange turn of events came to be owes much to Hastings' magnetic personality. He was a bright, articulate, persuasive speaker. At his trial he spoke convincingly on his own behalf, and the jury did not convict. The Senate trial was different.

A judicial inquiry had produced voluminous evidence that Hastings had solicited a $150,000 bribe from two racketeers. He had allegedly solicited it through an intermediary to maintain deniability, but an undercover agent impersonated one of the racketeers.

Balancing this damning information was the acquittal in court. The U.S. House of Representatives was faced with a dilemma. African-American Congressman John Conyers of Michigan was chosen to head the House's investigation. He gravely weighed the evidence and came to the conclusion that Hastings was guilty. Conyers addressed Congress and said, "We did not wage (the) civil rights struggle merely to replace one form of judicial corruption for another. . . . The principle of equality requires that a black public official be held to the same standard that other public officials are held to." The House voted 413 to 3 for impeachment.

Hastings' supporters were optimistic about the Senate vote. The Senate must vote to convict by a two-thirds majority before an official can be removed from office. The consensus was that Hastings could charm, cajole, and convince the requisite number of Senators to assure an acquittal.

The Senate, however, had to view the facts. The undercover agent testified that he asked the contact to demonstrate that he could get Hastings to do what he wanted; the contact arranged for Hastings to have dinner at a Miami hotel and appear in the lobby at a specific time. Hastings did just as the agent requested. When the money was paid, Hastings made his law clerk stay late to finish the paperwork releasing seized property belonging to the man the agent was impersonating.

In the end, despite the acquittal in court, the Senate voted to convict on October 20, 1989.[11] A visibly shaken Hastings left the chamber in tears. However, within a few years, he was elected to the House of Representatives from his south Florida district. Hastings now belongs to the body that voted for his impeachment.

When Congress began impeachment proceedings against President Clinton, it did not immediately establish its procedures. It did so only after receiving the report of Special Prosecutor Kenneth Starr. Congressional critics charged that Congress appeared to be shaping the procedures to the evidence, instead of designing them to impartially evaluate the evidence.

Impeachment in Congress is no guarantee that the elected official will not have to face charges in state or federal court. During President Nixon's impeachment ordeal, he faced a parallel prosecution in federal court. In fact, it was his loss before the U.S. Supreme Court that forced him to reveal the most damaging evidence against him, the Oval Office tapes. Had Mr. Nixon not resigned, those tapes would have been used against him in his Senate trial.

In the same vein, President Clinton was forced to relinquish his law license as part of the settlement of the perjury charges against him. President Clinton was accused of lying under oath concerning his affair with Monica Lewinsky during testimony in a civil suit brought against him for sexual harassment by Paula Jones.

AMBIGUITIES

Unlike criminal proceedings where the burden of proof is "guilt beyond a reasonable doubt," or civil actions where the "preponderance of evidence" standard applies, the burden of proof is not codified in impeachment proceedings. Congress has never specified what standard is to be used, but has left it up to the individual senator when voting to convict.

Additionally, the definition of "high crimes and misdemeanors" is nebulous. President Clinton's supporters argued that perjury in a civil case did not rise to the level of "high crimes and misdemeanors" as intended in the Constitution. They apparently convinced enough of the Senate to prevent conviction.

President Clinton's impeachment also raised another question. Can a president or federal judge be impeached for activities not related to the duties of his or her office?

President Clinton's questionable conduct was carried out as a private citizen. None of the impeachment articles alleged that he abused the privileges of his office. Almost all previous impeachments were prosecuted against office holders who acted illegally in the execution of their office.

CONCLUSION

Impeachment was designed to be a seldom-used tool. Despite having the form of a legal proceeding, it is in reality a political exercise. The Founding Fathers recognized this and put the safeguard of requiring a two-thirds majority to convict. Even though this section has focused on federal impeachment proceedings, the states each have impeachment proceedings.

Some states also use a process known as a recall vote. A recall vote is where the citizens choose to remove or recall an official through a referendum. Usually, it is necessary to get a certain number of signatures on a petition to get the issue on the ballot. If a majority of the citizens vote to recall the individual, he or she must leave office.

Impeachment is a process fraught with ambiguity. It can be open to political manipulation. In fact, no president has been impeached when his own party controlled Congress. Some historians have noted that when impeachment is abused, the public loses its appetite for it for years afterward.[42] House Minority Leader Richard Gephart referred to the Clinton impeachment as part of "the politics of personal destruction." Despite its possible misuse, impeachment is a process deeply ingrained in U.S. jurisprudence.

PRACTICE POINTERS

Legal professionals in paralegal or investigative positions who work for attorneys representing business owners, partnerships, and corporations will find themselves working on cases involving possible criminal charges typically considered "white-collar crimes." These clients pose special challenges since they are generally educated and understand how the legal system works. Many seek representation while the case is still under investigation or even before. Representation often involves cooperation with investigations and plea bargaining negotiation. These are processes in which members of the professional support staff often play a significant role.

Clients often want to know how likely it is that they could face charges. The U.S. Department of Justice has issued guidelines for their attorneys to use in determining when to start investigations, bring charges, or negotiate a plea agreement when a corporation and its owner or principal is the target.[43] These guidelines include:

- The nature and seriousness of the misconduct
- The pervasiveness of the wrongdoing
- The company's history of wrongdoing
- Cooperation by principals
- Voluntary disclosure of wrongdoing

- Willingness to make restitution
- Whether civil sanctions are enough

In the event federal charges are filed against a client, the odds of conviction after trial are high, often over 90 percent. If the case goes to trial, significant time and resources will be spent preparing documents and testimony to support efforts to reduce the sentence to be served. For example, you may be actively involved in seeking out mitigating factors that support an argument for deviation from the federal sentencing guidelines. This preparation may mean the difference between a prison sentence or supervised release and house detention.

The possible charges available to U.S. attorneys are far more extensive than those covered in this chapter. In addition to RICO charges, business owners may face mail and security fraud charges, accusations of environmental violations, antitrust and tax charges, and many more. Those investigating possible charges should remember that often there are also state crime code violations possible.

CHAPTER SUMMARY

The basis of civilization is the nation-state, or polis. The ancient Athenians had an almost poetic affection for the polis. At Pericles' funeral oration for Athens' honored war dead, he spoke of Athens as "a pattern to others" because Athenians were subservient to the rule of law.[44] Every democratic society since Athens has held that "no man is above the law." Unlike monarchies and oligarchies, the legitimacy of democratic government is based on the principle that a state's political leaders were ultimately answerable to the people.

Some 2,500 years after Pericles, another leader paid homage to a field of honored dead when he said "the government of the people, by the people, and for the people shall not perish from the earth."[45] To both Pericles and Lincoln, allegiance to the state was the highest duty of a citizen in a free society. The betrayal of that allegiance, whether that took the form of treason or simply bribery, profaned the graves of the men who had given their lives in its service.

Most of the criminal offenses described in this chapter are offenses against the rule of law in the sense that they go to the heart of the integrity of the system. Perjury, bribery, and obstruction of justice do more than harm an individual. Gone undetected and unpunished, they ultimately destroy the rule of law.

KEY TERMS

Bribery	Perjury	Subornation of
Contempt	Perjury Trap	Perjury
Impeachment	Recantation	Two-Witness Rule
Obstruction of Justice	RICO	

EXERCISE

1. In this chapter, you learned the story of Alcee Hastings, the former federal judge and present member of the U.S. House of Representatives. Mr. Hastings also holds an active license to practice law in Florida. He mentions in his official biography (see chapter Appendix) that he is a former federal judge but omits any reference to the impeachment he underwent. Would you send someone who had been impeached to the House of Representatives? Do you think he should be allowed to practice law? Has he been punished enough?

2. In this chapter, you also learned about I. "Scooter" Libby, who was convicted by a jury of one count of obstruction of justice, two counts of perjury, and one count of making false statements to federal investigators. He was sentenced to 30 months in prison, but President George W. Bush commuted his sentence to no jail time. Read the indictment, verdict, and notice of disbarment in the chapter Appendix and decide for yourself whether a commutation was appropriate.

DISCUSSION QUESTIONS

1. Should the government run "sting operations" where they offer bribes to politicians? Is this entrapment? Is this creating crime where none existed?

2. Do elected officials (or for that matter, attorneys) have a "higher duty" to the law than the average citizen? How would this apply to President Clinton's statements in Paula Jones' civil suit?

3. Should the RICO statutes be applied to areas other than just organized crime? Is that law written too broadly?

4. Does the U.S. Constitution's definition of "bribery, treason, high crimes, and misdemeanors" as the basis for impeachment refer to actions taken before an official took office? What level of offense meets this standard?

FOR FURTHER READING AND VIEWING

1. Mass, P. (1997). *Underboss: Sammy the Bull Gravano's Story of Life in the Mafia.* HarperCollins.

2. Jackson, D. D. (1973). *Judges: An Inside View of the Agonies and Excesses of an American Elite.* Antheneum.

3. Black, C. L. (1998). *Impeachment: A Handbook.* Yale University Press.

4. Caplan, G. M. (1983). *ABSCAM Ethics: Moral Issues and Deception in Law Enforcement.* HarperInformation.

5. Noonan, J. T. (1984). *Bribes.* Macmillan.

6. Wilson, J. C. (2004). *The Politics of Truth: Inside the Lies that Led to War and Betrayed My Wife's CIA Identity.* Carroll & Graf.

7. *And Justice for All.* (1979).
   This is the classic Al Pacino film about corruption in the legal system.

8. *The Firm* (1993).

    Tom Cruise and Gene Hackman star in this adaptation of the John Grisham novel, centering on corrupt lawyers, blackmail, and racketeering, with a satisfying and ironic ending.

ENDNOTES

1. *Ballentine's Law Dictionary.*

2. 18 P.S. § 4904.

3. 18 U.S.C. § 1623(e).

4. *United States v. Norris,* 300 U.S. 564 (1937).

5. 18 U.S.C. § 1623(d).

6. 18 U.S.C. § 1623(c).

7. *United States v. Gugliaro,* 501 F.2d 68 (2nd Cir. 1974).

8. M. Farmer, *The Long Arm of the Law* (Regia Anglorum Publications 1994) available at *http://www.ftecj.net/~regia/law.htm.*

9. *United States v. Wood,* 6 F.3d 692 (10th Cir. 1993).

10. 18 U.S.C. § 1515.

11. *United States v. Wood,* 6 F.3d 692 (10th Cir. 1993).

12. *United States v. Cammisano,* 917 F.2d 1057 (8th Cir. 1990).

13. "How Much Has Fred Zain Cost the State?" *Sunday Gazette-Mail,* September 23, 2001.

14. "Police Chemist's Missteps Cause Oklahoma Scandal," *Washington Post,* November 11, 2001.

15. Roadcap testified in cases the author prosecuted in the 1980s. So the author finds these later revelations particularly troublesome.

16. "'I Can Move On', Harrisburg, Man, State Settle Suits Claiming Frame-up in 1970 Murder," *Patriot News,* Harrisburg, PA, June 20, 2006.

17. *Ballentine's Law Dictionary.*

18. 18 U.S.C. § 401.

19. *In re Farquhar,* 160 U.S. App. DC 295, 492 F.2d 561 (1973).

20. *Floersheim v. Engman,* 161 U.S. App. DC 30, 494 F.2d 949 (1973).

21. *United States v. Seale,* 461 F.2d 345 (7th Cir. 1972).

22. Ibid.

23. "Lessons of the 60's: 'We'd Do It Again,' Say the Chicago Seven's Lawyers," *ABA Journal,* May 18, 1987.

24. *In re Bonanno,* 344 F.2d 830 (2nd Cir. 1965).

25. *Yates v. United States,* 355 U.S. 66 (1957).

26. *Bullock v. United States,* 265 F.2d 683 (6th Cir. 1959), *cert. denied,* 360 U.S. 909 (1959).

27. *United States v. Rollerson,* 145 U.S. App. DC 338, 449 F.2d 1000 (1971).

28. 28 C.F.R. 50.10(a).

29. J. C. Wilson, *The Politics of Truth: Inside the Lies that Led to War and Betrayed My Wife's CIA Identity* (Carroll & Graf 2004).

30. "How it Unfolded; CIA Leak Indictment," *Seattle Time,* October 29, 2005.

31. *Ballentine's Law Dictionary.*

32. *United States v. Hernandez*, 731 F.2d 1147 (5th Cir. 1984).

33. *United States v. Daniel*, 3 F.3d 775 (4th Cir. 1993).

34. *United States v. Kim*, 870 F.2d 81 (2nd Cir.1989).

35. 18 U.S.C. § 1961 et seq.

36. *Scheidler, et al. v. NOW Inc.*, 547 U.S. 9 (2006).

37. *Wilkie v. Robbins*, 127 S. Ct. 2588 (2007).

38. *Anza v. Ideal Steel Supply Corp.*, 126 S. Ct. 1991 (2006).

39. *Williams v. Mohawk Industries*, 465 F.3d. 1277 (2006).

40. United States Constitution, Article II, Section 4.

41. "Senate Convicts, Removes Hastings from Judgeship," *Wall Street Journal*, October 23, 1989.

42. M. J. Gerhardt, *Review: The Perils of Presidential Impeachment*, 67 U. Chi. L. Rev. 293.

43. J. M. Nolan, *White Collar Crime: Department of Justice Issues Guidance to U.S. Attorneys Regarding Criteria for Criminally Charging Corporations*, Findlaw Library, 2000, *http://www.findlaw.com.*

44. M. Cohen and N. Fermon, *Princeton Readings on Political Thought* (Princeton University Press, 1996).

45. A. Lincoln, *The Gettysburg Address.*

APPENDIX

ALCEE L. HASTINGS 23RD CONGRESSIONAL DISTRICT FLORIDA RULES COMMITTEE PERMANENT SELECT COMMITTEE ON INTELLIGENCE FLORIDA DELEGATION VICE CHAIRMAN UNITED STATES HELSINKI COMMISSION SENIOR DEMOCRATIC WHIP	PLEASE RESPOND TO: ☐ 2353 RAYBURN BUILDING WASHINGTON, DC 20515-0923 TELEPHONE: (202) 225-1313 FAX: (202) 225-1171 ☐ 2701 W. OAKLAND PARK BOULEVARD SUITE 200 FT. LAUDERDALE, FL 33311 TELEPHONE: (954) 733-2800 FAX: (954) 735-9444 ☐ 5725 CORPORATE WAY SUITE 208 WEST PALM BEACH, FL 33407 TELEPHONE: (561) 684-0565 FAX: (561) 684-3613 www.alceehastings.house.gov

Congress of the United States House of Representatives Washington, DC 20515-0923

United States Representative Alcee L. Hastings

Alcee L. Hastings represents his native state of Florida by serving as Congressman for District 23, which includes parts of Broward, Palm Beach, Hendry, Martin, and St. Lucie Counties. Congressman Hastings was first elected in 1992 and has been reelected seven times since, most recently in 2006. Born in Altamonte Springs, he attended Florida's public schools, and graduated from Fisk University in 1958. He earned his law degree from Florida A&M University in Tallahassee.

Known to many as "Judge," Alcee Hastings has distinguished himself as an attorney, civil rights activist, judge, and now Member of Congress. Appointed by President Jimmy Carter in 1979, he became the first African-American Federal Judge in the state of Florida, and served in that position for ten years. Since his election to Congress as the first African-American from Florida since the post-Civil War period, Congressman Hastings has been an outspoken advocate for making our country safer and more secure; ensuring that our election systems are easier and more fair; creating tax incentives for small businesses; expanding the Earned Income Tax Credit; providing job training and reeducation for displaced workers; banning assault weapons; funding Head Start and education programs; making Social Security an independent agency; advocating for environmental justice and providing family and medical leave to all workers. Known throughout the world as an expert in foreign policy, Mr. Hastings has introduced legislation advocating diplomacy before military action to settle disputes with established and emerging nations. Throughout his lifetime, Congressman Hastings has championed the rights of minorities, women, the elderly, children and immigrants.

Among Congress' most respected voices in international affairs, Congressman Hastings is the Chairman of the Commission on Security and Cooperation in Europe. Commonly referred to as the Helsinki Commission, this independent U.S. government agency was created in 1976 to monitor and encourage compliance with the landmark human rights and democracy-building treaty signed in Finland the previous year. Members of the Commission are appointed by the Speaker of the House, the Majority Leader of the Senate and the President. In 2007, Congressman Hastings became the first African-American to chair the Commission and continues his trailblazing work in the areas of human rights, economic development and parliamentary diplomacy.

Congressman Hastings is a senior Member of the House Permanent Select Committee on Intelligence (HPSCI) and a member of the powerful House Rules Committee. On the Rules Committee, Mr. Hastings is the Chairman of the Subcommittee on Legislative and Budget Process. This Subcommittee has general responsibility for measures or matters associated with the inter-branch relations of Congress and the Executive.

As a Senior Democratic Whip, Mr. Hastings is an influential member of the Democratic leadership. Moreover, underscoring his commitment to work closely on a bipartisan basis with his Florida colleagues, Hastings is the Co-Chairman of the Florida Delegation. Previously, Mr. Hastings served as Vice Chairman of the Democratic Select Committee on Election Reform. Congressman Hastings is the proud recipient of numerous honors and awards bestowed on him from organizations both at home and abroad. His governing philosophy is simple: he firmly believes that progress and change can be achieved through mutual respect and appreciation and that individuals and communities can see beyond the limits of parochialism, enabling them to better understand each other.

District of Columbia Court of Appeals

No.07-BG-179
In the Matter of
I. LEWIS LIBBY, JR.
A Member of the Bar of the
District of Columbia
Court of Appeals
Bar Registration No. 950758

BDN: 372-05

ORDER

It appearing that respondent was convicted in the United States District Court for the District of Columbia of obstruction of justice, making false statements to the Federal Bureau of Investigation, and two counts of perjury, having received certified copies of the indictment, docket, and verdict form, and it appearing that one or more of the offenses constitutes a "serious crime" as defined by D.C. Bar Rule XI, § 10 (b), it is

ORDERED pursuant to D.C. Bar Rule XI, § 10 (c), that the respondent, I. Lewis Libby, Jr., is suspended immediately from the practice of law in the District of Columbia pending resolution of this matter, and the Board on Professional Responsibility is directed to institute a formal proceeding for determination of the nature of the offenses for the purpose of determining whether or not the crimes involve moral turpitude within the meaning of D.C. Code § 11-2503 (a) (2001). It is

FURTHER ORDERED that respondent's attention is drawn to the requirements of D.C. Bar Rule XI, § 14 relating to suspended-attorneys and to the provisions of § 16 (c) dealing with the timing of eligibility for reinstatement based on compliance with § 14, including the filing of the required affidavit. It is

FURTHER ORDERED that Bar Counsel inform the Court if the matter is resolved without the necessity of further court action.

BY THE COURT:

ERIC T. WASHINGTON
Chief Judge

Garland Pinkston, Jr.
Clerk of the District of Columbia Court
of Appeals

By _____

IN THE UNITED STATES DISTRICT COURT FOR THE DISTRICT OF COLUMBIA

Holding a Criminal Term Grand Jury Sworn in on October 31, 2003

UNITED STATES OF AMERICA	) Criminal No.
	) GRAND JURY ORIGINAL
v.	) Count 1: Obstruction of Justice (18 U.S.C. § 1503)
	)
	) Counts 2-3: False Statements (18 U.S.C. § 1001(a)(2))
I. LEWIS LIBBY,	)
also known as "SCOOTER LIBBY"	) Counts 4-5: Perjury (18 U.S.C. § 1623)

INDICTMENT

COUNT ONE
(Obstruction of Justice)

THE GRAND JURY CHARGES:

1. At times material to this indictment:

Defendant's Employment and Responsibilities

a. Beginning on or about January 20, 2001, and continuing through the date of this indictment, defendant I. LEWIS LIBBY, also known as "SCOOTER LIBBY," was employed as Assistant to the President of the United States, Chief of Staff to the Vice President of the United States, and Assistant to the Vice President for National Security Affairs. In the course of his work, LIBBY had frequent access to classified information and frequently spoke with officials of the U.S. intelligence community, as well as other government officials, regarding sensitive national security matters.

b. In connection with his role as a senior government official with responsibilities for national security matters, LIBBY held security clearances entitling him to access to classified information. As a person with such clearances, LIBBY was obligated by applicable laws and regulations, including Title 18, United States Code, Section 793, and Executive Order 12958 (as modified by Executive Order 13292), not to disclose classified information to persons not authorized to receive such information, and otherwise to exercise proper care to safeguard classified information against unauthorized disclosure. On or about January 23, 2001, LIBBY executed a written "Classified Information Nondisclosure Agreement," stating in part that "I understand and accept that by being granted access to classified information, special confidence and trust shall be placed in me by the United States Government," and that "I have been advised that the unauthorized disclosure, unauthorized retention, or negligent handling of classified information by me could cause damage or irreparable injury to the United States or could be used to advantage by a foreign nation."

The Central Intelligence Agency

c. The Central Intelligence Agency (CIA) was an agency of the United States whose mission was to collect, produce, and disseminate intelligence and counterintelligence information to officers and departments of the United States government, including the President, the National Security Council, and the Joint Chiefs of Staff.

d. The responsibilities of certain CIA employees required that their association with the CIA be kept secret; as a result, the fact that these individuals were employed by the CIA was classified. Disclosure of the fact that such individuals were employed by the CIA had the potential to damage the national security in ways that ranged from preventing the future use of those individuals in a covert capacity, to compromising intelligence-gathering methods and operations, and endangering the safety of CIA employees and those who dealt with them.

Joseph Wilson and Valerie Plame Wilson

e. Joseph Wilson ("Wilson") was a former career State Department official who had held a variety of posts, including United States Ambassador. In 2002, after an inquiry to the CIA by the Vice President concerning certain intelligence reporting, the CIA decided on its own initiative to send Wilson to the country of Niger to investigate allegations involving Iraqi efforts to acquire uranium yellowcake, a processed form of uranium ore. Wilson orally reported his findings to the CIA upon his return.

f. Joseph Wilson was married to Valerie Plame Wilson ("Valerie Wilson"). At all relevant times from January 1, 2002 through July 2003, Valerie Wilson was employed by the CIA, and her employment status was classified. Prior to July 14, 2003, Valerie Wilson's affiliation with the CIA was not common knowledge outside the intelligence community.

Events Leading up to July 2003

2. On or about January 28, 2003, President George W. Bush delivered his State of the Union address which included sixteen words asserting that "The British government has learned that Saddam Hussein recently sought significant quantities of uranium from Africa."

3. On May 6, 2003, the New York Times published a column by Nicholas Kristof which disputed the accuracy of the "sixteen words" in the State of the Union address. The column reported that, following a request from the Vice President's office for an investigation of allegations that Iraq sought to buy uranium from Niger, an unnamed former ambassador was sent on a trip to Niger in 2002 to investigate the allegations. According to the column, the ambassador reported back to the CIA and State Department in early 2002 that the allegations were unequivocally wrong and based on forged documents.

4. On or about May 29, 2003, in the White House, **LIBBY** asked an Under Secretary of State ("Under Secretary") for information concerning the unnamed ambassador's travel to Niger to investigate claims about Iraqi efforts to acquire uranium yellowcake. The Under Secretary thereafter directed the State Department's Bureau of Intelligence and Research to prepare a report concerning the ambassador and his trip. The Under Secretary provided **LIBBY** with interim oral reports in late May and early June 2003, and advised **LIBBY** that Wilson was the former ambassador who took the trip.

5. On or about June 9, 2003, a number of classified documents from the CIA were faxed to the Office of the Vice President to the personal attention of **LIBBY** and another person in the Office of the Vice President. The faxed documents, which were marked as classified, discussed, among other things, Wilson and his trip to Niger, but did not mention Wilson by name. After receiving these documents, **LIBBY** and one or more other persons in the Office of the Vice President handwrote the names "Wilson" and "Joe Wilson" on the documents.

6. On or about June 11 or 12, 2003, the Under Secretary of State orally advised **LIBBY** in the White House that, in sum and substance, Wilson's wife worked at the CIA and that State Department personnel were saying that Wilson's wife was involved in the planning of his trip.

7. On or about June 11, 2003, **LIBBY** spoke with a senior officer of the CIA to ask about the origin and circumstances of Wilson's trip, and was advised by the CIA officer that Wilson's wife worked at the CIA and was believed to be responsible for sending Wilson on the trip.

8. Prior to June 12, 2003, Washington Post reporter Walter Pincus contacted the Office of the Vice President in connection with a story he was writing about Wilson's trip. LIBBY participated in discussions in the Office of the Vice President concerning how to respond to Pincus.

9. On or about June 12, 2003, LIBBY was advised by the Vice President of the United States that Wilson's wife worked at the Central Intelligence Agency in the Counterproliferation Division. LIBBY understood that the Vice President had learned this information from the CIA.

10. On June 12, 2003, the Washington Post published an article by reporter Walter Pincus about Wilson's trip to Niger, which described Wilson as a retired ambassador but not by name, and reported that the CIA had sent him to Niger after an aide to the Vice President raised questions about purported Iraqi efforts to acquire uranium. Pincus's article questioned the accuracy of the "sixteen words," and stated that the retired ambassador had reported to the CIA that the uranium purchase story was false.

11. On or about June 14, 2003, LIBBY met with a CIA briefer. During their conversation he expressed displeasure that CIA officials were making comments to reporters critical of the Vice President's office, and discussed with the briefer, among other things, "Joe Wilson" and his wife "Valerie Wilson," in the context of Wilson's trip to Niger.

12. On or about June 19, 2003, an article appeared in *The New Republic magazine* online entitled "The *First Casualty*: The *Selling of the Iraq War*." Among other things, the article questioned the "sixteen words" and stated that following a request for information from the Vice President, the CIA had asked an unnamed ambassador to travel to Niger to investigate allegations that Iraq had sought uranium from Niger. The article included a quotation attributed to the unnamed ambassador alleging that administration officials "knew the Niger story was a flat-out lie." The article also was critical of how the administration, including the Office of the Vice President, portrayed intelligence concerning Iraqi capabilities with regard to weapons of mass destruction, and accused the administration of suppressing dissent from the intelligence agencies on this topic.

13. Shortly after publication of the article in **The New Republic**, **LIBBY** spoke by telephone with his then Principal Deputy and discussed the article. That official asked **LIBBY** whether information about Wilson's trip could be shared with the press to re-but the allegations that the Vice President had sent Wilson. **LIBBY** responded that there would be complications at the CIA in disclosing that information publicly, and that he could not discuss the matter on a non-secure telephone line.

14. On or about June 23, 2003, **LIBBY** met with **New York Times** reporter Judith Miller. During this meeting **LIBBY** was critical of the CIA, and disparaged what he termed "selective leaking" by the CIA concerning intelligence matters. In discussing the CIA's handling of Wilson's trip to Niger, **LIBBY** informed her that Wilson's wife might work at a bureau of the CIA.

The July 6 "Op Ed" Article by Wilson

15. On July 6, 2003, the **New York Times** published an Op-Ed article by Wilson entitled "What I Didn't Find in Africa." Also on July 6, 2003, the **Washington Post** published an article about Wilson's 2002 trip to Niger, which article was based in part upon an interview of Wilson. Also on July 6, Wilson appeared as a guest on the television interview show "**Meet the Press**." In his Op-Ed

article and interviews in print and on television, Wilson asserted, among other things, that he had taken a trip to Niger at the request of the CIA in February 2002 to investigate allegations that Iraq had sought or obtained uranium yellowcake from Niger, and that he doubted Iraq had obtained uranium from Niger recently, for a number of reasons. Wilson stated that he believed, based on his understanding of government procedures, that the Office of the Vice President was advised of the results of his trip.

LIBBY's Actions Following Wilson's July 6 "Op Ed" Column

16. On or about July 7, 2003, **LIBBY** had lunch with the then White House Press Secretary and advised the Press Secretary that Wilson's wife worked at the CIA and noted that such information was not widely known.

17. On or about the morning of July 8, 2003, **LIBBY** met with **New York Times** reporter Judith Miller. When the conversation turned to the subject of Joseph Wilson, **LIBBY** asked that the information **LIBBY** provided on the topic of Wilson be attributed to a "former Hill staffer" rather than to a "senior administration official," as had been the understanding with respect to other information that **LIBBY** provided to Miller during this meeting. **LIBBY** thereafter discussed with Miller Wilson's trip and criticized the CIA reporting concerning Wilson's trip. During this discussion, **LIBBY** advised Miller of his belief that Wilson's wife worked for the CIA.

18. Also on or about July 8, 2003, **LIBBY** met with the Counsel to the Vice President in an anteroom outside the Vice President's Office. During their brief conversation, **LIBBY** asked the Counsel to the Vice President, in sum and substance, what paperwork there would be at the CIA if an employee's spouse undertook an overseas trip.

19. Not earlier than June 2003, but on or before July 8, 2003, the Assistant to the Vice President for Public Affairs learned from another government official that Wilson's wife worked at the CIA, and advised **LIBBY** of this information.

20. On or about July 10, 2003, **LIBBY** spoke to **NBC** Washington Bureau Chief Tim Russert to complain about press coverage of **LIBBY** by an **MSNBC** reporter. **LIBBY** did not discuss Wilson's wife with Russert.

21. On or about July 10 or July 11, 2003, **LIBBY** spoke to a senior official in the White House ("Official A") who advised **LIBBY** of a conversation Official A had earlier that week with columnist Robert Novak in which Wilson's wife was discussed as a CIA employee involved in Wilson's trip. **LIBBY** was advised by Official A that Novak would be writing a story about Wilson's wife.

22. On or about July 12, 2003, **LIBBY** flew with the Vice President and others to and from Norfolk, Virginia, on Air Force Two. On his return trip, **LIBBY** discussed with other officials aboard the plane what **LIBBY** should say in response to certain pending media inquiries, including questions from **Time** reporter Matthew Cooper.

23. On or about July 12, 2003, in the afternoon, **LIBBY** spoke by telephone to Cooper, who asked whether **LIBBY** had heard that Wilson's wife was involved in sending Wilson on the trip to Niger. **LIBBY** confirmed to Cooper, without elaboration or qualification, that he had heard this information too.

24. On or about July 12, 2003, in the late afternoon, **LIBBY** spoke by telephone with Judith Miller of the **New York Times** and discussed Wilson's wife, and that she worked at the CIA.

The Criminal Investigation

25. On or about September 26, 2003, the Department of Justice authorized the Federal Bureau of Investigation ("FBI") to commence a criminal investigation into the possible unauthorized disclosure of classified information regarding the disclosure of Valerie Wilson's affiliation with the CIA to various reporters in the spring of 2003.

26. As part of the criminal investigation, **LIBBY** was interviewed by Special Agents of the FBI on or about October 14 and November 26, 2003, each time in the presence of his counsel. During these interviews, **LIBBY** stated to FBI Special Agents that:

    a. During a conversation with Tim Russert of **NBC News** on July 10 or 11, 2003, Russert asked **LIBBY** if **LIBBY** was aware that Wilson's wife worked for the CIA. **LIBBY** responded to Russert that he did not know that, and Russert replied that all the reporters knew it. **LIBBY** was surprised by this statement because, while speaking with Russert, **LIBBY** did not recall that he previously had learned about Wilson's wife's employment from the Vice President.

    b. During a conversation with Matthew Cooper of **Time** magazine on or about July 12, 2003, **LIBBY** told Cooper that reporters were telling the administration that Wilson's wife worked for the CIA, but that **LIBBY** did not know if this was true; and

    c. **LIBBY** did not discuss Wilson's wife with **New York Times** reporter Judith Miller during a meeting with Miller on or about July 8, 2003.

27. Beginning in or about January 2004, and continuing until the date of this indictment, Grand Jury 03-3 sitting in the District of Columbia conducted an investigation ("the Grand Jury Investigation") into possible violations of federal criminal laws, including: Title 50, United States Code, Section 421 (disclosure of the identity of covert intelligence personnel); and Title 18, United States Code, Sections 793 (improper disclosure of national defense information), 1001 (false statements), 1503 (obstruction of justice), and 1623 (perjury).

28. A major focus of the Grand Jury Investigation was to determine which government officials had disclosed to the media prior to July 14, 2003 information concerning the affiliation of Valerie Wilson with the CIA, and the nature, timing, extent, and purpose of such disclosures, as well as whether any official making such a disclosure did so knowing that the employment of Valerie Wilson by the CIA was classified information.

29.   During the course of the Grand Jury Investigation, the following matters, among others, were material to the Grand Jury Investigation:

    i. When, and the manner and means by which, defendant **LIBBY** learned that Wilson's wife was employed by the CIA;

    ii. Whether and when **LIBBY** disclosed to members of the media that Wilson's wife was employed by the CIA;

    iii. The language used by **LIBBY** in disclosing any such information to the media, including whether **LIBBY** expressed uncertainty about the accuracy of any information he may have disclosed, or described where he obtained the information;

    iv. **LIBBY**'s knowledge as to whether any information he disclosed was classified at the time he disclosed it; and

    v. Whether **LIBBY** was candid with Special Agents of the Federal Bureau of Investigation in describing his conversations with the other government officials and the media relating to Valerie Wilson.

LIBBY's Grand Jury Testimony

30.   On or about March 5 and March 24, 2004, **LIBBY** testified before Grand Jury 03-3. On each occasion of **LIBBY**'s testimony, the foreperson of the Grand Jury administered the oath to **LIBBY** and **LIBBY** swore to tell the truth in the testimony he was about to give.

31.   In or about March 2004, in the District of Columbia.

I. LEWIS LIBBY,
also known as "**SCOOTER LIBBY**,"

defendant herein, did knowingly and corruptly endeavor to influence, obstruct and impede the due administration of justice, namely proceedings before Grand Jury 03-3, by misleading and deceiving the grand jury as to when, and the manner and means by which, **LIBBY** acquired and subsequently disclosed to the media information concerning the employment of Valerie Wilson by the CIA.

32.   It was part of the corrupt endeavor that during his grand jury testimony, defendant **LIBBY** made the following materially false and intentionally misleading statements and representations, in substance, under oath:

    a. When **LIBBY** spoke with Tim Russert of **NBC News,** on or about July 10, 2003:

      i. Russert asked **LIBBY** if **LIBBY** knew that Wilson's wife worked for the CIA, and told **LIBBY** that all the reporters knew it; and

      ii. At the time of this conversation, **LIBBY** was surprised to hear that Wilson's wife worked for the CIA;

    b. **LIBBY** advised Matthew Cooper of **Time** magazine on or about July 12, 2003, that he had heard that other reporters were saying that Wilson's wife worked for the CIA, and further advised him that **LIBBY** did not know whether this assertion was true; and

    c. **LIBBY** advised Judith Miller of the **New York Times** on or about July 12, 2003 that he had heard that other reporters were saying that Wilson's wife worked for the CIA but **LIBBY** did not know whether that assertion was true.

33.   It was further part of the corrupt endeavor that at the time defendant **LIBBY** made each of the above-described materially false and intentionally misleading statements and representations to the grand jury, **LIBBY** was aware that they were false, in that:

    a. When **LIBBY** spoke with Tim Russert of **NBC News** on or about July 10, 2003:

      i. Russert did not ask **LIBBY** if **LIBBY** knew that Wilson's wife worked for the CIA, nor did he tell **LIBBY** that all the reporters knew it; and

      ii. At the time of this conversation, **LIBBY** was well aware that Wilson's wife worked at the CIA; in fact, **LIBBY** had participated in multiple prior conversations concerning this topic, including on the following occasions:

- In or about early June 2003, **LIBBY** learned from the Vice President that Wilson's wife worked for the CIA in the Counterproliferation Division;
- On or about June 11, 2003, **LIBBY** was informed by a senior CIA officer that Wilson's wife was employed by the CIA and that the idea of sending him to Niger originated with her;
- On or about June 12, 2003, **LIBBY** was informed by the Under Secretary of State that Wilson's wife worked for the CIA;
- On or about June 14, 2003, **LIBBY** discussed "Joe Wilson" and "Valerie Wilson" with his CIA briefer, in the context of Wilson's trip to Niger;
- On or about June 23, 2003, **LIBBY** informed reporter Judith Miller that Wilson's wife might work at a bureau of the CIA;
- On or about July 7, 2003, **LIBBY** advised the White House Press Secretary that Wilson's wife worked for the CIA;
- In or about June or July 2003, and in no case later than on or about July 8, 2003, **LIBBY** was advised by the Assistant to the Vice President for Public Affairs that Wilson's wife worked for the CIA;

- On or about July 8, 2003, **LIBBY** advised reporter Judith Miller of his belief that Wilson's wife worked at the CIA; and

- On or about July 8, 2003, **LIBBY** had a discussion with the Counsel to the Office of the Vice President concerning the paperwork that would exist if a person who was sent on an overseas trip by the CIA had a spouse who worked at the CIA;

b. **LIBBY** did not advise Matthew Cooper, on or about July 12, 2003, that **LIBBY** had heard other reporters were saying that Wilson's wife worked for the CIA, nor did **LIBBY** advise him that **LIBBY** did not know whether this assertion was true; rather, **LIBBY** confirmed to Cooper, without qualification, that **LIBBY** had heard that Wilson's wife worked at the CIA; and

c. **LIBBY** did not advise Judith Miller, on or about July 12, 2003, that **LIBBY** had heard other reporters were saying that Wilson's wife worked for the CIA, nor did **LIBBY** advise her that **LIBBY** did not know whether this assertion was true;

In violation of Title 18, United States Code, Section 1503.

<u>**COUNT TWO**</u>
(False Statement)

THE GRAND JURY FURTHER CHARGES:

1. The Grand Jury realleges Paragraphs 1-26 of Count One as though fully set forth herein.
    2. During the course of the criminal investigation conducted by the Federal Bureau of Investigation and the Department of Justice, the following matters, among others, were material to that investigation:

> a. When, and the manner and means by which, defendant **LIBBY** learned that Wilson's wife was employed by the CIA;
> b. Whether and when **LIBBY** disclosed to members of the media that Wilson's wife was employed by the CIA;
> c. The language used by **LIBBY** in disclosing any such information to the media, including whether **LIBBY** expressed uncertainty about the accuracy of any information he may have disclosed, or described where he obtained the information; and
> d. **LIBBY**'s knowledge as to whether any information he disclosed was classified at the time he disclosed it.

3. On or about October 14 and November 26, 2003, in the District of Columbia,

I. LEWIS LIBBY,
also known as "**SCOOTER LIBBY**,"

defendant herein, did knowingly and willfully make a materially false, fictitious, and fraudulent statement and representation in a matter within the jurisdiction of the Federal Bureau of Investigation, an agency within the executive branch of the United States, in that the defendant, in response to questions posed to him by agents of the Federal Bureau of Investigation, stated that:

> During a conversation with Tim Russert of **NBC News** on July 10 or 11, 2003, Russert asked **LIBBY** if **LIBBY** was aware that Wilson's wife worked for the CIA. **LIBBY** responded to Russert that he did not know that, and Russert replied that all the reporters knew it. **LIBBY** was surprised by this statement because, while speaking with Russert, **LIBBY** did not recall that he previously had learned about Wilson's wife's employment from the Vice President.

4. As defendant **LIBBY** well knew when he made it, this statement was false in that when **LIBBY** spoke with Russert on or about July 10 or 11, 2003:

> a. Russert did not ask **LIBBY** if **LIBBY** knew that Wilson's wife worked for the CIA, nor did he tell **LIBBY** that all the reporters knew it; and
> b. At the time of this conversation, **LIBBY** was well aware that Wilson's wife worked at the CIA;

In violation of Title 18, United States Code, Section 1001(a)(2).

COUNT THREE
(False Statement)

THE GRAND JURY FURTHER CHARGES:

1. The Grand Jury realleges Paragraphs 1 and 2 of Count Two as though fully set forth herein.
    2. On or about October 14 and November 26, 2003, in the District of Columbia,

I. LEWIS LIBBY,
also known as **"SCOOTER LIBBY,"**

defendant herein, did knowingly and willfully make a materially false, fictitious, and fraudulent statement and representation in a matter within the jurisdiction of the Federal Bureau of Investigation, an agency within the executive branch of the United States, in that the defendant, in response to questions posed to him by agents of the Federal Bureau of Investigation, stated that:

> During a conversation with Matthew Cooper of **Time** magazine on July 12, 2003, **LIBBY** told Cooper that reporters were telling the administration that Wilson's wife worked for the CIA, but **LIBBY** did not know if this was true.

3. As defendant **LIBBY** well knew when he made it, this statement was false in that: **LIBBY** did not advise Cooper on or about July 12, 2003 that reporters were telling the administration that Wilson's wife worked for the CIA, nor did **LIBBY** advise him that **LIBBY** did not know whether this was true; rather, **LIBBY** confirmed for Cooper, without qualification, that **LIBBY** had heard that Wilson's wife worked at the CIA;

In violation of Title 18, United States Code, Section 1001(a)(2).

<u>COUNT FOUR</u>
(Perjury)

THE GRAND JURY FURTHER CHARGES:

1. The Grand Jury realleges Paragraphs 1-30 of Count One as though fully set forth herein.
  2. On or about March 5, 2004, in the District of Columbia,

I. LEWIS LIBBY,
also known as "**SCOOTER LIBBY**,"

defendant herein, having taken an oath to testify truthfully in a proceeding before a grand jury of the United States, knowingly made a false material declaration, in that he gave the following testimony regarding a conversation that he represented he had with Tim Russert of **NBC News,** on or about July 10, 2003 (underlined portions alleged as false):

.... <u>And then he said, you know, did you know that this—excuse me, did you know that Ambassador Wilson's wife works at the CIA? And I was a little taken aback by that. I remember being taken aback by it. And I said—he may have said a little more but that was—he said that. And I said, no, I don't know that. And I said, no, I don't know that intentionally because I didn't want him to take anything I was saying as in any way confirming what he said, because at that point in time I did not recall that I had ever known, and I thought this is something that he was telling me that I was first learning. And so I said, no, I don't know that because I want to be very careful not to confirm it for him, so that he didn't take my statement as confirmation for him.</u>

Now, I had said earlier in the conversation, which I omitted to tell you, that this—you know, as always, Tim, our discussion is off-the-record if that's okay with you, and he said, that's fine.

<u>So then he said—I said—he said, sorry—he, Mr. Russert said to me, did you know that Ambassador Wilson's wife, or his wife, works at the CIA? And I said, no, I don't know that. And then he said, yeah—yes, all the reporters know it. And I said, again, I don't know that. I just wanted to be clear that I wasn't confirming anything for him on this. And you know, I was struck by what he was saying in that he thought it was an important fact, but I didn't ask him anymore about it because I didn't want to be digging in on him,</u> and he then moved on and finished the conversation, something like that.

3. In truth and fact, as **LIBBY** well knew when he gave this testimony, it was false in that:

   a. Russert did not ask **LIBBY** if **LIBBY** knew that Wilson's wife worked for the CIA, nor did he tell **LIBBY** that all the reporters knew it; and
   b. At the time of this conversation, **LIBBY** was well aware that Wilson's wife worked at the CIA;

In violation of Title 18, United States Code, Section 1623.

<u>COUNT FIVE</u>
(Perjury)

THE GRAND JURY FURTHER CHARGES:

1. The Grand Jury realleges Paragraphs 1–30 of Count One as though fully set forth herein.
    2. On or about March 5, 2004 and March 24, 2004, in the District of Columbia,

I. LEWIS LIBBY,
also known as "**SCOOTER LIBBY**,"

defendant herein, having taken an oath to testify truthfully in a proceeding before a grand jury of the United States, knowingly made a false material declaration, in that he gave the following testimony regarding his conversations with reporters concerning the employment of Joseph Wilson's wife by the CIA (underlined portions alleged as false):

a. Testimony Given on or about March 5, 2004 Regarding a Conversation With Matthew Cooper on or About July 12, 2003:

Q. And it's your specific recollection that when you told Cooper about Wilson's wife working at the CIA, you attributed that fact to what reporters—

A. <u>Yes</u>.

Q. —plural, were saying. Correct?

A. <u>I was very clear to say reporters are telling us that because in my mind I still didn't know it as a fact. I thought I was —all I had was this information that was coming in from the reporters.</u>

. . . .

Q. And at the same time you have a specific recollection of telling him, you don't know whether it's true or not, you're just telling him what reporters are saying?

A. <u>Yes, that's correct, sir. And I said, reporters are telling us that, I don't know if it's true. I was careful about that because among other things, I wanted to be clear I didn't know Mr. Wilson. I don't know—I think I said, I don't know if he has a wife, but this is what we're hearing.</u>

b. Testimony Given on or about March 24,2004 Regarding Conversations With Reporters:

Q. And let me ask you this directly. Did the fact that you knew that the law could turn, the law as to whether a crime was committed, could turn on where you learned the information from, affect your account for the FBI when you told them that you were telling reporters Wilson's wife worked at the CIA but your source was a reporter rather than the Vice-President?

A. <u>No, it's a fact. It was a fact, that's what I told the reporters</u>.

Q. And you're, you're certain as you sit here today that every reporter you told that Wilson's wife worked at the CIA, you sourced it back to other reporters?

A. <u>Yes, sir</u>, because it was important for what I was saying and because it was—that's what — <u>that's how I did it.</u>

. . . .

Q. The next set of questions from the Grand Jury are—concern this fact. If you did not understand the information about Wilson's wife to have been classified and didn't understand it when you heard it from Mr. Russert, why was it that you were so deliberate to make sure that you told other reporters that reporters were saying it and not assert it as something you knew?

A. I want—I didn't want to—I didn't know if it was true and I didn't want people—I didn't want the reporters to think it was true because I said it. I—<u>all I had was that reporters are telling us that, and by that I wanted them to understand it wasn't coming from me and that it might not be true. Reporters write things that aren't true sometimes, or get things that aren't true. So I wanted to be clear they didn't, they didn't think it was me saying it. I didn't know it was true and I wanted them to understand that.</u> Also, it was important to me to let them know that because what I was telling them was that I don't know Mr. Wilson. We didn't ask for his mission. That I didn't see his report. <u>Basically, we didn't know anything about him until this stuff came out in June. And among the other things, I didn't know he had a wife. That was one of the things I said to Mr. Cooper, I don't know if he's married. And so I wanted to be very clear about all this stuff that I didn't, I didn't know about him. And the only thing I had, I thought at the time, was what reporters are telling us.</u>

. . . .

Well, talking to the other reporters about it, I don't see as a crime. What I said to the other reporters is what, you know—<u>I told a couple reporters what other reporters had told us,</u> and I don't see that as a crime.

3.   In truth and fact, as **LIBBY** well knew when he gave this testimony, it was false in that **LIBBY** did not advise Matthew Cooper or other reporters that **LIBBY** had heard other reporters were saying that Wilson's wife worked for the CIA, nor did **LIBBY** advise Cooper or other reporters that **LIBBY** did not know whether this assertion was true;

In violation of Title 18, United States Code, Section 1623.

A TRUE BILL:

_____

FOREPERSON

_____

PATRICK J. FITZGERALD
Special Counsel

UNITED STATES DISTRICT COURT
for the District of Columbia

UNITED STATES OF AMERICA

V.

I. LEWIS LIBBY

JUDGMENT IN A CRIMINAL CASE

Case Number: CR 05-394

USM Number: 28301-016

NANCY MAYER WHITTINGT0N,
CLERK U.S. DISTRICT COURT

Theodore Wells Jr and William Jeffress Jr.
Defendant's Attorney

THE DEFENDANT:

☐ pleaded guilty to count(s) _____

☐ pleaded nolo contendere to counl(s) _____
which was accepted by the court.

☑ was found guilty on count(s) after a plea of not guilty. Count 1, 2, 4 and 5 of the Indictment on March 6, 2007

The defendant is adjudicated guilty of these offenses:

Title & Section	Nature of Offense	Offense Ended	Count
18 USC 1503	Obstruction of Justice	Between October 14, 2003 and March 24, 2004	1

The defendant is sentenced as provided in pages 2 through __8__ of this judgment. The sentence is imposed pursuant to the Sentencing Reform Act of 1984.

☑ The defendant has been found not guilty on count(s) **Count 3 of the Indictment**

☐ Count(s) _____ is/are dismissed on the motion of the United States.

It is ordered that the defendant must notify the United States attorney for this district within 30 days of any change of name, residence, or mailing address until all fines, restitution, costs, and special assessments imposed by this judgment are fully paid. If ordered to pay restitution, the defendant must notify the court and United States attorney of material changes in economic circumstances.

6/14/07
Date of Imposition of Judgment

Signature of Judge

Reggie B. Walton   U.S. District Court Judge
Name of Judge   Title of Judge

6/22/07
Date

DEFENDANT: I. LEWIS LIBBY
CASE NUMBER: CR 05-394

ADDITIONAL COUNTS OF CONVICTION

Title & Section	Nature of Offense	Offense Ended	Count
False Statement	18 USC 1001(a)(2)	Between October 14, 2003 and November 26, 2003	2
Perjury	18 USC 1623	March 5, 2004	4
Perjury	18 USC 1623	Between March 5, 2204 and March 24, 2004	5

DEFENDANT: I. LEWIS LIBBY
CASE NUMBER: CR 05-394

IMPRISONMENT

The defendant is hereby committed to the custody of the United States Bureau of Prisons to be imprisoned for a total term of:

THIRTHY (30) months on Count 1; SIX (6) months on Count 2; TWENTY-FOUR (24) months on Count 4 and TWENTY-FOUR (24) months on Count 5 to run concurrent with each other;

☐ The court makes the following recommendations to the Bureau of Prisons:

☐ The defendant is remanded to the custody of the United States Marshal.

☐ The defendant shall surrender to the United States Marshal for this district:

    ☐ at _____ ☐ a.m. ☐ p.m. on _____.

    ☐ as notified by the United States Marshal.

☑ The defendant shall surrender for service of sentence at the institution designated by the Bureau of Prisons:

    ☐ before 2 p.m. on _____.

    ☐ as notified by the United States Marshal.

    ☑ as notified by the Probation or Pretrial Services Office.

RETURN

I have executed this judgment as follows:

Defendant delivered on _____ to _____
at _____, with a certified copy of this judgment.

_____
UNITED STATES MARSHAL

By _____
DEPUTY UNITED STATES MARSHAL

DEFENDANT: I. LEWIS LIBBY
CASE NUMBER: CR 05-394

SUPERVISED RELEASE

Upon release from imprisonment, the defendant shall be on supervised release for a term of:

TWO (2) years on Count 1; TWO (2) years on Count 2; TWO (2) years on Count 4 and TWO (2) years on Count 5 to run concurrent with each other.

The defendant must report to the probation office in the district to which the defendant is released within 72 hours of release from the custody of the Bureau of Prisons.

The defendant shall not commit another federal, state or local crime.

The defendant shall not unlawfully possess a controlled substance. The defendant shall refrain from any unlawful use of a controlled substance. The defendant shall submit to one drug test within 15 days of release from imprisonment and at least two periodic drug tests thereafter, as determined by the court.

☑ The above drug testing condition is suspended, based on the court's determination that the defendant poses a low risk of future substance abuse. (Check, if applicable.)

☐ The defendant shall not possess a firearm, ammunition, destructive device, or any other dangerous weapon. (Check, if applicable.)

☑ The defendant shall cooperate in the collection of DNA as directed by the probation officer. (Check, if applicable.)

☐ The defendant shall register with the state sex offender registration agency in the state where the defendant resides, works, or is a student, as directed by the probation officer. (Check, if applicable.)

☐ The defendant shall participate in an approved program for domestic violence. (Check, if applicable.)

If this judgment imposes a fine or restitution, it is a condition of supervised release that the defendant pay in accordance with the Schedule of Payments sheet of this judgment.

The defendant must comply with the standard conditions that have been adopted by this court as well as with any additional conditions on the attached page.

STANDARD CONDITIONS OF SUPERVISION

1) the defendant shall not leave the judicial district without the permission of the court or probation officer;

2) the defendant shall report to the probation officer and shall submit a truthful and complete written report within the first five days of each month;

3) the defendant shall answer truthfully all inquiries by the probation officer and follow the instructions of the probation officer;

4) the defendant shall support his or her dependents and meet other family responsibilities;

5) the defendant shall work regularly at a lawful occupation, unless excused by the probation officer for schooling, training, or other acceptable reasons;

6) the defendant shall notify the probation officer at least ten days prior to any change in residence or employment;

7) the defendant shall refrain from excessive use of alcohol and shall not purchase, possess, use, distribute, or administer any controlled substance or any paraphernalia related to any controlled substances, except as prescribed by a physician;

8) the defendant shall not frequent places where controlled substances are illegally sold, used, distributed, or administered;

9) the defendant shall not associate with any persons engaged in criminal activity and shall not associate with any person convicted of a felony, unless granted permission to do so by the probation officer;

10) the defendant shall permit a probation officer to visit him or her at any time at home or elsewhere and shall permit confiscation of any contraband observed in plain view of the probation officer;

11) the defendant shall notify the probation officer within seventy-two hours of being arrested or questioned by a law enforcement officer;

12) the defendant shall not enter into any agreement to act as an informer or a special agent of a law enforcement agency without the permission of the court; and

13) as directed by the probation officer, the defendant shall notify third parties of risks that may be occasioned by the defendant's criminal record or personal history or characteristics and shall permit the probation officer to make such notifications and to confirm the defendant's compliance with such notification requirement.

SPECIAL CONDITIONS OF SUPERVISION

That the defendant shall obtain and maintain full time employment. The circumstances of the defendant's employment shall be at the discretion of the Probation Office, but subject to review by the Court.

The defendant shall perform 400 hours of community service, as approved and directed by the Probation Office.

The Probation Department shall release the presentence investigation report to all appropriate agencies in order to execute the sentence of the Court. These agencies shall return the presentence report to the Probation Office upon completion and termination of the treatment involved.

DEFENDANT: I. LEWIS LIBBY
CASE NUMBER: CR 05-394

CRIMINAL MONETARY PENALTIES

The defendant must pay the total criminal monetary penalties under the schedule of payments on Sheet 6.

	Assessment	**Fine**	**Restitution**
TOTALS	$ 400.00	$ 250,000.00	$ 0.00

☐ The determination of restitution is deferred until _____. An **Amended Judgment in a Criminal Case** (A0 245C) will be entered after such determination.

☐ The defendant must make restitution (including community restitution) to the following payees in the amount listed below.

If the defendant makes a partial payment, each payee shall receive an approximately proportioned payment, unless specified otherwise in the priority order or percentage payment column below. However, pursuant to 18 U.S.C. § 3664(i), all nonfederal victims must be paid before the United States is paid.

Name of Payee	Total Loss*	Restitution Ordered	Priority or Percentage

TOTALS $ _____ 0.00 $ _____ 0.00

☐ Restitution amount ordered pursuant to plea agreement $ _____

☐ The defendant must pay interest on restitution and a fine of more than $2,500, unless the restitution or fine is paid in full before the fifteenth day after the date of the judgment, pursuant to 18 U.S.C. § 3612(f). All of the payment options on Sheet 6 may be subject to penalties for delinquency and default, pursuant to 18 U.S.C. § 3612(g).

☑ The court determined that the defendant does not have the ability to pay interest and it is ordered that:

☑ the interest requirement is waived for the ☑ fine ☐ restitution.

☐ the interest requirement for the ☐ fine ☐ restitution is modified as follows:

*Findings for the total amount of losses are required under Chapters 109A, 110,11OA, and 113 A of Title 18 for offenses committed on or after September 13, 1994, but before April 23, 1996.

DEFENDANT: I. LEWIS LIBBY
CASE NUMBER: CR 05-394

SCHEDULE OF PAYMENTS

Having assessed the defendant's ability to pay, payment of the total criminal monetary penalties are due as follows:

A ☐ Lump sum payment of $ _____ due immediately, balance due

☐ not later than _____, or
☐ in accordance ☐ C, ☐ D, ☐ E, or ☐ F below; or

B ☐ Payment to begin immediately (may be combined with ☐ C, ☐ D, or ☐ F below); or

C ☐ Payment in equal _____ (e.g., weekly, monthly, quarterly) installments of $ _____ over a period of _____ (e.g., months or years), to commence _____ (e.g., 30 or 60 days) after the date of this judgment; or

D ☐ Payment in equal _____ (e.g., weekly, monthly, quarterly) installments of $ _____ over a period of _____ (e.g., months or years), to commence _____ (e.g., 30 or 60 days) after release from imprisonment to a term of supervision; or

E ☐ Payment during the term of supervised release will commence within _____ (e.g., 30 or 60 days) after release from imprisonment. The court will set the payment plan based on an assessment of the defendant's ability to pay at that time; or

F ☑ Special instructions regarding the payment of criminal monetary penalties:

Special Assessment of 100.00 on Count 1; 100.00 on Count 2, 100.00 on Count 4 and 100.00 on Count 5 making a total of $400.00 which was due 30 days from the original 6/5/07 sentencing date. The payment of the special assessment and the fine are due immediately.

Unless the court has expressly ordered otherwise, if this judgment imposes imprisonment, payment of criminal monetary penalties is due during imprisonment. All criminal monetary penalties, except those payments made through the Federal Bureau of Prisons' Inmate Financial Responsibility Program, are made to the clerk of the court.

The defendant shall receive credit for all payments previously made toward any criminal monetary penalties imposed.

☐ Joint and Several

Defendant and Co-Defendant Names and Case Numbers (including defendant number), Total Amount, Joint and Several Amount, and corresponding payee, if appropriate.

☐ The defendant shall pay the cost of prosecution.

☐ The defendant shall pay the following court cost(s):

☐ The defendant shall forfeit the defendant's interest in the following property to the United States:

Payments shall be applied in the following order: (1) assessment, (2) restitution principal, (3) restitution interest, (4) fine principal, (5) fine interest, (6) community restitution, (7) penalties, and (8) costs, including cost of prosecution and court costs.

STATE OF NORTH CAROLINA

WAKE COUNTY

BEFORE THE
DISCIPLINARY HEARING COMMISSION
OF THE
NORTH CAROLINA STATE BAR
06 DHC 35

THE NORTH CAROLINA STATE BAR,

Plaintiff,

v.

MICHAEL B. NIFONG, Attorney,

Defendant.

AMENDED FINDINGS OF FACT,
CONCLUSIONS OF LAW AND
ORDER OF DISCIPLINE

The Hearing Committee on its own motion pursuant to Rule of Civil Procedure 60(a) enters the following Amended Findings of Fact, Conclusions of Law and Order of Discipline in order to correct a factual mistake in Findings of Fact Paragraph 43 of its original Order in this cause, and to add an additional Conclusion of Law (b):

A hearing in this matter was conducted on June 12 through June 16, 2007, before a Hearing Committee composed of F. Lane Williamson, Chair, and members Sharon B. Alexander and R. Mitchel Tyler. Plaintiff, the North Carolina State Bar, was represented by Katherine E. Jean, Douglas J. Brocker, and Carmen K. Hoyme. Defendant, Michael B. Nifong, was represented by attorneys David B. Freedman and Dudley A. Witt. Based upon the admissions contained in the pleadings and upon the evidence presented at the hearing, this Hearing Committee makes, by clear, cogent and convincing evidence, the following

FINDINGS OF FACT

1. Plaintiff, the North Carolina State Bar, is a body duly organized under the laws of North Carolina and is the proper party to bring this proceeding under the authority granted it in Chapter 84 of the General Statutes of North Carolina, and the Rules and Regulations of the North Carolina State Bar (Chapter 1 of Title 27 of the North Carolina Administrative Code).

2. Defendant, Michael B. Nifong, (hereinafter "Nifong"), was admitted to the North Carolina State Bar on August 19, 1978, and is, and was at all times referred to herein, an attorney at law licensed to practice in North Carolina, subject to the laws of the State of North Carolina, the Rules and Regulations of the North Carolina State Bar and the Revised Rules of Professional Conduct.

3. During all times relevant to this complaint, Nifong actively engaged in the practice of law in the State of North Carolina as District Attorney for the Fourteenth Prosecutorial District in Durham County, North Carolina.

4. Nifong was appointed District Attorney in 2005. In late March 2006, Nifong was engaged in a highly-contested political campaign to retain his office.

5. In the early morning hours of March 14, 2006, an exotic dancer named Crystal Mangum reported that she had been raped by three men during a party at 610 North Buchanan Boulevard in Durham. Ms. Mangum asserted that she had been vaginally, rectally, and orally penetrated with no condom used during the assault and with at least some of the alleged perpetrators ejaculating.

6. Various pieces of evidence were collected for later DNA testing, including evidence commonly referred to as a "rape kit," which contained cheek scrapings, oral, vaginal, and rectal swabs, a pubic hair combing, and a pair of Ms. Mangum's underwear.

7. The Durham Police Department (DPD) initiated an investigation in what would come to be known as "the Duke Lacrosse case" and executed a search warrant on the house at 610 North Buchanan Boulevard on March 16, 2006. The investigation revealed that the residents of 610 North Buchanan were captains of the Duke University lacrosse team, and that a majority of the other attendees at the March 13, 2006, party were members of the team.

8. On March 16, 2006, the three residents of 610 North Buchanan voluntarily assisted DPD in executing a search warrant at their residence. During the search, numerous pieces of evidence were seized for later testing. The three residents also provided voluntary statements and voluntarily submitted DNA samples for comparison testing purposes. One of the three residents was David Evans, who was later indicted for the alleged attack on Ms. Mangum.

9. On March 22, 2006, Nifong's office assisted a DPD investigator in obtaining a Nontestimonial Identification Order (NTO) to compel the suspects in the case to be photographed and to provide DNA samples.

10. On March 23, 2006, DNA samples from all 46 Caucasian members of the Duke University 2006 Men's Lacrosse Team were obtained pursuant to the NTO.

11. When Nifong learned of the case on March 24, 2006, he immediately recognized that the case would garner significant media attention and decided to handle the case himself, rather than having it handled by the assistant district attorney in his office who would ordinarily handle such cases.

12. On March 24, 2006, Nifong informed DPD that he was assuming primary responsibility for prosecuting any criminal charges resulting from the investigation and directed the DPD to go through him for direction as to the conduct of the factual investigation of those matters.

13. On March 27, 2006, the rape kit items and DNA samples from the lacrosse players were delivered to the State Bureau of Investigation (SBI) lab for testing and examination, including DNA testing.

14. On March 27, 2006, Nifong was briefed by Sergeant Gottlieb and Investigator Himan of the DPD about the status of the investigation to date. Gottlieb and Himan discussed with Nifong a number of weaknesses in the case, including that Ms. Mangum had made inconsistent statements to the police and had changed her story several times, that the other dancer who was present at the party during the alleged attack disputed Ms. Mangum's story of an alleged assault, that Ms. Mangum had already viewed two photo arrays and had not identified any alleged attackers, and that the three team captains had voluntarily cooperated with police and had denied that the alleged attack occurred.

15. During or within a few days of the initial briefing by Gottlieb and Himan, Nifong acknowledged to Gottlieb and Himan that the Duke Lacrosse case would be a very hard case to win in court and said "you know, we're fucked."

16. Beginning on March 27, within hours after he received the initial briefing from Gottlieb and Himan, Nifong made public comments and statements to representatives of the news media about the Duke Lacrosse case and participated in interviews with various newspapers and television stations and other representatives of news media.

17. Between March 27 and March 31, Nifong stated to a reporter for WRAL TV news that lacrosse team members denied the rape accusations, that team members admitted that there was underage drinking at the party, and that otherwise team members were not cooperating with authorities.

18. Between March 27 and March 31, 2006, Nifong stated to a reporter for ABC 11 TV News that he might also consider charging other players for not coming forward with information, stating "[m]y guess is that some of this stonewall of silence that we have seen may tend to crumble once charges start to come out."

19. Between March 27 and March 31, 2006, Nifong stated to a reporter for the New York Times, "There are three people who went into the bathroom with the young lady, and whether the other people there knew what was going on at the time, they do now and have not come forward. I'm disappointed that no one has been enough of a man to come forward. And if they would have spoken up at the time, this may never have happened."

20. Between March 27 and March 31, 2006, Nifong stated to a reporter for NBC 17 News that the lacrosse team members were standing together and refusing to talk with investigators and that he might bring aiding-and-abetting charges against some of the players who were not cooperating with the investigation.

21. Between March 27 and March 31, 2006, Nifong stated to a reporter for the Durham Herald Sun newspaper that lacrosse players still refused to speak with investigators.

22. Between March 27 and March 31, 2006, Nifong made the following statements to Rene Syler of CBS News: "The lacrosse team, clearly, has not been fully cooperative" in the investigation; "The university, I believe, has done pretty much everything that they can under the circumstances. They, obviously, don't have a lot of control over whether or not the lacrosse team members actually speak to the police. I think that their silence is as a result of advice with counsel"; "If it's not the way it's been reported, then why are they so unwilling to tell us what, in their words, did take place that night?"; that he believed a crime occurred; that "the guilty will stand trial"; and "There's no doubt a sexual assault took place."

23. Between March 27 and March 31, 2006, Nifong made the following statements to a reporter for NBC 17 TV News: "The information that I have does lead me to conclude that a rape did occur"; "I'm making a statement to the Durham community and, as a citizen of Durham, I am making a statement for the Durham community. This is not the kind of activity we condone, and it must be dealt with quickly and harshly"; "The circumstances of the rape indicated a deep racial motivation for some of the things that were done. It makes a crime that is by its nature one of the most offensive and invasive even more so"; and "This is not a case of people drinking and it getting out of hand from that. This is something much, much beyond that."

24. Between March 27 and March 31, 2006, Nifong stated to a reporter for ESPN, "And one would wonder why one needs an attorney if one was not charged and had not done anything wrong."

25. Between March 27 and March 31, 2006, Nifong stated to reporter for CBS News that "the investigation at that time was certainly consistent with a sexual assault having taken place, as was the victim's demeanor at the time of the examination."

26. Between March 27 and March 31, 2006, Nifong made the following statements to a reporter for MSNBC: "There is evidence of trauma in the victim's vaginal area that was noted when she was examined by a nurse at the hospital"; "her general demeanor was suggested—suggestive of the fact that she had been through a traumatic situation"; "I am convinced there was a rape, yes, sir"; and "The circumstances of the case are not suggestive of the alternate explanation that has been suggested by some of the members of the situation."

27. Between March 27 and March 31, 2006, Nifong stated to a reporter for the Raleigh News and Observer newspaper, "I am satisfied that she was sexually assaulted at this residence."

28. Between March 27 and March 31, 2006, Nifong stated to a reporter for the USA Today newspaper, "Somebody's wrong about that sexual assault. Either I'm wrong, or they're not telling the truth about it."

29. Between March 27 and March 31, 2006, Nifong made the following statements to a reporter for ABC 11 TV News: "I don't think you can classify anything about what went on as a prank that got out of hand or drinking that took place by people who are underage"; "In this case, where you have the act of rape—essentially a gang rape—is bad enough in and of itself, but when it's made with racial epithets against the victim, I mean, it's just absolutely unconscionable"; and "The contempt that was shown for the victim, based on her race was totally abhorrent. It adds another layer of reprehensibleness, to a crime that is already reprehensible."

30. Between March 27 and March 31, 2006, Nifong stated to a reporter for ABC News, "It is a case that talks about what this community stands for."

31. Between March 27 and March 31, 2006, Nifong stated to a reporter for the New York Times, "The thing that most of us found so abhorrent, and the reason I decided to take it over myself, was the combination gang-like rape activity accompanied by the racial slurs and general racial hostility."

32. Between March 27 and March 31, 2006, Nifong stated to a reporter for CBS News, "The racial slurs involved are relevant to show the mindset . . . involved in this particular attack" and "obviously, it made what is already an extremely reprehensible act even more reprehensible."

33. Between March 27 and March 31, 2006, Nifong stated to a reporter for WRAL TV News, "What happened here was one of the worst things that's happened since I have become district attorney" and "[w]hen I look at what happened, I was appalled. I think that most people in this community are appalled."

34. On or after March 27, 2006, Nifong stated to a reporter for the Charlotte Observer newspaper, "I would not be surprised if condoms were used. Probably an exotic dancer would not be your first choice for unprotected sex."

35. On or about March 29, 2006, Nifong stated during an interview with a reporter for CNN that "[i]t just seems like a shame that they are not willing to violate this seeming sacred sense of loyalty to team for loyalty to community."

36. On March 30, 2006, the SBI notified Nifong that the SBI had examined the items from the rape kit and was unable to find any semen, blood, or saliva on any of those items.

37. On March 31, 2006, Nifong stated to a reporter for MSNBC, "Somebody had an arm around her like this, which she then had to struggle with in order to be able to breathe . . . She was struggling just to be able to breathe" and "[i]f a condom were used, then we might expect that there would not be any DNA evidence recovered from say a vaginal swab."

38. In March or April, 2006, Nifong stated to a representative of the news media that a rape examination of Ms. Mangum done at Duke Medical Center the morning of the alleged attack revealed evidence of bruising consistent with a brutal sexual assault, "with the most likely place it happened at the lacrosse team party."

39. In April 2006, Nifong stated to a reporter for Newsweek Magazine that the police took Ms. Mangum to a hospital where a nurse concluded that she had suffered injuries consistent with a sexual assault.

40. In April 2006, Nifong stated to a reporter for the Raleigh News and Observer newspaper, "I would like to think that somebody [not involved in the attack] has the human decency to call up and say, 'What am I doing covering up for a bunch of hooligans?'"

41. In April 2006, Nifong stated to a reporter, "They don't want to admit to the enormity of what they have done."

42. In an April 2006 conversation with a representative of the Raleigh News and Observer newspaper, Nifong compared the alleged rape to the quadruple homicide at Alpine Road Townhouse and multiple cross burnings that outraged the city of Durham in 2005 and stated "I'm not going to let Durham's view in the minds of the world to be a bunch of lacrosse players from Duke raping a black girl in Durham."

43. On April 4, 2006, DPD conducted a photographic identification procedure in which photographs of 46 members of the Duke Lacrosse team were shown to Ms. Mangum. Ms. Mangum was told at the beginning of the procedure that DPD had reason to believe all 46 of the men depicted in the photographs she would view were present at the party at which she contended the attack had occurred. The procedure followed in this photographic identification procedure was conceived and/or approved by Nifong. During the photographic identification procedure, Ms. Mangum identified Collin Finnerty and Reade Seligman as her attackers with "100% certainty" and identified David Evans as one of her attackers with "90% certainty." Ms. Mangum had previously viewed photographic identification procedures which included photographs of Reade Seligman and David Evans and not identified either of them in the prior procedures.

44. On April 5, 2006, Nifong's office sought and obtained an Order permitting transfer of the rape kit items from the SBI to a private company called DNA Security, Inc. ("DSI") for more sensitive DNA testing than the SBI could perform. The reference DNA specimens obtained from the lacrosse players pursuant to the NTO were also transferred to DSI for testing, as were reference specimens from several other individuals with whom Ms. Mangum acknowledged having consensual sexual relations, including her boyfriend.

45. As justification for its Order permitting transfer of the evidence to DSI, the Court noted that the additional testing Nifong's office sought in its petition was "believed to be material and relevant to this investigation, and that any male cells found among the victim's swabs from the rape kit can be evidence of an assault and may lead to the identification of the perpetrator."

46. Between April 7 and April 10, 2006, DSI performed testing and analysis of DNA found on the rape kit items. Between April 7 and April 10, DSI found DNA from up to four different males on several items of evidence from the rape kit and found that the male DNA on the rape kit items was inconsistent with the profiles of the lacrosse team members.

47.   During a meeting on April 10, 2006 among Nifong, two DPD officers and Dr. Brian Meehan, lab director for DSI, Dr. Meehan discussed with Nifong the results of the analyses performed by DSI to that point and explained that DSI had found DNA from up to four different males on several items of evidence from the rape kit and that the DNA on the rape kit items was inconsistent with the profiles of all lacrosse team members.

48.   The evidence and information referred to above in paragraphs 46 and 47 was evidence or information which tended to negate the guilt of the lacrosse team members identified as suspects in the NTO.

49.   After the April 10, 2006 meeting with Dr. Meehan, Nifong stated to a reporter for ABC 11 TV News that DNA testing other than that performed by the SBI had not yet come back and that there was other evidence, including the accuser being able to identify at least one of the alleged attackers.

50.   While discussing DNA testing at a public forum at North Carolina Central University on April 11, 2006, in the presence of representatives of the news media, Nifong stated that if there was no DNA found "[i]t doesn't mean nothing happened. It just means nothing was left behind."

51.   On April 17, 2006, Nifong sought and obtained indictments against Collin Finnerty and Reade Seligman for first-degree rape, first-degree sex offense, and kidnapping. (The indicted members of the Duke lacrosse team are referred to collectively herein as "the Duke Defendants").

52.   Before April 17, 2006, Nifong refused offers from counsel for David Evans, who was eventually indicted, to consider evidence and information that they contended either provided an alibi or otherwise demonstrated that their client did not commit any crime.

53.   On April 19, 2006, two days after being indicted, Duke Defendant Reade Seligman through counsel served Nifong with a request or motion for discovery material, including, **inter alia,** witness statements, the results of any tests, all DNA analysis, and any exculpatory information.

54.   By April 20, 2006, DSI had performed additional DNA testing and analysis and found DNA from multiple males on at least one additional piece of evidence from the rape kit.

55.   By April 20, 2006, from its testing and analysis, DSI had determined that all the lacrosse players, including the two who had already been indicted, were scientifically excluded as possible contributors of the DNA from multiple males found on several evidence items from the rape kit.

56.   On April 21, 2006, Nifong again met with Dr. Meehan and the two DPD officers to discuss all of the results of the DNA testing and analyses performed by DSI to date. During this meeting, Dr. Meehan told Nifong that: (a) DNA from multiple males had been found on several items from the rape kit, and (b) all of the lacrosse players, including the two players against whom Nifong had already sought and obtained indictments, were excluded as possible contributors of this DNA because none of their DNA profiles matched or were consistent with any of the DNA found on the rape kit items.

57.   The evidence and information referred to above in paragraphs 54 through 56 was evidence or information which tended to negate the guilt of the Duke Defendants.

58.   At the April 21 meeting, Dr. Meehan told Nifong that DSI's testing had revealed DNA on two fingernail specimens that were incomplete but were consistent with the DNA profiles of two un-indicted lacrosse players, including DNA on a fingernail found in David Evans' garbage can which was incomplete but which was consistent with David Evans' DNA profile, and DNA from the vaginal swab that was consistent with the DNA profile of Ms. Mangum's boyfriend.

59.   During the April 21, 2006 meeting, Nifong notified Dr. Meehan that he would require a written report to be produced concerning DSI's testing that reflected the matches found between DNA on evidence items and known reference specimens. Nifong told Dr. Meehan he would let Dr. Meehan know when he needed the report.

60.   Sometime between April 21 and May 12, Nifong notified Dr. Meehan that he would need for him to prepare the written report for an upcoming court proceeding. As requested by Nifong, Dr. Meehan prepared a report that reflected the matches found by DSI between DNA found on evidence items and known reference specimens. This written report did not reflect that DSI had found DNA on rape kit items from multiple males who had not provided reference specimens for comparison ("multiple unidentified males") and did not reflect that all 46 members of the lacrosse team had been scientifically excluded as possible contributors of the male DNA on the rape kit items.

61.   In May, 2006, Nifong made the following statements to a reporter for WRAL TV News: "My guess is that there are many questions that many people are asking that they would not be asking if they saw the results"; "They're not things that the defense releases unless they unquestionably support their positions"; and "So, the fact that they're making statements about what the reports are saying, and not actually showing the reports, should in and of itself raise some red flags."

62.   On or before April 18, 2006, Nifong stated to a reporter for Newsweek Magazine that the victim's "impaired state was not necessarily voluntary . . . [I]f I had a witness who saw her right before this and she was not intoxicated, and then I had a witness who said that she was given a drink at the party and after taking a few sips of that drink acted in a particular way, that could be evidence of something other than intoxication, or at least other than voluntary intoxication?"

63.   On May 12, 2006, Nifong again met with Dr. Meehan and two DPD officers and discussed the results of DSI's testing to date. During that meeting, consistent with Nifong's prior request, Dr. Meehan provided Nifong a 10-page written report which set forth the results of DNA tests on only the three evidence specimens that contained DNA consistent with DNA profiles from several known reference specimens. The three items in DSI's written report concerned DNA profiles on two fingernail specimens that were incomplete but were consistent with the DNA profiles of two unindicted lacrosse players, including DNA on a fingernail found in

David Evans' garbage can which was incomplete but was consistent with David Evans' DNA profile, and DNA from the vaginal swab that was consistent with the DNA profile of Ms. Mangum's boyfriend. DSI's written report did not disclose the existence of any of the multiple unidentified male DNA found on the rape kit items, although it did list the evidence items on which the unidentified DNA had been discovered.

64.   Nifong personally received DSI's written report from Dr. Meehan on May 12, 2006, and later that day provided it to counsel for the two Duke Defendants who had been indicted and for David Evans, among others.

65.   When he received DSI's written report and provided it to counsel for the Duke Defendants, Nifong was fully aware of the test results that were omitted from the written report, including the test results revealing the existence of DNA from multiple unidentified males on rape kit items.

66.   Three days later, on May 15, 2006, Nifong sought and obtained an indictment against David Evans for first-degree rape, first-degree sex offense, and kidnapping.

67.   On May 17, Duke Defendant Collin Finnerty served discovery requests on Nifong, which specifically asked that any expert witness "prepare, and furnish to the defendant, a report of the results of **any** (not only the ones about which the expert expects to testify) examinations or tests conducted by the expert."

68.   On May 18, 2006, Nifong provided various discovery materials to all three Duke Defendants, including another copy of DSI's written report, in connection with a hearing in the case on that same day. The discovery materials Nifong provided on May 18 did not include any underlying data or information concerning DSI's testing and analysis. The materials Nifong provided also did not include any documentation or information indicating the presence of DNA from multiple unidentified males on the rape kit items. Nifong also did not provide in the discovery materials any written or recorded memorialization of the substance of Dr. Meehan's oral statements made during his meetings with Nifong in April and May 2006 concerning the results of all DSI's tests and examinations, including the existence of DNA from multiple unidentified males on the rape kit items ("memorializations of Dr. Meehan's oral statements").

69.   DSI's tests and examinations revealing the existence of DNA from multiple unidentified males on rape kit items and Dr. Meehan's oral statements regarding the existence of that DNA were evidence that tended to negate the guilt of the accused; Collin Finnerty, Reade Seligman and David Evans.

70.   Accompanying the discovery materials, Nifong served and filed with the Court written responses to the Duke Defendants' discovery requests. In these responses, Nifong stated: "The State is not aware of any additional material or information which may be exculpatory in nature with respect to the Defendant." In his written discovery responses, Nifong also identified Dr. Meehan and R.W. Scales, another person at DSI, as expert witnesses reasonably expected to testify at the trial of the underlying criminal cases pursuant to N.C. Gen. Stat. § 15A-903(a)(2). Nifong also gave notice in the written discovery responses of the State's intent to introduce scientific data accompanied by expert testimony. Nifong represented in the written discovery responses that all of the reports of those experts had been provided to the Duke Defendants.

71.   At the time he made these representations to the Court and to the Duke Defendants in his written discovery responses, Nifong was aware of the existence of DNA from multiple unidentified males on the rape kits items, was aware that DSI's written report did not reveal the existence of this evidence, and was aware that he had not provided the Duke Defendants with memorializations of Dr. Meehan's oral statements regarding the existence of this evidence.

72.   The representations contained in Nifong's May 18 written discovery responses were intentional misrepresentations and intentional false statements of material fact to opposing counsel and to the Court.

73.   At the May 18, 2006 hearing, the Honorable Ronald Stephens, Superior Court Judge presiding, asked Nifong if he had provided the Duke Defendants all discovery materials.

74.   In response to Judge Stephens' inquiry, Nifong stated: "I've turned over everything I have."

75.   Nifong's response to Judge Stephens' question was a misrepresentation and a false statement of material fact.

76.   On June 19, 2006, Nifong issued a press release to representatives of the news media stating, "None of the 'facts' I know at this time, indeed, none of the evidence I have seen from any source, has changed the opinion that I expressed initially."

77.   On June 19, 2006, counsel for the Duke Defendants requested various materials from Nifong, including a report or written statement of the meeting between Nifong and Dr. Meehan to discuss the DNA test results. This request was addressed at a hearing before Judge Stephens on June 22, 2006.

78.   In response to the Duke Defendants' June 19 discovery request and in response to Judge Stephens' direct inquiry, Nifong stated in open court that, other than what was contained in DSI's written report, all of his communications with Dr. Meehan were privileged "work product." Nifong represented to Judge Stephens, "That's pretty much correct, your Honor. We received the reports, which [defense counsel] has received, and we talked about how we would likely use that, and that's what we did."

79.   At the time Nifong made these representations to Judge Stephens on June 22, Nifong knew that he had discussed with Dr. Meehan on three occasions the existence of DNA from multiple unidentified males on the rape kits items, which evidence was not disclosed in DSI's written report, and knew that Dr. Meehan's statements to him revealing the existence of DNA from multiple unidentified males on the rape kits items were not privileged work product.

80.   Nifong's representations to Judge Stephens at the June 22 hearing were intentional misrepresentations and intentional false statements of material fact to the Court and to opposing counsel.

81.   During the June 22 hearing, Judge Stephens entered an Order directing Nifong to provide Collin Finnerty and later all the Duke Defendants with, among other things, "results of tests and examinations, or any other matter or evidence obtained during

the investigation of the offenses alleged to have been committed by the defendant" and statements of any witnesses taken during the investigation, with oral statements to be reduced to written or recorded form.

82.   Nifong did not provide the Duke Defendants with "results of tests and examinations, or any other matter or evidence obtained during the investigation of the offenses alleged to have been committed by the defendant" and did not provide the Duke Defendants with statements of any witnesses taken during the investigation, with oral statements reduced to written or recorded form.

83.   Nifong did not comply with Judge Stephens' June 22 Order.

84.   On August 31, 2006, the Duke Defendants collectively filed a Joint Omnibus Motion to Compel Discovery seeking, among other things, the complete file and all underlying data regarding DSI's work and the substance of any discoverable comments made by Dr. Meehan during his meetings with Nifong and two DPD officers on April 10, April 21, and May 12, 2006. The Joint Omnibus Motion was addressed by the Honorable Osmond W. Smith III, Superior Court Judge presiding, at a hearing on September 22, 2006.

85.   At the September 22 hearing, counsel for the Duke Defendants specifically stated in open court that the Duke Defendants were seeking the results of any tests finding any additional DNA on Ms. Mangum even if it did not match any of the Duke Defendants or other individuals for whom the State had provided reference DNA specimens for comparison.

86.   In response to a direct question from Judge Smith, Nifong represented that DSI's written report encompassed all tests performed by DSI and everything discussed at his meetings with Dr. Meehan in April and May 2006. The following exchange occurred immediately thereafter on the Duke Defendants' request for memorializations of Dr. Meehan's oral statements:

> Judge Smith: "So you represent there are no other statements from Dr. Meehan?"
> Mr. Nifong: "No other statements. No other statements made to me."

87.   At the time Nifong made these representations to Judge Smith, he was aware that Dr. Meehan had told him in their meetings about the existence of DNA from multiple unidentified males on the rape kit items, was aware that he had not provided the Duke Defendants with a written or recorded memorialization of Dr. Meehan's statements and was aware that the existence of that DNA was not revealed in DSI's written report.

88.   Nifong's statements and responses to Judge Smith at the September 22 hearing were intentional misrepresentations and intentional false statements of material fact to the Court and to opposing counsel.

89.   On September 22, Judge Smith ordered Nifong to provide the Duke Defendants the complete files and underlying data from both the SBI and DSI by October 20, 2006.

90.   On October 19, 2006 counsel for David Evans faxed to Nifong a proposed order reflecting Judge Smith's September 22 ruling. The proposed order stated, in paragraph 4, "Regarding the defendants' request for a report of statements made by Dr. Brian Meehan of DNA Security, Inc., during two separate meetings among Dr. Meehan, District Attorney Mike Nifong, Sgt. Mark Gottlieb, and Inv. Benjamin Himan in April 2006 . . . Mr. Nifong represented that those meetings involved the State's request for YSTR testing, Dr. Meehan's report of the results of those tests, and a discussion of how the State intended to use those results in the course of the trial of these matters. Mr. Nifong indicated that he did not discuss the facts of the case with Dr. Meehan and that Dr. Meehan said nothing during those meetings beyond what was encompassed in the final report of DNA Security, dated May 12, 2006. The Court accepted Mr. Nifong's representation about those meetings and held that there were no additional discoverable statements by Dr. Meehan for the State to produce."

91.   On October 24, 2006, Nifong responded by letter to defense counsel's October 19, 2006 letter and proposed order. In his response, Nifong identified two changes he believed were appropriate to two portions of the proposed order, made no mention of any changes he believed were appropriate to paragraph 4, and said "the proposed order seems satisfactory" and "it seems to reflect with acceptable accuracy the rulings of Judge Smith on September 22."

92.   On October 27, 2006, Nifong provided 1,844 pages of underlying documents and materials from DSI to the Duke Defendants pursuant to the Court's September 22, 2006 Order but did not provide the Duke Defendants a complete written report from DSI setting forth the results of all of its tests and examinations, including the existence of DNA from multiple unidentified males on the rape kit items, and did not provide the Duke Defendants with any written or recorded memorializations of Dr. Meehan's oral statements.

93.   After reviewing the underlying data provided to them on October 27 for between 60 and 100 hours, counsel for the Duke Defendants determined that DSI's written report did not include the results of all DNA tests performed by DSI and determined that DSI had found DNA from multiple unidentified males on the rape kit items and that such results were not included in DSI's written report.

94.   On December 13, 2006, the Duke Defendants filed a Motion to Compel Discovery: Expert DNA Analysis, detailing their discovery of the existence of DNA from multiple unidentified males on the rape kit items and explaining that this evidence had not been included DSI's written report. The motion did not allege any attempt or agreement to conceal the potentially exculpatory DNA evidence or test results. The Motion to Compel Discovery: Expert DNA Analysis was addressed by the Honorable Osmond W. Smith III, Superior Court Judge presiding, at a hearing on December 15, 2006.

95.   At the December 15 hearing, both in chambers and again in open court, Nifong stated or implied to Judge Smith that he was unaware of the existence of DNA from multiple unidentified males on the rape kit items until he received the December 13 motion and/or was unaware that the results of any DNA testing performed by DSI had been excluded from DSI's written report. Nifong stated to Judge Smith in open court: "The first I heard of this particular situation was when I was served with these reports—this motion on Wednesday of this week."

96. Nifong's representations that he was unaware of the existence of DNA from multiple unidentified males on the rape kit items and/or that he was unaware of the exclusion of such evidence from DSI's written report, were intentional misrepresentations and intentional false statements of material fact to the Court and to opposing counsel.

97. During the December 15 hearing, Dr. Meehan testified under oath to the following statements:

   a. he discussed with Nifong at the April 10, April 21, May 12 meetings the results of all tests conducted by DSI to date, including the potentially exculpatory DNA test results;

   b. he and Nifong discussed and agreed that "we would only disclose or show on our report those reference specimens that matched evidence items";

   c. DSI's report did not set forth the results of all tests and examinations DSI conducted in the case but was limited to only some results;

   d. the limited report was the result of "an intentional limitation" arrived at between him and Nifong "not to report on the results of all examinations and tests" that DSI performed;

   e. the failure to provide all test and examination results purportedly was based on privacy concerns; and

   f. he would have prepared a report setting forth the results of all DSI's tests and examinations if he had been requested to do so by Nifong or other representatives of the State of North Carolina at any time after May 12.

98. Immediately after the December 15 hearing, Nifong stated to a representative of the news media: "And we were trying to, just as Dr. Meehan said, trying to avoid dragging any names through the mud but at the same time his report made it clear that all the information was available if they wanted it and they have every word of it."

99. On January 12, 2007, Nifong recused himself from the prosecution of the Duke Defendants.

100. On January 13, 2007, the Attorney General of North Carolina took over the Duke Lacrosse case and began to review evidence and undertake further investigation.

101. After an intensive review of the evidence, the Attorney General concluded that Ms. Mangum's credibility was suspect, her various inconsistent allegations were incredible and were contradicted by other evidence in the case, and that credible and verifiable evidence demonstrated that the Duke Defendants could not have participated in an attack during the time it was alleged to have occurred.

102. Based on its finding that no credible evidence supported the allegation that the crimes occurred, the Attorney General declared Reade Seligman, Collin Finnerty, and David Evans innocent of all charges in the Duke Lacrosse case. The cases against the Duke Defendants were dismissed on April 11, 2007.

103. Nifong had in his possession, no later than April 10, 2006, an oral report from Dr. Meehan of the reports of test results showing the existence of DNA from multiple unidentified males on rape kit items.

104. From at least May 12, 2006 through January 12, 2007, Nifong never provided the Duke Defendants a complete report setting forth the results of all examinations and tests conducted by DSI and never provided the Duke Defendants with memorializations of Dr. Meehan's oral statements concerning the results of all examinations and tests conducted by DSI in written, recorded or any other form.

105. On or about December 20, 2006, Nifong received a letter of notice and substance of grievance from the Grievance Committee of the North Carolina State Bar alleging that: (a) he failed to provide the Duke Defendants with evidence regarding the existence of DNA from multiple unidentified males on the rape kit items; (b) he agreed with Dr. Meehan not to provide those results; and (c) he falsely represented to the Court that he was unaware of these results or their omission from DSI's report prior to receiving the Duke Defendants' December 13 motion to compel discovery.

106. Nifong initially responded to the Grievance Committee in a letter dated December 28, 2006, and supplemented his initial response, at the request of State Bar counsel, in a letter dated January 16, 2007.

107. In his responses to the Grievance Committee, Nifong: (a) acknowledged that he had discussed with Dr. Meehan during meetings in April and May 2006 the results of all DSI's testing, including the existence of DNA from multiple unidentified males on the rape kit items; (b) denied that he had agreed with Dr. Meehan to exclude the potentially exculpatory DNA test results from DSI's report; (c) stated that he viewed the evidence of DNA from multiple unidentified males on the rape kit items as "non-inculpatory" rather than as "specifically exculpatory"; and (d) represented that the discussion and agreement with Dr. Meehan to limit the information in DSI's report was based on privacy concerns about releasing the names and DNA profiles of the lacrosse players and others providing known reference specimens.

108. DSI's written report listed DNA profiles for Ms. Mangum, Ms. Mangum's boyfriend, and David Evans and Kevin Coleman, two lacrosse players who had not been indicted at the time the report was released, and listed the names of all 50 persons who had contributed reference DNA specimens for comparison.

109. Nifong further represented in his responses to the Grievance Committee that he did not realize that the existence of DNA from multiple unidentified males on the rape kit items was not included in DSI's report when he provided it to the Duke Defendants or thereafter, until he received defense counsel's December 13 motion to compel.

110. Nifong's representation to the Grievance Committee that he did not realize that the existence of DNA from multiple unidentified males on the rape kit items was not included in DSI's report from May 12 until he received the December 13 motion to compel was a false statement of material fact made in connection with a disciplinary matter, and was made knowingly.

111. Nifong also represented in his responses to the Grievance Committee that, by stating to the Court at the beginning of the December 15 hearing that the motion was the "first [he] heard of this particular situation," he was referring not to the existence of DNA from multiple unidentified males on the rape kit items but to the Duke Defendants' purported allegation that he had made an intentional attempt to conceal such evidence from them.

112. Counsel for the Duke Defendants did not allege any intentional attempt by Nifong to conceal the DNA evidence from them in either their December 13 motion to compel or their remarks to the Court prior to Nifong's statement.

113. Nifong's responses to the Grievance Committee set forth in paragraph 111 concerning his representations to the Court at the December 15, 2006, hearing were false statements of material fact made in connection with a disciplinary matter, and were made knowingly.

114. Nifong was required by statute and by court order to disclose to the Duke Defendants that tests had been performed which revealed the existence of DNA from multiple unidentified males on the rape kit items.

115. Nifong knew or reasonably should have known that his statements to representatives of the news media set forth in paragraphs 17–35, 37–42, 49–50, 61–62, and 76 above would be disseminated by means of public communication.

116. Nifong knew or reasonably should have known that his statements to representatives of the news media set forth in paragraphs 17–35, 37–42, 49–50, 61–62, and 76 above had a substantial likelihood of prejudicing the criminal adjudicative proceeding.

117. Nifong knew or reasonably should have known that his statements to representatives of the news media set forth in paragraphs 17–35, 37–42, 49–50, 61–62, and 76 above had a substantial likelihood of heightening public condemnation of the accused.

Based upon the preceding FINDINGS OF FACT, the Hearing Committee makes the following

CONCLUSIONS OF LAW

(a) By making statements to representatives of the news media including but not limited to those set forth in paragraphs 17–35, 37–42, 49–50, 61–62, and 76, Nifong made extrajudicial statements he knew or reasonably should have known would be disseminated by means of public communication and would have a substantial likelihood of materially prejudicing an adjudicative proceeding in the matter, in violation of Rule 3.6(a), and made extrajudicial statements that had a substantial likelihood of heightening public condemnation of the accused, in violation of Rule 3.8(f) of the Revised Rules of Professional Conduct.

(b) By instructing Dr. Meehan to prepare a report containing positive matches, Nifong knowingly disobeyed an obligation under the rules of a tribunal in violation of Rule 3.4(c) of the Revised Rules of Professional Conduct.

(c) By not providing to the Duke Defendants prior to November 16, 2006, a complete report setting forth the results of all tests and examinations conducted by DSI, including the existence of DNA from multiple unidentified males on the rape kit items and including written or recorded memorializations of Dr. Meehan's oral statements, Nifong:

   i. did not make timely disclosure to the defense of all evidence or information known to him that tended to negate the guilt of the accused, in violation of former Rule 3.8(d) of the Revised Rules of Professional Conduct; and

   ii. failed to make a reasonably diligent effort to comply with a legally proper discovery request, in violation of former Rule 3.4(d) of the Revised Rules of Professional Conduct;

(d) By never providing the Duke Defendants on or after November 16, 2006, and prior to his recusal on January 12, 2007, a report setting forth the results of all tests or examinations conducted by DSI, including the existence of DNA from multiple unidentified males on the rape kit items and including written or recorded memorializations of Dr. Meehan's oral statements, Nifong:

   i. did not, after a reasonably diligent inquiry, make timely disclosure to the defense of all evidence or information required to be disclosed by applicable law, rules of procedure, or court opinions, including all evidence or information known to him that tended to negate the guilt of the accused, in violation of current Rule 3.8(d) of the Revised Rules of Professional Conduct; and

   ii. failed to disclose evidence or information that he knew, or reasonably should have known, was subject to disclosure under applicable law, rules of procedure or evidence, or court opinions, in violation of current Rule 3.4(d)(3) of the Revised Rules of Professional Conduct.

(e) By falsely representing to the Court and to counsel for the Duke Defendants that he had provided all discoverable material in his possession and that the substance of all Dr. Meehan's oral statements to him concerning the results of all examinations and tests conducted by DSI were included in DSI's written report, Nifong made false statements of material fact or law to a tribunal in violation of Rule 3.3(a)(1), made false statements of material fact to a third person in the course of representing a client in violation of Rule 4.1, and engaged in conduct involving dishonesty, fraud, deceit or misrepresentation in violation of Rule 8.4(c) of the Revised Rules of Professional Conduct.

(f) By representing or implying to the Court that he was not aware of the existence on rape kit items of DNA from multiple unidentified males who were not members of the lacrosse team and/or that he was not aware of the exclusion of that evidence from DSI's written report at the beginning of the December 15, 2006, hearing, Nifong made false statements of material fact or law to a tribunal in violation of Rule 3.3(a)(1) and engaged in conduct involving dishonesty, fraud, deceit or misrepresentation in violation of Rule 8.4(c) of the Revised Rules of Professional Conduct.

(g) By falsely representing to the Grievance Committee of the State Bar that: (i) he did not realize that the test results revealing the presence of DNA from multiple unidentified males on the rape kit items were not included in DSI's report when he provided it to the Duke Defendants or thereafter, and (ii) his statements to the Court at the beginning of the December 15 hearing referred not to the existence of DNA from multiple unidentified males on the rape kit items but to the Duke Defendants' purported allegation that he had engaged in an intentional attempt to conceal such evidence, Nifong made knowingly false statements of material fact in connection with a disciplinary matter in violation of Rule 8.1(a), and engaged in conduct involving dishonesty, fraud, deceit or misrepresentation in violation of Rule 8.4(c) of the Revised Rules of Professional Conduct.

(h) Each of the violations set forth above separately, and the pattern of conduct revealed when they are viewed together, constitutes conduct prejudicial to the administration of justice in violation of Rule 8.4(d) of the Revised Rules of Professional Conduct.

Based upon the foregoing findings of fact and conclusions of law, the Hearing Committee makes by clear, cogent, and convincing evidence, the following additional

FINDINGS OF FACT REGARDING DISCIPLINE

1. Nifong's misconduct is aggravated by the following factors:

    a. dishonest or selfish motive;
    b. a pattern of misconduct;
    c. multiple offenses;
    d. refusal to acknowledge wrongful nature of conduct in connection with his handling of the DNA evidence;
    e. vulnerability of the victims, Collin Finnerty, Reade Seligman and David Evans; and
    f. substantial experience in the practice of law.

2. Nifong's misconduct is mitigated by the following factors:

    a. absence of a prior disciplinary record; and
    b. good reputation.

3. The aggravating factors outweigh the mitigating factors.

4. Nifong's misconduct resulted in significant actual harm to Reade Seligman, Collin Finnerty, and David Evans and their families. Defendant's conduct was, at least, a major contributing factor in the exceptionally intense national and local media coverage the Duke Lacrosse case received and in the public condemnation heaped upon the Duke Defendants. As a result of Nifong's misconduct, these young men experienced heightened public scorn and loss of privacy while facing very serious criminal charges of which the Attorney General of North Carolina ultimately concluded they were innocent.

5. Nifong's misconduct resulted in significant actual harm to the legal profession. Nifong's conduct has created a perception among the public within and outside North Carolina that lawyers in general and prosecutors in particular cannot be trusted and can be expected to lie to the court and to opposing counsel. Nifong's dishonesty to the court and to his opposing counsel, fellow attorneys, harmed the profession. Attorneys have a duty to communicate honestly with the court and with each other. When attorneys do not do so, they engender distrust among fellow lawyers and from the public, thereby harming the profession as a whole.

6. Nifong's misconduct resulted in prejudice to and significant actual harm to the justice system. Nifong has caused a perception among the public within and outside North Carolina that there is a systemic problem in the North Carolina justice system and that a criminal defendant can only get justice if he or she can afford to hire an expensive lawyer with unlimited resources to figure out what is being withheld by the prosecutor.

7. Nifong's false statements to the Grievance Committee of the North Carolina State Bar interfered with the State Bar's ability to regulate attorneys and therefore undermined the privilege of lawyers in this State to remain self-regulating.

8. This Hearing Committee has considered all alternatives and finds that no discipline other than disbarment will adequately protect the public, the judicial system and the profession, given the clear demonstration of dishonest conduct, multiple violations, the pattern of dishonesty established by the evidence, and Nifong's failure to recognize or acknowledge the wrongfulness of his conduct with regard to withholding of the DNA evidence and making false representations to opposing counsel and to the Court. Furthermore, entry of an order imposing discipline less than disbarment would fail to acknowledge the seriousness of the offenses committed by Nifong and would send the wrong message to attorneys regarding the conduct expected of members of the Bar in this State.

Based upon the foregoing findings of fact, conclusions of law and additional findings of fact regarding discipline, the Hearing Committee hereby enters the following

ORDER OF DISCIPLINE

1. Michael B. Nifong is hereby DISBARRED from the practice of law.

2. Nifong shall surrender his law license and membership card to the Secretary of the State Bar no later than 30 days from service of this order upon him.

3. Nifong shall pay the costs of this proceeding as assessed by the Secretary of the N.C. State Bar, including DHC costs and including costs of the transcription and depositions taken in this case as follows: court reporter costs; videographer and video-taping costs; transcription costs; shipping, handling, and transmittal costs; and witness costs. Defendant must pay the costs within 90 days of service upon him of the statement of costs by the Secretary.

4. Nifong shall comply with all provisions of 27 NCAC IB § .0124 of the North Carolina State Bar Discipline & Disability Rules ("Discipline Rules").

Signed by the Chair with the consent of the other hearing committee members, this the 24th day of July, 2007.

F. Lane Williamson
Chair, Disciplinary Hearing Committee

NORTH CAROLINA
WAKE COUNTY

BEFORE THE
DISCIPLINARY HEARING COMMISSION
OF THE
NORTH CAROLINA STATE BAR
06 DHC 35

THE NORTH CAROLINA STATE BAR,)
)
Plaintiff,)
)
)
v.)   H E A R I N G
)
)
MICHAEL B. NIFONG, Attorney,)
)
Defendant.)

June 16, 2007
Excerpt Transcript
Findings of Fact and Conclusions of Law
Order of Discipline
Third Floor Courtroom
Court of Appeals Building
One West Morgan Street
Raleigh, North Carolina

HEARING PANEL:
CHAIRMAN: F. Lane Williamson
                    212 S. Tryon Street, Suite 930
                    Charlotte, North Carolina 28281
ATTORNEY MEMBER: Sharon B. Alexander
                    240 Third Avenue W.
                    Hendersonville, North Carolina 28739
PUBLIC MEMBER: R. Mitchel Tyler
                    Post Office Box 222
                    Lake Waccamaw, North Carolina 28450
                    CAROL WILLIAMS WOLFF
                    CERTIFIED VERBATIM REPORTER

APPEARANCES

FOR THE PLAINTIFF:
KATHERINE E. JEAN, COUNSEL
CARMEN K. HOYME, DEPUTY COUNSEL
THE NORTH CAROLINA STATE BAR
208 Fayetteville Street
Raleigh, North Carolina 27601
DOUGLAS J. BROCKER, ESQUIRE
THE BROCKER LAW FIRM, P.A.
5540 Centerview Drive, Suite 200
Raleigh, North Carolina 27606
FOR THE DEFENDANT ATTORNEY:
DAVID B. FREEDMAN, ESQUIRE
DUDLEY A. WITT, ESQUIRE
CRUMPLER, FREEDMAN, PARKER & WITT
301 N. Main Street, Suite 1100
Winston-Salem, North Carolina 27101-3899

FINDINGS OF FACT AND CONCLUSIONS OF LAW

THE CHAIRMAN: The Hearing Committee has deliberated and has reached a unanimous conclusion as to each of the contested issues that have been submitted by the parties.

What I'm going to do is to read each of the contested issues that are listed in the Pre-trial Order, and then to indicate "yes" or "no," and in some cases with some explanation, but generally without any further elaboration. We'll have further elaboration at the conclusion of Phase Two as to certain matters.

And bear in mind that there are 19 issues, some of which are duplicative and some of which reflect that there were amendments to the applicable rules during the period we are talking about, so that you'll hear what sounds like pretty much the same thing.

A "yes" will signify that we have found the issue to by proved by clear, cogent and convincing evidence, which is the standard of proof applicable to the Bar's allegation.

A "no" simply means that there has been a failure or an absence of proof to the standard of clear, cogent and convincing evidence.

The first issue reads as follows:

"Did Defendant make extrajudicial statements to or in the presence of representatives of the news media, including those set forth in paragraphs 12 through 177 of the Amended Complaint?" Yes.

Two: "Did Defendant know or should Defendant reasonably have known that his extrajudicial statements set forth in paragraphs 12 through 177 of the Amended Complaint would be disseminated by means of public communication?" Yes.

"Did Defendant know or should Defendant reasonably have known that his extrajudicial statements set forth in paragraphs 12 through 177 of the Amended Complaint would have a substantial likelihood of materially prejudicing an adjudicative proceeding in the matter in violation of Rule 3.6(a)?" Yes.

Four: "Did Defendant's extrajudicial statements set forth in paragraphs 12 through 177 of the Amended Complaint have a substantial likelihood of heightening public condemnation of the accused in violation of Rule 3.8(f) of the Revised Rules of Professional Conduct?" Yes, with this further note of explanation. It will be necessary for us to have a finding, I believe, that the accused in this instance includes the set of suspects, that being the lacrosse players that were at the house on the night in question. It is not necessary for us to make a finding as a legal matter that they were actually indicted or criminal defendants at the time.

Five: "By making misleading statements to or in the presence of representatives of the news media did Defendant engage in conduct involving dishonesty, fraud, deceit or misrepresentation in violation of Rule 8.4(c) of the Revised Rules of Professional Conduct?" No. A word of explanation there. The one statement at issue there involving whether or not condoms might be involved is to our mind no worse than certain others that were not alleged to involve dishonesty, fraud, deceit or misrepresentation in violation of Rule 8.4(c); for instance, the statement to the effect that the accused were not cooperating.

And since it was not alleged that those statements involved an 8.4(c) violation, we do not think it is appropriate to pick out this particular one and say that it is. Although we have the option as a matter of law of finding some of the other statements to also include a Rule 8.4(c) violation, we decline to do so.

Number Six: "Did Defendant by not providing to the Duke defendants prior to November 16, 2006, a complete report setting forth the results of all tests or examinations conducted by DSI, including the potentially exculpatory DNA test results and evidence, a, fail to make timely disclosure to the Defense of all evidence or information known to him that tended to negate the guilt of the accused in violation of former Rule 3.8(d) of the Revised Rules of Professional Conduct?" Yes. "B"—cell phones off—"B, failed to make a reasonably diligent effort to comply with a legally proper discovery request in violation of former Rule 3.4(d) of the Revised Rules of Professional Conduct?" Yes.

"Did Defendant by not providing to the Duke defendants prior to November 16, 2006, memorializations of Dr. Meehan's oral statements concerning the results of all examinations and tests conducted by DSI in written, recorded or any other form, a, fail to make timely disclosure to the Defense of all evidence or information known to him that tended to negate the guilt of the accused in violation of former Rule 3.8(d) of the Revised Rules of Professional Conduct?" The answer is yes, with the proviso that the way that issue number 7 is worded with the word "memorializations" tends to imply that the violation is premised on violation of the Discovery Statute, rather than 3.8(d). We think for purposes of issue 7a it may be more appropriate to call that "communication in any form of Dr. Meehan's oral statements," and not just say "memorializations." "B, 7b, failed to make a reasonably diligent effort to comply with a legally proper discovery request, in violation of former Rule 3.4(d) of the Revised Rules of Professional Conduct?" That answer is no, based upon the converse of the distinction in "a;" that is, to the extent that is based upon compliance with the Discovery Statue. At the time, there was evidence that the Attorney General took the position that prosecutors did not have to provide such memorializations, and therefore there is a plausible reliance by the Defendant upon that position at the time, which is no longer the law, of the Attorney General. And that is the basis for saying no to 7b.

Eight: "Did Defendant by not providing to the Duke defendants after November 16, 2006, a complete report setting forth the results of all tests or examinations conducted by DSI, including the potentially exculpatory DNA test results in evidence, a, fail after a reasonably diligent inquiry to make timely disclosure to the Defense of all evidence or information required to be disclosed by applicable law, rules of procedure or court opinions, including all evidence or information known to him that tended to negate the guilt of the accused in violation of current Rule 3.8(d) of the Revised Rules of Professional Conduct?" The answer is yes. "B, failed to disclose evidence or information that he knew or reasonably should have known was subject to disclosure under applicable law, rules of procedure or evidence or court opinions in violation of current Rule 3.4(d)(3) of the Revised Rules of Professional Conduct?" The answer is yes.

Nine: "Did Defendant not providing to the Duke defendants after November 16, 2006, memorializations of Dr. Meehan's oral statements concerning the results of all examinations and tests conducted by DSI in written, recorded or any other form, a, fail after a reasonably diligent inquiry to make timely disclosure to the Defense of all evidence or information required to be disclosed by applicable law, rules of procedure or court opinions, including all evidence or information known to him that tended to negate the guilt of the accused in violation of current Rule 3.8(d) of the Revised Rules of Professional Conduct?" The answer is yes. "B, failed to disclose evidence or information that he knew or reasonably should have known was subject to disclosure under applicable law, rules of procedure or evidence or court opinion in violation of current Rule 3.4(d)(3) of the Revised Rules of Professional Conduct?" The answer is yes.

Number Ten: "Did Defendant by instructing Dr. Meehan to prepare a report containing positive matches, a, knowingly disobey an obligation under the rules of a tribunal in violation of Rule 3.4(c) of the Revised Rules of Professional Conduct?" The answer is yes. "B, request a person other than a client to refrain from voluntarily giving relevant information to another party in violation of Rule 3.4(f) of the Revised Rules of Professional Conduct?" That answer is no.

Eleven: "Did Defendant by representing to the Court that he had provided all potentially exculpatory evidence, a, make false statements of material fact or law to a tribunal in violation of Rule 3.3(a)(1)?" The answer is yes. "B, engage in conduct involving dishonesty, fraud, deceit or misrepresentation in violation of Rule 8.4(c) of the Revised Rules of Professional Conduct?" The answer is yes.

Twelve: "Did Defendant by representing to opposing counsel that he had provided all potentially exculpatory evidence, a, make false statements of material fact to a third person in the course of representing a client in violation of Rule 4.1?" The answer is yes. "B, engage in conduct involving dishonesty, fraud, deceit or misrepresentation in violation of Rule 8.4(c) of the Revised Rules of Professional Conduct?" The answer is yes.

Thirteen: "Did Defendant by representing to the Court that the substance of all Dr. Meehan's oral statements to him concerning the results of all examinations and tests conducted by DSI were included in DSI's report, a, make false statements of material fact or law to a tribunal in violation of Rule 3.3(a)(1)?" The answer is yes. "B, engage in conduct involving dishonesty, fraud, deceit or misrepresentation in violation of Rule 8.4(c) of the Revised Rules of Professional Conduct?" The answer is yes.

Fourteen: "Did Defendant by representing to opposing counsel that the substance of all Dr. Meehan's oral statements to him concerning the results of all examinations and tests conducted by DSI were included in DSI's report, a, make false statements of material fact to a third person in the course of representing a client in violation of Rule 4.1?" Yes. "B, engage in conduct involving dishonesty, fraud, deceit or misrepresentation in violation of Rule 8.4(c) of the Revised Rules of Professional Conduct?" The answer is yes.

Fifteen: "Did Defendant by representing or implying to the Court at the beginning of the December 15, 2006, hearing that he was not aware of the potentially exculpatory DNA results or alternatively was not aware of their exclusion from DSI's report, a, make false statements of material fact or law to a tribunal in violation of Rule 3.3(a)(1)?" The answer is yes. "B, engage in conduct involving dishonesty, fraud, deceit or misrepresentation in violation of Rule 8.4(c) of the Revised Rules of Professional Conduct?" The answer is yes.

"Did Defendant by representing to the Grievance Committee of the State Bar that the agreement with Brian Meehan to limit the information in DSI's report was based on privacy concerns of releasing the names and DNA profiles of individuals providing known reference specimens, a, knowingly make a false statement of material fact in connection with a disciplinary matter in violation of Rule 8.1(a)?" The answer is no. "B, engage in conduct involving dishonesty, fraud, deceit or misrepresentation in violation of Rule 8.4(c)?" The answer is no.

Seventeen: "Did Defendant by representing to the Grievance Committee of The State Bar that he did not realize that the potentially exculpatory DNA test results were not included in DSI's report when he provided it to the Duke defendants or thereafter, a, knowingly make a false statement of material fact in connection with a disciplinary matter in violation of Rule 8.1(a)?" The answer is yes. "B, engage in conduct involving dishonesty, fraud, deceit or misrepresentation in violation of Rule 8.4(c)?" The answer is yes.

Eighteen: "Did Defendant by representing to the Grievance Committee of the State Bar that his statements to the Court at the beginning of the December 15 hearing referred not to the existence of the potentially exculpatory DNA test results but to the Duke defendants' purported allegation that an intentional attempt had been made to conceal such evidence, a, knowingly make false statements of a material fact in connection with a disciplinary matter in violation of Rule 8.1(a)?" The answer is yes. "B, engage in conduct involving dishonesty, fraud, deceit or misrepresentation in violation of Rule 8.4(c)?" The answer is yes.

Here I wish to note the consensus of the Hearing Committee in regard to those issues that I have just read involving misrepresentations by the Defendant in his response to the Grievance Committee, we have some concern that those charges more or less as a matter of policy are perhaps not warranted from the standpoint that we have concerns that it is very rare that persons are charged with making false statements to the Grievance Committee in their responses, and that if defendants are charged with that, it may have a chilling effect upon defendants or respondents making a full and complete disclosure to Grievance Committee complaints if they are afraid that, well, if you just disagree with what I tell you, and that if we go to trial and I lose, then by necessity I have misrepresented something to you, that is perhaps unwise as a matter of a policy. Nevertheless, it is alleged here, and we do find that in certain instances there were violations. But we would simply note that in this particular case it may be at least in our view something of an instance of overcharging.

Nineteen: "Did Defendant through one of more of the above violations engage in conduct prejudicial to the administration of justice in violation of Rule 8.4(d)?" The answer is yes.

At the conclusion of Phase Two, we will provide certain additional reasoning for our findings and overall conclusions and, of course, as to the discipline imposed.

Looking forward to the conclusion of the proceedings, what we will do is, as we normally do, ask Counsel for the State Bar to prepare a proposed written order for us and to provide that to the Defendant's counsel for their review and submission to us. And, of course, we may make and probably will make a number of changes to it.

I'm saying that now so we don't have to go over that again.

At this time we'll go into Phase Two.

(End of excerpt portion of transcript, Findings of Fact and Conclusions of Law.)

ORDER OF DISCIPLINE

THE CHAIRMAN: Thank you for your patience.

The Hearing Committee has deliberated, and we are in unanimous agreement that there is no discipline short of disbarment that would be appropriate in this case given the magnitude of the offenses that we have found and the effect upon the profession and the public.

I do want to make some remarks as to why we reached that conclusion.

This matter has been a fiasco. There is no doubt about it. It has been a fiasco for a number of people, starting with the defendants, and moving out from there to the justice system in general.

We've heard evidence over the last several days of how that came about, and we are lawyers and a school administrator. We're not psychologists. You have to ask yourself why, why did we get to the place that we got?

It seems that at the root of it is self-deception arising out of self-interest. Mark Twain said that "when a person cannot deceive himself, the chances are against his being able to deceive other people." And what we have here, it seems, is that we had a prosecutor who was faced with a very unusual situation, in which the confluence of his self-interest collided with a very volatile mix of race, sex and class, a situation that if it were applied in a John Grisham novel would be considered to be perhaps too contrived. And at that time he was facing a primary, and, yes, he was politically naive. But we can draw no other conclusion but that those initial statements that he made were to further his political ambition. And having once done that, and having seen the facts as he hoped they would be, in his mind the facts remained that way in the face of developing evidence that was not in fact the case.

And even today, one must say that in the face of a declaration of innocence by the Attorney General of North Carolina, it appears the Defendant still believes the facts to be one way and the world now knows that is not the case.

We are required under our rules to consider certain aggravating and mitigating factors under Rule .0114(w), and those are set forth in the Rule, and I'm going to say what aggravating and mitigating factors we have found.

We have found as aggravating factors dishonest or selfish motive; a pattern of misconduct; multiple offenses; refusal to acknowledge wrongful nature of conduct in the respect of the handling of the DNA evidence. We do find that he has made some acknowledgement of his wrongful conduct in regards to the pre-trial statements. The vulnerability of the victim, or the victims in this case, and primarily the victims are the three young men who were wrongfully charged. And we find also as an aggravating factor substantial experience in the practice of law.

As mitigating factors we find absence of a prior disciplinary record and reputation for character.

We expressly find that the aggravating factors outweigh the mitigating factors.

This matter appears to be an aberration in a couple of respects. It appears to be an aberration in the life and career of Michael Nifong. It appears also to be an aberration in the way justice is handled in North Carolina. It's an illustration of the fact that character, good character, is not a constant. Character is dependent upon the situation. And probably any one of us could be faced with a situation at some point that would test our good character and we would prove wanting, and that has happened for Mike Nifong.

But the fact that it has happened and the fact that we have found dishonesty and deceitful conduct requires us in the interest of the protection of the public to enter the most severe sanction that we can enter, which is disbarment.

I want to say something about who the victims are here. The victims are the three young men to start with, their families, the entire lacrosse team and their coach, Duke University, the justice system in North Carolina and elsewhere. And indeed, prosecutors, honest, ethical, hardworking prosecutors throughout the Nation, as we've heard through anecdotal evidence, are victims of this conduct. And in particular, the justice system is a victim of the way this was taken out of, as Mr. Smith testified, taken out of the courtroom and put in the hands of the public. And not only the public in general, but into a media frenzy unprecedented in anyone's experience.

As I think anyone who has sat through this entire proceeding—and we've been here now on the fifth day—knows that you can't do justice in the media, you can't do justice on sound bites. The way to arrive at a determination of the facts is to hear in a fair and open proceeding all of the evidence, and then for the trier of fact to determine what the facts are. And we've done that this week. That did not happen and was not going to happen, apparently, in the Duke Lacrosse case.

The justice system righted itself somehow so that at the end of the day there was indeed a declaration of innocence of these three young men. But it was done with backup systems in a way that was never designed to work as the justice system should work.

Perhaps that was set in motion by the State Bar's initial complaint filed on December 28, 2006, that shortly thereafter led to the recusal of Mr. Nifong from the Duke Lacrosse cases. That was a controversial decision, I believe. It was certainly unprecedented that the State Bar would take disciplinary action against a prosecutor during the pendency of the case, when indeed the presiding judge had concurrent and coextensive disciplinary jurisdiction. That was a step—although we were not privy to the decision to do that—I am sure that was a matter of serious debate as to whether to do that, because that in itself took the justice system off track.

The other mechanism by which the system more or less righted itself was the involvement of the Attorney General and the special prosecutors, who looked at it from the standpoint of prosecutors who were cognizant of their duty, the duty that was described here by Marsha Goodenow from the Mecklenburg County District Attorney's Office, and whom we found to be a very persuasive witness. And that led to something really very extraordinary, a declaration of actual innocence of the three defendants, something that could never have been accomplished even if the criminal case had proceeded before Judge Smith. And while we don't know, it seems reasonably clear that one would predict that at the suppression hearing in February the case would have been dismissed. But it would have been dismissed with no declaration of innocence, and, indeed, this entire controversy regarding the wrongful prosecution still hanging over the heads of the defendants and of the justice system in North Carolina.

So perhaps that was the good thing that happened, If one can find much of anything good out of this situation. But the fact that if these extraordinary circumstances had not come to pass leading to that declaration of innocence raises another point that we should all be aware of, which is that the person who is the most powerful in the criminal justice system is not the judge, and except at the end of the process, it's not the jury. It's the prosecutor who makes the charging decision to start with.

The prosecutor, as any defense lawyer will tell you, is imbued with an aura that if he says it's so, it must be so. And even with all of the Constitutional rights that are afforded criminal defendants, the prosecutor, merely by asserting a charge against defendants, already has a leg up. And when that power is abused, as it was here, it puts Constitutional rights in jeopardy. We have a justice system, but the justice system only works if the people who participate in it are people of good faith and respect those rights.

And Mr. Nifong, it must be said, for whatever reason, it does appear to us to be out of self-interest, and self-deception, not necessarily out of an evil motive, but that his judgment was so clouded by his own self-interest that he lost sight of that and wandered off the path of justice. And it had to be put back on course again by, again, very extraordinary means.

This is also a case where due to the initial strong statements, unequivocal statements, made by Mr. Nifong there was a deception perpetrated upon the public, and many people were made to look foolish, because they simply accepted that if this prosecutor said it was true, it must be true. We all think back to those early days in the Spring of last year, and you think of how public opinion was so overwhelmingly against these defendants. And you think of the public approbation that they suffered, and then you look as to how the truth came out, slowly, in small increments. And look at the situation now as to what public opinion is. It is a 180 degree turn. And those who made a rush to judgment based upon an unquestioning faith in what a prosecutor had told them were made to look foolish, and many still do look foolish.

It is very difficult to find any good in this situation that brings us here. I can only think of a couple of things. One is that there are very few deterrents upon prosecutorial misconduct. For very good policy reasons, prosecutors are virtually immune from civil liability. About the worst that can happen to them in the conduct of a case is for the case to be overturned. The only significant deterrent upon prosecutors is the possibility of disciplinary sanction. And here the most severe sanction is warranted.

I want to briefly address a matter that was actually included in Mr. Nifong's initial Response to the State Bar Grievance, which was to the effect that the word on the street was that the State Bar was out to get a prosecutor, and citing a couple of well-publicized cases in recent years involving prosecutors, where it was widely perceived that there was insufficient discipline imposed.

And I just want to step back for a moment and speak not as the Chair of this Panel, but as the Chair of the Disciplinary Hearing Commission and note that in those two cases the situation was very different, although you could look at it and say the harm that was caused by the conduct was greater. In both of those cases someone was actually wrongfully convicted of a capital crime. But in one of those cases, when it was prosecuted, there was no contention that there was any misconduct on behalf of the prosecutor that extended beyond gross negligence. In other words, there was no allegation or proof of intentional wrongdoing. And under the restrictions that we are under in the case of State Bar versus Talford, probably the maximum discipline that could be imposed was imposed. And indeed, under the particular provision, the same one that we are dealing with here, Rule 3.8(d) as it was previously worded, the Panel held that there was a non-delegable duty to know what's in your file, and that under most jurisdictions or the majority view, actually no discipline would be imposed.

In the other case, which has recently been affirmed by the Court of Appeals, there was a dismissal based upon essentially the running of the limitations rule. And we did not address the merits. But we applied the rules.

We applied the rules in both of those cases and reached, in my opinion, the correct result, and in this case we have applied the rules and again we believe we have reached the correct result.

And every case is different, but the case we have here is a clear case of intentional prosecutorial misconduct.

So in addition to this being a deterrent to any prosecutorial misconduct, I would say that this should be a reminder to everyone that it's the facts that matter. It's not the allegations. And if you sit as a juror or if you sit at home watching your television about court proceedings, you have to carefully consider the facts and the evidence before you make the conclusion about something, and not just trust someone who tells you it is so because that is someone in a position who is supposed to know.

The other thing that may be good about this is to say this is another opportunity to acknowledge based upon the actual testimony that we have heard over the last several days, and to remind everyone, other than the testimony of Brian Meehan on

December 15, 2006, no one had given testimony in a public hearing under oath in this matter until this week. This has given an opportunity to air some, though not all, of the evidence that may relate to this matter. After all, our purpose is limited to the disciplinary matter before us and the specific allegations and only involves the law license of Michael Nifong. But we've had an opportunity over the last several days to hear additional evidence, and while it is really not within the purview of the Panel to make such a pronouncement, I want to say again that we acknowledge the actual innocence of the defendants, and there is nothing here that has done anything but support that assertion.

Finally, I want it to be noted—it may seem to be a subtle distinction—but it's an important one. It relates to this underlying case, which is, when this is reported, it should be noted not that the State Bar disciplined Michael Nifong, but that the Disciplinary Hearing Commission of the North Carolina State Bar, particularly this Panel of the Disciplinary Hearing Commission, disciplined Michael Nifong. That is important because it should illustrate to everyone that there has been a process here. The State Bar in secret did not decide to take away the license of Michael Nifong to practice law. The State Bar decided that they had evidence sufficient to go forward and seek to prove to an independent tribunal of triers of fact that his license should be taken away. And it took a long process, culminating to this point in order to do that. And that's due process, and that's what was nearly hijacked in the case of the Duke Lacrosse defendants.

That is about the only thing—those are the only things that come to mind that are good about this entire situation. It's been truly a—"fiasco" is not too strong a word. But it could have resulted from a lapse of character of practically anyone, not just in particular Mike Nifong. We've heard anecdotal evidence of the harm that it has caused. The actual harm is very difficult for one to get one's arms around. But I certainly hope that this process will help assuage the harm and stop the ripples that seemed to start when the stone was thrown in the pond. They just got bigger and bigger. But hopefully they will ebb from this point forward.

We expect to enter a written order in the near future. I won't put a timetable on it. It will take a little time. But again, that will be a final order, and I understand the Defendant has waived his right to appeal. So unless there's anything further for us to address, this proceeding is concluded. Thank you.

(End of excerpt transcript.)

Michael B. Nifong, 06/16/07
STATE OF NORTH CAROLINA
COUNTY OF WAKE

CERTIFICATE

I, Carol Williams Wolff, Certified Verbatim Reporter and Notary Public for the State of North Carolina, County of Wake, do hereby certify that the foregoing pages represent an excerpt transcript of the hearing held June 16, 2007, in the matter of The North Carolina State Bar versus Michael B. Nifong held before a Hearing Panel of the Disciplinary Hearing Commission of The North Carolina State Bar, and that these pages constitute a true and accurate transcript of an excerpt of the proceeding.

In witness whereof, I have hereunto affixed my hand this 19th day of June, 2007.

CAROL WILLIAMS WOLFF
Certified Verbatim Reporter
Notary Number 19941540100

CHAPTER 8

Social Crimes

CHAPTER CONTENTS

> *Of all tyrannies a tyranny sincerely exercised for the good of its victims may be the most oppressive. It may be better to live under robber barons than under omnipotent moral busybodies. The robber baron's cruelty may sometimes sleep, his cupidity may at some point be satiated; but those who torment us for our own good will torment us without end for they do so with the approval of their own conscience.*
>
> **James Madison,** *The Federalist No. 51*

CHAPTER OBJECTIVES

After studying this chapter, you should be able to:

- Understand the history of social crimes.
- Define prostitution and explain the elements required to be proven in a prosecution.
- Understand the history of laws criminalizing out-of-wedlock sexual relationships and their impact today.
- Understand the U.S. Supreme Court's position on sodomy and its impact.
- Describe some of the laws that regulate gambling.
- Understand the problem of drug abuse and law enforcement efforts to curtail the use and trafficking in illegal drugs.

INTRODUCTION

Every society has generally accepted rules of conduct for its members. Those rules vary from place to place and time to time. In some societies, the rules are strict and plentiful; while in others, they are few and far between. Conduct rules often have their roots in religious doctrines, but sometimes have more practical origins. For example, the prohibition against prostitution has its origin in religion, but some counties in the United States allow prostitutes to operate in licensed brothels where presumably regular health checks help prevent the spread of disease that might flourish in an unsupervised setting.

Most rules of conduct in modern societies don't carry criminal penalties but instead rely on self-censorship or public ostracism for enforcement. Some violations carry criminal sanctions, and it is to those we now turn our attention. The list of social offenses that have at one time or another been considered crimes include:

- Adultery and fornication
- Bestiality and buggery
- Miscegenation (mixed-race marriage)
- Seduction and alienation of affections

PROSTITUTION

Prostitution

Engaging in sexual intercourse or other sexual activity for pay.

Prostitution is generally defined as engaging in sexual intercourse or other sexual activity for pay. It can be engaged in by either sex, although most prostitutes are women. It was widespread across the ancient world in Greece, Egypt, and Rome and is sometimes referred to as the world's oldest profession. For some practitioners, selling sex acts supports a drug habit. Others who may have few job or social skills turn to prostitution for economic reasons. Still others are runaway teens who find themselves on the streets with no money or shelter and few support systems available. Prostitutes are also frequent targets for criminal acts, including murder. In fact, some of the most notorious serial killers in our history specifically targeted prostitutes.

Most states outlaw sex for money and make it a crime for both parties involved. It has long been a federal crime to transport someone over state lines for immoral purposes,[1] as the original language of the Mann Act is read. The law now defines "immoral purposes" with precision and provides that:

HISTORICAL HIGHLIGHT
Sex Workers Try to Dispel Stereotypes about Prostitution

Not everyone involved in prostitution and related activities do so out of desperation or the need to feed an addiction. Some claim to have chosen their profession freely and have formed organizations aimed at improving working conditions and gaining respect and legal protection for members. Many of these participants in prostitution and related acts such as acting in pornographic films, working in massage parlors, and dancing in strip clubs prefer to be called **sex workers.**

The North American Task Force on Prostitution is a network of sex workers and sex workers' rights organizations and individuals and organizations that support the rights of sex workers to ply their trades without interference from law enforcement and with the ability to organize into what amounts to trade unions or guilds. There are member organizations in many large cities offering education, health screening, and even legal assistance to sex workers.

Other groups operate on a model designed less to make prostitution a legitimate business and more to assure that sex workers are safe and healthy and able to receive medical treatment or drug counseling if desired. For example, in the nation's capital, HIPS (Helping Individual Prostitutes Survive) runs an outreach van nightly to assist sex workers. HIPS also operates a toll-free national hotline.

Sex Workers

A term preferred by some working in the sex industry such as prostitutes, porn actresses or actors, exotic dancers, and the like.

> Whoever knowingly transports any individual in interstate or foreign commerce, or in any Territory or possession of the United States, with intent that such individual engage in prostitution, or in any sexual activity for which any person can be charged with a criminal offense, or attempts to do so, shall be fined under this title or imprisoned not more than 10 years, or both.

At one point, the U.S. Supreme Court went as far as to say that a man who "transported a woman in interstate commerce so that she should become his mistress or concubine" was transporting her with an "immoral purpose" within the meaning of the Mann Act.[2] Over the years, the Act was also used to convict a Mormon practitioner of polygamy from bringing his brides home over state lines.[3] Eventually, the language was changed to its present wording to assure that only those transported over state lines to engage in the sale of sex for money would run afoul of the law.

State criminal laws outlawing prostitution generally outlaw two distinct behaviors: soliciting someone to engage in sex for money in a public place and working in a brothel or other private setting selling sex for money. For example, in Pennsylvania a person is guilty of prostitution if he or she:

> is an inmate of a house of prostitution or otherwise engages in sexual activity as a business; or loiters in or within view of any public place for the purpose of being hired to engage in sexual activity.[4]

Many states have graduated penalties for engaging in prostitution, with each additional conviction resulting in a longer prison term and fine. Many states, in recognition that prostitution can be a factor in the spread of sexually transmitted diseases, make selling sexual favors by those who know they are infected with the human immunodeficiency virus (HIV) a felony offense.

Those who hire prostitutes also commit a criminal offense in most states. In addition, anyone who works to procure clients for a prostitute (a **pimp**) can also be prosecuted. Although it was not always so, most states now punish pimps, prostitutes, and their clients equally. In addition, those who patronize prostitutes are sometimes subject to publicity.

Pimp

One who works to procure clients for a prostitute.

For example, in Pennsylvania, the second conviction for soliciting a prostitute carries with it a requirement that the conviction shall be published in a local newspaper (at the defendant's expense).[5]

There is only one state in the United States in which prostitution is legal. Since 1971, counties in Nevada have been able to elect to allow brothels within their borders.[6] The state requires that counties with brothels license their prostitutes and also requires that all clients wear condoms. It is still illegal to sell sex outside of brothels and in Las Vegas itself.

YOU MAKE THE CALL
THE DUKE RAPE CASE: DOES STRIPPING CONTRIBUTE TO PROSTITUTION OR SEXUAL VIOLENCE?

When three Duke lacrosse players were accused of raping a stripper they had hired for a party, it set off a storm of controversy. The stripper claimed she was stripping to support herself and her child while she attended school.

When the story first broke, civil rights leaders such as the Rev. Jesse Jackson decried a society where a woman would have to resort to stripping to get through college. He even offered to pay for her college education so that she would not have to strip.

The issue raised points to the very role of women, particularly young attractive women in our society. Is stripping just innocent fun? After all, male strippers often perform for women. Is stripping sexually exploitive in itself, and does it contribute to society viewing women as sex objects? If so, as sex objects are they more vulnerable to sexual violence? Should more restrictive laws governing the hiring of strippers be enacted? You make the call.

FORNICATION, ADULTERY, AND POLYGAMY/POLYANDRY

Fornication

Voluntary sexual intercourse between two unmarried persons.

Adultery

Sexual intercourse by a married person with someone not his or her spouse.

Both **fornication** and **adultery** were originally crimes in all states. Fornication is defined as voluntary sexual intercourse between two unmarried persons.[7] Adultery is sexual intercourse by a married person with someone not his or her spouse.[8]

Today, statutes criminalizing adultery and fornication are generally limited to situations where the acts take place between people who otherwise cannot marry and in cases where there is independent verification of the offense. For example, in Mississippi, it is a crime punishable by up to 10 years in prison to commit even one act of adultery or fornication with someone you could not marry because he or she was too close of a blood relative.[9] North Carolina outlaws fornication and adultery but does not allow the testimony of either of the participants against the other.[10] Those in the military can still face a court-martial for committing adultery under a section of the Uniform Code of Military Justice that prohibits conduct "prejudicial to good order and discipline."

Polygamy, or having several wives, and polyandry, or having several husbands, is a practice that today exists in some parts of the world, but it has been outlawed in every state in the Union. The term **bigamy** is used to describe the criminal act of marrying when one already has a spouse and applies to both polygamists and polyandrists. In the United States, it was officially practiced by Mormons until the Church of Jesus Christ of Latter-Day Saints prohibited it in 1890.[11] Outlawing polygamy was made a condition of joining the United States when western territories that had accepted the practice sought entry, as was the case for Utah's admission to the Union in 1896.

Some states even criminalize the teaching of bigamy. For example, in Mississippi, you may be fined up to $500 and imprisoned up to 6 months if you:

> teach another the doctrines, principles, or tenets, or any of them, of polygamy; or shall endeavor so to do; or shall induce or persuade another by words or acts, or otherwise, to embrace or adopt polygamy, or to emigrate to any other state, territory, district, or country for the purpose of embracing, adopting, or practicing polygamy.[12]

Bigamy

The criminal act of marrying when one already has a spouse.

Laws are made for the government of actions, and while they cannot interfere with mere religious belief and opinions, they may with practices.
Chief Justice Waite, in *Reynolds v. United States*, 98 U.S. 145 (1878)

HISTORICAL HIGHLIGHT
"Religious Duty" to Have Multiple Wives
Lands Man in Jail

Tom Green believes he has the religious duty to practice multiple marriage. To that end, he has been living in a polygamous household with five wives and several dozen children. The family lives in the Utah desert in a compound of trailers. But Mr. Green isn't shy about his unusual living arrangements. In fact, he touted what he calls his "original Mormonism" in daytime talk shows and challenged state prosecutors to charge him. They did.

When Green's case was tried, a jury took three hours to find him guilty of four counts of bigamy and one count of criminal failure to pay child support. On August 24, 2001, the 53-year-old was sentenced to five years in prison and ordered to repay $78,000 in welfare payments his wives and children had collected over the years. The Supreme Court of Utah upheld the conviction in 2004. He was then tried for the alleged rape of one of his wives—who was 13 when she gave birth to his child but is now his legal wife. A conviction netted him a second five-year prison term.

Green was released from prison on parole on August 7, 2007. He must register as a sex offender.[13]

Anyone charged under this act could likely defend by arguing that this statute is contrary to the First Amendment prohibition against curtailing free speech and religious freedom of thought, even though practicing bigamy may be punished. The U.S. Supreme Court early on upheld the right of a state to outlaw polygamy and bigamy even if it was practiced as part of a sincerely held religious belief.[14]

ABORTION

Abortion
The termination of pregnancy by something other than birth.

I will neither give a deadly drug to anybody if asked for it, nor will I make a suggestion to this effect. Similarly, I will not give to a woman an abortive remedy. Hippocratic Oath

Perhaps no issue divides the country as deeply as the legalization of **abortion**. Abortion is the termination of pregnancy by something other than birth (that is, when something goes spontaneously wrong or by intervention.) During most of the late nineteenth and in mid-twentieth century, states held that those who performed abortions were guilty of murder. These rigid rules have not historically been in place, however. Greek and Roman women practiced abortion without fear of retribution or punishment. However, the Hippocratic Oath, which has long been the source of medical ethics rules, does warn physicians not to induce abortions.

Nonetheless, abortion was not considered a violation of the Common Law in England. At Common Law, an abortion performed before "quickening" was not an indictable offense.[15] It wasn't until the mid-1800s that abortion became a crime, and then only after "quickening." Quickening was generally believed to occur around the fifteenth to eighteenth week of pregnancy and was the time a woman first felt her child move. But by the 1950s, virtually every state had enacted abortion laws outlawing all abortions that weren't performed to save the life of the mother. It is against this backdrop that the controversial U.S. Supreme Court abortion decisions were made.

Until the 1973 Supreme Court decision in *Roe v. Wade*,[16] every state but four had on its books laws that criminalized abortion. In *Roe*, the plaintiff was a pregnant woman who sought an abortion but could not get one in her home state of Texas because it was a criminal offense to procure an abortion if the mother's life was not in danger. She sued, arguing that the state law that would let her face possible criminal sanctions were she to procure an abortion in Texas violated her constitutional right to privacy.

The Supreme Court concluded that a woman's right to privacy and personal liberty encompassed allowing her to make the determination of whether she desires children. That right, however, was balanced against the state's right to protect her life and that of the fetus she carries by regulating the conditions under which she can seek an abortion. The Court came up with a three-prong decision, summarized as follows:

1. During the first trimester of pregnancy, the decision to have an abortion rests with the woman and her physician.
2. During the second trimester, the state can regulate the procedure in ways consistent with protecting maternal health.
3. During the final trimester, the state may prohibit abortions except to save the life of the mother.

The Court's decision in *Roe* has been one of the most controversial. In the nearly three decades since the initial decision, the Court has heard related cases many times and settled some questions left open. The Court has on several occasions refused to overrule itself. Since then, the Court has decided that a state cannot require notification to a husband as a condition for an abortion but has allowed to stand laws that require a short waiting period, parental notification with an alternative judicial petition in some cases, preabortion counseling and informed consent, and strict recordkeeping requirements.[17] It also removed the strict trimester approach and instead stated that abortion laws can't "unduly burden" a woman's right to choose. The Supreme Court also struck down a Nebraska law criminalizing so-called "partial-birth" abortions.[18] In response, Congress passed the Partial-Birth

Abortion Ban Act of 2003, which specifically defined partial birth abortion and provided exceptions to the ban for the mother's health. The law's constitutionality was almost immediately challenged, but the U.S. Supreme Court pointed to the law's specificity and safeguards for the mother's health when upholding the law in 2007.[19]

SODOMY

Sodomy is generally defined as sexual relations between members of the same sex, sexual conduct *per anus* or *per os* between unmarried persons of the opposite sex, and sexual intercourse with animals.[20] Historically, sodomy laws played a large role in controlling homosexual behaviors. The proscription of sodomy goes back at least as far as Roman times, where it was a capital offense.[21] In England, sodomy was an offense handled by the Catholic Church until the time of the Reformation when Henry VIII transferred all ecclesiastic offenses over to the King's Court.[22] All thirteen states made sodomy a crime at the time the Bill of Rights became the law of the land.[23] Many state laws criminalizing sodomy have been challenged on the basis that they interfere with the constitutional right to privacy.

The U.S. Supreme Court heard one such challenge in *Bowers v. Hardwick*.[24] In that case, Hardwick, the defendant, was charged with engaging in sodomy with another male in the privacy of his bedroom. Sodomy was against the law in Georgia. After his preliminary hearing on the charges, at which the district attorney announced he would not prosecute the case unless more evidence surfaced, Hardwick sued. He asserted that he was a practicing homosexual and that the Georgia sodomy statute placed him in imminent danger of arrest. He argued that the U.S. Constitution granted him a right to privacy in his bedroom and that the state had no business charging him with committing a sex act with another consulting adult. The Court, in a 5–4 vote, concluded that homosexuals did not have a constitutional right to violate state sodomy laws and that states were free to criminalize such behavior if they saw fit.

Many states then repealed their sodomy laws, making any kind of sexual contact (other than prostitution) between consenting adults of any sex legal. In 2003, the Supreme Court made an abrupt about-face on the question of criminalized sodomy. In a 6–3 decision, the Court overturned its decision in *Hardwick* and concluded that community standards have changed. They cited the states that had since decriminalized sodomy and found that remaining laws were unconstitutional as a denial of due process and violation of privacy. The case is *Lawrence v. Texas,* 539 U.S. 558 (2003). The decision is viewed by many as a milestone recognition by the Court of an inherent right to privacy.

PUBLIC INDECENCY OR LEWDNESS

All states have laws that criminalize behavior that constitutes **public indecency** or lewdness. Public indecency is generally defined as lewd or lascivious conduct that is open to public view.[25] Typical actions punished under these types of statutes include nude dancing, performing sex acts in a public place (where there is no reasonable expectation of privacy), and exposing one's genitals in a public place.

Sodomy
Sexual relations between members of the same sex, sexual conduct *per anus* or *per os* between unmarried persons of the opposite sex, and sexual intercourse with animals.

A crime not fit to be named.
William Blackstone, on the subject of sodomy

Public Indecency
Lewd or lascivious conduct that is open to public view.

Public indecency charges typically don't result in long sentences or large fines and tend to be viewed as catchall provisions of penal codes unless the defendant has been arrested on several occasions for the same conduct or appears to be threatening or dangerous. For example, a male suspect who makes it a habit to expose his genitalia to young children may have a greater likelihood of prosecution and punishment than a first-time offender caught masturbating in a dirty movie theater or engaging in sexual behavior in a parked car.

Perhaps the public lewdness case that has garnered the most publicity in recent history is that of children's program creator Pee Wee Herman, or Paul Reubens. In 1991, he was caught in an adult theater while allegedly exposing his genitals and masturbating. He later pleaded no contest to a charge of indecent exposure and was sentenced to perform 75 hours of community service and to pay a fine.[26] The episode lost him his television show and made him a social outcast for nearly a decade.

GAMBLING

Gambling

The act of taking a monetary risk on the chance of receiving a monetary gain.

Gambling and games of chance have been with us for most of history. Gambling is generally defined as the act of taking a monetary risk on the chance of receiving a monetary gain. Therefore, gambling involves chance, rather than skill.[27] It is the taking of a chance as opposed to the use of skill that distinguishes gambling from a game of skill or a contest. For example, suppose you wanted to sell your house in a hurry. If you held a raffle and charged every entrant $200, could you award the house to the lucky holder of the winning ticket? Probably not, because a game of chance, such as your raffle, would be gambling under most state laws (and as you will see later, might be a federal crime if you used the Internet to sell your raffle tickets).

But what if you held a contest with a $200 entry fee and awarded the house to the person who wrote the best essay? Would that qualify as a skill contest rather than a game of chance? The answer is unclear. At best the contest would have to comply with state sweepstakes and contest laws. But the owners would still risk having their raffle declared an illegal lottery or numbers game.

Today, most states[28] run their own gambling operations in the form of lotteries or otherwise permit limited legal gambling, while churches run bingo games and Monte Carlo nights regularly to raise funds. Some states have funded entire new social programs with lottery proceeds. For example, Pennsylvania's lottery provided nearly $16.5 billion in funding to programs that benefit older citizens in 2000, after taking in almost $3.07 billion in ticket sales. The programs funded include prescription drug discounts, transportation, and property tax breaks for senior citizens that might otherwise be funded with tax dollars. Gamblers buying tickets won back $1.8 billion in prizes.[29]

Gambling also takes place at racetracks, on Indian reservations that have established casinos, and in states that have legalized casinos and riverboat gambling. But legal gambling isn't the only form of gambling taking place. Many billions of dollars are spent every year on illegal games of chance, including Internet gambling. Internet gambling alone is expected to exceed $2 billion in 2001.[30]

What is the impact of gambling? In 1996, Congress wanted answers to that question and authorized the creation of the national Gambling Impact Study Commission. The commission released its study in June 1999, and made a number of findings and recommendations. These included:

- A recommendation that there be a moratorium on the expansion of gambling until a more complete assessment of the social harm that may result from expansion can be studied.
- A recommendation that federal law be considered to regulate the new area of Internet gambling, but that states, local authorities, and tribal leaders can best determine what restrictions should be placed on gambling within their jurisdictions.

In response, Congress tacked an Internet gambling ban on the SAFE Port Act of 2006. The ban allows courts and the Treasury department to block credit card usage for online gambling. Some estimates show the law has had little effect because Internet gambling grows at a rate of about 50 percent per year.[31]

States that have legalized some forms of gambling nonetheless regulate it carefully. Bingo and other small games of chance are generally allowed. Tempting as it might be to assume that legal, state-run, or state-supervised gambling would end criminal involvement in gambling, that does not appear to be the case. A significant amount of illegal gambling takes place as sports gambling, or gambling on the outcome of sporting events. Illegal gambling also takes the form of "numbers" games.[32] These illegal operations work much like the legal state-sponsored ones, except that the winnings aren't taxed, nor are the profits taxed or returned to the community in the form of social program funding or additions to the general funds.

In areas where legal casinos and legal lotteries exist, there is also a thriving illegal business in loan sharking, as gamblers seek ready access to cash.

Illegal gambling operations can be prosecuted under federal law if they meet the following criteria:

- The gambling operation violates state law where it is operated.
- It involves five or more persons who conduct, finance, manage, supervise, direct, or own all or part of the business.
- It has been or remains in substantially continuous operation for a period in excess of 30 days or has a gross revenue of $2,000 in any single day.[33]

The types of gambling operations covered by the law include lotteries, slot machines, pool selling, bookmaking, roulette wheels, and dice tables. The law also explicitly excludes bingo games and other similar gambling devices operated by organizations recognized as a tax-exempt organization by the Internal Revenue Service.

Another section of the U.S. Code has recently been used to prosecute those involved in Internet gambling. 18 U.S.C. § 1084 provides that:

> Whoever being engaged in the business of betting or wagering knowingly uses a wire communication facility for the transmission in interstate or foreign commerce of bets or wagers or information assisting in the placing of bets or wagers on any sporting event or contest, or for the transmission of a wire communication which entitles the recipient to receive money or credit as a result of bets or wagers, or for information assisting in the placing of bets or wagers, shall be fined under this title or imprisoned not more than two years, or both.

HISTORICAL HIGHLIGHT
Internet Gambling Operation Not Outside Reach of Federal Law

What happens when a bright young man working in the technology field decides he wants a piece of the Internet gold rush? If he sets up an overseas Internet sports bookmaking operation, he lands in jail. Consider the case of Jay Cohen. As a young man in San Francisco, he enjoyed a rewarding career as a derivatives trader. But in 1996, he saw that the Internet was about to take off and went in search of the fast lane. He dreamed of creating an e-company and settled on the idea of an offshore betting business model. He left his trading job and set up shop on the Caribbean island of Antigua.

There he started World Sports Exchange, a business organized solely to bookmake on American sporting events. The business operated like this: Customers opened an account with WSE in Antigua and deposited at least $300 in the account. To bet, customers would call or contact WSE on the Internet. WSE would confirm the bet and manage the details for a 10 percent commission or fee. Millions flowed into the operation. The operation was entirely legal on Antigua.

Federal Bureau of Investigation (FBI) agents then opened accounts, placed bets, and arrested Cohen. A jury convicted him of violating 18 U.S.C. § 1084, and the second Circuit Court of Appeals upheld the conviction.[34] The federal law, known as the Wire Communications Act, was enacted years before the birth of the Internet and was designed to prevent bookies from taking bets over the phone. Cohen was sentenced to 21 months in prison. Several other principals in the operation are still at large. The U.S. Supreme Court refused to hear his appeal.

Other federal laws that attempt to control illegal interstate gambling include 18 U.S.C. § 1952, which prohibits interstate or foreign travel to further gambling or other illegitimate business dealings, and 18 U.S.C. § 1953, which outlaws the interstate transportation of gambling paraphernalia.

DRUG PRODUCTION AND USE

Drug use in the United States is a considerable problem. According to the federal agency responsible for developing a national drug policy, the Office of National Drug Control Policy, in 2005, 9.9 percent of Americans aged 12 or older had used illegal drugs in the last month. Other statistics include:

- 2.1 million teens between the ages of 12 and 17 needed treatment for drug abuse in 2005.

- Children who smoke "pot" at an early age are less likely to finish school and more likely to commit crimes than those who don't.
- More than 1.35 million Americans were arrested for drug law violations in 2005.[35]

Clearly, illicit drug use and abuse is a serious problem for law enforcement. Today, the "war on drugs" has taken on a new urgency since it has become clear that terrorist organizations abroad have a hand in the production and distribution of illicit drugs in the United States. In turn, the profits from these operations may be providing valuable cash for terrorist organizations across the globe.

Those who use illicit drugs violate a variety of state and federal criminal laws, and those who produce, import, and sell those drugs face the harshest penalties. We will focus on federal drug laws, but every state has similar laws on its books. A few states have experimented with decriminalizing the usage, possession, and sale of some controlled substances, primarily marijuana.

A **controlled substance** is defined as a drug considered dangerous under the law because of its effects, including intoxication, stupor, or addictive potential.[36] That is, the drug is listed on either a state or federal directory of controlled substances and may in some cases be available by prescription to treat medical conditions. Examples include many commonly prescribed pharmaceuticals such as Dilantin and Ritalin. Some controlled substances are so dangerous that they are not legally available at all. Examples include heroin and, in most states, marijuana.

HISTORICAL HIGHLIGHT
DEA Reports on Drug Trafficking

Much of the job of ending drug trafficking into the United States falls on the Drug Enforcement Agency (DEA). Recently the agency released a report detailing how and from where illegal drugs not produced or grown domestically enter the country. The report calls the illegal drug market in the United States one of the most profitable in the world and claims it attracts the most ruthless, sophisticated, and aggressive drug traffickers.

Who is supplying the drug market in the United States? One source is South America, from where drug traffickers smuggle cocaine and heroin over land through Mexico and by sea through the Caribbean as well as via the air. Mexican criminal groups smuggle cocaine, heroin, methamphetamine, amphetamine, and marijuana through our southern border.

The source of Ecstacy (3, 4-methylenedioxymethamphetamine), a popular party drug, is now being smuggled into the country by Canadian-based Asian gangs who stepped in to fill the void created when law enforcement efforts destroyed Israeli and Russian drug syndicates. Heroin primarily enters the country from South America. Miami is the main port of entry, and then the drug is transported up Interstates 75 and 95 to the Eastern Seaboard and Midwest.[37]

It's so important for Americans to know that the traffic in drugs finances the work of terror, sustaining terrorists, that terrorists use drug profits to fund their cells to commit acts of murder. If you quit drugs, you join the fight against terror in America.
George W. Bush, President of the United States, December 14, 2001

Controlled Substance

A drug considered dangerous under the law because of its effects, including intoxication, stupor, or addictive potential.

We know that terrorist organizations routinely launder the proceeds from drug trafficking and use the funds to support and expand their operations internationally.
Senator Orrin Hatch (R-UT)

PENALTIES

Most criminal cases brought against drug abusers are state violations. As a practical matter, federal law enforcement officials handle cases involving trafficking of controlled substances across our borders and across state lines, while local law enforcement handles individual drug use and drug distribution and dealing on a local level. However, agents from federal agencies such as the Drug Enforcement Agency and the FBI work closely with state attorneys general and local police departments to coordinate the war on drugs. For example, in areas designated as High Intensity Drug Trafficking Areas (HIDTA), the federal government takes a lead role in coordinating federal, state, and local law enforcement efforts. There are 26 such areas in the United States.

Arrests for drug use are quite common. In 2005, there were over 1.8 million arrests by state and local law enforcement agencies.[38] More than four-fifths of drug law violation arrests are for possession violations, and drug abuse violations in 2005 accounted for 10.4 percent of all arrests. The most frequent drug possessed by the defendants was marijuana, followed by heroin and cocaine. Marijuana and heroin are Schedule I drugs (see the following list), while cocaine is a Schedule II drug. Approximately 92 percent of drug defendants handled by the court system during 2004 were convicted.[39]

There are five schedules of controlled substances catalogued by the federal drug laws, and additions are made when new drugs surface or a previously unscheduled drug is determined to belong on the list. Almost every state has adopted the same schedules. The penalty for possession of a substance on the list depends on which schedule the substance is on and how much of the substance with which the defendant was caught. The schedules can be found at 21 U.S.C. § 811 and at the DEA Web site, *www.dea.gov*. The major categories are:

Schedule I. (A) The drug or other substance has a high potential for abuse.

(B) The drug or other substance has no currently accepted medical use in treatment in the United States.

(C) There is a lack of accepted safety for use of the drug or other substance under medical supervision.

Schedule II. (A) The drug or other substance has a high potential for abuse.

(B) The drug or other substance has a currently accepted medical use in treatment in the United States or a currently accepted medical use with severe restrictions.

(C) Abuse of the drug or other substances may lead to severe psychological or physical dependence.

Schedule III. (A) The drug or other substance has a potential for abuse less than the drugs or other substances in Schedules I and II.

(B) The drug or other substance has a currently accepted medical use in treatment in the United States.

(C) Abuse of the drug or other substance may lead to moderate or low physical dependence or high psychological dependence.

Schedule IV. (A) The drug or other substance has a low potential for abuse relative to the drugs or other substances in Schedule III.

(B) The drug or other substance has a currently accepted medical use in treatment in the United States.

(C) Abuse of the drug or other substance may lead to limited physical dependence or psychological dependence relative to the drugs or other substances in Schedule III.

Schedule V. (A) The drug or other substance has a low potential for abuse relative to the drugs or other substances in Schedule IV.

(B) The drug or other substance has a currently accepted medical use in treatment in the United States.

(C) Abuse of the drug or other substance may lead to limited physical dependence or psychological dependence relative to the drugs or other substances in Schedule IV.

The statute then delineates the chemical name for each substance classified on the list. The penalties are found in 21 U.S.C. § 841 through § 863. For example, the penalty for simple possession of some controlled substance ranges from up to one year in prison for the first offense to a minimum of five years in prison for the possession of more than five grams of cocaine. For those engaged in trafficking in drugs, the penalties include life in prison. If the quantities are very high or if the defendant attempted to kill another to evade detection or arrest, the law authorizes the imposition of the penalty of death.[40] The average sentence in 2002 for drug trafficking was 55 months in prison.[41]

When crack cocaine hit the streets in the mid-1980s, Congress reacted with higher sentences for crack cocaine than for powder cocaine. Sentence guidelines suggested that judges count each gram of crack cocaine as 100 ounces of powder cocaine when calculating sentences. Since higher cocaine amounts require higher sentences, crack sellers and users were consistently being handed longer sentences. Critics argued the higher sentences disproportionately punished African–Americans because they more often used the cheaper crack cocaine.

In 2007, the Supreme Court ruled that sentence guidelines were advisory only, and judges who wished to consider crack and powder cocaine equally were free to do so.[42] Congress has suggested that the disparity be removed from the guidelines. While the guidelines are still on the books, judges are now free to ignore them if the case warrants it.

PRACTICE POINTERS

Some of the offenses described in this chapter will seldom be encountered by most legal professionals working in a private law firm. Those who work in state or local agencies, district attorneys' offices, or public defenders' offices may encounter cases involving defendants charged with sodomy, indecent exposure, and prostitution on a fairly regular basis. They should keep in mind that social offenses such as these aren't a priority for most law enforcement agencies.

Legal professionals working with firms, organizations, or agencies that provide abortion or abortion information need to familiarize themselves with the law in their state regarding abortion. For example, health clinics that provide abortions or assistance obtaining abortions must make sure they stay within the requirements of their state's abortion laws. If they do not, they risk criminal prosecution. In the area of abortion regulation, it is imperative that legal professionals keep up with legislative and judicial developments, since it is unlikely either those in favor of abortion rights or against such rights will let up their efforts to shape the debate in the legislature or the courts.

Legal professionals who work for firms or government agencies concerned with the gaming industry must be well versed in federal, state, and local laws on gambling. This is no small task. Every state has laws in place either outlawing all gambling, or authorizing limited gambling by the state or a state-supervised business, and outlawing all other forms of gambling. Prosecutors also appear willing to apply old laws to contests and variations on games of chance in an attempt to clarify what the rules are, especially on the Internet. They don't intend to wait until new legislation is passed. That means legal professionals researching the law of gambling need to think like a creative prosecutor. Try to imagine new uses for existing legislation, and you will serve the client well. New legislation is also likely as states grapple with the reality of gambling.

Legal professionals who work in the area of drug addiction and interdiction must keep abreast of changing laws and conditions in the war on drugs. Drugs, like fashion, go in and out of style, and the approach to charging or defending those involved in the trade changes accordingly. Expertise in pharmacology may be necessary in some cases involving clandestine laboratories and drug production. Cases involving trafficking in large amounts of dangerous drugs are the most difficult because penalties can include life in prison or even death. Those working with clients and attorneys to assess the likely outcome of drug cases will want to check with the Bureau of Justice Statistics. The agency's Web site provides access to a wealth of data, including information on the likelihood of prosecution, release on bond, conviction, and type and length of sentence. The Web site is *http://www.ojp.usdoj.gov/bjs.*

CHAPTER SUMMARY

In this chapter, we have explored social crimes. Many of these are what some refer to as "victimless" crimes. While that may be a fair characterization for crimes such as sodomy committed by consenting adults in the privacy of their bedroom, the reality is that many of the other offenses discussed in this chapter are associated with large-scale social problems such as drug addiction, gambling addiction, and the commission of petty crimes.

Prostitution is generally defined as engaging in sexual intercourse or other sexual activity for pay. It can be engaged in by either sex, although most prostitutes are women. Most states punish both prostitutes and those who patronize their services as well as anyone who works to procure clients for a prostitute. Prostitution is only legal in selected counties in Nevada.

Fornication and adultery are now seldom criminalized. Bigamy, or having more than one wife, is illegal in all states. It was once practiced by Mormons in the West but was outlawed as a condition of admission of those states to the Union. Today, there are still occasional prosecutions for bigamy.

Sodomy, defined as sexual relations between members of the same sex, sexual conduct *per anus* or *per os* between unmarried persons of the opposite sex, and sexual intercourse with animals, can and is still outlawed by some states. But in light of the U.S. Supreme Court decision in *Lawrence v. Texas*, many of those restrictions are bound to fall. States also have the right to punish public exposure or lewdness.

The Supreme Court has ruled that a woman may terminate a pregnancy but that states can set reasonable limits about the time, place, and conditions for abortion. States cannot unreasonably interfere with a woman's right to choose but can require her to receive counseling, notify parents or petition a court before the procedure is performed if she is a minor, and otherwise place administrative requirements on the process. States can also limit the right to an abortion if the pregnancy has progressed far into its term unless the mother's life is in danger. This is an area of the law that stirs emotions and is constantly undergoing challenge. The Supreme Court recently upheld the constitutionality of the Partial-Birth Abortion Ban Act of 2003 after previous similar laws had been struck down.

Gambling, which is defined as engaging in a game of chance by wagering money for the chance of a financial payoff, is now a source of revenue for most states. Gambling that isn't approved, controlled, or run by state governments is still illegal and can be a state or federal offense. Internet gambling has successfully been prosecuted under statutes forbidding the wagering of bets over telephone lines in states where wagering is illegal.

Illegal drug trafficking and use is a substantial problem in the United States today. State, local, and federal law enforcement agencies are working together to interdict drugs as they enter the United States and to prosecute those who traffic in controlled substances. The penalties for possession range from fines to short prison terms, while trafficking can net a defendant life in prison or even the death penalty.

KEY TERMS

Abortion	**Fornication**	**Public Indecency**
Adultery	**Gambling**	**Sex Workers**
Bigamy	**Pimp**	**Sodomy**
Controlled Substance	**Prostitution**	

EXERCISES

1. BetonSports.com was once advertised as "the largest online wagering service in the world" and allegedly allowed gamblers worldwide to place bets on professional and college sports. Now, the Web site greets visitors with the following message:

   > This website does not accept wagers on sports or sporting events from persons in the United States. It is a violation of United States law to transmit sports wagers or betting information to this website from the United States.

   Read the indictment in the chapter Appendix and answer the following questions:

   a. How would you approach the case if you were defending Gary Kaplan?

   b. A United States citizen and resident has asked you whether she can get in trouble for setting up an account with an online gaming company. What can you tell her about her risk?

   c. At the time of this writing, Kaplan had not yet been tried. His attorneys have, however, raised as a possible defense the fact that the offenses charged in the indictment took place before the passage of the SAFE Port Act (see preceding text). Is that a viable defense? Why or why not?

2. Some religions claim that a part of their religious practice requires the use of substances that otherwise would be illegal under federal and state controlled substances laws. Such was the case of the practitioners of a South American religion—who are, in the words of Chief Justice Roberts:

   > A religious sect with origins in the Amazon Rainforest receives communion by drinking a sacramental tea, brewed from plants unique to the region that contains a hallucinogen regulated under the Controlled Substances Act by the Federal Government.

   When their "tea" was seized by authorities, members of the church challenged the right of the federal government to confiscate what they claimed was sacramental materials. They cited the Religious Freedom Restoration Act, a 1993 law which prohibits the federal government from "unduly burdening" the exercise of religion. Of course, the United States raised the Controlled Substances Act as legal authority.

   a. How would you balance the right of the United States to control dangerous drugs with the right to the free exercise of religion? Should the church members be allowed to drink their hallucinogenic tea?

   b. Check your answer against the 8–0 Supreme Court decision (Alito did not participate) reproduced in the chapter Appendix. Were you right or wrong?

DISCUSSION QUESTIONS

1. Is prostitution a victimless crime? Why or why not?
2. Do you believe the U.S. Supreme Court went too far in its abortion decisions? Did it not go far enough?
3. Should states have the right to dictate what types of sexual activities go on between consenting adults in private? Would your answer change if the activity in question were dangerous or even deadly?

4. Should states be in the business of gambling?

5. Do states and the federal government do enough to curb the availability of illegal drugs?

6. Should casual drug users be imprisoned, or should they be required to undergo addiction treatment instead?

7. Should drug use be decriminalized?

FOR FURTHER READING AND VIEWING

1. Albert, A. (2001). *Brothel: Mustang Ranch and Its Women.* Random House.
   This book is an inside look at what went on at the Mustang Ranch in Nevada until it closed.

2. Solinger, R. (2001). *Abortion Wars: A Half Century of Struggle, 1950–2000.* University of California Press.
   A collection of essays on abortion by writers who are pro-choice; includes extensive discussion of *Roe v. Wade* and *Planned Parenthood v. Casey.*

3. Hull, N. E., and Hoffer, P. C. (2001). *Roe v. Wade: The Abortion Rights Controversy in American History.* University Press of Kansas.
   An overview of the abortion rights controversy.

4. Gordon, S. B. (2001). *The Mormon Question: Polygamy and Constitutional Conflict in Nineteenth-Century America.* University of North Carolina Press.
   A look at the history of polygamy in the West.

5. Goldstein, A. (2001). *Addiction: From Biology to Drug Policy.* Oxford University Press.
   Explores the nature of addiction to categories of drugs and the laws and policies needed to fight addiction.

6. Schlosser, E. (2003). *Reefer Madness: Sex, Drugs and Cheap Labor in the American Black Market.* Houghton Mifflin.
   An inside look at the illegal drug and adult entertainment industries and how demand has spurred a black market economy in sin.

7. Krakauer, J. (2003). *Under the Banner of Heaven: A Story of Violent Faith.* Doubleday.
   Exposé accent of religious fanaticism in the United States, especially in Utah.

8. *September Dawn* (2007).
   A film featuring John Voight about the September 11, 1857 massacre of a wagon train by Mormon activists in Utah.

ENDNOTES

1. Mann Act, 18 U.S.C. § 2421.

2. *Caminetti v. United States,* 242 U.S. 470 (1917).

3. *Cleveland v. United States,* 329 U.S. 14 (1946).

4. 18 P.S. § 5902.

5. 18 P.S. § 5902(e.2).

6. 15 N.R.S. § 201.354.

7. *Ballentine's Law Dictionary.*

8. *Ballentine's Law Dictionary.*

9. 97 Miss. Code § 97–29.5.

10. N.C. Gen. Stat. § 8–57.

11. *Toncray v. Budge,* 95 P. 26.

12. 97 Miss. Code § 97–29–43.

13. "Utah Polygamist Released from Prison on Parole after Serving 6 Years," CNN Online: *http://www.cnn.com/2007/US/08/07/polygamist.ap/index.html,* accessed August 19, 2007.

14. *Reynolds v. United States,* 98 U.S. 145 (1878).

15. W. Blackstone, *Commentaries.*

16. 410 U.S. 113 (1973).

17. *Planned Parenthood of Southeastern Pa. v. Casey,* 505 U.S. 833 (1992).

18. *Stenberg v. Carhart,* 530 U.S. 914 (2000).

19. *Gonzales v. Carjart et al,; Gonzales v. Planned Parenthood Federation of America,* 127 S. Ct. 1610 (2007).

20. *Ballentine's Law Dictionary.*

21. Code Theod. 9.7.6; Code Just. 9.9.31.

22. 25 Hen.VIII, ch. 6.

23. *Survey on the Constitutional Right to Privacy in the Context of Homosexual Activity,* 40 U. Miami L. Rev. 521 (1986).

24. *Bowers v. Hardwick,* 478 U.S. 186 (1984).

25. *Ballentine's Law Dictionary.*

26. B. Hardy, "Return from Planet Pee-wee," *Vanity Fair,* September 1999.

27. *Ballentine's Law Dictionary.*

28. Utah, Tennessee, and Hawaii are the holdouts.

29. *Pa. Lottery Annual Report,* June 30, 2007.

30. *National Gambling Impact Study Commission Final Report,* June 1999.

31. "Internet Gambling Soars in the US," *The register.com at http://www.co.uk/2006/05/10/internet_gambling_soars,* May 10, 2006.

32. R. Dunstan, *Gambling in California,* California Research Bureau, 1997.

33. 18 U.S.C. § 1955.

34. *USA v. Cohen,* F.3d (2nd Cir. 2001).

35. Office of National Drug Control Policy, *The National Drug Control Strategy: 2005 Annual Report.*

36. *Ballentine's Law Dictionary.*

37. Drug Enforcement Agency, *The National Drug Threat Assessment, 2006.*

38. Federal Bureau of Investigation, *Uniform Crime Reports, Crime in the United States,* 2005.

39. Department of Justice, Bureau of Justice Statistics, *Drug Crime and Facts.*

40. 18 U.S.C. § 3591.

41. Bureau of Justice Statistics, *Felony Sentences in State Court,* 2002.

42. *Kimbrough, v United States,* 128 S. Ct. 558 (2007).

APPENDIX

UNITED STATES DISTRICT COURT	
EASTERN DISTRICT OF MISSOURI	
EASTERN DIVISION	

UNITED STATES OF AMERICA,	)
	)
Plaintiff,	)
v.	)
	)
BETONSPORTS PLC, its predecessors,	) 18 U.S.C. § 1962(d) - Racketeering
holding companies, subsidiaries and associated	) Conspiracy [Count 1, pp. 1-17]
entities; GARY STEPHEN KAPLAN, also	) 18 U.S.C. § 1341- Mail Fraud
known as Greg Champion; NEIL SCOTT	) [Count 2, p. 18]
KAPLAN, also known as Scott Kaye; LORI	) 18 U.S.C. § 1084 - Transmission of
BETH KAPLAN MULTZ, also known as Beth;	) Wagers/Wagering Information
DAVID CARRUTHERS; PETER WILSON;	) [Counts 3-12, pp. 18-19]
NORMAN STEINBERG, also known as Tom	) 18 U.S.C. § 1953-Interstate
Miller and David Norman; TIM BROWN, also	) Transportation of Gambling Para.
known as Matt Brown; DIRECT MAIL	) [Count 13, p. 20]
EXPERTISE, INC.; DME GLOBAL	) 18 U.S.C. § 2 - Aiding and Abetting
MARKETING & FULFILLMENT, INC.;	) 26 U.S.C. § 7201- Tax Evasion
MOBILE PROMOTIONS, INC.; WILLIAM	) [Counts 14-16, p. 20-22]
HERNAN LENIS; WILLIAM LUIS LENIS;	) 26 U.S.C. § 7212(a) - Interference
MANNY GUSTAVO LENIS, and MONICA	) with Administration of Internal
LENIS,	) Revenue Laws [Counts 17-22, pp. 22-23]
Defendants.	) Forfeiture pursuant to: 18 U.S.C. §
	) 1963 [Forfeiture Count, p. 23]

INDICTMENT

FILED UNDER SEAL

UNITED STATES DISTRICT COURT
EASTERN DISTRICT OF MISSOURI
EASTERN DIVISION

UNITED STATES OF AMERICA,	)	
	)	
Plaintiff,	)	
v.	)	
	)	
BETONSPORTS PLC, its predecessors,	)	18 U.S.C. § 1962(d) - Racketeering
holding companies, subsidiaries and associated	)	Conspiracy [Count 1, pp. 1-17]
entities; GARY STEPHEN KAPLAN, also	)	18 U.S.C. § 1341 - Mail Fraud
known as Greg Champion; NEIL SCOTT	)	[Count 2, p. 18]
KAPLAN, also known as Scott Kaye; LORI	)	18 U.S.C. § 1084 - Transmission of
BETH KAPLAN MULTZ, also known as Both;	)	Wagers/Wagering Information
DAVID CARRUTHERS; PETER WILSON;	)	[Counts 3-12, pp. 18-19]
NORMAN STEINBERG, also known as Tom	)	18 U.S.C. § 1953 - Interstate
Miller and David Norman; TIM BROWN, also	)	Transportation of Gambling Para.
known as Matt Brown; DIRECT MAIL	)	[Count 13, p. 20]
EXPERTISE, INC.; DME GLOBAL	)	18 U.S.C. § 2 - Aiding and Abetting
MARKETING & FULFILLMENT, INC.;	)	26 U.S.C. § 7201 - Tax Evasion
MOBILE PROMOTIONS, INC.; WILLIAM	)	[Counts 14-16, p. 20-22]
HERNAN LENIS; WILLIAM LUIS LENIS;	)	26 U.S.C. § 7212(a) - Interference
MANNY GUSTAVO LENIS, and MONICA	)	with Administration of Internal
LENIS,	)	Revenue Laws [Counts 17-22, pp. 22-23]
Defendants.	)	Forfeiture pursuant to: 18 U.S.C. §
	)	1963 [Forfeiture Count, p. 23]

INDICTMENT

The Grand Jury charges that:

COUNT 1
(Racketeering Conspiracy)

At all times material to this Indictment, in the Eastern District of Missouri and elsewhere:

Introduction

1.   Beginning in approximately 1992, defendant GARY STEPHEN KAPLAN (hereafter "GARY KAPLAN") and others operated an illegal sports betting business in and near New York City. After GARY KAPLAN's arrest on New York State gambling charges in May of 1993, GARY KAPLAN relocated his illegal gambling operation to Florida, continuing to take sports wagers from bettors in New York by telephone. In approximately 1995, GARY KAPLAN moved the illegal gambling business to Aruba, in the West Indies, but continued to operate primarily in the United States. To facilitate its U.S. operations, the gambling businesses established and controlled toll-free telephone services and Internet web sites, and caused these services to accept sports wagers from gamblers in the United States. In about 1996-1997, GARY KAPLAN relocated the gambling operations to Antigua, and then to Costa Rica, leaving certain aspects of the financial operations in Antigua. Through all these relocations, GARY KAPLAN and the other defendants always operated, and caused the operation of their primary revenue-producing business, illegal sports wagering, in the United States.

2.   Among the first Internet gambling businesses operated by GARY KAPLAN was a computer-based sports book called the North American Sports Association International, or NASA, which evolved into BETonSPORTS.COM. GARY KAPLAN and the other defendants advertised BETonSPORTS.COM as the largest online wagering service in the world. BETonSPORTS.COM and the other gambling web sites operated by GARY KAPLAN and his co-defendants offered gamblers in the United States illegal wagering on professional and college football and basketball, as well as many other professional and amateur sporting events and contests. These Internet gambling web sites also advertised toll free telephone numbers for placing sports bets.

3.   In July of 2004, BETONSPORTS PLC, a holding company, was incorporated under the laws of England and the United Kingdom. Defendant GARY KAPLAN, through a holding company called Boulder Overseas, retained approximately 44% of the BETONSPORTS PLC stock. In July of 2005, defendant GARY KAPLAN sold and caused the sale of 23,000,000 shares of BETONSPORTS PLC, retaining ownership of 15% of the BETONSPORTS PLC stock through Boulder Overseas.

The Defendants

4.   Defendant GARY KAPLAN, also known as "Greg Champion" and "G," was the founder and primary operator of BETonSPORTS.COM and other Internet and telephone sports betting businesses.

5.   Defendant NEIL SCOTT KAPLAN (hereafter "NEIL KAPLAN"), also known as "Scott Kaye," is defendant GARY KAPLAN'S brother. NEIL KAPLAN was an agent and/or employee of BETonSPORTS.COM, and, among other things, handled purchasing of goods and services.

6.   Defendant LORI BETH KAPLAN MULTZ (hereafter "LORI KAPLAN MULTZ"), also known as "Beth," and "Beth Wilson," is GARY KAPLAN'S sister. LORI KAPLAN MULTZ was an employee and/or agent of BETonSPORTS.COM, who, among other things, arranged for advertising of the gambling web sites and telephone services.

7.   Defendant DAVID CARRUTHERS was the Chief Executive Officer of BETonSPORTS.COM, and a Director of BETONSPORTS PLC.

8.   Defendant PETER WILSON was the Media Director for BETonSPORTS.COM.

9.   Defendant NORMAN STEINBERG, also known as "Tom Miller" and "David Norman" owned and operated, with defendant GARY KAPLAN, a number of Internet and telephone service gambling web sites, collectively known as the Millennium Group.

10.   Defendant TIM BROWN, also known as "Matt Brown," is NORMAN STEINBERG's son-in-law, and, among other things, was an employee and/or agent of the Internet gambling web sites in the Millennium Group.

11.   Defendants MOBILE PROMOTIONS, INC., DIRECT MAIL EXPERTISE, INC., and DME GLOBAL MARKETING & FULFILLMENT (referred to in a group as "the Lenis Companies"), were all Florida corporations, which operated cooperatively and shared use of bank accounts and financing. These companies provided promotional services to the illegal gambling web sites and telephone services operated by GARY KAPLAN and the other defendants.

12.   Defendant WILLIAM HERNAN LENIS was an owner, officer and operator of the Lenis Companies.

13.   Defendant WILLIAM LUIS LENIS is the son of WILLIAM HERNAN LENIS, and was an officer and operator of the Lenis Companies.

14.   Defendant MONICA LENIS is the daughter of WILLIAM HERNAN LENIS, and was an officer and operator of the Lenis Companies.

15.   Defendant MANNY GUSTAVO LENIS is the nephew of WILLIAM HERNAN LENIS, and was an employee of the Lenis Companies.

16.   Defendant BETONSPORTS PLC is a publicly owned and traded holding company. BETONSPORTS PLC owned and operated BETonSPORTS.COM and other Internet and telephone sports gambling businesses operated illegally in the United States.

The Enterprise

17.   At least as early as 1992, and through the date of the filing of this Indictment, defendants GARY KAPLAN, NEIL KAPLAN, LORI KAPLAN MULTZ, DAVID CARRUTHERS, PETER WILSON, NORMAN STEINBERG, TIM BROWN, WILLIAM HERNAN LENIS, WILLIAM LUIS LENIS, MONICA LENIS, MANNY GUSTAVO LENIS, BETONSPORTS PLC, DIRECT MAIL EXPERTISE, INC., DME GLOBAL MARKETING FULFILLMENT & DISTRIBUTION, INC., MOBILE PROMOTIONS, INC. and others, known and

unknown, constituted an "enterprise" (hereafter referred to as the "KAPLAN GAMBLING ENTERPRISE," or the "ENTERPRISE"), as defined by Title 18, United States Code, § 1961(4); that is, a group of entities and individuals associated in fact. The KAPLAN GAMBLING ENTERPRISE constituted an ongoing organization, whose members functioned as a continuing unit, for the common purpose of achieving the objectives of the ENTERPRISE. The ENTERPRISE was engaged in, and its activities affected, interstate and foreign commerce.

18. The KAPLAN GAMBLING ENTERPRISE operated a number of Internet web sites, hosted on servers located outside the United States, that did business in the United States by, among other things, offering, facilitating and conducting unlawful computer and telephone service based sports betting, and other forms of gambling. The KAPLAN GAMBLING ENTERPRISE caused the operation of toll-free telephone services to facilitate sports gambling, and take sports bets. THE KAPLAN GAMBLING ENTERPRISE created and disseminated false and fraudulent advertising for its Internet gambling businesses throughout the United States.

19. In addition to the named defendants, members, associates and facilities of the KAPLAN GAMBLING ENTERPRISE included legal entities incorporated in the United States and other countries around the world. Some of these entities provided services to or otherwise supported the ENTERPRISE. The ENTERPRISE owned and controlled or had contractual rights entitling it to control domain names used to identify web sites that provided illegal gambling in the United States, or otherwise aided and abetted the ENTERPRISE's operations. These include:

(a) legal entities that operated as fronts for or supporters of the ENTERPRISE, and entities whose funding and services benefitted the ENTERPRISE's goals, included but were not limited to: BetonSports (Panama) S.A.; BetonSports (Costa Rica) S.A.; BetonSports (Antigua) Ltd. S.A.; BetonSports.com Ltd.; NASA International, Inc.; NASA Sports Books, Inc.; Millennium Sports; Mill Sports; Inversiones Millennium I y M S.A.; Corporation Moishe; B. Holdings, Inc.; Boulder Investment; Brentail International S.A.; J.S.I. Jaguar Sports Internacional S.A.; Fergrant International S.A.; Lansford Inc.; Sports on the Internet, Ltd.; Gibraltar Sports Corp.; Infinity Sports International Corp.; Rock Island, Inc.; Bettors Trust; Best Line Sports; MVP; I Q Ludorum; Domain Choices; the International Sportsbook Council (ISBC) and the Offshore Gaming Association (OSGA).

(b) Corporate entities owned and/or controlled by ENTERPRISE members, included, but were not limited to, World Wide Credit; Barrio Holdings; Iguana Azul S.A.; Insiders Publishing; and Boulder Overseas.

(c) Entities operated under Internet-associated brand or trade names belonging to or controlled by ENTERPRISE members, included but were not limited to: BETonSPORTS.COM (also known as BetonSports, BetonSports.com and BoS.com); BoS; Bestline Sports International; betmill.com; BetonFantasy.com; BetonSports.com; Bettorstrast.com; Blue Grass Sports; Gibraltar Sports; Infinity Sports International; Jagbet.com; MVP Bets.com; Millennium Sports; NASA International Sportsbook; Rock Island Sports; and Wagermall.com.

(d) Domain names currently and formerly used to operate web sites owned and controlled by ENTERPRISE members, or otherwise used by or related to the ENTERPRISE, included but were not limited to those listed in Attachment A, and herein incorporated by reference.

20. A principal goal of the KAPLAN GAMBLING ENTERPRISE was to make money for the ENTERPRISE, its employees, members and associates, by maximizing the number of individuals in the United States who opened wagering accounts and used those accounts to place illegal bets on sports and sporting events with ENTERPRISE-controlled telephone service and Internet gambling web sites. It was also a goal of the ENTERPRISE to make money by maximizing the number of individuals residing in the United States who opened wagering accounts and gambled on casino-type games offered on ENTERPRISE-controlled Internet web sites.

21. Another goal of the KAPLAN GAMBLING ENTERPRISE was to evade the payment of federal wagering excise taxes due to the United States from the employees, members and associates of the ENTERPRISE.

The Racketeering Conspiracy

22. Beginning no later than 1992 and continuing to the present, within the Eastern District of Missouri and elsewhere, defendants

GARY STEPHEN KAPLAN, also known as "Greg Champion;"
NEIL SCOTT KAPLAN, also known as "Scott Kaye;"
LORI BETH KAPLAN MULTZ; also known as "Beth;"
DAVID CARRUTHERS;
PETER WILSON;
NORMAN STEINBERG, also known as "Tom Miller" and "David Norman;"
TIM BROWN, also known as "Matt Brown;"
WILLIAM HERNAN LENIS, also known as "Bill Lenis;"
WILLIAM LUIS LENIS, also known as "Will Lenis";
MANNY GUSTAVO LENIS;
MONICA LENIS;

BETONSPORTS PLC, its predecessors, holding companies, and associated entities,
DIRECT MAIL EXPERTISE, a Florida corporation, its predecessors and successors;
DME GLOBAL MARKETING & FULFILLMENT, INC., a Florida corporation, its predecessors and successors;

MOBILE PROMOTIONS, INC., a Florida corporation, its predecessors and successors, together with other persons known and unknown, being persons employed by and associated with the KAPLAN GAMBLING ENTERPRISE, which engaged in, and the activities of which affected, interstate and foreign commerce, knowingly and intentionally conspired to violate Title 18, United States Code, § 1962(c), that is, to conduct and participate, directly and indirectly, in the conduct of the affairs of the ENTERPRISE through a pattern of racketeering activity consisting of multiple acts in violation of statutes in Missouri [Mo. Rev. Stat. §§ 572.020 and 572.030]; Florida [Fla. Stat. ch. 849.25]; New York [N.Y.Gen. Oblig. § 5-401 and N.Y. Penal § 225.10]; New Jersey [N.J. Stat. Ann. §2C:37-2]; Washington [Wash. Rev. Code §§ 9.46.220 to 221; and 9.46.180] and Illinois [720 I11. Comp. Stat. 5/28-I(a)(1 1)], and multiple acts indictable under:

(a) 18 U.S.C. § 1084 (the Wire Wager Act);
(b) 18 U.S.C. § 1341 (Mail Fraud);
(c) 18 U.S.C. § 1343 (Wire Fraud);
(d) 18 U.S.C. § 1952 (Interstate travel in aid of a Racketeering Enterprise);
(e) 18 U.S.C. § 1955 (Operation of an Illegal Gambling Business);
(f) 18 U.S.C. § 1953 (Interstate transportation of Gambling Paraphernalia); and
(g) 18 U.S.C. § 1956 (Money Laundering).

23.   It was part of the conspiracy that each defendant agreed that a conspirator would commit at least two acts of racketeering activity in the conduct of the affairs of the ENTERPRISE.

Manner, Method and Means of the Racketeering Conspiracy

24.   It was part of the conspiracy that the ENTERPRISE operated Internet web site and telephone gambling services from facilities physically located in San Jose, Costa Rica. The ENTERPRISE took wagers almost exclusively from gamblers in the United States. BETonSPORTS.COM promotional media materials, prepared and distributed by the ENTERPRISE, stated that in 2003, BETonSPORTS.COM had 100,000 active players, who placed 33 million wagers, worth over $1.6 billion dollars through the BETonSPORTS.COM web site. BETonSPORTS.COM promotional media materials prepared and distributed by the ENTERPRISE stated that in 2004, BETonSPORTS.COM had more than 2,000 inbound telephone lines, computer servers capable of handling 5,600 simultaneous web transactions, and more than 2,000 employees during peak gambling times such as the months preceding the Superbowl and March Madness. BETonSPORTS.COM promotional media materials publicly available in 2004 and 2005 stated that BETonSPORTS.COM had a state-of- the-art network infrastructure, and offered illegal Internet and telephone service gambling through sportsbooks, an online casino, and "proposition" bets. BETonSPORTS.COM promotional media materials available in 2004 and 2005 stated that the web site took in an average of 63 bets per minute, "24/7/52," 98 percent of which came from bettors in the United States. All wagering originating in the United States which occurred on ENTERPRISE web sites and telephone services was illegal under federal law.

25.   It was part of the conspiracy that in order to increase traffic and wagering on ENTERPRISE web sites and telephone services, the KAPLAN GAMBLING ENTERPRISE targeted U.S. gamblers, even though soliciting and accepting bets placed on sports and sporting events using interstate wire communications facilities was and is illegal in the United States, except where specifically authorized by federal law. The ENTERPRISE spent millions of dollars in the United States, advertising ENTERPRISE-controlled Internet web sites and telephone services in magazines, sports annuals and other sports publications, on sports radio, and on television.

26.   It was part of the conspiracy that the KAPLAN GAMBLING ENTERPRISE operated various illegal gambling businesses. The ENTERPRISE conducted illegal Internet and telephone gambling operations throughout the United States, in violation of the laws of the United States. The KAPLAN GAMBLING ENTERPRISE solicited millions of illegal bets on sports and sporting events from gamblers in the United States, twenty four hours a day, three hundred and sixty five days a year. These bets, and information related to illegal bets placed with the KAPLAN GAMBLING ENTERPRISE-controlled entities, were transmitted via interstate and international telephone lines, and computers connected to the Internet.

27. It was part of the conspiracy to develop a scheme to defraud gamblers in the United States, by inviting, inducing and persuading them to place bets with the KAPLAN GAMBLING ENTERPRISE through its various Internet web sites and telephone lines. As part of the scheme, the members and associates of the KAPLAN GAMBLING ENTERPRISE created and disseminated advertising throughout the United States, which falsely stated that Internet and telephone gambling on sporting events and contests was "legal and licensed." The KAPLAN GAMBLING ENTERPRISE concealed the fact that the multiple web sites and telephone services through which it offered sports and casino style gambling were all owned and operated by the ENTERPRISE, and used to conduct the ENTERPRISE's illegal gambling businesses that were in fact not legal or licensed in the United States.

28.   As part of the scheme to defraud, the KAPLAN GAMBLING ENTERPRISE used the United States mail system to deliver its fraudulent print advertising, and to cause bettors in the United States to send money to ENTERPRISE-controlled entities

for the purpose of placing illegal bets. The KAPLAN GAMBLING ENTERPRISE used radio and television to deliver fraudulent advertising, through broadcasts and cable casts in and across the United States.

29. As part of the scheme to defraud, the KAPLAN GAMBLING ENTERPRISE controlled, in whole or in part, two entities called the Offshore Gaming Association ("OSGA") and the International Sportsbook Council ("ISBC"). The OSGA and the ISBC were advertised and represented to gamblers in the United States as independent watchdog agencies, whose purpose was to monitor online gambling to protect the wagering public. The ENTERPRISE actually used the OSGA and ISBC web sites to direct U.S. gamblers to ENTERPRISE-controlled web and telephone gambling sites, and to inhibit loss of funds to the ENTERPRISE that might otherwise occur due to customer complaints or disputes.

30. It was part of the scheme to defraud and the conspiracy that the members and agents of the KAPLAN GAMBLING ENTERPRISE instructed individuals in the United States to send, or cause money to be sent to the ENTERPRISE, for the purpose of opening one or more gambling accounts. The ENTERPRISE instructed these individuals to send the money, intended to be used to place illegal wagers, to a named recipient other than directly to the ENTERPRISE web site or telephone line.

31. Another part of the conspiracy was to have the members and associates of the KAPLAN GAMBLING ENTERPRISE use interstate and international telephone and computer wire communications to illegally accept and record millions of sports wagers from gamblers in the United States, and to transmit information facilitating the acceptance of illegal wagers by KAPLAN GAMBLING ENTERPRISE web sites and gambling telephone services.

32. It was also part of the conspiracy that members and associates of the KAPLAN GAMBLING ENTERPRISE traveled and communicated across State and national borders, in aid of the ENTERPRISE and its operations, and purchased products and services in the United States, and caused them to be shipped to Costa Rica, and other locations outside the U.S. where the ENTERPRISE had physical facilities.

33. It was also part of the conspiracy that the members and associates of the KAPLAN GAMBLING ENTERPRISE transported gambling equipment across State and national borders, in aid of the ENTERPRISE and its operations.

34. Another component of the conspiracy was to have the members and associates of the KAPLAN GAMBLING ENTERPRISE launder money received by the ENTERPRISE in the form of illegal wagers and fees.

35. It was part of the conspiracy that the ENTERPRISE, its members and associates, used the U.S. and private mail services and wire transfer services to send money from ENTERPRISE components outside the United States to various recipients in the United States, and from the United States to recipients outside the United States, and between locations in the United States, in order to promote the ENTERPRISE's illegal telephone and Internet gambling operations.

Overt Acts

36. In furtherance of the conspiracy, and to accomplish the objects of the conspiracy, the defendants and their co-conspirators, committed, among others, the following acts within the Eastern District of Missouri and elsewhere:

(1) On or about January 31, 2002, the KAPLAN GAMBLING ENTERPRISE operated a telephone service and Internet gambling web site called Millennium Sportsbook, and transmitted to potential and actual bettors in the Eastern District of Missouri, instructions for opening a wagering account with Millennium Sportsbook. The instructions stated that the money was to be sent from the United States to "Rod Jones" in Ecuador.

(2) On or about February 6, 2002, the KAPLAN GAMBLING ENTERPRISE operated a telephone service and Internet gambling web site called Gibraltar Sportsbook, and transmitted to potential and actual bettors in the Eastern District of Missouri, instructions for opening a wagering account with Gibraltar Sportsbook. The instructions stated that the money was to be sent from the United States to "Thomas Navas" in Ecuador.

(3) On or about February 12, 2002, the KAPLAN GAMBLING ENTERPRISE operated a telephone service and Internet gambling web site called NASA, and transmitted to potential and actual bettors in the Eastern District of Missouri, instructions for opening a wagering account with NASA. The instructions stated that the money was to be sent from the United States to "David Allen" in Belize.

(4) On or about March 8, 2002, the KAPLAN GAMBLING ENTERPRISE operated a telephone service and Internet gambling web site called Gibraltar Sports, and transmitted to potential and actual bettors in the Eastern District of Missouri, instructions for opening a wagering account with Gibraltar Sports. The instructions stated that the money was to be sent from the United States to "Jerry Moore" in Ecuador.

(5) On or about March 8, 2002, the KAPLAN GAMBLING ENTERPRISE operated a telephone service and Internet gambling web site called Millennium, and transmitted to potential and actual bettors in the Eastern District of Missouri, instructions for opening a wagering account with Millennium. The instructions stated that the money was to be sent from the United States to "Kevin Green" in Ecuador.

(6) On or about March 12, 2002, the KAPLAN GAMBLING ENTERPRISE operated a telephone service and Internet gambling web site called Millennium Sportsbook, and transmitted to potential and actual bettors in the Eastern District of

Missouri, instructions for opening a wagering account with Millennium. The instructions stated that the money was to be sent from the United States to "Paul Rogers" in Ecuador.

(7) On or about March 13, 2002, the KAPLAN GAMBLING ENTERPRISE operated a telephone service and Internet gambling web site called Millennium Sports, and accepted an account inquiry via a telephone and Internet communication to an ENTERPRISE controlled Internet web site with the domain name of bet.wagermillennium.com.

(8) On or about April 25, 2002, the KAPLAN GAMBLING ENTERPRISE operated a telephone service and Internet gambling web site called Gibraltar Sports, and accepted a sports wager via a telephone and Internet communication to an ENTERPRISE-controlled Internet web site with the domain name of bettherock.com.

(9) On or about April 25, 2002, the KAPLAN GAMBLING ENTERPRISE operated a telephone service and Internet gambling web site called Millennium Sports, and accepted a sports bet via a telephone and Internet communication to an ENTERPRISE-controlled Internet web site with the domain name ofmillsports.com.

(10) On or about June 12, 2002, the KAPLAN GAMBLING ENTERPRISE operated a telephone service and Internet gambling web site called Millennium Sports, and accepted a request via telephone to withdraw money from a wagering account held by the KAPLAN GAMBLING ENTERPRISE.

(11) Between September 1 and October 30, 2003, the KAPLAN GAMBLING ENTERPRISE mailed brochures, magazines, coupons and flyers mailed from an address in Miami, Florida, to 12430 Tesson Ferry Road, St. Louis, Missouri.

(12) Between August 2002 and September 2003, the KAPLAN GAMBLING ENTERPRISE caused fraudulent radio advertisements to be broadcast by radio stations across the country.

(13) Between October 2001 and January 2002, the KAPLAN GAMBLING ENTERPRISE arranged for the telecast of a fraudulent television advertisement stating that its gambling telephone services and web sites were "legal and licensed."

(14) Between 2001 and the date of this Indictment, the KAPLAN GAMBLING ENTERPRISE transported and caused the transportation of gambling paraphernalia across state boundaries, and used the equipment to induce individuals to open betting accounts with various ENTERPRISE-controlled Internet sports gambling web sites.

(15) On or about November 24, 2003, defendant David Carruthers traveled to New York City, and met with employees of a media relations firm used by the ENTERPRISE to promote its operations.

(16) On or about February 20, 2004, employees, owners or agents of the Lenis Group of companies and employees and agents of the ENTERPRISE arranged for the shipment, from Miami, Florida to Costa Rica, of two automobiles, purchased with funds provided by the KAPLAN GAMBLING ENTERPRISE, for use by the ENTERPRISE.

(17) On or about September 6, 2000, the KAPLAN GAMBLING ENTERPRISE caused a check in the amount of $99,620.00 to be made out by American Media Communications, payable to One-on-One Sports, for the purchase of advertising for ENTERPRISE-controlled Internet gambling web sites on radio broadcasts.

(18) On or about December 11, 2000, the KAPLAN GAMBLING ENTERPRISE caused a check in the amount of $100,000 to be sent to Standard Register Company, to purchase services related to direct mail advertising of ENTERPRISE-controlled Internet gambling web sites.

(19) On or about April 11, 2001, the KAPLAN GAMBLING ENTERPRISE caused a check in the amount of $109,903.39 to be sent to Standard Register Company, to purchase services related to direct mail advertising of ENTERPRISE-controlled Internet gambling web sites.

(20) On or about September 2, 2003, the KAPLAN GAMBLING ENTERPRISE caused $90,000.00 to be sent from a bank located outside the United States via a wire transfer, to a bank account controlled by defendant DME GLOBAL located in Florida, to purchase advertising/promotional services on behalf of ENTERPRISE-controlled Internet gambling web sites.

(21) On or about August 4, 2004, the KAPLAN GAMBLING ENTERPRISE caused $61,962.00 to be sent from a bank located outside the United States via a wire transfer, to a bank account controlled by defendant DME GLOBAL located in Florida, to purchase advertising/promotional services on behalf of ENTERPRISE-controlled Internet gambling web sites.

(22) On or about December 28, 2005, BETONSPORTS PLC purchased three online sports books; MVPSportsbook, Player Super Book and V-Wager.

(23) On or about April 12, 2006, BETONSPORTS PLC owned web site BETonSPORTS.COM solicited and accepted wagers from an individual residing in the State of Washington, in violation of that State's laws.

All in violation of Title 18, United States Code, § 1962(d).

COUNT 2
(Scheme to Defraud - Mail)

37. The Grand Jury re-alleges paragraphs 25, 27 and 28 above, and further charges that on or about September 1 to October 30, 2003, in the Eastern District of Missouri and elsewhere, defendants BETONSPORTS PLC and DME GLOBAL MARKETING AND FULFILLMENT, INC, for the purpose of executing and attempting to execute the scheme to defraud, did knowingly cause to be delivered by mail, from Miami, Florida, to 12430 Tesson Ferry Road, St. Louis, Missouri, brochures, magazines, coupons and flyers, all in violation of Title 18, United States Code, §§1341 and 2.

COUNTS 3 to 12
(Use of a Communications Facility to Transmit Bets and Betting Information)

38. The Grand Jury re-alleges paragraphs 18, 26 and 31 above, and further charges that, on or about the dates listed below, in the Eastern District of Missouri and elsewhere, defendants GARY KAPLAN and NORMAN STEINBERG, and others known and unknown, being engaged in the business of betting and wagering, did knowingly use and cause the use of a wire communication facility, for the transmission in interstate and foreign commerce, between the State of Missouri and the country of Costa Rica, wagers on sporting events and contests, information assisting in the placing of bets and wagers on sporting events and contests, and a wire communication which entitled the recipient to receive money and credit as a result of bets and wagers, and information assisting in the placing of bets and wagers, in violation of Title 18, United States Code, §§ 1084 and 2.

Count	Date	Recipient	Defendant(s)	Communication
3	Jan. 31, 2002	Millennium Sportsbook	GARY KAPLAN & NORMAN STEINBERG	Call to 800-824-1637 transmitted instructions on opening a wagering account and instructions to send money to "Rod Jones" in Ecuador.
4	Feb. 6, 2002	Gibraltar Sportsbook	GARY KAPLAN & NORMAN STEINBERG	Call to 800-582-1381 transmitted instructions on opening a wagering account and instructions to send money to "Thomas Navas" in Ecuador.
5	Feb. 12, 2002	NASA	GARY KAPLAN	Call to 888-999-9238 transmitted instructions on opening a wagering account and instructions to send money to "David Allen" in Belize.
6	Mar. 8, 2002	Gibraltar Sports	GARY KAPLAN & NORMAN STEINBERG	Call to 800-582-1381 confirmed instructions to send money to "Jerry Moore" in Ecuador.
7	Mar. 8, 2002	Millennium	GARY KAPLAN & NORMAN STEINBERG	Call to 800-824-1637 transmitted instructions to send money to "Kevin Green" in Ecuador.
8	Mar. 12, 2002	Millennium Sportsbook	GARY KAPLAN & NORMAN STEINBERG	Call to 800-593-2915 transmitted instructions to send money to "Paul Rogers" in Ecuador.
9	Mar. 13, 2002	Millennium Sports	GARY KAPLAN & NORMAN STEINBERG	Internet communication to bet.wagermillennium.com confirmed account balance.
10	April 25, 2002	Gibraltar Sports	GARY KAPLAN & NORMAN STEINBERG	Internet communication to bettherock.com transmitted a bet.
11	April 25, 2002	Millennium Sports	GARY KAPLAN & NORMAN STEINBERG	Internet communication to millsports.com transmitted a bet.
12	June 12, 2002	Millennium Sports	GARY KAPLAN & NORMAN STEINBERG	Call to 800-824-1637 requested withdrawal of money from wagering account.

COUNT 13
(Interstate Transportation of Gambling Paraphernalia)

39.   The Grand Jury re-alleges paragraph 33 above, and further charges that on or about October 20, 2002, in the Eastern District of Missouri and elsewhere, defendants GARY KAPLAN, WILLIAM HERNAN LENIS, MONICA LENIS, MOBILE PROMOTIONS, INC. and others known and unknown, knowingly did carry and send in interstate commerce, from the State of Florida to the State of Missouri, laptop computers and software, used, and to be used and adapted, devised and designed for use in bookmaking, all in violation of Title 18, United States Code, §§ 1953 and 2.

COUNT 14
(Tax Evasion)

40.   The Grand Jury further charges that, in the Eastern District of Missouri and elsewhere:

During the time period from on or about January 29, 2001 to on or about February 3, 2002, BETonSPORTS.COM, BetonSports (Antigua), Millennium, Jaguar, Infinity, and Gibraltar, entities doing business in the United States, had and received taxable wagers in the sum of approximately $1,094,669,000.00; and defendant GARY KAPLAN, who owned and controlled BETonSPORTS.COM, BetonSports (Antigua), Millennium, Jaguar, Infinity, and Gibraltar, well-knowing and believing the foregoing facts, did willfully attempt to evade and defeat the said wagering excise tax due and owing by GARY KAPLAN, as the owner and operator of BETonSPORTS.COM, BetonSports (Antigua), Millennium, Jaguar, Infinity, and Gibraltar, to the United States of America for said time period, by failing to make any wagering excise tax returns on or before the last day of the month following the month the wagers were accepted, as required by law, to any proper officer of the Internal Revenue Service, by failing to pay to the Internal Revenue Service said wagering excise tax, and by directing that the wagering funds be sent outside the United States, all in violation of Title 26, United States Code, Section 7201, and Title 18, United States Code, Section 2.

COUNT 15
(Tax Evasion)

41.   The Grand Jury further charges that, in the Eastern District of Missouri, and elsewhere: During the time period from on or about February 4, 2002 to on or about February 2, 2003, BETonSPORTS.COM, BetonSports (Antigua), Jaguar, MVP, Millennium, Gibraltar, Infinity and Wagermall, entities doing business in the United States, had and received taxable wagers in the sum of approximately $1,228,874,000.00; and defendant GARY KAPLAN, who owned and controlled BETonSPORTS.COM, BetonSports (Antigua), Jaguar, MVP, Millennium, Gibraltar, Infinity and Wagermall, well-knowing and believing the foregoing facts, did willfully attempt to evade and defeat the said wagering excise tax due and owing by GARY KAPLAN as the owner and operator of BETonSPORTS.COM, BetonSports (Antigua),Jaguar, MVP, Millennium, Gibraltar, Infinity and Wagermall to the United States of America for said time period, by failing to make a wagering excise tax return on or before the last day of the month following the month wagers were accepted, as required by law, to any proper officer of the Internal Revenue Service, by failing to pay to the Internal Revenue Service said wagering excise tax, and by causing and directing that the wagering funds be sent outside the United States, all in violation of Title 26, United States Code, Section 7201, and Title 18, United States Code, Section 2.

COUNT 16
(Tax Evasion)

42.   The Grand Jury further charges that, in the Eastern District of Missouri, and elsewhere:
During the time period from on or about February 3, 2003 to on or about February 1, 2004, BETonSPORTS.COM, BetonSports (Antigua), Bettorstrust, Rockisland, Jaguar, MVP, Millennium, Gibraltar, Infinity and Wagermall, entities doing business in the United States, had and received taxable wagers in the sum of approximately $1,235,374,000.00; and defendant GARY KAPLAN, who owned and controlled BETonSPORTS.COM, BetonSports (Antigua), Bettorstrust, Rockisland, Jaguar, MVP, Millennium, Gibraltar, Infinity and Wagermall, well-knowing and believing the foregoing facts, did willfully attempt to evade and defeat the said wagering excise tax due and owing by GARY KAPLAN as the owner and operator of BETonSPORTS.COM, BetonSports (Antigua), Bettorstrust, Rockisland, Jaguar, MVP, Millennium, Gibraltar, Infinity and Wagermall to the United States of America for said time period, by failing to make wagering excise tax returns on or before the last day of the month following the month the wagers were accepted, as required by law, to any proper officer of the Internal Revenue Service, by failing to pay to the Internal Revenue Service said wagering excise tax, and by causing and directing that the wagering funds be sent outside the United States, all in violation of Title 26, United States Code, Section 7201, and Title 18, United States Code, Section 2.

COUNTS 17 to 22
(Interference With Administration of Revenue Laws)

43.   On or about the dates listed below, in the Eastern District of Missouri and elsewhere, defendants GARY KAPLAN, NORMAN STEINBERG and others known and unknown, did corruptly obstruct and impede and endeavor to obstruct and impede the due

administration of the internal revenue laws by directing that money for opening and funding sports wagering accounts, sent from the United States to unlawful Internet and telephone service gambling businesses located outside the United States, be directed to a third party recipient, all in violation of Title 26, United States Code, Section 7212(b), and Title 18, United States Code, Section 2, as follows:

COUNT 17 - January 31, 2002, Millennium Sportsbook employees gave instructions to an individual in the United States to send money to "Rod Jones" in Ecuador.

COUNT 18 - February 6, 2002, Gibraltar Sportsbook employees gave instructions to an individual in the United States to send money to open a wagering account to "Thomas Navas" in Ecuador.

COUNT 19 - February 12, 2002, NASA Sportsbook employees gave instructions to an individual in the United States to send money to open a wagering account to "David Allen" in Belize City.

COUNT 20 - March 8, 2002, Gibraltar Sportsbook employees gave instructions to an individual in the United States to send money to open an wagering account to "Jerry Moore" in Ecuador.

COUNT 21 - March 8, 2002, Millennium Sportsbook employees gave instructions to an individual in the Untied States to send money to "Kevin Green" in Quito, Ecuador.

COUNT 22 - March 12, 2002, Millennium Sportsbook employees gave instructions to an individual to send money to "Paul Rogers" in Ecuador.

RICO FORFEITURE

44.   The allegations contained in Count 1 of this Indictment are hereby repeated, realleged, and incorporated by reference herein as though fully set forth at length for the purpose of alleging forfeiture pursuant to the provisions of Title 18, United States Code, Section 1963. Pursuant to Rule 32.2, Fed. R. Crim. P., notice is hereby given to the defendants that the United States will seek forfeiture as part of any sentence in accordance with Title 18, United States Code, Section 1963 in the event of any defendant's conviction under Count 1 of this Indictment.

45.   The defendants,

GARY STEPHEN KAPLAN, also known as "Greg Champion;"
NEIL SCOTT KAPLAN, also known as "Scott Kaye;"
LORI BETH KAPLAN MULTZ; also known as "Beth;"
DAVID CARRUTHERS;
PETER WILSON;
NORMAN STEINBERG, also known as "Tom Miller and "Dave Brown;"
TIM BROWN, also known as "Matt Brown;"
WILLIAM HERNAN LENIS, also known as "Bill Lenis";
WILLIAM LUIS LENIS, also known as "Will Lenis";
MANNY GUSTAVO LENIS;
MONICA LENIS;
BETONSPORTS PLC, its predecessors, holding companies, and associated entities;
DIRECT MAIL EXPERTISE, a Florida corporation, its predecessors and successors;
DME GLOBAL MARKETING & FULFILLMENT, INC., a Florida corporation, its predecessors
and successors; and
MOBILE PROMOTIONS, INC., a Florida corporation, its predecessors and successors;

i. have acquired and maintained interests in violation of Title 18, United States Code, Section 1962, which interests are subject to forfeiture to the United States pursuant to Title 18, United States Code, Section 1963(a)(1);

ii. have an interest in, security of, claims against, and property and contractual rights which afford a source of influence over, the ENTERPRISE named and described herein which the defendants established, operated, controlled, conducted, and participated in the conduct of, in violation of Title 18, United States Code, Section 1962, which interests, securities, claims, and rights are subject to forfeiture to the United States pursuant to Title 18, United States Code,

iii. have property constituting and derived from proceeds obtained, directly and indirectly, from racketeering activity, in violation of Title 18, United States Code, Section 1962, which property is subject to forfeiture to the United States pursuant to Title 18, United States Code, Section 1963(a)(3),

46. The interests of the defendants subject to forfeiture to the United States pursuant to Title 18, United States Code, Section 1963(a)(1), (a)(2), and (a)(3), include but are not limited to:

a. at least $4.5 billion dollars; Recreational vehicle with VIN number 5B4MP67G023338413; Recreational vehicle with Florida license tag number S53-8XW; Recreational vehicle with Florida license tag number S79-7KJ; PT Cruiser with VIN number 3C8FY4BB41T586360; PT Cruiser registered to Mobile Promotions or William Lenis; PT Cruiser with Florida license tag number V65-TAG; Humvee with serial number 5GRGN23US4H116407; Humvee with serial number 5GRGN23US74H120068; Vehicle trailer VIN number 4DFTS10122N050735, Dell Latitude laptop computer, serial number 25633081; Gateway laptop computer, serial number 0027465903; Gateway laptop computer serial number 0015533205; Gateway laptop computer serial number 002804106; and Sprint cell phone assigned number 305-527-6674, forfeitable pursuant to Title 18, United States Code, Sections 1963(a)(1) and 1963(a)(3);

b. all right, title and interest in BETONSPORTS PLC and its subsidiaries and affiliates identified in paragraph 17 of this Indictment, forfeitable as each convicted defendant's interest in the ENTERPRISE pursuant to Title 18, United States Code, Section 1963(a)(2)(A);

c. all right, title and interest in those entities identified in paragraph 19 of this Indictment, forfeitable as each convicted defendant's interest in the ENTERPRISE pursuant to Title 18, United States Code, Section 1963(a)(2)(D);

47. If any of the property described in paragraphs (ii) and (iii) above, as a result of any act or omission of a defendant—

(1) cannot be located upon the exercise of due diligence;
(2) has been transferred or sold to, or deposited with, a third party;
(3) has been placed beyond the jurisdiction of the court;
(4) has been substantially diminished in value; or
(5) has been commingled with other property which cannot be divided without difficulty;

the court shall order the forfeiture of any other property of the defendants up to the value of any property set forth in paragraphs 45 and 46 above.

48. The above-named defendants, and each of them, are jointly and severally liable for the forfeiture obligations as alleged above.

All pursuant to Title 18, United States Code, Section 1963.

A TRUE BILL

FOREPERSON

CATHERINE L. HANAWAY
UNITED STATES ATTORNEY

MICHAEL K. FAGAN #6617
Assistant United States Attorney

MARTY WOELFLE AZ Bar #009363
Trial Attorney
Organized Crime and Racketeering Section

OCTOBER TERM, 2005

Syllabus

NOTE: Where it is feasible, a syllabus (headnote) will be released, as is being done in connection with this case, at the time the opinion is issued. The syllabus constitutes no part of the opinion of the Court but has been prepared by the Reporter of Decisions for the convenience of the reader. See *United States* v. *Detroit Timber & Lumber Co.,* 200 U. S. 321, 337.

SUPREME COURT OF THE UNITED STATES

Syllabus

GONZALES, ATTORNEY GENERAL, ET AL. *v.* O CENTRO ESPIRITA BENEFICENTE UNIAO DO VEGETAL ET AL.

CERTIORARI TO THE UNITED STATES COURT OF APPEALS FOR THE TENTH CIRCUIT

No. 04–1084.   Argued November 1, 2005—Decided February 21, 2006

Congress enacted the Religious Freedom Restoration Act of 1993 (RFRA) in response to *Employment Div., Dept. of Human Resources of Ore.* v. *Smith,* 494 U. S. 872, where, in upholding a generally applicable law that burdened the sacramental use of peyote, this Court held that the First Amendment's Free Exercise Clause does not require judges to engage in a case-by-case assessment of the religious burdens imposed by facially constitutional laws, *id.,* at 883–890. Among other things, RFRA prohibits the Federal Government from substantially burdening a person's exercise of religion, "even if the burden results from a rule of general applicability," 42 U. S. C. §2000bb–1(a), except when the Government can "demonstrat[e] that application of the burden to the person (1) [furthers] a compelling government interest; and (2) is the least restrictive means of furthering that... interest," §2000bb–1(b).

Members of respondent church (UDV) receive communion by drinking *hoasca,* a tea brewed from plants unique to the Amazon Rainforest that contains DMT, a hallucinogen regulated under Schedule I of the Controlled Substances Act, see 21 U. S. C. §812(c), Schedule I(c). After U. S. Customs inspectors seized a *hoasca* shipment to the American UDV and threatened prosecution, the UDV filed this suit for declaratory and injunctive relief, alleging, *inter alia,* that applying the Controlled Substances Act to the UDVs sacramental *hoasca* use violates RFRA. At a hearing on the UDVs preliminary injunction motion, the Government conceded that the challenged application would substantially burden a sincere exercise of religion, but argued that this burden did not violate RFRA because applying the Controlled Substances Act was the least restrictive means of advancing three compelling governmental interests: protecting UDV members' health and safety, preventing the diversion of *hoasca* from the church to recreational users, and complying with the 1971 United Nations Convention on Psychotropic Substances. The District Court granted relief, concluding that, because the parties' evidence on health risks and diversion was equally balanced, the Government had failed to demonstrate a compelling interest justifying the substantial burden on the UDV. The court also held that the 1971 Convention does not apply to *hoasca.* The Tenth Circuit affirmed.

Held: The courts below did not err in determining that the Government failed to demonstrate, at the preliminary injunction stage, a compelling interest in barring the UDV's sacramental use of *hoasca.* Pp. 6–19.

   1.   This Court rejects the Government's argument that evidentiary equipoise as to potential harm and diversion is an insufficient basis for a preliminary injunction against enforcement of the Controlled Substances Act. Given that the Government conceded the UDV's prima facie RFRA case in the District Court and that the evidence found to be in equipoise related to an affirmative defense as to which the Government bore the burden of proof, the UDV effectively demonstrated a likelihood of success on the merits. The Government's argument that, although it would bear the burden of demonstrating a compelling interest at trial on the merits, the UDV should have borne the burden of disproving such interests at the preliminary injunction hearing is foreclosed by *Ashcroft* v. *American Civil Liberties Union,* 542 U. S. 656, 666. There, in affirming the grant of a preliminary injunction against the Government, this Court reasoned that the burdens with respect to the compelling interest test at the preliminary injunction stage track the burdens at trial. The Government's attempt to limit the *Ashcroft* rule to content-based restrictions on speech is unavailing. The fact that *Ashcroft* involved such a restriction in no way affected the Court's assessment of the consequences of having the burden at trial for preliminary injunction purposes. Congress' express decision to legislate the compelling interest test indicates that RFRA challenges should be adjudicated in the same way as the test's constitutionally mandated applications, including at the preliminary injunction stage. Pp. 6–8.

   2.   Also rejected is the Government's central submission that, be cause it has a compelling interest in the *uniform* application of the Controlled Substances Act, no exception to the DMT ban can be made to accommodate the UDV. The Government argues, *inter alia,* that the Act's description of Schedule I substances as having "a high potential for abuse,"

GONZALES *v.* O CENTRO ESPIRITA BENEFICENTE UNIAO DO VEGETAL

Syllabus

"no currently accepted medical use," and "a lack of accepted safety for use ... under medical supervision," 21 U. S. C. §812(b)(1), by itself precludes any consideration of individualized exceptions, and that the Act's "closed" regulatory system, which prohibits all use of controlled substances except as the Act itself authorizes,see *Gonzales* v. *Raich,* 545 U. S.____, ____, cannot function properly if subjected to judicial exemptions. Pp. 8–16.

(a) RFRA and its strict scrutiny test contemplate an inquiry more focused than the Government's categorical approach. RFRA requires the Government to demonstrate that the compelling interest test is satisfied through application of the challenged law "to the person"—the particular claimant whose sincere exercise of religion is being substantially burdened. 42 U. S. C. §2000bb–1(b). Section 2000bb(b)(1) expressly adopted the compelling interest test of *Sherbert* v. *Verner,* 374 U. S. 398, and *Wisconsin* v. *Yoder,* 406 U. S. 205. There, the Court looked beyond broadly formulated interests justifying the general applicability of government mandates, scrutinized the asserted harms, and granted specific exemptions to particular religious claimants. *Id.,* at 213, 221, 236; *Sherbert, supra,* at 410. Outside the Free Exercise area as well, the Court has noted that "[c]ontext matters" in applying the compelling interest test, *Grutter v. Bollinger,* 539 U. S. 306, 327, and has emphasized that strict scrutiny's fundamental purpose is to take "relevant differences" into account, *Adarand Constructors, Inc.* v. *Peña,* 515 U. S. 200, 228. Pp. 9–10.

(b) Under RFRA's more focused inquiry, the Government's mere invocation of the general characteristics of Schedule I substances cannot carry the day. Although Schedule I substances such as DMT are exceptionally dangerous, see, *e.g., Touby* v. *United States,* 500 U. S. 160, 162, there is no indication that Congress, in classifying DMT, considered the harms posed by the particular use at issue. That question *was* litigated below. Before the District Court found that the Government had not carried its burden of showing a compelling interest in preventing such harm, the court noted that it could not ignore the congressional classification and findings. But Congress' determination that DMT should be listed under Schedule I simply does not provide a categorical answer that relieves the Government of the obligation to shoulder its RFRA burden. The Controlled Substances Act's authorization to the Attorney General to "waive the requirement for registration of certain manufacturers, distributors, or dispensers if he finds it consistent with the public health and safety," 21 U. S. C. §822(d), reinforces that Congress' findings with respect to Schedule I substances should not carry the determinative weight, for RFRA purposes, that the Government would ascribe to them. Indeed, despite the fact that everything the Government says about the DMT in *hoasca* applies in equal measure to the mescaline in peyote, another Schedule I substance, both the Executive and Congress have decreed an exception from the Controlled Substances Act for Native American religious use of peyote, see 21 CFR §1307.31; 42 U. S. C. §1996a(b)(1). If such use is permitted in the face of the general congressional findings for hundreds of thousands of Native Americans practicing their faith, those same findings alone cannot preclude consideration of a similar exception for the 130 or so American members of the UDV who want to practice theirs. See *Church of Lukumi Babalu Aye, Inc.* v. *Hialeah,* 508 U. S. 520, 547. The Government's argument that the existence of a *congressional* exemption for peyote does not indicate that the Controlled Substances Act is amenable to *judicially crafted* exceptions fails because RFRA plainly contemplates court-recognized exceptions, see §2000bb–1(c). Pp. 11–13.

(c) The peyote exception also fatally undermines the Government's broader contention that the Controlled Substances Act establishes a closed regulatory system that admits of no exceptions under RFRA. The peyote exception has been in place since the Controlled Substances Act's outset, and there is no evidence that it has undercut the Government's ability to enforce the ban on peyote use by non-Indians. The Government's reliance on pre-*Smith* cases asserting a need for uniformity in rejecting claims for religious exemptions under the Free Exercise Clause is unavailing. Those cases did not embrace the notion that a general interest in uniformity justified a substantial burden on religious exercise, but instead scrutinized the asserted need and explained why the denied exemptions could not be accommodated. See, *e.g., United States* v. *Lee,* 455 U. S. 252, 258, 260. They show that the Government can demonstrate a compelling interest in uniform application of a particular program by offering evidence that granting the requested religious accommodations would seriously compromise its ability to administer the program. Here the Government's uniformity argument rests not so much on the particular statutory program at issue as on slippery slope concerns that could be invoked in response to any RFRA claim for an exception to a generally applicable law, *i.e.,* "if I make an exception for you, I'll have to make one for everybody, so no exceptions." But RFRA operates by mandating consideration, under the compelling interest test, of exceptions to "rule[s] of general applicability." §2000bb–1(a). Congress' determination that the legislated test is "workable . . . for striking sensible balances between religious liberty and competing prior governmental interests," §200bb(a)(5), finds support in *Sherbert, supra,*at 407, and *Cutter* v. *Wilkinson,* 544 U. S. ____, ____. While there maybe instances where a need for uniformity precludes the recognition of exceptions to generally applicable laws under RFRA, it would be surprising to find that this was such a case, given the longstanding peyote exemption and the fact that the very reason Congress enacted RFRA was to respond to a decision denying a claimed right to sacramental use of a controlled substance. The Government has not shown that granting the UDV an exemption would cause the kind of administrative harm recognized as a compelling interest in, *e.g., Lee.* It cannot now compensate for its failure to convince the District Court as to its health or diversion concerns with the bold argument that there can be no RFRA exceptions at all to the Controlled Substances Act. Pp. 13–16.

3. The Government argues unpersuasively that it has a compelling interest in complying with the 1971 U. N. Convention. While this Court does not agree with the District Court that the Convention does not cover *hoasca,* that does not automatically mean that the Government has demonstrated a compelling interest in applying the Controlled Substances Act, which implements the Convention, to the UDV's sacramental use. At this stage, it suffices that the Government did not submit any evidence addressing the international consequences of granting the UDV an exemption, but simply relied on two affidavits by State Department officials attesting to the general (and undoubted) importance of honoring international obligations and maintaining the United States' leadership in the international war on drugs. Under RFRA, invocation of such general interests, standing alone, is not enough. Pp. 16–18.

389 F. 3d 973, affirmed and remanded.

ROBERTS, C. J., delivered the opinion of the Court, in which all other Members joined, except ALITO, J., who took no part in the consideration or decision of the case.

Cite as: 546 U. S. _____ (2006)

Opinion of the Court

NOTICE: This opinion is subject to formal revision before publication in the preliminary print of the United States Reports. Readers are requested to notify the Reporter of Decisions, Supreme Court of the United States, Washington, D. C. 20543, of any typographical or other formal errors, in order that corrections may be made before the preliminary print goes to press.

SUPREME COURT OF THE UNITED STATES

No. 04–1084

ALBERTO R. GONZALES, ATTORNEY GENERAL, ET AL., PETITIONERS *v.* O CENTRO ESPÍRITA BENEFICENTE UNIÃO DO VEGETAL ET AL.

ON WRIT OF CERTIORARI TO THE UNITED STATES COURT OF APPEALS FOR THE TENTH CIRCUIT

[February 21, 2006]

CHIEF JUSTICE ROBERTS delivered the opinion of the Court.

A religious sect with origins in the Amazon Rainforest receives communion by drinking a sacramental tea, brewed from plants unique to the region, that contains a hallucinogen regulated under the Controlled Substances Act by the Federal Government. The Government concedes that this practice is a sincere exercise of religion, but nonetheless sought to prohibit the small American branch of the sect from engaging in the practice, on the ground that the Controlled Substances Act bars all use of the hallucinogen. The sect sued to block enforcement against it of the ban on the sacramental tea, and moved for a preliminary injunction.

It relied on the Religious Freedom Restoration Act of 1993, which prohibits the Federal Government from substantially burdening a person's exercise of religion, unless the Government "demonstrates that application of the burden to the person" represents the least restrictive means of advancing a compelling interest. 42 U. S. C. §2000bb–1(b). The District Court granted the preliminary injunction, and the Court of Appeals affirmed. We granted the Government's petition for certiorari. Before this Court, the Government's central submission is that it has a compelling interest in the *uniform* application of the Controlled Substances Act, such that no exception to the ban on use of the hallucinogen can be made to accommodate the sect's sincere religious practice. We conclude that the Government has not carried the burden expressly placed on it by Congress in the Religious Freedom Restoration Act, and affirm the grant of the preliminary injunction.

I

In *Employment Div., Dept. of Human Resources of Ore.* v. *Smith,* 494 U. S. 872 (1990), this Court held that the Free Exercise Clause of the First Amendment does not prohibit governments from burdening religious practices through generally applicable laws. In *Smith,* we rejected a challenge to an Oregon statute that denied unemployment benefits to drug users, including Native Americans engaged in the sacramental use of peyote. *Id.,* at 890. In so doing, we rejected the interpretation of the Free Exercise Clause announced in *Sherbert* v. *Verner,* 374 U. S. 398 (1963), and, in accord with earlier cases, see *Smith,* 494 U. S., at 879–880, 884–885, held that the Constitution does not require judges to engage in a case-by-case assessment of the religious burdens imposed by facially constitutional laws. *Id.,* at 883–890.

Congress responded by enacting the Religious Freedom Restoration Act of 1993 (RFRA), 107 Stat. 1488, as amended, 42 U. S. C. § 2000bb *et seq.,* which adopts a statutory rule comparable to the constitutional rule rejected in *Smith.* Under RFRA, the Federal Government may not, as a statutory matter, substantially burden a person's exercise of religion, "even if the burden results from a rule of general applicability." §2000bb–1(a). The only exception recognized by the statute requires the Government to satisfy the compelling interest test—to "demonstrat[e] that application of the burden to the person—(1) is in furtherance of a compelling government interest; and (2) is the least restrictive means of furthering that compelling governmental interest." § 2000bb–1(b). A person whose religious practices are burdened in violation of RFRA "may assert that violation as a claim or defense in a judicial proceeding and obtain appropriate relief." § 2000bb–1(c).[1] 0(2000 ed.). Substances listed in Schedule I of the Act are subject to the

---

[1] As originally enacted, RFRA applied to States as well as the Federal Government. In *City of Boerne* v. *Flores,* 521 U. S. 507 (1997), we held the application to States to be beyond Congress' legislative authority under § 5 of the 14th Amendment.

GONZALES *v.* O CENTRO ESPÍRITA BENEFICENTE UNIÃO DO VEGETAL

Opinion of the Court

most comprehensive restrictions, including an outright ban on all importation and use, except pursuant to strictly regulated research projects. See §§823, 960(a)(1). The Act authorizes the imposition of a criminal sentence for simple possession of Schedule I substances, see §844(a), and mandates the imposition of a criminal sentence for possession "with intent to manufacture, distribute, or dispense" such substances, see §§841(a), (b).

O Centro Espírita Beneficente União do Vegetal (UDV) is a Christian Spiritist sect based in Brazil, with an American branch of approximately 130 individuals. Central to the UDV's faith is receiving communion through *hoasca* (pronounced "wass-ca"), a sacramental tea made from two plants unique to the Amazon region. One of the plants, *psychotria viridis*, contains dimethyltryptamine (DMT), a hallucinogen whose effects are enhanced by alkaloids from the other plant, *banisteriopsis caapi.* DMT, as well as "any material, compound, mixture, or preparation, which contains any quantity of [DMT]," is listed in Schedule I of the Controlled Substances Act. §812(c), Schedule I(c).

In 1999, United States Customs inspectors intercepted a shipment to the American UDV containing three drums of *hoasca*. A subsequent investigation revealed that the UDV had received 14 prior shipments of *hoasca*. The inspectors seized the intercepted shipment and threatened the UDV with prosecution.

The UDV filed suit against the Attorney General and other federal law enforcement officials, seeking declaratory and injunctive relief. The complaint alleged, *inter alia,* that applying the Controlled Substances Act to the UDV's sacramental use of *hoasca* violates RFRA. Prior to trial, the UDV moved for a preliminary injunction, so that it could continue to practice its faith pending trial on the merits.

At a hearing on the preliminary injunction, the Government conceded that the challenged application of the Controlled Substances Act would substantially burden a sincere exercise of religion by the UDV. See *O Centro Espírita Beneficente União do Vegetal* v. *Ashcroft*, 282 F. Supp. 2d 1236, 1252 (NM 2002). The Government argued, however, that this burden did not violate RFRA, because applying the Controlled Substances Act in this case was the least restrictive means of advancing three compelling governmental interests: protecting the health and safety of UDV members, preventing the diversion of *hoasca* from the church to recreational users, and complying with the 1971 United Nations Convention on Psychotropic Substances, a treaty signed by the United States and implemented by the Act. Feb. 21, 1971, [1979–1980], 32 U. S. T. 543, T. I. A. S. No. 9725. See 282 F. Supp. 2d, at 1252–1253.

The District Court heard evidence from both parties on the health risks of *hoasca* and the potential for diversion from the church. The Government presented evidence to the effect that use of *hoasca*, or DMT more generally, can cause psychotic reactions, cardiac irregularities, and adverse drug interactions. The UDV countered by citing studies documenting the safety of its sacramental use of *hoasca* and presenting evidence that minimized the likelihood of the health risks raised by the Government. With respect to diversion, the Government pointed to a general rise in the illicit use of hallucinogens, and cited interest in the illegal use of DMT and *hoasca* in particular; the UDV emphasized the thinness of any market for *hoasca*, the relatively small amounts of the substance imported by the church, and the absence of any diversion problem in the past.

The District Court concluded that the evidence on health risks was "in equipoise," and similarly that the evidence on diversion was "virtually balanced." *Id.,* at 1262, 1266. In the face of such an even showing, the court reasoned that the Government had failed to demonstrate a compelling interest justifying what it acknowledged was a substantial burden on the UDV's sincere religious exercise. *Id.,* at 1255. The court also rejected the asserted interest in complying with the 1971 Convention on Psychotropic Substances, holding that the Convention does not apply to *hoasca. Id.,* at 1266–1269.

The court entered a preliminary injunction prohibiting the Government from enforcing the Controlled Substances Act with respect to the UDV's importation and use of *hoasca*. The injunction requires the church to import the tea pursuant to federal permits, to restrict control over the tea to persons of church authority, and to warn particularly susceptible UDV members of the dangers of *hoasca*. See Preliminary Injunction ¶¶ 2, 5–12, 32–33, App. F to App. to Pet. for Cert. 249a, 250a–252a, 258a–259a. The injunction also provides that "if [the Government] believe[s] that evidence exists that *hoasca* has negatively affected the health of UDV members," or "that a shipment of *hoasca* contain[s] particularly dangerous levels of DMT, [the Government] may apply to the Court for an expedited determination of whether the evidence warrants suspension or revocation of [the UDV's authority to use *hoasca*]." *Id.,* at 257a, ¶29.

The Government appealed the preliminary injunction and a panel of the Court of Appeals for the Tenth Circuit affirmed, *O Centro Espírita Beneficente Uniao do Vegetal* v. *Ashcroft,* 342 F. 3d 1170 (2003), as did a majority of the Circuit sitting en banc, 389 F. 3d 973 (2004). We granted certiorari. 544 U. S. 973 (2005).

II

Although its briefs contain some discussion of the potential for harm and diversion from the UDV's use of *hoasca*, the Government does not challenge the District Court's factual findings or its conclusion that the evidence submitted on these issues was evenly balanced. Instead, the Government maintains that such evidentiary equipoise is an insufficient basis for issuing a preliminary injunction against enforcement of the Controlled Substances Act. We review the District Court's legal rulings *de novo* and its ultimate decision to issue the preliminary injunction for abuse of discretion. See *McCreary County* v. *American Civil Liberties Union*, 545 U. S. ____, ____ (2005) (slip op., at 19).

Cite as: 546 U. S. ____ (2006)

Opinion of the Court

The Government begins by invoking the well-established principle that the party seeking pretrial relief bears the burden of demonstrating a likelihood of success on the merits. See, *e.g., Mazurek* v. *Armstrong,* 520 U. S. 968, 972 (1997) *(per curiam); Doran* v. *Salem Inn, Inc.,* 422 U. S. 922, 931 (1975). The Government argues that the District Court lost sight of this principle in issuing the injunction based on a mere tie in the evidentiary record.

A majority of the en banc Court of Appeals rejected this argument, and so do we. Before the District Court, the Government conceded the UDV's prima facie case under RFRA. See 282 F. Supp. 2d, at 1252 (application of the Controlled Substances Act would (1) substantially burden (2) a sincere (3) religious exercise). The evidence the District Court found to be in equipoise related to two of the compelling interests asserted by the Government, which formed part of the Government's affirmative defense. See 42 U. S. C. §2000bb–1(b) ("Government may substantially burden a person's exercise of religion only if *it demonstrates* that application of the burden to the person—(1) is in furtherance of a compelling government interest . . ." (emphasis added)); § 2000bb–2(3) ("[T]he term 'demonstrates' means meets the burdens of going forward with the evidence and of persuasion"). Accordingly, the UDV effectively demonstrated that its sincere exercise of religion was substantially burdened, and the Government failed to demonstrate that the application of the burden to the UDV would, more likely than not, be justified by the asserted compelling interests. See 389 F. 3d, at 1009 (Seymour, J., concurring in part and dissenting in part) ("[T]he balance is between actual irreparable harm to [the] plaintiff and potential harm to the government which does not even rise to the level of a preponderance of the evidence").

The Government argues that, although it would bear the burden of demonstrating a compelling interest as part of its affirmative defense at trial on the merits, the UDV should have borne the burden of disproving the asserted compelling interests at the hearing on the preliminary injunction. This argument is foreclosed by our recent decision in *Ashcroft* v. *American Civil Liberties Union,* 542 U. S. 656 (2004). In *Ashcroft,* we affirmed the grant of a preliminary injunction in a case where the Government had failed to show a likelihood of success under the compelling interest test. We reasoned that "[a]s the Government bears the burden of proof on the ultimate question of [the challenged Act's] constitutionality, respondents [the movants] must be deemed likely to prevail unless the Government has shown that respondents' proposed less restrictive alternatives are less effective than [enforcing the Act]." *Id.,* at 666. That logic extends to this case; here the Government failed on the first prong of the compelling interest test, and did not reach the least restrictive means prong, but that can make no difference. The point remains that the burdens at the preliminary injunction stage track the burdens at trial.

The Government attempts to limit the rule announced in *Ashcroft* to content-based restrictions on speech, but the distinction is unavailing. The fact that *Ashcroft* involved such a restriction was the reason the Government had the burden of proof at trial under the First Amendment, see *id.,* at 665, but in no way affected the Court's assessment of the consequences of having that burden for purposes of the preliminary injunction. Here the burden is placed squarely on the Government by RFRA rather than the First Amendment, see 42 U. S. C. §§2000bb–1(b), 2000bb–2(3), but the consequences are the same. Congress' express decision to legislate the compelling interest test indicates that RFRA challenges should be adjudicated in the same manner as constitutionally mandated applications of the test, including at the preliminary injunction stage.

III

The Government's second line of argument rests on the Controlled Substances Act itself. The Government contends that the Act's description of Schedule I substances as having "a high potential for abuse," "no currently accepted medical use in treatment in the United States," and "a lack of accepted safety for use . . . under medical supervision," 21 U. S. C. §812(b)(1), by itself precludes any consideration of individualized exceptions such as that sought by the UDV. The Government goes on to argue that the regulatory regime established by the Act—a "closed" system that prohibits all use of controlled substances except as authorized by the Act itself, see *Gonzales* v. *Raich,* 545 U. S. _____, _____ (2005) (slip op., at 10)—"cannot function with its necessary rigor and comprehensiveness if subjected to judicial exemptions." Brief for Petitioners 18. According to the Government, there would be no way to cabin religious exceptions once recognized, and "the public will misread" such exceptions as signaling that the substance at issue is not harmful after all. *Id.,* at 23. Under the Government's view, there is no need to assess the particulars of the UDV's use or weigh the impact of an exemption for that specific use, because the Controlled Substances Act serves a compelling purpose and simply admits of no exceptions.

A

RFRA, and the strict scrutiny test it adopted, contemplate an inquiry more focused than the Government's categorical approach. RFRA requires the Government to demonstrate that the compelling interest test is satisfied through application of the challenged law "to the person"—the particular claimant whose sincere exercise of religion is being substantially burdened. 42 U. S. C. §2000bb–1(b). RFRA expressly adopted the compelling interest test "as set forth in *Sherbert* v. *Verner,* 374 U. S. 398 (1963) and *Wisconsin* v. *Yoder,* 406 U. S. 205 (1972)." 42 U. S. C. §2000bb(b)(1). In each of those cases, this Court looked beyond broadly formulated interests justifying the general applicability of government mandates and scrutinized the asserted harm of granting specific exemptions to particular religious claimants. In *Yoder,* for example, we permitted an exemption for Amish children from a compulsory school attendance law. We recognized that the State had a "paramount" interest in education, but held that "despite its

GONZALES *v.* O CENTRO ESPÍRITA BENEFICENTE UNIÃO DO VEGETAL

Opinion of the Court

admitted validity in the generality of cases, we must searchingly examine the interests that the State seeks to promote . . . and the impediment to those objectives that would flow from recognizing *the claimed Amish exemption."* 406 U. S., at 213, 221 (emphasis added). The Court explained that the State needed "to show with more particularity how its admittedly strong interest . . . would be adversely affected by granting an exemption *to the Amish."* *Id.,* at 236 (emphasis added).

In *Sherbert,* the Court upheld a particular claim to a religious exemption from a state law denying unemployment benefits to those who would not work on Saturdays, but explained that it was not announcing a constitutional right to unemployment benefits for "*all* persons whose religious convictions are the cause of their unemployment." 374 U. S., at 410 (emphasis added). The Court distinguished the case "in which an employee's religious convictions serve to make him a nonproductive member of society." *Ibid.;* see also *Smith,* 494 U. S., at 899 (O'Connor, J., concurring in judgment) (strict scrutiny "at least requires a case-by-case determination of the question, sensitive to the facts of each particular claim"). Outside the Free Exercise area as well, the Court has noted that "[c]ontext matters" in applying the compelling interest test, *Grutter* v. *Bollinger,* 539 U. S. 306, 327 (2003), and has emphasized that "strict scrutiny *does* take 'relevant differences' into account—indeed, that is its fundamental purpose," *Adarand Constructors, Inc.* v. *Peña,* 515 U. S. 200, 228 (1995).

B

Under the more focused inquiry required by RFRA and the compelling interest test, the Government's mere invocation of the general characteristics of Schedule I substances, as set forth in the Controlled Substances Act, cannot carry the day. It is true, of course, that Schedule I substances such as DMT are exceptionally dangerous. See, *e.g., Touby* v. *United States,* 500 U. S. 160, 162 (1991). Nevertheless, there is no indication that Congress, in classifying DMT, considered the harms posed by the particular use at issue here—the circumscribed, sacramental use of *hoasca* by the UDV. The question of the harms from the sacramental use of *hoasca* by the UDV *was* litigated below. Before the District Court found that the Government had not carried its burden of showing a compelling interest in preventing such harms, the court noted that it could not "ignore that the legislative branch of the government elected to place materials containing DMT on Schedule I of the [Act], reflecting findings that substances containing DMT have 'a high potential for abuse,' and 'no currently accepted medical use in treatment in the United States,' and that '[t]here is a lack of accepted safety for use of [DMT] under medical supervision.'" 282 F. Supp. 2d, at 1254. But Congress' determination that DMT should be listed under Schedule I simply does not provide a categorical answer that relieves the Government of the obligation to shoulder its burden under RFRA.

This conclusion is reinforced by the Controlled Substances Act itself. The Act contains a provision authorizing the Attorney General to "waive the requirement for registration of certain manufacturers, distributors, or dispensers if he finds it consistent with the public health and safety." 21 U. S. C. §822(d). The fact that the Act itself contemplates that exempting certain people from its requirements would be "consistent with the public health and safety" indicates that congressional findings with respect to Schedule I substances should not carry the determinative weight, for RFRA purposes, that the Government would ascribe to them.

And in fact an exception has been made to the Schedule I ban for religious use. For the past 35 years, there has been a regulatory exemption for use of peyote—a Schedule I substance—by the Native American Church. See 21 CFR §1307.31 (2005). In 1994, Congress extended that exemption to all members of every recognized Indian Tribe. See 42 U. S. C. §1996a(b)(1). Everything the Government says about the DMT in *hoasca*—that, as a Schedule I substance, Congress has determined that it "has a high potential for abuse," "has no currently accepted medical use," and has "a lack of accepted safety for use . . . under medical supervision," 21 U. S. C. §812(b)(1)— applies in equal measure to the mescaline in peyote, yet both the Executive and Congress itself have decreed an exception from the Controlled Substances Act for Native American religious use of peyote. If such use is permitted in the face of the congressional findings in §812(b)(1) for hundreds of thousands of Native Americans practicing their faith, it is difficult to see how those same findings alone can preclude any consideration of a similar exception for the 130 or so American members of the UDV who want to practice theirs. See *Church of Lukumi Babalu Aye, Inc.* v. *Hialeah,* 508 U. S. 520, 547 (1993) ("It is established in our strict scrutiny jurisprudence that 'a law cannot be regarded as protecting an interest 'of the highest order' . . . when it leaves appreciable damage to that supposedly vital interest unprohibited' " (quoting *Florida Star* v. *B. J. F.,* 491 U. S. 524, 541–542 (1989) (SCALIA, J., concurring in part and concurring in judgment))).

The Government responds that there is a "unique relationship" between the United States and the Tribes, Brief for Petitioners 27; see *Morton* v. *Mancari,* 417 U. S. 535 (1974), but never explains what about that "unique" relationship justifies overriding the same congressional findings on which the Government relies in resisting any exception for the UDV's religious use of *hoasca.* In other words, if any Schedule I substance is in fact *always* highly dangerous in any amount no matter how used, what about the unique relationship with the Tribes justifies allowing their use of peyote? Nothing about the unique political status of the Tribes makes their members immune from the health risks the Government asserts accompany any use of a Schedule I substance, nor insulates the Schedule I substance the Tribes use in religious exercise from the alleged risk of diversion.

The Government argues that the existence of a *congressional* exemption for peyote does not indicate that the Controlled Substances Act is amenable to *judicially crafted* exceptions. RFRA, however, plainly contemplates that *courts* would recognize exceptions—that is how the law works. See 42 U. S. C. § 2000bb–1(c) ("A person whose religious exercise has been burdened in

Cite as: 546 U. S. ____ (2006)

Opinion of the Court

violation of this section may assert that violation as a claim or defense in a judicial proceeding and obtain appropriate relief against a government"). Congress' role in the peyote exemption—and the Executive's, see 21 CFR §1307.31 (2005)—confirms that the findings in the Controlled Substances Act do not preclude exceptions altogether; RFRA makes clear that it is the obligation of the courts to consider whether exceptions are required under the test set forth by Congress.

C

The well-established peyote exception also fatally undermines the Government's broader contention that the Controlled Substances Act establishes a closed regulatory system that admits of no exceptions under RFRA. The Government argues that the effectiveness of the Controlled Substances Act will be "necessarily . . . undercut" if the Act is not uniformly applied, without regard to burdens on religious exercise. Brief for Petitioners 18. The peyote exception, however, has been in place since the outset of the Controlled Substances Act, and there is no evidence that it has "undercut" the Government's ability to enforce the ban on peyote use by non-Indians.

The Government points to some pre-*Smith* cases relying on a need for uniformity in rejecting claims for religious exemptions under the Free Exercise Clause, see Brief for Petitioners 16, but those cases strike us as quite different from the present one. Those cases did not embrace the notion that a general interest in uniformity justified a substantial burden on religious exercise; they instead scrutinized the asserted need and explained why the denied exemptions could not be accommodated. In *United States* v. *Lee,* 455 U. S. 252 (1982), for example, the Court rejected a claimed exception to the obligation to pay Social Security taxes, noting that "mandatory participation is indispensable to the fiscal vitality of the social security system" and that the "tax system could not function if denominations were allowed to challenge the tax system because tax payments were spent in a manner that violates their religious belief." *Id.,* at 258, 260. See also *Hernandez* v. *Commissioner,* 490 U. S. 680, 700 (1989) (same). In *Braunfeld* v. *Brown,* 366 U. S. 599 (1961) (plurality opinion), the Court denied a claimed exception to Sunday closing laws, in part because allowing such exceptions "might well provide [the claimants] with an economic advantage over their competitors who must remain closed on that day." *Id.,* at 608–609. The whole point of a "uniform day of rest for all workers" would have been defeated by exceptions. See *Sherbert*, 374 U. S., at 408 (discussing *Braunfeld*). These cases show that the Government can demonstrate a compelling interest in uniform application of a particular program by offering evidence that granting the requested religious accommodations would seriously compromise its ability to administer the program.

Here the Government's argument for uniformity is different; it rests not so much on the particular statutory program at issue as on slippery-slope concerns that could be invoked in response to any RFRA claim for an exception to a generally applicable law. The Government's argument echoes the classic rejoinder of bureaucrats throughout history: If I make an exception for you, I'll have to make one for everybody, so no exceptions. But RFRA operates by mandating consideration, under the compelling interest test, of exceptions to "rule[s] of general applicability." 42 U. S. C. §2000bb–1(a). Congress determined that the legislated test "is a workable test for striking sensible balances between religious liberty and competing prior governmental interests." §200bb(a)(5). This determination finds support in our cases; in *Sherbert*, for example, we rejected a slippery-slope argument similar to the one offered in this case, dismissing as "no more than a possibility" the State's speculation "that the filing of fraudulent claims by unscrupulous claimants feigning religious objections to Saturday work" would drain the unemployment benefits fund. 374 U. S., at 407.

We reaffirmed just last Term the feasibility of case-by-case consideration of religious exemptions to generally applicable rules. In *Cutter* v. *Wilkinson*, 544 U. S. ____ (2005), we held that the Religious Land Use and Institutionalized Persons Act of 2000, which allows federal and state prisoners to seek religious accommodations pursuant to the same standard as set forth in RFRA, does not violate the Establishment Clause. We had "no cause to believe" that the compelling interest test "would not be applied in an appropriately balanced way" to specific claims for exemptions as they arose. *Id.,* at ____ (slip op., at 12). Nothing in our opinion suggested that courts were not up to the task.

We do not doubt that there may be instances in which a need for uniformity precludes the recognition of exceptions to generally applicable laws under RFRA. But it would have been surprising to find that this was such a case, given the longstanding exemption from the Controlled Substances Act for religious use of peyote, and the fact that the very reason Congress enacted RFRA was to respond to a decision denying a claimed right to sacramental use of a controlled substance. See 42 U. S. C. §2000bb(a)(4). And in fact the Government has not offered evidence demonstrating that granting the UDV an exemption would cause the kind of administrative harm recognized as a compelling interest in *Lee, Hernandez,* and *Braunfeld.* The Government failed to convince the District Court at the preliminary injunction hearing that health or diversion concerns provide a compelling interest in banning the UDV's sacramental use of *hoasca*. It cannot compensate for that failure now with the bold argument that there can be no RFRA exceptions at all to the Controlled Substances Act. See Tr. of Oral Arg. 17 (Deputy Solicitor General statement that exception could not be made even for "rigorously policed" use of "one drop" of substance "once a year").

IV

Before the District Court, the Government also asserted an interest in compliance with the 1971 United Nations Convention on Psychotropic Substances, Feb. 21, 1971, [1979–1980], 32 U. S. T. 543, T. I. A. S. No. 9725. The Convention, signed by the United

GONZALES *v.* O CENTRO ESPÍRITA BENEFICENTE UNIÃO DO VEGETAL

Opinion of the Court

States and implemented by the Controlled Substances Act, calls on signatories to prohibit the use of hallucinogens, including DMT. The Government argues that it has a compelling interest in meeting its international obligations by complying with the Convention.

The District Court rejected this interest because it found that the Convention does not cover *hoasca*. The court relied on the official commentary to the Convention, which notes that "Schedule I [of the Convention] does not list . . . natural hallucinogenic materials," and that "[p]lants as such are not, and it is submitted are also not likely to be, listed in Schedule I, but only some products obtained from plants." U. N. Commentary on the Convention on Psychotropic Substances 387, 385 (1976). The court reasoned that *hoasca*, like the plants from which the tea is made, is sufficiently distinct from DMT itself to fall outside the treaty. See 282 F. Supp. 2d, at 1266–1269.

We do not agree. The Convention provides that "a preparation is subject to the same measures of control as the psychotropic substance which it contains," and defines "preparation" as "any solution or mixture, in whatever physical state, containing one or more psychotropic substances." See 32 U. S. T., at 546, Art. 1(f)(i); *id.,* at 551, Art. 3. *Hoasca* is a "solution or mixture" containing DMT; the fact that it is made by the simple process of brewing plants in water, as opposed to some more advanced method, does not change that. To the extent the commentary suggests plants themselves are not covered by the Convention, that is of no moment—the UDV seeks to import and use a tea brewed from plants, not the plants themselves, and the tea plainly qualifies as a "preparation" under the Convention.

The fact that *hoasca* is covered by the Convention, however, does not automatically mean that the Government has demonstrated a compelling interest in applying the Controlled Substances Act, which implements the Convention, to the UDV's sacramental use of the tea. At the present stage, it suffices to observe that the Government did not even *submit* evidence addressing the international consequences of granting an exemption for the UDV. The Government simply submitted two affidavits by State Department officials attesting to the general importance of honoring international obligations and of maintaining the leadership position of the United States in the international war on drugs. See Declaration of Gary T. Sheridan (Jan. 24, 2001), App. G to App. to Pet. for Cert. 261a; Declaration of Robert E. Dalton (Jan. 24, 2001), App. H, *id.,* at 265a. We do not doubt the validity of these interests, any more than we doubt the general interest in promoting public health and safety by enforcing the Controlled Substances Act, but under RFRA invocation of such general interests, standing alone, is not enough.[2]

* * *

---

[2]In light of the foregoing, we do not reach the UDV's argument that Art. 22, ¶5, of the Convention should be read to accommodate exceptions under domestic laws such as RFRA.

The Government repeatedly invokes Congress' findings and purposes underlying the Controlled Substances Act, but Congress had a reason for enacting RFRA, too. Congress recognized that "laws 'neutral' toward religion may burden religious exercise as surely as laws intended to interfere with religious exercise," and legislated "the compelling interest test" as the means for the courts to "strik[e] sensible balances between religious liberty and competing prior governmental interests." 42 U. S. C. §§2000bb(a)(2), (5).

We have no cause to pretend that the task assigned by Congress to the courts under RFRA is an easy one. Indeed, the very sort of difficulties highlighted by the Government here were cited by this Court in deciding that the approach later mandated by Congress under RFRA was not required as a matter of constitutional law under the Free Exercise Clause. See *Smith,* 494 U. S., at 885–890. But Congress has determined that courts should strike sensible balances, pursuant to a compelling interest test that requires the Government to address the particular practice at issue. Applying that test, we conclude that the courts below did not err in determining that the Government failed to demonstrate, at the preliminary injunction stage, a compelling interest in barring the UDV's sacramental use of *hoasca*.

The judgment of the United States Court of Appeals for the Tenth Circuit is affirmed, and the case is remanded for further proceedings consistent with this opinion.

It is so ordered.

JUSTICE ALITO took no part in the consideration or decision of this case.

CHAPTER 9

Common Law Defenses

CHAPTER CONTENTS

> *(The intoxicated) shall have no privilege by this voluntarily contracted madness, but shall have the same judgment as if he were in his right senses.*
>
> *M. Hale*

CHAPTER OBJECTIVES

After studying this chapter, you should be able to:

- Know the Common Law defenses and their essential elements.

- Understand the concept of self-defense and be able to explain when nondeadly and deadly force can be used.

- Explain under what circumstances consent is a defense.

- Explain when mistake of law and mistake of fact are defenses.

- Explain entrapment.

- Differentiate between the consequences of voluntary and involuntary intoxication.

- Explain the different standards for the insanity defense and how each operates.

INTRODUCTION

In every criminal trial, the prosecution has the burden of proof and must prove the case against the defendant beyond a reasonable doubt. The defendant isn't required to answer the charges except to plead not guilty or guilty.

As we have seen, every crime can be broken down into its essential elements, and the government is required to prove each element beyond a reasonable doubt. We have already examined the elements of many crimes. A prosecutor who proves these elements will generally get a conviction unless the defendant raises a defense to the crime. The law provides legitimate defenses that, if proven, dictate an acquittal.

Depending on the crime, a number of defenses may be available to defendants. Defenses take their legitimacy from Common Law, constitutional law, and statutory law. For instance, the insanity defense, known as the M'Naghten Rule, takes its name from the defendant in a nineteenth century English case that established the precedent. The defense became codified into law in the United States and has been altered by statute in some states. The *ex post facto* defense is written plainly in the Constitution. Anglo-American law has a rich tradition of limiting the power of the state, protecting the rights of the accused, and recognizing a defendant's right to use specific defenses to crimes.

JUSTIFICATION DEFENSES

Justification defenses can be used where the commission of the proscribed act is justified and therefore not appropriate for criminal sanctions. In other words, the person accused of the crime had a legitimate reason for committing the act and was therefore justified in committing an act that would otherwise be a crime. The justification defense most people are familiar with is **self-defense** in what would otherwise be a murder case. It is far from the only justification defense available.

Individuals have the right to defend themselves, innocent people, and their property from harm from others. Citizens trying to prevent a crime from occurring may also have a defense if their actions otherwise violate the law. Each case's circumstances dictate whether a justification defense protects the accused. There are no hard and fast rules; justification defenses are fact-driven affairs requiring the jury to decide whether the defendant's actions were reasonable under the circumstances.

A person may always use **nondeadly force** to prevent an attacker from committing a crime against them. The person may use a reasonable amount of force to restrain or render harmless the attacker. Persons using nondeadly force are not required to retreat at any time during the use of force. Consider this example. A woman walking down a busy street feels someone brush by her. She then feels her handbag's shoulder strap tighten and realizes the youth who brushed by her is trying to steal her purse. She can hit him over the head with her purse to subdue him, tie him to the nearest lamppost with her belt, and wait for the police to arrive. She has used nondeadly force to subdue and hold him and will be able to defend her actions if criminal assault and kidnapping charges are filed against her.

However, the use of **deadly force** is much more tightly controlled. A person may only use deadly force in self-defense when it reasonably appears necessary to prevent immediate death or serious injury or prevent the commission of a serious felony involving risk to

Justification Defenses

A legal excuse for committing an act that otherwise would be a tort or a crime.

Self-Defense

The use of force to protect oneself from death or imminent bodily harm at the hands of an aggressor.

Nondeadly Force

Force used to subdue a criminal or prevent a crime without risking death.

Deadly Force

Force intended to cause death or likely to result in death.

human life. Deadly force may only be used against an attacker who has initiated the aggression using unlawful force. Consider the following example. You are on a flight over the Atlantic when you notice that the man in the next seat is attempting to light his shoes. On closer observation, you notice that the shoelace resembles a fuse. You call attention to his behavior by summoning the cabin crew. Together, you and other passengers attempt to subdue the passenger, but he struggles to light the shoe. You hit him over the head with a wine bottle and kill him. It turns out his shoes were loaded with plastic explosives. Your actions involved the use of deadly force, but you were justified because it appeared he was attempting to blow up the plane. You used deadly force to prevent death and destruction. However, if the first blow knocked the passenger out and the rest of the crew tied him to a chair and removed his shoes, you cannot continue to hit him over the head until he is dead.

Often in deadly force situations, there is a question of whether a person could have or should have retreated from the situation when the opportunity arose. A **retreat rule** has grown out of Common Law decisions through the years. The rule has two parts:

- A person must retreat rather than use deadly force unless the person is at his or her home or business.
- Most states have adopted the rule that there is no duty to retreat unless the retreat can be made in complete safety.

Retreat Rule
The rule governing when a person must retreat rather than use deadly force.

Consider the shoe bomb case again. You were under no duty to retreat since to do so would be impossible. You can't get off the plane.

Oddly enough, aggressors can avail themselves of the self-defense argument under certain circumstances. Aggressors can regain the right to self-defense if they remove themselves from the fight. This is referred to as **withdrawal.**

Withdrawal
The act of removing oneself from a conflict.

Consider the following scenario. An armed gunman enters a store with the intent of robbing it. He pulls his gun and demands cash. The owner of the store instead pulls his gun. Shots are exchanged, but no one is hit. The gunman flees and throws his gun in a nearby dumpster. The storeowner pursues the gunman and begins firing at him. At this point, the gunman has regained his right to self-defense. The storeowner is now the aggressor.

Similarly, initial aggressors are protected under the doctrine of **sudden escalation.** If a fight that was not life threatening suddenly becomes life threatening, the initial aggressor can take whatever action is necessary to protect himself. As an example, one teenager approaches another and picks a fight. The second teenager at first defends himself in like fashion. However, at some point, the attacked teenager becomes enraged, picks up a sharp object lying nearby, and attacks the aggressor. The aggressor now has the right to take whatever steps necessary to defend himself. If the attacked teenager is now using deadly force, the initial aggressor may use deadly force to stop the attack.

Sudden Escalation
The concept that a conflict that was not life threatening escalates to the point that it is.

Another Common Law defense is the **defense of others.** A defendant can use the defense of others defense when he acts in the belief the intended victim had a legal right to act in his or her own defense. No special relationship need exist between the defendant and the intended victim. In this case, the defendant does not have to retreat unless he is sure the victim is safe.

Defense of Others
The defense used when otherwise criminal activities are done to save other people from harm.

This could be played out as follows. A man is walking down the street and sees a perpetrator attacking a woman. The man can use appropriate force to stop the attack. If the attacker is using deadly force, the man can use deadly force to stop him. However, if his initial interference is enough to drive off the attacker and the intended victim is now safe, the man may not pursue the attacker with the intent of doing him bodily harm.

The law delineates between what force may be used to defend people and what may be used to defend property. For instance, it is not permissible to kill an unarmed purse-snatcher. It is legal to try to catch him and hold him for police. Deadly force may only be used in property crimes where the aggressor is placing people in imminent danger.

Deadly force is permissible in the act of crime prevention if the crime is a serious felony that may endanger human life. For other less dangerous crimes, nondeadly force is appropriate. For example, you cannot rig a deadly trap to prevent break-ins to your home or hunting camp. In the classic case, *Katko v. Briney*, 183 N.W.2d 657 (1971), the Iowa Supreme Court let stand a jury verdict for actual and punitive damages against the owner of an abandoned farmhouse who had rigged a rifle to go off if an intruder entered. An intruder did and sued successfully when he was injured.

Necessity Defense

A defense where the defendant reasonably believes his or her action was necessary to avoid harm to society.

Sometimes breaking the law is necessary to protect human life or property. For instance, a person may trespass on a property to save a person from imminent danger. In order for the **necessity defense** to work, the defendant must reasonably believe his or her action was necessary to avoid harm to society, which is greater than any harm caused to the property. The necessity defense may never be used to justify a death to protect property. In any use of the necessity defense, the defendant must be without fault. For example, a co-conspirator to burn down a house cannot break into a neighbor's house to telephone the fire department.

Bear in mind that Common Law defenses may have been modified in your jurisdiction. Always check local laws before using or advising the use of deadly force to protect either people or property. There is also a growing trend, perhaps fueled by well-publicized mass killings such as those that occurred at Virginia Tech in 2007, to legalize the carrying and use of weapons in public places and to allow aggressive action in the defense of people and property, even in situations where there is the possibility of retreat.

YOU MAKE THE CALL

DOCTOR EUTHANIZES PATIENTS AS HURRICANE RAGES

Dr. Anna Pou was working at the Memorial Medical Center in New Orleans on August 29, 2005, as Hurricane Katrina hit the city. As the waters rose, hospital staff evacuated the lower floors. Eventually the wind and water knocked out the hospital's power.

Nurses had nowhere to empty bedpans and operated respirators manually. The temperature rose to 110 degrees inside the building. Despite pleas for help in evacuating patients, none had been moved by the morning of September 1. The situation was getting desperate.

Rose Savoie, age 90, Ireatha Watson, age 89, and Holis Alford, age 66, were among the suffering patients too sick to get out of bed. Emmett Everett Sr., age 61, presented particular challenges to the doctors. He weighed 380 pounds and was paralyzed. Evacuation efforts began at 11 AM on September 1. According to the Orleans Parish prosecutor, all four patients were alive at that time. By five o'clock that afternoon when the hospital had been completely evacuated, they were dead.

The prosecutor asserted that Dr. Pou and two nurses administered the four and possibly others a "lethal cocktail"[1] of morphine and midazolam hydrochloride. The four victims had never been prescribed these drugs, but they were found in their systems during their autopsy. After Dr. Pou was arrested in July 2006, the New Orleans medical community held protests claiming the charges were politically motivated, noting that Louisiana Attorney General Charles Foti who ran the investigation was seeking re-election.

Foti turned the case over to Orleans Parish prosecutor Eddie Jordon to handle. But Jordon wasn't as sure of the case. Even the Orleans Parish coroner said the evidence was inconclusive to tell whether the four were murdered, died accidentally, or died by natural causes. Jordon empaneled a grand jury to decide whether to indict the doctor and two nurses. The two nurses testified in return for immunity, and charges against them were dropped.

The grand jury ultimately decided not to charge Dr. Pou with anything. Attorney General Foti blamed Jordon for not presenting all the evidence including the conclusions of five forensic experts that not only these four patients, but also five others were murdered.[2]

Did Dr. Pou and the two nurses get away with murder? On the one hand, testimony from other doctors seemed to indicate Pou said she was willing to euthanize the suffering patients. Another doctor saw nurses with syringes in their hands. But no one saw Dr. Pou or the nurses inject the patients. Prosecutors point out that someone obviously did. Did the New Orleans jury just want the city to move on with rebuilding? Did a medical professional make an error of judgment while under extreme duress? Did Dr. Pou get away with murder? You make the call.

DURESS DEFENSES

Defendants sometimes commit acts under duress and can then use the **duress defense.** Duress is a defense if the defendant committed the crime out of a well-grounded fear of death or serious bodily harm. For instance, it would be illegal for a bank teller to hand a bag of cash to her best friend, but not to a robber with a gun in his hand. The difference is that the teller hands the money to the robber under duress. In these cases, the defendant is arguing that she is the victim of the crime, not the perpetrator. Hostages who are made to commit crimes such as bank robberies while under the control of their captors can also use the defense.

The following conditions must be met for the duress defense to apply:

- The actor was wrongfully threatened by another to perform an act that he or she otherwise would not have performed.
- The threat was of serious bodily harm or death to the person or an immediate family member.
- The threat was immediate, and there was no way for the threatened person to escape or avoid the threatened action.
- The harm threatened was greater than the harm from the crime committed.
- The threatened person wasn't intentionally involved in the situation.

Cases such as these are seldom prosecuted if the police and prosecutors are convinced that the hostage acted out of fear and the threat was real. The person in question must be under threat of death to herself or a family member. The threat must be immediate and real.

Duress Defense
The defense that a person acted under threat of bodily harm to themselves or a family member; it may not be used to justify killing; the crime committed must be less serious than the harm threatened.

The duress defense is generally not a defense to murder. That's because the crime committed under duress (murder) isn't greater than the harm threatened (death if the threatened person doesn't kill as ordered). In other words, you can't kill to avoid being killed, but you can rob to avoid being killed. Duress may be a defense to felony murder, if the person was under duress to commit the underlying felony. (See Chapter 3 for a discussion of the felony murder rule.)

The U.S. Supreme Court recently clarified the burden of proof for defendants using the duress defense. Keshia Dixon purchased firearms at gun shows using a false identity and address to conceal the fact that she was under a felony indictment at the time. She was caught and charged with illegally attempting to purchase a firearm. At trial, she claimed her purchases were made under duress because her boyfriend promised to hurt her children if she did not buy the guns. Her lawyer asked the judge to instruct the jury that unless the prosecutor had proved her claim was a lie beyond a reasonable doubt, then they had to acquit. The judge disagreed and instead told the jury that the defendant had to prove her duress story to be true by a preponderance of the evidence. Dixon appealed. Ultimately, the Supreme Court backed the judge. Defendants have the burden of proof in the duress defense, but they must only prove their story by a preponderance of the evidence.[3]

YOU MAKE THE CALL

CRIMINAL OR VICTIM? THE STRANGE CASE OF BRIAN WELLS

Brian Wells was a 46-year-old pizza delivery man in Erie, Pennsylvania, on August 28, 2003. An order for two large sausage and pepperoni pizzas came into Mama Mia's Pizza during the lunchtime rush. Brian took the order and went to deliver the pies a little over one mile down the road. When he didn't return right away, shop owner Tony Ditmo became concerned. Brian was one of his most reliable workers.

Ditmo's concern turned to bewilderment at two o'clock as he watched Brian on television pleading with the state trooper pointing the gun at him to get some help. According to the news reports, Brian had robbed a bank and had some sort of device around his neck that Brian claimed was a bomb that was going to go off. After asking the policeman, "Why is it nobody trying to come get this thing off me? I don't have a lot of time," Brian pulled a pin out of the device starting a timer. "It's gonna go off. I'm not lying. Did you call my boss?" Then came the explosion. Brian fell backward and died as confused police looked on.

Four years of investigation have shed some light on that afternoon's events, but whether Brian Wells was a betrayed accomplice or innocent victim is still a debateable issue. Investigators have found this string of facts. A caller ordered the pizzas from a pay phone at a gas station and asked that it be delivered to an address of a nearby television station satellite dish. Investigators believe the man who called was 60-year-old William Rothstein, a shop teacher and engineer who lived near both the gas station and pizza delivery site.

Police would come to know Rothstein better after he called them on September 21, 2003, to tell them about the murder victim stored in his freezer. Rothstein told them that the victim was James Roden, who had the bad fortune to have been the boyfriend of Marjorie Diehl-Armstrong. Diehl-Armstrong had been engaged to Rothstein twice in the 35 years they had known each other. The broken engagements appear to be the only reason Rothstein was still alive.

Diehl-Armstrong shot an ex-boyfriend, but at her trial claimed she was a victim of domestic abuse. The jury acquitted her. Her first husband hung himself. Her second died from head injuries after a fall at home. Rothstein told the police that Diehl-Armstrong shot Roden with a shotgun in bed in her home and asked him to dispose of the body, paying him $2,000 for his efforts. Rothstein measured the body and bought the appropriate size freezer for storage. But when Diehl-Armstrong insisted he run the body through an ice grinder to dispose of it, Rothstein balked.

In exchange for immunity, he testified against Diehl-Armstrong. She is currently serving a 20-year sentence. But police still believed Rothstein and Diehl-Armstong were connected to Brian Wells' death and the botched bank robbery. One reason for their suspicion was that the Federal Bureau of Investigation (FBI) profiler assigned to the case believed that more than one person was behind the plan. The team would need someone sadistic and controlling and a mechanical genius who could build the complicated device and provide the complex directions Brian was to follow. When investigators found that Brian had gone fishing with Diehl-Armstrong, they felt they had a connection to tie him to the crime.[4] Were the elaborate directions just a ruse allowing Brian to claim innocence? Could Rothstein and Diehl-Armstrong been on the way to get the money from Brian when the police caught him? At least one eyewitness describes a car carrying both Diehl-Armstrong and Rothstein going the wrong way down a nearby highway that day. Rothstein has since died, so his story will never be told. The question is how much did Brian Wells know as he sat there pleading for help? Was he a criminal or a victim?

OTHER COMMON LAW DEFENSES

The **mistake of fact** defense can be used when a defendant honestly believes something to be true that isn't. For instance, a person retrieving a piece of luggage at an airport that looks exactly like his or hers may be guilty of not checking the claim check, but not of stealing someone's luggage. The mistake of fact defense applies to different crimes differently. For instance, for general intent crimes the mistake must be a reasonable mistake. But for specific intent crimes, any mistake of fact may be used as a defense. You could not form the specific intent to commit a crime if you are mistaken about the facts. For example, in a hypothetical jurisdiction it is a specific intent crime to have sexual contact with a brother or sister. You and your twin brother were separated at birth and placed in different foster homes. Thirty years later, you meet but do not know you are related. You fall in love and have sexual relations. The fact that you don't realize you are related is a defense to criminal charges of incest. Once you find out you are sister and brother, however, the defense is no longer available. The mistake of fact defense may not be used for strict liability crimes.

The **mistake of law** defense can generally be used when a person in good faith relied on an interpretation of law from a person charged with administering the law. For instance, an IRS official tells you that the cost of your "Home of the Whopper" boxer shorts are a legitimate entertainment deduction. You take the deduction, but it is later disallowed. You could use the mistake of law defense to avoid any criminal penalty. Most likely you will have to pay the tax due.

The mistake of law defense can also be used if an interpretation of the law changed. For instance, in the preceding scenario the IRS agent was accurate at the time he gave you the interpretation, but the interpretation changed the following year to only allow deductions for Elvis "Hunka Hunka Burning Love" boxers. If this were the case, you could

Mistake of Fact
A defense used when a defendant honestly believes something to be true that isn't.

Mistake of Law
A defense used when a person in good faith relied on an interpretation of law from a person charged with administering the law.

Entrapment

A defense used when law enforcement officials lure a person into committing a crime.

Government agents may not originate a criminal design, implant in an innocent person's mind the disposition to commit a criminal act, and then induce commission of the crime so that the Government may prosecute.

Justice White, in *Jacobson v. United States,* 503 U.S. 540 (1992)

Subjective Standard (or Majority Rule) for Entrapment

Asks the question: "Was the defendant predisposed to commit the crime?"

Objective Standard (or Minority Rule) for Entrapment

Asks the question: "Would an innocent person be induced to commit the crime by the officer's acts?"

avoid criminal liability for deducting the "Whopper" boxers. The mistaken interpretation of law may not come from an attorney.

Entrapment is a defense used when law enforcement officials lure a person into committing a crime. Most frequently, this occurs in bribery cases. To work, the entrapment defense must pass a two-prong test. First, the criminal design must have originated with law enforcement. Second, the defendant must not be predisposed to commit the crime.

Depending on the case law in your jurisdiction, one of two tests for predisposition is used. Most jurisdictions use the **subjective standard,** also known as the **majority rule.** The subjective standard revolves around the answer to one question: "Was the defendant predisposed to commit the crime?" Other jurisdictions use the **objective standard** or the **minority rule.** The objective standard focuses on the government's inducement and asks the question: "Would an innocent person be induced to commit the crime by the officer's acts?"

The U.S. Supreme Court answered that question in a case involving the receipt of child pornography. It ruled that the entrapment defense prohibited prosecution of a defendant who ordered child pornography after a 26-month mail campaign by the government to induce him to order a catalog. The campaign included personal letters from a postal inspector posing as another male interested in seeing nude teenage boys, solicitations to join associations dedicated to freedom of the press, and requests that he purchase magazines depicting boys. When his order from the sting operation arrived, he was arrested. A search of his house turned up nothing but the materials the government had sent him. The Supreme Court ruled that the government's campaign to get him to order was entrapment.[5]

A defendant may use the victim's **consent** as a defense in some circumstances. For instance, a defendant accused of rape is not guilty if the sex was consensual. The consent defense is unavailable for statutory rape. A victim's consent is not valid if:

- The victim is a minor.
- The victim has a mental disease or defect.
- The victim is intoxicated to the point he or she is unable to make a reasonable judgment.
- Consent is obtained by force or duress.
- Consent is obtained by fraudulent or deceptive means.
- The victim has been judged to be legally incompetent.
- The law in question precluded the consent defense.

Generally, consent is not a defense to crimes involving grievous bodily harm or death. For example, it isn't a defense to murder that the victim wanted to die or a defense to assault that the victim wanted to be beaten or disfigured. These acts would be crimes whether the victim wanted the acts to take place or not, unlike rape, which wouldn't be a crime if the other party consented.

CAPACITY DEFENSES

Capacity defenses may be used when the defendant lacks the capacity or ability to control his or her actions or understand that the act was criminal in nature. Age, mental disabilities, intoxication, and insanity can affect the ability to understand the law and control one's actions. Capacity defenses shield from liability those who can't understand right from wrong or control their actions.

INFANCY DEFENSE

For instance, debate rages about how to try minors who commit violent crimes. Under the Common Law, children of tender age could not be held liable for criminal acts under the presumption that they lacked the capacity to tell right from wrong. Although some states have sought to modify the standard by statute, the Common Law standard for the **infancy defense** is as follows:

- Children under 7 years of age are conclusively presumed to be incapable of knowing the wrongfulness of their crimes.
- Children 7 to 14 years of age have a rebuttable presumption of incapacity. The burden of proof is on the prosecutor to prove beyond a reasonable doubt that the defendant appreciated the quality and nature of his or her actions.
- Children over 14 were treated as adults and presumed to fully appreciate the difference between right and wrong.

Keep in mind that capacity is only part of the story. Children who have the capacity to commit crimes can be tried in the state's juvenile court system or in the adult system. Before a child is tried in adult court, a hearing is held. That hearing may include a discussion of the child's capacity as well as an examination of the charges and any prior record. Some states have recently enacted legislation that allows more children to be charged as adults in response to demands by the public that "doing adult crime ought to mean doing adult time." A full discussion of the treatment of juveniles as adults is beyond the scope of this text.

INTOXICATION DEFENSE

The intoxication defense is most successfully used in cases of **involuntary intoxication.** This happens when a person unknowingly ingests an intoxicating substance. Date rape drugs are an example of this. This defense may be made to both specific and general intent crimes. Persons who are involuntarily intoxicated are treated the same as insane defendants. They must meet whatever test the jurisdiction uses for insanity. (See the Insanity section in this chapter.)

Voluntary intoxication is quite another matter. It may never be used as a defense to a general intent crime. It also cannot be used as an excuse or justification of a crime of homicide. It cannot be used as a defense to crimes involving negligence, recklessness, or strict liability. Voluntary intoxication has been used as a defense to specific intent crimes where the intoxication prevents the defendant from formulating the requisite intent. If successful, this can reduce a charge of first-degree murder to second-degree murder.

INSANITY

Courts have long wrestled with the concept of trying the mentally ill or handicapped. Just as young children do not understand the nature of their actions, mentally ill or handicapped people may not either. Over the years, courts have recognized several defenses based on the defendant's inability to distinguish right from wrong when committing a crime.

The most common of these defenses is the **insanity defense.** In essence, a defendant using the insanity defense is claiming he or she lacked the mental state to understand the nature and consequences of the crime. Federal law requires defendants to show by clear and

Consent

A defense usually used in rape cases; argues the defendant had the "victim's" consent to perform the acts.

Infancy Defense

The defense that a child is too young to either be prosecuted or stand trial as an adult.

Involuntary Intoxication

The condition of a person who unknowingly ingests an intoxicating substance; generally treated like insanity.

Voluntary Intoxication

The condition where a person knowingly ingests an intoxicating substance; not a defense to murder or most crimes.

Insanity Defense
States that the defendant lacked the mental state to understand the nature and consequences of the crime.

convincing evidence that they were insane at the time of the crime.[6] The insanity defense is often used when the evidence against the defendant is overwhelming. Under these circumstances, the defendant cannot deny committing the crime but can argue insanity. If the defendant were successful, he or she would be committed to a mental hospital rather than prison. The defendant would remain there until the state determined the person to be sane.

HISTORICAL HIGHLIGHT
The Move Away from Capital Punishment for the Mentally Retarded

In 2002, Virginia became the eighteenth state to outlaw execution of the mentally retarded. Under Virginia law, convicts with an IQ below 70 may not be executed. Twelve other states have no capital punishment. Virginia's decision may have tipped the scales for the U.S. Supreme Court. Later the same year, the Court ruled that applying the death penalty to mentally retarded persons was cruel and unusual punishment in violation of the Eighth Amendment. The case was *Atkins v. Virginia*, 536 U.S. 304 (2002). States who still have the death penalty will now have to come up with standards to determine who is mentally retarded and who is not.

Several high-profile executions of prisoners with very low IQs brought the capacity question to the fore of the debate over capital punishment. Since people with very low IQs never develop the equivalent of "adult minds," the question of whether they can form intent or understand the consequences of their actions cannot be answered clearly. Some even argue that trying and convicting these people amounts to trying a child in an adult court.

Additionally, the deterrent aspects of capital punishment may very well be lost on a person who neither understands what he is doing or its consequences. Nor is there a general deterrent effect that would likely dissuade other mentally retarded persons to refrain from criminal acts, given diminished capacity to understand the connection between the criminal act and the consequences. Persons with low IQs may also lack the ability to aid their own defense at trial, resulting in false convictions. Given the permanent nature of the death penalty, life imprisonment would seem a better alternative.[7] The Supreme Court seems to agree. For a fuller discussion of the death penalty, see Chapter 13.

M'Naghten Rule
Holds that a defendant "is presumed to be sane and to possess a sufficient degree of reason to be responsible for his crimes, until the contrary be proved to (the jury's) satisfaction" beyond a reasonable doubt.

The insanity defense was first used successfully in 1843. The defendant in that case was named Daniel M'Naghten. Hence, future insanity cases would be governed by the **M'Naghten rule**. If a defendant at the time of the crime was "laboring under such a defect of reason, from diseases of the mind, as not to know the nature and quality of the act he was doing, or, if he did know it, that he did not know that what he was doing was wrong," no conviction is warranted. The burden of proof for the insanity defense is as follows:

> Every man is presumed to be sane and to possess a sufficient degree of reason to be responsible for his crimes, until the contrary be proved to (the jury's) satisfaction; and that to establish a defense on the ground of insanity, it must be clearly proved.[9]

HISTORICAL HIGHLIGHT
Guns and Alcohol: The James Allen Egelhoff Story

James Allen Egelhoff was camping and picking mushrooms in northwestern Montana when he met Roberta Pavlova and John Christenson. They sold their mushrooms and went to a bar for some drinks. After drinking at the bar, they proceeded to a private party where more drinking occurred. Sometime during the evening Egelhoff gave his gun to Pavlova to store in the car's glove compartment.

That night around midnight Montana state troopers were called to the scene of a car that had gone off the road into a ditch. In the front seat were Pavlova and Christenson. Each had been shot in the head once and killed. In the back seat was Egelhoff, yelling obscenities and behaving wildly. His gun lay on the floor at his feet with two discharged rounds.

The policemen arrested Egelhoff. His hands tested positive for gunshot residue, and his blood alcohol level an hour after his arrest was .36, over four times the intoxication level.

Egelhoff was charged with two counts of deliberate homicide. However, he had no memory of committing the crimes. Under Montana law, a person is guilty of deliberate homicide if he purposely or knowingly causes the death of another human being.

At trial, Egelhoff maintained that he was so drunk that he could not have committed the crimes. He argued that some fourth person must have pulled the trigger and he was too intoxicated to remember the incident. In the charge to the jury, the judge informed them that they could not take Egelhoff's intoxication into account when "determining the existence of a mental state which is an element of the offense." The jury convicted him of both homicides and sentenced him to 84 years in prison.

Egelhoff appealed to the Montana Supreme Court. He argued that his intoxication was relevant to his ability to form intent. If he could not form intent, he was not guilty of deliberate homicide, but some lesser offense such as manslaughter. The Montana Supreme Court agreed and reversed the conviction. The case was appealed to the U.S. Supreme Court.

This case proved to be a very divisive one for the justices. At issue was whether excluding the intoxication evidence from consideration as it affected his ability to form intent was a denial of due process. By a 5–4 margin, the Court ruled that the trial judge had not erred in instructing the jury to determine Egelhoff's intent without taking his intoxication into account. In other words, his voluntary intoxication could never be an excuse for committing homicide.[8]

BEYOND M'NAGHTEN

Some U.S. states have modified the M'Naghten rule. In 1886, Alabama adopted the more liberal "irresistible impulse" test. In effect, this created a "temporary insanity" for people who committed "crimes of passion."[10]

HISTORICAL HIGHLIGHT
The M'Naghten Case

Sir Robert Peel was the British Home Secretary in the mid 1840s. Mr. Peel was a crusader in the fight against crime. In fact, he is generally considered to be the father of the British police—hence, the nickname "Bobbies."

Of course, not everyone appreciated Sir Robert's passion. One individual in particular did not take kindly to the war on crime. His name was Daniel M'Naghten, and he believed that Sir Robert Peel was the head of a conspiracy to kill him. In his paranoid rage, he shot and killed Edward Drummond, Peel's private secretary. M'Naghten mistook Drummond for Peel.

At trial, his attorney argued that M'Naghten was insane at the time he shot Drummond and should be hospitalized, not imprisoned. The jury agreed, and M'Naghten was found "not guilty by reason of insanity."

Durham Test

Test of insanity that only requires a "substantial lack of capacity" on the part of the defendant.

Guilty, but Mentally Ill

Defendants who do not meet the complete lack of capacity standard but fall under the substantial lack of capacity standard are convicted and sent to a mental hospital; if they recover, they are sent to prison for the rest of their term.

M'Naghten was expanded even further in the 1954 *Durham v. United States,* 94 U.S. App. D. C. 228, 214 F.2d 862 (1954), case. In this case, the District of Columbia Appeals Court ruled "an accused is not criminally responsible if his unlawful act was the product of mental disease or defect."[11] Where M'Naghten required a complete lack of capacity, the **Durham test** only required a "substantial lack of capacity." The "substantial lack of capacity" test is part of the Model Penal Code but has not been adopted by all states.

GUILTY, BUT MENTALLY ILL

The insanity defense debate has paralleled the capital punishment debate in the United States for most of its history. Very shortly after the U.S. Supreme Court outlawed the death penalty as it was practiced in 1972, states began working on new death penalty laws and tighter restrictions on the insanity defense.

Illinois enacted a "**guilty, but mentally ill**" statute in the wake of the acquittal of a defendant by reason of insanity and subsequent repeat murders. But the national spotlight shone on the subject after the 1980 assassination of John Lennon by a deranged fan and the 1981 attempt on President Reagan's life by the delusional John Hinckley. The thought of releasing either Hinckley or Lennon's assassin, Mark David Chapman, was more than many could bear. In response, several states enacted "guilty, but mentally ill" statutes.

Under "guilty, but mentally ill" laws, defendants who do not meet the M'Naghten standard of a complete lack of capacity but fall under the substantial lack of capacity standard are convicted and sent to a mental hospital. If they recover, they are sent to prison for the rest of their term.

COMPETENCY TO STAND TRIAL

A variation on the insanity defense is to claim that the defendant is **incompetent to stand trial.** Common Law has long held that a person must be able to understand the proceedings against him and be able to interact with his attorneys in order have a fair trial. However, a defendant who is incompetent today may be competent tomorrow. Can the state hold someone indefinitely until they can stand trial?

This question came before the U.S. Supreme Court in 1972. In that case, *Indiana v. Jackson*, 406 U.S. 715 (1972), the Court ruled that defendants could only be held for a reasonable amount of time. Subsequent decisions have generally held that defendants cannot be held more than the lesser of 18 months or the maximum sentence for the crime with which they are charged. At that point, the state must:

- Try the defendant, if he or she is competent to stand trial,
- Dismiss the charges, or
- Commence civil proceedings to have the defendant committed to a mental institution.[12]

The standard for competency in many jurisdictions comes from Justice Thurgood Marshall's dissent in *White v. Estelle*, 459 U.S. 1118 (1983), where he stated: "This Court has approved a test of incompetence which seeks to determine whether the defendant 'has sufficient present ability to consult with his lawyer with a reasonable degree of rational understanding—and whether he has a rational as well as factual understanding of the proceedings against him'" [*Dusky v. United States*, 362 U.S. 402 (1960)].[13]

In recent years, older defendants have avoided trial temporarily or permanently due to their health condition. Often this is a combination of senility or overall health condition. This concept is recognized in international law as well. In 2000, former Chilean dictator Augusto Pinochet was arrested in England for crimes committed during his reign. A Spanish court had issued the indictment. An English judge ruled that the man was in too ill health to stand trial and released him.

In the United States, the cases of Thomas E. Blanton Jr. and Bobby Frank Cherry, accused of bombing the 16th Street Baptist Church in Birmingham, Alabama, in 1963, were delayed because of the defendant's age. Blanton was not convicted until 2001, and Cherry's trial was delayed when he was at first ruled incompetent to stand trial and later ruled competent.

In addition to poor physical health, defendants may have mental health problems that prevent them from fully participating in their defense. People with schizophrenia or psychosis may experience hallucinations or hear voices, making their perception of the proceedings unreliable. In one case, Charles Thomas Sell, a federal defendant with a long history of mental illness, was found to be competent for trial when taking his medication, but not at other times. However, Sell was less than religious in taking his medication.

Sell was held at a mental hospital until he could be deemed competent to stand trial. He refused his medication. His psychiatrist asked for a hearing in order to obtain permission to provide involuntary medication to Sell, arguing that Sell was a danger to himself and others. Sell's attorney appealed, and the district magistrate found that Sell was not dangerous, but that medicating him was appropriate to make him competent to stand trial. The Appeals Court agreed. The case was appealed to the U.S. Supreme Court who ruled that it was appropriate to medicate federal prisoners involuntarily to render them competent to

Incompetent to Stand Trial

A person unable to understand the proceedings against him and unable to interact with his attorneys.

Where does the violet tint end and the orange tint begin? Distinctly we see the difference of the colors, but where exactly does the one first blending enter into the other. So with sanity and insanity.
Herman Melville

HISTORICAL HIGHLIGHT
Bombingham: The Death Throes of Segregation

It was April 1963. Dr. Martin Luther King Jr. set his sights on Birmingham, Alabama, the last bastion of southern segregation. Almost nine years after the famous *Brown v. Board of Education* decision, Birmingham's schools were still segregated. Neither the city nor downtown merchants employed African-Americans. In addition to segregated drinking fountains, restrooms, and dressing rooms, local ordinances required separate taxi cabs, ambulances, hospitals, cemeteries, elevators, eating places, hotels, and theaters. Marriage between the races was a felony.

Dr. King's arrival was designed to help the city's already growing civil rights movement headed by local minister Rev. Fred Shuttlesworth. At the time, local officials and members of the Ku Klux Klan were terrorizing the African-American community. Black homes were frequently bombed leading to the city's nickname "Bombingham." King's plan was to train large groups of protesters to protest nonviolently and be arrested in large numbers. The mass arrests would overwhelm local law enforcement and focus national attention on segregation.

Shuttlesworth's church, the 16th Street Baptist Church, was the epicenter of the movement. After Dr. King was arrested for illegally demonstrating, teenagers left the church in waves of 50, only to be arrested. As each group was arrested, another took their place. Eventually, the city had to turn fire hoses and dogs on the protesters because they had no place to incarcerate them. When it happened, the television cameras were rolling.

City merchants, fearing the city's reputation would be forever sullied, relented. They met with Dr. King and ended the protests, as well as the accompanying Black boycott of the stores. But the segregationists were not finished. That September, Klansmen set off a bomb in the basement of the 16th Street Baptist Church, killing four young girls.

Law enforcement officials suspected four men, Robert "Dynamite Bob" Chambliss, Herman Cash, Thomas E. Blanton Jr., and Bobby Frank Cherry. Chambliss was the first to go to trial and was convicted in 1977. Herman Cash was never charged and died in 1994. The case seemed dead until the FBI received new evidence in 1997. Charges were eventually brought against Blanton and Cherry. Blanton was convicted in 2001 and sentenced to life in prison. Cherry was charged based partly on evidence provided by his son, who claimed Cherry was not home the night before the bombing as he had told police.[14]

However, Cherry was now old and in poor health. Initially, Cherry was found incompetent to stand trial. After receiving medical treatment, his condition improved. Cherry's case went to trial in 2002. He was found guilty and sentenced to life in prison. He died in prison in 2004. The story of Cherry's relationship with his son is told in the television movie *Sins of the Father.*

stand trial. However, hearings must be held focusing on the competency issue to make that determination.[15]

Can someone be competent to stand trial, but not competent to represent himself? That is a question before the U.S. Supreme Court during the 2007–2008 term. Ahmad Edwards stole a pair of shoes from an Indiana store. A store security guard confronted him and Edwards fired three shots from a gun he was carrying wounding a person on the street. An off-duty FBI agent chased Edwards and arrested him.

Edwards has a long history of schizophrenia. Several psychiatrists found him incompetent to stand trial. After several years of delay, he was eventually tried. Edwards petitioned the court to represent himself. The court refused because Edwards had already indicated he wished to use the insanity defense. Edwards was convicted of criminal recklessness and theft, but the jury could not decide on the attempted murder charge. The court declared a mistrial on the attempted murder charge.

For the new trial, Edwards again asked to represent himself, and the court again refused. He was convicted and appealed. He argued before the appeals court that the same competency standard applies to standing trial and representing oneself. Therefore, if he was competent to stand trial, he was competent to represent himself. The Appeals Court agreed with Edwards and remanded the case for a new trial. The State of Indiana appealed to the U.S. Supreme Court to decide if the same standard applies to both being tried and representing oneself.[16]

INCAPACITY AND PUNISHMENT

In cases where the death penalty has already been imposed, convicts can postpone execution by claiming **insanity just prior to execution.** The Common Law basis for this defense also goes back to England. The legal scholar Blackstone opined that this safeguard was necessary because the condemned prisoner may be able to produce some valid reason that execution should be stayed. In the United States, the U.S. Supreme Court upheld this standard in 1958.[17]

Prisons tend to have a damaging effect on a person's sanity. Consequently, prisoners may become insane during their prison term. Should **insanity during incarceration** occur, prisoners are moved to a psychiatric hospital for the remainder of their term. Should they still be insane at the end of their term, they may be committed to a mental hospital until they recover.

Insanity Just Prior to Execution

Most jurisdictions will not execute an insane person; persons whose sanity returns are rewarded with death.

Insanity during Incarceration

Prisoners who become insane are generally removed to mental hospitals; if they are still insane at the conclusion of their prison term, they are generally committed.

PRACTICE POINTERS

Every criminal charge should be examined closely for the possibility of raising a defense to the charges. This is true whether you are working for the prosecution or the defense. In many cases, the evidence will be strong enough to assure a conviction, but for the assertion of a defense. The examination process should proceed as follows:

- Examine the charges and outline the essential elements of each charge. Evaluate the evidence and determine whether it appears the prosecution can prove every element of the offense beyond a reasonable doubt. It may help to use a checklist and check off each element.

- List possible defenses based on your knowledge of the defendant and the allegations made by the police. Is there a question of self-defense? Is there evidence of entrapment? Does the defendant suffer from a mental impairment?
- Once you have identified possible defenses, list the elements required to prove the defense and outline the facts you believe will prove the defense.
- If you believe a defense is available, but you don't yet have the evidence needed to support the defense, come up with an investigative plan to gather the evidence.
- Be sure to check the law in your jurisdiction. Some states require prior notification to the prosecution if certain defenses such as the insanity defense will be used.

CHAPTER SUMMARY

Common Law has carved out several defenses for defendants who would otherwise be found guilty. Justification defenses can be used where the person accused of the crime had a legitimate reason for committing the act. The most common justification defense in murder cases is the self-defense justification. Individuals have the right to defend themselves, innocent people, and their property. Individuals also have some protection when they are attempting to prevent a criminal act from occurring. A person may use nondeadly force to prevent an attacker from committing a crime against him or her.

A person may only use deadly force in self-defense when it reasonably appears necessary to prevent immediate death or serious injury or prevent the commission of a serious felony involving risk to human life. The retreat rule defines criminal behavior when the option of using deadly force or retreating exists. The rule has two parts:

1. A person must retreat rather than use deadly force unless the person is at his or her home or business.
2. Most states have adopted the rule that there is no duty to retreat unless the retreat can be made in complete safety.

Aggressors who withdraw from a fight may defend themselves from subsequent charges by showing they backed down. Aggressors may also protect themselves from the sudden escalation of a fight. The defense of others defense allows defendants to protect innocent citizens from criminal attack.

Deadly force may only be used in property crimes where the aggressor is placing people in imminent danger. Deadly force is permissible in the act of crime prevention if the crime is a serious felony that may endanger human life. A person may use the necessity defense when the crime was committed in the process of saving human life or property.

Defendants may use the duress defense if someone is threatening to kill the person or a family member if the crime is not committed.

The mistake of fact defense can be used when a defendant honestly believes something to be true that isn't. The mistake of fact defense may not be used for strict liability crimes. Similarly, the mistake of law defense can generally be used when a person in good faith relied on an interpretation of law from a person charged with administering the law. The mistaken interpretation of law may not come from an attorney.

Entrapment is a defense used when law enforcement officials lure a person into committing a crime. The entrapment defense must pass a two-prong test. First, the criminal design must have originated with law enforcement. Second, the defendant was not predisposed to commit the crime.

A defendant may use the victim's consent as a defense in some circumstances. For instance, a defendant accused of rape is not guilty if the sex was consensual. The consent defense is unavailable for statutory rape and crimes involving death or serious bodily injury.

Capacity defenses may be used when the defendant lacks the capacity or ability to control his or her actions or understand that the act was criminal in nature. The Common Law standard for the infancy defense says that children under 7 years of age may not be tried, and children 7 to 14 years of age have a rebuttable presumption of incapacity. The prosecutor must prove beyond a reasonable doubt the defendant appreciated the quality and nature of his or her actions. Children over 14 are treated as adults for purposes of capacity. Juvenile courts may authorize trying the defendant as an adult.

Involuntary intoxication occurs when a person unknowingly ingests an intoxicating substance. This defense may be made to both specific and general intent crimes. Persons who are involuntarily intoxicated are treated the same as insane defendants. They must meet whatever test the jurisdiction uses for insanity.

Voluntary intoxication may never be used as a defense to a general intent crime. It cannot be used as an excuse or justification of a specific intent crime such as murder. It cannot be used as a defense to crimes involving negligence, recklessness, or strict liability.

Under the insanity defense, a defendant claims he or she lacked the mental state to understand the nature and consequences of the crime. The Common Law insanity defense derives from the M'Naghten case. The M'Naghten rule states that a defendant "is presumed to be sane and to possess a sufficient degree of reason to be responsible for his crimes, until the contrary be proved to (the jury's) satisfaction" beyond a reasonable doubt.

Some U.S. states have modified the M'Naghten rule employing the "irresistible impulse" or "temporary insanity" defense for people who committed "crimes of passion." More liberal interpretations include the Durham test, which is the "substantial lack of capacity" test.

Some states have a "guilty, but mentally ill" statute where defendants who do not meet the M'Naghten standard of a complete lack of capacity but fall under the substantial lack of capacity standard are convicted and sent to a mental hospital. If they recover, they are sent to prison for the rest of their term.

Some defendants are judged to be incompetent to stand trial. Generally, defendants cannot be held more than the lesser of 18 months or the maximum sentence for the crime with which they are charged. At that point, the state must try the defendant, if he or she is competent to stand trial, dismiss the charges, or commence civil proceedings to have the defendant committed to a mental institution.

The standard for competency in many jurisdictions is whether the defendant "has sufficient present ability to consult with his lawyer with a reasonable degree of rational understanding—and whether he has a rational as well as factual understanding of the proceedings against him."

Older defendants may not be competent for trial due to their overall health condition. They have the same rights as other defendants judged to be incompetent to stand trial.

In cases where the death penalty has already been imposed, convicts can postpone execution by claiming "insanity just prior to execution." Prisoners who become insane during their prison term are moved to a psychiatric hospital for the remainder of their term. Should they still be insane at the end of their term, they may be committed to a mental hospital until they recover.

KEY TERMS

Consent

Deadly Force

Defense of Others

Duress Defense

Durham Test

Entrapment

Guilty, but Mentally Ill

Incompetent to Stand Trial

Infancy Defense

Insanity Defense

Insanity during Incarceration

Insanity Just Prior to Execution

Involuntary Intoxication

Justification Defenses

M'Naghten Rule

Mistake of Fact

Mistake of Law

Necessity Defense

Nondeadly Force

Objective Standard (or Minority Rule) for Entrapment

Retreat Rule

Self-Defense

Subjective Standard (or Majority Rule) for Entrapment

Sudden Escalation

Voluntary Intoxication

Withdrawal

EXERCISE

1. This chapter briefly described how consent may be a defense to some criminal charges, such as an allegation of rape. But in the United States, there are very few instances in which the victim's request to become a victim (i.e., consent to be harmed) will operate as a valid defense. Consider the following example and determine whether you believe consent should be a valid defense. An individual responds to an online invitation to be killed, dismembered, and cannibalized. The gruesome event is videotaped so that authorities have a clear record of both the consent and the specific acts. Should consent be a defense to charges of murder?[18]

DISCUSSION QUESTIONS

1. Explain the differences between the M'Naghten rule, the Durham test, and guilty, but mentally ill. If you were advising a client who wants to raise the insanity defense, which defense would be most advantageous for her?
2. Research the insanity defense in your jurisdiction. Which defense or defenses does your jurisdiction use?
3. When is the defense of entrapment available in your jurisdiction?
4. Explain when you can use nonlethal force and when you can use lethal force to protect yourself from criminal activity.
5. Should the insanity defense be eliminated?

FOR FURTHER READING

1. Smith, R. (1981). *Trial by Medicine: The Insanity Defense in Victorian England.* Edinburgh University Press.

      Discusses the advances in the jurisprudence of insanity in Victorian England.

2. Moran, R. (1981). *Knowing Right from Wrong: The Insanity Defense of Daniel M'Naghten.* Free Press.

      Recounts the story of the insanity defense.

3. Bonnie, R. (1986). *Trial of John W. Hinckley, Jr.: A Case Study in the Insanity Defense.* Foundation Press.

ENDNOTES

1. CNN.com, *"They Pretended They Were God" Doctor, 2 Nurses Allegedly Killed Patients with Lethal Drug Dose,* accessed at *http://www.cnn.com/2006/LAW/07/18/hospital. deaths/index.html.*

2. Foti Defends How Office Handled Investigation; Says Grand Jury Didn't See Evidence, *Times-Picayune* (New Orleans), July 25, 2007.

3. *Dixon v. United States,* 126 S. Ct. 2437 (2006).

4. Kiley, S., Crime: After the Homemade Bomb Chained around Bank Robber Brian Wells's Neck Exploded, Baffled Police in the Pretty Lakeside Town or Erie Found Detailed Instructions to a Bizarre Treasure Hunt, *Observer Magazine,* July 22, 2007.

5. *Jacobson v. United States*, 503 U.S. 540 (1992).

6. 18 U.S.C.A. 17 (2000); *United States v. Cameron,* 907 F.2d 1051, 1061 (11th Cir. 1990).

7. "Va. Moves to Limit Executions: Senate Approves Shielding Retarded," *Washington Post,* February 9, 2002.

8. *Montana v. Egelhoff,* 518 U.S. 116 (1996).

9. *Rex v. M'Naghten,* House of Lords, 10 Cl. & F. 200, 8 Eng. Rep. 718.

10. *Parsons v. State*, 81 Ala. 577, 2 So. 854 (1887).

11. *Durham v. United States*, 94 U.S. App. D. C. 228, 214 F.2d 862 (1954).

12. *Indiana v. Jackson,* 406 U.S. 715 (1972).

13. *White v. Estelle*, 459 U.S. 1118 (1983).

14. Editorial, "1963 Birmingham Bombing: Another Man's Time to Answer," The Durham Herald (Durham, NC), January 7, 2002.

15. *Sell v. United States,* 539 U.S. 166 (2003).

16. *Caritativo v. California*, 359 U.S. 549 (1958).

17. Leavitt, N., "Is It Always Torture to Dismember and Eat a Conscious Human Being?" Findlaw commentary, *http://writ.news.findlaw.com/commentary/ 20040108_leavitt.htm,* accessed August 19, 2007.

18. *Edwards v. Indiana,* 866 N.E. 2d 252, (2007) *cert granted* U.S. Supreme Court 128 S. Ct. 741 (2007).

CHAPTER 10

Constitutional Rights before Arrest

CHAPTER CONTENTS

> The poorest man may in his cottage bid defiance to all the forces of the Crown. It may be frail, its roof may shake, the wind may blow through it, the storm may enter, the rain may enter, but the King of England cannot enter! All his forces dare not cross the threshold of the ruined tenement.
>
> *William Pitt the Elder, Lord Chatham, English statesman, in a speech, 1763*

> The right of the people to be secure in their persons, houses, papers, and effects, against unreasonable searches and seizures, shall not be violated, and no Warrants shall issue, but upon probable cause, supported by Oath or Affirmation, and particularly describing the place to be searched, and the persons or things to be seized.
>
> *U.S. Constitution, Fourth Amendment, 1791*

CHAPTER OBJECTIVES

After studying this chapter, you should be able to:

- Explain the constitutional protection against unreasonable searches and seizures.
- Give examples of searches that violate the Fourth Amendment.
- Explain what proof law enforcement must have before a search warrant will be issued.
- Explain the steps that law enforcement officers must take in order to get a search warrant issued.

- List areas that can be searched without a warrant.
- Explain probable cause.
- Explain the exclusionary rule.
- Explain the right to remain silent.
- Explain double jeopardy.
- Define and explain *ex post facto* laws and bills of attainder.
- Explain the right to bail.

INTRODUCTION AND HISTORICAL BACKGROUND

A right is not what someone gives you; it's what no one can take from you.
Ramsey Clark, former U.S. attorney general, *New York Times,* October 2, 1977

Unreasonable Searches and Seizures

The rule, based on the Fourth Amendment, that police must obtain a warrant before searching a home or arresting a suspect; the rule has numerous exceptions.

The U.S. Constitution is more than just a framework for government. It is in fact a series of limitations on governmental power. Like many documents, the Constitution was a product of its time. When the constitutional convention convened in 1787, British abuses of power were still fresh in the Founding Fathers' memories. But they also understood that a weak central government invited foreign attack and domestic instability. The constitutional framers set out to balance these two concerns.

When it came to protecting individual rights, the framers thought specifically of abuses suffered under British rule. In the 1760s, it was common practice for British agents to enter American buildings and homes searching for goods on which customs taxes hadn't been paid. These searches took place without the British having to state a reason for suspecting that they would find contraband in the house.

The American colonists resented the expanding British control over numerous aspects of American life, ranging from religious practices to where and how the colonists were tried if charged with a crime. Put in its simplest terms, the colonists wanted to be left alone. Once they freed themselves from Britain's yoke, they were reluctant to replace the harness with a new one. One reflection of the American spirit of independence is the Constitution's guarantee that the government can't conduct **unreasonable searches and seizures** or arrest citizens except upon probable cause.

So strong is the populace's resistance to governmental intrusions that evidence obtained in violation of the prohibition against unreasonable searches and seizures generally can't be admitted into evidence, no matter how incriminating the evidence turns out to be. If the police don't follow the law, the consequence may well be that a guilty man or woman goes free.

The Constitution also protects citizens from being tried repeatedly for the same crime after being acquitted, or **double jeopardy**. In the United States, citizens also can't be tried for acts committed before the behavior was made a criminal offense; the government is prohibited from making *ex post facto* laws. Nor can governments pass **bills of attainder**. Bills of attainder are criminal laws that apply only to named individuals or specific, identified groups. These three Constitutional protections help assure that citizens aren't harassed or oppressed by their government through the use of the criminal process and assure that the laws are applied uniformly and fairly.

The Constitution also protects persons charged with crimes from having to incriminate himself or herself through oral testimony or a confession. The right against **self-incrimination** is an important safeguard that prevents, for example, the use of torture to extract confessions. Persons charged with crimes are also entitled to effective assistance of counsel and a reasonable opportunity to post **bail** so that he or she can assist in the preparation for trial.

As you study this chapter, think about the liberties accorded to all citizens and ask yourself whether the great legal scholar William Blackstone was right when he said "it is better that ten guilty persons escape than that one innocent suffer." Is that the price we all must pay in order to live in a free society? Does the price become too high in time of war?

WHAT IS AN UNREASONABLE SEARCH?

The Fourth Amendment to the U.S. Constitution provides that "the right of the people to be secure in their persons, houses, papers, and effects, against unreasonable searches and seizures, shall not be violated." This right has evolved over the years to protect citizens from overzealous law enforcement officers and judges eager to secure criminal convictions. One of the key words in the Fourth Amendment is "unreasonable." "Reasonable" searches and seizures are allowed; it's only unreasonable ones that are unconstitutional.

EXPECTATION OF PRIVACY

Searches are unreasonable if they unduly interfere with the people's expectations of privacy. Thus, it can be said that people, not places, are protected from unreasonable searches. That is, if a person has a reasonable expectation of privacy in a place, the place may not be searched without a warrant. However, if he or she does not have a reasonable expectation of privacy in a place, the area can be searched without a warrant.

Courts have long held that people have an expectation of privacy in their homes. Police must either get permission to search a home, be in hot pursuit of someone, or obtain a warrant. The U.S. Supreme Court has held that "except in certain carefully defined classes of cases, a search of private property without proper consent is 'unreasonable' unless it has been authorized by a valid search warrant."[1] (For an explanation of the requirements for obtaining a warrant, see the discussion on probable cause later in this chapter.) Simply put, unless an officer gets permission to enter, is acting in an exigent situation, or gets a search warrant, it's illegal for him or her to enter someone's home or apartment.

Double Jeopardy
The rule, based on the Fifth Amendment, that a person can only be tried once for the same offense; the rule has several exceptions.

For my part I think it less evil that some criminals should escape, than that the government should play some ignoble part.
Oliver Wendell Holmes Jr., in *Olmstead v. United States,* 1928

***Ex Post Facto* Law**
The rule that a person cannot be charged with a crime that became a crime after he committed the act made illegal.

The right to be let alone is indeed the beginning of all freedoms.
William O. Douglas, 1952

Bill of Attainder

A law passed that singles out a person or persons as the only individuals affected by a criminal law; originally, a bill of attainder singled out an individual for capital punishment without benefit of a trial.

Self-Incrimination

The act of giving testimony against one's penal interest; generally, persons have a right to withhold information that may incriminate and to refuse to answer questions that incriminate; the right does not generally extend to giving DNA samples or submitting to blood alcohol testing or withholding other physical evidence.

Bail

Money or other guarantee posted to assure a defendant who is released from custody pending trial or appeal will appear when called or forfeit the security posted.

HISTORICAL HIGHLIGHT
The Right to Privacy

The word "privacy" does not appear in the U.S. Constitution. So where does the "right to privacy" come from? It is a legal construct based on various amendments to the Constitution. The "right to be let alone" was first noted by Justice Louis Brandeis in a 1928 case challenging the government's right to tap phones.[2]

Brandeis' "right to be let alone" wasn't applied to sexual or reproductive matters. Brandeis specifically refused to invoke it in a case deciding whether the state could forcibly sterilize a "promiscuous" girl. Brandeis concurred in the majority opinion allowing sterilization, apparently with no qualms about its effect on the "right to be let alone."[3]

However, the seed was planted. When the state of Oklahoma wanted to sterilize a career criminal (whose last conviction was for chicken theft), Justice William O. Douglas ruled that the right to have children was a "basic liberty."[4]

In 1961, the U.S. Supreme Court was faced with a challenge to a Connecticut law that forbade doctors to distribute contraceptives. Noted conservative jurist John Harlan cited the Oklahoma case when he wrote that the due process clause in the Fourteenth Amendment protected the "privacy of the home." When the same doctor challenged the Connecticut law four years later, Justice Douglas wrote that the state could not violate the "zone of privacy" surrounding the marital bedroom.[5]

This right to privacy was further enlarged in the case of *Roe v. Wade*, when the right to privacy was expanded to include a woman's right to have an abortion under certain circumstances.[6]

There have been limits placed on this right to privacy. Subsequent decisions have failed to expand the right. Other types of sexual activity have been ruled to not be covered by the "right to privacy" until recently.

In 1986, a homosexual male sought unsuccessfully to have Georgia's sodomy law overturned. The plaintiff had been arrested for engaging in oral sex with another man in his own apartment. If convicted under Georgia's 1816 anti-sodomy law, he would have faced up to 20 years in prison. The district attorney dropped the charges, but the plaintiff sought to have the law declared unconstitutional. The Supreme Court ruled against him on a 5–4 vote, arguing that moral concerns outweighed the "right to privacy" in this case. In effect, the Supreme Court ruled that it was a matter left to the states to regulate.[7]

Recently, the Supreme Court revisited the matter and overturned its earlier ruling in a 6–3 decision. The Court concluded that the right to privacy includes what consenting adults do in the privacy of their own home, and due process protects them from criminal prosecution for that conduct, however offensive it may be to other members of the community.[8] The case is seen by some as a major step forward for the gay rights movement.

The law gets more complicated, however, when the area to be searched isn't the suspect's own home or apartment. For example, when can police search a car? Can they search your desk at work? What about listening in on the calls you make from a public telephone booth? Can they read your e-mail? What if you're a guest at someone's home? What about your backyard? Your luggage? The Supreme Court has considered these and other cases on a case-by-case basis.

For example, what happens if a wife calls the police to report her husband's illegal drug use? The police show up, and the wife invites the police in to show them evidence of her husband's drug use. The husband refuses to consent to the search. Can the police go in? The Supreme Court addressed this situation recently and determined that when police encountered this situation and entered the property and eventually charged the man with cocaine possession, they acted illegally. The Court ruled the husband's refusal barred the police from entering unless they had a warrant.[9]

Essentially, the higher the reasonable expectation of privacy, the greater the likelihood that the police can't invade that privacy. For example, a conversation overheard by an off-duty police officer at a restaurant in which the dining companions discuss a murder-for-hire scheme wouldn't be protected, but the same conversation in the privacy of the conspirators' home would be. In the first, the diners have no reasonable expectation that their conversation is private since they are in public. In the last, the speakers can reasonably expect that their conversations aren't being monitored. It is the cases that fall between these extremes that have called for judicial interpretation.

For example, in *Mancusi v. De Forte,*[10] the Supreme Court held that a union official had an expectation of privacy in an office he shared with other workers. The warrantless search of his office space was a violation of the Fourth Amendment. For the search to have been valid, the police officers needed to get a warrant or the consent of the employer. They had done neither. However, the Supreme Court recently refused to review an Alaska case in which a worker complained that a secret video camera was aimed at her desk. The

YOU MAKE THE CALL

THE DUKE RAPE CASE—WARRANTLESS SEARCH OF STUDENT DORMS

According to one news report, police investigating the Duke University rape case entered a campus dormitory where several of the lacrosse players lived without a warrant. For security reasons, anyone entering the building had to swipe a Duke ID card through an electronically locked door to gain access. Police allegedly waited until a student opened the door and then followed the student in. The police spoke with several lacrosse players and entered at least one lacrosse player's dorm room.[12]

Did the police violate the dormitory residents' civil rights? If so, at what point? Do dormitory residents in a building where a key card is necessary for entry have an expectation of privacy? Are dormitory halls public or private space? Should the police need a warrant to enter them uninvited? At the time, many of the lacrosse players had retained legal counsel. Should the police have contacted the attorneys to speak with the players? Was this just a case of police intimidation of young men who feared their lack of cooperation would make them look guilty?

Consider all of these questions and you make the call.

college where she worked suspected she was stealing money from the college theatre, and local police crawled through the vents in the ceiling and installed a video camera aimed at her desk, all without a warrant. She was caught on tape taking money from an office moneybag and putting it in her purse. She asked the Court to suppress the evidence, but the Alaska Supreme Court concluded she had no expectation of privacy in her desk, since it was in an area accessible to other workers.[11]

In another case, *Minnesota v. Olson*,[13] a suspected driver of the getaway car used in a murder took refuge in an apartment rented by two female friends. The police surrounded the apartment and called the occupants. When one of the women answered, police heard a male voice say "tell them I left." Although they had the apartment surrounded, the officers stormed the apartment and arrested Olson. He challenged his arrest, arguing that the officers should have obtained a warrant or permission from the women before entering. The Supreme Court agreed. Olson, as an overnight guest, had a reasonable expectation of privacy. The Court wrote:

> To hold that an overnight guest has a legitimate expectation of privacy in his host's home merely recognizes the everyday expectations of privacy that we all share. Staying overnight in another's home is a longstanding social custom that serves functions recognized as valuable by society. We stay in others' homes when we travel to a strange city for business or pleasure, when we visit our parents, children, or more distant relatives out of town, when we are in between jobs or homes, or when we housesit for a friend. We will all be hosts and we will all be guests many times in our lives. From either perspective, we think that society recognizes that a houseguest has a legitimate expectation of privacy in his host's home.

Minnesota v. Olson, 495 U.S. 91, 99 (1990)

Persons who use a pay telephone and close the door behind them to make a call have a reasonable expectation of privacy. Their conversation can't be intercepted by police officers without a warrant.[14] But no one has a reasonable expectation of privacy in things that are in plain view. For example, if an officer walking down the street sees a marijuana plant growing next to the petunias in your flowerbed, he can use the plants as evidence without a warrant. But he can't knock your door down and seize the plants you were also growing in the basement.

Nor can police use a heat-sensing device to sniff out energy use as a way to get probable cause to search for marijuana plants. That's what the Supreme Court ruled in a 5–4 decision in *Kyllo v. United States*.[15] In that case, the Court concluded that the warrantless use of a thermal-imaging device aimed at a private home from a public street to detect relative amounts of heat within a home was an unlawful search within meaning of the Constitution's Fourth Amendment. Justice Scalia, who wrote the Court's opinion, concluded that a device that could tell "at what hour each night the lady of the house takes her daily sauna and bath" surely violated the right to privacy in one's home.

As you can see, each case is evaluated on its own merits. Because the standard of "reasonable expectation" is subjective, search-and-seizure questions are frequently raised in criminal cases. Many of these have reached the Supreme Court. Consider that from 1969 through 1986 the Supreme Court under Chief Justice Warren Burger decided 130 search-and-seizure cases.

PROBABLE CAUSE

How exactly does a police officer go about getting a search warrant? The details of the procedure vary from jurisdiction to jurisdiction, but generally the officer must present enough evidence to a magistrate to show there is probable cause to make an arrest or search the premises for evidence of criminal wrongdoing. While open to interpretation, "probable cause" generally means enough evidence to conclude that it is more likely than not that a crime was committed or that the place to be searched is connected with a crime. It is more than a suspicion but less than that needed for a conviction.[16]

EXCEPTIONS TO THE RULE

There are several exceptions to the rule that a search requires a warrant. The most obvious exception is consent. If the person whose home or possessions were searched gave his permission for the search, then the search does not violate the Fourth Amendment. Unsophisticated defendants who are politely asked if the officers can "look around" have waived any right to later object. The police are not required to educate you that you have the right to refuse a search or a stop and frisk if they come without a warrant. It is expected that any reasonable person would know that they have the right to refuse the search.[17]

The same holds true if the owner of the premises you are visiting or someone else in charge such as an employer gives permission. But landlords generally can't give consent to the search of a renter's apartment.[18] Three other exceptions we will consider are the automobile exception, the **exigent circumstances** exception, and the **stop and frisk** exception.

Automobiles are by their nature mobile. With a few exceptions such as large travel trailers, automobiles are generally not homes. There is therefore a reduced expectation of privacy associated with cars and other motorized vehicles. As a result, courts considering whether automobiles could be searched early on concluded that a lower standard was appropriate. Although a man's home may be his castle, his car is only transportation.

The first Supreme Court case to consider a search of an automobile was decided in 1925.[19] The case, *Carroll v. Illinois*, held that if the officer conducting the search had "probable cause" to have a warrant issued but didn't ask for one, the search was still valid. The chief reason was the mobility of automobiles. By the time the officer could have gotten a warrant, the car, unlike a house, would be long gone.

Over the years, the Supreme Court has continued to allow warrantless searches of automobiles, trunks, and glove compartments on the premise that the car is mobile and that there is a reduced expectation of privacy. This is true even if the car has been impounded and the owner jailed. As the Court wrote in *United States v. Ross:*[20]

> In many cases, however, the police will, prior to searching the car, have cause to arrest the occupants and bring them to the station for booking. In this situation, the police can ordinarily seize the automobile and bring it to the station. Because the vehicle is now in the exclusive control of the authorities, any subsequent search cannot be justified by the mobility of the car. Rather, an immediate warrantless search of the vehicle is permitted because of the second major justification for the automobile exception: the diminished expectation of privacy in an automobile.

Under the law, the police seize the driver of a car they pull over for purposes of searching it. The Fourth Amendment protects the driver from unreasonable searches. But what about passengers? Police pulled over a California man to "check his registration." The police recognized a passenger in the car as a parole violator. They used his parole status as justification to search the car where they found drugs and drug paraphernalia. At his trial, the passenger argued the police lacked probable cause to pull the car over and all

Exigent Circumstances
Situations that require urgent action, sufficient to excuse delay to get a warrant issued.

Stop and Frisk
Police officers may briefly stop, identify, and frisk persons reasonably believed to have committed a crime during the course of an investigation.

evidence found in the search should be suppressed. But the government argued they only pulled over the driver, in effect seizing him within the meaning of the Fourth Amendment. The passenger was not seized and could have left at any time. In other words, by remaining in the car, he agreed to be searched. The Supreme Court disagreed. They ruled the man was seized by the police because no reasonable person would believe the police would allow him to leave the scene. As a result, he could challenge whether the search was legal.[21]

Another issue that arises with some frequency is the question of whether a roadblock set up by police to stop motorists is a legitimate practice or violates the Fourth Amendment. In 2000, the Supreme Court ruled 6–3 in *Indianapolis v. Edmond*[22] that many such police checkpoints violate the Fourth Amendment. In that case, the Indianapolis police created a roadblock program that was designed to interdict illegal drug activity. The police set up six roadblocks between August and November 1998 on city roads. All told, they stopped 1,161 vehicles and made 104 arrests, 55 for drug-related offenses and the remainder for other crimes. Edmond challenged the roadblocks as warrantless and without probable cause. The Supreme Court agreed, writing:

> The Fourth Amendment requires that searches and seizures be reasonable. A search or seizure is ordinarily unreasonable in the absence of individualized suspicion of wrongdoing. . . . We have never approved a checkpoint program whose primary purpose was to detect evidence of ordinary criminal wrongdoing. Rather, our checkpoint cases have recognized only limited exceptions to the general rule that a seizure must be accompanied by some measure of individualized suspicion.

The Supreme Court decided another roadblock case in early 2004. The question posed was whether the police can set up a roadblock at the site of an earlier accident in order to attempt to find a motorist who might have witnessed an earlier fatal accident. The case, *Illinois v. Lidster*, involved a motorist who was arrested for drunk driving after he stopped at the roadblock. This time, a unanimous Court sided with the police. It distinguished earlier cases by pointing out that the police weren't searching for a suspect in the earlier crime but were simply asking if anyone had information about the crime. It was more akin to police officers asking people in a crowd what they may have observed.[23] Similarly, police may stop vehicles in emergency situations such as stopping vehicles when a flood has washed out a bridge. Stops at border crossings or for regulatory purposes such as emissions testing are permissible without warrants.

Because nearly one hundred cases involving the Fourth Amendment and the search of automobiles have been decided by the Supreme Court since 1925, any questions about the legality of automobile searches and seizures should be carefully researched before concluding that the search was or wasn't legal.

Exigent circumstances sometimes justify a search and seizure without a warrant. Generally speaking, exigent circumstances are those situations in which the law enforcement officer believes that getting a warrant will create the risk of injury or death or result in the destruction of evidence. One example is blood alcohol testing following an accident or arrest, since the level of alcohol in the blood may fall by the time a warrant can be obtained. Blood alcohol levels are considered **evanescent evidence,** meaning they are evidence that will change or evaporate in a manner that will destroy its evidentiary value. You will learn more about blood testing and breath analysis in Chapter 11.

Evanescent Evidence

Evidence that will change or evaporate in a manner that will destroy its evidentiary value.

The Supreme Court recently addressed a case where police entered a home to prevent bodily harm to an individual and ended up arresting those in the home. The situation began with a 3 AM call from a neighbor complaining about a loud party in the neighborhood. Police from the Brigham City, Utah, police department arrived to investigate. The police saw two underage individuals drinking beer in the backyard. The police entered the yard and looked in the house where they saw four adults and one juvenile arguing. When the juvenile hit one of the adults in the face hard enough to force the victim to spit blood into the sink, the police moved in announcing their presence. Ultimately, they arrested three of the adults and charged them with contributing to the delinquency of a minor, disorderly conduct, and intoxication.

At trial, the accused moved to have all evidence seized during the search of the home suppressed because the police lacked warrants or any viable reason to enter the house. The Utah State Supreme Court agreed, noting that the police could not have been there to assist the injured adult because they provided him no aid and therefore entered the house without either warrant or probable cause. The city appealed to the Supreme Court, who ruled the officers acted within the law because they "had an objectively reasonable basis for believing that an occupant was seriously injured or imminently threatened with such an injury.[24]

The most obvious situation that qualifies as exigent is when a police officer is in hot pursuit of a defendant, either on foot or in an automobile. Obviously, the suspect will get away if the officer had to first get a warrant from a magistrate. However, the circumstance must truly be an emergency or involve the destruction of evidence. Like other search-and-seizure cases, exigent circumstances cases are fact driven; that is, each case is decided on its unique facts. For example, the Supreme Court recently concluded that there is no bright line between conducting a warrantless search of a car with the driver still in the car or outside it. In *Thornton v. United States*,[25] the defendant parked his car before a police officer had a chance to stop him. The defendant got out of the car and was stopped by the officer. Because the defendant had drugs in his pocket, the officer arrested him and then searched the parked car. The officer found a handgun and added a firearms charge.

Thornton asked the Court to suppress the gun evidence on the premise that a warrantless search of a parked car was illegal. The Court disagreed and ruled 7–2 that officers can search a parked car when the occupant recently left the car. Would the result be the same if the driver had parked in his own driveway and had entered his house before the officer pulled up? It's hard to say. The Supreme Court seems to decide a case on the limits of exigent automobile cases every year.

What happens if the car you are riding in is pulled over by police for speeding and during the course of the stop an officer finds illegal drugs? Can the officer arrest all passengers and wait for one to confess? That's the question the Supreme Court tackled in *Maryland v. Pringle*.[26] In that case, police became suspicious when the driver reached into the glove compartment for his registration information, revealing a wad of cash. He asked the driver if he could look around and was given permission. The officer found cocaine under the back seat armrest. Pringle, who was seated in the front passenger seat, was arrested along with the driver and another passenger. Pringle finally confessed that the drugs were his and was eventually convicted and sentenced to ten years in prison. He now alleges that the officer had no probable cause to arrest all three and did so only to coerce a confession. The Supreme Court decided the case in late December 2003, again unanimously.

The Court wrote it was reasonable to arrest all three in the car on the premise that they were engaged in a common criminal enterprise. That the others were released after Pringle confessed was immaterial.[27]

Police officers can also stop and frisk suspicious individuals.[28] In *Terry v. Ohio*, a police officer noticed two African-American men in downtown Cleveland in the late afternoon in 1963. The officer later said that they "didn't look right to me." After observing the men looking in windows and pacing back and forth many times, he stopped them and frisked one man. In the man's coat he found a gun. The defendant argued that he had been searched in violation of the Fourth Amendment. The Supreme Court disagreed and upheld the stop and frisk as constitutional.

Since then, the right to stop and frisk has been limited. Officers must have more than a suspicion about an individual; they must describe specific suspicious actions. Police can't stop individuals because of their race or appearance unless they match the description of individuals wanted by the police or seen leaving the scene of a crime.[29] In other words, law enforcement officials must have more than a hunch that someone is engaged in criminal activity.

However, the Supreme Court recently explained that citizens are not free to refuse to give police their identity. If an officer conducts a *Terry* stop, the citizen stopped must provide his or her name and faces criminal penalties if uncooperative. The case *Hiibel v. Nevada*[30] involved a police officer responding to a report that a woman was being assaulted in a car. The officer responded to the reported location and stopped Hiibel outside a car with a woman inside. The officer asked Hiibel his name and arrested Hiibel when he refused to identify himelf. Hiibel's attorney argued that his client's Fourth Amendment rights included the right to refuse to give his name when he believed he wasn't engaging in criminal conduct. The Supreme Court disagreed and ruled that states can charge uncooperative persons criminally if they refuse to disclose their name. As long as the stop meets *Terry* standards for reasonableness, the suspect is required to identify himself.

One area of stop and frisk that has recently expanded is that of airport searches. This is partly in response to increased terrorist attacks and partly as a result of increased drug smuggling. Generally, persons entering the country can be frisked and even strip-searched, based upon nothing more than their appearance and point of origin.[31]

EXECUTING SEARCH WARRANTS

Once officers have a warrant in hand, they are supposed to "knock and announce" their presence. That is, the right to privacy includes the right to not be surprised by officers who knock down your door and storm in. A case recently decided by the U.S. Supreme Court tested the limits of the "knock and announce" requirement. During an afternoon, North Las Vegas police officers in SWAT uniforms raided the apartment of Lashawn Banks, whom they suspected was a drug dealer. Warrant in hand, they knocked and waited about 15 seconds before using a battering ram to gain entrance. Banks, who was showering, heard the loud noise and ran into the living room. There he was ordered to the floor by police officers wearing hoods. He claimed that their actions violated his right to privacy and that the evidence the officers found should be suppressed.

The Ninth Circuit sided with Banks, and the police appealed. A unanimous Supreme Court ruled in late 2003 that under the circumstances, the police were justified in breaking the door down. Given that the officers were executing a warrant for possession of cocaine, they could reasonably have suspected that the defendant's brief delay in answering the door was due to his efforts to dispose of the evidence.[32]

Police frequently work with informants and others whose reputations for honesty and integrity are suspect. So police may be on shaky ground when seeking a warrant based on the word of an informant. When weighing whether to issue the warrant, the court uses a totality of the circumstances test.

The case that set the standard involved an anonymous letter received by police. The letter claimed that a husband-and-wife team would transport a large amount of drugs in an automobile. The husband was to fly down to Florida while the wife drove the automobile. In Florida, the car was to be loaded with drugs, and the husband was to drive the car back. Acting on the information in the letter, the police found that the husband had reservations to fly to Florida. Acting with Florida police, they discovered that he and a female did drive a car back from Florida. When the couple arrived home, the police were waiting.

The couple challenged the warrant on the basis that the informant was unknown. But the Supreme Court, adopting the totality of the circumstance test, upheld the warrant since independent police work confirmed the information provided in the letter.[33] To meet Constitutional standards, a search warrant must describe specifically "the place to be searched and the persons or things to be seized."[34]

THE EXCLUSIONARY RULE

To discourage the abuse of the rules against unreasonable searches and seizures, the Supreme Court adopted the **exclusionary rule**. The rule makes any evidence seized in violation of the Fourth Amendment inadmissible in court. The Court, in *Mapp v. Ohio*, 367 U.S. 643 (1961), ruled that such evidence is like the "fruit of a poisonous tree" and can't be used against the defendant. The rule has since been modified so that evidence obtained through search warrants obtained in good faith, but which are invalidated for technical reasons, can be used at trial.[35]

Exclusionary Rule
The "fruit of the poisonous tree" doctrine that prohibits the admission of evidence obtained illegally at a defendant's criminal trial; the rule does allow the use of evidence obtained with a technically defective warrant, but in good faith.

HISTORICAL HIGHLIGHT
Police Can Search Indian Reservation with Warrant

Native American members of the Paiute-Shoshone tribe run the Paiute Palace Casino in Bishop, California, on tribal lands. The casino has 300 slot machines and seven game tables and provides much-needed jobs to tribe members. Police in Inyo County became suspicious that some tribe members were collecting welfare benefits while working at the casino and obtained a warrant to search the premises for evidence of welfare fraud. The casino had previously refused to turn over records, citing confidentiality.

The police officers raided the casino offices and seized employment records. No evidence of fraud was discovered, but the police threatened to enter tribal lands again. That's when tribal leaders sued in federal court, alleging that the police were violating the tribe's sovereign immunity. The tribe won in the Ninth Circuit but lost in the Supreme Court, 9–0. Police can, using a warrant, enter and search tribal lands. The case is *Inyo County v. Paiute-Shoshone Indians*, 538 U.S. 701 (2003).

TECHNOLOGY AND SEARCHES

Only one of the Founding Fathers had any real experience with electricity. But Ben Franklin's kite flying is as removed from modern electronic communications as the caveman's wheel is from the space shuttle. The U.S. Constitution's framers concept of searches consisted largely of broken-in doors and ransacked homes. Modern electronics provide far more information with less violence.

WIRETAPS

Law enforcement officers recognized early on that listening in on telephone conversations could yield valuable evidence. No law existed governing telephone taps in the 1920s, and most jurisdictions treated telephone taps like any other search. When Seattle police shut down the operation of a bootlegger named Olmstead using evidence from wiretaps, Olmstead challenged the wiretaps' legality. The prosecutor in the case argued that since government officials did not access the telephone calls, no law was broken. The case eventually landed in the U.S. Supreme Court, where the Court said that no law forbade law enforcement officials from using information obtained by nongovernment actors, even if obtained illegally. (Seattle police hired a lineman to tap the telephones by accessing lines running through publicly accessible areas to skirt the Fourth Amendment. However, Washington state law at the time made it a misdemeanor to listen in on someone else's telephone conversation.) The opinion practically begged Congress and state legislatures to pass laws to guide law enforcement officers.[36]

In response, Congress passed the Federal Communications Act of 1934, which prohibited wiretapping without a court order.[37] Rules for how to obtain such a court order were left to the states. New York State's law required law enforcement officers to provide a state judge (not just any magistrate) with the target's name and the reason why the wiretap was needed. Unless renewed, wiretaps expired in 60 days.[38]

The law was challenged as unconstitutional, and the challenge eventually reached the Supreme Court, who struck it down as too vague.[39] Congress then passed the Omnibus Crime Control and Safe Streets Wiretap Act of 1968. Title III of the Act regulates the interception of all oral and wire communications. To obtain authorization for a wiretap under Title III:

1. The law enforcement officer must show that normal investigative procedures have been tried and failed, are unlikely to succeed, or are dangerous;[40]
2. The surveillance must be conducted in a way that minimizes the interception of irrelevant information;[41]

3. There must be probable cause to believe the interception will reveal evidence of one of a list of specific predicate crimes;[42]

4. The order must be authorized by a high-level Justice Department official and signed by a federal judge;[43] and

5. The order is time-limited to thirty days (the government can request an extension).[44]

Federal courts later brought warrant requests for video surveillance under Title III requirements as well.[45] In 1986, Congress passed the Electronics Communications Privacy Act, which extended Title III to cover e-mails and other electronic messages.[46]

Following the terror attacks of September 11, 2001, Congress passed the Uniting and Strengthening America by Providing Appropriate Tools Required to Intercept and Obstruct Terrorism Act of 2001. Commonly known as the Patriot Act, the law supersedes Title III in many ways including:

- Expanding federal law enforcement authority to monitor e-mail and other electronic communications by treating stored voicemail messages like e-mail instead of telephone conversations. No warrant is necessary to access stored voice or e-mail.
- Federal courts can issue pen register and trap orders (devices that catalog the telephone numbers or e-mail addresses contacted by a particular person) throughout the nation.
- Law enforcement officials can now catalog the Web addresses visited by a computer without a warrant if they can show the information is "relevant to an ongoing investigation."
- Roving wiretaps, where multiple telephones used by the same person may be tapped, eliminating the need to get a new court order each time a person of interest obtained a new cell phone.
- The Patriot Act created several new crimes including money laundering in support of terrorism or cybercrime, overseas use of fraudulent U.S. credit cards, terrorist attacks on mass transit, and harboring terrorists.
- The Act also increased penalties for counterfeiting.
- Law enforcement agencies are now permitted to share grand jury testimony and wiretap information with intelligence agencies if it meets the definition of "foreign intelligence."

One of the more controversial Patriot Act provisions allows federal agents to enter a home without a warrant to "look around" and then seek a warrant if they find any evidence. This "sneak a peek" provision became a central theme in the Brandon Mayfield saga. (See the following Historical Highlight.)

> Those who would give up essential liberty to purchase a little temporary safety deserve neither safety nor liberty.
> Benjamin Franklin

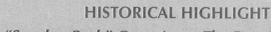

HISTORICAL HIGHLIGHT
"Sneak-a-Peek" Gone Awry: The Brandon Mayfield Saga

Spanish police found a fingerprint in the aftermath of the 2004 Madrid train bombing they believed belonged to one of the terrorists. They shared the fingerprint with the Federal Bureau of Investigation (FBI). After running it through the national fingerprint database, the FBI thought they had a match. They sent the matching fingerprint back to Spanish authorities. But the Spanish weren't so sure and concluded there was no match.

Undeterred, the FBI checked out the owner of their "matching" fingerprint. He was Portland, Oregon, attorney Brandon Mayfield. The FBI also learned the attorney was a convert to Islam. How did the FBI come to have Mayfield's fingerprint? Mayfield had served in the military, and the fingerprint was in the database from his time in the U.S. Army.

Since leaving the military, Mayfield met an Egyptian woman, converted to Islam, married, had two children, and opened a small law office. Through his local mosque, Mayfield met several Arab Americans, some of whom he represented in family court matters.

To the FBI, the matching fingerprint, the conversion to Islam, and identifying one of Mayfield's clients as being on a terror watch list added up to a likely participant in the Madrid bombing. Under the Patriot Act, the FBI did a sneak-a-peek investigation of Mayfield's home, took over 300 pictures, and planted listening devices.

The Mayfields began to find clues someone had been in their house. The deadbolt they never locked would be locked when they returned home at the end of the day. Even though they never wore shoes in the house, muddy shoe prints appeared in one of their children's bedrooms.[47]

On May 6, 2004, the FBI arrested Mayfield. Almost immediately the FBI was unable to answer obvious questions. Mayfield's passport showed he had not left the country. The FBI maintained he must have done so using someone else's passport. The FBI produced papers with words written in Spanish seized from the Mayfields' home. It turned out to be one of the Mayfield children's Spanish homework. (Imagine telling your teacher the FBI seized your homework.) The Spanish authorities again told the FBI the fingerprint did not match.

By the time Mayfield was released, he had been held in jail for two weeks. He claimed he was subject to "lockdowns, strip searches, sleep deprivation, unsanitary living conditions, shackles and chains, threats, physical pain and humiliation." Mayfield sued the Attorney General, and the Justice Department settled the case for $2 million. Mayfield retained his right to challenge the constitutionality of the Patriot Act.[48]

The FBI's misidentification of the fingerprint arose from the image being flipped when faxed to the United States. They were looking at a mirror image. The agency has apologized.

The Department of Justice conducted an investigation into the botched investigation. You can review the report at *http://www.usdoj.gov/oig/special/s0601/Chapter1.pdf.*

DOUBLE JEOPARDY

The Fifth Amendment to the U.S. Constitution provides that no person shall "be subject for the same offense to be twice put in jeopardy of life or limb." Its roots can be traced to Roman times, when the Emperor Justinian declared "the governor should not permit the same person to be again accused of crime of which he has been acquitted."[49] This Constitutional provision assures that no one can be put on trial a second time for the same offense after a court or jury has decided that the government was unable to prove its case beyond a reasonable doubt. In other words, it doesn't matter if the defendant, after being acquitted, takes out a full-page ad in the local paper declaring that he "did it." He can't be tried again after the jury has spoken.

Prosecutors only have one opportunity to present the case to a jury; if the case is botched or if evidence is uncovered later, the opportunity has been lost. As a practical matter, this means that the government must bring all possible charges arising out of one incident against an individual at one time. For example, the government can't first try a defendant for murder and later try him for possession of a firearm during the robbery in which the murder took place. If it fails to convict on the murder charge, it can't retry on the weapons charge. "All the charges against a defendant that grow out of a single criminal act, occurrence, episode, or transaction" must be tried together.[50]

The guarantee, however, has several well-established exceptions. These include the government's:

- Right to retry a suspect if the jury is deadlocked, or "hung"
- Right to retry a suspect when an appellate court has ordered a retrial because of some error in an earlier trial
- Right to try a suspect in federal court on federal criminal charges if a state court acquitted on state charges and vice versa or to try and convict an individual in both state and federal courts if the same act violated both state and federal laws
- Right on retrial to ask for and get the death penalty if the defendant was originally sentenced to life in prison but appealed the conviction and won a new trial.

Each of these exceptions is discussed following.

RETRIAL AFTER HUNG JURY

When a jury is unable to reach a verdict of guilty or not guilty, the defendant may be, and often is, retried. There is no violation of the double jeopardy clause because both the defendant and the government are entitled to a jury's decision on the case. The U.S. Supreme Court explained the issue this way:

> The double-jeopardy provision of the Fifth Amendment, however, does not mean that every time a defendant is put to trial before a competent tribunal he is entitled to go free if the trial fails to end in a final judgment. Such a rule would create an insuperable obstacle to the administration of justice in many cases in which there is no semblance of the type of oppressive practices at which the double-jeopardy prohibition is aimed. There may be

unforeseeable circumstances that arise during a trial making its completion impossible, such as the failure of a jury to agree on a verdict. In such event the purpose of law to protect society from those guilty of crimes frequently would be frustrated by denying courts power to put the defendant to trial again.

Wade v. Hunter, 336 U.S. 684 (1949)

RETRIAL AFTER REVERSAL ON APPEAL

When a judge or jury finds a criminal defendant guilty of a crime, the defendant may appeal the decision to an appellate court if he or she believes an error occurred during the trial. Errors include incorrect rulings on the admissibility of testimony, ineffective assistance of counsel, violation of a Constitutional right, and the like. Only the criminal defendant can appeal a conviction; the government can't appeal an acquittal.[51]

The remedy ordered by the appellate court is typically a new trial. That new trial allows the defendant to exclude the erroneously admitted evidence the second time around, to have the assistance of effective counsel, to have evidence admitted, or the like. In other words, the new trial gives the defendant another opportunity for acquittal. Only in rare circumstances will an appellate court find that the errors in the first trial are so egregious that a second trial would be double jeopardy. (See Historical Highlight: Commonwealth v. Smith, *Suppressed Evidence Taken with a Grain of Sand.*)

Before going to prison I believed that criticism of the criminal justice system for its treatment of the poor was so much liberal bleating and bunk. I was wrong. G. Gordon Liddy, 1977

Trial in Both State and Federal Court for the Same Act   Another exception to the rule against double jeopardy is a second trial in the event a defendant violates the laws of two or more jurisdictions by one act. The double jeopardy clause doesn't prevent both state and federal courts from prosecuting, convicting, and sentencing the same defendant for committing one act that is both a federal and a state crime. For example, if a defendant makes moonshine that violates both a state law against home brewing and federal laws against producing moonshine for transportation across state lines, he or she can be punished under both laws. That's because each jurisdiction has the right to enforce its criminal laws.[52] If he or she was acquitted of state charges, he or she can also still be convicted on the federal charges.

A number of crimes have both state and federal consequences. For example, both the federal government and the individual states have laws against the sale and distribution of

HISTORICAL HIGHLIGHT
Commonwealth v. Smith, *Suppressed Evidence Taken with a Grain of Sand*

Susan Reinert had reason to be happy in the summer of 1979. She was engaged to a fellow teacher, William Bradfield, and was to be married that summer. She also had reason to be afraid. Bradfield and Smith, the assistant principal of the school where Reinert and Bradfield taught, may have planned to murder her and her children. The possible reason was the $730,000 of insurance Bradfield had persuaded her to purchase, naming him as the beneficiary.

Ms. Reinert and her two children left their home on the evening of June 22, and were not seen alive again. Reinert's nude and beaten body was discovered in the trunk of a car parked in a hotel parking lot 100 miles away from her home. Her children's bodies were never found.

According to the prosecution, Bradfield and Smith had planned to kill Reinert and her children for the insurance money. The prosecution also showed that the two had previously engaged in a criminal conspiracy. In 1977, Smith had been accused of theft, but Bradfield provided an alibi for him. Despite Bradfield's testimony, Smith was convicted, and was due to start his sentence on June 26, 1979, the day after Reinert's body was discovered.

The prosecution theorized that it was a double cross. Bradfield was to kill Reinert, and Smith was to dispose of the children. The bodies were not supposed to be found, and after the seven-year waiting period, the two would share in the insurance money. Smith would have the alibi of being incarcerated at the time of the "disappearance." Perhaps, the prosecution argued, Bradfield realized that Smith would be in jail, and if Reinert's body was discovered, he could collect the money right away and be long gone by the time Smith finished his sentence.

Both men were eventually charged with the murders, and they were tried separately. Bradfield was convicted and sentenced to three life terms. He died in prison in 1998. Smith was convicted and sentenced to death.

However, the prosecution had suppressed a piece of evidence at Smith's trial. The state police had lifted grains of sand from Reinert's feet. Smith had maintained as his defense that Bradfield had taken Reinert to the New Jersey shore and killed her there. Despite the fact that several other key pieces of physical evidence tied Smith to Reinert's death, the Pennsylvania Supreme Court ruled that the suppression of evidence was prosecutorial misconduct. Normally, this would mean a new trial, but the high court went further. They ruled that the conduct was so egregious that to try Smith again would violate the Constitutional prohibition against double jeopardy. The conviction was overturned, and Smith was set free.

In 1998, Smith sued prosecutors, policemen, and author Joseph Wambaugh, who wrote a best seller about the case, *Echoes in the Darkness*, alleging they violated his civil rights. Smith claimed Wambaugh had offered to pay a Pennsylvania state police officer if his book was a success. Attorneys for the prosecutors and policemen argued in the civil trial that the "grains of sand" were quartz that could have come from anywhere. Thus, they were not deemed important at the time of trial. The jury apparently was convinced by this argument but was skeptical of Smith's explanation of how one of his combs was found under Reinert's body and how pieces of her clothing were discovered in his car.

Smith is free. This case shows that even in cases where there is strong evidence pointing to a person's guilt, the Constitutional protection against double jeopardy can prevent the state from trying that person again.

controlled substances. In most cases, the state laws are virtually identical to the federal law. A defendant who sells heroin violates two criminal laws with each sale and can be prosecuted in both state and federal courts. As a practical matter, most defendants are prosecuted under either state or local laws, not under both. This is due in part to the "petite policy," a policy developed by the Department of Justice that essentially prohibits federal prosecutors from prosecuting a defendant on state charges if the federal law violated is substantially similar to a state one and the state has prosecuted the defendant on the state charges.

Only in cases that would create a manifest injustice if the defendant were allowed to go free does the federal government prosecute an individual who has already been tried and convicted or acquitted of an act that is a state crime and also a federal crime. You may recall from Chapter 1 that the police officers who were acquitted of beating Rodney King were later tried and convicted in federal court for violating Mr. King's civil rights. The unique fact situation of the Rodney King beatings and the riots that followed the acquittal of the police officers caught on camera was such a circumstance warranting another prosecution.

Retrial and the Death Penalty   What happens if a murder defendant is convicted and sentenced to life in prison but receives a new trial? Can the prosecution seek the death penalty? The answer was until recently "no." The Supreme Court had ruled that to do so would be double jeopardy.[53] But in 2003, a divided Court concluded the opposite. The case involved a Pennsylvania defendant who was convicted of murder by a jury for killing a restaurant worker during a robbery. The jury was unable to agree on whether the defendant should receive death or life in prison. Because it was deadlocked, Pennsylvania law dictated he be sentenced to life. He appealed and was granted a new trial based on other defects in the trial. The prosecution again sought death, and this time the jury was willing to order it. The Supreme Court ruled that there was no double jeopardy in this case but left open the possibility that had the first jury voted for life rather than being unable to agree, the prosecution would be barred from seeking death.[54] When the case was remanded to state court, the court let the death sentence stand.[55]

EX POST FACTO LAWS AND BILLS OF ATTAINDER

Two rights granted by the U.S. Constitution that are rarely the subject of controversy in criminal law deserve at least a brief mention, if only to illustrate the mind-set of the Founding Fathers and the tyranny from which they sought to protect the citizens of their new nation. These two concepts are the prohibition against the passage of *ex post facto* laws and bills of attainder. *Ex post facto* laws are laws that criminalize behavior after the behavior has already taken place. Bills of attainder are criminal statutes passed that make behavior a crime for only some persons and not others.

Ex Post Facto Laws

The Constitution outlaws *ex post facto* laws. That is, neither the federal government nor a state or local government can pass a law that makes an act a crime that was not a crime when the defendant committed the act. Nor can a legislature pass laws that increase the penalty for a crime that was committed before the law was passed. "The Constitution forbids the application of any new punitive measure to a crime already consummated, to the detriment or material disadvantage of the wrongdoer."[56]

The reason for the prohibition is rooted in the criminal law concept that holds crimes are intentional acts in disobedience of the law. A person can't disobey a law that does not yet exist. It would be patently unfair for the justice system to punish people after the fact. There is an exception. So-called "three times, you're out" recidivism statutes aren't *ex post facto,* even if the first two crimes were committed before the passage of the recidivism law went into effect, as long as the third strike happened after the recidivism law went into effect. In other words, a defendant must be on notice that another conviction will mean a longer sentence than the third conviction ordinarily would carry but for his or her prior record.

What about a prisoner sentenced to a lengthy term who would have had a parole hearing every year until the law changed the interval between hearings? The U.S. Supreme Court has ruled that since the change doesn't affect the original sentence, only his potential early release, the change wasn't an *ex post facto* law.[57]

A recent Supreme Court opinion clarified how far the legislature can go to punish behavior that occurred a long time ago. The case involved a 70-year-old grandfather who was charged with sexual offenses against minors—something that happened over 50 years earlier. In response to complaints that the state's statute of limitations for sex crimes for minors was too short (it had been three years for some time), the California legislature authorized prosecutors to charge defendants up to one year from the time they were notified by a victim that the assault had taken place. The law was passed in part to help victims of childhood sexual abuse who may have feared coming forward for years.

The Supreme Court ruled that the law violated the prohibition against *ex post facto* laws and threw out the conviction by a 5–4 vote.[58] The decision put in question the arrest and conviction of a number of priests accused of abusing young boys in their charge. In states that have changed their statute of limitations since the abuse occurred, no prosecution seems likely.[59]

HISTORICAL HIGHLIGHT
Ex Post Facto *and Sex Offender Registration*

Perhaps no crime strikes greater fear in the community than violent offenses against children. Children who are victims of rape or other forms of sexual abuse are understandably sympathetic victims. Likewise, their assailants are almost universally reviled, even among other criminal offenders. So deep does the prohibition against harming defenseless children go that prisons almost always separate child abusers from the rest of the inmate population to protect the abusers from harm.

It should come as no surprise that laws designed to identify criminals who prey on children are popular in many communities. So-called sexual predator laws typically require those convicted of sexual offenses involving children to register their addresses. Usually referred to as Megan's Laws, because they were inspired by the tragic death of Megan Kanka at the hands of a sexual predator who lived in her neighborhood, the laws require community notification when a sex offender moves into a neighborhood. Presumably, parents and other adults will be more vigilant when they know their neighbor has a history of violent sexual crimes.

Sexual predator registration laws have been challenged by offenders who argue that having to register as predators is additional punishment inflicted after they have served their sentences, especially for those who committed their crimes before the laws were passed. They argue Megan's Laws amount to *ex post facto* laws and violate the Constitution.

When Alaska passed a version of Megan's Law, two former sex offenders sued. They argued that registering after they had served their sentences was additional punishment for a crime they had committed long before the law was passed. The Alaska Sex Offender Registration Act required that the former offender's name, address, place of employment, conviction and sentence, driver's license information, and photograph be published on the Internet. One offender had been convicted of sexually abusing his daughter from age 9 through 11, and the other had pled no contest to charges he had sexually abused a 14-year-old teen.

The Supreme Court, in a 6–3 decision, upheld the legislation. Although registering might subject the offenders to shame, the majority reasoned that was not punishment as contemplated by the *ex post facto* clause. The Court wrote that:

> The purpose and the principal effect of notification are to inform the public for its own safety, not to humiliate the offender. Widespread public access is necessary for the efficacy of the scheme, and the attendant humiliation is but a collateral consequence of a valid regulation.

> Smith v. Doe, 538 U.S. 1009 (2003)

BILLS OF ATTAINDER

Bills of attainder are criminal laws passed that only apply to a specific person or specific group of persons. In England, bills of attainder originally singled out individuals for capital punishment without benefit of a trial. The term now refers to any law that targets a specific individual or group for criminal punishment. For example, assume a local city government passed an ordinance that made it a crime for John Smith to smoke in public. Since the law names an individual, it is a bill of attainder. Everyone else can smoke in public, except John Smith. Laws also can't designate an identifiable group as the subject. For example, a law banning all Communist Party members from holding union offices unfairly singled out a specific group for special treatment and was ruled a bill of attainder.[60] In short, a law is a bill of attainder if it singles out either a specific person or a group of persons for prosecution or other punishment.

PRESUMPTION OF INNOCENCE

Each person is presumed to be innocent until proven guilty of the charges against him or her in court. The presumption of innocence is therefore a **rebuttable presumption,** meaning that the prosecution can present evidence showing that presumption is false, and if the evidence proves guilt beyond a reasonable doubt, then the defendant is no longer presumed innocent.

Some presumptions are **irrebuttable presumptions**. For instance, it is presumed child under age 7 cannot commit a felony because the child lacks mens rea. No evidence the prosecution presents can prove the child committed the felony.

The presumption of innocence stays with the defendant after arrest and throughout the trial. As a result, the prosecution must prove all elements of the crime to secure a conviction. Savvy defendants often refuse to speak with investigators out of fear they will provide evidence that may overcome their presumption of innocence.

RIGHT TO REMAIN SILENT

The Fifth Amendment provides that no person "shall be compelled in any criminal case to be a witness against himself." The right against self-incrimination, or the **right to remain silent**, is fundamental to the U.S. system of justice. It reflects the fundamental belief of the Founding Fathers that it's the government that has the burden of proof in criminal cases and that the accused can't be forced to do the prosecutor's job. Simply put, a defendant cannot be compelled to confess to a crime or to provide testimony against himself. Of course, he may do so voluntarily.

Police have an obligation to inform suspects in custody or under arrest of the right to remain silent, among other rights. Since the U.S. Supreme Court's decision in *Miranda v. Arizona*,[61] law enforcement officers routinely read suspects their rights. This has become known as "Mirandizing" a suspect. *Miranda's* effect after arrest is discussed in Chapter 11.

However, there are several exceptions to the rule. Volunteered statements defendants make when not under interrogation are not covered by *Miranda*. The courts do not require investigators to interrupt a defendant's confession to read him his rights. It would be both rude and poor law enforcement technique.

The courts also do not recognize routine questions such as requests for name, address, age, and so forth as interrogation requiring the police to Mirandize the person being questioned. Police interrogations at routine traffic stops do not trigger *Miranda*. So you can refuse to answer when the police officer asks "did you see that stop sign," if you think it will help.

Police can also ask questions in the interest of public safety without reading the person his rights. For example, police at a fire do not need to Mirandize the captured arsonist before asking if anyone is inside the building.

Rebuttable Presumption

A presumption that can be overcome by presenting evidence to the contrary.

Irrebuttable Presumption

A presumption that cannot be disproved regardless of the amount or quality of evidence to the contrary.

Even an attorney of moderate talent can postpone doomsday year after year, for the system of appeals that pervades American jurisprudence amounts to a legalistic wheel of fortune, a game of chance, somewhat fixed in the favor of the criminal, that the participants play interminably. Truman Capote, *In Cold Blood,* 1965

Right to Remain Silent

The right of all persons not to testify against their own interests when suspected of or charged with a crime; the right to remain silent is rooted in the belief that it is the government's obligation to prove guilt.

Similarly, undercover officers do not have to read anyone their rights. Obviously, doing so would blow their cover and shorten their career. Courts do not consider undercover situations covered by *Miranda* because no one is in custody and they do not take place in a "police-dominated atmosphere."[62] However, once someone is in custody, the police may not use undercover agents to elicit information.

THE ROLE OF POLYGRAPH

Polygraphs or lie detectors are machines that measure heart, respiration, and perspiration rates based on the theory that people will display stress reactions when they lie. Most polygraph results are inadmissible in court because of their unreliability. Defense attorneys often use polygraph results to bolster the defendant's credibility.

A professionally performed polygraph test will start with some routine questions that both the interrogator and the person being questioned know the answers to, such as name, address, date and place of birth, and so forth. This provides the interrogator with baseline readings when the subject is relating truthful answers. Significant deviations from these readings are assumed to be false answers, or some tests may be ruled inconclusive. Defense attorneys whose tests indicate their clients may be lying are often reported as "inconclusive."[63]

Because polygraph results are inadmissible, defense attorneys seldom let police or prosecutors conduct them on their clients. Polygraph tests can be subject to abuse. In her days as a prosecutor, the author heard the story of police running some wires from a kitchen colander to a copy machine and telling a suspect the contraption was a lie detector machine. They placed the colander on his head and interrogated him. When he gave what they thought to be an untruthful answer, they would press the copy button that always printed a sheet that said "LIE" on it. The author never actually saw this polygraph in action and hopes the police officers were making it all up. She did tell them that this method should not be used.

In recent years voice stress tests have gained some acceptance. Like polygraphs, voice stress tests operate on the premise that stress will show up in measurable form when someone lies. Interrogations are recorded, and experts examine the recording to detect stress. Voice stress tests are also generally inadmissible in court.[64]

Right to Bail

The limited right to be released from prison pending trial after posting enough security to assure appearance at the time of trial; the right is subject to limitation in cases of murder or where release has been shown to pose a threat to the public.

RIGHT TO REASONABLE BAIL

Another fundamental right enjoyed by Americans is the Eighth Amendment guarantee against excessive bail. Though not without limits, defendants are generally entitled to bail pending trial. Release from prison before trial serves several purposes. First, it serves as an incentive for the government to bring cases to closure. If defendants could be indefinitely detained in prison pending trial, there would be little incentive to moving the case forward. Second, the **right to bail** allows the defendant to fully participate in his or her defense, something difficult to do from the inside of a prison cell. Coupled with the right to a speedy trial (discussed in Chapter 11), the right to bail helps grease the wheels of justice.

The amount of bail set is intended as a guarantee that the defendant will show up for trial. Bail generally is set in an amount that will guarantee that the defendant doesn't skip town. Since 1987, however, bail can be denied altogether if the defendant poses a danger to the community. Bail can be denied in capital cases, in cases where the defendant may intimidate witnesses, or in cases where the public's safety is at stake. A hearing is required before bail can be denied, and the government must show that the defendant poses a public threat that no conditions of release can change.[65]

CHAPTER SUMMARY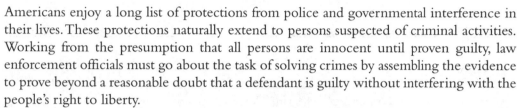

Americans enjoy a long list of protections from police and governmental interference in their lives. These protections naturally extend to persons suspected of criminal activities. Working from the presumption that all persons are innocent until proven guilty, law enforcement officials must go about the task of solving crimes by assembling the evidence to prove beyond a reasonable doubt that a defendant is guilty without interfering with the people's right to liberty.

All persons are accorded the right to be free from unreasonable searches and seizures. The U.S. Constitution protects the public's reasonable expectation of privacy, whether at home, at work, or in a closed telephone booth along the interstate. Police can only search private places with either consent or a search **warrant**. A search warrant requires that police officers obtain one from a neutral magistrate or judge after presenting probable cause that the place to be searched will yield evidence of a crime or the person to be detained has committed a crime.

Warrant
A document issued by a magistrate or judge authorizing the search of a place or the arrest of a person.

Officers can detain, search, and arrest individuals without a warrant, but with probable cause, if certain circumstances mitigate against obtaining a search warrant from a magistrate or judge. These include the searching of an automobile stopped for reasons that amount to probable cause, exigent circumstances such as the pursuit of a suspect on foot or in a car, and the temporary detainment, identification, and search of an individual in a stop and frisk.

If a defendant can show that the police violated his or her right to be free of unreasonable searches and seizures, the remedy may be that the evidence obtained cannot be used in court. This is the exclusionary rule.

In the U.S. system of justice, the government has only one opportunity to try a suspect; if a jury acquits him, he is free to go, even if later he shouts his guilt from the highest rooftop. Double jeopardy protects him and all others from repeated attempts at conviction for the same offense. It does not mean that a defendant who wins an appeal can't be retried. Nor does it prevent another trial if the jury is unable to reach a verdict. Defendants can also be tried in both state and federal courts for activities that violate both state and federal laws.

The rule against *ex post facto* laws prevents the government from punishing persons who committed acts that were legal at the time but were made illegal later. The rule against bills of attainder prevent the government from passing laws that apply only to certain individuals or specific groups of people.

Finally, defendants and suspects have the right to legal counsel to represent them at most stages of a criminal prosecution and the right to remain silent throughout the process.

KEY TERMS

Bail

Bill of Attainder

Double Jeopardy

Evanescent Evidence

Ex Post Facto Law

Exclusionary Rule

Exigent Circumstances

Irrebuttable
  Presumption

Rebuttable Presumption

Right to Bail

Right to Remain Silent

Self-Incrimination

Stop and Frisk

Unreasonable Searches
  and Seizures

Warrant

EXERCISE

1. Do you carry a cell phone? Most students do. If you want to be absolutely sure no one is listening in on your conversation—or anyone else's conversation in the room—remove the battery. That's right. Your trusty communications device may be a bug. That's what the world learned when a federal judge considering a criminal case against a purported member of the Genovese crime family ruled that the FBI was free to reprogram cell phones as roving electronic eavesdropping bugs. Here's how it supposedly works. Technology is available in software form that switched on the microphone in recent model cell phones, even when the cell phone is powered off. For example, this allows persons sitting in a FBI cubicle in Washington, DC, to listen in on live conversations anywhere in the world. Nextel, Samsung, and Motorola Razr cell phones are reportedly the easiest to "tap" this way. The only way to defeat the "bug" is to remove the battery from the handset.

   Read Judge Kaplan's opinion in the chapter Appendix and consider under what circumstances you think such roving bugs should be approved. Knowing what you know, do you think it would be a good idea to have clients, investigators, and attorneys who meet to discuss a case remove the batteries from their cell phones? What are the implications of a roving bug on attorney-client privilege and the right to an attorney?

DISCUSSION QUESTIONS

1. Discuss the right to privacy in one's home and in other places discussed in this chapter. Does the system provide sufficient safeguards against unreasonable searches, or does it hamper law enforcement to the detriment of law-abiding citizens' rights to be free from crime?

2. You have been stopped by a police officer because your brake light is out. Your brother, whom you suspect has a drug problem, throws something under your seat. The officer asks if he can look around. What do you do?

3. A trend in recent years has been for state legislatures to pass laws that require sex offenders who have served their sentences to register their address with the police

and for the government to notify communities that a convicted sex offender is now their neighbor. What arguments would you make on behalf of a sex offender who committed the offense before the passage of the registration law?

4. How intrusive a search are you willing to undergo in order to fly? Does your tolerance for searches change if instead of flying you are taking the train? A bus? A taxi? Entering a sporting event?

FOR FURTHER READING AND VIEWING

READING

1. Alderman, E., & Kennedy, C. (1997). *The Right to Privacy*. Vintage Books.
   Examines the origin of the right to privacy and its application in civil and criminal law through case studies such as the story of the routine strip searching performed on women arrested for minor traffic violations.

2. Alderman, E., & Kennedy, C. (1992). *In Our Defense: The Bill of Rights in Action*. Avon Books.
   Explores the origin and history of the Bill of Rights using case examples.

3. Amar, A., & Hirsch, A. (1998). *For the People: What the Constitution Really Says About Your Rights*. Free Press.
   Provides an alternative interpretation of the history of the U.S. Constitution and the Bill of Rights that focuses on the rights of the collective "we the people" rather than on the rights of the individual.

4. Katz, L., & Shepard, T. (1994). *Know Your Rights*. Banks–Baldwin.
   This practical legal guide answers questions such as what to do when stopped by a police officer on the road or when you are arrested.

5. Moore, W. (1996). *Constitutional Rights and Powers of the People*. Princeton University Press.
   This book examines how the social and political climate of the time affects the interpretation of the U.S. Constitution.

VIEWING

1. *The Bourne Ultimatum* (2007).
   Action thriller staring Matt Damon as Jason Bourne, based on the novel by Robert Ludlum. The film features lots of real-time cell phone tracing and bugging as the Central Intelligence Agency (CIA) tries to track Bourne across the world.

2. *The Star Chamber* (1983).
   This film stars Michael Douglas and centers on a secret justice system that "tries" defendants released on a technicality in the real justice system.

3. *Cape Fear* (1991).
   Nick Nolte stars as a former defense attorney who allowed evidence he should have moved to exclude go forward, resulting in the conviction of the character played by Robert DeNiro. DeNiro seeks revenge for the legal malpractice and stalks the attorney's family.

ENDNOTES

1. *Camara v. Municipal Court*, 387 U.S. 523 (1967).
2. *Olmstead v. United States*, 277 U.S. 438 (1928).
3. *Buck v. Bell*, 274 U.S. 200 (1927).
4. *Skinner v. Oklahoma Ex rel. Williamson, Attorney General*, 316 U.S. 535 (1942).
5. *Griswold et al. v. Connecticut*, 381 U.S. 479 (1965).
6. *Roe v. Wade*, 410 U.S. 113 (1973).
7. *Bowers, Attorney General of Georgia v. Hardwick et al.*, 478 U.S. 186 (1986).
8. *Lawrence v. Texas*, 539 U.S. 558 (2003).
9. *Georgia v. Randolph*, 547 U.S. 103 (2006).
10. *Mancusi v. De Forte*, 392 U.S. 364 (1968).
11. *Cowles v. Alaska*, 23 P.3d 1168 (2001), *cert. denied*, 2002 U.S. Lexis 701.
12. Bernstein, V., "Police Enter Dormitory at Duke to Query Players in Rape Case," *New York Times*, April 15, 2006.
13. *Minnesota v. Olson*, 495 U.S. 91 (1990).
14. *Katz v. United States*, 389 U.S. 347 (1967).
15. *Kyllo v. United States*, 533 U.S. 27 (2001).
16. *Brinegar v. United States*, 338 U.S. 160 (1949).
17. *United States v. Drayton et al.*, 536 U.S. 194 (2002).
18. *Chapman v. United States*, 365 U.S. 610 (1961).
19. *Carroll v. Illinois*, 267 U.S. 132 (1925).
20. *United States v. Ross*, 456 U.S. 798 (1982).
21. *Brendlin v. California*, 127 S. Ct. 2400 (2007).
22. *Indianapolis v. Edmond*, 531 U.S. 32 (2000).
23. *Illinois v. Lidster*, 540 U.S. 419 (2004).
24. *Brigham City, Utah v. Charles W. Stuart*, 126 S. Ct. 1943 (2006).
25. *Thornton v. United States*, 124 S. Ct. 2127 (2004).
26. *Maryland v. Pringle*, 370 Md. 525, 805 A.2d 1016 (2002), *aff'd*, 540 U.S. 366 (2003).
27. *Maryland v. Pringle*, 540 U.S. 366 (2003).
28. *Terry v. Ohio*, 392 U.S. 1 (1968).
29. *Brignoni-Ponce v. United States*, 422 U.S. 873 (1975).
30. *Hiibel v. Nevada*, 124 S. Ct. 2451 (2004).
31. *United States v. Sokolow*, 490 U.S. 1 (1989).
32. *United States v. Banks*, 540 U.S. 31 (2003).
33. *Illinois v. Gates*, 462 U.S. 213 (1983).
34. U.S. Constitution, Fourth Amendment.
35. *Illinois v. Krull*, 480 U.S. 340 (1987).

36. *Olmstead et al. v. United States*, 277 U.S. 438.

37. 47 U.S.C. 605 (2004).

38. N.Y. Crim. Proc. 813-a (1958), overturned by *Berger v. New York,* 388 U.S. 41, 59 (1967).

39. *Berger v. New York,* 388 U.S. 41, 59 (1967).

40. 18 U.S.C. 2518 (3)(c) (2000).

41. 18 U.S.C. 2518 (5) (2000).

42. 18 U.S.C. 2518 (4)(c) (2000).

43. 18 U.S.C. 2516 (2000).

44. 18 U.S.C. 2518 (5) (2000).

45. *United States v. Torres*, 751 F.2d. 875 (7th Cir. 1984).

46. Pub. L. No. 99-508, 100 Stat. 1848 (1986).

47. Rose, J., "Mayfields' Home Goes from Safe to Sinister," *The Oregonian,* December 1, 2006.

48. "Lawyer Falsely Jailed for Bombing Wins $2m," *The Australian.* December 1, 2006.

49. *Digest of Justinian*: Digest 48.2.7.2, translated in 11 Scott, The Civil Law.

50. *Ashe v. Swenson*, 397 U.S. 436 (1970).

51. *Benton v. Maryland*, 395 U.S. 784 (1969).

52. *United States v. Lanza*, 260 U.S. 377 (1922).

53. *Bullington v. Missouri*, 451 U.S. 430 (1981).

54. *Sattazahn v. Pennsylvania*, 537 U.S. 101 (2003).

55. *Commonwealth v. Sattazahn,* 869 A.2d 529 (2006).

56. *Kring v. Missouri*, 107 U.S. 221 (1883).

57. *California Dept. of Corrections v. Morales*, 513 U.S. 1074 (1995).

58. *Stogner v. California*, 123 S. Ct. 2446 (2003).

59. Goodyear, C., and Podger, P., "California Molestation Law Struck Down," *San Francisco Chronicle,* June 27, 2003.

60. *United States v. Brown*, 381 U.S. 437 (1965).

61. *Miranda v. Arizona*, 384 U.S. 436 (1966).

62. *Illinois v. Perkins,* 496 U.S. 292 (1990).

63. The author sat in on a polygraph session with another attorney's client to understand the process.

64. *United States v. Traficant,* 566 F. Supp. 1046 (N.D. Ohio 1983); *State v. Thompson*, 381 So. 2d 823 (1980); *Smith v. State*, 355 A.2d. 527 (1976).

65. *United States v. Salerno*, 481 U.S. 739 (1987).

APPENDIX

UNITED STATES DISTRICT COURT
SOUTHERN DISTRICT OF NEW YORK   S2 06 Crim. 0008 (LAK)
--X
UNITED STATES OF AMERICA,

     -against-

JOHN TOMERO, et al.,
         Defendants.
--X

MEMORANDUM OPINION

Appearances:

Jonathan Kolodner
Eric Snyder
Assistant United States Attorneys
MICHAEL J. GARCIA
UNITED STATES ATTORNEY

Richard A. Rehbock
Attorney for Defendant Ardito

Vincent J. Martinelli
Attorney for Defendant Larca

Michael Rosen
Jean Graziano
Attorneys for Defendant Fiorino

James B. Lebow
Attorney for Defendant Russo

Diarmuid White
Attorney for Defendant Tranquillo

Michael A. Marinaccio
Attorney for Defendant De Luca

Michael J. Gilbert
Attorney for Defendant Facciano

Louis Aidala
Attorney for Defendant Galiano

Nick Pinto
Attorney for Defendant Caponigro

Vincent L. Bricetti
Bricetti Calhoun & Lawrence, LLP
Attorney for Defendant Faella

LEWIS A. KAPLAN, *District Judge*
    . Thirty-four defendants are charged with various criminal acts associated with the operations of the Genovese organized crime family. Ten move to suppress conversations intercepted by listening devices, colloquially known as "roving bugs," installed in cellular telephones.

Background

A. *The Investigation*
    1. *The Traditional Intercepts*
        The indictment stems from a three-year investigation into the criminal activity of members and associates of the Genovese organized crime family. The investigation initially focused on the crew of John Ardito, a high-ranking member of the family. The FBI learned from cooperating witnesses that Ardito's crew met regularly at a restaurant called Brunello Trattoria in New Rochelle, New York, to conduct family business. In December 2002, the Honorable Barbara S. Jones of this Court authorized the interception of oral communications of Ardito and other subjects at this location.
        The intercepted conversions revealed that Ardito and his crew met at three additional restaurants, in part because they were suspicious of law enforcement surveillance. The government applied for, and Judge Jones authorized, the interception of conversations at these three restaurants as well as continued interception at Brunello Trattoria. In July 2003, however, Ardito's crew found the listening devices in three of the restaurants and became even more wary of surveillance whenever they returned to their usual meeting places.

    2. *The Roving Intercepts*
      a. *Ardito's Cellular Telephone*
        Based on physical surveillance and the conversations previously intercepted, the FBI learned that Ardito's crew no longer conducted meetings exclusively at the four restaurants, but met also in twelve additional restaurants, automobiles, Ardito's home, an auto store, an insurance office, a jewelry store, a doctor's office, a boat, and public streets.

The government applied for a "roving bug," that is, the interception of Ardito's conversations at locations that were "not practical" to specify, as authorized by 18 U.S.C. § 2518(11)(a). Judge Jones granted the application, authorizing continued interception at the four restaurants and the installation of a listening device in Ardito's cellular telephone.[1] The device functioned whether the phone was powered on or off, intercepting conversations within its range wherever it happened to be.

b. Peluso's Cellular Telephone

By February 2004, the government had learned that Peter Peluso, an attorney and close associate of Ardito, was relaying messages to and from high-ranking family members who were wary of government listening devices and who used Peluso as a messenger to avoid meeting together directly. In a renewal application dated February 6, 2004, the government sought, and Judge Jones in due course granted, authority to install a roving bug in Peluso's cellular telephone.[2] This order was renewed several times throughout 2004, as the government continued to identify locations where Peluso and Ardito discussed family matters and learned that the subjects were growing increasingly cautions of government surveillance.

In January 2005, Peluso agreed to cooperate with the government's investigation. At that point the government removed the listening device in his cellular telephone and Peluso began recording conversations with family members consensually by wearing a microphone. On July 7, 2005, Peluso pleaded guilty, pursuant to a cooperation agreement with the government, to a four-count information, charging him with, among other things, engaging in a pattern of racketeering activity.

3. This Motion

By the conclusion of the Investigation, the government had intercepted hundreds of hours of Ardito's and Peluso's conversations with each other and with other defendants, including Claudio Caponigro, Pasquale De Luca, Albert Faella, Albert Facciano, Gerald Fiorino, Walter Galiano, Salvatore Larca, Vincent Russo, and Albert Tranquillo, Jr.

On February 14, 2006, a grand jury returned a 42-count indictment charging 32 defendants with wide-ranging racketeering crimes and other offenses spanning more than a decade. On April 3, 2006, the grand jury returned a 45-count superceding indictment naming two additional defendants. Defendants now seek suppression of the conversations intercepted by the listening devices in the Ardito and Peluso cellular telephones.

Discussion

Title III of the Omnibus Crime Control and Safe Streets Act ("Title III")[3] sets forth procedures for the interception of oral communications. Sections 2518(1)(b)(ii) and (3)(d) require, respectively, that an application for electronic surveillance include "a particular description of the nature and location of the facilities from which or the place where the communication is to be intercepted"[4] and be based on "probable cause for belief that the facilities from which, or the place where, the wire, oral, or electronic communications are to be intercepted are being used, or about to be used, in connection with the commission of" an offense.[5]

In 1986, Congress amended Title III to "update and clarify Federal privacy protections and standards in light of dramatic changes in new computer and telecommunications technologies."[6] One of the amendments was Section 2518(11), which permits "roving" electronic surveillance. It provides that

"The requirements of subsections (1)(b)(ii) and (3)(d) of this section relating to the specification of the facilities from which, or the place where, the communication is to be intercepted do not apply if—

"(a)	in the case of an application with respect to the interception of an oral communication—
"(i)	the application is by a Federal investigative or law enforcement officer and is approved by the Attorney General, the Deputy Attorney General, the Associate Attorney General, an Assistant Attorney General, or an acting Assisting Attorney General;
"(ii)	the application contains a full and complete statement as to why such specification is not practical and identifies the person committing the offense and whose communications are to be intercepted; and
"(iii)	the judge finds that such specification is not practical"[7]

Section 2518(12) further provides that an agent implementing a roving intercept under subsection 11 must ascertain the place of the communication in advance of interception.[8]

---

[1]The order prohibited interception unless "the agents and officers conducting the interception have reason to believe, through physical surveillance, source information, prior interceptions or conduct, or other facts revealed during the course of the investigation that Ardito and other SUBJECTS or other members and associates of [the family] are engaging in conversations regarding the SUBJECT OFFENSES." *E.g.*, Application, Sept. 3, 2003 ¶ 8.
[2]Like the one installed in Ardito's phone, the device operated whether or not the phone was in use.
[3]18 U.S.C. § 2510 *et seq*.
[4]*Id*. § 2518(1)(b)(ii).
[5]*Id*.§ 2518(3)(d).
[6]S. Rep. No. 541, 99th Cong., 2d Scss. 32, *reprinted* in 1986 U.S.C.C.A.N. 3555, 3555.
[7]18 U.S.C. § 2518(11).
[8]*See id*. § 2518(12).

A. *Constitutionality of Section 2518(11)*
1. *Facial Challenge*

Defendants argue that the roving bug provision of Title III is unconstitutional because it fails to comport with the Fourth Amendment's requirement that a warrant "particularly describ[e] the place to be searched."[9] In other words, by allowing the government to intercept communications without identifying the place of interception in advance, the statute authorizes general warrants.

In *United States v. Bianco,*[10] the Second Circuit upheld Section 2518(11) against an identical constitutional challenge.[11] That holding is binding here. The facial challenge therefore is foreclosed.

2. *As-Applied Challenge*

Defendants argue that *Bianco* is distinguishable. The argument, however, is unpersuasive.

a. *Mobile Interception Devices*

Defendants point first to the fact that the order in *Bianco* authorized the placement of listening devices only in buildings whereas the order here authorized placement in mobile telephones. But the argument misses the point.

The essence of the motion to suppress is that the statute unconstitutionally permits interception in the absence of any specification of the place where communications are to be intercepted. In *Bianco,* the Second Circuit rejected precisely this argument. The fact that the unspecified location in *Bianco* happened to be in a building had nothing to do with the holding. Furthermore, while a mobile device makes interception easier and less costly to accomplish than a stationary one, this does not mean that it implicates new or different privacy concerns. It simply dispenses with the need for repeated installations and surreptitious entries into buildings. It does not invade zones of privacy that the government could not reach by more conventional means.

b. *Particular Conversations*

Defendants next seek to distinguish *Bianco* on the ground that the government in that case had a particular meeting in mind when it sought authorization to intercept. Again, the distinction is irrelevant. Nothing in Bianco suggests that the constitutionality of the statute and the order hinged on the fact that the government knew that a particular meeting was to take place. The issue was whether it knew the location of the anticipated meeting when it obtained the order. It did not, but the order nevertheless was held constitutional.

c. *Ten-Day Status Reports*

Finally, defendants argue that *Bianco* is distinguishable because the order in that case required status reports every seven days instead of every ten. This difference is immaterial. A progress report every ten days was sufficient to keep the issuing court appraised of the status of the investigation and to alert it to any potential government overreaching. Like the issuing judge in *Bianco,* had Judge Jones suspected any government misconduct, she could have revoked or revised the order at any time.[12]

B. *Section 2518 Requirements*
1. *Other Investigative Procedures*

An application for electronic surveillance must include, among other things, "a full and complete statement as to whether or not other investigative procedures have been tried and failed or why they reasonably appear to be unlikely to succeed if tried or to be too dangerous."[13] Defendants argue that the application failed adequately to do so.

As this Court had held, Section 2518(3)(c)'s exhaustion requirement "is far from an insurmountable hurdle. The government must demonstrate only that normal investigative techniques would prove difficult."[14] All that is required is "a reasoned explanation, grounded in the facts of the case, and which squares with common sense."[15] Moreover, as with the issuing judge's determination of probable cause, "a determination that the government has made this showing is entitled to substantial deference from a reviewing court."[16]

---

[9]U.S. CONST. amend. IV.

[10]998 F.2d 1112 (2d Cir. 1993).

[11]*Id.* at 1124.

[12]*See Bianco*, F. 2d at 1125.

[13]Id. § 2518(1)(c).

[14]United States v. Bellomo, 954 F. Supp. 630, 638-39 (S.D.N.Y. 1997); see also United States v. Torress, 901 F.2d 205, 231 (2d Cir. 1990) ("the purpose of the statutory requirements is not to preclude resort to electronic surveillance until after all other possible means of investigation have been exhausted by investigative agents; rather, they only require that the agents inform the authorizing judicial officer of the nature and progress of the investigation and of the difficulties inherent in the use of normal law enforcement methods.").

[15]Bellomo, 954 F. Supp. at 639 (quoting United States v. Ianniello, 621 F. Supp. 1455, 1465 (S.D.N.Y. 1985)).

[16]Id. (citing Ianniello, 621 F. Supp. at 1465).

Defendants contend that there was no "'genuine need' for either the Peluso or the Ardito roving bug."[17] They suggest that the government could have relied on its confidential informants, preexisting warrants, or an undercover agent in order to obtain the information it sought.

The government addressed these possibilities in its applications. First, it stated that its confidential informants were unhelpful to the investigation because they were not privy to relevant conversations, in part because the defendants changed meeting locations frequently. In addition, one such informant was unwilling to wear a microphone or testify in court.[18]

Second, the government explained that physical surveillance had been useful in "placing people with each other" and observing that meetings took place, but that it "provide[d] limited evidence of the purpose of the meetings or the content of [the subjects'] conversations."[19]

Third, the government asserted than an undercover operation was "not feasible due, in part, to the unwillingness of the SUBJECTS to deal extensively with outsiders who are not members or associates of' the family or related organizations.[20]

Finally, the government explained why more traditional methods of surveillance than roving intercepts were insufficient. It stated that wiretaps on the Ardito and Peluso cellular telephones were not successful because the subjects "were extremely careful and guarded on the cellphone, [and] recognize[d] the potential for electronic interception."[21] Further, the conversations intercepted at the four restaurants painted a limited picture of the subjects' criminal activity because defendants were aware of the listening devices there and held meetings in other places, such as public streets, where the risk of surveillance was low.[22]

The applications made a sufficient case for electronic surveillance. They indicated that alternative methods of investigation either had failed or were unlikely to produce results, in part because the subjects deliberately avoided government surveillance.

2. Identification of Interceptees

Defendants argue also that the order is invalid because the government failed to identify "the person . . . whose communications are to be intercepted."[23] They point to the fact that the government's applications named specific subjects, but referred also to "others as yet unknown."

The statute limits interception to situations where "a particular identified individual or individuals can be expected to use numerous telephones or locations to discuss their crimes as a means of evading surveillance."[24] It does not require the government to name every person whose voice it will capture, however. Rather, use of the singular "person" indicates that the government must identify a main subject whose communications it will intercept. It then may intercept conversations between the subject and interlocutors whose identities may not be known.[25] In other words, the statute prevents the interception of communications between two unknowns, not between a known subject and an unknown interlocutor.[26]

3. Impracticality

Finally, defendants argue that it was practical to specify the locations of interceptions because Peluso had a propensity to frequent certain location, and he and Ardito were not entirely successful in evading surveillance.

Title III does not require the government to show complete unpredictability in the movement of the subjects, that other methods of surveillance have failed or would fail, or that the subjects were successful in avoiding interception.[27] It was required to

---

[17]Fiorino Br. 14 (quoting *United States v. Dalia*, 441 U.S. 238, 250 (1979)).

[18]*See e.g.*, Application, Sept. 3, 2003 ¶ 66(a).

[19]*Id.* ¶ 66(b).

[20]*Id.* ¶ 66(e).

[21]*Id.* ¶ 66(g).

[22]*Id.* ¶ 66(h). The defendants are incorrect to claim that the intercept order was unlawful merely because other investigative techniques has been helpful to the investigation. The government did not seek information it already had obtained through other means. Rather, it sought to "intercept conversations thought necessary to explore matters that the government had not succeeded in investigating through available means." *United States v. Scala*, 388 F. Supp. 396. 404 (S.D.N.Y. 2005).

[23]18 U.S.C. § 2518(11)(a)(ii).

[24]United States v. Ferrara, 771 F. Supp. 1266, 1318 (D. Mass. 1991) (noting that § 2518(11)(a)(ii)'s requirement is more stringent than that of § 2518(1)(b)(iv), which requires identification of subjects, "if known").

[25]*Id.* ("It is, however, permissible for the government to use a roving intercept order to capture criminal conversation between an anticipated participant who has been targeted by name in a roving order and another individual, whether or not the other person was previously known to the government.").

[26]*Id.*

[27]Defendants point to the language of § 2518(11)(b), which outlines procedures for roving wiretaps. That section is similar to § 2518(11)(a), but instead of requiring impracticality, requires a showing that the subject's "actions could have the effect of thwarting interception from a specified facility." 18 U.S.C. § 2518(11)(b)(ii). Defendants claim that this additional requirement indicates a lower standard for obtaining a wiretap than an oral intercept. The standard, however, is not necessarily higher or lower; it simply is more specific. A roving wiretap may be obtained only on a showing of an attempt to thwart surveillance. A roving oral intercept, on the other hand, may be obtained on any showing of impracticality, which *may* include the subject's efforts to evade. Indeed, as the Second Circuit noticed in *Bianco*, effort to evade is probative of impracticality. *See Bianco*, 998 F. 2d at 1123 (quoting S. Rep. No. 54, 99th Cong., 2d Sess. 32, *reprinted* in U.S.C.C.A.N. 3555, 3586).

show only that the defendants moved often enough that the regular procedures for obtaining a warrant would inhibit the interception of some conversations needed for the investigation.[28]

The government satisfied this burden. It determined that Ardito and Peluso met at dozens of locations and frequently were on the move because of their concern about surveillance. It stated in its application for the roving intercept that the subjects "conduct their meetings . . . in cars, at several different restaurants, on the street during 'walks and talks' . . . and in offices."[29] Moreover, the government was conducting a wide-ranging investigation into a sprawling set of alleged conspiracies spanning more than a decade. Conversations relevant to the case potentially occurred numerous times daily. It would have been impractical for the government to predict their time and location in advance.[30]

C. Good Faith

Finally, even if the order failed to comply with Title III's requirements, nothing in the record suggests that the government implemented it in bad faith.

In *United States v. Leon*,[31] the Supreme Court held that suppression is not proper where the government conducted a search in good faith reliance on a facially valid warrant.[32] This good-faith exception to the exclusionary rule applies in Title III cases.[33]

Conclusion

Defendants' motions to suppress conversations intercepted pursuant to 18 U.S.C. § 2518 are denied.[34]

SO ORDERED
Dated: November 27, 2006.

---

[28]Defendants claim that the government "jumpe[d] from interception order to interception order without meaningful and continual reassessment of necessity." Fiorino Br. 15. The Title III applications in this case, however, reveal the opposite. The government began with a traditional intercept order for Brunello Trattoria. When this proved insufficient, it sought to install listening devices in three additional restaurants. Only when this failed did it apply for the roving intercept order on Ardito and eventually Peluso. The government expanded the investigation slowly and deliberately, each time determining that its preexisting warrants were insufficient for intercepting all of Ardito's and Peluso's relevant conversations.

[29]*See, e.g.*, Application, Sept. 3, 2003 ¶ 66(h).

[30]Defendants argue also that the order failed to comply with § 2518(12), which provides that no interception by a roving intercept may begin "until the place where the communication is to be intercepted is ascertained by the person implementing the interception order," 18 U.S.C. § 2518(12). Defendants contend that this section was violated because the "[o]rders are [sic] boilerplate. It includes no such finding [of advance ascertainment]. It simply authorizes Interceptions at locations 'that are impractical to specify,'" Fiorino Br. 12.

This argument is mistaken. § 2518(12) does not require the order to specify a location in advance, but requires the officer implementing the order to do so. Defendants do not argue, and the record does not indicate, that the officers implementing the order violated this provision.

[31]468 U.S. 897 (1984).

[32]*Id.* at 922 ("We conclude that the marginal or nonexistent benefits produced by suppressing evidence obtained in objectively reasonable reliance on a subsequently invalidated search warrant cannot justify the substantial cost of exclusion.").

[33]*See, e.g.*, *Bellomo*, 954 F Supp. at 638 (citing cases where courts applied the good-faith exception to Title III cases). *See also Scala*, 388 F. Supp. 2d at 403.

[34]Defendants assert in their brief, without explanation, that the government violated Judge Jones's intercept order and misled her about the extent of the surveillance. Fiorino Br. 2 They do not address these contentions, however, let alone provide support for them in the remainder of their brief. Nor does the record indicate that these assertions are true. Accordingly, the claims are disregarded.

United States Attorney
Southern District of New York

FOR IMMEDIATE RELEASE
APRIL 27, 2007.

CONTACT:

U.S. ATTORNEY'S OFFICE
YUSILL SCRIBNER
REBEKAH CARMICHAEL
PUBLIC INFORMATION OFFICE
(212) 637-2600

GENOVESE ORGANIZED CRIME FAMILY SOLIDER AND ASSOCIATES SENTENCED TO PRISON TERMS FOR OFFENSES INCLUDING RACKETEERING, EXTORTION, OBSTRUCTION OF JUSTICE, NARCOTICS TRAFFICKING AND FIREARMS TRAFFICKING.

MICHAEL J, GARCIA, the United States Attorney for the Southern District of New York, announced that 14 defendants were sentenced recently in Manhattan federal court. As alleged in the associates of the Genovese Organized Crime Family. These defendants were originally charged in Manhattan federal court in a 42-count Indictment, captioned *United States v. Liborio S. Bellomo, et al.,* S1 06 Cr. 08 (LAK) (the "Indictment") which charged 34 defendants, including an Acting Boss and various members and associates of the Genovese Organized Crime Family of La Cosa Nostra, with wide-ranging racketeering crimes and other offenses spanning more than a decade, including murder, violent extortions of various individuals and businesses, labor racketeering, obstruction of justice, narcotics trafficking, money laundering, and firearms trafficking. The Indictment targeted factions of the Genovese Organized Crime Family based in the Bronx, East Harlem, and Westchester, and was the result of a Federal investigation that began in 2003, and a related investigation by state authorities in Westchester County that began in 2005.

On April 13, 2007, four of the 14 defendants were sentenced. These defendants included Genovese Family Soldier Salvatore Larca, and Genovese Family associates Albert "Allie Boy" Tranquillo, Albert Faella, and John Tomero. Larca pleaded guilty to Racketeering crimes including labor racketeering, firearms trafficking and obstruction of justice. He was sentenced to, among other things, 63 months' imprisonment and he forfeited $10,000 on the date of sentencing. Tranquillo pleaded guilty to two separate extortion conspiracies involving violent beatings of the extortion victims. Tranquillo was sentenced to, among other things, 100 months' imprisonment and he forfeited $250,000 on the date of sentencing. Faella pleaded guilty to obstruction of justice and he was sentenced to, among other things, 30 days' incarceration to be served on weekends. Finally, Tomero pleaded guilty to a narcotics trafficking conspiracy and the use of a firearm in furtherance of that conspiracy. Tomero was sentenced to, among other things, 87 months' imprisonment.

On April 26 and 27, 2007, nine other defendants were sentenced. These defendants included Genovese Family associate Tomes Terraciano, as well as Andrew Shea, Eric Cmiel, Joseph Lanza, Raymond Delarcsa, Brian Falco, Samuel Lopez, Mark Fiore, and Louis Grillo. Terraciano pleaded guilty to obstruction of justice and was sentenced to, among other things, 12 months' imprisonment. Shea, Cmiel, Lanza, Delarosa, Falco, Lopez, Fiore, and Grillo all pleaded guilty to a narcotics trafficking conspiracy and received sentences ranging from 60 to 120 months' imprisonment.

In addition to the sentences described above, on February 26, 2007, after pleading to a narcotics trafficking conspiracy, Joseph Derosa was sentenced to, among other things, 30 months' imprisonment.

All of the above defendants were sentenced by the Honorable Lewis A. Kaplan, District Judge of the United States District Court for the Southern District of New York.

Mr. GARCIA praised the efforts of the Federal Bureau of Investigation, the Westchester County District Attorney's Office, and the New York City Police Department, in this investigation. In addition, Mr. GARCIA expressed his appreciation to the Putnam County District Attorney and the Putnam County Sheriff's Offices for their assistance in this investigation.

Assistant United States Attorneys MIRIAM E. ROCAH, JONATHAN S. KOLODNER AND ERIC SYNDER are in charge of this prosecution.

07-104   ###

CHAPTER 11

Constitutional Rights after Arrest

CHAPTER CONTENTS

> *Every society gets the kind of criminal it deserves. What is equally true
> is that every community gets the kind of law enforcement it insists on.*
>
> *Robert Kennedy,* **The Pursuit of Justice**

> *If one really wishes to know how justice is administered in a country, one
> does not question the policemen, the lawyers, the judges, or the protected
> members of the middle class. One goes to the unprotected, those, precisely,
> who need the law's protection most! And listens to their testimony.*
>
> *James Baldwin,* **The Price of the Ticket,** *1972*

CHAPTER OBJECTIVES

After studying this chapter, you should be able to:

- Explain the *Miranda* warning.
- Explain when a criminal defendant has a right to counsel.
- Explain the rights of indigent defendants to a public defender.
- Explain the right against self-incrimination.
- List and explain the circumstances under which a person can be compelled to testify against himself.
- Explain the attorney-client privilege, husband-wife privilege, and priest-penitent privilege.
- Explain when physical evidence can be compelled from defendants without violating the right against self-incrimination.
- Explain the right to a speedy trial.
- Distinguish statutes of limitations from the Constitutional right to a speedy trial.

INTRODUCTION AND HISTORICAL BACKGROUND

As you have learned in the last few chapters, many of the rights we accord persons charged with crimes stem from abuses suffered by the colonists at the hand of the British crown. The U.S. Constitution and the Bill of Rights serve as reminders that our forefathers vowed that never again would they be subjected to the whims of a monarch and that the right to a prompt, fair, public trial and adequate legal representation would be sacrosanct. In this chapter, we will explore the defendants' rights in the crucial time between arrest and trial.

Most importantly, defendants have the right to an attorney who will represent their interests as the case winds its way through the court system. Since many defendants lack financial resources, the right to counsel includes the right to a court-appointed attorney for poor defendants.

Defendants also have the right to remain silent, that is, the right to compel the government to prove the case against him or her. As we will see, that right is limited to testimonial silence. In some circumstances, defendants can also prevent others from providing testimony.

The right to remain silent is not absolute. The government can compel the production of some forms of physical evidence. Similarly, a person can also be compelled to testify if he or she has received immunity from prosecution or the statute of limitations has expired.

ARREST

Arrest

The official taking of a person to answer criminal charges.

In Chapter 10, you learned that law enforcement officers must establish probable cause to obtain a search warrant from the court. Similarly, officers must also have probable cause to believe an individual committed a crime before making an **arrest.** An arrest is the official taking of a person to answer criminal charges. The person is detained and is not free to perform his or her normal daily duties. Usually, the person is handcuffed or otherwise restrained.

Police officers or other law enforcement personnel carry out most arrests. An officer need not be in uniform or on duty to make an arrest. Many states authorize citizens to make arrests in certain circumstances.

Often states have different sets of rules governing citizens' arrest depending on whether the crime was a felony or misdemeanor. Generally, citizens may arrest anyone they witness committing a crime. However, if the citizen only hears of a crime being committed, most states will not allow him to arrest the person if the crime is a misdemeanor. Citizens are always free to arrest someone to prevent a felony, but not always a misdemeanor. Check the laws in your state, and always be ready to dial 911.

CUSTODY

Courts consider a person to be in custody when he or she is not free to leave. Defendants can be in **custody** even if they are not in jail. In one case, the U.S. Supreme Court ruled a defendant was in custody when being questioned in his own bedroom.[1] Courts look at the totality of circumstances in each case. As soon as the defendant is not free to leave, police must read the defendant the *Miranda* rights and affirm that the defendant understands the rights. Any statements made by the defendant between being placed in custody and acknowledging understanding the rights are not admissible.

Custody

The state of being detained by law enforcement officers; a person is in custody when that person is not free to leave.

BAIL

The first legal proceeding after a person is arrested is the **initial appearance,** where the accused is informed of the seriousness of the charge, the consequences of the initial appearance and future hearings, and their right to have counsel represent them. If the defendant cannot afford an attorney, he or she can request one at this initial appearance. The practice varies from jurisdiction to jurisdiction, but attorneys can be appointed for defendants before or at the initial appearance.

Initial Appearance

A court proceeding shortly after a suspect's arrest where the suspect is informed of specific rights.

Shortly after the initial appearance, the court holds a bail or bond hearing. Judges often weigh the seriousness of the charge and the chance the defendant will flee rather than face charges in court when setting bail. In very serious cases or when the judge feels the flight risk is very high, the magistrate can refuse to set bail, and the defendant must remain in custody until trial. Often the time served counts toward fulfilling the defendant's sentence if convicted.

The U.S. Constitution offers specific prohibitions against setting excessive bail. Consequently, the defendant can challenge an extremely high bail.

Most defendants do not have enough cash on hand to post bail. Bail bondsmen often step in to fill this gap. Most bail bondsmen take a 10 percent nonrefundable deposit to post a defendant's bail. If the defendant doesn't show up for trial, the bail bondsman forfeits the full amount of the bond until the defendant is brought in. As a result, bail bondsmen are very highly motivated to find fugitive defendants. Judges have sole discretion over whether bail is forfeited and often allow bail bondsmen to get their bond back once the fugitive is brought in.

Some jurisdictions limit the types of cases for which certain courts can set bail. Often bail for murder and other serious crimes is set by higher court judges.

PRELIMINARY HEARINGS

Preliminary hearings are held within a short time of the defendant's arrest. Some jurisdictions have specific time limits prosecutors must meet. Preliminary hearings are held to determine whether the state has probable cause for the defendant's arrest. The state must show by a preponderance of the evidence that the defendant committed the crime.

This standard is different than the beyond a reasonable doubt standard necessary to convict the defendant at trial. As a result, prosecutors will often only present enough evidence to show that it is more likely than not that the defendant committed the crime.

Defendants can waive a preliminary hearing if they so choose. Often, this is a matter of negotiation between the defendant's attorney and the prosecutor. The prosecutor may agree to a lower bail request in return for waiving the preliminary hearing.

The preliminary hearing is less formal than a full trial. Similarly, evidentiary rules are more lax. Hearsay testimony is acceptable at a preliminary hearing but would not be at trial. The hearing is before a judge, not a jury. The judge will make the decision whether to bind the case over for trial.

If the judge believes the prosecution has made its case, it will issue a **binding**, transferring the case to another court for trial.

Binding

An order holding an accused person for trial.

True Bill

An indictment voted on by a grand jury where the jury has found that it is more likely than not that a crime has been committed and that the person being charged committed it.

GRAND JURY AND INDICTMENT

In most felony cases, a grand jury must issue a **true bill** charging the defendant with the felony. Grand juries date back to English law and are specifically mentioned in the Fifth Amendment to the U.S. Constitution. Grand juries are selected from the general population in the jurisdiction prosecuting the case. For example, federal grand juries are drawn from people living in the federal district. The grand jury system serves as a check on governmental power by ensuring the prosecution has evidence against the accused.

Despite its role in limiting governmental power, grand juries can be very one-sided affairs. The old saw that a "grand jury would indict a ham sandwich" has some basis in fact, largely because, only the prosecution can present its case to the grand jury. The defense never appears.

Part of the reason for this is that grand juries are often investigatory bodies. The prosecutor presents the known facts of the crime and the evidence against the defendant. But the grand jury can subpoena witnesses, grant immunity to witnesses, and take the investigation into areas the prosecutor never intended.

The basic grand jury procedure dictates that the prosecutor presents an indictment to the grand jury accusing the defendant(s) of a crime or crimes. The grand jury investigates the prosecutor's claims and decides first, whether it was more likely than not that a crime was committed and second, if it is more likely than not that the defendant committed the crime. If the answer to both questions is yes, they vote to issue a true bill.

Even though the defendant's lawyers cannot participate in the grand jury process, there are ways to combat a true bill filed against their defendant. If the defendant believes the grand jury acted in an unconstitutional manner, he or she can move to have the indictment **quashed**. The court will rule on the motion, and if the indictment is quashed, then the charges against the defendant are dropped. The defendant is not necessarily out

Quash

To annul.

of the woods yet. Jeopardy does not attach just because a person has been accused. Indictments can only be quashed because of procedural issues. The grand jury can reconvene, or another one can be empanelled and issue another true bill.

YOU MAKE THE CALL
THE DUKE RAPE CASE: MISUSE OF THE GRAND JURY?

2006 was an election year in Durham County, North Carolina. District Attorney Mike Nifong faced a stiff challenge for the Democratic nomination, and in Durham County, winning the Democratic nomination virtually assured winning the general election.

On March 13, 2006, two cocaptains of the Duke University lacrosse team held a party at an off-campus house. They hired two exotic dancers for $800. The next day one of the dancers, who was black, told police she had been beaten and raped by three white team members. The Durham County Court compelled all white team members to provide DNA samples.

Before the test results were back, Nifong labeled the assailants as "hooligans" and promised the DNA evidence would show "precisely who was involved." On April 10, the DNA test results came in, and no match was found among the team members. One week after the results came in, a grand jury indicted two lacrosse players, Collin Finnerty and Reade Seligmann, charging them with rape, sexual offense, and kidnapping.

Since the defense does not put on a case before a grand jury, Mike Nifong was the only one presenting evidence to the grand jury. Because grand jury proceedings are sealed, we may never know whether Nifong revealed the DNA results to the grand jury. One thing we do know is that at the time the grand jury issued the true bill, Nifong had not turned over the DNA test results to the players' defense attorneys.

On May 2, Mike Nifong won the Democratic primary election. It was only after the general election that he revealed the test results to the defense. By then he was facing sanctions from the courts.[2] Did Nifong manipulate the grand jury for political purposes? What safeguards could be put in place to prevent this behavior? Can grand juries perform their constitutional function of preventing malicious or politically-based prosecutions if they don't hear the defense's side of the story? You make the call!

THE RIGHT AGAINST SELF-INCRIMINATION

Throughout the criminal investigation process, police, investigators, or even the grand jury can interrogate a defendant. Defendants do not have to answer questions that may incriminate them. The right against self-incrimination is enshrined in the Fifth Amendment to the U.S. Constitution as: "No person . . . shall be compelled in any criminal case to be a witness against himself." A person who refuses to answer questions about alleged criminal activities is said to "plead the Fifth." No right is fundamentally more representative of the U.S. justice system. The government's prosecutor and police officers must prove a person guilty of a crime. Defendants do not have to prove their innocence. To protect that fundamental right, no person can be compelled to help the government by being forced to give evidence against himself or herself.

Confessions may only be used against a defendant if the prosecution can show that they followed the procedures laid out in *Miranda* and that they did not coerce or otherwise extract a confession from the defendant. All confessions must be voluntary and have been given after notification of the right to remain silent.

The right to remain silent is not without limits. In some circumstances, there is no risk associated with speaking. In that case, prosecutors and others can compel testimony. That's because the right to remain silent is the **right against self-incrimination**. That is, in order for the right to apply, the act of speaking must be related to the possibility of criminal prosecution. If that possibility doesn't exist, there is no potential self-incrimination. For example, if the statute of limitations has expired, there is no restriction on what can be asked. There is also nothing to prevent police or others from demanding sworn testimony under oath when the defendant's criminal trial has already ended and he or she has been sentenced or acquitted. That's because he or she no longer faces the possibility of the testimony being used against him or her. In addition, if a defendant has been given immunity, testimony can be compelled. Immunity is explored later in this chapter.

Right against Self-Incrimination

The right embodied in the Fifth Amendment to the U.S. Constitution that allows an accused person to remain silent; its corollary is "innocent until proven guilty."

POSTARREST INTERROGATION

Once a defendant has been arrested and has been read his or her rights, police may begin interrogation. Under Miranda, the defendant has the right to remain silent and the right to have an attorney present during questioning. Once the defendant acknowledges that he or she understands the Miranda rights, any statement made is presumed to be voluntary.

HISTORICAL HIGHLIGHT
The Christian Burial Speech

Skilled interrogators will often use tricks or bring psychological pressure to bear to get the defendant to make voluntary statements. But courts place limits on what interrogators can do.

An example of both skilled interrogation technique and violating a prisoner's rights is the "Christian Burial" case. In this Iowa case, recently released mental patient Robert Williams was suspected of abducting and killing ten-year-old Pamela Powers on Christmas Eve 1968. The abduction occurred in Des Moines, and Williams' abandoned car was found 160 miles east in Davenport. Based on eyewitness accounts linking Williams and his car to the abduction, police issued a warrant for his arrest.

Williams contacted Des Moines attorney, Henry McKnight, who advised him to turn himself in to the Davenport police. Williams turned himself in, and the Davenport police spoke with the attorney by telephone and agreed not to interrogate Williams until he was returned to Des Moines, where the attorney could be present. A Davenport attorney reiterated the agreement to the policemen transporting Williams.

Despite these warnings, the police tried to engage Williams in a conversation about the girl. Each time, he rebuffed them stating, "When I get to Des Moines and see Mr. McKnight, I am going to tell you the whole story." Finally, one of the detectives started talking about other issues including religion. When he ascertained that Williams was a religious man, he gave what came to be known as the "Christian Burial" speech, where he asked Williams to observe the worsening weather conditions of sleet and freezing rain and that several inches of snow were forecast for the evening. He told Williams that since he was the only person who knew where the body was, he should tell them now so they could find it before the snow piled up. He concluded by saying, "I feel that we could stop and locate the body so that the parents of this little girl should be entitled to a Christian burial for the little girl who was snatched away from them on Christmas Eve and murdered." Williams agreed to show them the body's location.

Prior to his trial, his attorney moved to have all evidence of the car ride conversation suppressed, but the motion was denied. Williams was convicted of first-degree murder. On appeal, the court ruled Williams waived his right to remain silent by volunteering the information. The Iowa Supreme Court affirmed, but the U.S. Supreme Court saw it differently.

The Court ruled that questioning Williams without counsel present after he had repeatedly asked for it violated both his Sixth and Fourteenth Amendment rights to counsel.[3]

THE INTERROGATORS TOOLS: TRICKERY AND DECEIT

Police are free to trick defendants into confessing within limits. Anyone who watches police shows on television knows some of the more familiar tricks such as telling a defendant someone else is blaming him for the crime when that is not true. Police tricks often provoke court scrutiny and skirt the borders of legality.

For instance, telling a defendant his statements are "off the record" is not allowed. Obviously, threats of or actual torture to obtain a confession or testimony are illegal and will result in the evidence being excluded. Similarly, depriving a defendant of sleep, food, drink, or other necessities of life in order to obtain a confession is illegal.

CONFESSIONS

Because no one can be compelled to testify against himself, the state must prove that the defendant gave the **confession** voluntarily. If the defense can prove otherwise, the confession can be excluded. Courts have a specific procedure for evaluating whether confessions are to be entered into evidence.

The quality of a nation's civilization can be largely measured by the methods it uses in the enforcement of its criminal law.
Harvard Professor Schaefer

Pain forces even the innocent to lie.

Publilius Syrus, first century BC

Confession

A voluntary statement by a person that he or she is guilty of a crime or any admission of wrongdoing.

Holding cell in London's Savile Row Police Station.

Jackson-Denno Hearing

A hearing designed to determine whether law enforcement officers violated a defendant's rights in securing a confession.

Before a defendant's confession can be entered into evidence, the court will hold a **Jackson-Denno hearing.** The hearing takes its name from a landmark U.S. Supreme Court case, *Jackson v. Denno,*[4] where the issue was first addressed.

At a Jackson-Denno hearing, the state must prove the confession was offered voluntarily. Usually, the police who obtained the confession will testify about the events leading to the confession, noting exactly where in the sequence the defendant acknowledged understanding the Miranda rights, whether the defendant asked for an attorney, and when the confession began.

Because many cases hinge on the admissibility of confessions, many jurisdictions have taken to recording confessions with either audio or video equipment. In fact, European Union (EU) countries are required to allow arrested defendants to have eight hours of sleep and a meal before they are interrogated. All interrogations in the EU are videotaped with an attorney present.[5] Increasingly, federal judges have looked to the EU to judge the U.S. criminal justice system's fairness.

In addition to fairness issues, prosecutors and police have found that recordings of interrogations provide strong evidence that confessions were voluntary. The audiotapes or videotapes can bolster police testimony in a Jackson-Denno hearing.

THE CONSTITUTIONAL RIGHT TO COUNSEL IN CRIMINAL CASES

The Sixth Amendment of the U.S. Constitution states that: "In all criminal prosecutions, the accused shall enjoy the right . . . to have the Assistance of Counsel for his defense." Given the complexity of the legal system and the high stakes for a defendant, very few persons accused of a crime elect to represent themselves. Most prefer to have a trained attorney at their side. But the right to assistance of counsel wasn't widespread until this century, at least in "minor" criminal cases.

For many years, the right to be represented by a member of the bar was limited to capital cases (cases where the death penalty was sought by the prosecution). In 1932, the U.S. Supreme Court wrote that a layman:

> lacks both the skill and knowledge adequately to prepare his defense, even though he has a perfect one. He requires the guiding hand of counsel at every step ... without it, though he is innocent, he faces the danger of conviction because he does not know how to establish his innocence.[6]

By 1938, the right was extended to all federal felony cases. By 1963, defendants charged with any felony, state or federal, were entitled to counsel regardless of their ability to pay for one.[7] By 1964, the Supreme Court had ruled that confessions obtained after police didn't tell the defendant he was entitled to counsel or refused to let him talk to his attorney are not admissible.[8]

The right to counsel isn't limited to having an attorney to represent you at trial. A defendant has a right to counsel at his or her arraignment, preliminary hearing, during most police questioning, during a lineup, at trial, and at sentencing. In addition, he or she has a right to counsel for his or her first appeal.

The right to counsel means little if the defendant is ignorant of his right to counsel. Therefore, the Supreme Court decided in the *Miranda* case that police have an obligation to inform a suspect of his rights under the Constitution.

Police must inform any person put under arrest or held in a custodial interrogation, such as at a police station, that he has the following rights before questioning begins:

1. That he has the right to remain silent,
2. That anything he says can and will be used against him,
3. That he has the right to an attorney during questioning,
4. That if he can't afford one, one will be appointed at no charge before questioning, and
5. That at any time during the questioning, he can stop, and the interrogation will end.

HISTORICAL HIGHLIGHT
The Scottsboro Boys: The Right to Counsel

On March 31, 1931, a train was rolling through the Alabama countryside. As was often the case during the Depression, many drifters were riding in the train's boxcars. This train had a group of young black boys, ages 12 to 19, and a group of white boys along with two white girls. A fight broke out among the boys, and all the white boys except for one were thrown from the train. They immediately alerted the authorities, and at the next stop, the blacks were arrested after the girls accused them of rape.

As a group, these boys had little or no education. All were illiterate, and not one of them was an Alabama native. By the time they were in custody, word had spread of the incident, and a large angry crowd awaited them at Scottsboro. The local sheriff called for the state militia to help protect the boys.

The trial was set for a week after the indictment. The local judge appointed all members of the local bar to assist in the boys' defense but charged no one attorney in particular to represent them. A Tennessee attorney was contacted by the families of one of the defendants and appeared at the first day of trial, offering to assist the court-appointed attorney. Although some members of the local bar had spoken with the defendants, none were prepared to conduct their defense. The Tennessee attorney was given the opportunity to represent them by himself, but explained that he wasn't prepared for trial, and was unfamiliar with court practices in Alabama. Eventually, one of the local attorneys was appointed, and the Tennessee attorney assisted him.

The defendants were tried as three groups and, with the exception of the 12-year-old defendant, separately sentenced to death. The trials lasted one day each. The convictions were upheld by the appeals court and the Alabama Supreme Court, and only Chief Justice Anderson dissented, stating he did not feel the boys received a fair trial.

The International Labor Defense, a Communist organization, represented the boys when the case was appealed to the U.S. Supreme Court. The case was appealed on three grounds: (1) they were not given a fair, impartial, and deliberate trial; (2) they were denied the right of counsel, with the accustomed incidents of consultation and opportunity of preparation of trial; and (3) they were tried before juries from which qualified members of their own race were systematically excluded.[9]

The Supreme Court dealt only with the second charge, the denial of right to counsel. The High Court, citing the Sixth Amendment, reaffirmed the right to counsel for all citizens accused of a crime and described the type of defense afforded the Scottsboro boys as "rather pro forma than zealous and active."[10] The Court noted the lack of time for the defense to prepare for trial and the lack of time for the defendants, all of whom lived out of state, to secure counsel of their own choice as sufficient to invalidate their defense. The Court reversed the convictions and sent the cases back to be retried with adequate counsel.

At the second trial, the boys were convicted, but the judge found the testimony of the girls unbelievable and set aside the verdict and ordered a new trial. He was defeated in the next election.[11]

The Scottsboro boys' saga dragged on for many years. None of them were ever executed, but all spent time in prison. The last one, Clarence Norris, was finally pardoned by Governor George Wallace in 1976.[12]

Miranda is discussed more fully in the Historical Highlight: *How Mirandizing Became a Verb*. In 1968, Congress passed a law that essentially intended to gut the *Miranda* decision. This law (18 U.S.C.S. § 3501) provided that as long as the defendant's confession was voluntary, it needn't be preceded by the *Miranda* warning. In 2000, the Supreme Court had an opportunity to consider *Miranda* again. In that case, the defendant had been indicted for a bank robbery. He confessed to the crime when asked by the Federal Bureau of Investigation (FBI) and then moved to strike his confession because he gave it without being warned as required by *Miranda*. The government argued that under 18 U.S.C.S. § 3501, it wasn't required to warn him.

The trial judge suppressed the confession, but the Fourth Circuit Court of Appeals reversed. The defendant appealed to the Supreme Court. The Court, in a strongly worded opinion, ruled that it meant what it said in *Miranda* and ordered the confession suppressed. The Court found the warning to be a fundamental constitutional right.[13]

What happens if a police officer deliberately doesn't read a suspect her Miranda rights, gets her to confess, then Mirandizes her, and gets the confession the second time? That was the issue before the Court in a 2004 case involving a mother who allegedly conspired to commit arson to cover up a child's natural death. Unfortunately, the cover-up arson went badly and killed another youth. The officer who questioned her claimed to have learned the double confession trick at a training seminar. The Court ruled 5–4 that the tactic was illegal, and the second confession was invalid.[14]

The Supreme Court recently heard another case involving double confessions. In that case, the officers came to the defendant's house and asked him if he had been involved in illegal drug use after telling him he had been indicted. He confessed and was taken to the police station, where he was read his *Miranda* rights and again confessed. On appeal, he argued both confessions should be thrown out because he had not been read his rights. A unanimous Supreme Court sent the case back to the lower court, stating that the real question was whether the defendant's Sixth Amendment rights to counsel had been violated in that he had not been offered the opportunity to have his lawyer present.[15]

The issue is one that doesn't seem to want to go away. On the same day it concluded that the arson-setting mother's confession was illegal, the Court also decided that a gun found after a defendant admitted he had one can be used as evidence, even though the admission came after the police failed to read the suspect his *Miranda* rights. The case involved a defendant who, when arrested, stopped the officer from reading the *Miranda* warning because he claimed to know it already. The confession he made was suppressed, but the gun the police seized was allowed into evidence. The Court, in another 5–4 decision, upheld the use of physical evidence found as a result of information gleaned from an illegal confession.[16]

THE POOR AND THE RIGHT TO COUNSEL

A criminal defendant is entitled to more than just an attorney to represent him or her. The defendant has the right to effective assistance of counsel. Effective counsel is competent counsel.[17] Obviously, the right to counsel would mean very little if a defendant doesn't have the means to retain an attorney. After all, the government expends a vast amount of money on its police force, district attorneys, judges, and other court personnel. As the U.S. Supreme Court pointed out in *Gideon v. Wainwright,* the fact that "[t]he government hires lawyers to prosecute and defendants who have the money hire lawyers to defend are the strongest indications of a widespread belief that lawyers in criminal courts are necessities, not luxuries."[18]

The need for counsel in order to protect the privilege [against self-incrimination] exists for the indigent as well as the affluent.
Chief Justice Earl Warren, *Miranda v. Arizona* (1969)

Indigent defendants have the right to court-appointed counsel at no charge. Since 1964, when the Criminal Justice Act of 1964 was passed into law, defendants charged with federal crimes are entitled to a federal public defender. The states have passed similar legislation to assure a supply of experienced criminal law attorneys are available to those who cannot afford an attorney. Most public defender offices also have available professional investigators who can assist in preparing cases for trial.

HISTORICAL HIGHLIGHT
How Mirandizing Became a Verb

Watch any police show on television and invariably at some point a police officer will read a defendant or suspect his rights. You can probably recite the warning verbatim yourself, so often have you heard it. "You have the right to remain silent and the right to consult an attorney. Anything you say can and will be used against you in a court of law. . . ."

The warning has almost become a police officer's mantra. In fact, almost every police officer carries a copy of the *Miranda* warning with him or her. That's not because he or she is likely to forget to inform a defendant of a right. Rather, it reflects an easy way for officers to testify later. Sometime in the future, the officer will be asked whether he or she read the defendant his rights. The officer is unlikely to remember the exact details of an arrest or interrogation that happened months, even years, earlier. Instead, the officer will testify that he did read the suspect his rights by pulling out the card and reading it to him word for word. The officer will tell the court how he Mirandized the defendant.

Just how did Mirandizing become a verb? The term is derived from the 1966 U.S. Supreme Court decision in *Miranda v. Arizona*. The case actually involved not just Ernesto Miranda, the Arizona defendant who lent his name to the legal warning. In the same decision, the Court also decided that Michael Vignera, a New Yorker, Carl Calvin Westover of Kansas City, and Roy Allen Stewart of Los Angeles had confessed without knowing their constitutional rights.

Together, their cases served to highlight just how common the police practice of extracting quick confessions from suspects unfamiliar with their rights was. All gave confessions after lengthy interrogations. At least one confession declared that the statement was made "with full knowledge of my rights." Another confessed after a series of interrogations that spanned five days. Together, their cases convinced the Court that something as simple as a warning was needed to curb the widespread denial of suspects' right to remain silent. Ever since, police officers Mirandize suspects.

Judges sometimes appoint and the government pays for experienced private attorneys in complex or serious cases where the local public defender office is short-staffed or lacks an attorney with specific expertise. Court-appointed private counsel is generally reserved for high-profile capital cases such as the Oklahoma City bombing cases. The right to counsel continues after trial through the posttrial appeals and any direct appellate appeals.

ARRAIGNMENT

Once a grand jury has issued a felony indictment, the defendant must then attend an arraignment. At the arraignment, the court reads the charges against the defendant, and the defendant pleads guilty or not guilty to the charges. If the defendant is still without representation at this point, he or she can request the court to appoint an attorney.

Defendants are usually notified of their arraignment date when they post bail or through certified mail from the prosecutor. Defendants who fail to appear for their arraignment may be required to forfeit their bail. In that case, the judge will issue a **bench warrant** giving the police the power to arrest the defendant. Once the defendant is arrested, he will sit in jail until the next scheduled arraignment.

Depending on the jurisdiction, the arraignment gives defendants and their attorneys a glimpse of the prosecution's case. At minimum, the prosecution must provide the indictment and a list of state witnesses who will be called to testify. Some states require one or both sides to serve discovery documents at the arraignment.

Bench Warrant

A warrant issued by a judge ordering law enforcement officers to arrest a specific person.

PLEA BARGAINING

Not all cases go to trial. In fact, most cases are resolved through plea bargaining. Plea bargaining reduces case loads for prosecutors and judges in return for a reduced sentence for the defendant. Public defenders who often have more cases than they can realistically handle like plea bargaining because it lightens their load.

Plea bargaining is not always in the defendant's best interest. Sometimes the prosecutor offers a plea bargain because his case is weak. The defendant may be able to be acquitted if he doesn't agree to the deal. This is where an experienced attorney can help a defendant by understanding the prosecution's case well enough to advise the client.

Ultimately, the decision to plea or not to plea is up to the defendant. Attorneys and prosecutors can bring pressure to bear, but it is the defendant who lives with the conviction for the rest of his life.

If the defendant and the prosecutor come to an agreement, they will meet with the judge in a **bench conference.** The judge must sign off on the agreement before it becomes effective. Sometimes, the judges' record of plea agreements can become an election issue, so judges are ever mindful of the political ramifications of plea agreements.

Once the plea is agreed upon, the judge will question the defendant in open court to ensure the defendant understands the sentence he is receiving and the rights he has forfeited, specifically the right to trial, by agreeing to the plea arrangement. The judge will also ask if the agreement is voluntary.

Plea agreements are between prosecutors and defendants. They are not binding on judges. As a result, plea agreements only contain a recommendation for sentencing. Whether that is the sentence the defendant gets is up to the judge. Most of the time, the

Bench Conference

A conference called among the judge and attorneys for both sides and possibly the accused to discuss matters without the jury hearing it.

judge will agree to the sentence in the agreement, having worked out the details at the bench conference. But defendants should understand that judges are under political pressure and do not have to take the sentencing recommendation.

Once a defendant has pled guilty, he gives up many constitutional protections. In addition to relinquishing his right to a trial by jury, he is no longer presumed innocent. Further, he no longer has the right to appeal his conviction and sentence.

Instead of pleading guilty, a defendant can plead nolo contendere or no contest to a charge. From a criminal standpoint, the nolo contendere plea is substantially the same as a guilty plea. But in cases where a civil suit may arise out of the same circumstances as the criminal charge, a nolo contendere plea does not require the defendant to admit wrongdoing. A litigant could use a guilty plea as an admission of guilt, but not a nolo contendere plea. Some states only allow nolo contendere pleas for some crimes.

Alford Plea

A plea entered where the accused maintains his innocence but agrees to be sentenced as if guilty.

Another plea possibility is the **Alford Plea**, named for the U.S. Supreme Court case *North Carolina v. Alford*.[19] Under an Alford plea, the defendant pleads guilty but maintains his innocence. Defendants facing a strong government case may elect this plea to get a lighter sentence.

In the Alford case, North Carolina law at the time called for the death penalty for first-degree murder convictions unless the jury voted for life imprisonment. Facing strong evidence of his guilt, Alford pled guilty to second-degree murder but stated in court the only reason for doing so was his fear of the death penalty. He then appealed claiming the plea had been made under duress, specifically the state's threat of execution. The Supreme Court ruled the plea was valid even though the defendant maintained his innocence.

IMMUNITY

It has long been the rule that a person who receives immunity can be compelled to testify, no matter how personally embarrassing or humiliating testifying may be. As long as the prospect of criminal prosecution is absent, there is no right to "plead the Fifth." That's been the rule since 1888.[20]

USE IMMUNITY

Use Immunity

A limited form of immunity where the person's testimony cannot be used as evidence against him or her.

Immunity falls into two different categories. The first is **use immunity**. If a defendant is granted use immunity, anything he says to investigators cannot be directly used against him in a later trial. That is, the prosecutor can't use his direct words or anything the prosecution discovers that was related to the testimony. For example, assume that a defendant was granted use immunity in exchange for testimony about a murder. If the defendant testifies that he threw the weapon in the Susquehanna River, police can't dredge the river for the gun and use the weapon as evidence. However, if a bather, independent of the government, stumbles upon the gun and turns it in, the gun can be used against the defendant. The key is that independent evidence gathered by the police or others can be used even if immunity has been granted as long as it can be shown that it wasn't the testimony that led to the discovery of the evidence.

HISTORICAL HIGHLIGHT
Suspected Nazi War Criminal Must Sing

In this chapter, you have learned that the right to remain silent protects defendants from having to provide testimony that can be used against themselves in a criminal proceeding. You have also learned that the rule against self-incrimination applies to the states, not just the federal government. Defendants also can't be forced to testify in a federal criminal case if they face the reasonable prospect of having that testimony used against them in a state criminal case. But what happens if the information requested places the defendant in danger of prosecution in a foreign nation? Can the defendant refuse to testify in that situation?

The U.S. Supreme Court answered that question in 1998 in *United States v. Balsys.* The real and substantial fear of prosecution in a foreign nation does not mean that a defendant can refuse to answer on the ground that his answer may incriminate him.

Balsys involved a resident alien who had been admitted to the United States in 1961 under the Immigration and Nationalization Act. All applicants for resident status under that law must provide sworn information about his or her criminal past, if he or she has one. The application Balsys signed in 1961 provided that if he provided false or misleading information, he would be subject to criminal prosecution in the United States and face deportation. In his application, Balsys swore that he had served in the Lithuanian Army from 1934 through 1940 and had lived in hiding from the start of World War II to 1944.

More than 35 years after his admission to the United States, the Justice Department began an investigation into whether Balsys had participated in Nazi persecution of Jews and other groups during World War II. If he had, he would be subject to deportation. When he was subpoenaed, he refused to answer questions about his alleged Nazi past on the grounds that it would subject him to criminal prosecution in Israel or Lithuania as a war criminal. He didn't claim any fear of prosecution in the United States because the statute of limitations on falsifying his immigration application had passed. Therefore, he had no valid fear of prosecution in this country.

After the Supreme Court ruling, Balsys faced the prospect of being held in criminal contempt if he continued to refuse to answer questions about his alleged Nazi past or answering and being deported to face a war crimes trial.

TRANSACTIONAL IMMUNITY

Transactional immunity is the preferred form of immunity for defendants. With transactional immunity, the government is forever barred from prosecuting the defendant for the crime from which he or she was granted immunity. No amount of independently

Transactional Immunity

A broad form of immunity where the person cannot be prosecuted for any action related to the testimony as long as the person testifies truthfully.

gathered evidence can support a prosecution. The defendant, in exchange for testimony, is guaranteed that he or she will never be prosecuted for the crime about which he or she testified.

PRIVILEGE AND THE RIGHT TO KEEP OTHERS SILENT

A concern for the sanctity and privacy of personal conversations and actions is inherent in the U.S. Constitution and the Bill of Rights. The focus on privacy can be seen in the reluctance to allow unfettered police access to our homes and possessions and in the recognition of a number of testimonial privileges that prevent the prosecution from compelling attorneys, spouses, and others from testifying about private conversations.

ATTORNEY-CLIENT PRIVILEGE

A privilege has long existed in conversations between counsel and client. The attorney-client privilege is one of the oldest recognized privileges for confidential communications.[21] The privilege is intended to encourage full and frank communication between attorneys and their clients. Without the guarantee that what is said to one's attorney is confidential, few faced with difficult circumstances would avail themselves of the right to counsel. The privilege applies to the attorney and anyone else on his or her staff.

In order for attorney-client privilege to apply, there must be an underlying agreement that the attorney has been retained to represent the defendant. If not, there is no privilege. Attorneys and their office staff should consult their state bar association for specific guidance on what is necessary for the formation of an attorney-client relationship and to learn under what circumstances attorneys are required to withdraw from representation if the client reveals he or she will lie under oath.

The attorney-client privilege does not extend to an attorney's participation in a crime. For example, an attorney can't hold the murder weapon in his or her safe or conceal and destroy records that have been entrusted to his or her care. The attorney-client privilege does protect notes that attorneys make memorializing client discussions and outlining the course of action recommended. The **work product rule** protects from disclosure any material the attorney created to prepare for trial.

Work Product Rule

The rule that protects material produced by an attorney in preparation for a trial, or the work product, from discovery.

Marital Privilege

The right of a person to refuse to testify against his or her spouse.

SPOUSAL PRIVILEGE

Another well-established privilege available to criminal defendants is the spousal privilege. This privilege is meant to protect private conversations between husband and wife and to protect marriages from the destructive effects of being compelled to testify against a husband or wife. This rule, like so many others, is not without limits.

As with many other Common Law rules, spousal privilege has a long history, springing from medieval society. Two justifications for the **marital privilege** developed over time. First was the rule that a defendant can't or shouldn't be compelled to testify against himself. Second, because husband and wife were regarded as one and since a wife had no recognized separate legal existence, if a wife were compelled to testify, it would be the same as if the husband were the one forced to speak. Thus, what was inadmissible from the lips of the defendant's husband was also inadmissible from his wife.

For many years, courts assumed that the marital privilege meant that neither husband or wife could be compelled to testify against each other and that each could prevent the other from testifying against the other. That changed in 1980 when the U.S. Supreme Court decided *Trammel v. United States.*[22] Elizabeth Trammel traveled to Thailand where she bought heroin. She then boarded a plane for the United States with several ounces of heroin on her person. During a routine customs stop in Hawaii, she was searched, the heroin was discovered, and she was arrested. She made a deal with the Drug Enforcement Agency in which she received immunity in exchange for her testimony against her husband. He claimed that her testimony violated the marital privilege.

HISTORICAL HIGHLIGHT
Attorney-Client Privilege Survives Death

In 1993, shortly after the beginning of William Clinton's first term as president of the United States, employees who worked for the White House Travel Office were discharged en masse. At the time, there was a great deal of speculation in the press about who ordered the firings and why. The White House conducted its own internal investigation into the firings. Shortly after, several investigations were initiated as to whether anyone in the White House involved with the investigation had committed criminal acts. Deputy White House Counsel Vincent W. Foster Jr., a personal friend and former law partner of First Lady, Hillary Clinton, was involved in the investigation.

On July 20, 1993, Vince Foster took his own life in a public park in Washington, DC. Nine days earlier Foster had met with James Hamilton, an attorney at the law firm of Swidler & Berlin in Washington, DC. Vince Foster sought the firm's representation and asked whether the conversation would be covered by the attorney-client privilege. James Hamilton took three pages of handwritten notes during the meeting, all under the heading "privileged."

By December 1995, an Independent Counsel, Kenneth Starr, had been appointed to investigate potential wrongdoing by the White House, including the circumstances surrounding the Travel Office firings. At Starr's request, a federal grand jury subpoenaed James Hamilton's handwritten notes. The law firm filed a motion to quash the subpoena. A motion to quash is a request to a court to be excused from complying with a subpoena. The firm argued that the notes were protected by attorney-client privilege. The Independent Counsel argued that the privilege dies with the client, and Vince Foster was dead.

> The U.S. Supreme Court took up the novel question and issued an expedited opinion. On June 25, 1998, the Court issued an opinion that declared that the attorney-client privilege survives death. The Court wrote:
>
> Knowing that communication will remain confidential even after death encourages the client to communicate fully and frankly with counsel.... Clients may be concerned about reputation, civil liability, or possible harm to friends or family. Posthumous disclosure of such communications may be as feared as disclosure during the client's lifetime.
>
> *Swidler & Berlin and Hamilton v. United States*, 524 U.S. 399 (1998)

The Supreme Court disagreed and ruled that a spouse who voluntarily chooses to testify against her husband may do so. The privilege belongs to the person speaking, not to the other spouse. The Court reasoned that women are no longer considered an extension of their husbands, but individual human beings. Presumably that means they can use that individuality to decide for themselves whether they will protect their spouse or cut a deal with the prosecutor.

Additionally, in state and local jurisdictions, this rule can have multiple variations. For example, Pennsylvania does not afford spousal privilege in cases "in which one of the charges pending against the defendant includes murder, involuntary deviate sexual intercourse or rape."[23]

PRIEST-PENITENT PRIVILEGE

Priest-Penitent Privilege

The right of confidentiality accorded members of the clergy for conversations held during the ritual of confession.

At Common Law, there also existed a **priest-penitent privilege.** Its intent was to keep secret statements made in the confessional. The privilege has been mentioned in passing in several Supreme Court decisions, but the Court has never faced the question of its continued relevance. An attempt to call a priest or other religious figure to the stand to testify would likely be met with opposition. The issue may be raised in criminal prosecutions of Catholic priests accused of molesting boys in their parishes. It remains to be seen if those to whom the priests confessed within the Church hierarchy will be forced to testify later.

PATIENT-COUNSELOR PRIVILEGE

Patient-Counselor Privilege

The right of confidentiality accorded counselors for conversations held in the course of mental health treatment.

Another privilege recognized by the Supreme Court, the **patient–counselor privilege,** is the right to keep confidential conversations between a patient and his or her psychotherapist. For example, in one case the Supreme Court ruled that a police officer's social worker could not be compelled to testify in a civil suit brought by the family of a man killed by a female police officer responding to a call. She had received extensive counseling after the shooting. The family had sued the officer for allegedly violating the dead man's civil rights. The Court concluded that "[t]he psychotherapist privilege serves the public interest by facilitating the provision of appropriate treatment for individuals suffering the effects of a mental or emotional problem. The mental health of our citizenry, no less than its physical health, is a public good of transcendent importance."[24]

COMPELLING THE PRODUCTION OF PHYSICAL EVIDENCE, INCLUDING DNA TESTING

The right against self-incrimination doesn't apply to physical evidence. That is, the government can make a suspect produce physical evidence of guilt as long as the method used isn't unreasonably intrusive. Defendants can be made to try on items of clothing, such as a shirt or a glove.[25] But taking a suspect to the hospital and making him vomit up evidence by pumping his stomach is unreasonably intrusive.[26]

Defendants can be brought down to the police station and be made to stand in a lineup. That's because the U.S. Constitution only protects a defendant against "being compelled to testify against himself, or otherwise provide the State with evidence of a testimonial or communicative nature."[27] A lineup merely serves as a way for the police to determine if the suspect is likely to be the individual sought. The state will still have to show beyond a reasonable doubt that he committed the crime, and defendants are entitled to have an attorney present during the lineup.

Defendants can also be compelled to submit to fingerprinting, photographing, and measuring. They can also be forced to provide writing and voice samples, and the results can be introduced in court.

YOU MAKE THE CALL

THE DUKE RAPE CASE: THE PHOTO LINEUP

You may recall the case of the alleged rape of an exotic dancer at a party attended by members of the Duke University lacrosse team. As is typical of such cases, law enforcement officials asked the victim to identify the assailant. In this case, police demanded that all 46 players have their pictures taken. They did.

Then the exotic dancer was twice shown a PowerPoint presentation of the photos and picked out three men as her assailants, including one who could show he was not at the party.

Defense counsel asked that her identification be suppressed, based on the fact that two other men who were at the party but were not members of the team were not included in the photo lineup. Should the identification have been suppressed? You make the call.

If the glove doesn't fit, you must acquit.
Johnny Cochran, in closing argument to the jury, *California v. O. J. Simpson*

BREATH ANALYSIS, BLOOD, AND DNA EVIDENCE

Physical evidence obtained by reasonable means can be used against a suspect. For example, most state driving under the influence laws provide that motorists stopped on suspicion of driving under the influence of drugs or alcohol must submit to a Breathalyzer test or forfeit their license to operate a motor vehicle. The results of the test can be admitted at a criminal trial. He or she can also be compelled to take a blood test to determine the amount and kind of intoxicant in the body.[28]

Again, the evidence can be used for trial. However, defendants and suspects can't be compelled to take physical tests that seek to measure physiological responses that the examiner can claim indicate guilt or a state of mind. Thus, suspects can't be made to take a lie detector test.

Since the middle of the twentieth century, blood evidence compelled from a suspect has been available in court. With the advent of new, more sophisticated analysis of blood, the justice system has increased its use of such evidence. For example, DNA evidence is now routinely used to solve rape and murder cases. DNA analysis can exclude suspects altogether or provide compelling odds that the defendant committed the crime. Defendants in both civil and criminal cases are finding it hard to argue that DNA evidence doesn't prove either beyond a reasonable doubt or by a preponderance of the evidence (the criminal and civil standards of proof) that the defendant left the genetic material in question.[29]

An interesting twist on compelling physical evidence came in a recent U.S. Supreme Court case. The City of Charleston, South Carolina, decided something had to be done to combat cocaine use by pregnant women. Working with the local police department, the public hospitals in town drew urine tests on pregnant women without their consent and without a search warrant and tested for cocaine use. Positive test results were referred to the police department for prosecution. The case ended up before the Supreme Court, which ruled that nonconsensual urine tests violated the Fifth Amendment's prohibition against unreasonable searches.[30]

THE RIGHT TO A SPEEDY TRIAL

The Sixth Amendment to the U.S. Constitution guarantees a defendant the right to a "speedy and public" trial. The Amendment prevents defendants from being left in jail to rot pending trial or from enjoying years of freedom outside prison if he or she has been able to make bail.

The Supreme Court has ruled that the right to a speedy trial is flexible, with no fixed number of days or weeks dictating whether the right has been denied.[31] Instead, the Court suggested that state and federal legislatures pass laws setting time limits, if they choose. As a result, most states have laws on the books that set strict time limits for bringing defendants to trial, usually within one year of being formally charged and arrested.

The Speedy Trial Act of 1974[32] sets strict time limits for bringing federal defendants to trial. The Act has a built-in mechanism for dealing with requests for continuances and other common delays. The penalty for violating the right to a speedy trial is dismissal of the charges.

Don't confuse the right to a speedy trial with statutes of limitations. Each state and the federal government has set time limits for the initiation of criminal proceedings against persons suspected of committing crimes. These limits range from a few years for minor crimes to indefinitely for murder. In effect, statutes of limitations set a deadline for the commencement of criminal actions, while the right to a speedy trial dictates how soon the trial must begin after a suspect has formally been charged with that crime. For example, a woman who murders her boyfriend at 18 can be charged with that murder at age 80, but is then guaranteed a speedy trial within her state's time limits.

PRACTICE POINTERS

Anyone who works in the criminal justice system must be fully prepared to keep up on the latest technologies and police methods. It's also crucially important to keep up on the development of criminal procedure and constitutional law at both the state and federal levels. For example, each year the U.S. Supreme Court decides about one dozen criminal law and procedure cases.

You can follow the Supreme Court at Northwestern University's "On the Docket" Web site. The site includes background information on all the pending cases written by journalism students at the university's Medill School of Journalism. You can access the site at *http://docket.medill.northwestern.edu.*

You can also track the current Supreme Court term through the American Bar Association's Web site at *http://www.abanet.org/publiced/preview.*

Other good sources for the latest information on evidence, confessions, and other investigative techniques include:

- The Innocence Project—a nonprofit legal clinic run through the Benjamin Cardozo School of Law in New York City. The Web site is *http://www. innocenceproject.org.*
- The Innocence Network—tries to connect defendants with pro bono help. The Web site is *http://www.innocencenetwork.org.*
- The President's DNA Initiative—This is a five-year program funded with $1 billion to increase the use of DNA technology in the criminal justice system. The Web site provides information on training and education in scientific evidence and is located at *http://www.dna.gov.*

CHAPTER SUMMARY

For a person charged with a crime, one of the most important constitutional guarantees is the right to counsel. Without counsel, a defendant would be left to navigate a complicated labyrinth without a guide. The right to counsel is so crucial to the legitimacy of the criminal law system that all persons, whether rich or indigent, are entitled to the services of a competent attorney. Those without adequate resources to retain private counsel are entitled to the services of a state or federal public defender or other court-appointed counsel.

A criminal suspect or defendant is also entitled to remain silent. In the U.S. justice system, all persons are presumed innocent until the state or federal government proves beyond a reasonable doubt that the suspect is guilty. No defendant is required to help the prosecutor prove his case through his own words. The right to remain silent and the exclusionary rule, which prevents prosecutors from using confessions or evidence obtained in violation of constitutional rights, serve to curb possible police abuses. Confessions beaten out of defendants can't be used to convict them.

The right to remain silent has several significant limitations. First, an individual who faces no possibility of having his or her words used against him or her cannot "plead the Fifth." For example, a person who has already been convicted of a crime no longer faces the possibility that his words will be used to convict. Persons granted immunity can also be forced to testify, since they don't face the possibility of having their words used against them either.

In our legal system, some relationships are regarded as inviolate. Therefore, confidences expressed in private with attorneys, counselors, a spouse, or a spiritual advisor are generally protected by a privilege against compelled revelation.

However, the privilege against self-incrimination doesn't apply to physical characteristics or evidence that is obtained in a reasonable fashion. For example, DNA and fingerprint evidence are standard fare in criminal prosecutions.

The right to remain silent and the right to counsel would mean little if persons charged with crimes were unaware of those rights. Therefore, law enforcement officers are required to tell a suspect or person under arrest that he has those rights and the right to have counsel appointed if indigent. The *Miranda* warning has become the standard method for police to convey those rights.

Defendants are also entitled to a speedy trial. Prisoners are not allowed to linger in prison awaiting trial or remain out on bail indefinitely.

KEY TERMS

Alford Plea	Initial Appearance	Right against Self-incrimination
Arrest	Jackson-Denno Hearing	
Bench Conference	Marital Privilege	Transactional Immunity
Bench Warrant	Patient-counselor Privilege	True Bill
Binding		Use Immunity
Confession	Priest-penitent Privilege	Work Product Rule
Custody	Quash	

EXERCISES

1. Read the Advancing Justice through DNA Technology guidelines in the chapter Appendix and answer the following questions:

   a. What are some examples of the use of DNA to clear crimes in which no suspect has been identified?

   b. What new technologies are under development, and how might they help law enforcement or those on the defense side prepare cases?

   c. What are some examples of DNA being used to free innocent persons who did not commit the crime for which they were imprisoned?

2. We have covered confessions and the conditions under which a confession is freely given. You may also recall that the U.S. military and others may be engaged in interrogations of certain high-value detainees held at Guantanamo in Cuba and in the custody of other nations, perhaps in secret prisons around the world. Look over the approved techniques in the chapter Appendix (note Vice President Cheney's handwritten note on the approved list) and answer the following questions based on what you have learned in this chapter:

   a. You represent a U.S. citizen who was held at Guantanamo before being transferred to civilian authorities. He was captured in Afghanistan shortly after the U.S.-led invasion, allegedly on the battlefield. He has been charged with aiding and abetting a terrorist organization, and the prosecution claims to have a written confession from the client. The client says he was tortured and lied to stop the torture. How would you go about challenging the admissibility of his confession?

b. You work for the prosecutor's office and have received a motion to suppress the preceding confession. How do you respond?

DISCUSSION QUESTIONS

1. Several states have recently started DNA databases. These are similar to the fingerprint databases kept by the FBI to aid in the solving of crimes. By using DNA taken from prisoners, agencies hope to be able to match prisoners with unsolved crimes still on the books and to be able to match future unsolved crimes to past prisoners. Discuss the legal and ethical implications of this trend.
2. Computer technology has grown by leaps and bounds in the last decade. As the new technologies develop, criminals are using more sophisticated encryption tools to safeguard the contents of their e-mail and the documents on their hard drives. Assuming that police had a valid warrant to seize and search a suspect's hard drive for evidence of criminal activity, can the suspect be compelled to give police the key to his encryption program so that they may have access to his records?
3. Indigent defendants are entitled to a public defender in criminal cases, but not in civil cases. Building on what you have learned in the previous chapters, why do you think this is so?
4. What methods and procedures do you think should be in place in a law firm to protect the confidentiality of information obtained from persons who have an attorney-client relationship with attorneys in the firm?
5. You have learned about the Miranda warning. Do you think the warning is sufficient to convey constitutional rights?

FOR FURTHER READING AND VIEWING

READING

1. Lewis, A. (1989). *Gideon's Trumpet*. Vintage Books.
   This book details the landmark case of *Gideon v. Wainwright* that established the right to legal counsel for everyone.
2. Leo, R. A., Thomas, G. C., III, and Thomas, G. C. (Eds.). (1998). *The Miranda Debate: Law, Justice, and Policing.* Northeastern University Press.
   This is a collection of essays from across the political spectrum about the *Miranda* decision and its impact on law enforcement and society.
3. Horne, G. (1997). *Powell v. Alabama: The Scottsboro Boys and American Justice (Historic Supreme Court Cases)*. Franklin Watts Publishing. This book is geared toward young adults, but tells the story of the Scottsboro boys in detail, and explains the importance of the case in legal and historical context.

VIEWING

1. *Gideon's Trumpet* (1980).
   The story of Clarence Earl Gideon's case as it went to the U.S. Supreme Court, starring Henry Fonda, José Ferrer, and John Houseman.

2. *Judge Horton & the Scottsboro Boys* (1976).

A made-for-television movie about the Scottsboro boys episode. The two women who claimed they were raped by the boys filed suit over this presentation. The suit was dismissed.

ENDNOTES

1. *Orozco v. Texas,* 394 U.S. 324.
2. Mallia, J., "Innocent Duke Charges Dropped; 395 Days: Key Dates in the Case," *Newsday* (New York), April 12, 2007.
3. 430 U.S. 387.
4. 378 U.S. 368.
5. Information provided by London Metropolitan Police officers during author's visit to London in January 2005.
6. *Powell v. Alabama,* 287 U.S. 45 (1932).
7. *Gideon v. Wainwright,* 372 U.S. 335 (1963).
8. *Escobedo v. Illinois,* 378 U.S. 478 (1964).
9. *Powell et al. v. State of Alabama,* 287 U.S. 45 (1932).
10. Ibid.
11. *Famous American Trials: The Scottsboro Boys, http://www.law.umkc.edu/ftrials/scotboro. Trials 1931–1937.*
12. Ibid.
13. *Dickerson v. United States,* 530 U.S. 428 (2000).
14. *Missouri v. Seibert,* 124 S. Ct. 2601 (2004).
15. *Fellers v. United States,* 124 S. Ct. 1019 (2004).
16. *United States v. Patane,* 124 S. Ct. 2620 (2004).
17. *McMann v. Richardson,* 397 U.S. 759 (1970).
18. *Gideon v. Wainwright,* 372 U.S. 335 (1963).
19. 400 U.S. 25.
20. *Hunt v. Blackburn,* 128 U.S. 464 (1888).
21. *Brown v. Walker,* 161 U.S. 591 (1896).
22. *Trammel v. United States,* 445 U.S. 40 (1980).
23. 42 Pa. Cons. Stat. § 5914, Act 16 of 1989.
24. *Jaffee v. Redmond,* 516 U.S. 1091 (1996).
25. *Holt v. United States,* 218 U.S. 245 (1910).
26. *Rochin v. California,* 342 U.S. 165 (1952).
27. *Schmerber v. California,* 384 U.S. 757 (1966).
28. Ibid.
29. For example, DNA comparison testing of a stain found on Monica Lewinsky's now-infamous navy blue dress with a blood sample obtained from President Bill Clinton revealed a probability of 1 out of 7.87 trillion that the stain was left by a Caucasian other than the president.

30. *Fergusen v. City of Charleston,* 532 U.S. 67 (2001).
31. *Barker v. Wingo,* 407 U.S. 514 (1972).
32. Speedy Trial Act, 18 U.S.C.S. § 3161.

APPENDIX

UNCLASSIFIED

GENERAL COUNSEL OF THE DEPARTMENT OF DEFENSE
1600 DEFENSE PENTAGON
WASHINGTON, D.C. 20301-1600

ACTION MEMO

2002 Dec 2 AM 11: 03   November 27, 2002 (1:00 PM)
OFFICE OF THE SECRETARY OF DEFENSE   DEPSEC_____

FOR: SECRETARY OF DEFENSE

FROM: William J. Haynes II, General Counsel

SUBJECT: Counter-Resistance Techniques

- The Commander of USSOUTHCOM has forwarded a request by the Commander of Joint Task Force 170 (now JTF GTMO) for approval of counter-resistance techniques to aid in the interrogation of detainees at Guantanamo Bay (Tab A).

- The request contains three categories of counter-resistance techniques, with the first category the least aggressive and the third category the most aggressive (Tab B).

- I have discussed this with the Deputy, Doug Feith and General Myers. I believe that all join in my recommendation that, as a matter of policy, you authorize the Commander of USSOUTHCOM to employ, in his discretion, only Categories I and II and the fourth technique listed in Category III ("Use of mild, non-injurious physical contact such as grabbing, poking in the chest with the finger, and light pushing").

- While all Category III techniques may be legally available, we believe that, as a matter of policy, a blanket approval of Category III techniques is not warranted at this time. Our Armed Forces are trained to a standard of interrogation that reflects a tradition of restraint.

RECOMMENDATION: That SECDEF approve the USSOUTHCOM Commander's use of those counter-resistance techniques listed in Categories I and II and the fourth technique listed in Category III during the interrogation of detainees at Guantanamo Bay.

SECDEF DECISION:

Approved _~~signature~~_____   Disapproved _____ Other _____

Attachments
As stated However, I stand for 8-10 hours A day. Why is standing limited to 4 hours?

cc: CJCS, USD(P)

Declassified Under Authority of Executive Order 12958
By Executive Secretary, Office of the Secretary of Defense
William P. Marriott, CAPT, USN
June 18, 2004

UNCLASSIFIED

DEPARTMENT OF DEFENSE
UNITED STATES SOUTHEHH COMMAND
OFFICE OF THE COMMANDER
2511 NW 91ST AVENUE
MIAMI, FL 33172-1217

SCCDR   25 October 2002

MEMORANDUM FOR Chairman of the Joint Chiefs of Staff, Washington, DC 20318-9999

SUBJECT: Counter-Resistance Techniques

    1.   The activities of Joint Task Force 170 have yielded critical intelligence support for forces in combat, combatant commanders, and other intelligence/law enforcement entities prosecuting the War on Terrorism. However, despite our best efforts, some detainees have tenaciously resisted our current interrogation methods. Our respective staffs, the Office of the Secretary of Defense, and Joint Task Force 170 have been trying to identify counter-resistant techniques that we can lawfully employ.

    2.   I am forwarding Joint Task Force 170's proposed counter-resistance techniques. I believe the first two categories of techniques are legal and humane. I am uncertain whether all the techniques in the third category are legal under US law, given the absence of judicial interpretation of the US torture statute. I am particularly troubled by the use of implied or expressed threats of death of the detainee or his family. However, I desire to have as many options as possible at my disposal and therefore request that Department of Defense and Department of Justice lawyers review the third category of techniques.

    3.   As part of any review of Joint Task Force I70's proposed strategy, I welcome any suggested interrogation methods that others may propose. I believe we should provide our interrogators with as many legally permissible tools as possible.

    4.   Although I am cognizant of the important policy ramifications of some of these proposed techniques, I firmly believe that we must quickly provide Joint Task Force 170 counter-resistance techniques to maximize the value of our intelligence collection mission.

                                             James T. Hill
                                          General, US Army
                                          Commander

Encls
1. JTF 170 CDR Memo
    dtd 11 October, 2002
2. JTF 170 SJA Memo
    dtd 11 October, 2002
3. JTF 170 J-2 Memo
    dtd 11 October, 2002

Declassify Under the Authority of Executive Order 12958
By Executive Secretary, Office of the Secretary of Defense
By William P. Marrion, CAPT. USN
June 21, 2004

DEPARTMENT OF DEFENSE
JOINT TASK-FORCE 170
GUANTANAMO BAY, CUBA
APO AE 09880

JTF 170-CG

11 October 2002

MEMORANDUM FOR Commander, United States Southern Command, 3511 NW 91st Avenue, Miami, Florida 33172-1217

SUBJECT: Counter-Resistance Strategies

    1. Request that you approve the interrogation techniques delineated in the enclosed Counter-Resistance Strategies memorandum. I have reviewed this memorandum and the legal review provided to me by the JTF-170 Staff Judge Advocate and concur with the legal analysis provided.

    2. I am fully aware of the techniques currently employed to gain valuable intelligence in support of the Global War on Terrorism. Although these techniques have resulted in significant exploitable intelligence, the same methods have become less effective over time. I believe the methods and techniques delineated in the accompanying J-2 memorandum will enhance our efforts to extract additional information. Based on the analysis provided by the JTF-170 SJA, I have concluded that these techniques do not violate U.S. or international laws.

    3. My point of contact for this issue is LTC Jerald Phifer at DSN 660-3476.

2 Encls
1. JTF 170-J2 Memo,
   11 Oct 02
2. JTF 170-SJA Memo,
   11 Oct 02

MICHAEL B. DUNLAVER
Major General, USA
Commanding

DEPARTMENT OF DEFENSE
JOINT TASK FORCE 170
GUANTANAMO BAY, CUBA
APO AE 05360

JTF 170-SJA   11 October 2002

MEMORANDUM FOR Commander, Joint Task Force 170

SUBJ: Legal Review of Aggressive Interrogation Techniques

    1.   I have reviewed the memorandum on Counter-Resistance Strategies, dated 11 Oct 02, and agree that the proposed strategies do not violate applicable federal law. Attached is a more detailed legal analysis that addresses the proposal.

    2.   I recommend that interrogators be property trained in the use of the approved methods of interrogation, and that interrogations involving category II and III methods undergo a legal review prior to their commencement.

    3.   This matter is forwarded to you for your recommendation and action.

2 Encls
1. JTF 170-J2 Memo,
    11 Oct 02
2. JTF 170-SJA Memo,
    11 Oct 02

                           DIANE E. BEAVER
                           LTC, USA
                           Staff Judge Advocate

UNCLASSIFIED

DEPARTMENT OF DEFENSE
JOINT TASK FORCE 170
GUANTANAMO BAY, CUBA
APO AE 09860

JTF 170-SJA

11 October 2002

MEMORANDUM FOR Commander, Joint Task Force 170

SUBJECT: Legal Brief on Proposed Counter-Resistance Strategies

(1) (U) ISSUE: To ensure the security of the United States and its Allies, more aggressive interrogation techniques than the once presently used, such as the methods proposed in the attached recommendation, may be required in order to obtain information from detainees that are resisting interrogation efforts and are suspected of having significant information essential to national security. This legal brief references the recommendations obtained in the JTF-170-J2 memorandum, dated 11 October 2002.

(2) (U) FACTS: The detainees currently held at Guantanamo Bay, Cuba (GTMO), are not protected by the Geneva Conventions (GC). Nonetheless, DoD interrogations trained to apply the Geneva Conventions have been using commonly approved methods of interrogation such as support building through the direct approach, rewards, the multiple interrogator approach, and the use of deception. However, because detainees have been able to communicate among themselves and debrief each other about their respective interrogations, their interrogation resistance strategies have become more sophisticated. Compounding this problem is the fact that there is no established clear policy for interrogation limits and operations at GTMO, and many interrogations have felt in the past that they could not do anything that could be considered "controversial." In accordance with President Bush's 7 February 2002 directive, the detainees are not Enemy Prisoners of War (EPW). They must be treated humanely and, subject to military necessary, in accordance with the principles of GC.

(3) (U) DISCUSSION: The Office of the Secretary of Defense (OSD) has not adopted specific guidelines regarding interrogation techniques for detainee operations at GTMO. While the procedures outlined in, Army FM 34-52 Intelligence Interrogation (28 September 1992), are utilized, they are constrained by, and conform to the GC and applicable international law, and therefore are not binding. Since the detainees are not HPWs, the Geneva Conventions limitations that ordinarily would govern captured enemy personnel interrogations are not binding on U.S. personnel conducting detainee interrogations at GTMO, Consequently, in the absence of specific binding guidance, and in accordance with the President's directive to treat the detainees humanely, we must look to applicable international and domestic law in order to determine the legality of the more aggressive interrogation techniques recommended in the J2 proposal.

a. (U) International Law: Although no international body of law directly applies, the more notable international treaties and relevant law are listed below.

(1) (U) In November of 1994, the United States ratified The Convention Against Torture and Other Cruel, Inhumane or Degrading Treatment or Punishment. However, the United States took a reservation to Article 16, which defined cruel, inhumane and degrading treatment or punishment, by instead deferring to the current standard articulated in the 8th Amendment to the United States Constitution. Therefore, the United States is only prohibited from committing those acts that would otherwise be prohibited under the United States Constitutional Amendment against cruel and unusual punishment. The United States satisfied the treaty with the understanding that the convention would not be self-executing, that is, that it would not create a private cause of action in U.S. Courts. This convention is the principal U.N. treaty regarding torture and other cruel, inhumane, or degrading treatment.

(2) (U) The International Covenant on Civil and Political Rights (ICCPR), ratified by the United States in 1992, prohibits inhumane treatment in Article 7, and arbitrary arrest and detention in Article 9. The United States ratified it on the condition that it would not be self-executing, and it took a reservation to Article 7 that we would only be bound to the extent that the United States Constitution prohibits cruel and unusual punishment.

(3) (U) The American Convention on Human Rights forbids inhumane treatment, arbitrary imprisonment, and requires the state to promptly inform detainees of the charges against them, to review their pretrial confinement, and to conduct a trial within a reasonable time. The United States signed the convention on 1 June 1977, but never ratified it.

(4) (U) The Rome Statute established the International Criminal Court and criminalized inhumane treatment, unlawful deportation, and imprisonment. The United States not only failed to ratify the Rome Statute, but also later withdrew from it.

(5) (U) The United Nations' Universal Declaration of Human Rights, prohibits insurance or degrading punishment, arbitrary arrest, detention, or exile. Although international declarations may provide evidence of customary international law (which is considered binding on all nations even without a treaty), they are not enforceable by themselves.

(6) (U) There is some European case law stemming from the European Court of Human Rights on the issue of torture. The Court ruled on allegations of torture and other forms of inhumane treatment by the British in the Northern Ireland conflict. The British authorities developed practices of interrogation such as forcing detainees to stand for long hours, placing black hoods over their heads, holding the detainees prior to interrogation in a room with continuing loud noise and depriving them of sleep, food, and water. The European Court contained that these acts did not rise to the level of torture as defined in the Convention Against Torture, because torture was defined as an aggravated form of cruel, inhuman or degrading treatment or punishment. However, the Court did find that these techniques constituted cruel, inhumane, and degrading treatment. Nonetheless, and as previously mentioned, not only is the United States not a part of the European Human Rights Court, but as previously stated, it only ratified the definition of cruel, inhuman, and degrading treatment consistent with the U.S. Constitution. See also Mehinovic v. Vuckovic, 198 F. Supp. 2d 1322 (N.D. Geor. 2002); Committee Against Torture v. Israel, Supreme Court of Israel, 6 Sep 99, 7 BHRC 31; Ireland v. UK (1978), 2 EHRR 25.

a. (U) Domestic Law: Although the detainee interrogations are not occurring in the continental United States, U.S. personnel conducting said interrogations are still bound by applicable Federal Law, specifically, the Eight Amendment of the United States Constitution, 18 U.S.C. § 2340, and for military interrogators, the Uniform Code of Military Justice (UCMJ).

(1) (U) The Eighth Amendment of the United States Constitution provides that excessive bail shall not be required, nor excessive fines imposed, nor cruel and unusual punishment inflicted. There is a lack of Eighth Amendment case law relating in the context of interrogations, as most of the Eighth Amendment litigation in federal court involves either the death penalty, or 42 U.S.C. § 1983 actions from inmates based on prison conditions. The Eighth Amendment applies as to whether or not torture or inhumane treatment has occurred under the federal torture statute.[1]

(a) (U) A principal case in the confinement context that is instructive regarding Eighth Amendment analysis (which is relevant because the United States adopted the Convention Against Torture, Cruel, Inhumane and Degrading Treatment, it did so deferring to the Eighth Amendment of the United States Constitution) and conditions of confinement if a U.S. court were to examine the issue is Hudson v. McMilban, 503 U.S. 1 (1992). The issue in Hudson stemmed from a 42 U.S.C. § 1983 action alleging that a prison inmate suffered minor bruises, facial swelling, loosened teeth, and a cracked dental plate resulting from a beating by prison guards while he was cuffed and shackled. In this case the Court held that there was no governmental interest in beating an inmate in such a manner. The Court further ruled that the use of excessive physical force against a prisoner might constitute cruel and unusual punishment, even though the inmate does not suffer serious injury.

(b) (U) In Hudson the Court relied on Whitley v. Albers, 475 U.S. 312 (1986), as the seminal case that establishes whether a constitutional violation has occurred. The Court stated that the extent of the injury suffered by an inmate is only one of the factors to be considered, but that there is no significant injury requirement in order to establish an Eighth Amendment violation, and that the absence of serious injury is relevant to, but does not end, the Eighth Amendment inquiry. The Court based its decision on the ". . . settled rule that the unnecessary and various infliction of pain . . . constitutes cruel and unusual punishment forbidden by the Eighth Amendment." Whitley at 319, quoting Ingraham v. Wright, 430 U.S. 651, 670 (1977). The Hudson Court then held that in the excessive force or conditions of confinement context, the Eighth Amendment violation test delineated by the Supreme Court in Hudson is that when prison officials maliciously and sadistically use force to cause harm, contemporary standards of decency are always violated, whether or not significant injury is evident. The extent of injury suffered by an inmate is one factor that may suggest whether the use of force could plausibly have been thought necessary in a particular situation, but the question of whether the measure taken inflicted unnecessary and want on pain and suffering, ultimately turns on whether force was supplied in a good faith effort to maintain or restore discipline, or maliciously and sadistically for the very (emphasis added) purpose of causing harm. If so, the Eighth Amendment claim will prevail.

(c) (U) At the District Court level, the typical conditions-of-confinement claims involve a disturbance of the inmate's physical comfort, such as sleep deprivation or load noise. The Eighth Circuit ruled in Singh v. Holcomb, 1992 U.S. App. LEXIS 24790, that an allegation by an inmate that he was constantly deprived of sleep which resulted in emotional distress, loss of memory, headaches, and poor concentration, did not show either the extreme deprivation level, or the officials' culpable state of mind required to fulfill the objective component of an Eighth Amendment conditions-of-confinement claim.

---

[1]Notwithstanding the argument that U.S. personnel are bound by the Constitution, the detainees confined at GTMO have no jurisdictional standing to bring a section 1983 action alleging an Eighth Amendment violation in U.S. Federal Court.

(d) (U) In another sleep deprivation case alleging an Eighth Amendment violation, the Eighth Circuit established a totality of the circumstances test, and stated that if a particular condition of detention is reasonably related to a legitimate governmental objective, it does not, without more, amount to punishment. In Ferguson v. Cape Girardean County, 88 F.3d 647 (8th Cir. 1996), the complainant was confined to a 5-½ by 5-½ foot cell without a toilet or sink, and was forced to sleep on a mat on the floor under bright lights that were on twenty-four hours a day. His Eighth Amendment claim was not successful because he was able to sleep at some point, and because he was kept under those conditions due to a concern for his health, as well as the perceived danger that he presented. This totality of the circumstances test has also been adopted by the Ninth Circuit. In Green v. CSO Strack, 1995 U.S. App. LEXIS 14451, the Court held that threats of bodily injury are insufficient to state a claim under the Eighth Amendment, and that sleep deprivation did not rise to a constitutional violation where the prisoner failed to present evidence that he either lost sleep or was otherwise harmed.

(e) (U) Ultimately, an Eighth Amendment analysis is based primarily on whether the government had a good faith legitimate governmental interest, and did not act maliciously and sadistically for the very purpose of causing harm.

(2) (U) The torture statute (18 U.S.C. § 2340) is the United States' codification of the signed and ratified provisions of the Convention Against Torture and Other Cruel, Inhuman or Degrading Treatment or Punishment, and pursuant to subsection 2340B, does not create any substantive or procedural rights enforceable by law by any party in any civil proceeding.

(a) (U) The statute provides that "whoever outside the United States commits or attempts to commit torture shall be fined under this title or imprisoned not more than 20 years, or both, and if death results to any person from conduct prohibited by this subsection, shall be punished by death or imprisoned for any term of years or for life."

(b) (U) Torture is defined as "an act committed by a person acting under color of law specifically intended (emphasis added) to inflict severe physical or mental pain or suffering (other than pain or suffering incident to lawful sanctions) upon another person within his custody or physical control." The statute defines "severe mental pain or suffering' as "the prolonged mental harm caused by or resulting (emphasis added) from the intentional infliction or threatened infliction of severe physical pain or suffering; or the administration or application, or threatened administration or application, of mind-altering substances or other procedures calculated to disrupt profoundly the senses of the personality; or the threat of imminent death; or the threat that another person will imminently be subjected to death, severe physical pain or suffering, or the administration or/application of mind-altering substances or other procedures calculated to disrupt profoundly the senses or personality."

(c) (U) Case law in the context of the federal torture statute and interrogations is also lacking, as the majority of the case law involving torture relates to either the illegality of brutal tactics used by the police to obtain confessions (in which the Court simply states that these confessions will be deemed as involuntary for the purposes of admissibility and due process, but does not actually address torture or the Eighth Amendment), or the Alien Torts Claim Act, in which federal courts have defined that certain uses of force (such as kidnapping, beating and raping of a bad with the consent or acquiescence of a public official. See Ortiz v. Gramsio, 886 F.Supp. 162 (D. Mass. 1995)) constituted torture. However, no case law on point within the context of 18 USC 2340.

(3) (U) Finally, U.S. military personnel are subject to the Uniform Code of Military Justice. The punitive articles that could potentially be violated depending on the circumstances and results of an interrogation are: Article 93 (cruelty and maltreatment), Article 118 (murder), Article 119 (manslaughter), Article 124 (maiming), Article 128 (assault), Article 134 (communicating a threat, and negligent homicide), and the inchoate offenses of attempt (Article 80), conspiracy (Article 81), accessory after the fact (Article 78), and solicitation (Article 82), Article 128 is the article most likely to be violated because a simple assault can be consummated by an unlawful demonstration of violence which creates in the mind of another a reasonable apprehension of receiving immediate bodily harm, and a specific intent to actually inflict bodily harm is not required.

4. (U) ANALYSIS: The counter-resistance techniques proposed in the JTF-170-J2 memorandum are lawful because they do not violate the Eighth Amendment to the United States Constitution or the federal torture statute as explained below. An international law analysis is not required for the current proposal because the Geneva Conventions do not apply to these detainees since they are not HPWs.

(a) (U) Based on the Supreme Court framework utilized to assess whether a public official has violated the Eighth Amendment, so long as the force used could plausibly have been thought necessary in a particular situation to achieve a legitimate governmental objective, and it was applied in a good faith effort and not maliciously or sadistically for the very purpose of causing harm, the proposed techniques are likely to pass constitutional master. The federal torture statute will not be violated so long as any of the proposed strategies are not specifically intended to cause severe physical pain or suffering or prolonged mental harm. Assuming that severe physical pain is not inflicted, absent any evidence that any of these strategies will in fact cause prolonged and long lasting mental harm, the proposed methods will not violate the statute.

(b) (U) Regarding the Uniform Code Military Justice, the proposal to grab, poke in the chest, push lightly, and place a wet towel or hood over the detainee's head would constitute a per se violation of Article 128 (Assault). Threatening a detainee with death may also constitute a violation of Article 128, or also Article 134 (communicating a threat). It would be advisable to have permission or immunity in advance from the convening authority, for military members utilizing these methods.

(c) (U) Specifically, with regard to Category I techniques, the use of mild and fear related approaches such as yelling at the detainee is not illegal because in order to communicate a threat, there most also exist an intent to injure. Yelling at the detainee is legal so long as the yelling is not done with the intent to cause severe physical damage or prolonged mental harm. Techniques of deception such as multiple interrogator techniques, and deception regarding interrogator identity are all permissible methods of interrogation, since there is no legal requirement to be truthful while conducting an interrogation.

(d) (U) With regard to Category II methods, the use of stress positions such as the proposed standing for four hours, the use of isolation for up to thirty days, and interrogating the detainee in an environment other than the standard interrogation booth are all legally permissible so long as no severe physical pain is inflicted and prolonged mental harm intended, and because there is a legitimate governmental objective in obtaining the information necessary that the high volume detainees on which these methods would be utilized possess, for the protection of the national security of the United States, its citizens, and allies. Furthermore, these methods would not be utilized for the "very malicious and sadistic purpose of causing harm," and absent medical evidence to the contrary, there is no evidence that prolonged mental harm would result from the use of these strategies. The use of falsified documents is legally permissible because interrogation may use deception to achieve their purpose.

(e) (U) The deprivation of light and auditory stimuli, the placement of a hood over the detainee's head during transportation and questioning, and the use of 20 hour interrogations are all legally permissible so long as there is an important governmental objective, and it is not done for the purpose of causing harm or with the intent to cause prolonged mental suffering. There is no legal requirement that detainees must receive four hours of sleep per night, but if a U.S. Court ever had to rule on this procedure, in order to pass Eighth Amendment scrutiny, and as a cautionary measure, they should receive some amount of sleep so that no severe physical or mental harm will result. Removal of comfort items is permissible because there is no legal requirement to provide comfort items. The requirement is to provide adequate food, water, shelter, and medical care. The issue of removing published religious items or materials would be relevant if these were United States citizens with a First Amendment right. Such is not the case with the detainees. Forced grooming and removal of clothing are not illegal, so long as it is not done to punish or cause, harm, as there is a legitimate governmental objective to obtain information, maintain health standards in the camp and protect both the detainees and the guards. There is no illegality in removing hot meals because there is no specific requirement to provide hot meals, only adequate food. The use of the detainee's phobias is equally permissible.

(f) (U) With respect to the Category III advanced counter-resistance strategies, the use of scenarios designed to convince the detainee that death or severely painful consequences are imminent is not illegal for the same aforementioned reasons that there is a compelling governmental interest and it is not done intentionally to cause prolonged harm. However, caution should be utilized with this technique because the torture statute specifically mentions making death threats as an example of inflicting mental pain and suffering. Exposure to cold weather or water is permissible with appropriate medical monitoring. The use of a wet towel to induce the misperception of suffocation would also be permissible if not done with the specific intent to cause prolonged mental harm, and absent medical evidence that it would. Caution should be exercised with this method, as foreign courts have already advised about the potential mental harm that this method may cause. The use of physical contact with the detainee, such as pushing and poking will technically constitute an assault under Article 128, UCMJ.

5. (U) RECOMMENDATION: I recommend that the proposed methods of interrogation be approved, and that the interrogators be properly trained in the use of the approved methods of interrogation. Since the law requires examination of all facts under a totality of circumstances test, I further recommended that all proposed interrogations involving category II and III methods must undergo a legal, medical, behavioral science, and intelligence review prior to their commencement.

6. (U) POC: Captain Michael Borders, X3536.

DIANE E. BEAVER
LTC, USA
Staff Judge Advocate

UNCLASSIFIED

DEPARTMENT OF DEFENSE
JOINT TASK FORCE 170
GUANTANAMO BAY, CUBA
APO AE 9960

JTF-J2   11 October 2002

MEMORANDUM FOR Commander, Joint Task Force 170

SUBJECT: Request for Approval of Counter-Resistance Strategies

1. (U) PROBLEM: The current guidelines for interrogation procedures at GTMO limit the ability of interrogators to counter advanced resistance.

2. (U) Request approval for use of the following interrogation plan.

    a. Category I techniques. During the initial category of interrogation the detainee should be provided a chair and the environment should be generally comfortable. The format of the interrogation is the direct approach. The use of rewards like cookies or cigarettes may be helpful. If the detainee is determined by the interrogator to be uncooperative, the interrogator may use the following techniques.

    (1) Yelling at the detainee (not directly in his ear or to the level that it would cause physical pain or hearing problems)

    (2) Techniques of deception:

    (a) Multiple interrogator techniques.

    (b) Interrogator identity. The interviewer may identify himself as a citizen of a foreign nation or as an interrogator from a country with a reputation for harsh treatment of detainees.

    b. Category II techniques. With the permission of the GIC, Interrogation Section, the interrogator may use the following techniques.

    (1) The use of stress positions (like standing), for a maximum of four hours.

    (2) The use of falsified documents or reports.

    (3) Use of the isolation facility for up to 30 days. Request must be made to the OIC, Interrogation Section, to the Director, Joint Interrogation Group (JIG). Extensions beyond the initial 30 days must be approved by the Commanding General. For selected detainees, the OIC, Interrogation Section, will approve all contacts with the detainee, to include medical visits of a non-emergent nature.

    (4) Interrogating the detainee in an environment other than the standard interrogation booth:

    (5) Deprivation of high and auditory stimuli

    (6) The detainee may also have a hood placed over his head during transportation and questioning. The hood should not restrict breathing in any way and the detainee should be under direct observation when hooded.

    (7) The use of 20 hour interrogations:

    (8) Removal of all comfort items (including religions items):

    (9) Switching the detainee from hot rations to MREs.

    (10) Removal of clothing.

    (11) Forced grooming (shaving of facial hair etc . . .)

    (12) Using detainees individual phobias (such as fear of dogs) to induce stress.

c. Category III techniques. Techniques in this category may be used only by submitting a request through the Director. JTG, for approval by the Commanding General with appropriate legal review and information to Commander, USSOUTHCOM. These techniques are required for a very small percentage of the most uncooperative detainees (less than 3%). The following techniques and other aversive techniques, such as those used in U.S. military interrogation resistance training or by other U.S. government agencies, may be utilized in a carefully coordinated manner to help interrogate exceptionally resistant detainees. Any or these techniques that require more than light grabbing, poking, or pushing, will be administered only by individuals specifically trained in their safe application.

(1) The use of scenarios designed to convince the detainee that death or severely painful consequences are imminent for him and/or his family.

(2) Exposure to cold weather or water (with appropriate medical monitoring).

(3) Use of a wet towel and dripping water to induce the misperception of suffocation.

JTF 170-J2
SUBJECT: Request for Approval of Counter-Resistance Strategies

(4) Use of mild, non-injurious physical counter such as grabbing, poking in the chest with the finger, and light pushing.

3. (U) The POC for this memorandum is the undersigned at x3476.

JERALD PHIFER
LTC, USA
Director, J2

ADVANCING JUSTICE

THROUGH

DNA TECHNOLOGY

MARCH 2003

Advancing Justice Through DNA Technology

TABLE OF CONTENTS

Advancing Justice Through DNA Technology

EXECUTIVE SUMMARY

DNA technology is increasingly vital to ensuring accuracy and fairness in the criminal justice system. DNA can be used to identify criminals with incredible accuracy when biological evidence exists, and DNA can be used to clear suspects and exonerate persons mistakenly accused or convicted of crimes.

The current federal and state DNA collection and analysis system needs improvement. In many instances, public crime labs are overwhelmed by backlogs of unanalyzed DNA samples. In addition, these labs may be ill-equipped to handle the increasing influx of DNA samples and evidence. The problems of backlogs and the lack of up-to-date technology result in significant delays in the administration of justice. More research is needed to develop faster methods for analyzing DNA evidence. Professionals involved in the criminal justice system need additional training and assistance in order to ensure the optimal use of DNA evidence to solve crimes and assist victims. And the criminal justice system needs the means to provide DNA testing in appropriate circumstances for individuals who assert that they have been wrongly convicted.

President Bush believes we must do more to realize the full potential of DNA technology to solve crime and protect the innocent. The President has proposed $232.6 million in federal funding in FY 2004 for his initiative, *Advancing Justice Through DNA Technology*, and calls for continuing this level of funding for five years—a total commitment of over $1 billion. Under the President's initiative, the Attorney General will improve the use of DNA in the criminal justice system—especially in federal, state, and local forensic laboratories—by providing funds, training and assistance to ensure that this technology reaches its full potential. The President's initiative promotes:

✓ **Using DNA to Solve Crimes**: When used to its full potential, DNA technology will permit the criminal justice system to identify criminals quickly and accurately. More crimes will be solved and persons mistakenly accused or convicted of crimes will be cleared if the criminal justice system is provided with the necessary funding, technology, and assistance it needs to reap the benefits of DNA technology. Under the President's initiative, the Attorney General will:

- **Eliminate Backlogs**: The initiative provides funding to eliminate, within five years, the current backlogs of unanalyzed DNA samples for the most serious violent offenses—rapes, murders, and kidnappings—and for convicted offender samples needing testing.

- **Strengthen Crime Laboratory Capacity**: The initiative provides funding to improve the analysis capacity of federal, state, and local crime labs so they can process DNA samples efficiently and cost-effectively and help prevent future backlogs.

- **Stimulate Research and Development:** The initiative provides resources to stimulate innovative research in order to develop, among other things, more rapid and less costly methods of DNA analysis and the ability to analyze smaller and more degraded samples.

- **Provide Training**: The initiative provides training on the collection and use of DNA evidence to the wide variety of professionals involved in using DNA evidence in the criminal justice system—police officers, prosecutors, defense attorneys, judges, forensic scientists, medical personnel, victim service providers, corrections officers, and probation and parole officers.

✓ **Using DNA to Protect the Innocent:** Under the President's initiative, the Attorney General will advance the use of DNA technology to protect the innocent from wrongful prosecution. The initiative supports providing access to post-conviction DNA testing in appropriate circumstances for state or federal inmates who may have been wrongly convicted, and establishes a grant program to assist states in providing post-conviction testing.

✓ **Using DNA to Identify Missing Persons:** The events of September 11, 2001 demonstrated on a national scale the potential for anguish when the remains of a missing person go unidentified. In order to help provide closure for families of missing persons, the President's initiative provides education and outreach to medical examiners, coroners, law enforcement officers, and victims' families on the use of DNA to identify missing persons.

USING DNA TO SOLVE CRIMES

The past decade has seen great advances in a powerful criminal justice tool: deoxyribonucleic acid, or DNA. DNA can be used to identify criminals with incredible accuracy when biological evidence exists. By the same token, DNA can be used to clear suspects and exonerate persons mistakenly accused or convicted of crimes. In all, DNA technology is increasingly vital to ensuring accuracy and fairness in the criminal justice system.

News stories extolling the successful use of DNA to solve crimes abound. For example, in 1999, New York authorities linked a man through DNA evidence to at least 22 sexual assaults and robberies that had terrorized the city. In 2002, authorities in Philadelphia, Pennsylvania, and Fort Collins, Colorado, used DNA evidence to link and solve a series of crimes (rapes and a murder) perpetrated by the same individual. In the 2001 "Green River" killings, DNA evidence provided a major breakthrough in a series of crimes that had remained unsolved for years despite a large law enforcement task force and a $15 million investigation.

DNA is generally used to solve crimes in one of two ways. In cases where a suspect is identified, a sample of that person's DNA can be compared to evidence from the crime scene. The results of this comparison may help establish whether the suspect committed the crime. In cases where a suspect has not yet been identified, biological evidence from the crime scene can be analyzed and compared to offender profiles in DNA databases to help identify the perpetrator. Crime scene evidence can also be linked to other crime scenes through the use of DNA databases.

For example, assume that a man was convicted of sexual assault. At the time of his conviction, he was required to provide a sample of his DNA, and the resulting DNA profile was entered into a DNA database. Several years later, another sexual assault was committed. A Sexual Assault Nurse Examiner worked with the victim and was able to obtain biological evidence from the rape. This evidence was analyzed, the resulting profile was run against a DNA database, and a match was made to the man's DNA profile. He was apprehended, tried, and sentenced for his second crime. In this hypothetical case, he was also prevented from committing other crimes during the period of his incarceration.

DNA evidence is generally linked to DNA offender profiles through DNA databases. In the late 1980s, the federal government laid the groundwork for a system of national, state, and local DNA databases for the storage and exchange of DNA profiles. This system, called the Combined DNA Index System (CODIS), maintains DNA profiles obtained under the federal, state, and local systems in a set of databases that are available to law enforcement agencies across the country for law enforcement purposes. CODIS can compare crime scene evidence to a database of DNA profiles obtained from convicted offenders. CODIS can also link DNA evidence obtained from different crime scenes, thereby identifying serial criminals.

In order to take advantage of the investigative potential of CODIS, in the late 1980s and early 1990s, states began passing laws requiring offenders convicted of certain offenses to provide DNA samples. Currently all 50 states and the federal government have laws requiring that DNA samples be collected from some categories of offenders.

When used to its full potential, DNA evidence will help solve and may even prevent some of the Nation's most serious violent crimes. However, the current federal and state DNA collection and analysis system needs improvement:

(1) In many instances, public crime labs are overwhelmed by backlogs of unanalyzed DNA samples.

(2) In addition, these labs may be ill-equipped to handle the increasing influx of DNA samples and evidence. The problems of backlogs and lack of up-to-date technology result in significant delays in the administration of justice.

(3) More research is needed to develop faster methods for analyzing DNA evidence.

(4) Professionals working in the criminal justice system need additional training and assistance in order to ensure the optimal use of DNA evidence to solve crimes and assist victims.

President Bush believes we must do more to realize the full potential of DNA technology to solve crime and protect the innocent. Under the President's initiative, the Attorney General will improve the use of DNA in the criminal justice system by providing funds and assistance to ensure that this technology reaches its full potential to solve crimes.

1. Eliminating Backlogs

One of the biggest problems facing the criminal justice system today is the substantial backlog of unanalyzed DNA samples and biological evidence from crime scenes, especially in sexual assault and murder cases. Too often, crime scene samples wait unanalyzed in police or crime lab storage facilities. Timely analysis of these samples and placement into DNA databases can avert tragic results. For example, in 1995, the Florida Department of Law Enforcement linked evidence found on a rape-homicide victim to a convicted rapist's DNA profile just eight days before he was scheduled for parole. Had he been released prior to being linked to the unsolved rape-homicide, he may very well have raped or murdered again.

By contrast, analysis and placement into CODIS of DNA profiles can dramatically enhance the chances that potential crime victims will be spared the violence of vicious, repeat offenders. The President's initiative calls for $92.9 million to help alleviate the current backlogs of DNA samples for the most serious violent offenses—rapes, murders, and kidnappings—and for convicted offender samples needing testing. With this additional federal backlog reduction funding, the funding provided by this initiative to improve crime laboratory capacity, and continued support from the states, the current backlogs will be eliminated in five years.

Understanding the Backlog

The state and local backlog problem has two components: (1) "***casework sample backlogs***," which consist of DNA samples obtained from crime scenes, victims, and suspects in criminal cases, and (2) "***convicted offender backlogs***," which consist of DNA samples obtained from convicted offenders who are incarcerated or under supervision. The nature of the DNA backlog is complex and changing, and measuring the precise number of unanalyzed DNA samples is difficult.

- Casework Sample Backlogs: In a 2001 survey of public DNA laboratories, the Bureau of Justice Statistics (BJS) found that between 1997 and 2000, DNA laboratories experienced a 73% increase in casework and a 135% increase in their casework backlogs. Many casework samples go unanalyzed for lack of a suspect to which to compare the biological evidence from the crime scene. These are often referred to as "no-suspect" cases. Based on an ongoing assessment of crime laboratories and law enforcement agencies, the National Institute of Justice (NIJ) estimates that the current backlog of rape and homicide cases is approximately 350,000. The initiative calls for $76 million in FY 2004 to help eliminate these backlogs over five years.

- Convicted Offender Backlogs: States are increasing the number of convicted offenders required to provide DNA samples. Currently, 23 states require all convicted felons to provide DNA samples. Preliminary estimates by NIJ place the number of collected, untested convicted offender samples at between 200,000 and 300,000. NIJ also estimates that there are between 500,000 and 1,000,000 convicted offender samples that are owed, but not yet collected. The initiative calls for $15 million in FY 2004 to help eliminate convicted offender backlogs over five years.

The federal government also faces a high demand for analysis of casework and convicted offender DNA samples. The FBI has two DNA casework analysis units (see page 5). The first unit, which focuses on analyzing nuclear DNA, has a backlog of approximately 900 cases. The second unit, which focuses on analyzing mitochondrial DNA (mtDNA), has a backlog of roughly 120 cases.

The federal government also collects DNA samples from persons convicted of offenses in certain categories, including crimes of violence or terrorism. The FBI currently has a backlog of approximately 18,000 convicted offender samples. The initiative calls for $1.9 million in FY 2004 to fund the federal convicted offender program; some of these funds will be devoted to eliminating the federal convicted offender backlog.

Effect of Clearing the Backlog

The results of addressing backlogs are dramatic, as the two examples below illustrate:

- In September 1993, a married couple was attacked on a jogging trail in Dallas by a man with a gun who sexually assaulted the woman after shooting the man. No suspect was ever positively identified, although police investigated over 200 leads and 40 potential suspects. In August 2000, evidence from the case was analyzed using current DNA technology. Then, in February 2001, the DNA sample was matched to an individual who was already serving a five-year sentence for an unrelated 1997 sexual assault of a child. The man has since been convicted of capital murder and aggravated sexual assault.

- In March 1992, an Alexandria, Virginia shop owner was stabbed more than 150 times in her home. There were no witnesses to the crime. For years, detectives had no leads, but they did have traces of someone's blood, apparently from the fierce struggle between the victim and the killer. Meanwhile, in 1996, a man pleaded guilty to robbing a gas station, and his DNA was collected for analysis and inclusion in the Virginia DNA database. Because of the backlog, the man's sample was not immediately analyzed. In the summer of 2000, the sample was analyzed and matched through the database to the evidence from the Alexandria woman's murder. In April 2001, almost nine years after the commission of this brutal crime, the man was sentenced to life in prison.

Several law enforcement agencies, prosecutors' offices, and crime labs across the country have established innovative programs to review old cases. Often called "cold case units," these programs have enabled criminal justice officials to solve cases that have languished for years without suspects. Most frequently, DNA evidence has been the linchpin in solving these cases. For instance, this past July, a California man was found guilty of the 1974 rape-homicide of a 19 year-old pregnant woman—a case that was solved through DNA evidence nearly thirty years after the crime was committed.

Prior Federal Support of State DNA Backlog Reduction

In recent years, the federal government has strongly supported states in their efforts to eliminate backlogs of convicted offender and casework DNA samples. Since the creation in 2000 of the Department of Justice's (DOJ's) Convicted Offender DNA Backlog Reduction Program, more than 493,600 offender samples from 24 states have been analyzed. Since the creation in 2001 of the No Suspect Casework DNA Backlog Reduction Program, federal funds have been provided to support the analysis of approximately 24,800 cases. States have analyzed evidence in an additional 18,000 "no-suspect" cases as a result of a match requirement of Convicted Offender DNA Backlog Reduction funding.

In 2002 and 2003 combined, the President requested and Congress appropriated $70.8 million to fund these DNA backlog reduction programs. Additionally, Attorney General John Ashcroft also made available $25 million in Asset Forfeiture funds to address the backlog of convicted offender and "no suspect" casework samples. Thus, the Bush Administration already has devoted more than $95 million to reducing DNA backlogs.

2. Strengthening Crime Laboratory Capacity

At present, many of our Nation's crime laboratories do not have the capacity necessary to analyze DNA samples in a timely fashion. Many have limited equipment resources, outdated information systems, and overwhelming case management demands. As a result, the criminal justice system as a whole is unable to reap the full benefits of DNA technology. The President's initiative will provide federal funding to further automate and improve the infrastructure of federal, state, and local crime labs so they can process DNA samples efficiently and cost-effectively. These infrastructure improvements are critical to preventing future DNA backlogs, and to helping the criminal justice system realize the full potential of DNA technology.

Increasing the Analysis Capacity of Public Crime Labs

The President's initiative will provide significant support to public crime labs so that these labs can update their infrastructure, automate their DNA analysis procedures, and improve their retention and storage of forensic evidence. The initiative calls for $60 million in FY 2004 funding, which will be dedicated to:

- Providing Basic Infrastructure Support: Some public crime laboratories still need assistance to help them obtain equipment and material to conduct the basic processes of DNA analysis—extraction, quantitation, amplification and analysis—and to help them meet various accreditation requirements.

- Building Infrastructure through Laboratory Information Management Systems: Laboratory Information Management Systems, or "LIMS," are designed to automate evidence handling and casework management, to improve the integrity and speed of evidence handling procedures, and to ensure proper chain of custody. DOJ estimates that only 10 percent of the public DNA laboratories have LIMS systems.

- Providing Automation Tools to Public DNA Laboratories: To streamline aspects of the DNA analysis procedure that are labor and time-intensive, crime laboratories should have automated systems, such as robotic DNA extraction units. Automated DNA analysis systems increase analyst productivity, limit human error and reduce contamination.

- Providing Support for the Retention and Storage of Forensic Evidence: Forensic evidence must be stored in a manner that ensures its integrity and maintains its availability throughout criminal investigations and judicial proceedings. Appropriate evidence storage conditions require costly equipment such as security systems, environmental control systems, ambient temperature monitors, and de-humidifiers. The initiative will support the improvement of evidence storage capabilities.

Funding the FBI Forensic Analysis Programs

The FBI Laboratory runs several different programs for the analysis of DNA information. The Nuclear DNA Program supports federal, state, local, and international law enforcement agencies by providing advanced technical assistance within the forensic biology discipline and sub-disciplines through interrelated capabilities and expertise. The Mitochondrial DNA (mtDNA) Analysis Program is responsible for performing mtDNA analysis of forensic evidence containing small or degraded quantities of DNA on items of evidence submitted from federal, state, and local law enforcement agencies. Mitochondrial DNA is a powerful tool available for investigating cases of kidnapping, missing persons, and skeletal remains where nuclear DNA is not present. The initiative will provide funds to these two existing programs to permit them to continue their important work. In addition, the initiative will provide funds to the FBI to further expand regional mtDNA labs that will provide an alternative source for mtDNA analysis to state and local law enforcement, and allow the FBI laboratory to concentrate more of its efforts on federal cases. The initiative calls for $20.5 million in FY 2004 to fund these programs.

Funding the Combined DNA Index System

The Combined DNA Index System (CODIS), administered by the FBI, maintains DNA profiles obtained through federal, state, and local DNA sample collection programs, and makes this information available to law enforcement agencies across the country for law enforcement identification purposes. Currently, the National DNA Index System (NDIS) of CODIS contains about 1.7 million

DNA profiles. The President's initiative includes funding to complete a general redesign and upgrade of CODIS, which will increase the system's capacity to 50 million DNA profiles, reduce the search time from hours to microseconds for matching DNA profiles, and enable instant, real-time (as opposed to weekly) searches of the database by participating forensic laboratories. The initiative calls for $9.9 million in FY 2004 to fund this program.

3. Stimulating Research and Development

In order to improve the use of DNA technology to advance the cause of justice, the Attorney General will stimulate research and development of new methods of analyzing DNA samples under the President's initiative. Also, the President has asked the Attorney General to establish demonstration projects under the initiative to further study the public safety and law enforcement benefits of fully integrating the use of DNA technology to solve crimes. Finally, the President has directed the Attorney General to create a National Forensic Science Commission to study rapidly evolving advances in all areas of the forensic sciences and to make recommendations to maximize the use of the forensic sciences in the criminal justice system. In all, the President's initiative will devote $24.8 million in FY 2004 to fund advances in the use of DNA technology.

Improving DNA Technology

Forensic DNA analysis is rapidly evolving. Research and development of tools that will permit crime laboratories to conduct DNA analysis quickly is vital to the goal of improving the timely analysis of DNA samples. Smaller, faster, and less costly analysis tools will reduce capital investments for crime laboratories while increasing their capacity to process more cases. Over the course of the next several years, DNA research efforts will focus on the following areas:

- The development of "DNA chip technology" that uses nanotechnology to improve both speed and resolution of DNA evidence analysis. This technology will reduce analysis time from several hours to several minutes and provide cost-effective miniaturized components.

- The development of more robust methods to enable more crime labs to have greater success in the analysis of degraded, old, or compromised items of biological evidence.

- Advanced applications of various DNA analysis methods, such as automated Short Tandem Repeats (STRs), Single Nucleotide Polymorphisms (SNPs), mitochondrial DNA analysis (mtDNA), and Y-chromosome DNA analysis.

- The use of animal, plant, and microbial DNA to provide leads that may link DNA found on or near human perpetrators or victims to the actual perpetrator of the crime.

- Technologies that will enable DNA identification of vast numbers of samples occasioned by a mass disaster or mass fatality incident.

- Technologies that permit better separation of minute traces of male sexual assailant DNA from female victims.

The initiative devotes $10 million in FY 2004 funding to benefit the state and local criminal justice community through DNA research and development. It also requests $9.8 million in FY 2004 funding to further expand the FBI's DNA research and development program.

Establishing DNA Demonstration Projects

To further research the impact of increased DNA evidence collection on public safety and law enforcement operations, the Attorney General will conduct rigorous scientific research through demonstration projects on the use of DNA evidence under the initiative. This research will help determine the scope of public safety benefits that result when police are trained to more effectively collect DNA evidence and prosecutors are provided with training to enhance their ability to present this evidence in court.

Several jurisdictions will be selected to incorporate core training and evidence collection requirements in their daily operations. At each site, one or more law enforcement agencies will be chosen to implement extensive training on the collection of DNA evidence and to increase the resources devoted to the investigation and prosecution of these cases. Prosecutors will also receive training on how to more effectively present DNA evidence and how forensic DNA technology may be used to solve current and "cold" cases. Jurisdictions that received increased training and resources will be compared with jurisdictions that did not receive these benefits.

The resulting comparison will measure the impact of increased DNA evidence collection on public safety and law enforcement operations. For example, projects will examine whether there are increased crime clearance rates, whether DNA aided investigations, the number of cases successfully prosecuted, the number of cases where guilty pleas were obtained due to the presence of DNA evidence, any financial savings resulting from the use of forensic evidence, and increased responsiveness to victims. The information obtained will allow state and local governments to make more informed decisions regarding investment in forensic DNA as a crime-fighting tool. The initiative calls for $4.5 million in FY 2004 to fund these projects.

Creating a National Forensic Science Commission

To facilitate the ability of policymakers to assess the needs of the forensic science community, and to stimulate public awareness of the uses of forensic technology to solve crimes, the President has directed the Attorney General to create a National Forensic Science Commission. The Commission will be charged with two primary responsibilities: (1) developing recommendations for long-term strategies to maximize the use of current forensic technologies to solve crimes and protect the public, and (2) identifying potential scientific breakthroughs that may be used to assist law enforcement.

The Attorney General will appoint Commission members from professional forensic science organizations and accreditation bodies and from the criminal justice community. These individuals will have broad knowledge and in-depth expertise in the criminal justice system and in various areas of the forensic sciences such as analytical toxicology, trace evidence, forensic biology, firearms and toolmark examinations, latent fingerprints, crime scene analysis, digital evidence, and forensic pathology, in addition to DNA. Judges, prosecutors, attorneys, victim advocates, and other members of the criminal justice system will also be represented on the Commission.

The Commission will study advances in all areas of the forensic sciences and make recommendations on how new and existing technologies can be used to improve public safety. The Commission will also serve as an ongoing forum for discussing initiatives and policy, and may issue recommendations that will assist state and local law enforcement agencies in the cost-effective use of these technologies to solve crimes. The initiative devotes $500,000 in FY 2004 to the establishment of the Commission.

4. *Training the Criminal Justice Community*

In order to maximize the use of DNA technology, under the President's initiative, the Attorney General will develop training and provide assistance regarding the collection and use of DNA evidence to the wide variety of professionals involved in the criminal justice system, including police officers, prosecutors, defense attorneys, judges, forensic scientists, medical personnel, victim service providers, corrections officers, and probation and parole officers.

Key players in the criminal justice system should receive additional training in the proper collection, preservation, and use of DNA evidence. Fundamental knowledge of the capabilities of DNA technology is essential for police officers to collect evidence properly, prosecutors and defense attorneys to introduce and use it successfully in court, and judges to rule correctly on its admissibility. Victim service providers and medical personnel likewise need to understand DNA technology in order to encourage more successful evidence collection and to be fully responsive to the needs of victims.

Law Enforcement Training

As the first responders to crime scenes, law enforcement officers should be able to identify, collect and preserve probative biological evidence for submission to crime laboratories. Improper collection can mean that valuable evidence is missed or rendered unsuitable for testing. The initiative devotes $3.5 million in FY 2004 to assist law enforcement in meeting the following training needs:

- Basic "awareness training" on DNA evidence for patrol officers and other first-responders;

- Intensive training on identifying, collecting, and preserving potential DNA evidence for evidence technicians, investigators, and others processing crime scenes;

- Training and education for investigators and responding officers on DNA databases and their potential to provide leads in current and "cold" cases; and

- Training and information for law enforcement leadership and policymakers to facilitate more informed decisions about effective DNA evidence collection and testing.

Training Prosecutors, Defense Attorneys, and Judges

In order to achieve just results in cases involving DNA evidence, prosecutors, defense attorneys, and judges should receive proper training on the use and presentation of DNA evidence. The initiative devotes $2.5 million in FY 2004 to support:

- Training and technical assistance for prosecutors to learn about solving "cold cases" with DNA evidence, responding to post-conviction DNA testing requests, and developing innovative legal strategies to optimize the power of forensic DNA technology. Grant funds will be available for state and local prosecutors' organizations for the development and delivery of training materials to assist prosecutors in presenting this evidence before courts and juries, and in understanding more about the value of DNA evidence in particular cases.

- Training for defense counsel handling cases involving biological evidence on the applications and limitations of DNA evidence. Grant funds will be made available to continuing legal education programs or bar associations to provide training and resources on forensic DNA technology.

- Training for judges, who must be equipped with sufficient technical and scientific knowledge to make appropriate rulings in cases involving DNA evidence. Grant funds will be available to national judicial conferences and organizations.

Training For Probation and Parole Officers and Corrections Personnel

Probation and parole officers play a critical role in ensuring that offenders are complying with their statutory obligations to provide DNA samples. Corrections personnel often are responsible for obtaining DNA samples from inmates required by law to submit such samples. Through training and education programs, these professionals will be better equipped to ensure that samples are taken from all individuals who are required by law to provide them. The initiative calls for $1 million in FY 2004 to support this training.

Training for Forensic Scientists

The forensic science community has a critical need for trained forensic scientists in public crime laboratories. The initiative will assist the development of comprehensive training programs for a new generation of forensic scientists, enabling new forensic scientists to receive in-depth training to prepare them for analyzing actual casework in a crime laboratory. The initiative calls for $3 million in FY 2004 to support this training.

Training for Medical Personnel

The initiative will also provide $5 million in FY 2004 to support the development of training and educational materials for doctors and nurses involved in treating victims of sexual assault. Trained medical personnel are needed to effectively collect usable DNA evidence, while safeguarding the privacy rights and addressing the needs of rape victims requiring sexual assault exams. These programs will specifically target underserved areas of the country. Funding may also be used to support the development of SANE (Sexual Assault Nurse Examiner), SAFE (Sexual Assault Forensic Examiner), and SART (Sexual Assault Response Team) programs.

Training for Victim Service Providers

Victims and those who advocate on their behalf must have access to information about the investigative and courtroom uses of forensic DNA evidence. Victims should be properly informed about how DNA evidence may impact their cases. In situations involving post-conviction DNA testing, victim service providers must be able to assist victims through the often-painful process of newly-ordered DNA tests and re-opened court proceedings. To address the concerns of victims, the initiative would develop additional DNA education and training programs for victim advocates and victim service providers so that they may better assist victims in all cases involving DNA evidence. The initiative calls for $5 million in FY 2004 to support this training.

USING DNA TO PROTECT THE INNOCENT

DNA technology is increasingly vital to ensuring fairness in the criminal justice system. Every effort that is made to reduce backlogs of untested evidence, to better equip forensic laboratories, to develop faster methods of analyzing samples, and to better train professionals in the use of DNA technology, will improve the accuracy of the criminal justice system. Accordingly, the measures described in the previous sections will not only help solve crimes and keep dangerous offenders off the streets, but will also help minimize the risk that innocent individuals are wrongly accused or convicted.

Post-conviction DNA testing has received considerable attention in recent years. Since the advent of forensic DNA analysis, a number of individuals convicted of crimes have been subsequently exonerated through DNA analysis of crime scene evidence that was not tested at the time of trial. The following are two recent reported examples:

- In February 2003, a Hampton Roads, Virginia man was released from prison after post-conviction DNA tests proved that he did not rape a nursing student in 1981. The man had spent two decades in prison after being convicted of breaking into the woman's apartment and raping her. Two juries failed to reach a verdict, but a third jury found him guilty. From the time of his arrest, however, the man maintained his innocence. Last year, a Virginia crime lab located evidence in the man's case in a file maintained by a forensic scientist who had since died. DNA tests conducted on this evidence proved that he was not the perpetrator, and have preliminarily linked the crime scene evidence to a felon whose DNA sample was maintained in the Virginia DNA database. The Norfolk Commonwealth Attorney supported the man's immediate release from prison after learning of the DNA test result. Law enforcement authorities are following up on the "cold hit."

- A Maryland man served 20 years of a 30-year sentence after being convicted of a 1982 home invasion rape of a schoolteacher. Through post-conviction DNA testing, the man was exonerated in 2002. When the crime scene profile was uploaded to CODIS, it was preliminarily linked to a felon whose DNA profile was maintained in a DNA database. This man has subsequently been arrested and charged for the 1982 crime, and is awaiting trial later this year. The original defendant was pardoned in January 2003.

Many states have already enacted provisions that allow convicted offenders in certain cases to seek post-conviction DNA testing of evidence collected in those cases. Currently, 31 states have enacted special statutory provisions providing post-conviction DNA testing, and additional states make post-conviction testing available through other procedures. Federal law also should provide for post-conviction DNA testing in appropriate cases.

To demonstrate support for appropriate post-conviction testing of DNA evidence, the Attorney General will create a $5 million grant program under the President's initiative to help states defray the costs of post-conviction DNA testing. In order to receive this funding, state programs will be required to meet criteria established by the Department of Justice. These criteria will require that DNA testing be performed by an accredited forensic laboratory, and will encourage states to develop plans that ensure prompt DNA testing of persons who may be wrongly convicted and discourage frivolous testing that may cause unnecessary expense and needless harm to crime victims.

USING DNA TO IDENTIFY MISSING PERSONS

Families of missing persons who are presumed dead face tremendous emotional turmoil when they are unable to learn about the fates of their loved ones. The events of September 11, 2001 demonstrated on a national scale the potential for anguish when the remains of a missing person go unidentified. In the wake of this tragedy, the Department of Justice brought together DNA experts from across the country to develop improved DNA analysis methods identifying the World Trade Center victims.

Despite tremendous scientific advancements, DNA technology is not routinely used in missing persons cases. According to statistics maintained by the FBI's National Crime Information Center (NCIC), there are nearly 5,000 reported unidentified persons in the United States. This element of the President's initiative will help identify the missing, and in doing so, will provide an increased sense of closure to their families.

The FBI's Missing Persons DNA Database Program currently provides the essential infrastructure for identifying human remains. This database maintains two indices of DNA samples. The first index contains DNA profiles of relatives of missing persons and the second contains DNA profiles of unidentified human remains. Successful identifications require that both profiles be entered. Currently, this database is not used to its full potential. States have only recently begun to conduct DNA analysis on human remains and to submit the results to the FBI for inclusion in its database. Many unidentified human remains continue to be disposed of without the collection of DNA samples. Further, even when the samples are collected, many crime labs lack the capacity to conduct timely analysis, especially where the biological sample is old or degraded. In addition, many family members and law enforcement officials lack sufficient information about the existence of the program and how to participate.

The President's initiative will help ensure that DNA forensic technology is used to its full potential to identify missing persons. The initiative will:

- Provide outreach and education to medical examiners, coroners, and law enforcement officers about the use of DNA to identify human remains and to aid in missing persons cases;

- Make DNA reference collection kits available to these state and local officials;

- Support the development of educational materials and outreach programs for families of missing children and adults;

- Encourage states to collect DNA samples before any unidentified remains are disposed;

- Strengthen crime lab capacity (see page 4) to enable more state and local labs to conduct timely DNA analysis of biological samples from unidentified human remains;

- Provide for the analysis of degraded and old biological samples through the FBI's Mitochondrial DNA Analysis Program (see page 5);

- Provide technical assistance to state and local crime labs and medical examiners on the collection and analysis of degraded remains through the FBI and the National Institute of Justice; and

- Support research and development of more robust methods for analyzing degraded, old, or compromised biological samples (see page 6).

The President's initiative will devote $2 million in FY 2004 for outreach programs and the development of educational materials and reference collection kits.

FUNDING

The President's DNA Initiative, *Advancing Justice Through DNA Technology*, calls for $232.6 million in federal funding for FY 2004. This includes $100.7 million in new funding. In addition, as part of the $232.6 million, the Justice Department is targeting $13.5 million in FY 2004 funding from existing programs within the Office of Justice Programs to support the DNA Initiative.*

Element of the Initiative	2004 Budget Request (millions of dollars)
USING DNA TO SOLVE CRIMES	
Eliminating Backlogs	**$92.9**
State Casework Backlogs	$76.0
State Convicted Offender Backlogs	$15.0
Funding the Federal Convicted Offender Program	$1.9
Strengthening Crime Lab Capacity	**$90.4**
Increasing the Analysis Capacity of Public Crime Labs	$60.0
Funding FBI Forensic Analysis Programs	$20.5
Funding the Combined DNA Index System	$9.9
Stimulating Research and Development	**$24.8**
Improving DNA Technology	$10.0
FBI Research and Development	$9.8
DNA Demonstration Projects	$4.5
The National Forensic Science Commission	$0.5
Training the Criminal Justice Community	**$17.5**
Law Enforcement	$3.5
Prosecutors, Defense Attorneys, and Judges	$2.5
Probation & Parole Officers, Corrections Personnel	$1.0
Forensic Scientists	$3.0
Medical Personnel	$5.0
Victim Service Providers	$2.5
USING DNA TO PROTECT THE INNOCENT	**$5.0**
USING DNA TO IDENTIFY MISSING PERSONS	**$2.0**
TOTAL FUNDING	**$232.6**

*These funds must be used in accordance with the applicable programs' authorizing statutes.

GTMO Interrogation Techniques

<u>**Approved by SECDEF in Dec 2002:**</u>
Category I
—Incentive
—Yelling at Detainee
—Deception
—Multiple Interrogator techniques
—Interrogator identity

Category II
—Stress positions for a maximum of four
  hours (e.g., standing)
—Use of falsified documents or reports
—Isolation up to 30 days (requires notice)
—Interrogation booth
—Interrogation outside of the standard
—Deprivation of light and auditory stimuli
—Hooding during transport & interrogation
—Use of 20 hour interrogations
—Removal of all comfort items
—Switching detainee from hot meal to MRE
—Removal of clothing
—Forced grooming (e.g., shaving)
—Inducing stress by use of detainee's fears (e.g., dogs)

Category III
—Use of mild, non-injurious physical contact

<u>**Used Dec 2002 through 15 Jan 2003:**</u>
Category I
—Yelling (Not directly into ear)
—Deception (Introducing of confederate detainee)
—Role-playing interrogator in next cell

Category II
—Removal from social support at Camp Delta
—Segregation in Navy Brig
—Isolation in Camp X-Ray
—Interrogating the detainee in an environment
  other than standard interrogation room at
  Camp Delta (i.e., Camp X-Ray)
—Deprivation of light (use of red light)
—Inducing stress (use of female interrogator)
—Up to 20-hour interrogations
—Removal of all comfort items, including religious items
—Serving MRE instead of hot rations
—Forced grooming (to include shaving facial hair
  and head—also served hygienic purposes)
—Use of false documents or reports

CHAPTER 12

The Constitutional Right to Trial by Jury

CHAPTER CONTENTS

In all criminal prosecutions the accused shall enjoy the right to a speedy and public trial, by an impartial jury of the state and district wherein the crime shall have been committed.

U.S. Constitution, Eighth Amendment, 1791

The jury is both the most effective way of establishing the people's rule and the most efficient way of teaching them how to rule.

Alexis De Tocqueville, Democracy in America, 1835

Jury

A group of men and women from the community selected to determine the truth; while the judge is responsible for interpreting the law, the jury is charged with the task of finding the facts of the case. The right to trial by jury is guaranteed by the U.S. Constitution in all serious criminal cases. A jury decides what the facts of the case are and applies those facts to the law. Juries must be convinced beyond a reasonable doubt that the defendant broke the law.

Magna Carta

The Great Charter, a document that was signed by King John of England in 1215; it guaranteed the noblemen under the king's jurisdiction life, liberty, and property. Many of the promises made in the Magna Carta became the basis of the guarantees found in the U.S. Constitution and the constitutions of the states.

CHAPTER OBJECTIVES

After studying this chapter, you should be able to:

- Explain the history of the right to trial by jury in criminal cases.
- Define **jury.**
- List and explain the provisions in the U.S. Constitution that require trial by jury in criminal cases.
- Explain how the members of a jury pool are selected.
- Explain the process of *voir dire.*
- List some reasons a potential juror can be excused for cause.
- Explain sequestration.
- List some reasons for a change of **venue** and change of *venire.*
- Explain what "beyond a reasonable doubt" means.
- List and explain some differences between federal juries and state juries.

INTRODUCTION AND HISTORICAL BACKGROUND

Every year, all across the United States, millions of very ordinary citizens are called to **jury** duty. For a brief time, 12 men and women gather together to render judgment on a fellow human being. Once judgment has been passed, they part company as abruptly as they came together. These ordinary men and women perform an extraordinary task that many see as an essential component of U.S. democracy. As jurors, they are the fact finders in both criminal and civil cases. That is, they decide what witness and what evidence is worthy of belief. In this chapter, we will explore the origin of the jury system, its modern use, and its role in bringing criminal defendants to justice and judgment.

One of the earliest known uses of ordinary citizens as fact finders is the use of volunteers in ancient Greece. These volunteers were collectively referred to as the dicastery. From this pool of citizens, individual dicasts would be picked to decide the fate of fellow citizens.

The Vikings, whose warriors spread fear and destruction through Europe and the British Isles during the centuries between 900 AD and about 1300 AD, also had a well-developed internal system of justice. The *Thing* (pronounced Ting), a group of Viking citizens, met to mete out justice.

England traces the right to trial by jury as far back as Henry II's Constitutions of Clarendon in 1164 and the **Magna Carta** in 1215. Its usage grew and developed so that by the eighteenth century the great legal commentator, William Blackstone, could write: ". . . the truth of every accusation . . . should afterwards be confirmed by . . . twelve of his equals and neighbors."[1]

Trial by jury replaced two earlier methods for determining guilt in medieval England, trial by battle and trial by ordeal. In trial by battle, the defendant and his accuser fought to the death. **Trial by battle** was essentially used when a private individual believed himself or his clan wronged by the accused in some way. These cases were generally civil rather than criminal in nature. As early as 1110, Henry I ordered lords who could not settle their differences to do so by duel. Trial by battle in the form of the duel survived well into the nineteenth century. For example, in 1801, Alexander Hamilton was killed in a duel with Aaron Burr.

HISTORICAL HIGHLIGHT
Socrates Condemned to Death by Jury
for Corrupting Youth

Socrates was a Greek philosopher and teacher who lived in Athens from about 469 BC to 399 BC. Students of the law may be most familiar with him through a teaching method he is credited with inventing. The Socratic method is a staple of many law school classes. It involves the instructor questioning and challenging students to come up with answers rather than the teacher lecturing on the subject matter. Through the Socratic method, facts particular to the subject being taught are discussed. From the discussion, students draw conclusions that are general or universal, not just pertinent to the particular facts at hand. For example, a student may discuss a case that involves an automobile running a red light, causing an accident. The driver is found to have been negligent. Using the Socratic method, students may conclude that any person who violates a law and, because of the violation, causes damage to another is negligent. From the specific facts, the student generalizes about negligence in any case.

So popular was Socrates among young people and so unpopular were his views that he was brought to trial. He was charged with undermining democracy in Athens. He was tried before a jury consisting of volunteers who swore to uphold the laws of Athens, much the same way a modern jury is sworn. A jury of citizens of Athens found him guilty and sentenced him to death. He died after drinking a cup of poison made from the bark of the hemlock tree, surrounded by the young people he was charged with corrupting. An account of the trial and Socrates' last days can be found in Plato's *Apology.*

Trial by Battle
A method of determining guilt in medieval England; usually reserved for civil cases, in trial by battle the winner of the battle won the lawsuit.

No freeman shall be taken, or imprisoned, or outlawed, or exiled, . . . except by the legal judgment of his peers or by the law of the land.
Magna Carta, Clause 39, 1215

Trial by Ordeal
A method of determining guilt in medieval England; in trial by ordeal, the defendant was made to perform a physical task, such as holding a hot piece of iron. If the wound healed without becoming infected, the accused was innocent; if it became infected, he was guilty (and ill).

Trial by ordeal involved having the accused perform some physical task. If he survived unharmed, he was innocent. For example, the accused was made to carry a red hot piece of iron for a short distance or to dip his hand in a pot of boiling water long enough to pull out a stone. After performing the feat, his hand was bandaged. If after three days there was no sign of infection, the accused was declared innocent.[2]

The right to a jury trial came to America with the English colonists. The settlers demanded that they be tried in America, not back in England. They also insisted that the jury consist of fellow colonists, not Englishmen.[3]

After the American Revolution, the right to a jury trial in a criminal case was specifically provided for in the U.S. Constitution, not once, but twice. First, Article III, Section 2 of the Constitution states that "[t]he Trial of All Crimes, Except in Cases of Impeachment, shall be by Jury; and such Trial shall be held in the State Where the Said Crimes have been committed." Then, the **Sixth Amendment** reiterates the right by providing that "[i]n all criminal prosecutions, the accused shall enjoy the right to a speedy and public trial, by an impartial jury of the State and district wherein the crime shall have been committed."

Sixth Amendment

The provision of the Bill of Rights that originally guaranteed all federal criminal defendants the right to trial by jury; it has since been applied to the states through the Fourteenth Amendment, which guarantees all citizens equal protection of the laws of the United States.

Over the last two centuries, our courts have refined the right to a jury trial in many important ways. Through judicial interpretation, the right to a jury trial has been expanded and refined. It is now clear that every criminal defendant who is accused of a crime punishable by more than six months in prison can demand a jury trial. Both states and the federal government must provide juries for criminal defendants who want them. Ordinary citizens are finding it more difficult than ever before to avoid jury duty. That's because the U.S. Supreme Court has set strict standards for the composition of juries so that they reflect the philosophy that citizens must be tried by a "jury of one's peers" and that the pool from which a jury is picked was assembled in a nondiscriminatory way.

DEFINING THE RIGHT TO TRIAL BY JURY

WHO CAN DEMAND TRIAL BY JURY?

The federal government has always allowed defendants in criminal cases to have their case heard by juries. In addition, every state constitution provides some type of guarantee that criminal defendants may have their case heard by a jury. But until 1968, it was unclear if persons charged with state crimes had the exact same right to a jury trial as a person charged with a federal crime. For example, some state constitutions only provided for the right to a jury trial in cases where the punishment was death or imprisonment at hard labor for a long period of time. One such state was Louisiana.

The case that firmly established that the Sixth Amendment's guarantee of a jury trial applied to the states was *Duncan v. Louisiana*.[4] *Duncan* involved a young man charged with simple battery. He asked for a jury trial but instead was tried by a judge. The crime carried a possible penalty of up to two years in prison, although young Duncan received a sentence of 60 days. He appealed to the U.S. Supreme Court. The Court wrote that the Sixth Amendment applied to states, too, not just to the federal government. "Our conclusion," wrote the Court, "is that in the American States, as in the federal judicial system, a general grant of jury trial for serious offenses is a fundamental right, essential for preventing miscarriages of justice and for assuring that fair trials are provided for all defendants."[5]

But not every state crime requires a jury trial. Petty, or minor, offenses can be tried before a judge or even a district magistrate or justice of the peace. Generally, if the punishment possible under a criminal law is six months or less in prison, there is no right to a jury trial.[6] If the defendant faces the possibility of more than six months in prison, he or she has the right to demand a jury trial. The choices are: plead guilty, be tried by a judge, or be tried by a jury.

Recently some state legislatures have discussed changing their state constitutions to guarantee the prosecution the right to have criminal cases heard by juries. In *United States v. United States District Court*, the prosecution petitioned for a writ of mandamus to require the U.S. District Court for the Eastern District of California to grant a jury trial in a case involving sexual abuse of children. Michael and Juliette Labrecque of Fort Worth, Texas, and Allen Harrod and Irene Hunt of Sacramento, California, were charged with ten years of ritualistic sexual abuse upon the defendants' five children. The defendants requested a nonjury trial. The district court granted the defendants' request, noting "the heinous and repugnant conduct of the defendants, both charged and uncharged, which will be vividly apparent to the jury from the evidence to be presented, would render it 'impossible or unlikely' that ordinary jurors would be able to dispassionately listen to and consider defendants' more technical arguments." But the Ninth Circuit Court of Appeals reversed the district court's decision, granting the prosecution its jury trial.[7] The court quoted *Singer v. United States,* stating "there is no federally recognized right to a criminal trial before a judge sitting alone,"[8] and noted that granting a defendant a jury trial fulfills his or her constitutional rights. It remains to be seen whether the Supreme Court will agree.

PLEA BARGAINING AND TRIAL BY JURY

As a practical matter, not every criminal defendant gets a jury trial. According to U.S. Courts Federal Judicial Caseload Statistics for the year ending March 31, 2005, in 9 percent of federal cases, charges are dropped. Among defendants sentenced for a federal crime, 95 percent plead guilty, with only 5 percent of defendants in federal courts going to trial before a judge or jury.[9] Of those who go to trial, 87 percent are convicted.

These figures may reflect the prevalence of the practice of plea bargaining. Many courts have crowded dockets, and criminal cases must be moved through the system. Criminal defendants are entitled to a speedy trial (see Chapter 11). Therefore, most courts sanction the practice of plea bargaining. A plea bargain is an agreement between the prosecutor and a criminal defendant that calls for the defendant to plead guilty in exchange for receiving a lighter sentence than he might have received had the case gone to trial or in exchange for a reduction in the type or number of charges.

For example, let's assume that a defendant is charged with 12 counts of forgery. In this example, each count represents one forged check written on a pack of stolen checks. If the defendant were convicted of all 12 counts, he would face the sentence for forgery mutiplied twelvefold. A two- to five-year sentence could become 24 to 60 years. If he chooses a jury trial, he runs the risk of a substantial sentence. If he makes a **plea bargain** (in street parlance, if he "cops a plea"), he may be able to reduce the possibility of a long sentence. Through his attorney, he may agree to plead guilty to one count, and the prosecutor drops the remaining 11 counts. Now his possible sentence is two to five years. What's in this for the prosecutor and the court? For one thing, jury trials are expensive and time-consuming. A jury trial may tie up the court for one week or more; a plea of guilty can take 10 minutes. But perhaps most important, a plea of guilty is final. As long as all the parties fulfill the terms of the plea agreement, the defendant can't appeal his case. Plea bargaining is a common and accepted means of dealing with criminal court backlogs among the members of the legal community. Members of the public frequently criticize the practice as being "easy on crime."

On the federal level, plea bargaining came under attack in 2003, when former U.S. Attorney General John Ashcroft issued a new, more stringent policy for federal prosecutors accepting pleas. At the time more than 90 percent of all criminal cases were resolved by plea bargaining. A tough-on-crime lawyer, Mr. Ashcroft's new policy included the following requirements. First, with only a few, specific exceptions, federal prosecutors must pursue "the most serious readily provable chargeable offense." Second, prosecutors may not "charge bargain" or drop from the most serious provable offense, in accordance with the first requirement, to a lesser charge when negotiating guilty pleas. Instead, the defendant must either plead guilty to the most serious charge or face trial. Finally, at the sentencing stage,

Plea Bargain

In a criminal case, an agreement between the prosecuting attorney and the defendant for the defendant to plead guilty in exchange for some benefit or advantage such as a reduction in the kind or number of charges or a reduced sentence; most criminal cases are settled with some form of a plea bargain.

Ashcroft's policy required federal prosecutors to actively oppose defense requests for "downward departures" from the sentencing range prescribed by the U.S. Sentencing Guidelines, with a few exceptions. For example, it provided for downward departures when the defendant has cooperated with the government's criminal investigation.

The policy essentially forced federal prosecutors to be aggressive in charging and accepting pleas from defendants. One benefit of such a policy is that it brings all prosecutors in line with one another by trimming their personal discretion. It also centralizes control over sentencing by bringing prosecutors throughout the country under a common federal standard, which some considered inappropriate.

At the same time, Ashcroft, backed by a Republican Congress, launched a campaign to pressure federal judges to refrain from downward departures. They published statistics on sentences by judges they felt were granting too many downward departures in an attempt to pressure them into tougher sentencing. Critics felt this was an assault on the independence of the judiciary, a fundamental element of our democracy.[10]

Trial by Judge

A defendant may choose to be tried by a judge rather than by a jury or rather than pleading guilty; when a judge tries a case, he or she decides both the facts and the law.

Petit Jury

A trial jury; in criminal cases, the petit jury determines the facts of the case, applies those facts to the law as given them by the judge, and decides if the state has proven beyond a reasonable doubt that the defendant committed the crime with which he or she was charged. Federal juries consist of 12 jurors; state juries can consist of as few as six jurors.

TRIAL BY JUDGE

Sometimes the defendant and his counsel are unable to reach an agreement that will dispose of the case without trial. That doesn't mean that the case will always be heard by a jury. In a few cases, trial may be by a judge. A defendant may choose **trial by judge** if the case involves facts that might inflame a jury. For example, cases involving child sexual abuse or abuse of elderly citizens may make it difficult for a jury of everyday citizens to be impartial. However, judges have heard it all before. A defendant charged with crimes most jurors would find abhorrent may not want to plead guilty but might want to take a chance on a judge. When a judge hears a case, he or she assumes the role the jury would have fulfilled, by deciding what the facts of the case are and by applying those facts to the law.

Trial by judge has another advantage. Unlike a guilty plea, the decision can be appealed to a higher court.

HOW THE JURY POOL IS SELECTED

GRAND AND PETIT JURIES

There are two types of juries: grand and **petit**. Each has distinct features and functions. One serves as a mechanism for bringing criminal charges, and the other decides whether the accused is guilty as charged or innocent of the charges against him.

A grand jury is a group of people selected to decide whether a prosecutor has enough evidence to charge an individual with a crime. The grand jury hears evidence and decides if the accused should be indicted and tried. If the grand jury finds there is probable cause to believe the defendant committed a crime, he or she is indicted. To find probable cause, the grand jurors must believe that the alleged facts are probably true. A grand jury usually consists of 23 members, thus, the name "grand." The Fifth Amendment to the U.S. Constitution guarantees that no person can be charged with a serious federal crime unless a grand jury authorizes a federal prosecutor to charge him or her.[11] Grand juries may meet over the course of many weeks or months on a complex case. For example, some federal grand jurors are required to meet once per week for one year to hear evidence in one or more cases that a federal prosecutor is investigating.

A petit jury is the trial jury. In a criminal case, the petit jury decides whether the government has proven beyond a reasonable doubt that the accused is guilty of the crime with which he was charged. Essentially, petit juries are fact finders; they decide collectively what the facts are in a case. Petit juries usually consist of 12 or fewer members, thus the term "petit."

Grand juries hear requests for permission to file serious criminal charges from federal prosecutors. Some states also use their own versions of grand juries to bring charges in criminal cases or as investigative bodies. Other states give their district attorneys or attorneys general the authority to bring charges without the use of a grand jury. There is no requirement that states use grand juries to authorize serious criminal prosecutions. For more information on the criminal trial process, see Chapter 1.

HOW JURORS ARE CALLED

The group of people from which a jury is selected is referred to by many names. The group is variously known as the jury pool, array, panel, or **venire**. The pool from which jurors are to be picked is drawn from the local population. The U.S. Constitution requires that jurors be selected from "the State and district wherein the crime shall have been committed" and that "such Trial shall be held in the State where the said Crimes shall have been committed."[12] In other words, the venire members must at the very least come from the state where the crime was committed. This guarantees that a Virginian will not be judged by jurors from Alaska or another distant community whose mores and standards of conduct may differ considerably. For a discussion on change of venue and change of venire, see the discussion later in this chapter.

The jury pool must be varied enough to allow the jury selected from the pool to be a "representative cross section of the community."[13] Selection for a federal jury is governed by the Federal Jury Selection and Service Act of 1968, which requires that both grand juries and petit juries be selected at random from a fair cross section of the community.[14]

States differ in the ways that they select community members to serve on jury duty. Most jurisdictions use a combination of methods to secure jurors for the pool. These include using voter registration lists, tax records, and driver's license records. At Common Law, the sheriff was authorized to conscript jurors from those passing by. States can use any method that does not exclude from selection an identifiable group or class such as women or minorities.

The U.S. Supreme Court has consistently upheld the right of all groups or classes of citizens to serve on juries. For example, in 1998, the Court decided that the apparent systematic exclusion of blacks as grand jury forepersons violated the due process clause of the Fourteenth Amendment. In that case, a white defendant challenged the Louisiana method of choosing the foreperson. The selection was made by the judge, and in the last 20 years, there had never been an African-American selected even though more than 20 percent of the registered voters in the district were African-American. The Court concluded that if the selection "process is infected with racial discrimination, doubt is cast over the fairness of all subsequent decisions."[15] The decision is the latest in a long line of cases that have held African-Americans cannot be excluded from the jury pool because the Fourteenth Amendment prohibits unequal treatment and discrimination on the basis of race. As early

Venire

A group of individuals from the community from whom the petit jury that will hear a criminal case is drawn; also referred to as the jury panel, pool, or array.

Jury service is an exercise in responsible citizenship by all members of the community, including those who might not have the opportunity to contribute to our civic life.
Justice Antonin Kennedy

HISTORICAL HIGHLIGHT
Don't Venture Near the Courthouse;
You May End Up on a Jury!

A little-known power of county sheriffs is the right to literally "pull people off the street" to empanel a jury. This power dates back to medieval England. Modern-day usage is rare, and it often meets with an angry response.

In Pennsylvania, a retrial of a murder case exhausted the pool of potential jurors for that month. The judge ordered the sheriffs to go out in the night and bring in people scheduled for the following month's pool. When they knocked on the door of one of the potential jurors, his wife slammed the door in the sheriff's face. After some persistent knocking and cajoling, the door opened, and the sheriff took the man to court.[17]

A Texas couple was at a grocery store when they observed constables roaming through the parking lot talking to people. When they were approached, they were informed that the night court needed one more juror to try a misdemeanor speeding case, and one of them would have to go. She went and was elected jury foreperson.

The constables reported that not everyone was quite as amiable. Some people had to be shown the writ issued by the judge. Others were simply incredulous that people were being brought in to try a speeding case. When the judge needed a jury for a second case, he suggested sending the constables out "shopping" again. The deputy sheriff spoke with the judge, and it was decided the trial could wait another day.

Dragging in jurors off the streets is one of the long-held powers of local sheriffs. In colonial New England, sheriffs could draft townsmen to help in any emergency, and they could be fined if they refused. Although modern methods of jury pool selection make these sheriffs' surprise visits rare, it might be a good idea to avoid the courthouse area if you have plans for the evening.

as 1880, the Supreme Court ruled that a fair trial demanded that all racial groups be included in the pool of potential jurors and that all groups have the opportunity to serve on juries.[16]

EMPANELING THE JURY

EXCUSING JURORS FOR HARDSHIP

The next step in the jury selection process is excluding potential jurors who can't serve for business, personal, or some other reason. Some jurisdictions allow potential jurors to request exemptions as soon as they receive written notice to appear for jury duty. Others require all jurors to appear before the trial judge to request an exemption.

Common reasons cited by potential jurors include health conditions, running a small business, being the caregiver for young children, farming during planting season or the harvest, and being in a profession that requires long and irregular hours such as medicine. Note that these reasons have nothing to do with the particular case being tried. Jurors excused from service for these personal reasons claim they can't serve on any jury because of competing obligations. Granting every request tends to concentrate those with "free time" on juries, usually the retired, the unemployed, and students. In recent years, judges have grown less tolerant of requests to be excused.[18]

VOIR DIRE

Those accused of committing crimes are entitled to an impartial jury selected from a jury pool that is representative of the community. Note that the actual jury need not be representative of the community, only that the pool from which they are selected is representative. One reason for that is that it is difficult, if not impossible, to find 12 jurors who are impartial and who also mirror the racial, ethnic, sexual, and religious composition of the community for every case.

When the court or attorneys involved in a case question potential jurors about their ability to serve as impartial jurors, the process is called voir dire. Voir dire literally means "to speak the truth." Jurors are asked a series of questions about their ability to decide the case based on what they hear as evidence in the case and not based on what they read in the paper or saw on the six o'clock news. Voir dire also helps weed out those who may be prejudiced against the defendant because of his race, religion, or national origin.

If, during voir dire, attorneys for either the state or the defense find that the answers a juror gives indicates that he or she may not be able to render an impartial verdict, the attorney will ask the trial judge to strike the juror from consideration. This can be done through either a challenge for cause or the use of a peremptory challenge.

> We have a criminal jury system which is superior to any in the world; and its efficiency is only marred by the difficulty of finding twelve men every day who don't know anything and can't read.
> Mark Twain, Fourth of July speech, 1873

HISTORICAL HIGHLIGHT
The Right of Women to Serve on Juries

As a group, women have only recently begun to secure equal rights and privileges on a par with those accorded men. Women saw African-American males given equal protection of the laws long before females were granted the right to vote. It wasn't until 1920 that Congress saw fit to give all citizens a say in choosing their government. The Nineteenth Amendment to the U.S. Constitution provides that "[t]he right of citizens of the United States to vote shall not be denied by the United States or by a State on account of sex." It would be another 55 years before jury service by women was recognized as a fundamental privilege of citizenship. Women's quest for equal political status has met with considerable opposition over the years.

Consider the Equal Rights Amendment. The Equal Rights Amendment would have extended equal rights to women on the same basis as the Fourteenth Amendment did for African-Americans in 1868. It was passed by Congress in 1972, but never ratified by the required 38 states (3/4) to become effective. It expired in 1982, just two states short of ratification. Women have had to rely on state legislatures and the U.S. Congress to provide equal rights in the workplace. Some federal statutes that protect women include the Equal Pay Act, the Civil Rights Act of 1964, and the Pregnancy Discrimination Act. The U.S. Supreme Court's interpretation of the Fourteenth Amendment's equal protection clause has also helped broaden women's rights.

Fifty-five years after women were granted the right to vote, a Sixth Amendment case provided the Supreme Court with an opportunity to address the right of women to fully participate in the nation's political life through jury service. The case was *Taylor v. Louisiana,* 419 U.S. 522 (1975). Ironically, it was a male who secured a woman's right to jury duty. He argued that Louisiana's exclusion of women from petit (trial) juries violated his right to be tried by citizens representing a cross section of the community. Until *Taylor,* female jurors were often the exception rather than the rule. Women's rights to jury service evolved slowly.

In 1789, Congress passed the first law regulating the selection of juries for federal trials. Jurors were to be picked based on the rules in the state where the federal court was located. Since no state allowed women as jurors, federal jurors were also all male. As states added women to the list of eligible jurors, more federal courts also did. The first state to allow women jurors was Utah, in 1898. By mid-century, Congress changed the 1789 law. The Civil Rights Act of 1957 finally allowed women to serve on all federal juries. But many states still excluded women well into the later part of this century.

Taylor involved a male who was charged with kidnaping in a Louisiana state court. At that time, women were called to jury duty only if they asked to serve, while men were simply ordered to serve. The Supreme Court ruled that by systematically excluding a group that made up 53 percent of the population, Louisiana had violated the defendant's right to a jury drawn from a fair cross section of the community.

HISTORICAL HIGHLIGHT
Oklahoma City Jurors Make Excuses

THE SEARCH FOR UNBIASED JURORS

Few events in recent history shocked Americans more than the events of April 19, 1995. At 9:03 AM, as federal workers grabbed the first cup of coffee of the day and children settled into their daily routine at the on-site child care center in the Alfred P. Murrah Federal Building in Oklahoma City, Oklahoma, a powerful explosion shattered the morning calm. Before nightfall, the death toll was staggering.

In all, 168 people were dead, and over 500 more were injured. Like the John F. Kennedy assassination in 1963, the *Challenger* accident in 1986, and September 11, 2001, almost every American old enough to remember vividly recalls where he was and how he felt when the news broke.

How the judicial system found jurors to serve in the Oklahoma City bombing cases is a classic example of how difficult it is to guarantee all criminal defendants a trial by an unbiased jury of peers. Both Timothy McVeigh and Terry Nichols chose trial by jury. Finding willing jurors was a daunting task.

The problem became particularly acute in Terry Nichols' trial after the national publicity McVeigh's conviction and death sentence received. Over 500 potential jurors were summoned to a state fairground for the first round of selection. There they filled out detailed questionnaires about their background, exposure to pretrial publicity, and attitudes. Apparently, many of the potential jurors called for the jury pool concluded that they could avoid jury duty by providing the "wrong" answers on voir dire.

One potential juror announced that she was psychic and heard messages from time to time. Nichols' attorney asked that she be excused even though she had promised to tell the court if she received any messages from the hereafter. His request was granted.

Another juror expressed faith of another kind, in technology. He proclaimed that all he had to do to arrive at the "correct" decision on guilt or innocence was to put the "facts" into his laptop computer, which he conveniently carried with him. The following exchange took place between the potential juror and the court:

THE COURT: Now, you know, this isn't like computers. This isn't like feeding a lot of stuff into a database and pulling it up. This involves human judgment. That's what being on a jury is. Human judgment. That's why we don't have computers deciding cases. There's quite a difference. Do you agree?

A: Maybe we should look into computers. I would agree, yes, sir.

THE COURT: Would you like to be judged by a computer?

A: Depending on the given parameters.

THE COURT: Parameters of judgment as to whether what a witness says is true? Do you think that's a human function, to judge the truth of what another person says?

A: It would be impartial and unbiased.

Another was convinced that Nichols was hiding something because of a particular look in his eyes. She couldn't be persuaded to set aside her belief. She was also removed from the pool.

A jury of seven women and five men was finally chosen. They spent two months together considering the evidence against Nichols before convicting him of conspiracy to bomb the Murrah building and manslaughter in the death of the federal agents killed in the blast. After the verdict, the foreperson received death threats. She explained that if she had it to do over again, she would try to avoid jury duty.[19]

THE CHALLENGE FOR CAUSE

Challenge for Cause

If a juror can't be impartial because he or she knows about the case, knows the defendant's family, knows the victim or any of the people involved in the case, has already made a decision about the defendant's guilt or innocence, or admits to prejudice, he or she can be challenged for cause; there are an unlimited number of challenges for cause available. Any potential juror who can't be impartial can be stricken for cause.

When making a **challenge for cause,** the attorney states his or her reasons for believing that the jury pool member is unable to be an impartial judge of the facts of the case. That belief may be based on the juror's religion, nation of origin, race, gender, or relationship to the defendant, judge, attorneys, or victim in the case. For example, if the potential juror is married to a police officer and the case involves the brutal murder of a police officer, the spouse may not be impartial. The judge in a case may strike as many jurors from consideration for cause as is necessary. That's because every defendant is guaranteed an impartial jury.

THE PEREMPTORY CHALLENGE

A **peremptory challenge** involves striking a juror from consideration as a juror for any reason, or no reason at all. In most courts, only a few peremptory challenges are allowed for each side. Peremptory challenges allow attorneys to help mold a jury into a group each presumes will be inclined to convict or acquit. It was designed, in the words of the Supreme Court, "to eliminate persons thought to be inclined against their interests . . . ."[20] Since no reason needs to be given, an attorney defending someone charged with the rape of a young girl may try to exclude potential jurors with daughters or granddaughters the age of the victim.

A word of caution is due here. The courts have warned attorneys, especially prosecutors, against using peremptory challenges to strike potential jurors of one race or another in order to get a racially pure jury. For example, prosecutors can't strike all black jurors to get an all-white jury or all women to get a male jury. That would be a violation of the juror's Fourteenth Amendment right to equal protection and equal participation in civic life and would taint the perception of the justice system as fair and impartial. It doesn't matter whether the defendant is black or white.[21]

Recently the Supreme Court considered just such a case. In *Miller-El v. Dretke,* a case involving a black defendant who faced death, Texas prosecutors allegedly followed an informal practice of striking potential jurors who were black on the assumption they were less willing to punish a black defendant. The 6–3 decision overturned the death sentence based in part on the fact that prosecutors in the case had used their peremptory strikes to exclude 91 percent of the eligible black venire members and noted "happenstance was unlikely to produce this disparity."

The Court also relied on the Supreme Court's 1986 decision in *Batson v. Kentucky,* which established a three-step process for evaluating whether a particular peremptory challenge violates the defendant's Fourteenth Amendment rights. The steps are as follows:

1. The defendant must make a prima facie case that the peremptory challenge was based on race.
2. If the defendant shows racial bias according to (1), then the prosecutor must offer a race-neutral basis for striking the juror in question.
3. In light of both parties' submissions, the trial court must determine whether the strike was discriminatory.

The Court was also convinced that race had been significant in peremptory strikes of two particular black jurors. Justice Breyer, concurring, wrote that the case "suggested the need to confront the choice between the right of a defendant to have a jury chosen in conformity with the requirements of the Fourteenth Amendment and the right to challenge peremptorily" and suggested it "was necessary to reconsider the Batson test, and the peremptory challenge system as a whole."[22]

In deciding *Batson v. Kentucky*, Supreme Court Justice Thurgood Marshall wrote "the decision today will not end the racial discrimination that peremptories inject into the jury-selection process. That goal can be accomplished only by eliminating peremptory challenges entirely."[23]

HISTORICAL HIGHLIGHT
Shackles Prejudice Jurors

In July 1996, Carman Deck and his sister knocked on the home of an elderly couple, Zelma and James Long, and asked for directions. The Longs invited them in and gave them the directions they had asked for, but instead of leaving, Deck drew a pistol and ordered them to lie face down on their beds. The Longs did so, offering them money and whatever valuables were in the house.

After Deck finished robbing the house, he stood at the edge of the bed, deliberating for ten minutes while they pleaded with him. He shot them each twice in the head. Deck later told police he shot them because he thought they might be able to identify him later.

In 1998, the State of Missouri tried Deck. During the trial, the state required Deck to wear leg braces that were not visible to the jury. Deck was convicted and sentenced to death. The sentence was overturned on appeal.

During the second sentencing proceedings, the state brought Deck into the courtroom shackled with leg irons, handcuffs, and a belly chain. Deck's counsel objected several times to the use of the leg irons during voir dire and moved to strike the jury panel because "the fact that Mr. Deck is shackled in front of the jury . . . makes them think that he is . . . violent today."[24] This time, the jury recommended two death sentences, which the trial court imposed.

Deck appealed, claiming, among other things, that being shackled violated his due process rights. The Supreme Court agreed and overturned his sentence, ruling that visible shackling undermines the presumption of innocence and quoting from "Pleas of the Crown," which provided that a defendant "ought not be brought to the Bar in a contumellious Manner; as with his Hands tied together, or any other Mark of Ignominy and Reproach . . . unless there be some Danger of a Rescous [rescue] or Escape."[25]

Peremptory Challenge

Attorneys are allowed a number of peremptory challenges when selecting jurors; the number varies from court to court. Peremptory challenges are without cause; that is, the attorney making the challenge need not state the reason for eliminating the potential juror. Caution must be used when peremptory challenges follow a pattern that seems race- or gender-based.

DEATH QUALIFYING JURORS

There are special rules for selecting members of a jury who will hear a capital case. A capital case is a case in which the possible penalty is death. A jury that will hear a death penalty case must be *Witherspoon* qualified. The term comes from the Supreme Court case *Witherspoon v. Illinois.*[26] In that case, the Court ruled that members of the jury pool can't be automatically excluded from a jury because they are conscientiously opposed to the death penalty. They must be asked whether they are able to follow the court's instructions on the law and can vote for death if the facts are appropriate. If they answer "yes," they are *Witherspoon* qualified. Similarly, jurors who say they don't have a conscientious objection to the death penalty must assure the court that they won't automatically impose the death penalty.[27] (See Chapter 13 for more information about the death penalty.)

HOW MANY JURORS DOES A JURY MAKE?

In federal criminal cases, a jury must have 12 members. That's been the law of the land since 1898, when the Supreme Court decided *Thompson v. Utah.*[28] *Thompson* involved a livestock thief who was tried twice. Utah was still a federal territory at the time of the first trial. The first jury consisted of 12 men. He won an appeal that gave him a new trial. Meanwhile, Utah became a state. Under Utah's new constitution, he was allowed only eight jurors. When he was again found guilty, he claimed he had been denied his Sixth Amendment rights to a jury of 12.

When the case was heard by the Supreme Court, he argued that the theft happened when Utah was still a territory under the federal government's control. The case was therefore a federal, not a state, matter. The Supreme Court agreed. The Sixth Amendment right to trial by jury was a part of the Common Law as brought to America by the colonists. Since according to English Common Law, a jury contained 12 members, so must a federal jury.

However, criminal trials in state courts can use a lesser number of jurors. In 1970, the Supreme Court held that six jurors were a sufficient number. By the time of the decision in *Williams v. Florida,* the Court concluded that "the fact that the jury at common law was composed of precisely 12 is a historical accident, unnecessary to effect the purposes of the jury system and wholly without significance except to mystics."[29]

Five jurors are too few. That's what the Supreme Court concluded a few years later in *Ballew v. Georgia.*[30] The case involved the Paris Adult Theatre in Atlanta. In 1973, two county investigators saw the film *Behind the Green Door* at the theater. The film was an "adult" picture featuring Marilyn Chambers, a former mainstream model. After getting a warrant, they saw the movie again and then promptly seized it as evidence. The owner was charged with violating the Georgia obscenity laws, which were misdemeanor criminal offenses. Under Georgia law, defendants charged with misdemeanors were entitled to a jury of five. *Ballew* argued that a jury of five couldn't be expected to assess what were the contemporary standards of the community, which is required in order to convict on an obscenity charge. He was convicted and appealed the use of a five-person jury.

The Supreme Court relied on a number of studies on jury deliberations and group dynamics. These studies concluded that as the size of the jury shrinks from twelve to fewer

---

Witherspoon Qualified

A jury in a capital case who have stated they will consider imposing the death penalty even if they are opposed to the death penalty.

For as Christ and his twelve apostles were finally to judge the world, so human tribunals should be composed of the King and twelve wise men.

Credited to Morgan of Gla-Morgan, King of Wales, 725 AD

than six jurors, the dynamics change. In fact, one study cited by the Court found that the likelihood of convicting an innocent person rises as the size of the jury shrinks, while the risk of not convicting a guilty person rises as the size of the jury gets larger. Based upon the studies and the arguments of the attorneys in the case, the Supreme Court held that six is the minimum number of jurors allowed on a criminal petit jury.

PRETRIAL PUBLICITY, CHANGE OF VENUE OR VENIRE, AND SEQUESTRATION

THE MEDIA AND FINDING IMPARTIAL JURORS

As we have learned in this chapter, the U.S. Constitution requires that an impartial jury decide whether the government has proven beyond a reasonable doubt that the defendant is guilty of the crime with which he was charged. A century ago finding a jury that hadn't heard the details about a criminal case was relatively easy. There was no television news, no Internet news reports delivered worldwide in an instant, and no satellite communications. Today the details of crimes are known to millions of people almost as soon as they happen. If you have any doubt about the speed and distance news travels, ask yourself if you would have known the details of the following crimes and news events had you lived in the 1800s:

- The Virginia Tech massacre
- Andrea Yates' drowning her five children in the bathtub
- The kidnapping of Elizabeth Smart from her bedroom
- The Washington Beltway sniper
- The Nickel Mines Amish school shooting

Juries are obligated to judge defendants impartially. Jurors can only consider the evidence presented at trial. They can't consider what they may have learned about the case from newspaper or television reports. The more publicity a case has received before trial, the more likely a potential juror may have prejudged the case. The ideal juror knows absolutely nothing about the defendant, the victim, or the case. But the ideal juror doesn't exist in the age of electronic communications.

The courts have come up with several ways to minimize the impact of pretrial publicity on potential jurors, to judge whether pretrial publicity will affect a juror's ability to be impartial, and to assure that jurors decide the case only on the evidence they hear and see in the courtroom. These methods include change of venue, change of venire, and sequestration.

CHANGE OF VENUE AND VENIRE

Many crimes receive intense media coverage locally, but little mention statewide or nationally. The victim or the accused may be well known in their community, but unknown in other geographic areas. If a defendant claims he or she can't get an impartial jury, the case can be moved to another location for trial if the court agrees. This usually involves trying the case in another county if it is a state case or another federal courthouse in the same judicial district if it's a federal case. For example, the Oklahoma City bombing trials

Venue

The county or judicial district in which a case is tried; in criminal cases, the venue is usually where the crime was committed.

were moved to Denver from Oklahoma City. Moving the case to another geographic area is called a change of **venue**. Depending on the complexity of the case, number of witnesses, and how long the trial will last, a change of venue can be expensive. A request for change of venue is seldom granted.

Another way of finding impartial jurors is through a change of venire. Sometimes the court concludes that impartial local jurors are hard to come by because of extensive pre-trial publicity but doesn't want to require witnesses, prosecutors, and defense attorneys to travel to another location. In that case, the simplest solution may be to bring the jurors in from another location. In other words, the jury pool or venire, is brought in from out of town. This solution may be attractive when trial publicity will be extensive and the court anticipates sequestering the jury anyway. (See the following discussion.)

HISTORICAL HIGHLIGHT
Change of Venue Cannot Change
Scott Peterson's Fate

On April 13, 2002, the body of a male fetus, umbilical cord still attached, washed ashore in San Francisco Bay. The next day, a partial female torso missing its hands, feet, and head washed ashore in the same area. The bodies were later identified as Laci Peterson and her unborn child, Connor. Decomposition made an autopsy difficult, but the medical examiner noted three broken ribs on Laci's body that could not have come from being dragged over the rocks in the bay. An investigation by the FBI and Modesto Police Department pointed to Laci's husband of five years, fertilizer salesman Scott Peterson. The authorities quickly discovered that Peterson had been engaged in an affair with Amber Frey, a massage therapist from Fresno. Frey told the police Peterson had implied that he was a widower, telling her he had "lost his wife" two weeks before Laci's disappearance. Frey became a critical prosecution witness and even let investigators tape conversations with Peterson, which revealed that just days after Laci went missing, Peterson had claimed to be celebrating the holidays in Paris.

Peterson was arrested on April 18, 2003, in La Jolla, California, carrying $15,000 in cash, four cell phones, multiple credit cards belonging to family members, camping equipment, knives, a gun, a map to Frey's workplace, sleeping pills, Viagra, and his brother's driver's license. His hair and beard were bleached blonde, the effect, he said, of chlorine from swimming.

The case was circumstantial, but very convincing. It was also front-page news in Modesto and throughout the country. By his trial date, the hostility toward him in his wife's hometown of Modesto was so high his attorney, Mark Geragos, said his tires were slashed while he visited Peterson in jail. "The extent and intensity of the publicity in this case is of unprecedented proportions in Northern California," Geragos said.[31] In his request for a new venue, Geragos quipped that the prosecution's argument "can be boiled down to the old adage, 'Sure we can give him a fair trial, then we will take him out and hang him.'" Stanislaus County Superior Court Judge Al Girolami agreed. The trial was moved to Redwood City, California.

In the end, the change of venue failed to change Peterson's fate. A jury convicted Peterson of first-degree murder with special circumstances for Laci Peterson's death and second-degree murder for the death of unborn Connor. Peterson's defense filed a request for another change of venue before the sentencing phase of the trial and a change of jurors as well. Judge Alfred A. Delucchi denied the motions saying, "Where could I send this case in the state of California that hasn't been inundated with the media coverage?"

On March 16, 2005, Judge Delucchi sentenced Peterson to death by lethal injection. He denied a defense request for a new trial and ordered Peterson to pay $10,000 toward his wife's funeral. He remains on death row in San Quentin State Prison, which overlooks the bay where Laci's body washed ashore.[32]

SEQUESTRATION

Once a trial starts, jurors are told to disregard anything they hear about the case other than in the courtroom. Jurors are told not to read about the case, not to listen to news reports about the case, and not to discuss the case with anyone until it's time to deliberate. They are also told not to discuss the case among themselves until they retire to the jury room to decide the defendant's fate. Since most trials last only a day or two, jurors generally don't have too much trouble following the court's directions. But in cases heavily covered by the media or that will take a long time to try, it may be impossible to avoid hearing about the case from other sources.

To minimize the possibility of exposure to facts outside the courtroom, juries can be sequestered. **Sequester** means to separate. When jurors are sequestered, they are housed and fed at government expense until the case is over. Usually, sequestered jurors have only very limited contact with their families and are guarded by the local sheriff and deputies. Their mail, telephone calls, and reading materials are censored.

Sequestration is used very rarely because it is expensive and very disruptive. But some jurors have been sequestered for months or longer. For example, the jurors in the O. J. Simpson murder case were sequestered for over one year. For many, sequestration represents a real hardship, both financial and personal. Consider how hard it would be to be away from your family, friends, school, or job for months.

"No, no!" said the Queen, "Sentence first, verdict afterwards."
Lewis Carroll, *Alice in Wonderland,* 1865

Sequester

To separate jurors in order to assure that they will remain impartial during the trial and deliberations.

WHAT PRICE, DUTY? FEES PAID FOR JURY SERVICE NATIONWIDE

Jurisdiction	Juror Fees Per Day	Jurisdiction	Juror Fees Per Day
Federal	$40.00[a]	Missouri	$6.00
Alabama	10.00	Montana	12.00[p]
Alaska	12.50[b,c]	Nebraska	35.00
Arizona	12.00[d]	Nevada	9.00[q]
Arkansas	5.00[e]	New Hampshire	10.00[b]
California	15.00[f]	New Jersey	(r)

(Continued)

Jurisdiction	Juror Fees Per Day	Jurisdiction	Juror Fees Per Day
Colorado	(g)	New Mexico	(s)
Connecticut	(h)	New York	(t)
Delaware	20.00[i]	North Carolina	12.00[u]
District of Columbia	30.00[j]	North Dakota	25.00
Florida	(k)	Ohio	10.00[l,v]
Georgia	5.00[l]	Oklahoma	12.50
Hawaii	30.00	Oregon	10.00
Idaho	10.00[b]	Pennsylvania	(w)
Illinois	4.00[l]	Rhode Island	15.00
Indiana	15.00[m]	South Carolina	10.00
Iowa	10.00	South Dakota	10.00[x]
Kansas	10.00	Tennessee	10.00
Kentucky	12.50	Texas	6.00[l,y]
Louisiana	12.00	Utah	(z)
Maine	10.00	Vermont	30.00
Maryland	15.00[l,n]	Virginia	30.00
Massachusetts	(g)	Washington	10.00[l]
Michigan	7.50[b]	West Virginia	40.00
Minnesota	30.00[o]	Wisconsin	8.00[b,l]
Mississippi	15.00	Wyoming	30.00[aa]

Note: Daily juror fees are set by State statutes and do not include any mileage payments to jurors.

a May be raised to $50.00 per day after 30 days of service upon discretion of the judge.

b Half-day rate.

c Anchorage provides $5.00 half-day rates for the first day, then $12.50 per half-day after the first day.

d No fee for the first day (discretionary); $12.00 per day thereafter.

e $20.00 per day while actually serving (sworn).

f No fee for first day; $15.00 per day thereafter.

g No fee for the first 3 days; $50.00 per day thereafter. Expenses for unemployed available. Employers must pay employees for first 3 days while serving.

h No fee for first 5 days; $50.00 per day thereafter. Expenses for unemployed available. Employers must pay employees for first 5 days while serving.

i No fee for first day; $20.00 per day thereafter.

j No fee for first day; $30.00 per day thereafter.

k If employer pays salary or wages of person on jury duty, there is no fee paid for 3 days; then $30 per day thereafter. If individual is not employed or employer does not pay salary, fee is $15.00 per day for first 3 days; then $30.00 per day thereafter.

l Fees vary among counties.

m $40.00 per day while actually serving (sworn).

n Provided as an expense; not reported as income.

o Child care expenses available

p $25.00 per day while actually serving (sworn).

q $15.00 per day while actually serving (sworn). $30.00 per day after 5 days of service. $9.00 per day if not sworn.

r $5.00 for first 3 days; $40.00 per day thereafter.

s $5.15 per hour, established by minimum wage law.

t If employer has more than 10 employees, must pay at least $40.00 per day for the first 3 days. After 3 days, the court must pay $40.00 per day. If juror is not employed or if employer has less than 10 employees, then court must pay $40.00 per day from day 1.

u $30.00 per day after 5 days of service.

v County commission shall fix the compensation not to exceed $40.00. After 10 days of actual service, compensation to be one and a half times the daily rate—minimum of $15.00. Maximum may be set by county not to exceed twice the daily rate for service of less than 10 days.

w $9.00 for first 3 days; $25.00 per day thereafter.

x $50.00 maximum per day while actually serving (sworn).

y $30.00 maximum per day while actually serving (sworn).

z 18.50 for first day; $49.00 per day thereafter.

aa May be raised to $50.00 per day after 4 days of service upon discretion of the judge.

Source: Sourcebook of Criminal Justice Statistics.

YOU MAKE THE CALL

SHOULD JURORS BE ALLOWED TO CASH IN ON VERDICTS?

On June 13, 2005, a California jury acquitted entertainer Michael Jackson of charges of lewd conduct with a child younger than 14, administering alcohol to facilitate child molestation, conspiracy to commit child abduction, and related child abuse charges. Fans inside and outside the courtroom cheered and wept as the verdicts were read: not guilty of all charges. After the verdicts, the judge read a statement from the jury, which said "We the jury feel the weight of the world's eyes upon us," and asked that they be allowed to return to their "private lives as anonymously as we came."[33]

On August 8, 2005, less than two months after the trial ended, two of the jurors, Eleanor Cook and Ray Hultman, made the startling announcements that they regretted the verdicts. As it turned out, each was promoting a book on the subject, Cook's entitled *Guilty as Sin, Free as a Bird* and Hultman's entitled *The Deliberator*. They were also working together on a combined made-for-television movie.[34]

Being called to jury duty on a high-profile or celebrity case, in our media-saturated culture, has become a ticket to celebrity, in a practice that's perfectly legal, but that many consider perfectly hazardous to the system of justice. Consider that in the Michael Jackson case, the media was speculating before the verdicts ever came in that the first juror to write a book following the case could expect to earn at least $1 million, especially if the verdict were guilty.

That's the real hazard of the practice. Critics warn that jurors, dreaming of seven-figure book deals, might lean toward the verdict with the greatest personal profit potential. The profit potential might also make would-be jurors deliberately give answers during voir dire that they think will land them a spot in the jury box.

In California, Penal Code Section 1122 states "after the jury has been sworn and before the people's opening address, the court shall instruct the jury . . . that prior to, and within 90 days of, discharge, they shall not request, accept, agree to accept, or discuss with any person receiving or accepting, any payment or benefit in consideration for supplying any information concerning the trial."[35] Clearly Cook and Hultman were in violation of the California Penal Code. Could their puzzling about-face have anything to do with the fact that it injected a feeling of controversy into what was otherwise a rather bland story? Michael Jackson, innocent and set free, is perhaps not as exciting a story as Jackson, child molester, set free to molest again due to a dreadful miscarriage of justice.

Most states have similar statutes limiting, but not outlawing, jury book and movie deals. California's Penal Code goes on to state in Section 1122.5 that "the Legislature recognizes that the appearance of justice, and justice itself, may be undermined by any juror who, prior to discharge, accepts, agrees to accept, or benefits from valuable consideration for providing information concerning a criminal trial." Should jurors be forbidden to write about their experience? You make the call.

RENDERING THE VERDICT BEYOND A REASONABLE DOUBT

WHAT IS REASONABLE DOUBT?

Chapter 1 covered the essential differences between civil law and criminal law. One of those differences is the burden of proof that the prosecutor or the plaintiff must meet in order to prevail. Recall that in a civil case, the plaintiff must prove his or her case by a preponderance of the evidence. In a criminal case, the burden of proof is considerably higher. The state must prove that the defendant is guilty of a crime beyond a reasonable doubt. If the legal scales of justice must tip ever so slightly in favor of the plaintiff in a civil case, in a criminal case they must tip heavily in favor of guilt.

HISTORICAL HIGHLIGHT
Can the Prosecution Put Away Two Different People for the Same Crime?

On May 14, 1984, John David Stumpf, Clyde Daniel Wesley, and a companion were traveling along Interstate 70 through Guernsey County, Ohio. Needing gas money, the men stopped the car along the highway. Stumpf and Wesley knocked on the door of Norman and Mary Jane Stout and asked to use the telephone. Once inside, Stumpf held the pair at gunpoint while Wesley ransacked the house. When Norman Stout made a move toward Stumpf, he shot him twice in the head. Mr. Stout fell unconscious and revived in time to hear the four gunshots that killed his wife.

The third man was arrested shortly after the shooting and implicated Stumpf and Wesley. Stumpf denied any knowledge of the crime until he learned that Norman Stout had survived. He then admitted shooting Mr. Stout but said Wesley had shot Mrs. Stout. Stumpf was charged with aggravated murder, attempted aggravated murder, aggravated robbery, and two counts of grand theft. Three of the statutory specifications of the aggravated murder charge made Stumpf eligible for the death penalty.

Stumpf accepted a plea agreement. He pled guilty to aggravated murder and attempted aggravated murder, with the other charges being dropped. In the aggravated murder charge, the prosecution dropped two of the three capital specifications. The third specification meant Stumpf was still eligible for the death penalty.

Pleading mitigating circumstances before a three-judge panel, Stumpf argued that he had participated only at the urging of Wesley and that Wesley had fired the fatal shots at Mrs. Stout. Stumpf hoped this would spare him the death penalty. However, the prosecution argued that Stumpf had indeed shot Mrs. Stout. The prosecution also noted that Ohio law does not restrict the death penalty to those who commit murder by their own hands—an accomplice to murder could also receive it. The three-judge panel found that Stumpf "was the principle offender" in the murder and sentenced Stumpf to death.

Afterward, Wesley was extradited to Ohio for a jury trial before the same prosecutor and one of the same judges who had convicted Stumpf. The prosecution had new evidence. Wesley's cellmate testified that Wesley had admitted firing the shots that killed Mrs. Stout. The prosecution argued that Wesley was the principle offender in Mrs. Stout's murder. During the trial, the defense noted that the prosecutor had taken a contrary stance in Stumpf's trial and that Stumpf had already been sentenced to death for the crime. Wesley was sentenced to life imprisonment with the possibility of parole.

Stumpf, with an appeal pending in the Ohio Court of Appeals, returned to the Court of Common pleas with a motion to withdraw his guilty plea or vacate his death sentence, arguing that the state's case against Wesley had cast doubt on his own conviction and sentence. The Court of Common Pleas rejected his motion. However, the U.S. Court of Appeals for the Sixth Circuit reversed, concluding that habeas corpus relief was warranted because Stumpf's plea appeared ill informed; the court believed Stumpf did not understand that he was pleading to intentionally murdering Mrs. Stout. Second, the appellate court found that "Stumpf's due process rights were violated by the state's deliberate action in securing convictions of both Stumpf and Wesley for the same crime, using inconsistent theories."[36]

The U.S. Supreme Court reinstated Stumpf's guilty plea, ruling "a plea's validity may not be collaterally attacked merely because the defendant made what turned out, in retrospect, to be a poor deal." The Court also ruled that Stumpf's conviction of aggravated murder was valid, despite the prosecution's conflicting arguments about which of the two men, Wesley or Stumpf, had shot Mrs. Stout, noting "the precise identity of the triggerman was immaterial to Stumpf's conviction for aggravated murder."

However, the court did rule that the prosecution's conflicting theories may have more directly affected Stumpf's sentence and remanded the death sentence for further consideration. The Supreme Court noted in its ruling that Stumpf's case raised the legitimate question of "whether a death sentence could be allowed to stand when the sentence had been imposed in response to a factual claim that the prosecution had necessarily contradicted in subsequently arguing for a death sentence in the case of a codefendant."[37]

When a jury hears a criminal case, the jury must decide if there is enough evidence to prove beyond a reasonable doubt that a crime was committed and the defendant did it. The court defines reasonable doubt for the jury before it begins deliberations. Reasonable doubt is perhaps best defined by what it is not. It is not without any doubt. If that were the case, few convictions would be possible. Jurors are only required to decide that they are convinced that the defendant did it. Reasonable doubt is somewhere between more likely than not that the defendant did it and absolute certainty that he did. A reasonable doubt is a fair doubt based upon common sense.

Jury Instructions

The directions the judge gives jurors about how they are to come to a verdict; jury instructions typically include an explanation of the law and what must be proven to convict the defendant.

Juries are told before they begin deliberation that their function is to decide what the facts are and then to apply the law to those facts. These are the **jury instructions**. The court tells the jury what the law is. Juries are also told that they must apply the law as it is, even if they think it's an unjust, unfair, or stupid law. In other words, the jury only decides the facts, not what is the law. However, there have been many cases where juries have seemingly ignored the law and refused to convict a defendant. This is referred to as jury nullification.

Recent rulings have indicated increasing intolerance of jury nullification among judges. In 1997, in *U.S. v. Thomas*, the Second Circuit ruled that jurors can be removed if there is evidence that they intend to nullify the law. The California Supreme Court took a further step in *People v. Williams*, a statutory rape case. On the first day of jury deliberations, the foreperson informed the judge that one of the jurors refused to follow instructions because he believed the law was wrong. The judge replaced the juror. The defendant appealed, arguing that jury nullification is acceptable. The California Supreme Court unanimously upheld the conviction. Chief Justice Ronald M. George wrote: "A nullifying jury is essentially a lawless jury."[38] The ruling led to a new jury instruction that requires jurors to inform the judge whenever a fellow panelist appears to be deciding a case based on his or her dislike of the law.

JURY UNANIMITY, HUNG JURIES, AND REASONABLE DOUBT

In federal criminal trials, the jury must reach a unanimous decision. That is, all 12 jurors must agree that the defendant is guilty beyond a reasonable doubt. But just as state criminal juries don't need to have more than six jurors, neither do state juries have to reach a unanimous verdict. The U.S. Supreme Court has upheld a state law that required only 9 out of 12 jurors to agree on conviction or acquittal.[39] The fewer members there are on a jury, the more likely it is that the members must make a unanimous decision. In 1979, the Supreme Court ruled that juries of six (the smallest criminal jury allowed) must reach a unanimous decision.[40]

Most states do require a unanimous jury decision. In those states, if all jurors don't agree on the defendant's guilt or acquittal, the jury is said to be a hung jury. A defendant can be retried if the jury is unable to convict or acquit him or her. (See Chapter 10 for a discussion of why a retrial isn't double jeopardy.)

THE ROLE OF THE JURY AND THE ROLE OF THE JUDGE

It is important to understand how the responsibilities of the judge differ from the responsibilities of the juror, since their roles are distinctly separate. The judge is charged with the task of interpreting and determining what is law. The jury is given the role of finding the facts in a case.

The Supreme Court ruling in *Apprendi v. New Jersey*[41] illustrates this distinction. Early on December 22, 1994, Charles Apprendi Jr. fired several shots into the home of an African-American family. He pled guilty to second-degree possession of a firearm for an unlawful purpose, which carries a prison term of 5 to 10 years. During the sentencing phase of this case, the prosecution presented evidence to the judge that Apprendi's crime

HISTORICAL HIGHLIGHT
William Penn and Jury Nullification

One of the most famous jury trials in history involved William Penn, the founder of the Colony of Pennsylvania. William Penn was a Quaker at a time when England was intolerant of religious beliefs other than the Church of England's. Quakers were seen as dangerous radicals. Their religious services, held in "meeting houses," were closed by the government. They were forbidden to meet or to preach in the streets. In 1670, William Penn and a fellow Quaker, William Mead, defied the king of England and were arrested. They were accused of trying to incite a riot.

A jury of 12 men was selected to hear the case. Four of the 12 refused to find Penn and Mead guilty. The judge ordered them all to continue deliberating until they reached the proper and correct verdict. What happened next illustrates the idea of jury nullification. Jurors are generally told by the judge before they begin deliberations that they must follow the law. For example, jurors are instructed that they cannot refuse to find a defendant guilty because they believe the law they are applying to the facts is an unjust or immoral law. **Jury nullification** occurs when a jury deliberately ignores the court's instructions to apply the law, however unjust, to the facts.

In William Penn's case, the jurors were denied food, drink, and tobacco until they reconsidered. After a few days, the 12 jurors united. Now the vote was unanimous. Penn and Mead were not guilty! The judge finally accepted their verdict but jailed the jurors for rendering an improper verdict. They won on appeal. The case helped establish the sanctity of jury verdicts, even when that verdict seems contrary to law or common sense. A jury has the last word since defendants can't be tried again. A second trial would be double jeopardy.

Jury Nullification
A decision by a jury to ignore the law or the judge's instructions when deliberating; for example, jurors who believe the law is unjust may refuse to convict the defendant even if it is clear that he broke the law.

had been racially motivated, including Apprendi's confessing to police shortly after the shooting that he didn't want the family in his neighborhood because of their race. Under New Jersey law, a judge was given the ability to increase the maximum sentence for a crime motivated by racial biases. The judge sentenced Apprendi to 12 years, two more than the maximum for the weapons crime of which he was convicted. The Supreme Court overturned the sentence, ruling that "the Constitution requires that any fact that increases the penalty for a crime beyond the prescribed statutory maximum, other than the fact of a prior conviction, must be submitted to a jury and proved beyond a reasonable doubt."

In *Ring v. Arizona,*[42] the Supreme Court affirmed their previous decision in *Apprendi*. Timothy Stuart Ring had been convicted of felony murder, which had taken place in the course of an armed robbery. After being convicted by a jury, the judge held a separate sentencing hearing and reviewed evidence of aggravating circumstances.[43] The judge then increased Ring's possible maximum sentence, giving him the death penalty. Upon appeal, the Supreme Court ruled that allowing a judge to determine aggravating circumstances, which would increase the defendant's possible sentence beyond the maximum, would violate the defendant's Sixth Amendment right to a jury trial. However, the Court refused to apply the rule in *Ring* retroactively to others on death row sentenced under the procedure the Court found deficient in its earlier decision.[44]

PRACTICE POINTERS

Defendants who have concluded it is not in their best interest to plead guilty should be counseled in what lies ahead—whether they will be best off with trial by judge or trial by jury. That means the defense team will have to weigh factors such as pretrial publicity, the facts of the case and their potential emotional impact on jurors, and the record of the judge if trial by judge is a possibility.

Choosing a jury may be one of the most important decisions in a criminal trial. That's one reason both the prosecution and the defense team members need to take the matter seriously, especially if the case is a capital one. If there are the financial means to do so, the defense team may want to consider hiring a jury consultant who can advise on what makes a good defense jury. If not, the defense team will have to diligently review the juror questionnaires and compose appropriate questions to ferret out bias, prejudice, or other factors that can negatively impact the outcome and verdict.

Defendants should also be coached on how to look and act before a jury. That's especially true if the defendant plans to take the stand. Defendants should dress respectfully and may need help selecting appropriate clothing. They should also be advised on proper courtroom etiquette and behavior as well as demeanor.

CHAPTER SUMMARY

Juries are an old legal tradition going back at least to the ancient Greeks. In England, the jury traces its roots to the time of Henry II and King John. When King John signed the Magna Carta in 1215, he agreed that his subjects would be judged by their peers and the law of the land rather than simply by royal command. The jury grew to be an important buffer between the people and the will of the government.

The colonists took English Common Law with them when they colonized North America. One of these traditions was the right to trial by jury. Every state constitution contains a provision for trial by jury. The U.S. Constitution guarantees the right to trial by jury in federal criminal cases in Article III and in the Sixth Amendment. This protection also extends to the states through the Fourteenth Amendment. In every criminal case where the defendant faces the possibility of imprisonment for more than six months, he or she is guaranteed a trial by jury.

The right to request trial by jury rests with the accused. When charged with a crime, a defendant faces several choices. He or she can demand a trial by jury, plead guilty, or request a trial by judge. Few cases are actually tried by juries. Most defendants plead guilty, usually after making a plea bargain. Plea bargains are agreements between the government and the defendant that usually involve a reduction in the kind or number of charges or the length of the sentence in exchange for a plea of guilty. One advantage of plea bargaining is finality. A defendant who voluntarily pleads guilty can't appeal his conviction to a higher court. Another advantage is cost. Jury trials are very expensive, especially if the members of the jury have to be sequestered.

There are two types of juries: petit and grand. A grand jury hears evidence and decides if there is enough evidence to charge someone with a crime. A grand jury may have 23 members. A petit jury is a trial jury. It usually has 12 members, but some states allow petit juries to have as few as six members. A petit jury actually hears the criminal case and decides if the defendant is guilty beyond a reasonable doubt.

The group from which a petit jury is selected is known as the jury pool, array, panel, or venire. The members of the pool must be selected in a way that creates a pool that is representative of the community where the defendant allegedly committed the crime. Therefore, methods of calling potential jurors that eliminate segments of the community from the pool are illegal. Many jurisdictions use methods to locate jurors that are race, sex, color, and national origin blind. Some common techniques are to use voter registration records, tax records, license records, and the like in order to create a representative jury pool.

Defendants are guaranteed that the jury pool is representative of the community but have no constitutional right to a jury that is representative of the community. That is, it's enough that the jury pool is representative, but the actual jury picked doesn't have to mirror the community. Attorneys must be careful in how they exclude potential members of the jury. For example, a prosecutor can't strike all African-Americans from the jury through the use of his or her peremptory strikes.

Jurors can be removed from the jury pool for hardship, for cause, or through the use of a peremptory strike. Courts sometimes excuse jurors for hardships such as illness, financial need, family obligations, and business obligations. Courts will eliminate jurors for cause if there is a reason that the juror can't be impartial. Reasons include being acquainted with the parties or victim, having independent knowledge of the case or the evidence, and having prejudged the defendant's guilt or innocence. In contrast, peremptory challenges are challenges for which the attorneys don't have to provide a specific reason. Most courts limit the number of peremptory challenges. Challenges for cause are unlimited in number. A process called voir dire is used to select those potential jurors who will serve. During voir dire, potential jurors are asked questions by the court or the attorneys that are intended to identify jurors who can't be impartial.

In federal criminal cases, the jury must have 12 members, and the jury must reach a unanimous verdict. In some state courts, the jury may have as few as six members. In addition, state juries don't have to make unanimous decisions unless the jury has only six members.

Defendants are guaranteed an impartial jury. Pretrial publicity can make it difficult to find jurors who haven't prejudged the case. If the publicity has been intense, the court may change the venue, or move the case to another geographic location. Another solution is to bring in a jury pool from another location. This is a change of venire. To prevent jurors from receiving outside information about the case, the court can also sequester the jury away until the case is over.

Juries are obligated to convict a defendant when they conclude that he or she is guilty beyond a reasonable doubt. Beyond a reasonable doubt is a heavy burden but doesn't require that the jury be absolutely certain that the defendant did it.

KEY TERMS

Challenge for Cause	Petit Jury	Trial by Ordeal
Jury	Plea Bargain	Venire
Jury Instructions	Sequester	Venue
Jury Nullification	Sixth Amendment	*Witherspoon* Qualified
Magna Carta	Trial by Battle	
Peremptory Challenge	Trial by Judge	

EXERCISE

1. Review the juror questionnaire used in the Scott Peterson case (reproduced in the chapter Appendix). Do you think the questions helped screen out potential jurors who knew too much about the case? Are there any additional questions you would have liked to see asked?

DISCUSSION QUESTIONS

1. What are the provisions in the U.S. Constitution that require trial by jury in criminal cases?
2. How are the members of a jury pool selected?
3. What information would you like to get from a potential juror during voir dire?
4. What are some reasons a potential juror can be excused for cause?
5. What are the advantages and disadvantages of sequestration for the prosecution? The defense?
6. Why would a defense attorney want a change of venue or change of venire?
7. Explain what "beyond a reasonable doubt" means.
8. List and explain some differences between federal juries and state juries.

FOR FURTHER READING AND VIEWING

READING

1. Grisham, J (1996). *The Runaway Jury.* Century Books, LTD.
   Legal thriller recounting what happens when a man with a vendetta wants to be on a jury to hear a landmark tobacco liability case.

VIEWING

1. *To Kill a Mockingbird.* (1962).
   Adaptation of the novel by Harper Lee. A small-town lawyer in the South defends a black man accused of raping a white woman; starring Gregory Peck.

2. *My Cousin Vinny.* (1992).

New York lawyer goes to Wahzoo, Alabama, to defend his cousin and his friend on murder charges; starring Marisa Tomei and Joe Pesci.

3. *Inherit the Wind.* (1960).

Midwestern school teacher is put on trial for teaching Darwin's theory of evolution; starring Gene Kelly, Dick York, and Spencer Tracey.

4. *Class Action.* (1991).

Father and daughter, both lawyers, serve on opposite sides of a case; starring Gene Hackman.

5. *Judgment at Nuremberg.* (1961).

Four German judges are put on trial for compromising their integrity for the Nazis; starring Judy Garland, Montgomery Clift, Marlene Dietrich, Burt Lancaster, Spencer Tracey, and Maximilian Schell.

6. *The Verdict.* (1982).

A drunkard attorney sobers up long enough to seek justice for comatose victim of a hospital's carelessness; starring Paul Newman.

7. *Twelve Angry Men.* (1957).

A courtroom drama in which one jury member holds out against the rest of the jury's desire for a quick conviction; starring Henry Fonda and Jack Klugman. If you see no other film on the jury system, see this one.

8. *The Runaway Jury.* (2003).

John Cusack stars in this adaptation of the Grisham book. The movie version changes the case from one about tobacco to one about guns.

ENDNOTES

1. W. Blackstone, *Commentaries on the Laws of England,* Cooley, ed., (1899).

2. V. P. Hans and L. Vidmar, *Judging the Jury* (New York: Plenum Press, 1986).

3. R. Perry, ed., *Sources of Our Liberties* (1959).

4. *Duncan v. Louisiana,* 391 U.S. 145 (1968).

5. Ibid.

6. *Blanton v. North Las Vegas,* 489 U.S. 538 (1989).

7. *United States v. United States District Court,* No. 06-72498, D.C. No. CR-03-00384-WBS, Opinion (2006).

8. *Singer v. United States,* 380 U.S. 25–26 (1965).

9. "U.S. District Courts—Criminal Defendants Disposed of, by Type of Disposition and Major Offense (excluding Transfers), During the 12-Month Period Ending March 31, 2006," U.S. Courts Federal Judicial Caseload Statistics, *www.uscourts.gov,* March 31, 2006.

10. "Attorney General Ashcroft's New Charging, Plea Bargaining, and Sentencing Policies: Though Consideration Is Needed, Criticism Has Been Overstated," former federal prosecutor Edward Lazarus, Esq., *FindLaw Legal News and Commentary,* October 2, 2003.

11. U.S. Constitution, Fifth Amendment.

12. U.S. Constitution, Sixth Amendment and U.S. Constitution, Article 3.

13. *Taylor v. Louisiana,* 419 U.S. 522 (1975).

14. Federal Jury Selection and Service Act of 1968, 28 U.S.C. § 1861.

15. *Campbell v. Louisiana,* 523 U.S. 392 (1998).

16. *Strauder v. West Virginia,* 100 U.S. 303 (1880).

17. As recounted by the author's husband, who served on the sequestered jury; the gentleman in question became an alternate juror.

18. However, the author would welcome the opportunity to serve on a jury. She was once sent a selection notice that asked for her occupation, and she responded that she was a Pennsylvania licensed attorney who had served as an assistant attorney in another county at the beginning of her career. She was never called for the jury pool. Recently, she received another selection notice. This time she put her occupation as "writer." To her surprise and delight, she was called shortly after—for an 18-month investigative grand jury. She was selected despite revealing that she is the author of this textbook and a former prosecutor. But before the first official session, she received a note informing her that her services were not needed.

19. *Holland v. Illinois,* 493 U.S. 473 (1990).

20. *Powers v. Ohio,* 499 U.S. 400 (1991).

21. *Miller-El v. Dretke,* 545 U.S. 231 (2005).

22. *Batson v. Kentucky,* 476 U.S. 79 (1986).

23. *Carman L. Deck v. Missouri,* 544 U.S. 622 (2005).

24. *Deck v. Missouri,* quoting 2 W. Hawkins, Pleas of the Crown, Ch. 28, § 1, p. 308 (1716–1721), section on arraignments.

25. *Witherspoon v. Illinois,* 391 U.S. 510 (1968).

26. *Morgan v. Illinois,* 504 U.S. 719 (1992).

27. *Thompson v. Utah,* 170 U.S. 343 (1898).

28. *Williams v. Florida,* 399 U.S. 78 (1970).

29. *Ballew v. Georgia,* 435 U.S. 223 (1978).

30. "Change of Venue Sought in Trial of Scott Peterson," Cable News Network, *www.CNN.com,* December 15, 2003.

31. *People of the State of California v. Scott Lee Peterson,* Case No. 1056770 (2003).

32. "Jackson Not Guilty," Cable News Network, *www.CNN.com,* June 13, 2005.

33. "2 Jurors Say They Regret Jackson's Acquittal," Associated Press, August 9, 2005.

34. California Penal Code § 1122.

35. *Stumpf v. Mitchell,* 367 F.3d 594, 596 (2004).

36. *Warden v. Stumpf,* 545 U.S. 175 (2005).

37. *People v. Williams,* 01 C.D.O.S. 3577 (2001).

38. *Johnson v. Louisiana,* 406 U.S. 356 (1972) and *Apodaca v. Oregon,* 406 U.S. 404 (1972).

39. *Burch v. Louisiana,* 441 U.S. 130 (1979).

41. *Apprendi v. New Jersey,* 530 U.S. 466 (2000).

42. *Ring v. Arizona,* 122 S. Ct. 2428 (2002).

43. An aggravating circumstance is a fact in a case that may make sentencing more severe. Examples of aggravating circumstances may include the commission of a crime in conjunction with another crime, murder in the course of an armed robbery, past criminal record, or likelihood to present future danger to society.

44. *Schriro v. Summerlin,* 124 S. Ct. 2519 (2004).

APPENDIX

JUROR ID: _____

JUROR QUESTIONNAIRE

TO ALL PROSPECTIVE JURORS:

The process of jury selection will take place in two stages. The first stage will be the completion of this questionnaire. The second stage will consist of a period of question and answer which will be conducted in person. The use of this questionnaire in the first stage will shorten the process of jury selection. <u>YOUR WRITTEN RESPONSES ARE NOT CONFIDENTIAL BECAUSE THE QUESTIONNAIRES ARE PUBLIC RECORDS</u>.

When answering these questions, please keep in mind that you are sworn to tell the truth and that your answers are given under penalty of perjury. It is important that you answer the questions as completely and as honestly as possible. This will reduce the time necessary for questioning in court. You will be given an opportunity to further explain and clarify your answers when being questioned by the lawyers. If you do not understand a question, please so indicate on your questionnaire.

It is extremely important that your answers be your own. You must personally fill out the questionnaire without discussing the questions or your answers with any other person.

Please do not speculate about the evidence to be presented in this case based on any question or set of questions contained in this questionnaire. If you are selected to serve, you will be given all of the facts during the trial.

Thank you for your cooperation.

PLEASE NOTE THAT THERE IS A BLANK PAGE AT THE END OF THIS QUESTIONNAIRE THAT WELL GIVE YOU ROOM TO FULLY ANSWER ALL QUESTIONS ASKED BELOW. PLEASE RECALL THAT IF YOU REQUEST CONFIDENTIALITY AS TO ANY ANSWER, YOU MUST SO INDICATE.

1. Juror Number: _____

2. Gender: _____ Male _____ Female

3. Age: _____

4. Place of birth: _____

5. Where did you grow up (City, State, Country)? _____

6. Race or ethnic background you most identify with: (Check one)

_____ African American   _____ Native American
_____ Caucasian   _____ Asian (specify: _____)
_____ Pacific Islander   _____ Hispanic (specify: _____)
_____ Other (specify: _____)

7. Where were your parents born? (City, State, Country)

Father: _____

Mother: _____

8. If they were not born in the United States, when did they come to this country?

Mother: _____   Father: _____

9. Do you have a religious preference? _____ YES _____ NO

If yes, please name: _____

Are you active? _____

10. Would your religious or philosophical beliefs interfere with your ability to serve as a juror in this case? _____ YES _____ NO

If yes, please explain: _____

_____

11. In terms of your religious beliefs, do you think of yourself as:

_____ Very religious   _____ Somewhat religious
_____ Moderately religious   _____ Not very religious
_____ Not religious at all

RESIDENCE

12. How long have you lived in San Mateo County? _____ In California? _____

13. What is your current <u>area</u> (i.e. city) of residence?

_____

14. How long have you lived at your current residence? _____

15. Do you: _____ own _____ rent _____ neither (Check one)

FAMILY

16. Marital Status:

_____ Single   _____ Married
_____ Separated   _____ Divorced
_____ Widowed   _____ Living with significant other

How many times have you been married? _____

How many times have you been divorced? _____

17. If married, how long have you been married? _____

If living with a significant other, how long have you lived with this person?

_____

18. If married or living with another person, what is your spouse's or significant other's job or occupation? _____

   a) Job Description _____

   b) Educations Background _____

19. If he or she is retired or unemployed, what was his or her occupation before retiring or being unemployed?

   _____

20. If previously married, what was your former spouse's occupation: _____

21. Do you have children?

   _____ Yes, and at least one lives at home
   _____ Yes, but none live at home
   _____ No

22. Please list the age, sex, occupation (or area of study), and marital status of each of your children or stepchildren:

Age	Male/Female	Occupation (or area of study)	Marital Status
____	_____	_____	_____
____	_____	_____	_____
____	_____	_____	_____
____	_____	_____	_____
____	_____	_____	_____

23. Have you or any relative or close friend ever lost a child? (Miscarriage, accident, crime, etc.)

   ___ YES ___ NO

24. What are/were your parents' occupations? _____

   _____

25. If anyone else is living in your home, what is their <u>relationship</u> to you, <u>age</u> and <u>occupation</u>?

   _____

   _____

   _____

26. Do you have any opinions about people involved in extramarital affairs?

   _____ YES _____ NO

   If yes, please explain _____

   _____

EDUCATION

27. What is your highest level of education completed?

   _____ Less Than High School   _____ Tech School Degree
   _____ Some High School   _____ College Degree
   _____ High School Degree   _____ Some Graduate School
   _____ Some College or Tech School   _____ Post-Graduate Degree

   Please list all degrees, certificates, licenses, and major areas of study, telling when and from what institution _____

   _____

28. Have you ever studied or received training in medicine, psychology, psychiatry, social work, sociology, or counseling?

   _____ YES _____ NO

   If yes, please explain _____

   _____

29. Do you have any friends who are physicians, psychiatrists or psychologists? ____ YES ____ NO

30. If yes, do you discuss their work with them? _____ YES _____ NO

31. Have you received any training in law, law enforcement or criminology? _____ YES _____ NO

    If yes, please explain. _____

    _____

32. Have you ever had any training, education or jobs or have you ever done any volunteer work in any of the following areas? (Check each one that applies to you.)

    _____ Banking/Finance   _____ Correctional/Jail/Prison   _____ Counseling
    _____ Drugs/alcohol   _____ Firearms/Guns   _____ Forensic Science
    _____ Genetics/DNA   _____ Handwriting analysis   _____ Investigations
    _____ Justice systems/courts   _____ Laboratory   _____ Law
    _____ Medicine/nursing   _____ Local/state government   _____ Police procedures
    _____ Mental Health   _____ Pathology   _____ Law enforcement
    _____ Psychology   _____ Science or biology   _____ Security
    _____ Telecommunications   _____ TV/radio   _____ Statistics
    _____ Victims of crimes

    If YES to any of these, please explain: _____

    _____

33. Are you related to or close friends with anyone who works or has special training in any of the following areas? Check each one that applies to them.

    _____ Banking/Finance   _____ Correctional/Jail/Prison   _____ Forensic Science
    _____ Drugs/alcohol   _____ Firearms/Guns   _____ Investigations
    _____ Genetics/DNA   _____ Handwriting analysis   _____ Law
    _____ Justice systems/courts   _____ Laboratory   _____ Police procedures
    _____ Medicine/nursing   _____ Local/state government   _____ Law enforcement
    _____ Mental Health   _____ Pathology   _____ Security
    _____ Psychology   _____ Science or biology   _____ Statistics
    _____ Telecommunications   _____ TV/radio
    _____ Victims of crimes   _____ Counseling

    If YES to any of these, please explain: _____

    _____

34. Do you have further education plans for the future? _____ YES _____ NO
    If YES, please explain: _____

EMPLOYMENT

35. What is your present job or occupation? _____

    _____ Full Time   _____ Part Time
    _____ Unemployed   _____ Disabled
    _____ Retired   _____ Homemaker
    _____ Student

    If you are retired, what was your last job or occupation? _____

    _____

    If you are currently unemployed, what is your customary work? _____

    _____

36. By whom are/were you last employed? _____

    Length of employment: _____

37. What are/were your duties and responsibilities? _____

    _____

    _____

38. How long have you worked at your present employment or last employment? _____

    _____

39. Do/did you supervise others? _____ YES _____ NO

    If so, how many? _____

40. How do/did you feel about supervising others? _____

    _____

41. Do/did you make policy decisions? _____ YES _____ NO

    If yes, how do you feel about this responsibility? _____

    _____

42. Do/did you have authority to hire and fire employees? _____ YES _____ NO

43. Number of people who work for your employer:

    _____ Large business (employing over 250 people)
    _____ Medium-sized business (employing 50–249 people)
    _____ Small business (employing fewer than 50 people)
    _____ Federal Government
    _____ State Government
    _____ Local Government

44. Have you ever considered or pursued a career in law enforcement? _____ YES _____ NO

    If yes, please explain: _____

    _____

PERSONAL

45. Do you have a bumper sticker on your car? _____ YES _____ NO

    If yes, please describe: _____

    _____

46. In terms of your political outlook, do you usually think of yourself as:

    _____ very conservative   _____ somewhat liberal
    _____ somewhat conservative   _____ very liberal
    _____ middle of road

47. What would you describe as your hobbies? _____

    _____

48. Have you ever or do you currently participate in any of the following recreational activities? (<u>Check</u> each one that applies to you.)

    a) Hiking   _____ YES, currently   _____ YES, past   _____ NO
    b) Golf   _____ YES, currently   _____ YES, past   _____ NO
    c) Fishing (Ocean)   _____ YES, currently   _____ YES, past   _____ NO
    d) Fishing (Freshwater) _____ YES, currently   _____ YES, past   _____ NO
    e) Boating   _____ YES, currently   _____ YES, past   _____ NO

    If yes to any of the above, please describe your involvement in the activity/ies:

    _____

    _____

    _____

49. Do you have any knowledge of boats? _____ YES _____ NO

    If YES, please describe your experience with boats: _____

    _____

50. Do you currently own a gun? _____ YES _____ NO

    If YES, for what reason (i.e. hunting, protection)? _____

    _____

51. To what clubs or organizations do you belong?. _____
_____

52. Have you ever held a leadership position in these organizations? _____
_____

53. Have you ever belonged to or attended a grief/loss counseling group or organization? _____ YES _____ NO

    If YES, please describe: _____
    _____

54a. Have you ever been involved in a lawsuit (other than divorce proceedings)? _____ YES _____ NO

54b. If yes, were you: _____ The plaintiff _____ The defendant _____ Both
    Please explain: _____

55. What is your main source of news? (Check only one)

    _____ Television   _____ Radio
    _____ Newspapers   _____ Internet
    _____ Friends   _____ I DO NOT FOLLOW THE NEWS

56. What kind of books do you regularly read? _____
_____

57. If you read magazines, which ones do you prefer to read? (<u>Check</u> each one that applies to you.)

    _____ Architectural Digest   _____ Car & Driver
    _____ Business Week   _____ Consumer Reports
    _____ Cosmopolitan   _____ Field & Stream
    _____ Forbes   _____ Ladies Home Journal
    _____ National Enquirer   _____ Newsweek
    _____ People   _____ Popular Mechanics
    _____ Reader's Digest   _____ Sports Illustrated
    _____ Martha Stewart   _____ U.S. News and World Reports
    _____ Golf Digest   _____ Golf Magazine
    _____ American Angler   _____ California Game & Fish
    _____ Good Housekeeping   _____ Money Magazine
    _____ Others (Please List Here)

    _____

58. What television and radio programs do you view or listen to on a regular basis?
_____
_____

59a. Do you use a computer? _____ YES _____ NO

59b. How often do you access the Internet?

    _____ Multiple times a day   _____ Monthly
    _____ Once or twice a day   _____ I only use the Internet for e-mail
    _____ Once or twice a week   _____ I do NOT use the Internet

59c. If you access the Internet, what web sites do you typically visit? _____
_____

59d. Do you log-on to internet chat rooms? _____ YES _____ NO

    If YES, what Topics? _____
    _____

60. How often do you read a newspaper?
    ____ Daily
    ____ Several times a week
    ____ Seldom or never
    ____ Only on Sundays

61. Which section of the newspaper do you typically read first?

_____ Front Section   _____ Sports Section
_____ Calendar/Events Section   _____ Business Section
_____ Other

62a. How often, if at all, do you tune in to cable news programs on TV?

_____ Daily
_____ Several times a week
_____ Seldom
_____ Never

62b. Have you seen any movies in the last six (6) months depicting the law or legal system, excluding this case?

_____ YES   _____ NO

If yes, please list: _____

_____

62c. Do you, or anyone in your household, watch such television shows as Larry King, Greta Van Susteren, or Geraldo Rivera?

_____ Yes (self)   _____ Yes (other)   _____ Yes (both)   _____ No

If yes, about how often?   _____ Daily
_____ Several times a week
_____ A few times a month
_____ A few times a year

63. Do you currently or have you in the past owned any pets?

_____ Yes, currently
_____ Yes, in the past
_____ No

If yes, please note what kind of pet: _____

_____

MILITARY

64. Were you ever in the military?

_____ YES   _____ NO

If yes, answer the following. If no skip to question 67a

a. What branch? _____
b. Date of service? _____
c. Rate or rank? _____
d. Where were you stationed? _____
e. Character of discharge (honorable, general, etc.)? _____
f. Reason for discharge? _____
g. Reason for discharge? _____

65. Were you ever involved in any way with military law enforcement, non-judicial punishment, courts martial, or administrative boards or hearings?

_____ YES   _____ NO

66. Were you ever in combat?   _____ YES   _____ NO

If YES, when and where were you in combat? _____

_____

LAW ENFORCEMENT AND JUDICIAL CONTACTS

67a. Have you, any friends or relatives ever been involved in law enforcement (for example, F.B.I., D.E.A., Sheriffs Department, County Prosecutor's Office, California State Police, Attorney General's Office, United States Attorneys Office) or been employed by any such agency? _____ YES _____ NO

If yes, please explain. _____

_____

67b. Have you, any of your family members or close friends ever been employed by or volunteered in any aspect of criminal defense work, including any Public Defender's office, a Legal Aid, or with a related support or advocacy group having to do with the rights of people charged with crimes?

_____ YES _____ NO

If yes, who (relationship to you): _____

If yes, please explain: _____

67c. Have you, a family member or close friend ever belonged to, donated money to, signed a petition for, or otherwise supported an advocacy group(s) for people accused of crimes or people who are in prison?

_____ YES _____ NO

If yes, who (relationship to you): _____

Which group(s)? _____

_____

68. Have you, any relatives, or friends ever been arrested, charged with a criminal offense (other than minor traffic violations), or convicted of a crime? _____ YES _____ NO

If so, explain who, when, the charges and the outcome. _____

_____

69. If you answered yes to the previous question, please explain how you feel about the way each matter was handled by the police, prosecution, defense attorney, court, probation department and others involved in the law enforcement and judicial systems: _____

_____

70. Are you personally acquainted with any judges, prosecuting attorneys, or criminal defense attorneys? _____ YES _____ NO

If yes, please give the name and position of the person(s), how you came to know them, and the extent of your relationship with them: _____

_____

71. Are you a member of a Neighborhood Watch, M.A.D.D., or any other program devoted to crime prevention or victims' rights? _____ YES _____ NO
If yes, please explain. _____

_____

72. Have you ever participated in a trial as a party, witness, or interested observer? _____ YES _____ NO
If yes, please explain: _____

_____

73. What is your attitude, in general, toward law enforcement officers? _____

_____

74. Have you, or any member of your family, or close friends, ever been the VICTIM or WITNESS to any crime? _____ YES _____ NO

If yes, please explain. _____

_____

How did you feel about what happened? _____

_____

75. If you answered yes to the previous question, was the crime reported to the police? _____ YES _____ NO

   If yes, how do you feel about the way the police handled the case? _____

   _____

CRIMINAL JUSTICE SYSTEM

76. Do you have any, for whatever reason, negative feelings toward any law enforcement or prosecution agency including but not limited to San Mateo or Stanislaus County? _____ YES _____ NO

   If yes, please name the agency and explain why you feel this way: _____

   _____

   _____

77. Do you have any feelings/opinions about the effectiveness of law enforcement in California? _____ YES _____ NO

   Please explain: _____

   _____

78. Would your attitudes on our criminal justice system influence you to favor the prosecution or the defense before hearing all of the evidence? _____ YES _____ NO

   Please explain: _____

   _____

79. If selected as a juror in this case, will you be able to follow the Court's instruction that a defendant arrested for any offense is presumed innocent? _____ YES _____ NO

80. If selected as a juror in this case, will you be able to follow the Court's instruction that such a defendant is innocent until the State proves guilt beyond a reasonable doubt? _____ YES _____ NO

81. Police officers are more likely to tell the truth than other witnesses.

   _____ Strongly Agree   _____ Slightly Disagree
   _____ Agree   _____ Disagree
   _____ Slightly Agree   _____ Strongly Disagree

82. The police are too quick to arrest a suspect in cases where there is a significant amount of publicity or pressure to find a perpetrator?

   _____ Strongly agree   _____ Somewhat disagree
   _____ Somewhat agree   _____ Strongly disagree

83. How much confidence do you have in the following types of evidence?

	A lot	Some	Not much	Undecided
Eyewitness testimony	_____	_____	_____	_____
DNA	_____	_____	_____	_____
Forensic evidence	_____	_____	_____	_____
Chemical residue	_____	_____	_____	_____
Fibers	_____	_____	_____	_____
Hairs	_____	_____	_____	_____
Fingerprints	_____	_____	_____	_____
Circumstantial evidence	_____	_____	_____	_____
Documentary evidence	_____	_____	_____	_____
Originals	_____	_____	_____	_____
Photocopies	_____	_____	_____	_____
Expert witness testimony	_____	_____	_____	_____
Photographs	_____	_____	_____	_____

   If you checked "Some" or "Not much," please explain why: _____

   _____

   _____

JURY SERVICE

84. Have you ever served on a jury or a grand jury? ____ YES   ____ NO

85. If you have served on a jury before, please answer the following:

Year	Criminal or Civil	Charge or Issue	Were you Foreperson	Was verdict reached Y/N

86. How did your jury service affect your opinions about the jury system? _____
_____
_____
_____

87. Do you know or recognize the defendant, Scott Peterson, the prosecutors, the defense attorneys, the judge or any other court personnel involved in this case? ____ YES   ____ NO

If yes, please explain. _____
_____

MISCELLANEOUS

88. There are two types of evidence: direct evidence and circumstantial evidence. Do you have any attitudes or beliefs that would prevent you from relying on circumstantial evidence in a murder case? ____ YES   ____ NO

89. The judge will instruct you that both direct and circumstantial evidence are entitled to equal weight. Will you follow the court's instruction in that regard? ____ YES   ____ NO

PUBLICITY

90. Do you know, or have you read, seen, or heard <u>anything</u> about this case? ____ YES   ____ NO

91. If yes, what have you read, seen or heard about this case? _____
_____
_____

92. If yes, when did you first hear, see or read <u>anything</u> about this case? _____
_____

Please explain: _____
_____

93. If yes, please indicate where you have heard something about this case:

TV: Which stations: _____
Radio News: Which stations: _____
Radio Talk Shows: Which ones: _____
Newspaper: Which ones: _____
Magazines: Which ones: _____
Internet Chat Rooms: Which ones: _____
Conversations with others: Who: _____
Other: Who: _____

94. If you have been exposed to pre-trial publicity about this case, it would be natural to form some opinions about what you have heard. Have you formed any preliminary opinions about this case? ____ YES   ____ NO

If you answered yes to the previous questions, please explain what they are.

_____
_____

95. Have you formed or expressed any opinions about the guilt or innocence of the defendant, Scott Peterson?

_____ YES, guilt _____ YES, innocence _____ Not enough information to decide

Please explain: _____

_____

96. Has anyone expressed any opinion as to his guilt or innocence to you?

_____ YES, guilt _____ YES, innocence _____ NO

97a. The jurors that sit on this case will be instructed that they must base their decision entirely on the evidence produced in court, <u>not</u> from any outside source or preexisting opinion or attitudes. Can you do that, despite what you have read, heard, or seen about this case?

_____ YES _____ NO

Please explain: _____

_____

97b. Do you think the news media always presents the story accurately? _____ YES _____ NO

98. If you have already formed opinions about this case, can you set them aside and base your decision entirely on the evidence presented in this courtroom, even if it conflicts with what you have previously heard? _____ YES _____ NO

99. Despite anything you may have heard, read or seen about this case, can you still be fair to the prosecution and the defense? _____ YES _____ NO

100. If selected as a juror in this case, will you be able to follow the court's instruction to avoid any news coverage about this case beginning today? _____ YES _____ NO

101. Is there anything else that you feel the court should know about your qualifications as a juror? _____ YES _____ NO
If yes, please explain. _____

_____

_____

102. Is there any reason you would not be a fair juror in this case? _____ YES _____ NO
If yes, please explain. _____

_____

103. a. If after hearing all of the evidence in this case you are convinced beyond a reasonable doubt that the defendant is guilty of one or more of the counts of the Information, would you be able to return a verdict of guilty on that count or counts? _____ YES _____ NO

b. If after hearing all of the evidence in this case you are not convinced beyond a reasonable doubt that the defendant is guilty of one or more of the counts of the Information, would you be able to return a verdict of not guilty on that count or counts? _____ YES _____ NO

104. During the trial you may become aware that members of the defendant's family and/or members of the victim's family will generally be present in the courtroom during the proceedings. Will you be able to ignore their presence and consider only the evidence in determining the defendant's innocence or guilt? _____ YES _____ NO

105. Have you seen the movie "The Perfect Husband: The Laci Peterson Story"? _____ YES _____ NO

106. If so, how has it affected your views and/or opinions about the case, if at all? _____

VIEWS ON THE DEATH PENALTY AND THE PENALTY OF LIFE IN PRISON
WITHOUT THE POSSIBILITY OF PAROLE

The court is asking the following questions regarding your feelings about the death penalty because one of the possible sentences for a person convicted of the charges the prosecution has filed is the death penalty. Therefore, the court must know whether you could be fair to both the prosecution and the defense on the issue of punishment if you reach that issue. By asking these questions, the court is not suggesting that you will ever need to decide this question because the court has no way of knowing what the evidence in this case will be, or whether or not you will find the defendant guilty of anything at all. In other words, the only way the issue of punishment will be decided by the jury is if it should find the defendant guilty beyond a reasonable doubt of first degree murder of at least one count, and guilty of first or second degree murder on the other count, and the alleged special circumstance true beyond a reasonable doubt.

By asking about your views on penalty now, the court is <u>not</u> suggesting that the jury in this case will find the defendant guilty.

    A. Will asking questions concerning your views about the death penalty and the penalty of life in prison without possibility of parole suggest to you that the defendant must be guilty?

_____

_____

    B. Do you understand that the only task jurors are asked to perform during the first phase of trial is to judge guilt or innocence?

_____

_____

Do you understand that if there is a penalty trial, the only two possible sentences will be the death penalty and life in prison without the possibility of parole?

_____

_____

107. What are your feelings regarding the death penalty? _____

_____

_____

108. What are your feelings regarding life in prison without the possibility of parole?

_____

_____

109. How would you rate your attitude towards the death penalty?

    ____ Strongly Oppose   ____ Weakly Support

    ____ Oppose   ____ Support

    ____ Weakly Oppose   ____ Strongly Support

110. Would it be difficult for you to vote for the death penalty if the crime was the guilty party's first offense? ____ YES ___ NO ____ Depends on the Evidence

111. Briefly describe any article, book, or news programs that influenced your feelings about the death penalty: _____

_____

112. Have you ever been involved in any way, such as circulating a petition, in support of the death penalty? ____ YES ____ NO

    If yes, please explain: _____

_____

113. Have you ever been involved in any way, such as circulating a petition in opposition to the death penalty? ____ YES ____ NO

114. Over the last ten years, have your views on the death penalty changed? ____ YES ____ NO

    If yes, please explain: _____

_____

115. Do you have any moral, religious, or philosophical opposition to the death penalty so strong that you would be unable to impose the death penalty regardless of the facts? ____ YES ____ NO

    If yes, please explain: _____

_____

116. Do you have any moral, religious, or philosophical beliefs in favor of the death penalty so strong that you would be unable to impose life without possibility of parole regardless of the facts? ____ YES ____ NO

    If yes, please explain: _____

_____

I declare under penalty of perjury that the answers set forth on this Jury Questionnaire are true and correct to the best of my knowledge, information, and belief.

Executed on _____, 2004, in San Mateo County, California.

_____

                 Prospective Juror Number

DECLARATION UNDER PENALTY OF PERJURY

REGARDING REQUEST FOR HARDSHIP DISQUALIFICATION

TO: Judge Alfred A. Delucchi

JUROR ID NUMBER: _____

REQUEST FOR HARDSHIP DISQUALIFICATION

REASON:

_____

_____

_____

_____

_____

_____

The following is a list of the individuals (i.e. the law firms, attorneys, witnesses, and defendant) involved in this case. Please <u>circle</u> any of the names that you, or any member of your family, <u>know personally</u> or have done business with:

<u>**EXPLANATION SHEET**</u>

If you feel that in the spaces provided, you were unable to sufficiently answer any particular question, please use this area to provide that information. Thank you very much for your cooperation.

_____

_____

_____

_____

_____

_____

_____

_____

_____

_____

_____

_____

_____

_____

I certify, under penalty of perjury, that the foregoing is true and correct, and that I have received no assistance from any other person in completing this questionnaire.

Executed in the County of San Mateo on _____

Date

_____

JUROR ID and INITIALS
(Do NOT write your name)

CHAPTER 13

Constitutional Rights Postconviction

CHAPTER CONTENTS

> *Thou shalt give life for life, eye for eye, tooth for tooth, hand for hand, foot for foot, burning for burning, wound for wound.*
>
> Bible, King James Version, Exodus 21:23–25

> *Excessive bail shall not be required nor excessive fines imposed, nor cruel and unusual punishments inflicted.*
>
> U.S. Constitution, Eighth Amendment, 1791

CHAPTER OBJECTIVES

After studying this chapter, you should be able to:

- Explain the history of the Eighth Amendment to the U.S. Constitution.
- Define criminal punishment.
- List and explain the two requirements that must be satisfied before a punishment is cruel and unusual.
- Explain why capital punishment is not unconstitutional as cruel and unusual punishment.
- Explain what procedural protection is required before the death penalty can be carried out.

- Define aggravating and mitigating circumstances.
- List the classifications of persons who can be executed.
- List the crimes that are punishable by death.
- Explain the U.S. Supreme Court's position on life in prison for repeat offenders.
- List and describe two current trends in punishment.

INTRODUCTION AND HISTORICAL BACKGROUND

Throughout history men have experimented with various forms of punishment for those who fail to conform to society's expectations. Lawbreakers have been punished in many ways. In ancient Rome, condemned prisoners did battle with wild beasts in arenas while the public watched from the stands.[1]

Punishment in England was often equally harsh and public. During the seventeenth through the early nineteenth century, criminals in England were frequently punished harshly, sometimes for what are today considered minor offenses. Dozens of prisoners were hung at a time for offenses ranging from murder to horse thievery and housebreaking. In light of the penal practices of the day, it was little wonder that the criminal law was popularly known as the **Bloody Code**.[2]

Executions were often great public spectacles. Such a scene was recorded by Samuel Pepys (1633–1703), who served as the English Secretary of the Admiralty. He kept a diary covering his life from 1660 through 1669. His entry for October 13, 1660 reads:

> I went out to Charing Cross to see Maj.-Gen. Harrison hanged, drawn and quartered— which was done there—he looked as cheerful as any man could in that condition. He was presently cast down and his head and his heart shown to the people, at which there was great shouts of joy.[3]

Prisons were reserved for very minor offenses, and stays there were short.

An alternative to hanging or a short prison stay was the practice of transportation.[4] **Transportation** was a form of banishment or exile. Criminals were shipped to the American colonies, often for life. The practice did not end until the American Revolution, when the colonies were no longer a practical dumping ground for prisoners. England's temporary solution was to turn abandoned ships into floating prisons moored on the Thames.[5]

Bloody Code

Popular name for England's criminal laws because of their harshness and the long list of crimes classified as capital offenses.

Transportation

The practice of exiling or expelling a prisoner from his homeland as punishment.

THE HUNG
DRAWN AND QUARTERED
I WENT TO SEE
MAJOR GENERAL HARRISON
HUNG DRAWN AND QUARTERED
HE WAS LOOKING AS CHEERFUL
AS ANY MAN COULD
IN THAT CONDITION
SAMUEL PEPYS
13TH OCTOBER 1660

A tavern now stands on the site where Major Harrison met his end.

It is against this background that we examine the meaning and application of the U.S. Constitution's prohibition against **cruel and unusual punishment.**

The Eighth Amendment's language was taken from a provision of the Virginia Declaration of Rights of 1776. Virginia borrowed the provision from the English Bill of Rights of 1689, which was passed by Parliament upon the ascent of William and Mary. The English Bill of Rights was an attempt to curb the royal misuse of punishment in criminal cases during the reign of King James II. It provided that "excessive Baile ought not be required nor excessive Fines imposed nor cruel and unusual Punishments inflicted."[6] The law was based on an earlier document, the Magna Carta of 1215, in which the noblemen forced King John to agree that "amercements" would not be excessive.[7]

The Eighth Amendment was not a part of the original Constitution as ratified in 1789. Rather, it is a part of the Bill of Rights, added in response to concerns that the new Constitution provided few protections for accused criminals. The Bill of Rights was added to the Constitution in 1791.

As we explore the meaning of cruel and unusual punishment you may want to keep three questions in mind. They are:

1. What types of penalties are considered punishments within the meaning of the Eighth Amendment?
2. What punishments arc outlawed because they are cruel and unusual?
3. Who is protected from cruel and unusual punishment?

Cruel and Unusual Punishment

Punishment which violates the Eighth Amendment and which violates evolving standards of decency.

DEFINING PUNISHMENT

Is a junior high student who is paddled by his teacher so hard that a hematoma[8] develops on his buttocks, causing him to miss school for several days, protected by the Eighth Amendment? The U.S. Supreme Court has said no. **Corporal punishment** of children is not the sort of punishment protected by the Eighth Amendment.[9]

The Eighth Amendment only applies to punishment for criminal behavior. Ask yourself: Is this punishment for the commission of a crime? If the punishment is not for the commission of a crime, the individual punished is not protected by the Eighth Amendment.[10] That is not to say that corporal punishment may not be a crime. A teacher who paddles a child may face criminal charges of assault, child abuse, or reckless endangerment, among other possibilities.

Therefore, we must first determine if the individual being punished has committed a crime. A crime is defined as a breach of a law made for the public good that is punishable by public law, or simply, an offense against society.[11] Most of the time the question is answered by looking at the law the defendant is accused of breaking. If the government has classified the offense as a crime, the punishment the statute imposes must meet Eighth Amendment standards.

Sometimes a criminal statute is challenged because the statute makes a crime of an action that is not properly a crime. If the act or behavior being punished is not properly a crime, its criminalization is in and of itself cruel and unusual and therefore improper. For example, a California law that made being a drug addict a crime punishable by imprisonment was a violation of the ban on cruel and unusual punishment because it criminalized a status or condition, not behavior.[12] As Justice Stewart wrote in that case, "Even one day in prison would be cruel and unusual punishment for the 'crime' of having a common cold."[13] Legislatures cannot create crimes of conditions such as being HIV positive or being an alcoholic. It is not a crime to be sick or to have an addiction.

CRUEL AND UNUSUAL PUNISHMENTS

We now turn to determining what criminal punishments are cruel and unusual. The U.S. Supreme Court has held that the Eighth Amendment outlaws a punishment as cruel and unusual if the punishment itself involves unnecessary infliction of pain or if the punishment is grossly disproportionate to the nature or severity of the crime. To be excluded, a punishment must have been considered cruel and unusual at the time the Bill of Rights was adopted in 1791[14] or be contrary to the "evolving standards of decency that mark the progress of a maturing society."[15]

We will first consider capital punishment; second, life imprisonment; third, prison conditions; and finally, chemical castration and sex offender registration.

THE DEATH PENALTY

Capital punishment is not **per se** cruel and unusual punishment. The U.S. Constitution implicitly assumes executions are an allowable punishment. It provides that "no person shall be held to answer for a capital or otherwise infamous crime unless on a presentment or indictment of a Grand Jury."[16] Therefore, we can assume that the Founding Fathers accepted capital punishment.

Corporal Punishment

Punishment inflicted on the body, such as paddling, whipping, or caning.

Per Se

Latin; by itself, in and of itself.

Thirty-eight states and the federal government currently authorize the death penalty, while 12 states plus the District of Columbia do not.[17] Generally, the death penalty only applies to cases where the defendant deliberately killed another human being[18] or where the defendant was a major participant in a felony murder.[19] In addition, federal law authorized death for certain federal offenses such as espionage and treason. At the end of 2005, the latest year for which national figures are available, there were 3,254 individuals on Death Row, including 52 women.[20] In 2006, 53 inmates were executed, all of them men. Texas executed 24 of them.

Death is an accepted and acceptable sanction under the Constitution. It is the way that the death penalty is carried out that is subject to scrutiny under the Eighth Amendment. As the Supreme Court wrote in *Louisiana ex rel. Francis v. Resweber:*

> The cruelty against which the Constitution protects a convicted man is cruelty in the method of punishment, not the necessary suffering involved in any method employed to extinguish life humanely.[21]

We will consider the procedural safeguards required before an execution can take place and what methods can be used to "extinguish life humanely."

PROCEDURAL SAFEGUARDS REQUIRED BY THE EIGHTH AMENDMENT

In recent years, the U.S. Supreme Court has focused on the procedures used by states to arrive at death as the sanction for criminal behavior rather than on the continued use of the death penalty by the criminal justice system. This is despite the fact that Amnesty International, the Roman Catholic Church, and various other human rights groups condemn death as a sanction, and many modern nations have abolished it altogether.[22] For example, the European Union makes it a condition of membership that nations abolish the death penalty.

The Supreme Court has never ruled that the death penalty is always unconstitutional. However, the Court will invalidate state statutes that do not provide enough procedural safeguards for defendants facing death. For example, in the 1972 case of *Furman v. Georgia,*[23] the Supreme Court effectively halted the death penalty temporarily. The Court ruled that Georgia's statute was so procedurally flawed that the penalty was arbitrarily and capriciously imposed. As a practical matter, no executions were carried out between 1972 and 1976, when the Supreme Court again considered the issue.

As a result of the Supreme Court's decision in *Furman,* many states revamped their death penalty laws. In 1976, the Supreme Court again considered the death penalty, this time reviewing new state statutes designed to overcome the Court's earlier objections. The Court concluded in *Gregg v. Georgia*[24] that execution remains a constitutionally sanctioned punishment, given the existence of certain procedural safeguards. These can include:

1. A bifurcated trial, in which the jury first decides whether the defendant is guilty, and a sentencing stage, at which the jury determines punishment after hearing evidence of **aggravating** or **mitigating circumstances.** The condemned prisoner must be given an opportunity to present mitigating factors in his defense, no matter how heinous his crime. The sentence of death cannot be automatic.[25]
2. An automatic appeal to the state supreme court of all sentences of death, at least if an appeal is requested by the condemned prisoner.

Death is . . . different. Death is irremedial. Death is unknowable; it goes beyond this world. It is a legislative decision to do something, and we know not what we do.
Anthony Amsterdam, oral argument before the U.S. Supreme Court in *Gregg v. Georgia,* March 30, 1976

Aggravating Circumstance

Act or conduct that increases the seriousness of an act, often resulting in a harsher punishment.

Mitigating Circumstance

Act or conduct that lessens or reduces the punishment for a crime, such as lack of a criminal record, state of mind, or youth.

The Supreme Court has considered what information jurors are entitled to receive when weighing whether a defendant should be put to death. In *Kelly v. South Carolina,* 534 U.S. 246 (2002), the Court ruled that in the penalty phase of a death penalty case where the choice is between life in prison with no possibility of parole or death, the jury must be told that life in prison means just that. In that way, those concerned about recidivism won't feel compelled to choose death because they fear the defendant will be freed at some point, possibly to kill again.

In October 2006, the Supreme Court ruled in *Abdul-Kabir (fka Cole) v. Quarterman* that juries weighing a death sentence must be allowed "to give meaningful consideration and effect to all mitigating evidence that might provide a basis for refusing to impose the death penalty." The decision struck down jury instructions given by the Fifth Circuit Court to evaluate mitigating circumstances only on the basis of two "special issues" as sanctioned by the state of Texas for capital sentencing: one, the deliberateness of the crime, and two, the future dangerousness of the criminal. Abdul-Kabir's defense offered evidence that he was neurologically damaged as a result of childhood abuse and abandonment. The Supreme Court noted that such evidence was "double-edged," in that it was intended to reduce the defendant's culpability, but also implied he would be dangerous in the future. By allowing the jury to consider that evidence only as it applied to the deliberateness of the crime and Abdul-Kabir's future dangerousness and limiting the jurors' responses to "yes or no" answers to each of those two questions, the Fifth Circuit Court had not allowed them to give full, meaningful consideration to the evidence.[26] The Court relied on *Penry v. Lynaugh*, which required that juries be instructed to consider a defendant's mitigating evidence and give a reasoned, moral response to that evidence in recommending a death sentence.[27]

Since the Supreme Court's decision in *Gregg* on July 2, 1976, 1,089 executions have been carried out.[28] Ten of the executed prisoners were women. The annual number rose sharply, from 1 in 1977 to a high of 98 in 1999, and then leveled off. In 2004, 59 death sentences were carried out. In 2005, 60 prisoners were executed. The number of executed prisoners fell to 53 in 2006.

NUMBER OF PERSONS EXECUTED BY YEAR SINCE 1930

1930: 155	1948: 119	1966: 1	1992: 31
1931: 153	1949: 119	1967: 2	1993: 38
1932: 140	1950: 82	1968–1976: 0	1994: 31
1933: 160	1951: 105	1977: 1	1995: 56
1934: 168	1952: 83	1978: 0	1996: 45
1935: 199	1953: 62	1979: 2	1997: 74
1936: 195	1954: 81	1980: 0	1998: 68
1937: 147	1955: 76	1981: 1	1999: 98
1938: 190	1956: 65	1982: 2	2000: 85
1939: 160	1957: 65	1983: 5	2001: 66
1940: 124	1958: 49	1984: 21	2002: 71
1941: 123	1959: 49	1985: 18	2003: 65
1942: 147	1960: 56	1986: 18	2004: 59
1943: 131	1961: 42	1987: 25	2005: 60
1944: 120	1962: 42	1988: 11	2006: 53
1945: 117	1963: 21	1989: 16	
1946: 131	1964: 15	1990: 23	
1947: 153	1965: 7	1991: 14	

Source: United States Department of Justice Bureau of Justice Statistics, 2007.

APPROPRIATE METHODS OF DEATH

Generally, the sanction of death may be imposed in any way that is not unnecessarily cruel. The U.S. Supreme Court held *In re Kimmler*[29] that "[p]unishments are cruel when they involve torture or a lingering death." Thus, firing squads are permissible,[30] as are electrocutions, lethal gas, and lethal injections. In one case the Supreme Court ruled that it was not cruel and unusual punishment to attempt to execute the same person twice. Willie Francis was convicted of murder and sentenced to death by electrocution in September 1945. On May 3, 1946, Francis was placed in the electric chair. The executioner threw the switch, but the apparatus failed. Francis was returned to his cell, and a new death warrant was signed, setting his execution for May 9, 1946. He appealed this second attempt to kill him, alleging that two attempts at electrocution was cruel and unusual punishment. The Supreme Court disagreed, writing that "[t]he fact that an unforeseeable accident prevented the prompt consummation of the sentence cannot, it seems to us, add an element of cruelty to a subsequent execution."[31]

Equipment malfunctions still occasionally happen. For example, on March 25, 1997, during the successful execution of convicted killer Pedro Medina in Florida, witnesses reported that a six-inch flame erupted from the head of the prisoner, filling the execution chamber with smoke and the smell of burning flesh.[32] The Florida State Attorney General commented that "[p]eople who wish to commit murder, they better not do it in the state of Florida because we may have a problem with our electric chair."[33]

Of the 1,089 prisoners executed between 1977 and July 2007, 920 were killed by lethal injection, 153 by electrocution, 11 by lethal gas, 3 by hanging, and 2 by firing squad.[34] The trend has been away from electrocution toward lethal injection. All of the executions carried out in 2005, 2006, and the first half of 2007 were by lethal injection; in 2004, all but one were by lethal injection, with one inmate electrocuted.[35] In 37 of the 38 states that use capital punishment, lethal injection is the prescribed method of death.

YOU MAKE THE CALL

IS LETHAL INJECTION PAINLESS?

On January 26, 2006 at 6:00 PM, Clarence Hill, 48, convicted of the 1982 murder of a Pensacola police officer, was strapped to a gurney, a needle in his arm, when the U.S. Supreme Court stayed his execution. While the Court refused to hear Hill's claim that lethal injection was cruel and unusual, it agreed to hear a narrower claim, which had been rejected by a federal appeals court in Atlanta, that the lethal injection formula would cause him excessive pain. That evening, the Court issued stays of execution for Hill plus two other inmates.

The next day the Court's unanimity broke down. It allowed an Indiana execution, challenged on similar grounds, to proceed, and executions by lethal injection continued, despite pleas identical to Hill's from many other death row inmates. But Hill's stay signaled the Supreme Court's willingness to consider the constitutionality at least of the lethal injection formula.

Lethal injection uses a three-drug protocol infused via intravenous lines. The first drug is sodium thiopental, an anesthetic which puts the inmate to sleep. Second, pavulon or pancurium bromide is administered to paralyze the inmate and stop his breathing. Finally, potassium chloride is administered to stop the heart.

Though touted as painless, lethal injection can be problematic, partly because medical ethics prevent doctors from administering the drugs. Instead, technicians or orderlies perform the injections, often with mixed results. In June 1997, Michael Eugene Elkins waited for an hour while executioners tried to find a suitable vein. As they probed for a vein, he asked, "Should I lean my head down a little bit?" They finally found one in Elkin's neck. In 1998, Texas inmate Joseph Cannon made his final statement, and the execution began. One of Cannon's veins collapsed, and the needle popped out. Cannon lay back, closed his eyes, and said, "It's come undone." Officials pulled back the curtain, worked on him for fifteen minutes, and then reopened it. A weeping Cannon made his second final statement, and the execution resumed.

Many journalists come to an execution by lethal injection expecting to see a quick and painless death and are mortified by five- to ten-minute death throes. Florida prisoner Angel Diaz, executed in December 2006, continued to move after the first injection was administered. A second dose was administered, which took 34 minutes to kill him, causing Florida Governor Jeb Bush to call for an investigation into the method. Texas inmate Stephen McCoy had such a violent reaction to the drugs, including heaving chest, gasping, and choking, that a male witness fainted, knocking over another witness.[36]

The U.S. Supreme Court has accepted several cases examining the lethal injection question. At press time, they are yet to rule on them.[37]

Is lethal injection cruel and unusual? You make the call!

PERSONS WHO CAN BE EXECUTED

Minor

A person who has not yet reached legal age, typically 18.

Although death itself may not be cruel and unusual punishment, it has been argued that it may be cruel and unusual to impose death on particular classes of individuals. These include the mentally ill, mentally retarded, and those who were **minors** at the time of the commission of the offense for which death is the sentence.

MENTALLY ILL AND MENTALLY RETARDED

In *Ford v. Wainwright*, the U.S. Supreme Court has ruled that a state may not execute a prisoner who is mentally incompetent at the time of execution.[38] The Court concluded that the execution of an individual who is insane violates the Eighth Amendment because the defendant is either unaware of his impending execution or the reason for it. The defendant, Alvin Bernard Ford, did not believe he would be executed because he had delusions that he owned the prison and could control the governor through "mind waves." The Supreme Court wrote: "the Eighth Amendment prohibits a State from carrying out a sentence of death upon a prisoner who is insane. Whether its aim is to protect the condemned from fear and pain without comfort of understanding, or to protect the dignity of society itself from the barbarity of exacting mindless vengeance, the restriction finds enforcement in the Eighth Amendment."[39]

However, prison officials can force an otherwise mentally incompetent individual to receive medication to restore his competence even if the prisoner objects.[40] The question the Supreme Court has not addressed is whether a prisoner facing execution can be forced to take medication to restore his competence long enough to be executed. The Court refused to hear *Perry v. Louisiana,* in which the State of Louisiana argued that a defendant could be forced to receive medication to restore his mental state to normal long enough to carry out the sentence of death.[41] The Supreme Court of Louisiana later rejected that notion and concluded it was a clear violation of the U. S. Constitution to force someone to take drugs long enough to be executed.[42]

On February 20, 2002, the Georgia parole board stayed the execution of a killer who was allegedly so psychotic he believed that actress Sigourney Weaver was God. The prisoner, Alexander Williams, claimed that he had been forcibly medicated to make him eligible for execution. His attorneys had appealed to the Supreme Court, but his sentence was commuted to life in prison without the possibility of parole by the state's parole board before the Supreme Court could make any decisions.[43]

The following year, the Court did hear a case involving a man charged with less serious crimes who did not want to be medicated. The state wanted to medicate him so that he could become competent to stand trial. In a 6–3 decision, the Court ruled that the state cannot medicate a prisoner solely to stand trial but can do so "if the treatment is medically appropriate, is substantially unlikely to have side effects that may undermine the trial's fairness, and, taking account of less intrusive alternatives, is necessary significantly to further important governmental trial–related interests." In this case, the government had not met its burden of showing that the medication would not interfere with the defendant's ability to prepare his defense.[44]

In October 2003, the Supreme Court refused, without comment, to hear the case of Charles Singleton, a schizophrenic man sentenced to death for murder. At age 19, Singleton had stabbed a grocery store owner during an attempted robbery in Hamburg, Arkansas. In 1997, while on death row, Singleton was diagnosed with paranoid schizophrenia. A prison review panel ordered Singleton to take antipsychotic drugs. The medication reduced Singleton's psychotic symptoms, and Arkansas proceeded with plans to execute him.

Singleton's attorney filed a lawsuit arguing the state could not force his client to take medication to restore his competency in order to execute him. In October 2001, a panel of the Eighth U.S. Circuit Court of Appeals ruled that Singleton should be sentenced to life in prison without possibility of parole, but in 2004, a sharply divided full Eighth Circuit Court lifted the stay of execution. The court noted that by this time Singleton was taking the antipsychotic medications voluntarily, and since the state had an interest in having sane inmates, the side effect of sanity should not affect Singleton's sentence. Singleton was executed by lethal injection on January 6, 2004.[45]

The Supreme Court will have to weigh in on the issue directly in the case of Seven Staley, a Texas death row inmate who murdered a Forth Worth restaurant manager during an attempted holdup. Staley refuses to regularly take his antipsychotic medication, claiming his doctors are trying to poison him. When off his medication, he is ostensibly delusional and incoherent. District Judge Wayne Salvant ordered that Staley be forcibly medicated to render him competent for execution. Assistant Tarrant County District Attorney Charles Mallin said, "You should not be able to circumvent the judgment of a jury by not taking your medication, and thus escape the consequences of your actions." On Staley's appeal to the Supreme Court, Mallin said, "There is no Texas law, and the Supreme Court of the United States has never decided this issue. We're out on the cutting edge here. We have nothing to lose."[46]

At one time, many states allowed the execution of the mentally retarded. Some states, including Colorado, Indiana, Kansas, and New York, prohibited the execution of defendants shown to be mentally retarded.[47] The Supreme Court had ruled in *Penry v. Lynaugh* that the Eighth Amendment did not bar a retarded individual from death but required that he be treated like any other defendant. He could only attempt to use his retardation as mitigating evidence.[48]

Interestingly, the same case resurfaced in the Supreme Court in 2001. The defendant, John Paul Penry, whose IQ has been tested at 56, was retried and again convicted. This time, he argued that the jury that decided whether he would live or die wasn't given enough information about his disability. The Supreme Court agreed and reversed his sentence. His death sentence was overturned a third time since, and he still awaits resentencing. The case is *Penry v. Johnson,* 532 U.S. 782 (2001).

In 2002, the Supreme Court ruled in *Atkins v. Virginia* that executing the mentally retarded does violate the prohibition against cruel and unusual punishment. The Court found that contemporary standards of what is appropriate have changed and that the mentally retarded, with limited ability to understand the consequences of the punishment they face, should not be subjected to execution.

HISTORICAL HIGHLIGHT
Executing the Mentally Retarded—Cruel
or Unusual?

Terry Washington had organic brain damage. He had the mind of a 6-year-old but managed to work in a restaurant as a dishwasher. This was no easy task, for his condition would sometimes cause him to have violent seizures and foam at the mouth. Unfortunately, one night after an argument with his supervisor, Terry murdered him.

Little doubt exists that Terry Washington killed the man. The trial was an open-and-shut case, and the jury voted to give Washington the death penalty. However, the jurors were never told that Washington was severely retarded.

Washington invoked his Fifth Amendment right not to testify during the trial. His attorneys never raised the issue during the determination of guilt phase of the trial or the sentencing phase. On May 6, 1998, Washington became one of the approximately 25 mentally retarded people to be executed since the death penalty was reinstated in 1976.

The U.S. Supreme Court had ruled previously that the execution of mentally retarded convicts was not cruel and unusual punishment per se. But the decision left the door open when it said "a national consensus against execution of the mentally retarded may someday emerge reflecting the evolving standards of decency that mark the progress of a maturing society."[49]

The landscape of the death penalty has changed dramatically since then with the Supreme Court's ruling that execution of the mentally retarded violates the Eighth Amendment protection against cruel and unusual punishment. Daryl Atkins, who was convicted of murder and sentenced to death, had an IQ estimated at 59. He appealed his death sentence. The Supreme Court found that a national consensus against execution of the mentally retarded had finally emerged based upon a majority of states having laws prohibiting such executions. The Court relied on information about changes to some state laws since it last reviewed a similar case. Using that information, the Court concluded that the nation's mood had changed and what was acceptable just a few years earlier was no longer acceptable.[50]

More recently, the Court rejected a Texas scheme that made low intelligence an aggravating rather than a mitigating factor in a jury's decision whether to order the death penalty or life in prison. The Court ruled that low intelligence may only be considered a mitigating factor, not a ground to execute a defendant.[51]

MINORS

The U.S. Supreme Court had ruled in 1988 that it was cruel and unusual punishment to impose the death penalty on persons who committed their offense while 15 years of age or younger. However, the next year the same Court concluded, in *Thompson v. Oklahoma,* that a youth 16 or 17 at the time of the offense could be sentenced to death,[52] thereby setting the lower limit for capital crimes at 16. That decision stood until 2005, when the Supreme Court heard the case of *Roper v. Simmons*.

Christopher Simmons, of Fenton, Missouri, was 17 in September 1993, when he came up with a plan to break into someone's home, tie the person up, and throw the person off a bridge. Simmons recruited two younger friends to help him carry out his plan, one of whom backed out at the last minute. Simmons and his remaining friend broke into the home of Shirley Crook. They found her in bed, bound her with duct tape, and taped her eyes and mouth shut. Then they put her in the back of her van and drove to Castlewood State Park. On arriving they realized Crook had unbound her hands and removed some of the duct tape from her mouth. Simmons used her bathrobe tie, her purse strap, a towel, and some electrical wire he found nearby to bind her hands and feet. They covered her face completely with the duct tape. Then they pushed her off a railroad trestle into the river below. Her body was found the following day.

Simmons confessed to the murder and was sentenced to death. Simmons appealed on the basis of the *Atkins v. Virginia* decision, arguing that juveniles should have the same protections as the mentally retarded. His case put an end to the juvenile death penalty in the United States on March 1, 2005, when the Supreme Court ruled in a 5–4 decision that imposing the death penalty on defendants who were under the age of 18 when they committed their offense violated the Constitution's Eighth Amendment protection against cruel and unusual punishment. At the time, 71 people were on death row for juvenile crimes, ranging in age from 18 to 43 at the time of the court's decision.[53]

The Supreme Court based its decision on numerous factors. The court cited evidence of a national consensus against executing minor offenders, similar to the consensus cited in *Atkins* against executing the mentally retarded. The Court noted that thirty states had already prohibited the juvenile death penalty, including 12 that had abandoned the death penalty altogether. Among the 20 states that still permitted juvenile executions, the practice was infrequent. The Court also found that when enacting the Federal Death Penalty Act (18 U.S.C.S. § 3591) in 1994, Congress had determined that the death penalty should not extend to juveniles. The immaturity of juveniles made them less culpable, the Court reasoned. The Court also noted that the United States was the only country in the world that continued to sanction the juvenile death penalty.

O'Connor dissented, arguing that "the court had adduced no evidence impeaching the seemingly reasonable conclusion reached by many state legislatures that at least some 17-year-old murderers were sufficiently mature to deserve the death penalty." Scalia, joined by Rehnquist and Thomas, also dissented, writing that the court "had proclaimed itself the sole arbiter of the nation's moral standards" and "in the course of discharging that responsibility, had purported to take guidance from the views of foreign courts,"[54] never a popular position in the U.S.

Between 1976 and *Roper v. Simmons*, 22 juvenile offenders had been executed, about two percent of all executions during that time.

HISTORICAL HIGHLIGHT
A Killer Called "Youngster"

At age 17, Anzel Keon Jones was a sophomore in North Lamar High School in Paris, Texas. He was a mediocre student but an accomplished athlete who ran track and played receiver and running back on the football team. His only brush with the law before the morning of May 2, 1995, was an appearance in juvenile court the year before for stealing cigarettes.

"I'm sort of a people person," he said in an interview from the Texas Department of Criminal Justice Prison, where he was known by his fellow inmates on death row as "Youngster."

J. Kerye Ashmore, an assistant district attorney who prosecuted Jones, described him differently. "This is what I can tell you about Anzel Keon Jones,"

Ashmore said. "He went into a backyard, took a nearly 50-year-old woman and beat her with a gun, cut her throat in front of her mother, then sexually assaulted her mother in every way imaginable, including perforating her organ with an antenna, cut her throat, attempted to burn the house down and fled. He doesn't deserve to be in society ever again. He needs to be executed. Twelve people heard the evidence, including his age, and didn't feel that it mitigated his crime."

Asked why he did it, Jones said, "I sit back nights, actually years, and I just can't think of anything." Anzel was one of 28 Texas death row inmates whose sentence was commuted to life in prison following the U.S. Supreme Court decision to abolish the death penalty for prisoners who had been younger than 18 at the time they committed their crimes.

OFFENSES PUNISHABLE BY DEATH

Generally, most states reserve the death penalty for murder or felony murder, at least where the defendant was substantially involved in the victim's death.[55] Whether someone is substantially involved in a murder depends on the facts of the case. For example, substantial involvement was not found in a case where the defendant did not intend to kill anyone, did not know that his codefendant would do so, and only drove the getaway car.[56] However, when another defendant, along with other family members, planned his father's escape from prison and watched his father kill and rob a family of four during the getaway, the defendant was sentenced to death. The father was serving a life sentence because he had killed a guard in a previous, unsuccessful escape attempt. The son's sentence was upheld by the U.S. Supreme Court in *Tison v. Arizona*.[57]

A few states add treason as a capital offense. One state, Louisiana, specifies death for the aggravated rape of a victim under age 12. If the rape involves an adult, the death penalty is improper. In *Coker v. Georgia*, the Supreme Court ruled that death for rape is unconstitutional.[58] The defendant, while serving a life sentence for murder, rape, kidnapping, and aggravated assault, escaped from a Georgia prison and raped an adult woman. In *Coker,* the Supreme Court ruled that the Eighth Amendment bars not only punishments that are barbaric, but also those that are excessive. The Court wrote:

> [a] punishment is "excessive" and unconstitutional if it makes no measurable contribution to acceptable goals of punishment and hence is nothing more than purposeless and needless imposition of pain and suffering or is grossly out of proportion to the severity of the crime.[59]

Under federal law, death is an allowable sanction for a number of offenses, including the taking of a human life, espionage terrorist acts, and treason.[60] The Supreme Court has upheld death for espionage.[61]

HISTORICAL HIGHLIGHT
Death for Corruption?

For as long as the debate about capital punishment has raged, the question of when to use it has been at the forefront. In the days of segregation, crimes committed by African-Americans were capital crimes, while the same crime committed by a Caucasian only brought a jail sentence. This clearly unfair application of capital punishment fed the movement against capital punishment in the late 1960s and early 1970s.

There are some who believe in the death penalty but don't like the way it is applied. Some believe that chronic sex offenders should receive the death penalty, while teenagers who commit violent crimes should not. They reason that the violent teenagers are more likely to be rehabilitated than the sex offenders.

In an interesting twist in the debate, Pennsylvania Supreme Court nominee John A. Maher advocated the death penalty for corrupt politicians during his confirmation hearings in 1997. Understandably, the Pennsylvania state senators who had to confirm Maher in order for him to take a seat on the high court were less than enthusiastic about his views.

Maher was quoted by the *Philadelphia Inquirer* as saying, "I think the highest crime is the sale of office, and I am always offended as a citizen when I read the sale of office accompanied by a two-year probation. I'm not against capital punishment. I just think we should be more careful about what we give it for. The sale of office is an offense against the very existence of society."[62]

Maher's position was seen as too extreme, certainly for the politicians passing judgment on him, and he was not confirmed. At Maher's request, then Pennsylvania Governor Tom Ridge withdrew his name from consideration.

HISTORICAL HIGHLIGHT
Julius and Ethel Rosenberg Executed for Espionage

Julius and Ethel Rosenberg are the only Americans to receive the death penalty during peacetime for the crime of espionage. They were executed in New York's electric chair at Sing Sing Prison on June 19, 1953, after last-minute appeals to the U.S. Supreme Court were turned down and President Dwight Eisenhower denied a plea for executive clemency. They left behind two young sons, Robert, age 6, and Michael, age 10. Both boys were later relocated and placed in an adoptive home.

The Rosenbergs were accused of giving the Soviet Union top secret information about the United States' development of an atomic bomb during World War II. The program, code-named the Manhattan Project, led to the end of the war with Japan after the atomic bomb was dropped on Japanese civilians in the cities of Nagasaki and Hiroshima. Many of the scientists working on the project were refugees from wartime Europe. One of them, German-born, lifelong Communist Klaus Fuchs provided secret data to the Russians.

Klaus Fuchs was arrested and convicted of espionage in Great Britain in 1949. He received a 15-year jail term in exchange for providing information about other spies. He provided authorities the name of American Harry Gold. In turn, Gold implicated David Greenglass as another spy for the Soviets. Greenglass was Ethel's brother. In exchange for a guarantee that his wife would not be prosecuted and no prison sentence for himself, he implicated his sister and her husband, Julius. He claimed they had recruited him for the Soviets. He testified against them at their trial.

Both Ethel and Julius insisted that they were innocent but were convicted of espionage by a jury. Although urged to do so, they would not cooperate and name others as spies. They were sentenced to death. Up until the hour of their executions, they were offered clemency if they would name others in their alleged spy ring. Recently declassified information in both the United States and the former Soviet Union indicate that Julius, but not Ethel, may have been involved in low-level espionage but does not implicate them in passing atomic secrets.

LIFE IN PRISON

According to the Federal Bureau of Investigation (FBI), there were 11.6 million crimes reported to law enforcement officials in 2005. These included 16,692 murders, 93,934 forcible rapes, and about 2 million burglaries.[63] The numbers of both violent and nonviolent crimes have decreased since the early 1990s, and the rates of each have also declined. Still, roughly two-thirds of offenders released from prison are rearrested within three years. In response, many legislatures have passed laws requiring long sentences for recidivists. So-called "three strikes and you're out" legislation has been popular with many state lawmakers. These laws attempt to eliminate recidivism by providing that repeat offenders be imprisoned for life.

The U.S. Supreme Court has upheld some forms of repeat offender legislation as a legitimate use of state police powers, writing that states have an "interest expressed in all recidivism statutes, in dealing in a harsher manner with those who by repeated criminal acts have shown that they are simply incapable of conforming to the norms of society."[64]

Prisoners have argued that mandatory life in prison for repeat offenders is cruel and unusual punishment, especially when applied to relatively minor crimes. Two such cases have reached the Supreme Court. In 1980, the Court concluded that life in prison for three nonviolent crimes was not unconstitutional as long as the prisoner was at some point eligible for parole. The case involved the following three convictions:

1. Credit card theft, $80.00
2. Forged check, $28
3. False pretenses, $120

The defendant was therefore given a life sentence as a recidivist for the theft of $228 over a nine-year period.[65]

However, in 1983, the Supreme Court struck down a similar law in a case where a defendant was sentenced to life in prison with no chance of parole for writing a bad check for $100, his third petty offense. Because he was never eligible for parole, the Court ruled the punishment cruel and unusual.[66]

HISTORICAL HIGHLIGHT
That's the Way the Cookie Crumbles

A parolee, Kevin Weber, broke into a restaurant to steal chocolate chip cookies and was sentenced to 25 years to life. The sentence may seem a little stiff, but the judge had no choice. Under California's "three strikes, you're out" law, any third felony conviction sends the felon away for a long time. Weber's intention was to rob the restaurant's safe, but he was unable to open it before he set off the burglar alarm. Apparently, somewhere along the way he decided he needed a snack and picked up some chocolate chip cookies. When police arrested him, he had the cookies in his pockets.[67]

Critics of the "three strikes, you're out" law argue that it ties judges' hands when sentencing offenders and makes no distinction between violent felons and nonviolent cookie snatchers. However, supporters of the law feel that anyone who is convicted of a third felony is a career criminal and should be locked away.

This case and others like it received much publicity. In fact, California has sentenced over 300 petty criminals to life in prison under the three strikes law. When the Ninth Circuit Court of Appeals got a case testing the constitutionality of California's three strike law, it concluded the law was unconstitutional as applied to convictions for shoplifting that resulted in a term of life in prison. The February 7, 2002 decision affects only those whose third convictions are for shoplifting. The same court ruled earlier that the law applied to the theft of videotapes was unconstitutional as cruel and unusual punishment. California appealed both cases to the U.S. Supreme Court.[68] The Court agreed to hear arguments on both cases in the 2002–2003 term.[69] On March 5, 2003, the Court by a 5–4 vote upheld the sentences.

PRISON CONDITIONS

Generally, the punishments prohibited by the Eighth Amendment are those considered to be torture or otherwise barbarous. The U.S. Constitution prohibits the "wanton and unnecessary infliction of pain."[70] Imprisonment itself obviously carries with it some control over the day-to-day lives of the inmates, including confinement and physical coercion when necessary. These are not constitutionally prohibited unless they rise to a level that can cause serious illness or injury. Thus, double bunking in prison is allowable.[71] However, conditions cannot be so poor that inmates are allowed to prey on each other and prisoners suffer malnutrition.[72] In addition, adequate medical care must be provided for inmates.[73]

HISTORICAL HIGHLIGHT
The Hitching Post Meets the Eighth Amendment

In June 1995, Larry Hope, an inmate at the Limestone Prison in Alabama, received the usual punishment for disruptive behavior. He was confined to a hitching post, a bar placed approximately 57 inches above the ground.

While being taken to his chain gang's work site, Hope made vulgar remarks and wrestled with a prison guard. The guards transported him back to the prison in handcuffs and shackles. Upon arrival, they removed Hope's shirt and handcuffed him to the hitching post. He remained shirtless, in a standing position with his hands above his shoulders, for seven hours in the hot Alabama sun. During his time on the hitching post, Hope was offered water only once or twice and was given no bathroom breaks. One guard even taunted him about being thirsty.

In 2002, the U.S. Supreme Court ruled in Hope's favor in a civil suit against the three guards who participated in his punishment. Citing precedence from *Ort v. White,*[74] the justices held that "physical abuse directed at [a] prisoner after he terminates his resistance to authority would constitute an actionable Eighth Amendment violation." The Court also ruled that the guards were not entitled to qualified immunity—they could be held liable in Hope's suit against them—because any reasonable person could have determined that this type of punishment is cruel and unusual.

EMERGING TRENDS

Two trends in punishment have recently received widespread press coverage and attention from state and federal legislators. Both attempt to deal with repeat offenders.

PREDATORY SEX OFFENDER REGISTRATION

Every state now has predatory sex offender registration laws mandating that prisoners who are released from prison after violent sexual offenses or those involving children must register their address and make public their presence in the community where they live after release. These laws are generally referred to as Megan's Laws. Named for Megan Kanka, a young girl who was raped and murdered by a repeat sexual offender, these new laws are causing controversy. Federal law establishes a national database at the FBI designed to track every person who has been convicted of a criminal offense against a minor, a sexually violent offense, or who is a sexually violent "predator."

Offenders are categorized by the severity of their crimes and the likelihood of their reoffending. Level One offenders are first-time offenders considered a lower risk to society. Level Two offenders are convicted of multiple or more serious offenses and are considered a higher risk. Level Three offenders are repeat offenders or those committing the most serious offenses and are considered to pose the highest risk of reoffending. Offenders must register with the National Sex Offender Registry and keep their registrations up to date, Level One offenders for 15 years from release, Level Two for 25 years, and Level Three for life. In addition, federal law requires that state and local governmental officials release relevant information deemed necessary to protect the public from predators.[75] It is up to the states to decide how much information to publish and about what levels of offenders. Some states send photo postcards to neighborhoods to announce the presence of violent sexual predators. Each state has its own requirements for registration, and most have searchable sites on the World Wide Web, many complete with pictures, names, and addresses. Some, such as Maine, have been criticized for including addresses of all offenders. On the other hand, Pennsylvania has been criticized for not giving addresses of any offenders, which some feel make its registry useless.

Recently, states have been improvising ways to monitor offenders. Delaware provides for the letter "Y" to be imprinted on the driver's license of all monitored sex offenders. Some states have residency requirements that forbid sex offenders from living within a prescribed distance from schools, pools, and day care centers. After 9-year-old Jessica Lunsford was abducted, raped, and buried alive by a repeat sex offender in Homosassa, Florida, a public outcry led to the introduction of Global Positioning System (GPS) monitoring in Florida. Several states followed suit. Ohio's law requires GPS monitoring for life for sexually violent offenders; Oklahoma's law imposes lifetime monitoring on all habitual offenders.[76]

YOU MAKE THE CALL

MEGAN'S LAW: OPEN SEASON FOR VIGILANTES?

On August 26, 2005, Michael Mullen went to the home of three men living together in Bellingham, Washington, who were listed as Level Three offenders on the state's sex offender registry. Dressed in a black cap and blue jumpsuit, Mullen identified himself as an FBI agent there to warn them of an Internet "hit list" targeting sex offenders. One of the roommates left for work while Mullen was in the house. When he came home the next morning, he found both of his roommates dead from gunshot wounds.

Calling himself "Agent Life," Mullen posted messages online and sent letters to the media following the attack, saying he was responsible "for the deaths of two level three pedophiles in Bellingham, Washington" and adding "they are not the last to be executed unless things change for the better."[77] Subsequent investigation revealed that Mullen had been sexually abused as a child. He faces two charges of aggravated first-degree murder and a possible death sentence.

Eight months later, Stephen Marshall of Nova Scotia, armed with two handguns and a list of registered sex offenders loaded into his laptop, drove to Corinth, Maine, and shot William Elliott dead. He then drove to Milo to the home of 57-year-old Joseph Gray and shot him through a window as his wife watched terrified. When police caught up with Marshall aboard a bus in Boston, he killed himself.

The mother of Marshall's first victim, William Elliott, said her son was 19 when he had sex with his girlfriend, who was a couple of weeks shy of her sixteenth birthday. She said he was in love and wanted to have a family with her. Marshall had access online to Elliott's name and address, the charges, sexual abuse of a minor, and the time served, four months.[78]

Is Megan's Law safe? Is it constitutional? John La Fond, a retired professor from the University of Missouri Law School and author of *Preventing Sexual Violence: How Society Should Cope with Sex Offenders*, has said, "These laws are almost a confession by the state that we have done all we can, you must now take the defense of your family into your own hands."[79] Kansas City civil rights attorney Arthur Benson, who has challenged Missouri's lifetime sexual offender registry, says, "While these laws are often couched in terms of protecting the public against repeat offenses, at heart they are vengeful, punishing acts."[80]

On the other hand, roughly 69 percent of sexual assault victims are juveniles. Children 17 and under comprise approximately 84 percent of victims of forcible fondling, 79 percent of forcible sodomy victims, and 75 percent of victims of sexual assault with an object.[81] One in 5 violent state prisoners reported a victim under age 18.[82]

Are sex offender registries the modern equivalent of the Scarlet Letter? Do they protect children from dangerous predators? You make the call!

HISTORICAL HIGHLIGHT

Prisoners Are Covered by the Americans with Disabilities Act

Ronald Yeskey was a prisoner in a state prison in Pennsylvania when he heard about a program the state offered first-time offenders like himself. It was a motivational boot camp that allowed qualified prisoners to have their sentences reduced upon completion. Yeskey applied for the program but was rejected because of his history of high blood pressure.

Yeskey claimed that he was being discriminated against because of his disability. In effect, he said he would have to stay in prison longer because of his disability. He filed suit against the Commonwealth of Pennsylvania under the Americans with Disabilities Act (ADA).

The ADA prohibits discrimination against "qualified persons with disabilities" by any "public entity." The case went all the way to the U.S. Supreme Court, who ruled in Yeskey's favor. In their ruling, they stated that the ADA's wording was very clear that "all public entities" were covered by the ADA.[83]

In *United States v. Georgia et al.,* the Supreme Court also found in favor of a disabled inmate asserting ADA rights, relying in part on its ruling in *Yeskey*. Tony Goodman, a paraplegic inmate in a Georgia state prison, claimed that his cell was too small to allow him to turn his wheelchair around and that he lacked accessible toilet and shower facilities. He also claimed he was denied physical therapy and medical treatment, as well as access to prison programs and services because of his disability.

The Supreme Court held that Goodman's treatment, which forced him to sit in his own bodily waste at times, violated his Fourteenth Amendment protections against cruel and unusual punishment and remanded his ADA case for further consideration. The ruling granted Congress the authority to apply the ADA to prisons in cases where Fourteenth Amendment violations could be shown. However, it did not go beyond that to grant Congress full authority to apply the ADA to prisons more generally.[84]

The U.S. Supreme Court has twice in the last few years addressed whether convicted sex offenders who have served their sentences can be further confined. In *Kansas v. Hendricks,* 521 U.S. 346 (1997), the Court concluded that the Kansas Sexually Violent Predator Act was constitutional. The Act allowed involuntary confinement of persons with a mental abnormality or personality disorder who were found to be dangerous by a jury. The Court also ruled that confinement after serving a sentence for sex offenses wasn't double jeopardy. Nor was the law an *ex post facto* law, since it was not criminal, but civil in nature. In *Kansas v. Crane,* 534 U.S. 407 (2002), the Court clarified that the state must show at a minimum that the person they want to confine must have at least some difficulty controlling his urges but wasn't required to show that it would be impossible to control those urges.

In 2003, the Court considered whether the registration laws are in effect *ex post facto* laws[85] and held that they were not.[86] So far, Megan's Laws have held up to a multitude of legal challenges.

HISTORICAL HIGHLIGHT
Convicted Sex Offender Programs and Self-Incrimination

The state of Kansas offers convicted sex offenders an opportunity to participate in a Sexual Abuse Treatment Program (SATP), which requires participating inmates to complete a sexual history form revealing all of their prior sexual activities. This list of activities could include any activities that may constitute a criminal offense for which an inmate has never been charged. Kansas makes no promise that the information will never be used against them. Inmates who refuse to participate in the program may have a reduction in their prison privileges and could be transferred to a potentially more dangerous maximum security area.

Robert G. Lile, a Kansas prisoner, was facing the dilemma of choosing between improved prison privileges and disclosing potentially incriminating information about his past that could lead to further criminal charges. He filed an action for injunctive relief on the grounds that participating in Kansas' SATP would violate his Fifth Amendment protection against compelled self-incrimination.

The Tenth Circuit decided that because refusing to participate in the program would result in an automatic reduction of Mr. Lile's privileges and housing accommodations, the penalty would have a sufficiently substantial impact on him that it would constitute a compelling reason to release information that could create a risk of further prosecution. However, the U.S. Supreme Court overturned this decision on appeal, stating that the consequences for refusing to participate were not great enough to compel a prisoner to abandon his or her right against self-incrimination.[87]

The question still remains of how broadly Megan's Law may be applied. Louis Rocco of Scranton, Pennsylvania, never actually had any physical contact with any of his victims. He admitted to making numerous telephone calls and leaving notes threatening violent sexual acts. Although Rocco's case is pending, prosecutors have expressed their intent to try to have Megan's Law applied to his case. Dana Oxley, Assistant District Attorney for Lackawanna County, said, "To me, if there was ever a case for Megan's Law, this is it, despite the lack of physical contact. The psychological terror he inflicted on his victims matches or possibly exceeds physical terror."[88]

CHEMICAL CASTRATION

Chemical castration of sex offenders is also gaining in popularity. Both surgical castration and chemical castration have been used in Norway, Sweden, Denmark, and Switzerland for a number of years. Now several states in the United States have followed suit. California[89] and Georgia[90] have passed laws making chemical castration a condition of parole for sex offenses, especially those involving a child victim. Chemical castration is accomplished by the injection of the chemical medroxyprogesterone acetate, commonly referred to by its trade name, Depo-Provera. The drug reduces the level of testosterone and decreases the male sex drive.

Chemical castration is likely to be challenged on Eighth Amendment grounds as cruel and unusual punishment.

HISTORICAL HIGHLIGHT
Not All Sexual Predators Are Male

A Tacoma, Washington, woman is listed as a sexual predator under the provisions of that state's Megan's Law. In 1990, Laura Faye McCollum was convicted of raping a 3-year-old girl. She completed her 5½-year sentence in 1995 and has been housed at a treatment center ever since. She remains confined voluntarily.

McCollum is aware of her condition but is almost helpless to stop her own actions if left unsupervised. One of her counselors described her as "an obsessive and compulsive child molester who is particularly attracted to preverbal and barely verbal children ages 2 to 4."

This type of obsessive behavior is more commonly found in males, but at least one other woman has made the sexual predator list. Minnesota also has a woman sex offender on that state's list.[91]

In fact, there were enough female sex offenders listed in the Georgia state registry that someone dedicated an Internet Web site to them. Miss Georgia's Sex Offenders 2004 Pageant featured photos of 18 female sex offenders culled from the registry, including the women's names, ages, and crimes under headings such as "Most Swine-Like," "Miss Herpes," and "Most Likely to be Mistaken for Jabba the Hut."[92]

Women make up 1 to 2 percent of sex offenders.[93] With 550,000 registered offenders in the United States,[94] that makes between 5,000 and 10,000 female sex offenders.

HISTORICAL HIGHLIGHT
Study Blasts Death Penalty

There has been a real resurgence in the past few years in popular opposition to the imposition of the death penalty. A rash of cases in which death row inmates have been proven not guilty through DNA analysis of evidence has shaken some in the legal community. Since 1989, more than 100 people have been released from prison because of DNA tests, 12 of them from death row.[95] As yet, there has been no definitive cases clearing a defendant who has already been executed. However, there have been enough cases of wrongful conviction to worry even staunch supporters of the death penalty.

Adding to the public discourse is a study by Columbia Law School faculty and researchers. Released February 11, 2002, the study reports that of all capital cases analyzed between 1973 and 1995, 68 percent were reversed on appeal due to serious, reversible error. The study concludes that the "U.S. legal system is collapsing under the weight of error-filled death penalty cases" and recommends the imposition of a new standard of evidence in capital cases. Instead of finding a defendant guilty beyond a reasonable doubt, the researchers call for finding guilt beyond any doubt. The study is *A Broken System, Part II: Why There Is So Much Error in Capital Cases and What Can Be Done About It.*

HISTORICAL HIGHLIGHT
Governor Ryan Has Death Penalty Doubts

Following the release of a thirteenth exonerated death row inmate since the reinstatement of the death penalty in 1977, Illinois Governor George Ryan declared a statewide moratorium on executions on January 31, 2002. Ryan appointed a commission to study Illinois' death penalty administration. In April 2002, the Commission of Capital Punishment presented a report suggesting over 80 changes that Illinois could implement to make their death penalty system less likely to convict and execute innocent suspects. These suggestions included establishing a panel to review prosecutorial decisions to seek the death penalty before the case goes to trial, having the police videotape all interrogations of homicide suspects rather than solely the confession, and giving judges the ability to reverse a jury's death sentence if the verdict seems improper. Best-selling author Scott Turow was a member of the commission, and the work he did served as a catalyst for his legal thriller, *Reversible Errors.* He has also written a short book, *Ultimate Punishment: A Lawyer's Reflections on Dealing with the Death Penalty.*

In a similar situation, Maryland's release of their hundredth innocent death row inmate prompted Governor Paris N. Glendening to declare a moratorium and order a study done on racial bias in the Maryland capital punishment administration. As death penalty activists see that the U.S. Supreme Court is susceptible to arguments that evolving community standards may require it to shift its stand on capital punishment, calls for moratoriums are gaining ground.

HISTORICAL HIGHLIGHT
What If MySpace Flagged You as a Sexual Predator?

Jessica Davis, a 29-year-old University of Colorado student, was shocked one day in May 2007, when she was kicked off of the Web site MySpace.com on the grounds that she was a registered sex offender. Davis, as she immediately told MySpace, had no idea what they were talking about. An English major on her way to studying law, Davis insisted she had no criminal record and was not a sex offender.

Several days later, MySpace responded by saying it did not keep records of removed profiles. It took several days before Sentinel Corporation, which built the database for MySpace, acknowledged that the system had flagged her because there was a registered sex offender with the same name and a birth date two years and two days off from Davis'.[96] Sounds close, until you consider that there are over one-half million registered sex offenders in this country.

MySpace had introduced the database in 2006, after journalist Kevin Poulsen published an investigative report saying he had crossed MySpace member profiles against the National Sex Offender Registry and found 744 verified matches. Poulsen wrote that one registered offender was "actively trolling for underage boys" on MySpace. That offender was later arrested. MySpace responded by hiring a background check company, Sentinel Tech Holding Corp., to conduct a similar search.

Within the next year, My Space removed 29,000 offenders from its Web site, out of a total of more than 180 million profiles. After news of the Web site's discoveries were made public, eight attorneys general sent a letter to MySpace expressing concern over the Web site's design, particularly that it did not require parental permission before minors could create a profile. The attorneys general also asked MySpace to provide the names of the registered sex offenders the company had removed from the site.[97]

Jessica Davis, who hopes to work in public service, is concerned that her close call with the National Sex Offender Registry will come back to haunt her. "I don't want to have to explain to people that there's this Web site MySpace, and they screwed this up," Davis said. "I don't want to have to defend my innocence."

PRACTICE POINTERS

Whether you work in law enforcement or on a defense team, you will probably find that the most stressful cases are those involving the death penalty. Fortunately, such cases don't come along frequently and are likely to fall into the hands of experienced prosecutors and defense counsel who have handled difficult cases.

The stakes are high, for both the victim's family and for the defendant. If the prosecution is wrong and an innocent person is convicted and executed, the public's confidence in the legal system will suffer, and the system will have been responsible for a tragic and irreversible miscarriage of justice. Needless to say, everyone involved in the process must approach the case with integrity.

Fortunately, there are resources available to help assure justice. You learned about some in Chapter 12, particularly the use of forensic evidence such as DNA analysis to produce physical evidence of guilt.

There is also specialized training available. Just about every state with the death penalty requires attorneys to get specialized training. That's one way to assure that defendants, no matter their income or socioeconomic status, get a fair trial. Some resources include:

- Federal Judicial Center—provides resources for federal judges and their support staff who are handling a death penalty case. More information is available at *www.fjc.gov*.
- U.S. Department of Justice—provides resources for U.S. attorneys handling death penalty cases. More information is available at *http://www.usdoj.gov/usao/eousa/foia_reading_room/usam/title9/10mcrm.htm*.
- Northeastern University Capital Jurors Project—provides information on how jurors arrive at decisions in capital cases. More information is available at *http://www.cjp.neu.edu*.
- National Center for State Courts—resources for defense counsel. More information is available at *http://www.ncsconline.org/wc/CourTopics/ResourceGuide.asp?topic=CapPun*.
- Capital Defense Weekly—provides up-to-date information for defense counsel. More information is available at *http://capitaldefenseweekly.com*.
- Cornell Death Penalty Project—provides information on the death penalty. More information is available at *http://library2.lawschool.cornell.edu/death/default.htm*.

CHAPTER SUMMARY

The Eighth Amendment has historical roots reaching back at least as far as the Magna Carta of 1215. Transplanted to the United States by English colonists, it serves as the minimum standard by which criminal punishments are measured.

Capital punishment has provided a fertile ground for interpretation of the ban on cruel and unusual punishment. For a brief period of time it seemed as if the death penalty would expire, beginning with the 1972 U.S. Supreme Court decision in *Fuhrman v. Georgia*. But rather than signaling its death rattle, proponents came back with new and improved legislation. In 1976, the Supreme Court revisited its 1972 decision and upheld a death penalty statute that provided procedural safeguards against arbitrary and capricious imposition of the penalty.

Life in prison is not cruel and unusual punishment for numerous offenses, including those committed by both violent and nonviolent offenders. For nonviolent offenders, a recidivism statute may not forever foreclose the possibility of parole.

Generally, prison conditions are not cruel and unusual punishment unless they reach the level of wanton and unnecessary infliction of pain.

Two areas of punishment likely to receive review under the Eighth Amendment are lifetime sex offender registration and castration of sex offenders.

KEY TERMS

Aggravating Circumstance	Cruel and Unusual Punishment	Per Se Transportation
Bloody Code	Minor	
Corporal Punishment	Mitigating Circumstance	

EXERCISE

1. In 1965, Edward "Teddy" Deegan was shot in an alley. At the time, the FBI's priority was its war against the Mafia. When a mob hit man, who had been working with the FBI, told local prosecutors that the killers were Joseph Salvati, Peter Limone, Henry Tameleo, and Louis Greco, the four were charged with murder. The FBI agents didn't tell authorities that they knew the hit man was lying, and the four were convicted. In reality, the hit man and apparently the FBI knew the identity of the real killer.

   Two of the defendants died in prison, while Salvati and Limone were freed after 30 years in prison. Limone had spent part of his prison time on death row. The truth came to light when memos surfaced during another unrelated investigation into FBI misconduct.

   The surviving men and the estates of the men who died in prison sued the FBI for wrongful conviction. They were awarded approximately $1 million for each year spent in prison, or a total of $102,000 million. Was the verdict fair?

   Now consider the case of a Hanover, Pennsylvania, man who spent 16 years in prison for a crime he did not commit. In 1987, Berry Laughman was convicted of murder and had allegedly confessed to state trooper John J. Holtz that he had raped and murdered 85-year-old Edna Laughman, a distant relative. At the time, the prosecution sought the death penalty, but a jury spared his life.

   At trial, state police chemist Janice Roadcap (see references to Roadcap from previous chapters) offered explanations for why Laughman's blood type differed from that of the semen found on the victim. DNA testing was not yet possible at the time, so no tests absolutely ruled out Laughman. But the DNA was saved, and a news reporter tracked the sample down in 2003. Tests revealed Berry was not the source of the semen, and he was freed.

   Berry Laughman has sued Roadcap, Holtz, and a third trooper, alleging that they concocted the confession and that Roadcap falsely testified about the physical evidence, casting doubt where there was no scientific reason for doubt.[98] At the time of this writing, a trial was scheduled. If the defendants are shown to have concocted false evidence, what do you think an appropriate punishment would be?

DISCUSSION QUESTIONS

1. Explain the history of the Eighth Amendment to the U.S. Constitution.
2. Define criminal punishment.
3. List and explain the two requirements that must be satisfied before a punishment is cruel and unusual.

4. Explain why capital punishment is not unconstitutional as cruel and unusual punishment.
5. Explain what procedural protection is required before the death penalty can be carried out.
6. Define aggravating and mitigating circumstances.
7. List the classifications of persons who can be executed.
8. List the crimes that are punishable by death.
9. Explain the U.S. Supreme Court's position on life in prison for repeat offenders.
10. List and describe two current trends in punishment.

FOR FURTHER READING AND VIEWING

READING

1. Meeropol, R., and Meeropol, M. (1975). *We Are Your Sons: The Legacy of Ethel and Julius Rosenberg.* Houghton Miffllin.
   Written by the sons of Ethel and Julius Rosenberg, who were made orphans by the execution of their parents. This book tells the story of the trial, conviction, and execution of the Rosenbergs through the eyes of 6- and 9-year-old Robert and Michael. It includes death row correspondence from their parents.
2. Prejean, H. (1993). *Dead Man Walking.* Random House.
   Recounts a Roman Catholic nun's work with Louisiana death row inmates. The book has been made into a major movie starring Susan Sarandon and Sean Penn.
3. Radelet, M. L., Hugo, A. B., and Putnam, C. (1992). *In Spite of Innocence: Erroneous Convictions in Capital Cases.* Northeastern University Press.
   Studies the cases of 400 Americans who have been convicted of capital crimes and either were executed or incarcerated. The authors argue all were innocent of the crimes charged.
4. Roberts, S. (2001). *The Brother: The Untold Story of Atomic Spy David Greenglass and How He Sent His Sister, Ethel Rosenberg, to the Electric Chair.* Random House.
   After years of silence, a *New York Times* reporter gets Ethel's brother to confess his involvement in the Rosenberg case.
5. Turow, S. (2002). *Reversible Errors.* Farrar Straus Giroux.
   Tells the fictional story of a corporate attorney appointed to represent a death row inmate who just possibly might be innocent of the triple murder he was sentenced to death for committing.
6. Turow, S. (2003). *Ultimate Punishment: A Lawyer's Reflections on Dealing with the Death Penalty.* Farrar Straus Giroux.
   Tells of Turow's involvement with the Illinois Commission of Capital Punishment.
7. LaFond, J. (2005). *Preventing Sexual Violence: How Society Should Cope with Sex Offenders.* American Psychological Association.

VIEWING

1. *The Green Mile.* (2000). Warner.
   A film starring Tom Hanks and featuring life on death row.

2. *Monster.* (2003).

The role of Aileen Wuornos, a prostitute executed in 2002 for a series of murders in Florida, won actress Charlize Theron the 2003 Best Actress Academy Award. The film attempts to explain Aileen's horrific childhood and gradual transformation into a serial killer.

ENDNOTES

1. L. O. Pike, *A History of Crime in England* (London: Elder & Co., 1973).

2. M. Ignatieff, *A Just Measure of Pain; the Penitentiary in the Industrial Revolution, 1750–1850* (New York: Pantheon, 1978).

3. M. R. Latham, and W. Matthews, eds., *The Diary of Samuel Pepys, A New and Complete Transcription* (Berkeley: University of California Press, 1978).

4. Ignatieff, *A Just Measure of Pain.*

5. Ibid.

6. 1 Wm. & Mary, sess. 2, ch. 2 (1689).

7. Magna Carta (1215).

8. *Webster's New World/Stedman's Medical Dictionary,* 1st ed., 1987, defines hematoma as "a localized mass of extravasated, usually clotted, blood confined within an organ, tissue or space."

9. *Ingraham v. Wright,* 430 U.S. 651 (1977).

10. There are other remedies available under the law. For example, school children who are paddled or slapped may be able to recover damages for the torts of assault and battery, and the punishment may constitute criminal assault or child abuse.

11. *Black's Law Dictionary.*

12. *Robinson v. California,* 370 U.S. 660 (1962).

13. *Robinson v. California,* 370 U.S. 660, 668 (1962).

14. *Ford v. Wainwright,* 477 U.S. 399 (1986).

15. *Trop v. Dulles,* 356 U.S. 86 (1958).

16. U.S. Constitution, Fifth Amendment.

17. Alaska, District of Columbia, Hawaii, Iowa, Maine, Massachusetts, Michigan, Minnesota, North Dakota, Rhode Island, Vermont, West Virginia, and Wisconsin.

18. *Edmund v. Florida,* 458 U.S. 782 (1982).

19. *Tison v. Arizona,* 481 U.S. 137 (1987). See Chapter 14 for an explanation of the felony murder rule.

20. Bureau of Justice Statistics, U.S. Department of Justice, *Capital Punishment 2000,* December 31, 2000.

21. *Louisiana ex rel. Francis v. Resweber,* 329 U.S. 459 (1947).

22. R. Hood, *The Death Penalty, A World Wide Perspective,* 2nd ed. (Oxford: Clarendon Press, 1996).

23. *Furman v. Georgia,* 408 U.S. 238 (1972).

24. *Gregg v. Georgia,* 428 U.S. 153 (1976).

25. *Roberts v. Louisiana,* 431 U.S. 633 (1977) and *Roberts v. Louisiana,* 428 U.S. 325 (1976). Although both cases involve an automatic death sentence for cop killers, the two defendants are not related. They only share the same name, crime, and sentence.

26. *Abdul-Kabir (fka Cole) v. Quarterman,* 550 U.S. (2007).

27. *Penry v. Lynaugh,* 492 U.S. 302.

28. "Executions in the United States in 2007," Death Penalty Information Center, July 2007.

29. *In re Kimmler,* 136 U.S. 436 (1890).

30. *Wilkerson v. Utah,* 99 U.S.1130 (1879).

31. *Louisiana ex rel. Francis v. Resweber,* 329 U.S. 459, 465 (1947).

32. D. P. Baker, *Washington Post,* March 26, 1997, p. A01.

33. M. Clay, "Flames Leap from Inmate's Head at Execution," *Los Angeles Times,* March 26, 1997.

34. Ibid.

35. Ibid.

36. "Some Examples of Post–Furman Botched Executions," Death Penalty Information Center, May 24, 2007.

37. *Baze v. Rees,* 128 S.Ct. 34 (2007)

38. *Ford v. Wainwright,* 477 U.S. 399 (1986).

39. Ibid.

40. *Washington v. Harper,* 494 U.S. 210 (1990).

41. *Perry v. Louisiana,* 498 U.S. 38 (1990).

42. *State v. Perry,* 610 So. 2d 757 (1992).

43. "Death Sentence Commuted for Mentally Ill Man," CNN Online, February 26, 2002.

44. *Sell v. United States,* 539 offenses punishab U.S. 166 (2003).

45. "Arkansas

46. "Forced into Sanity before Death," *San Antonio Express-News,* April 17, 2006.

47. Bureau of Justice Statistics, U.S. Department of Justice, *Capital Punishment 1996.*

48. *Penry v. Lynaugh,* 492 U.S. 302 (1989).

49. Ibid.

50. *Atkins v. Virginia,* 536 U.S. 304 (2002).

51. *Tennard v. Dretke,* 124 S. Ct. 2562 (2004).

52. *Thompson v. Oklahoma,* 487 U.S. 815 (1988).

53. "Juvenile Defenders Who Were On Death Row," Death Penalty Information Center, 2007.

54. *Roper v. Simmons,* 543 U.S. 551 (2005).

55. Murder committed during the commission of a felony, such as rape or armed robbery, even if not personally committed by the defendant. See Chapter 14 for a more complete discussion.

56. *Edmund v. Florida,* 458 U.S. 782 (1982).

57. *Tison v. Arizona,* 481 U.S. 137 (1987).

58. *Coker v. Georgia,* 433 U.S. 584 (1977).

59. *Coker,* at 593.

60. 18 U.S.C. § 7794; 18 U.S.C. § 2381.

61. *Rosenberg v. United States,* 346 U.S. 273 (1953).

62. "Professor Withdraws as High-Court Nominee: Supreme Court Nominee John Maher Had Said Corrupt Politicians Deserve to Die," *Philadelphia Inquirer,* March 19, 1997. Professor Maher taught the author everything she knows about corporate and antitrust law while she was a student at the Dickinson School of Law.

63. "Reported Crime in United States," U.S. Department of Justice, Bureau of Justice Statistics, 2007.

64. *Rummel v. Estelle,* 445 U.S. 263 (1980).

65. "Cookie Burglar Gets at Least 25 Years," CNN Online, October 27, 1995.

66. *Rummel v. Estelle,* 445 U.S. 263 (1980).

67. *Solem v. Helm,* 463 U.S. 277 (1983).

68. B. Egelko, "Three Strikes Ruled Unjust in Shoplifting Convictions," *San Francisco Chronicle,* February 8, 2002.

69. *California v. Andrade,* 538 U.S. 63 (2002) and *Ewing v. California,* 538 U.S. 11 (2003).

70. *Hutto v. Finney,* 437 U.S. 678 (1978).

71. *Bell v. Wollfish,* 441 U.S. 520 (1979).

72. *Hutto v. Finney,* 437 U.S. 678 (1978).

73. *Estelle v. Gamble,* 429 U.S. 97 (1976).

74. *Ort v. White,* 813 F.2d 318 (1987).

75. Public Law, 104–105 (April 17, 1996) and 104–236 (October 3, 1996).

76. "States Move on Sex Offender GPS Tracking," Associated Press, Jefferson City, MO, via FoxNews.com, August 17, 2005.

77. "Bellingham Suspect Could Face Death Penalty," Mike Carter, *Seattle Times,* September 8, 2005.

78. Andrew Buncombe, "The Bitter Legacy of Megan's Law," *The Independent* (London, England), June 24, 2006, p. 29.

79. Gregory D. Kesich, "Killings Rekindle Vigilante Debate," *Portland Press Herald,* April 19, 2006.

80. "States Move on Sex Offender GPS Tracking," Associated Press, Jefferson City, MO, via FoxNews.com, August 17, 2005.

81. "Sexual Assault of Young Children as Reported to Law Enforcement, Victim, Incident, and Offender Characteristics," A NIBRS Report, U.S. Department of Justice, Bureau of Justice Statistics, July 2000.

82. "Child Victimizers: Violent Offenders and Their Victims," U.S. Department of Justice, Bureau of Justice Statistics, August 12, 1998.

83. *Pennsylvania Department of Corrections v. Yeskey,* 524 U.S. 206 (1998).

84. *United States v. Georgia et al.,* No. 04-1203 (2006).

85. *Otte v. Doe,* 534 U.S. 1126 (2002).

86. *Smith v. Doe,* 538 U.S. 84 (2003).

87. *McKune et al. v. Lile,* 536 U.S. 24 (2002).

88. "Megan's Law Labels Stalker: Man Only Used Frightful Words," *Patriot News* (Harrisburg, PA), July 30, 2002.

89. D. Norton, "Wilson to Sign Castration Bill," *San Francisco Chronicle,* September 17, 1996.

90. G. Lucas, "Chemical Castration Bill Passes," *Augusta Chronicle,* February 12, 1997.

91. Bill Savitsky Jr., and Pete Shellem, "Woman Held as a Sex Predator: Designation Is State's First," *Seattle Times,* January 22, 1997.

92. "Miss Georgia's Sex Offenders 2004 Pageant, *www.porkdisco.com.*

93. Donna M. Vandiver, Jeffery T. Walker, "Female Sex Offenders: An Overview and Analysis of 40 Cases," *Criminal Justice Review,* Vol. 27 No. 2, Georgia State University, 2002, pp. 284–300.

94. "Adam Walsh Act Becomes Law," America's Most Wanted, FoxNews.com, July 25, 2006.

95. Anthony Brooks, "DNA, the Law, and the Politics of the Death Penalty Debate," WBUR.org, National Public Radio, Boston, MA.

96. Kevin Poulsen, "MySpace Labels Innocent Woman as Sex Offender," Wired.com, May 25, 2007.

97. Kevin Poulsen, "Attorneys General Give Up Sex Offenders," Wired.com, May 14, 2007.

98. Cassidy, C., "Freed Man Alleges Conspiracy in Slaying Case," *Patriot News* (Harrisburg, PA), August 21, 2007.

APPENDIX
The Constitution of the United States of America

WE THE PEOPLE of the United States, in Order to form a more perfect Union, establish Justice, insure domestic Tranquility, provide for the common defence, promote the general Welfare, and secure the Blessings of Liberty to ourselves and our Posterity, do ordain and establish this Constitution for the United States of America.

ARTICLE ONE

Section 1.

All legislative powers herein granted shall be vested in a Congress of the United States, which shall consist of a Senate and House of Representatives.

Section 2.

The House of Representatives shall be composed of members chosen every second year by the people of the several States, and the electors in each State shall have the qualifications requisite for electors of the most numerous branch of the State legislature.

No Person shall be a Representative who shall not have attained to the age of twenty five years, and been seven years a citizen of the United States, and who shall not, when elected, be an inhabitant of that State in which he shall be chosen.

Representatives and direct taxes shall be apportioned among the several States which may be included within this Union, according to their respective numbers, which shall be determined by adding to the whole number of free persons, including those bound to service for a term of years, and excluding Indians not taxed, three fifths of all other persons. The actual enumeration shall be made within three years after the first meeting of the Congress of the United States, and within every subsequent term of ten years, in such manner as they shall by law direct. The number of Representatives shall not exceed one for every thirty thousand, but each State shall have at least one Representative; and until such enumeration shall be made, the State of New Hampshire shall be entitled to choose three, Massachusetts eight, Rhode Island and Providence Plantations one, Connecticut five, New York six, New Jersey four, Pennsylvania eight, Delaware one, Maryland six, Virginia ten, North Carolina five, South Carolina five and Georgia three. When vacancies happen in the Representation from any State, the executive authority thereof shall issue writs of election to fill such vacancies.

The House of Representatives shall choose their Speaker and other officers; and shall have the sole power of Impeachment.

Section 3.

The Senate of the United States shall be composed of two Senators from each State, chosen by the legislature thereof, for six years; and each Senator shall have one Vote.

Immediately after they shall be assembled in consequence of the first election, they shall be divided as equally as may be into three classes. The seats of the Senators of the first class shall be vacated at the expiration of the second year, of the second class at the expiration of the fourth year, and of the third class at the expiration of the sixth year, so that one third may be chosen every second year; and if vacancies happen by resignation, or otherwise, during the recess of the legislature of any State, the executive thereof may make temporary appointments until the next meeting of the legislature, which shall then fill such vacancies.

No person shall be a Senator who shall not have attained to the age of thirty years, and been nine years a citizen of the United States, and who shall not, when elected, be an inhabitant of that State for which he shall be chosen.

The Vice-President of the United States shall be President of the Senate, but shall have no vote, unless they be equally divided.

The Senate shall choose their other officers, and also a President pro tempore, in the absence of the Vice-President, or when he shall exercise the office of President of the United States.

The Senate shall have the sole power to try all impeachments. When sitting for that purpose, they shall be on oath or affirmation. When the President of the United States is tried, the Chief Justice shall preside: And no Person shall be convicted without the concurrence of two thirds of the members present.

Judgment in cases of impeachment shall not extend further than to removal from office, and disqualification to hold and enjoy any office of honor, trust or profit under the United States: but the party convicted shall nevertheless be liable and subject to indictment, trial, judgment and punishment, according to law.

Section 4.

The times, places and manner of holding elections for Senators and Representatives, shall be prescribed in each State by the legislature thereof; but the Congress may at any time by law make or alter such regulations, except as to the places of choosing Senators.

The Congress shall assemble at least once in every year, and such meeting shall be on the first Monday in December, unless they shall by law appoint a different day.

Section 5.

Each house shall be the judge of the elections, returns and qualifications of its own members, and a majority of each shall constitute a quorum to do business; but a smaller number may adjourn from day to day, and may be authorized to compel the attendance of absent members, in such manner, and under such penalties as each house may provide.

Each house may determine the rules of its proceedings, punish its members for disorderly behavior, and, with the concurrence of two-thirds, expel a member.

Each house shall keep a journal of its proceedings, and from time to time publish the same, excepting such parts as may in their judgment require secrecy; and the yeas and nays of the members of either house on any question shall, at the desire of one fifth of those present, be entered on the journal.

Neither house, during the session of Congress, shall, without the consent of the other, adjourn for more than three days, nor to any other place than that in which the two Houses shall be sitting.

Section 6.

The Senators and Representatives shall receive a compensation for their services, to be ascertained by law, and paid out of the Treasury of the United States. They shall in all cases, except treason, felony and breach of the peace, be privileged from arrest during their attendance at the session of their respective houses, and in going to and returning from the same; and for any speech or debate in either house, they shall not be questioned in any other place.

No Senator or Representative shall, during the time for which he was elected, be appointed to any civil office under the authority of the United States which shall have been created, or the emoluments whereof shall have been increased during such time; and no person holding any office under the United States, shall be a member of either house during his continuance in office.

Section 7.

All bills for raising revenue shall originate in the House of Representatives; but the Senate may propose or concur with amendments as on other bills.

Every bill which shall have passed the House of Representatives and the Senate, shall, before it become a law, be presented to the President of the United States; If he approve he shall sign it, but if not he shall return it, with his objections to that house in which it shall have originated, who shall enter the objections at large on their journal, and proceed to reconsider it. If after such reconsideration two thirds of that house shall agree to pass the bill, it shall be sent, together with the objections, to the other house, by which it shall likewise be reconsidered, and if approved by two thirds of that house, it shall become a law. But in all such cases the votes of both houses shall be determined by yeas and nays, and the names of the persons voting for and against the bill shall be entered on the journal of each house respectively. If any bill shall not be returned by the President within ten days (Sundays excepted) after it shall have been presented to him, the same shall be a law, in like manner as if he had signed it, unless the Congress by their adjournment prevent its return, in which case it shall not be a law.

Every order, resolution, or vote to which the concurrence of the Senate and House of Representatives may be necessary (except on a question of adjournment) shall be presented to the President of the United States; and before the same shall take effect, shall be approved by him, or being disapproved by him, shall be repassed by two thirds of the Senate and House of Representatives, according to the rules and limitations prescribed in the case of a bill.

Section 8.

The Congress shall have power to lay and collect taxes, duties, imposts and excises, to pay the debts and provide for the common defence and general welfare of the United States; but all duties, imposts and excises shall be uniform throughout the United States; To borrow money on the credit of the United States; To regulate commerce with foreign nations, and among the several States, and with the Indian tribes; To establish an uniform rule of naturalization, and uniform Laws on the subject of bankruptcies throughout the United States; To coin money, regulate the value thereof, and of foreign coin, and fix the standard of weights and measures; To provide for the punishment of counterfeiting the securities and current Coin of the United States; To establish post-offices and post-roads; To promote the progress of science and useful arts, by securing for limited times to authors and inventors the exclusive right to their respective writings and discoveries; To constitute tribunals inferior to the Supreme Court; To define and punish piracies and felonies committed on the high seas, and offenses against the law of nations; To declare war, grant letters of marque and reprisal, and make rules concerning captures on land and water; To raise and support armies, but no appropriation of money to that use shall be for a longer term than two years; To provide and maintain a navy; To make rules for the government and regulation of the land and naval forces; To provide for calling forth the militia to execute the laws of the union, suppress insurrections and repel invasions; To provide for organizing, arming, and disciplining, the militia, and for governing such part of them as may be employed in the service of the United States, reserving to the States respectively, the appointment of the officers, and the authority of training the militia according to the discipline prescribed by Congress; To exercise exclusive legislation in all cases whatsoever, over such district (not exceeding ten miles square) as may, by cession of particular States, and the acceptance of Congress, become the seat of the Government of the United States, and to exercise like authority over all places purchased by the consent of the legislature of the State in which the same shall be, for the erection of forts, magazines, arsenals, dock-yards, and other needful Buildings; and To make all laws which shall be necessary and proper for carrying into execution the foregoing powers, and all other powers vested by this Constitution in the Government of the United States, or in any department or officer thereof.

Section 9.

The migration or importation of such persons as any of the States now existing shall think proper to admit, shall not be prohibited by the Congress prior to the Year one thousand eight hundred and eight, but a tax or duty may be imposed on such importation, not exceeding ten dollars for each person.

The privilege of the writ of habeas corpus shall not be suspended, unless when in cases of rebellion or invasion the public safety may require it.

No bill of attainder or ex post facto law shall be passed.

No capitation, or other direct tax shall be laid, unless in proportion to the census or enumeration herein before directed to be taken.

No tax or duty shall be laid on articles exported from any State.

No preference shall be given by any regulation of commerce or revenue to the ports of one State over those of another: nor shall vessels bound to, or from, one State, be obliged to enter, clear, or pay duties in another.

No money shall be drawn from the Treasury, but in consequence of appropriations made by law; and a regular statement and account of the receipts and expenditures of all public money shall be published from time to time.

No title of nobility shall be granted by the United States; and no person holding any office of profit or trust under them, shall, without the consent of the Congress, accept of any present, emolument, office, or title, of any kind whatever, from any king, prince or foreign State.

Section 10.

No State shall enter into any treaty, alliance, or confederation; grant letters of marque and reprisal; coin money; emit bills of credit; make anything but gold and silver coin a tender in payment of debts; pass any bill of attainder, ex post facto law, or law impairing the obligation of contracts, or grant any title of nobility.

No State shall, without the consent of the Congress, lay any imposts or duties on imports or exports, except what may be absolutely necessary for executing its inspection laws: and the net produce of all duties and imposts, laid by any State on imports or exports, shall be for the use of the Treasury of the United States; and all such laws shall be subject to the revision and control of the Congress.

No State shall, without the consent of Congress, lay any duty of tonnage, keep troops, or ships of war in time of peace, enter into any agreement or compact with another State, or with a foreign power, or engage in war, unless actually invaded, or in such imminent danger as will not admit of delay.

ARTICLE TWO

Section 1.

The executive power shall be vested in a President of the United States of America. He shall hold his office during the term of four years, and, together with the Vice-President chosen for the same term, be elected, as follows:

Each State shall appoint, in such manner as the legislature thereof may direct, a number of electors, equal to the whole number of Senators and Representatives to which the State may be entitled in the Congress: but no Senator or Representative, or person holding an office of trust or profit under the United States, shall be appointed an elector.

The electors shall meet in their respective States, and vote by ballot for two persons, of whom one at least shall not lie an inhabitant of the same State with themselves. And they shall make a list of all the persons voted for, and of the number of votes for each; which list they shall sign and certify, and transmit sealed to the seat of the government of the United States, directed to the President of the Senate. The President of the Senate shall, in the presence of the Senate and House of Representatives, open all the certificates, and the votes shall then be counted. The person having the greatest number of votes shall be the President, if such number be a majority of the whole number of electors appointed; and if there be more than one who have such majority, and have an equal number of votes, then the House of Representatives shall immediately choose by ballot one of them for President; and if no person have a majority, then from the five highest on the list the said House shall in like manner choose the President.

But in choosing the President, the votes shall be taken by States, the representation from each State having one vote; a quorum for this purpose shall consist of a member or members from two thirds of the States, and a majority of all the States shall be necessary to a choice. In every case, after the choice of the President, the person having the greatest number of votes of the electors shall be the Vice-President. But if there should remain two or more who have equal votes, the Senate shall choose from them by ballot the Vice-President.

The Congress may determine the time of choosing the electors, and the day on which they shall give their votes; which day shall be the same throughout the United States.

No person except a natural born citizen, or a citizen of the United States, at the time of the adoption of this Constitution, shall be eligible to the office of President; neither shall any person be eligible to that office who shall not have attained to the age of thirty five years, and been fourteen years a resident within the United States.

In case of the removal of the President from office, or of his death, resignation, or inability to discharge the powers and duties of the said office, the same shall devolve on the Vice-President, and the Congress may by law provide for the case of removal, death, resignation or inability, both of the President and Vice President, declaring what officer shall then act as President, and such officer shall act accordingly, until the disability be removed, or a President shall be elected.

The President shall, at stated times, receive for his services, a compensation, which shall neither be increased nor diminished during the period for which he shall have been elected, and he shall not receive within that period any other emolument from the United States, or any of them.

Before he enter on the execution of his office, he shall take the following oath or affirmation:

"I do solemnly swear (or affirm) that I will faithfully execute the office of President of the United States, and will to the best of my ability, preserve, protect and defend the Constitution of the United States."

Section 2.

The President shall be Commander-in-Chief of the Army and Navy of the United States, and of the militia of the several States, when called into the actual service of the United States; he may require the opinion, in writing, of the principal officer in each of the executive departments, upon any subject relating to the duties of their respective offices, and he shall have power to grant reprieves and pardons for offenses against the United States, except in cases of impeachment.

He shall have power, by and with the advice and consent of the Senate, to make treaties, provided two thirds of the Senators present concur; and he shall nominate, and by and with the advice and consent of the Senate, shall appoint ambassadors, other public ministers and consuls, judges of the Supreme Court, and all other officers of the

United States, whose appointments are not herein otherwise provided for, and which shall be established by law: but the Congress may by law vest the appointment of such inferior officers, as they think proper, in the President alone, in the courts of law, or in the heads of departments.

The President shall have power to fill up all vacancies that may happen during the recess of the Senate, by granting commissions which shall expire at the end of their next session.

Section 3.

He shall from time to time give to the Congress information of the State of the Union, and recommend to their consideration such measures as he shall judge necessary and expedient; he may, on extraordinary occasions, convene both houses, or either of them, and in case of disagreement between them, with respect to the time of adjournment, he may adjourn them to such time as he shall think proper; he shall receive ambassadors and other public ministers; he shall take care that the laws be faithfully executed, and shall commission all the officers of the United States.

Section 4.

The President, Vice-President and all civil officers of the United States, shall be removed from office on impeachment for, and conviction of, treason, bribery, or other high crimes and misdemeanors.

ARTICLE THREE

Section 1.

The judicial power of the United States, shall be vested in one Supreme Court, and in such inferior courts as the Congress may from time to time ordain and establish. The judges, both of the supreme and inferior courts, shall hold their offices during good behavior, and shall, at stated times, receive for their services, a compensation, which shall not be diminished during their continuance in office.

Section 2.

The judicial power shall extend to all cases, in law and equity, arising under this Constitution, the laws of the United States, and treaties made, or which shall be made, under their authority; to all cases affecting ambassadors, other public ministers and consuls; to all cases of admiralty and maritime jurisdiction; to controversies to which the United States shall be a party; to controversies between two or more States; between a State and citizens of another State; between citizens of different States; between citizens of the same State claiming lands under grants of different States, and between a State, or the citizens thereof, and foreign States, citizens or subjects.

In all cases affecting ambassadors, other public ministers and consuls, and those in which a State shall be party, the Supreme Court shall have original jurisdiction. In all the other cases before mentioned, the Supreme Court shall have appellate jurisdiction, both as to law and fact, with such exceptions, and under such regulations as the Congress shall make.

Trial of all crimes, except in cases of impeachment, shall be by jury; and such trial shall be held in the State where the said crimes shall have been committed; but when not committed within any State, the trial shall be at such place or places as the Congress may by law have directed.

Section 3.

Treason against the United States, shall consist only in levying war against them, or in adhering to their enemies, giving them aid and comfort. No person shall be convicted of treason unless on the testimony of two witnesses to the same overt act, or on confession in open court.

The Congress shall have power to declare the punishment of treason, but no attainder of treason shall work corruption of blood, or forfeiture except during the life of the person attainted.

ARTICLE FOUR

Section 1.

Full faith and credit shall be given in each State to the public acts, records, and judicial proceedings of every other State. And the Congress may by general laws prescribe the manner in which such acts, records and proceedings shall be proved, and the effect thereof.

Section 2.

The citizens of each State shall be entitled to all privileges and immunities of citizens in the several States.

A person charged in any State with treason, felony, or other crime, who shall flee from justice, and be found in another State, shall on demand of the executive authority of the State from which he fled, be delivered up, to be removed to the State having jurisdiction of the crime. No person held to service or labor in one State, under the laws thereof, escaping into another, shall, in consequence of any law or regulation therein, be discharged from such service or labor, But shall be delivered up on claim of the party to whom such service or labor may be due.

Section 3.

New States may be admitted by the Congress into this Union; but no new States shall be formed or erected within the jurisdiction of any other State; nor any State be formed by the junction of two or more States, or parts of States, without the consent of the legislatures of the States concerned as well as of the Congress.

The Congress shall have power to dispose of and make all needful rules and regulations respecting the territory or other property belonging to the United States; and nothing in this Constitution shall be so construed as to prejudice any claims of the United States, or of any particular State.

Section 4.

The United States shall guarantee to every State in this Union a republican form of government, and shall protect each of them against invasion; and on application of the legislature, or of the executive (when the legislature cannot be convened) against domestic violence.

ARTICLE FIVE

The Congress, whenever two thirds of both houses shall deem it necessary, shall propose amendments to this Constitution, or, on the application of the Legislatures of two thirds of the several States, shall call a convention for proposing amendments, which, in either case, shall be valid to all intents and purposes, as part of this Constitution, when ratified by the Legislatures of three fourths of the several States, or by conventions in three fourths thereof, as the one or the other mode of ratification may be proposed by the Congress; provided that no amendment which may be made prior to the Year One thousand eight hundred and eight shall in any manner affect the first and fourth Clauses in the Ninth Section of the first Article; and that no State, without its consent, shall be deprived of its equal suffrage in the Senate.

ARTICLE SIX

All debts contracted and engagements entered into, before the adoption of this Constitution, shall be as valid against the United States under this Constitution, as under the Confederation.

This Constitution, and the laws of the United States which shall be made in pursuance thereof; and all treaties made, or which shall be made, under the authority of the United States, shall be the supreme law of the land; and the judges in every State shall be bound thereby, anything in the Constitution or laws of any State to the contrary notwithstanding.

The Senators and Representatives before mentioned, and the members of the several State Legislatures, and all executive and judicial officers, both of the United States and of the several States, shall be bound by oath or affirmation, to support this Constitution; but no religious test shall ever be required as a qualification to any office or public trust under the United States.

ARTICLE SEVEN

The ratification of the Conventions of nine States, shall be sufficient for the establishment of this Constitution between the States so ratifying the same.

BILL OF RIGHTS

AMENDMENT I (1791)

Congress shall make no law respecting an establishment of religion, or prohibiting the free exercise thereof; or abridging the freedom of speech, or of the press; or the right of the people peaceably to assemble, and to petition the government for a redress of grievances.

AMENDMENT II (1791)

A well regulated militia, being necessary to the security of a free State, the right of the people to keep and bear arms, shall not be infringed.

AMENDMENT III (1791)

No soldier shall, in time of peace be quartered in any house, without the consent of the owner, nor in time of war, but in a manner to be prescribed by law.

AMENDMENT IV (1791)

The right of the people to be secure in their persons, houses, papers, and effects, against unreasonable searches and seizures, shall not be violated, and no warrants shall issue, but upon probable cause, supported by Oath or affirmation, and particularly describing the place to be searched, and the persons or things to be seized.

AMENDMENT V (1791)

No person shall be held to answer for a capital, or otherwise infamous crime, unless on a presentment or indictment of a Grand Jury, except in cases arising in the land or naval forces, or in the militia, when in actual service in time of war or public danger; nor shall any person be subject for the same offence to be twice put in jeopardy of life or limb; nor shall be compelled in any criminal case to be a witness against himself, nor be deprived of life, liberty, or property, without due process of law; nor shall private property be taken for public use, without just compensation.

AMENDMENT VI (1791)

In all criminal prosecutions, the accused shall enjoy the right to a speedy and public trial, by an impartial jury of the State and district wherein the crime shall have been committed, which district shall have been previously ascertained by law, and to be informed of the nature and cause of the accusation; to be confronted with the witnesses against him; to have compulsory process for obtaining witnesses in his favor, and to have the assistance of counsel for his defence.

AMENDMENT VII (1791)

In suits at common law, where the value in controversy shall exceed twenty dollars, the right of trial by jury shall be preserved, and no fact tried by a jury, shall be otherwise re-examined in any court of the United States, than according to the rules of the common law.

AMENDMENT VIII (1791)

Excessive bail shall not be required, nor excessive fines imposed, nor cruel and unusual punishments inflicted.

AMENDMENT IX (1791)

The enumeration in the Constitution, of certain rights, shall not be construed to deny or disparage others retained by the people.

AMENDMENT X (1791)

The powers not delegated to the United States by the Constitution, nor prohibited by it to the States, are reserved to the States respectively, or to the people.

AMENDMENT XI (1798)

The judicial power of the United States shall not be construed to extend to any suit in law or equity, commenced or prosecuted against one of the United States by Citizens of another State, or by citizens or subjects of any foreign State.

AMENDMENT XII (1804)

The electors shall meet in their respective States, and vote by ballot for President and Vice-President, one of whom, at least, shall not be an inhabitant of the same State with themselves; they shall name in their ballots the person voted for as President, and in distinct ballots the person voted for as Vice-President, and they shall make distinct lists of all persons voted for as President, and of all persons voted for as Vice-President and of the number of votes for each, which lists they shall sign and certify, and transmit sealed to the seat of the Government of the United States, directed to the President of the Senate; The President of the Senate shall, in the presence of the Senate and House of Representatives, open all the certificates and the votes shall then be counted; the person having the greatest number of votes for President, shall be the President, if such number be a majority of the whole number of Electors appointed; and if no person have such majority, then from the persons having the highest numbers not exceeding three on the list of those voted for as President, the House of Representatives shall choose immediately, by ballot, the President. But in choosing the President, the votes shall be taken by States, the representation from each State having one vote; a quorum for this purpose shall consist of a member or members from two-thirds of the States, and a majority of all the States shall be necessary to a choice. And if the House of Representatives shall not choose a President whenever the right of choice shall devolve upon them, before the fourth day of March next following, then the Vice-President shall act as President, as in the case of the death or other constitutional disability of the President.

The person having the greatest number of votes as Vice-President, shall be the Vice-President, if such number be a majority of the whole number of Electors appointed, and if no person have a majority, then from the two highest numbers on the list, the Senate shall choose the Vice-President; a quorum for the purpose shall consist of two-thirds of the whole number of Senators, and a majority of the whole number shall be necessary to a choice. But no person constitutionally ineligible to the office of President shall be eligible to that of Vice-President of the United States.

AMENDMENT XIII (1865)

Section 1.

Neither slavery nor involuntary servitude, except as a punishment for crime whereof the party shall have been duly convicted, shall exist within the United States, or any place subject to their jurisdiction.

Section 2.

Congress shall have power to enforce this article by appropriate legislation.

AMENDMENT XIV (1868)

Section 1.

All persons born or naturalized in the United States, and subject to the jurisdiction thereof, are citizens of the United States and of the State wherein they reside. No State shall make or enforce any law which shall abridge the privileges or immunities of citizens of the United States; nor shall any State deprive any person of life, liberty, or property, without due process of law; nor deny to any person within its jurisdiction the equal protection of the laws.

Section 2.

Representatives shall be apportioned among the several States according to their respective numbers, counting the whole number of persons in each State, excluding Indians not taxed. But when the right to vote at any election for the choice of Electors for President and Vice-President of the United States, Representatives in Congress, the executive and judicial officers of a State, or the members of the Legislature thereof, is denied to any of the male inhabitants of such State, being twenty-one years of age, and citizens of the United States, or in any way abridged, except for participation in rebellion, or other crime, the basis of representation therein shall be reduced in the proportion which the number of such male citizens shall bear to the whole number of male citizens twenty-one years of age in such State.

Section 3.

No person shall be a Senator or Representative in Congress, or elector of President and Vice-President, or hold any office, civil or military, under the United States, or under any State, who, having previously taken an oath, as a member of Congress, or as an officer of the United States, or as a member of any State legislature, or as an executive or judicial officer of any State, to support the Constitution of the United States, shall have engaged in insurrection or rebellion against the same, or given aid or comfort to the enemies thereof. But Congress may by a vote of two-thirds of each House, remove such disability.

Section 4.

The validity of the public debt of the United States, authorized by law, including debts incurred for payment of pensions and bounties for services in suppressing insurrection or rebellion, shall not be questioned. But neither the United States nor any State shall assume or pay any debt or obligation incurred in aid of insurrection or rebellion against the United States, or any claim for the loss or emancipation of any slave; but all such debts, obligations and claims shall be held illegal and void.

Section 5.

The Congress shall have power to enforce, by appropriate legislation, the provisions of this article.

AMENDMENT XV (1870)

Section 1.

The right of citizens of the United States to vote shall not be denied or abridged by the United States or by any State on account of race, color, or previous condition of servitude.

Section 2.

The Congress shall have power to enforce this article by appropriate legislation.

AMENDMENT XVI (1913)

The Congress shall have power to lay and collect taxes on incomes, from whatever source derived, without apportionment among the several States and without regard to any census or enumeration.

AMENDMENT XVII (1913)

The Senate of the United States shall be composed of two senators from each State, elected by the people thereof, for six years; and each Senator shall have one vote. The electors in each State shall have the qualifications requisite for electors of the most numerous branch of the State legislature. When vacancies happen in the representation of any State in the Senate, the executive authority of such State shall issue writs of election to fill such vacancies: Provided, That the legislature of any State may empower the executive thereof to make temporary appointments until the people fill the vacancies by election as the legislature may direct.

    This amendment shall not be so construed as to affect the election or term of any senator chosen before it becomes valid as part of the Constitution.

AMENDMENT XVIII (1919)

Section 1.

After one year from the ratification of this article, the manufacture, sale, or transportation of intoxicating liquors within, the importation thereof into, or the exportation thereof from the United States and all territory subject to the jurisdiction thereof for beverage purposes is hereby prohibited.

Section 2.

The Congress and the several States shall have concurrent power to enforce this article by appropriate legislation.

Section 3.

This article shall be inoperative unless it shall have been ratified as an amendment to the Constitution by the legislatures of the several States, as provided in the Constitution, within seven years from the date of the submission hereof to the States by Congress.

AMENDMENT XIX (1920)

The right of citizens of the United States to vote shall not be denied or abridged by the United States or by any States on account of sex. The Congress shall have power by appropriate legislation to enforce the provisions of this article.

AMENDMENT XX (1933)

Section 1.

The terms of the President and Vice-President shall end at noon on the twentieth day of January, and the terms of Senators and Representatives at noon on the third day of January, of the years in which such terms would have ended if this article had not been ratified; and the terms of their successors shall then begin.

Section 2.

The Congress shall assemble at least once in every year, and such meeting shall begin at noon on the third day of January, unless they shall by law appoint a different day.

Section 3.

If, at the time fixed for the beginning of the term of the President, the President-elect shall have died, the Vice-President-elect shall become President. If a President shall not have been chosen before the time fixed for the beginning of his term, or if the President-elect shall have failed to qualify, then the Vice-President-elect shall act as President until a President shall have qualified; and the Congress may by law provide for the case wherein neither a President-elect nor a Vice-President-elect shall have qualified, declaring who shall then act as President, or the manner in which one who is to act shall be selected, and such person shall act accordingly until a President or Vice-President shall have qualified.

Section 4.

The Congress may by law provide for the case of the death of any of the persons from whom the House of Representatives may choose a President whenever the right of choice shall have devolved upon them, and for the case of the death of any of the persons from whom the Senate may choose a Vice-President whenever the right of choice shall have devolved upon them.

Section 5.

Sections 1 and 2 shall take effect on the 15th day of October following the ratification of this article.

Section 6.

This article shall be inoperative unless it shall have been ratified as an amendment to the Constitution by the legislatures of three-fourths of the several States within seven years from the date of its submission.

AMENDMENT XXI (1933)

Section 1.

The eighteenth article of amendment to the Constitution of the United States is hereby repealed.

Section 2.

The transportation or importation into any State, Territory, or possession of the United States for delivery or use therein of intoxicating liquors, in violation of the laws thereof, is hereby prohibited.

Section 3.

The article shall be inoperative unless it shall have been ratified as an amendment to the Constitution by conventions in the several States, as provided in the Constitution, within seven years from the date of the submission hereof to the States by the Congress.

AMENDMENT XXII (1951)

Section 1.

No person shall be elected to the office of the President more than twice, and no person who has held the office of President, or acted as President for more than two years of a term to which some other person was elected President shall be elected to the office of the President more than once. But this Article shall not apply to any person holding the office of President when this Article was proposed by the Congress, and shall not prevent any person who May be holding the office of President, or acting as President, during the term within which this Article becomes operative from holding the office of President or acting as President during the remainder of such term.

Section 2.

This article shall be inoperative unless it shall have been ratified as an amendment to the Constitution by the legislatures of three-fourths of the several States within seven years from the date of its submission to the States by the Congress.

AMENDMENT XXIII (1961)

Section 1.

The District constituting the seat of government of the United States shall appoint in such manner as the Congress may direct:

A number of electors of President and Vice-President equal to the whole number of Senators and Representatives in Congress to which the District would be entitled if it were a State, but in no event more than the least populous State; they shall be in addition to those appointed by the States, but they shall be considered, for the purposes of the election of President and Vice-President, to be electors appointed by a State; and they shall meet in the district and perform such duties as provided by the twelfth article of amendment.

Section 2.

The Congress shall have power to enforce this article by appropriate legislation.

AMENDMENT XXIV (1964)

Section 1.

The right of citizens of the United States to vote in any primary or other election for President or Vice-President, for electors for President or Vice-President, or for Senator or Representative in Congress, shall not be denied or abridged by the United States or any State by reason of failure to pay any poll tax or other tax.

Section 2.

The Congress shall have power to enforce this article by appropriate legislation.

AMENDMENT XXV (1967)

Section 1.

In case of the removal of the President from office or of his death or resignation, the Vice-President shall become President.

Section 2.

Whenever there is a vacancy in the office of the Vice-President, the President shall nominate a Vice-President who shall take office upon confirmation by a majority vote of both Houses of Congress.

Section 3.

Whenever the President transmits to the President pro tempore of the Senate and the Speaker of the House of Representatives his written declaration that he is unable to discharge the powers and duties of his office, and until he transmits to them a written declaration to the contrary, such powers and duties shall be discharged by the Vice-President as Acting President.

Section 4.

Whenever the Vice-President and a majority of either the principal officers of the executive departments or of such other body as Congress may by law provide, transmit to the President pro tempore of the Senate and the Speaker of the House of Representatives their written declaration that the President is unable to discharge the powers and duties of his office, the Vice-President shall immediately assume the powers and duties of the office as Acting President.

Thereafter, when the President transmits to the President pro tempore of the Senate and the Speaker of the House of Representatives his written declaration that no inability exists, he shall resume the powers and duties of his office unless the Vice-President and a majority of either the principal officers of the executive department or of such other body as Congress may by law provide, transmit within four days to the President pro tempore of the Senate and the Speaker of the House of Representatives their written declaration that the President is unable to discharge the powers and duties of his office. Thereupon Congress shall decide the issue, assembling within forty-eight hours for that purpose if not in session. If the Congress, within twenty-one days after receipt of the latter written declaration, or, if Congress is not in session, within twenty-one days after Congress is required to assemble, determines by two-thirds vote of both Houses that the President is unable to discharge the powers and duties of his office, the Vice-President shall continue to discharge the same as Acting President; otherwise, the President shall resume the powers and duties of his office.

AMENDMENT XXVI (1971)

Section 1.

The right of citizens of the United States, who are eighteen years of age or older, to vote shall not be denied or abridged by the United States or by any State on account of age.

Section 2.

The Congress shall have power to enforce this article by appropriate legislation.

GLOSSARY

Abduction   The illegal carrying away of a person by force or coercion, generally with the intent to do harm to the victim. Today, the same criminal statute generally covers kidnapping and abduction.

Abortion   The termination of pregnancy by something other than birth.

Actual Possession   Physically having the item on one's person, directly under physical control, or within reach.

Actus Reus   A wrongful action.

Adultery   Sexual intercourse by a married person with someone not his or her spouse.

Advise and Consent   The constitutional relationship of the Senate to the president regarding the selection of federal judges and other duties.

Advocating Overthrow of Government   Speaking in favor of rebellion or insurrection.

Aggravating Circumstance   Act or conduct that increases the seriousness of an act, often resulting in a harsher punishment.

Alford Plea   A plea entered where the accused maintains his innocence but agrees to be sentenced as if guilty.

Analytical School   The school of jurisprudence thought that believes laws are based on logic.

Arraignment   A judicial proceeding where an accused hears the charges against him and enters a plea of guilty or not guilty; the stage of a criminal case at which the defendant is first formally charged with a specific crime.

Arrest   The official taking of a person to answer criminal charges.

Arrest Warrant   Document approved by a magistrate or judge attesting that there is probable cause to believe that someone has committed a specific crime and authorizing that person's arrest.

Arson   The intentional and malicious burning of a structure. At Common Law, it was the malicious burning of the dwelling house of another.

Assault   An act of force or threat of force intended to inflict harm upon a person or to put the person in fear that such harm is imminent.

Bail   Money or other guarantee posted to assure a defendant who is released from custody pending trial or appeal will appear when called or forfeit the security posted.

Bench Conference   A conference called among the judge and attorneys for both sides and possibly the accused to discuss matters without the jury hearing it.

Bench Warrant   A warrant issued by a judge ordering law enforcement officers to arrest a specific person.

Beyond a Reasonable Doubt   The burden of proof the prosecution must meet in a criminal case in order to convict the accused; the prosecutor is required to prove beyond a reasonable doubt that the defendant committed the crime with which he or she was charged. A reasonable doubt is a fair doubt based upon common sense.

Bigamy   The criminal act of marrying when one already has a spouse.

Bill of Attainder   A law passed that singles out a person or persons as the only individuals affected by a criminal law; originally, a bill of attainder singled out an individual for capital punishment without benefit of a trial.

Binding   An order holding an accused person for trial.

Bloody Code   Popular name for England's criminal laws because of their harshness and the long list of crimes classified as capital offenses.

Bot   Compensation paid for minor injuries.

Bourgeoisie   In Marxist theory, the class in society that controls the means of production.

Bribery   The crime of giving something of value with the intention of influencing the action of a public official.

Burden of Proof   The duty to go forward to prove an allegation with facts.

Burglary   At Common Law, the breaking and entering of the dwelling house of another at night with the intent to commit a felony inside. Today, burglary is the forcible entry into a structure with the intent to commit a felony once inside.

But For Rule   The rule that states but for the defendant's actions, the harm would not have occurred.

Causation   The requirement that the act must cause the harm.

Challenge for Cause   If a juror can't be impartial because he or she knows about the case, knows the defendant's family, knows the victim or any of the people involved in the case, has already made a decision about the defendant's guilt or innocence, or admits to prejudice, he or she can be challenged for cause; there are an unlimited number of challenges for cause available. Any potential juror who can't be impartial can be stricken for cause.

Chattel   Personal property.

Checks and Balances   The system of restraints built into the U.S. Constitution that prevents one branch of government from dominating the others.

Child Abuse   Child abuse is the label given to crimes that are either committed against minors or crimes created to protect children who cannot act in their own best interest. Examples include statutory rape, incest, and child medical neglect.

Child Molestation or Child Sexual Abuse   The engaging of a child in sexual activities that the child cannot comprehend, for which the child is developmentally unprepared and cannot give informed consent, and/or that violate the social and legal taboos of society. The sexual activity may include all forms of oral, genital, or anal contact by or to the child, or non-touching abuses, such as exhibitionism, voyeurism, or using the child in the production of pornography.

Command School   The school of jurisprudence thought that posits that laws are dictated to society by the ruling class of that society.

Commerce Clause   The clause of the U.S. Constitution that gives the federal government the right to regulate interstate commerce; Article I, Section 8, Clause 3.

Common Law   The system of jurisprudence, originated in England and later applied in the United States, that is based on judicial precedent rather than legislative enactments.

Concurrent Jurisdiction   Jurisdiction shared by two or more courts.

Confession   A voluntary statement by a person that he or she is guilty of a crime or any admission of wrongdoing.

Confirmation   The process of approval of presidential nominees by the Senate.

Consensus Theory   A theory developed by Emile Durkheim that postulates that laws develop out of a society's consensus of what is right and wrong.

Consent   A defense usually used in rape cases; argues the defendant had the "victim's" consent to perform the acts.

Conspiracy   An agreement between two or more persons to engage in a criminal act; it requires at least one overt act and is punished as if the parties accomplished the objective of their agreement.

Constructive Intent   The concept that some actions are so likely to cause a specific result that the law treats that result as intended, whether the person meant to cause it or not.

Constructive Possession   The concept that extends liability to people who have some control over an item without possessing it.

Contempt   Conduct that brings the authority and administration of the law into disrespect or that embarrasses or obstructs the court's discharge of its duties.

Controlled Substance   A drug considered dangerous under the law because of its effects, including intoxication, stupor, or addictive potential.

Corporate Liability   The legal concept that allows employers to be charged with a crime resulting from their employees' actions while carrying out corporate business.

Corpus Delicti   Literally "the body of the crime;" the fact that a crime has been committed.

Corporal Punishment   Punishment inflicted on the body, such as paddling, whipping, or caning.

Crime   A wrong against society or the public interest.

Criminal Homicide   A killing that breaks the law, designated as either murder or manslaughter.

Criminal Negligence Manslaughter   The crime of causing the death of a person by negligent or reckless conduct.

Criminal Solicitation   The act of when one person requests or encourages another to perform a criminal act.

Crits   A short term for the School of Critical Legal Studies who see the legal system as arbitrary and artificial.

Cross-Examination   Questioning of a witness put on the stand by the other side following direct examination.

Cruel and Unusual Punishment Punishment which violates the Eighth Amendment and which violates evolving standards of decency.

Custody The state of being detained by law enforcement officers; a person is in custody when that person is not free to leave.

Deadly Force Force intended to cause death or likely to result in death.

Deadly Weapon Doctrine Use of a deadly weapon is proof of intent to kill.

Defendant In a civil case, the person against whom a suit is filed. In a criminal trial, the person accused of a crime.

Defense of Others The defense used when otherwise criminal activities are done to save other people from harm.

Degree A measure of severity for crimes with first degree crimes being the most severe and warranting stronger punishments.

Diplomatic Immunity The courtesy afforded all diplomats while in foreign countries that allows them to be immune from prosecution for crimes they commit.

Direct Cause The case where there is a clear link between the criminal act and the effect.

Direct Examination The initial questioning of one's own witness.

Domestic Terrorism Activities that occur primarily within U.S. jurisdiction, that involve criminal acts dangerous to human life, and that appear to be intended to intimidate or coerce a civilian population, to influence government policy by intimidation or coercion, or to affect government conduct by mass destruction, assassination, or kidnapping.

Domestic Violence Assault, battery, aggravated assault, harassment, stalking, and other crimes involving physical or mental injury to a victim when perpetrated by the victim's partner.

Double Jeopardy The rule, based on the Fifth Amendment, that a person can only be tried once for the same offense; the rule has several exceptions.

Dual Sovereignty The legal doctrine that allows a person to be prosecuted by different sovereigns or governmental entities for the same action or set of actions; most commonly prosecution by both the federal and state government for the same action.

Duress Defense The defense that a person acted under threat of bodily harm to themselves or a family member; it may not be used to justify killing; the crime committed must be less serious than the harm threatened.

Durham Test Test of insanity that only requires a "substantial lack of capacity" on the part of the defendant.

Duty An obligation to perform an action.

Duty by Contract A duty voluntarily assumed through an agreement.

Duty by Relationship A duty expected of certain people, such as parents, by virtue of their connection with the person owed the duty, such as the parents' children.

Duty by Statute A duty imposed by law.

Elder Abuse Syndrome Similar to battered wife syndrome, it is a psychological condition where elder persons learn to accept the abuse they receive.

Elite Theory Also known as the ruling class theory, it is the theory put forth by Karl Marx that postulates laws exist only as a means of class oppression.

Embezzlement   The use, conversion, or retention of property legally possessed by the perpetrator, but belonging to another.

Eminent Domain   The state's power to take private property for a public use or public purpose without the owner's consent. The U.S. Constitution requires that property can only be taken after due process of law.

English Bill of Rights   A precursor to the U.S. Bill of Rights, it guarantees due process and bars cruel and unusual punishment.

Entrapment   A defense used when law enforcement officials lure a person into committing a crime.

Enumerated Powers   The powers explicitly given to the federal government in the U.S. Constitution.

Espionage   Knowingly and willfully communicating, furnishing, transmitting, or otherwise making available to an unauthorized person, or publishing, or using in any manner prejudicial to the safety or interest of the United States, or for the benefit of any foreign government to the detriment of the United States, any classified information; spying; selling or giving secrets to another government.

Euthanasia   The act of causing death to end pain and distress; also called mercy killing.

Evanescent Evidence   Evidence that will change or evaporate in a manner that will destroy its evidentiary value.

Ex Post Facto Law   The rule that a person cannot be charged with a crime that became a crime after he committed the act made illegal.

Exclusionary Rule   The "fruit of the poisonous tree" doctrine that prohibits the admission of evidence obtained illegally at a defendant's criminal trial; the rule does allow the use of evidence obtained with a technically defective warrant, but in good faith.

Exclusive Jurisdiction   A court with exclusive jurisdiction is the only court that can hear the case.

Executive   One of the three branches of government; the branch charged with enforcing the law.

Exigent Circumstances   Situations that require urgent action, sufficient to excuse delay to get a warrant issued.

Extradition   The process of returning an accused criminal to the jurisdiction in which he or she is charged.

Federal Circuit   One of 13 federal judicial districts, each with a U.S. District Court and a U.S. Court of Appeals.

Federal System   A system of governing where government is divided into different levels.

Fee Simple   The legal term for ownership of the entire bundle of rights that go with a piece of property.

Felonies   The most serious classification of crimes punishable by long prison sentences or death.

Felony Murder Rule   The rule that a death occurring by accident or chance during the course of the commission of a felony is first-degree murder.

Fem-Crits   A school of jurisprudence that holds the legal system perpetuates the oppression of women in society.

First Degree   Under the Model Penal Code, crimes that are committed willfully.

First-degree Murder   Murder committed deliberately with malice aforethought, that is, with premeditation.

Forgery   The fraudulent making or altering of any writing in a way that alters the legal rights and liabilities of another.

Fornication   Voluntary sexual intercourse between two unmarried persons.

Fourth Degree Offences   Under the Model Penal Code, crimes that are committed negligently.

Gambling   The act of taking a monetary risk on the chance of receiving a monetary gain.

General Intent   The type of intent where the person intended an action only and not the results of the action.

Grand Jury   A body of citizens, usually 23, whose job it is to determine if a crime has been committed and if a person should be charged with that crime based on probable cause.

Guilty, but Mentally Ill   Defendants who do not meet the complete lack of capacity standard but fall under the substantial lack of capacity standard are convicted and sent to a mental hospital; if they recover, they are sent to prison for the rest of their term.

Habeas Corpus   Literally meaning "you have the body," a judicial process for determining the legality of a particular person's custody. The "Great Writ," which orders another authority to bring a person held to the court. It was originally used to prevent kings from simply making enemies disappear.

Harm   Injury or damage.

Hate Crimes   Offenses motivated by hatred against a victim based on his or her race, religion, sexual orientation, handicap, ethnicity, or national origin.

Heat of Passion   The expression for a mental state on the part of a criminal defendant adequate in law to reduce the crime from murder to manslaughter.

Historical School   The school of jurisprudence thought that believes that law is an accumulation of societal traditions.

Homicide   The killing of a human being.

Homicide by Vehicle   A form of criminal negligence manslaughter reserved for a person operating a motor vehicle.

Hung Jury   A jury that is unable to reach a verdict.

Impeachment   The process by which Congress may charge a sitting judge, president, or vice president with "high crimes and misdemeanors" and convict that person in a trial before the Senate; a conviction results in removal from office.

In Loco Parentis   Acting in the role of parents.

Incest   Sexual activity between relatives within a prescribed degree of sanguinity or affinity.

Inchoate   Incomplete.

Incompetent to Stand Trial   A person unable to understand the proceedings against him and unable to interact with his attorneys.

Indecent Assault or Indecent Touching   An attack on a person in which there is groping or other offensive touching, but no sexual act is performed or attempted.

Indictment   A written accusation claiming that a specific person committed a specific crime or crimes; prosecutors present indictments to grand juries so the jury can vote on whether the indictment is a true bill.

Infancy Defense   The defense that a child is too young to either be prosecuted or stand trial as an adult.

Infanticide   The murder of a newborn or very young child.

Information   A formal document signed and filed by a district attorney or prosecutor that charges an individual with a specific crime.

Initial Appearance   A court proceeding shortly after a suspect's arrest where the suspect is informed of specific rights.

Insanity Defense   States that the defendant lacked the mental state to understand the nature and consequences of the crime.

Insanity During Incarceration   Prisoners who become insane are generally removed to mental hospitals; if they are still insane at the conclusion of their prison term, they are generally committed.

Insanity Just Prior to Execution   Most jurisdictions will not execute an insane person; persons whose sanity returns are rewarded with death.

Intent to Do Serious Bodily Harm   A defendant's plan to injure another.

Intent to Kill   The plan, course, or means a person conceives to take another life.

International Terrorism   Activities that occur primarily outside U.S. jurisdiction and involve criminal acts dangerous to human life, including acts of mass destruction, intended to influence the policy of a government by intimidation or coercion or to affect the conduct of a government by assassination or kidnapping.

Interstate Commerce   Commerce that occurs between states as opposed to strictly within a state's borders.

Intervening Causes   Complications that arise between a criminal act and all of its consequences.

Intrastate   Occurring within a state's border.

Involuntary Intoxication   The condition of a person who unknowingly ingests an intoxicating substance; generally treated like insanity.

Involuntary Manslaughter   The unintentional killing of a human being by a person engaged in doing some unlawful act not amounting to a felony, or in doing some lawful act in a manner tending to cause death or great bodily injury.

Irrebuttable Presumption   A presumption that cannot be disproved regardless of the amount or quality of evidence to the contrary.

Jackson–Denno Hearing   A hearing designed to determine whether law enforcement officers violated a defendant's rights in securing a confession.

Joint Tenancy with Right of Survivorship   Form of ownership in which the joint tenant receives the property should the other die. Either may sell their share before death, and the new owners then become tenants in common.

Judicial   One of the three branches of government; the branch charged with interpreting the law.

Jurisdiction   The power to hear and decide a case; jurisdiction can be divided as to subject matter, parties, or territory.

Jurisprudence   The study of law.

Jury   A group of men and women from the community selected to determine the truth; while the judge is responsible for interpreting the law, the jury is charged with the task of finding the facts of the case. The right to trial by jury is guaranteed by the U.S. Constitution in all serious criminal cases. A jury decides what the facts of the case are and applies those facts to the law. Juries must be convinced beyond a reasonable doubt that the defendant broke the law.

Jury Instructions   The directions the judge gives jurors about how they are to come to a verdict; jury instructions typically include an explanation of the law and what must be proven to convict the defendant.

Jury Nullification   A decision by a jury to ignore the law or the judge's instructions when deliberating; for example, jurors who believe the law is unjust may refuse to convict the defendant even if it is clear that he broke the law.

Justifiable Homicides   Those killings committed out of duty with no criminal intent.

Justification Defenses   A legal excuse for committing an act that otherwise would be a tort or a crime.

Kidnapping   The crime of taking and detaining a person against his will by force, intimidation, or fraud. Holding the victim for ransom is not required.

Knowing Possession   The condition existing when a person possesses and holds onto an item intentionally.

Law   The body of rules of conduct created by government and enforced by the authority of government.

Legislative   One of the three branches of government; the one charged with making the law.

Letters of Marque and Reprisal   A letter from a government formerly used to grant a private person the power to seize the subjects of a foreign state.

Living Will   A document in which a person sets forth directions regarding medical treatment to be given if he or she becomes unable to participate in decisions regarding his or her health care.

M'Naghten Rule   Holds that a defendant "is presumed to be sane and to possess a sufficient degree of reason to be responsible for his crimes, until the contrary be proved to (the jury's) satisfaction" beyond a reasonable doubt.

Magna Carta   The Great Charter, a document that was signed by King John of England in 1215; it guaranteed the noblemen under the king's jurisdiction life, liberty, and property. Many of the promises made in the Magna Carta became the basis of the guarantees found in the U.S. Constitution and the constitutions of the states.

Mala In Se   According to Blackstone, a category of crimes that are bad in and of themselves.

Mala Prohibita   According to Blackstone, a category of crimes that are crimes because society has decided they are crimes.

Malice Aforethought   Intent to kill or injure, or the deliberate commission of a dangerous or deadly act.

Malicious Mischief   Also known as criminal mischief, it is defined as the criminal offense of intentionally destroying another person's property.

Marital Privilege   The right of a person to refuse to testify against his or her spouse.

Mens Rea   A wrongful mind.

Mere Possession   The condition occurring when a person possesses an item unawares.

Military Actions   Actions carried out by members of the armed services under the direction of appropriate civilian authorities.

Military Tribunal   A military court convened in times of emergency to try those accused of war-related crimes, such as terrorism, espionage, or treason.

Minor   A person who has not yet reached legal age, typically 18.

Miranda **Warning**   The warning given suspects upon arrest informing of their constitutional rights.

Misdemeanors   Crimes punishable by relatively short prison sentences or fines; misdemeanors are less serious than felonies.

Mistake of Fact   A defense used when a defendant honestly believes something to be true that isn't.

Mistake of Law   A defense used when a person in good faith relied on an interpretation of law from a person charged with administering the law.

Mitigating Circumstance   Act or conduct that lessens or reduces the punishment for a crime, such as lack of a criminal record, state of mind, or youth.

Model Penal Code and Commentaries   Code that attempts to unify state penal codes. Legislatures often look to it when drafting legislation.

Moral Theory of Law   A theory subscribed to by Natural Law adherents stating that laws are based on the moral code of the society.

Motive   The reason a person commits a crime.

Napoleonic Code   The French system of laws developed by Napoleon I, it is the basis of Louisiana law.

Natural Law School   The school of jurisprudence thought that teaches that laws are based on morality and ethics and that people have natural rights.

Necessity Defense   A defense where the defendant reasonably believes his or her action was necessary to avoid harm to society.

Nolo Contendere   Latin for "I will not contest this," also called "no contest"; a plea entered that admits no wrongdoing but allows the court to sentence the defendant as if guilty.

Nondeadly Force   Force used to subdue a criminal or prevent a crime without risking death.

Objective Intent   What a reasonable person should have known or thought at the time of the event.

Objective Standard (or Minority Rule) for Entrapment   Asks the question: "Would an innocent person be induced to commit the crime by the officer's acts?"

Obstruction of Justice   The crime of impeding or hindering the administration of justice in any way.

Omission   The failure to perform a duty.

Opening Statements   The statements made by prosecuting or defense attorneys at the beginning of a trial outlining what the lawyer hopes to prove during the trial.

Parens Patriae   Common Law rule that requires that the Crown protect those most vulnerable in society when they cannot protect themselves.

Parental Liability   The responsibility parents have for the actions of their minor children.

Patient-Counselor Privilege   The right of confidentiality accorded counselors for conversations held in the course of mental health treatment.

Peremptory Challenge   Challenge to seating a juror that cannot be challenged. Generally each side is allowed a fixed number of peremptory challenges.

Perjury   Giving false testimony in a judicial or administrative proceeding; lying under oath as to a material fact; swearing to the truth of anything one knows or believes to be false.

Perjury Trap   A situation where a grand jury subpoenas a witness for the sole purpose of obtaining perjured testimony.

Personal Property   All property other than real property.

Personal Status   Generally current laws do not view personal status as an act, but historically personal status has been seen as a criminal act.

Per Se   Latin; by itself, in and of itself.

Petit Jury   A trial jury; in criminal cases, the petit jury determines the facts of the case, applies those facts to the law as given them by the judge, and decides if the state has proven beyond a reasonable doubt that the defendant committed the crime with which he or she was charged. Federal juries consist of 12 jurors; state juries can consist of as few as six jurors.

Petition for *Certiorari*   Request by a litigant that the U.S. Supreme Court hear his or her appeal.

Phishing   The attempt to obtain personal identifying information by posing as a bank or financial institution in an e-mail communication.

Pimp   One who works to procure clients for a prostitute.

Plaintiff   The party who files a lawsuit.

Plea   A formal response to criminal charges; a plea may be not guilty, guilty, *nolo contendere,* or not guilty by reason of insanity.

Plea Bargain   In a criminal case, an agreement between the prosecuting attorney and the defendant for the defendant to plead guilty in exchange for some benefit or advantage such as a reduction in the kind or number of charges or a reduced sentence; most criminal cases are settled with some form of a plea bargain.

Plea Bargaining   The process of negotiating the settlement of criminal charges without a trial.

Police Power   The power of a government to enforce laws and regulate the health, safety, morals, and welfare of the population.

Possession   Dominion or control over property.

Power to Declare War   The power reserved by Congress in the U.S. Constitution. Congress can declare war on a belligerent, and then the Executive Branch conducts the war.

Precedent   Prior decision that a court must follow when deciding a new, similar case.

Preemption Doctrine   The concept that federal law must take precedence over state and local law.

Preliminary Arraignment   An accused's first official notification of the charges against him or her; preliminary arraignment generally occurs shortly after arrest.

Preliminary Hearing   A formal hearing that is the first occasion at which the government must produce evidence against the defendant; the prosecutor must convince the judge or magistrate hearing the case that it is more likely than not that the defendant committed the crime with which he or she is charged.

Preponderance of the Evidence   Evidence that is more convincing than the opposing evidence; enough evidence to tip the scales of justice.

Priest-Penitent Privilege   The right of confidentiality accorded members of the clergy for conversations held during the ritual of confession.

Primogeniture   The ancient common law of descent where all the father's property went to the oldest son. Also the law of succession to the English throne.

Principle of Legality   The theory that an action is not a crime unless it is prohibited by law and assigned a punishment by the state.

Probable Cause   A low standard of proof in a criminal case used to justify an arrest or hold a defendant over for trial after a preliminary hearing; the standard requires that there be sufficient proof to convince a reasonable person that it is more likely than not that he or she committed the crime charged. The amount of proof required before an officer can obtain a search warrant, stop a suspect, or make an arrest; enough evidence from which a reasonable person could conclude that the facts alleged are probably true.

Proletariat   In Marxist theory, the working class who must sell their labor in order to survive.

Property Rights   A bundle of rights, including the right to possess, use and enjoy, and dispose of something. It is not a material object itself, but a person's right to do what he or she wishes with that object, subject to limitations provided in the law.

Prostitution   Engaging in sexual intercourse or other sexual activity for pay.

Proximate Cause   An act that sets in motion a chain of events leading to harm.

Public Indecency   Lewd or lascivious conduct that is open to public view.

Quash   To annul.

Rape   Traditionally defined as forced sexual intercourse with a woman, not one's wife. Modern rape definitions don't distinguish between male or female victims and have expanded the types of sexual contact that are included in the definition. Most states also allow at least a limited right to bring rape charges against a spouse and no longer require the use of direct force or physical harm.

Rape Shield Law   Codified rule of evidence that provides for the exclusion of a rape victim's sexual history unless it is directly relevant to his or her consent or other evidence in the case.

Real Property   Consists of land and everything permanently attached to it. It includes land, subsurface rights, air rights, timbering and harvesting rights, and any buildings and structures permanently attached to the land.

Realists   Belonging to the Sociological School of jurisprudence; realists believe that the purpose of law is to shape societal behavior.

Rebellion or Insurrection   An attempt to overthrow the government by force or unconstitutional means.

Rebuttable Presumption   A presumption that can be overcome by presenting evidence to the contrary.

Recantation   The retraction of testimony.

Recross Examination   Questioning of a witness called by the other side following redirect examination.

Redirect Examination   Questioning of one's own witness following cross-examination.

Res Gestae Theory   Literally "the acts of the thing"; the acts or words through which an event speaks.

Respondeat Superior   A term literally meaning "let the superior respond" it refers most commonly to employer liability for employee action when the employee is acting as an agent of the employer.

Retreat Rule   The rule governing when a person must retreat rather than use deadly force.

RICO   The Racketeering Influenced and Corrupt Organizations Act is legislation that enables the government to prosecute individuals and organizations for a pattern of criminal activity; originally meant to target organized crime.

Right Against Self-Incrimination   The right embodied in the Fifth Amendment to the U.S. Constitution that allows an accused person to remain silent; its corollary is "innocent until proven guilty."

Right to Bail   The limited right to be released from prison pending trial after posting enough security to assure appearance at the time of trial; the right is subject to limitation in cases of murder or where release has been shown to pose a threat to the public.

Right to Remain Silent   The right of all persons not to testify against their own interests when suspected of or charged with a crime; the right to remain silent is rooted in the belief that it is the government's obligation to prove guilt.

Robbery   The taking of personal property from the person of another against his will, by either force or threat of force.

Scienter   A necessary element to prove in some crimes where the offender knew a certain fact or understood the law being broken.

Second Degree   Under the Model Penal Code, crimes that are committed knowingly.

Sedition   A conspiracy to overthrow, put down, or to destroy by force the Government of the United States, or levy war against them, or to oppose the authority thereof, or by force to prevent, hinder, or delay the execution of any law of the United States, or by force to seize, take, or possess any property of the United States contrary to the authority thereof.

Self-Defense   The use of force to protect oneself from death or imminent bodily harm at the hands of an aggressor.

Self-Incrimination   The act of giving testimony against one's penal interest; generally, persons have a right to withhold information that may incriminate and to refuse to answer questions that incriminate; the right does not generally extend to giving DNA samples or submitting to blood alcohol testing or withholding other physical evidence.

Sequester   To isolate jurors in order to assure that they will remain impartial during the trial and deliberations.

Sex Workers   A term preferred by some working in the sex industry such as prostitutes, porn actresses or actors, exotic dancers, and the like.

Sine Qua Non   Literally, without which, not; the Latin term for the "but for rule."

Sixth Amendment   The provision of the Bill of Rights that originally guaranteed all federal criminal defendants the right to trial by jury; it has since been applied to the states through the Fourteenth Amendment, which guarantees all citizens equal protection of the laws of the United States.

Sociological School   Adherents of the Sociological School of jurisprudence believe that the purpose of law is to shape societal behavior; believers are called realists.

Sodomy   Sexual relations between members of the same sex, sexual conduct *per anus* or *per os* between unmarried persons of the opposite sex, and sexual intercourse with animals.

Sovereign Immunity   The protection from lawsuits government agencies enjoy.

Specific Intent   The type of intent where the person commits an act designed to cause a specific criminal result.

Stare Decisis   To stand by that which was decided; rule by which courts decide new cases based on how they previously decided similar cases.

Statutory Rape   Sexual intercourse with a victim below the age of consent or unable to consent due to a physical or mental impairment. The crime is commonly referred to as statutory rape because it is the statute that defines what may otherwise seem to be a consensual act as a crime. The legislative presumption is that some persons cannot give meaningful consent.

Stop and Frisk   Police officers may briefly stop, identify, and frisk persons reasonably believed to have committed a crime during the course of an investigation.

Strict Liability   The legal responsibility for damage or injury, even if you are not at fault or negligent.

Subjective Intent   The offender's conscious intentions at the time of the crime.

Subjective Standard (or Majority Rule) for Entrapment   Asks the question: "Was the defendant predisposed to commit the crime?"

Subornation of Perjury   Convincing or seeking to convince another person to commit perjury.

Sudden Escalation   The concept that a conflict that was not life threatening escalates to the point that it is.

Summary Offenses   Minor offenses such as parking tickets or minor traffic violations.

Supremacy Clause   The clause in the U.S. Constitution that states that the Constitution, federal law, and treaties are the supreme law of the land; Article VI, Section 2.

Tenancy by the Entirety   The legal joint ownership in which both spouses own an undivided interest in the whole property and in which neither spouse can sell his or her interest without the consent of the other.

Tenancy in Common   Form of joint ownership in which each owns an undivided interest in the whole property.

Terrorism   The unlawful use or threat of violence, especially against the state or the public as a politically motivated means of attack or coercion.

Theft   The taking and carrying away of another's personal property with the intent to deprive him or her of it permanently.

Third Degree   Under the Model Penal Code, crimes that are committed recklessly.

Tort   A private or civil wrong or injury independent of contract, resulting from a breach of a legal duty.

Tort Feasor   A person who commits a tort.

Transactional Immunity   A broad form of immunity where the person cannot be prosecuted for any action related to the testimony as long as the person testifies truthfully.

Transferred Intent   The type of intent where a person tries to harm one person and as a result harms someone else.

Transportation   The practice of exiling or expelling a prisoner from his homeland as punishment.

Treason   Levying war against the United States, or in adhering to their enemies, giving them aid and comfort. Treason must be proven by the testimony of two witnesses to the same overt act, or the defendant's confession in open court; transferring loyalty or allegiance to the enemy.

Trial by Battle   A method of determining guilt in medieval England; usually reserved for civil cases, in trial by battle the winner of the battle won the lawsuit.

Trial by Judge   A defendant may choose to be tried by a judge rather than by a jury or rather than pleading guilty; when a judge tries a case, he or she decides both the facts and the law.

Trial by Ordeal   A method of determining guilt in medieval England; in trial by ordeal, the defendant was made to perform a physical task, such as holding a hot piece of iron. If the wound healed without becoming infected, the accused was innocent; if it became infected, he was guilty (and ill).

True Bill   An indictment voted on by a grand jury where the jury has found that it is more likely than not that a crime has been committed and that the person being charged committed it.

Two-Witness Rule   The Common Law rule that requires two witnesses to testify to another's perjury in order for a conviction to take place.

U.S. Courts of Appeals   The federal court system's intermediate appellate courts.

U.S. District Courts   The federal court system's trial courts.

U.S. Supreme Court   The highest court in the United States.

Unlawful Act Manslaughter   Where the defendant committed a crime that resulted in the death of a person.

Unreasonable Searches and Seizures The rule, based on the Fourth Amendment, that police must obtain a warrant before searching a home or arresting a suspect; the rule has numerous exceptions.

Use Immunity A limited form of immunity where the person's testimony cannot be used as evidence against him or her.

Venire A group of individuals from the community from whom the petit jury that will hear a criminal case is drawn; also referred to as the jury panel, pool, or array.

Venue The county or judicial district in which a case is tried; in criminal cases, the venue is usually where the crime was committed.

Verdict A judge or jury's decision at the end of a trial; the verdict in a civil case must be by at least a preponderance of the evidence, while the verdict in a criminal case must be beyond a reasonable doubt.

Vicarious Liability Where one person is held responsible for someone else's actions.

Violence Against Women Act (VAWA) The Violence Against Women Act, a federal law criminalizing interstate acts of domestic violence and funding research and education programs.

Voir Dire From the French meaning "to speak the truth," it refers to the examination of citizens to ascertain their fitness for serving on a jury; during the voir dire phase of a criminal trial, the attorneys or the judge ask questions of the jury pool. These are designed to ferret out those jurors who can't be impartial or who can't serve on the jury because of illness or other obligations and to help the attorneys in the case decide where and when to use available peremptory challenges.

Voluntary Act The actus reus element of a crime; a crime must be a voluntary act.

Voluntary Intoxication The condition where a person knowingly ingests an intoxicating substance; not a defense to murder or most crimes.

Voluntary Manslaughter A homicide committed with the intent to kill, but without deliberation, premeditation, or malice.

War on Terror The term commonly used to refer to the aftermath of the September 11, 2001 attacks and efforts to bring the masterminds of the attacks to justice.

Warrant A document issued by a magistrate or judge authorizing the search of a place or the arrest of a person.

Wergild Compensation paid to a family group if a member of that family was killed or suffered severe injury.

Wite A public fine payable to a lord or tribal chieftain.

Withdrawal The act of removing oneself from a conflict.

Witherspoon **Qualified** A jury in a capital case who have stated they will consider imposing the death penalty even if they are opposed to the death penalty.

Work Product Rule The rule that protects material produced by an attorney in preparation for a trial, or the work product, from discovery.

Writ of Certiorari Notice from the U.S. Supreme Court that the court will hear a case.

INDEX

References are to pages.